~
ORIGINS
OF THE
Ñuu

~ ORIGINS
OF THE
Ñuu

Archaeology in the Mixteca Alta, Mexico

Stephen A. Kowalewski ♦ Andrew K. Balkansky
Laura R. Stiver Walsh ♦ Thomas J. Pluckhahn ♦ John F. Chamblee
Verónica Pérez Rodríguez ♦ Verenice Y. Heredia Espinoza ♦ Charlotte A. Smith

UNIVERSITY PRESS OF COLORADO

© 2009 by the University Press of Colorado

Published by the University Press of Colorado
5589 Arapahoe Avenue, Suite 206C
Boulder, Colorado 80303

 The University Press of Colorado is a proud member of
the Association of American University Presses.

The University Press of Colorado is a cooperative publishing enterprise supported, in part,
by Adams State College, Colorado State University, Fort Lewis College, Mesa State College,
Metropolitan State College of Denver, Regis University, University of Colorado, University of
Northern Colorado, and Western State College of Colorado.

∞ The paper used in this publication meets the minimum requirements of the American
National Standard for Information Sciences—Permanence of Paper for Printed Library Materials.
ANSI Z39.48-1992

Library of Congress Cataloging-in-Publication Data

Origins of the Ñuu : archaeology in the Mixteca Alta, Mexico / Stephen A. Kowalewski . . . [et
al.].
    p. cm.
Includes bibliographical references and index.
ISBN 978-0-87081-929-2 (alk. paper) — 978-1-60732-103-3 (pbk : alk. paper)
1. Mixtec Indians—Origin. 2. Mixtec Indians—History. 3. Mixtec Indians—Antiquities. 4.
Oaxaca (Mexico)—Antiquities. I. Kowalewski, Stephen A.

F1219.8.M59O75 2008
972'.7401—dc22

                                                                    2008041565

Design by Daniel Pratt

To our teacher Ron Spores, in admiration of
his leadership and superlative contributions to
the anthropology of the Mixteca.

Contents

Chapter 3: Greater Teposcolula 81

Chapter 4: Greater Huamelulpan 157

Chapter 5: The Inner Basin 183

Chapter 6: Greater Tlaxiaco 255

Chapter 7: The Polities of the Early and Middle Formative 285

Figures

Tables

xix

Preface

We are most grateful that the National Science Foundation (NSF) funded our 1999 fieldwork. The Instituto Nacional de Antropología e Historia (INAH) authorized this research and gave its institutional backing. INAH and NSF together should be credited for their achievements in advancing archaeological research in Mexico. Among many INAH colleagues we owe special thanks to Joaquín García Bárcena, Eduardo López Calzada, Raúl Matadamas, and Nelly Robles García. The Foundation for the Advancement of Mesoamerican Research also helped with travel support.

To the thousands of friendly and welcoming people of the Mixteca Alta, and to all their elected authorities in the dozens of municipalities in which we had the plea-sure of working, our saludos and heartfelt thanks. In Tlaxiaco the Santos and Cruz families helped out in many ways and we appreciate their friendship. Since well-fed surveyors are happy surveyors, we happily thank our fine cook, Rosa Fátima Múrcio Jiménez. We had excellent help in the field and lab from visiting students Xochitl Bautista, Minerva Delgado, Aline P. Lara Galicia, Joel Torrices, and Naoli Victoria

Lona. Dmitri Beliaev and Roberto Santos Pérez were full-time participants in the 1999 field- and lab work and they contributed greatly to the success of the project. Xinyu Ren digitized Figure 1.3 and helped with the settlement-pattern analysis.

The paper and electronic topographic information comes from the Instituto Nacional de Estadística Geografía e Informática (INEGI), and we very much appreciate the consultations offered by numerous INEGI representatives. We thank Charles S. Spencer (American Museum of Natural History) and Arthur Demarest (Vanderbilt University) for arranging the assistance of their institutions. The University of Georgia's Department of Anthropology supplied resources and the Georgia Museum of Natural History gave us laboratory space. Members of the Center for Applied Spatial Analysis at the University of Arizona lent their technical expertise in the making of the settlement-pattern maps. Katy McNulty and Matt Powers are appreciated for providing a place to work on Tybee Island, Georgia.

All the authors contributed their field, laboratory, and analytical expertise as well as their ideas to this book and each made additional contributions. Andrew Balkansky brought the Huamelulpan project to completion and in 1999 he was our excellent field director and chief ceramicist. Laura Stiver Walsh was in charge of the admirable Teposcolula survey and wrote the ceramic chronology chapter. As crew chief, Thomas Pluckhahn was a key organizer in the field, he led the mountain brigade, and he wrote the section on the Sierra de Nochixtlán. John Chamblee created and managed the database and GIS—almost all the settlement-pattern maps and tables in this book are his work. Verónica Pérez Rodríguez was our lama-bordo analyst and wrote the Spanish summary. Verenice Heredia became our expert on intrasite artifact analysis and moved the whole project along by taking a lot of the responsibility for our final report to INAH. Charlotte Smith was our superior lab organizer, artifact photographer, and macroregional analyst; all the architectural renderings are her work.

We most gratefully credit John Christopher Burns (jcbD) for the elegant visual presentation of the archaeological data in this book. John's support has been amazingly generous. He created the design and the look and feel of every map and drawing and spent long, long hours transforming each crude draft into a professional-quality figure.

Many colleagues offered their good advice and we especially thank Richard E. Blanton, Gary Feinman, Laura Finsten, Jackie Saindon, Charles R. Spencer, Ron Spores, and Mark Williams. We sincerely thank Blanton and three anonymous reviewers for their thoughtful, helpful, and much-appreciated comments on the manuscript. We thank Darrin Pratt and the University Press of Colorado for their confidence in the idea of this book and the fact that they made it happen.

This volume differs from conventional archaeological survey reports in its reliance on the graphic display of information (thank you again, John Christopher Burns). We do not describe individual sites one after another. Verbal descriptions of 999 sites and 1,668 components would be lengthy and numbingly redundant. Yet we wanted to let readers appreciate the richness of the archaeological detail and we wanted to make the data available and useful for future researchers. Our solution is

Chapters 2–6, which describe in words and graphics batches of similar sites as they occur in subregions. Together, the narrative, tables, settlement-pattern maps, site plans, and photographs provide descriptive, quantitative, and visual details relevant for understanding theme and variation. Specialists needing the complete ceramic, lithic, and site data sets can use our report to the Instituto Nacional de Antropología e Historia (Kowalewski et al. 2006). Scholars wishing to use the database in electronic form should contact Kowalewski or Chamblee.

~ ORIGINS
OF THE
Ñuu

CHAPTER ONE

Regional Study of Ancient Societies in the Mixteca Alta

The Mixteca Alta in the state of Oaxaca, Mexico, was an important region in the center of Mesoamerica (Figure 1.1). But compared to the better-known Maya lowlands and the Aztec heartland, the Mixteca Alta has received much less archaeological attention. This was a magnificent land with wonderful archaeological sites. The Spanish conquerors in the sixteenth century described it as well-populated, rich, and prosperous. Today it is notoriously eroded and poor; the Mixteca's major export is its own people. This volume sheds light on what happened to the Mixteca Alta.

To do so, we consider the fundamental question: What were the prehispanic societies (the organized groups of people) of this area and how did they change over time? To address this problem, we begin with settlement patterns (where people lived and worked). Rather than concentrating on a single settlement we take a regional approach.

Since the Mixteca Alta is a place where most archaeological sites can be readily seen on the surface without excavation, we carried out fieldwork designed to find

1

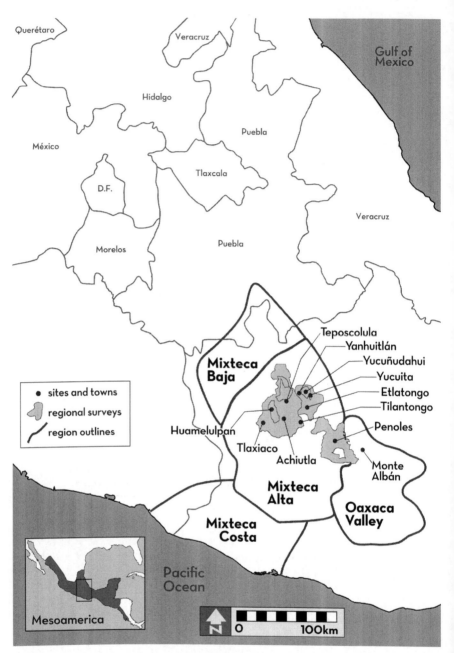

1.1 *Regions, survey areas, important sites, and modern towns.*

all the visible remains of settlements and other ancient features over an area large enough to contain many autonomous societies. This was full-coverage regional surface survey. Trained crews walked systematically over the whole area (1,622 km²) to locate, map, describe, and collect from all archaeological sites (we found 999). In the last thirty years, similar regional surveys have fundamentally altered and improved explanations about the rise of civilization and the nature of urbanism. When combined with finer-scale excavation and other data, surveys have proven to be very productive to gather new information on past civilizations and the relationships between people and environments.

The study region, which we call the Central Mixteca Alta, when added to the other survey projects in highland Oaxaca provides nearly continuous coverage of a swath 170 km in length, a total area of about 8,000 km². This unusually extensive coverage opens up new perspectives. Archaeologists can now move beyond debating about single places of origin or centers of influence to examining Mesoamerica or other civilizations as social systems. We can identify multiple societies and track each over time. We can also see how large-scale phenomena affected local events (and vice versa). We are beginning to understand the key processes of change at local, regional, and macroregional scales. The difference between the older culture-history approach to civilization and the developing macroregional perspective based on regional surveys is similar to that between guessing a whole picture from a few pieces of a jigsaw puzzle versus assembling all the pieces. Today we still do not have all the pieces, but we have enough to know which method offers the better chance to see the whole picture.

PLAN OF THE BOOK

The book builds from particular archaeological facts toward the bigger picture. This chapter describes the Central Mixteca Alta and our field and lab methods. Chapters 2–6 display the archaeological sites and settlement patterns, phase by phase, for the twenty-six subregions or small valleys in the large area we surveyed. The subregions fall into five groups that have much in common geographically and historically. The order of presentation is by these five groups, from east to west, beginning in Chapter 2 with the western edge of the Nochixtlán Valley, that is, the eastern flanks of the Sierra de Nochixtlán. Then we take up the major kingdom of Teposcolula and its satellites (Chapter 3). We next move to a key place in the emergence of state and urbanism in the Mixteca Alta, Huamelulpan and its dependencies (Chapter 4). Chapter 5 displays the settlement patterns of seven subregions in a rich and dynamic region we call the "inner basin." We describe the core of the major *cacicazgo* of Tlaxiaco in the southwestern part of the study area in Chapter 6. Chapters 2–6 show all the variations that allowed us to apprehend a broad pattern of development as well as showing how the ideal pattern played out on the ground in specific environmental and social contexts.

Chapters 7–10 unify all the localities to illuminate the regional patterns in the earlier Formative, later Formative, Classic, and Postclassic. These discussions bring together the archaeology of the Mixteca Alta's petty kingdom or state—*ñuu*—and its predecessors. Chapter 11 discusses these findings in a broader anthropological context. To make our point in another way, Chapter 12 sums up in Spanish.

ORIGINS OF URBANISM AND THE STATE

How and why states and cities developed is one of the classic problems of history and the social sciences. For social scientists the state generally means a hierarchically organized bureaucratic governing institution that claims sovereignty within a territory. The common archaeological markers of states are deep settlement and civic-ceremonial hierarchies and sometimes written texts or special buildings that are the manifestations of hierarchical governance. Cities are the top-ranking places in central-place hierarchies; they have relatively high populations and notable internal differentiation.

The problem of state and urban origins is a classic one in the sense that it is the laboratory or proving ground for major theories of social science. Class conflict, population pressure, war, long-distance trade, central-place theory, the social contract, the urban cosmovision—these and various other ideas have been promoted and then criticized using the comparative record of human history. Our study describes a sequence that runs from the first farming villages to the origins of the state and urbanism and their subsequent developments. The Mixteca Alta case is one in which new social institutions developed in situ yet with much trouble, conflict, and contingency. The transition to the state took place about 2,000 years ago within one cultural, demographic, and environmental setting but it was accomplished by an emphatic punctuation that ended one equilibrium and began another.

Our perspective differs from that of other scholars who have addressed this classic problem. In Oaxaca multiple adjoining regions have now been subjected to systematic archaeological survey. This allows us to see change in neighboring regions simultaneously over more than 3,000 years. Aside from the story of the Mixteca Alta, itself fascinating and important, our more general contribution to the problem of state and urban origins comes from our perspective of a macroregion composed of interacting regional societies. This vantage has several theoretical implications. First, the story of state origins in any one of the regions was rather different from that of its neighboring regions. Yet these varying stories are not competing or inconsistent explanations because each regional trajectory was the particular outcome of a common, overarching, macroregional process. Second, the important causal factors were different not only at the same scale (each region looks different) but also the causes of the macroregional movements were not the same as these but were of a different order. Different causal factors operate at different scales (in space and time). Third, good explanation should comprehend what went on at multiple scales. The rise of the state and urbanism can best be explained by integrating macroregional, regional, and lower-level variation. Propositions like these are similar to what the historian Braudel (1972) said about particular events and long-term structures or what ecologists sometimes refer to as "hierarchical patch dynamics" (Wu and Loucks 1995).

Having multiple regional surveys as well as smaller-scale studies means that we have instruments big enough to see multiple neighboring states and discerning enough to see a level or two below to the cities and towns within these states.

THE CENTRAL MIXTECA ALTA

Oaxaca is the mountainous tangle where Mexico's Sierra Madre del Sur and Sierra Madre Occidental intersect like ragged scissor blades. It was a multilingual, populous region in the heart of Mesoamerican civilization between the Aztecs of Central Mexico and the Maya of the east. The Mixtec languages, a branch of the Otomanguean family, predominate in western Oaxaca. The Mixteca Alta is the high country above 1,500 m asl (above sea level) (Tamayo 1950:96) at the upper reaches of the Río Balsas and the Río Verde, which run to the Pacific, and the Río Papaloapan, which flows through the deep valley called the Cañada to the Gulf of Mexico.

In the sixteenth century the Dominicans considered the area so rich and important that they established major monasteries at Yanhuitlán, Coixtlahuaca, Teposcolula, Achiutla, and Tlaxiaco. Palerm and Wolf (1957) wrote that the Mixteca Alta was one of Mesoamerica's key areas that persisted, period after period, and encompassed regions of demographic power and centers of economic networks that organized diverse environments. The Mixteca Alta is known for its codices, which are precolumbian and Colonial painted manuscripts, and for its native cacicazgos, petty kingdoms ruled by hereditary noble families. Abundant archaeological remains reveal a long tradition of complex urban culture.

The Mixteca underwent two major evolutionary transformations. Around 1300 BC the way of life shifted from hunting and gathering to sedentary agricultural villages (a Neolithic revolution). The second major change began around 300 BC and after several centuries saw the birth of urbanism and the state. Like other urban systems, those in the Mixteca Alta also underwent dramatic collapse, which happened here at the end of the Classic period. But after AD 1200 the region experienced its greatest population growth and prosperity. A few decades before the Spanish invasion the area had become tributary provinces of the expanding Aztec empire (the Aztec presence left only the slightest archaeological imprint).

Our Central Mixteca Alta study area is a portion of the whole cultural region, but it is a significant part because it contains all of several native cacicazgos, large portions of others, and many of the peripheries and boundaries in between. Our area covers all or parts of the politically and demographically important realms of Teposcolula, Yanhuitlán, Tilantongo, Achiutla, Huamelulpan, and Tlaxiaco, as well as smaller polities. This book combines three projects: Andrew Balkansky's (1998b) survey of the Huamelulpan Valley, Laura Stiver Walsh's (2001) survey of the Teposcolula Valley, and our 1999 survey, in which all of us worked together. These projects were carried out using similar procedures, which made it relatively easy to combine our data.

1.2 Planting trees to help retain soil. A portion of the mural at the palacio municipal, San Agustín Tlacotepec.

Environment

The following sections describe natural factors important in human/environmental interaction and settlement history. Local details are in Chapters 2–6. Environmental change is the product of natural processes and human action. In the Mixteca Alta the great weight was on the human side of this equation. Again and again since the origin of sedentary villages, human action changed the environment. People cleared the land of its forest and grasses. Clearing caused rapid soil loss because the best soils were also the most prone to erode (Figure 1.2). Yet by capturing soil on the move, people created verdant, moist, lush, productive, and sustainable gardens, orchards, and fields. Many places like this can be seen today alongside eroded hillsides that look like mine tailings on the moon.

The key to this paradox is human input and its opposite, lack of human input (Spores 1969). Active retention of soil creates fertile places. Unprotected by natural or cultivated vegetation, soil will depart en masse on a downhill train powered by summer thunderstorms and gravity. Retaining walls and vegetation held the soil to its station. When retaining walls were neglected or vegetation removed, erosion began and soil washed down onto valley floors. Farmers could semi-deliberately move soil from upper slopes and catch it behind retaining walls on lower slopes.

Geology

Our understanding of bedrock and soils comes from the informative Carta Geológica series (INEGI 1984; Figure 1.3) and Michael Kirkby's geomorphological study of the Nochixtlán Valley (1972). Highland Oaxaca has several widely spaced mountain ridges of Cretaceous limestone. Between these, in the Tertiary era, were lacustrine basins, which filled with reddish beds of limestone or sandstone cobbles loosely cemented by carbonates in a fine-grained matrix. There is variation in the makeup of these beds but they are generally referred to as the Yanhuitlán and Jaltepec formations (Figure 1.4). These were the preferred soils for agriculture and the most erodible. When weathered these soils produce a calcareous (calcrete) layer that can be cut to make building blocks (*endeque*) (Kirkby 1972:14–15). Volcanic flows and dikes extruded into the basins in mid-Tertiary times, forming cones, precipices, and ridges as high as the limestone crests and breaking the terrain into small pockets surrounded by mountains.

Climate

The area has a humid-temperate climate (Tamayo 1950; Carta de Climas 1970; INEGI 1988; Alvarez 1998). Measured mean annual temperatures are about 16–17°C. Annual rainfall averages over 900 mm in the south (Tlaxiaco) but the north is drier, with Teposcolula receiving about 650 mm of precipitation on average. This is a summer-dominated rainfall regime. Localized rain shadows and year-to-year and month-to-month variability in rainfall and frosts combine to produce substantial local variation. Risks to dry farming place a premium on other adaptations such as retaining moisture by terracing, irrigating, making use of altitudinal variation, and planting varied cultigens.

Garvin's (1994:21–51) compilation of data from twenty-three weather stations in the Mixteca and the Valley of Oaxaca shows no correlation between elevation and precipitation. Local variations must override general patterns. For farmers, adaptations to local rainfall and watershed conditions were most significant.

Vegetation

Today the valleys and hills are almost entirely cleared for agriculture and grazing up to about 200 m in elevation above the local valley floor. Above this level pine predominates in the mountain forests; oak and juniper are common at lower elevations. Usually there is a mix of pine and oak. Disturbance history is a major factor in forest composition and in the prevalence of grasses. The most luxuriant pine forests grow along the eastern mountain ridges but upper slopes and ridge crests throughout the area are covered with mixed pine and oak. Pine needle litter can cover the ground surface and make artifacts hard to find but in most circumstances grazing, plowing, logging, or erosion exposes artifacts, and stone architecture is visible in any case.

Hot-climate cultigens like sugarcane and bananas will grow at low elevations in the south of our study area, around San Mateo Peñasco (1,800 m asl), but not in Teposcolula where the valley floor is at 2,200 m. Xerophytic cultigens (e.g., agave, cactus, yucca) are economically important everywhere.

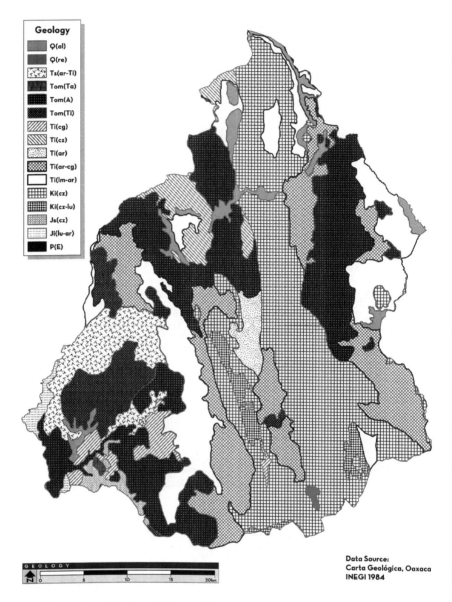

Geology
- Q(al)
- Q(re)
- Ts(ar-Ti)
- Tom(Ta)
- Tom(A)
- Tom(Ti)
- Ti(cg)
- Ti(cz)
- Ti(ar)
- Ti(ar-cg)
- Ti(lm-ar)
- Ki(cz)
- Ki(cz-lu)
- Js(cz)
- Ji(lu-ar)
- P(E)

GEOLOGY

0   5   10   15   20km

Data Source:
Carta Geológica, Oaxaca
INEGI 1984

1.3 *Surface geology of the Central Mixteca Alta.*

Land Use

There is a general pattern of intensive infield cultivation in and around settlements; less intensive, sometimes dry-farmed fields at a distance from settlements; and sporadic special use of outlying uplands. Today's villages and small towns tend

1.4 Soil profile in the Yanhuitlán Formation in the Nochixtlán Valley. Note that an A-horizon has formed in the center of the picture. On top of the hill is a layer of caliche.

to have dispersed houses with fields between. Valley floors are agricultural; uplands have only a few fields. Sheep, goats, cattle, and burros graze everywhere. Uplands are for grazing and wood cutting. Historically, landed haciendas were not as important in the Mixteca Alta compared to other regions in Mexico but our area did have fixed and transhumant livestock haciendas. Sometimes herds of 10,000 or more animals were moved seasonally over long distances (Romero 1990:323–354). Today outside timber and charcoal businesses sometimes are permitted to harvest large tracts. Mines in this part of Oaxaca were always small in scale. Limestone products (cement, cal) are extracted near Teposcolula and east of Tlaxiaco and there is a salt source in the Teposcolula Valley. There is very little industry.

Present land use is only a partial clue about past land use. What today is barren badlands may have been a rich and productive agricultural terrace system in the past. Today's pine-dominated forest may have been fields or a more diverse forest in the past. Five centuries of livestock grazing have depleted grasses and contributed to unchecked erosion.

Ancient, historic, and present-day agricultural terraces are prominent features of the landscape (Figures 1.5, 1.6). *Lama-bordos* are chains of agricultural terraces built in drainages. There are also contour terraces on hillsides. Terracing dramatically increases yields and sustainability and is an important factor in cultural and demographic development.

1.5 Santo Domingo Huendio, from SDH 1 north to SDH 2. The modern settlement is in the upper end of a lama bordo. Note the milpas on the terraces with tree-lined retaining walls.

History and Ethnography

The Mixteca Alta was the subject of Woodrow Borah's and Sherburne Cook's seminal studies in historical geography that linked the region's erosion to its population history (Cook 1949; Borah and Cook 1960; Cook and Borah 1968). Good overviews of the Colonial and recent history of the Mixteca Alta have been written by Dahlgren (1954) and Spores (1967, 1984); Terraciano's (2001) and Pastor's (1987) historical studies are essential. Major ethnographic studies of villages include Butterworth's (1975) on Tilantongo in our study area, Romney and Romney's (1966) on Juxtlahuaca, and Monaghan's (1995) on Nuyoo, south of Tlaxiaco.

Before the Spanish conquest everyone in the Mixteca Alta spoke one dialect or another of the Mixtec language (the largest in number of speakers and geographical extent), Trique (southwest of Tlaxiaco), or Chocho (around Coixtlahuaca and Tamazulapan). A specifically Mixtec ethnic or political identity was never as strongly expressed as loyalty to one's home community. During Colonial times many indigenous-language speakers were drawn into new towns and they ceased to speak their local dialect in favor of Spanish. This loss of indigenous language—part of a process sometimes called "depeasantization"—continues today as labor markets pull people away from the Mixteca Alta. Yet the Mixtec language still thrives in many places. Many people are bilingual, speaking Mixtec and Spanish, and some of those who have dealings with the north are trilingual, adding English to their repertoire.

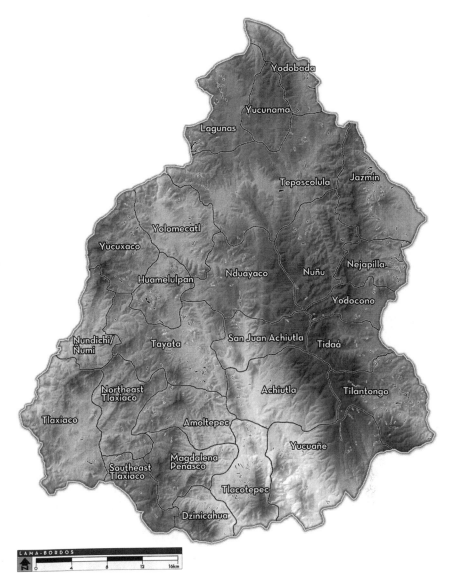

1.6 Regional distribution of lama-bordos. From our field observations and air photos.

In 1912 twenty-three-year-old José López Alavez, a native of Huajuapan in the Mixteca Baja who was studying in Mexico City, wrote the popular song "Canción Mixteca," which still brings forth tears from migrants who long for their *patria chica*:

Que lejos estoy del suelo donde he nacido!
Inmensa nostalgia invade mi pensamiento.
Y al verme tan solo y triste, cual hoja al viento.
Quisiera llorar, quisiera morir de sentimiento.

Over the past century the flow of people out of the Mixteca has been significant. With cash a necessity today it is difficult to make a living by family farming, and tens of thousands of people have migrated permanently or temporarily to Puebla, Mexico City, and the United States. Their remittances are used to embellish houses, public buildings, and churches. But even with this new money rural communities, whether Mixtec or mestizo, are poor, and with their eighteen- to forty-five-year-old men and women away, they are demographically hollow.

Mixtec-speaking villages and villages where only Spanish is spoken are not outwardly different (in our study area most but not all villages are Mixtec speaking). All are rural communities that have public schools, churches, cemeteries, basketball courts, municipal offices, small jails, a few small stores, electricity, a few paved streets, public faucets with running water, and satellite dishes for television. They have participatory local governments and an annual round of church ceremonies and festivals—the civic-ceremonial system seen in many middle-American communities. Religious beliefs and practices are a syncretic blend of indigenous and Catholic.

All rural communities here are more or less closed and corporate—they defend the land that is their means of livelihood and they do so in collective ways that tend to exclude outsiders. All adult men must provide *tequio* (labor) to the community. Ties of labor sharing, food exchange, and ritual bind households together. Yet sometimes villages are almost paralyzed by grievances and factional disputes among their members.

In Mixtec-speaking communities an intensely local, territorial ideology is still expressed in oral histories, myths, rituals, prayers, place-names, and cosmologies, all encoded in the indigenous dialect. All over the Mixteca Alta there are hundreds of tiny shrines that families use for curing and to pray for rain (the practices are syntheses of the Catholic and the indigenous). The oral traditions and place-names often match in specific detail scenes in the Mixtec codices, the painted folded-screen manuscripts of precolumbian and early Colonial times. Thus the names used by Mixtec speakers today for important archaeological sites, mountains, and caves can be an aid to reading the prehispanic codices.

In the Colonial period the Spanish authorities had a policy of *congregación*, meaning that native settlements in the hills or dispersed over the countryside were to be abandoned and their inhabitants brought down to the valley floor and concentrated in "proper" towns. In some ways the effects of congregación can be seen today but in fact the policy had quite mixed results (Spores 2005). Modern towns such as Teposcolula, Yanhuitlán, and Tlaxiaco were new centers created in the sixteenth century by resettlement. Most communities do have a central settlement with streets laid out on a grid. Yet throughout Colonial and recent times there has been a strong centrifugal tendency. Today's central settlements often have fewer than half of a community's members—the rest of the people are dispersed in widely scattered villages, hamlets, and single houses. Tilantongo, Nduayaco, Yucuxaco, and other communities have markedly dispersed settlement, and indeed most communities are in some degree dispersed. The modern settlement pattern is not vastly different from that of late prehispanic times. In most places there are specific similarities in the pattern of settlement between the Postclassic and the present day, although as we shall see, prehispanic populations were often larger than today's.

European plants, animals, and diseases, the sixteenth-century demographic and economic collapse, and the incorporation of the Mixteca Alta into the modern world system wrought enormous change. Indigenous self-rule has been gone for 500 years. Exploitation has drained off wealth and created poverty. Natural resources have been depleted by overgrazing and erosion. Peasantization, depeasantization, and migration often broke the close links among social groups, local territory, Mixtec language, and culture. These transformations severed the transmission of knowledge and history from one generation to the next. Breaking off the past from the present had profound intellectual and practical consequences.

Yet again and again people in the Mixteca Alta have made adjustments and created institutions that resemble in some ways long-standing prehispanic adaptations. For example, popular markets, which had been important in prehispanic times, have been irrepressible. Tequio is still an important institution and people today sometimes speak of "working for the *presidente municipal*" (the elected mayor) in the same terms they used when they were rendering tribute labor to a native lord. The very local territorial community persisted or was created again in many places even as its internal organization took different forms. The urban centers of prehispanic times disappeared, but left to itself, rural settlement tended to recreate the rural aspect of Classic and Postclassic settlement systems. The cycles of erosion, soil capture, cultivation, and abandonment play out again in our lifetime. Through all of these continuities we hear the uniformitarian chorus: the processes that we see happening today occurred also in the past and shaped the land and the history of its people.

Political Divisions and Population

Our area lies at the intersection of three districts: Teposcolula, Tlaxiaco, and Nochixtlán (García 1998). In Mexico the basic municipal and territorial political unit is the *municipio*, which has a political center, the *cabecera*. Legally there are various types of places subordinate to a cabecera municipal but here we refer to them all as *agencias*. In our combined project we surveyed in twenty-nine municipios (see Table 1.1; the locations of these places are shown on the settlement pattern maps in Chapters 2–6). We surveyed only parts of some jurisdictions. This means that some of the total municipio population in Table 1.1 is not in our study area. There are also small census locations we surveyed that are not listed in the 1990 agencia population column in Table 1.1. In all, our study area had about 45,000 to 50,000 inhabitants in 1990.

The recent population is relatively sparse and dispersed. Notice the large number of small settlements in Table 1.1. Population fell over the thirty years from 1960 to 1990 in most rural places but it grew in the city of Tlaxiaco. The totals for the whole area in 1960 and 1990 are almost the same. As our results show, the population at AD 1500 and at AD 400 was much higher than that of today and there were more cities. Even in 200 BC the population may have been about the same as that of the twentieth century.

Prior Archaeological Research

This project would not have been possible without the foundational work of Ron Spores (1967, 1972, 1974). Studies of Formative sites in the Mixteca have been carried out by Jorge Acosta and Javier Romero (1992) at Monte Negro, Margarita Gaxiola (1984) at Huamelulpan, Roberto Zárate (1987) and Jeffrey Blomster (1998) at Etlatongo, and Nelly Robles (1988) and Patricia Plunket (1983) at Yucuita. These researchers describe the farming villages of Early Formative times and the growth of social differentiation and political centers in the Middle Formative (Winter et al. 1984; Winter 1994). The site of Yucuñudahui in the Nochixtlán Valley (Caso 1938, 1942; Spores 1972) has been considered the archetypical Classic center in the Mixteca Alta. Yucuita (Plunket 1983) also had substantial Classic occupation.

Excavations by Ignacio Bernal (1949) at Coixtlahuaca and Michael Lind (1977) in Nochixtlán describe social variation in major Postclassic centers. In many instances the local archaeological record can be linked securely to sixteenth-century descriptions and to codices (Byland and Pohl 1994). Spores (1967:90–104), Rodolfo Pastor (1987), Charlotte Smith (1993), and John Monaghan (1994) have described variation in the scale, internal organization, and economic activities of Postclassic kingdoms. Study of the Mixtec codices by Alfonso Caso (1977), Emily Rabin (1979), and many other modern students (see Smith 1973, 1998; Jansen and Reyes García 1997) have established the historicity of the Mixtec kingdom as the form of the state in the Postclassic period.

Balkansky's (1998a) review of all the settlement pattern surveys in the Mixteca Alta identified the major outstanding issues and controversies. We have drawn heavily on the surveys of adjoining and nearby areas: Bruce Byland (1980) in Tamazulapan/Tejupan, Spores (1972) in Nochixtlán, Plunket (1983) in Yucuita, and Byland and John Pohl (1994) in Jaltepec/Tilantongo.

Chronology

Chapter 1 of an archaeological report should always have a chronological table (Table 1.2). Appendix 1 illustrates diagnostic pottery types and outlines the ceramic sequence (see Stiver 2001 for a fuller treatment). Our chronology is derived from those of previously known regions just to the east. We owe a great deal to Spores's and Marcus Winter's superb ceramic knowledge. Plunket's work (1983) also contributed to refining the chronology. Balkansky and Stiver Walsh worked with Huamelulpan and Teposcolula collections for several years before the 1999 project. In addition to the published literature we were helped by study of Mixteca collections at the American Museum of Natural History in New York City, ceramic workshops sponsored by the Instituto Nacional de Antropología e Historia (INAH) in Oaxaca, stratigraphic tests at selected sites carried out by INAH and Spores in the 1990s, and Spores's earlier surface collections from sites in the Mixteca Alta and Baja (Spores 1996). Through study of these collections and ceramics from the Peñoles area it is apparent that even in economically marginal areas where decorated pottery is less frequent, careful attention to surface finish and the details of vessel shape and rim profile often permit discrimination to the time scale of the archaeological periods and phases recognized in the better-documented regions of central Oaxaca (Kowalewski 2003a). Nevertheless the sequence begs for refinement, especially from the Classic through the Postclassic.

SURVEY

Our objective was to produce data on settlements and agricultural and other cultural features comparable to the full-coverage surveys in other parts of the Mesoamerican highlands. One way of conceiving objectives and methods, which we used in our research proposal, was to list the tangible research products stated in terms of systematic data sets. The data sets we proposed and produced were INAH site forms, 1:50,000 maps locating all sites, maps showing survey coverage, sketches of sites having preserved architecture, a ceramic data set listing numbers of each artifact type for each collection area, a lithic data set, measurements for each class of architectural feature (e.g., terrace, mound, plaza, walled structure), map of lama-bordos, photo list, a list of Mixtec toponyms, reports in Spanish for each community, and a final report to INAH (Kowalewski, Heredia et al. 2006).

Field Procedures

The field objectives were to locate and describe all visible archaeological sites (places having the remains of past human facilities), especially (but not limited to) habitation areas, fortifications, and agricultural features; to describe the environmental contexts of sites (topography, soils, water, vegetation, land use, special resources); to place in time sites and components thereof using existing ceramic chronologies; to measure, map, and describe architectural and agricultural features; to examine gully profiles and roadcuts for evidence of buried sites and soils; and to make collections of pottery and stone artifacts roughly and preliminarily representing the main stylistic, functional, and chronological variation present. It was also our objective to train archaeologists from the United States and Mexico in every aspect of diplomatic, field, laboratory, and analytical procedure so that they could carry out systematic regional surveys that meet the highest current standards.

The remainder of this section is a detailed description of field procedures. It will show what data were, how they were collected, and the limitations of these methods.

This section will also serve as an overview of current standards for systematic full-coverage regional settlement pattern survey in this part of the world.

We lived in Tlaxiaco on the western edge of the survey area. Tlaxiaco had more services than any other town, including the biggest, sloppiest hamburgers in Mesoamerica, sold by a man on the plaza. For a time when we were surveying on the eastern side of the area, some of us stayed at a hotel in Nochixtlán. The mountain crew sometimes camped for five days running in the Sierra de Nochixtlán. It was good that the project director was mainly absent and only visited periodically, leaving matters in the competent hands of the field director and crew.

Survey projects run up a lot of vehicle miles. We had two used Jeep Cherokees with "Universidad de Georgia—Departamento de Antropología" logos on the doors so we would not be taken for police, government officials, or *narcotraficantes*. One Jeep worked, the other's problems took us months to diagnose and fix.

Local diplomacy is time-consuming, anxiety-producing, frustrating, and sometimes fun. Permissions must be obtained well in advance of survey. The Centro INAH Oaxaca provided us with letters addressed individually to each district, municipio, and sometimes agencia, directed to the municipal authorities and the Comisariado de Bienes Comunales (in most towns both sets of authorities had to be contacted) (Figure 1.7). Permission also had to be obtained from most agencias—the municipal head town's permission was not sufficient. Diplomatic visits were best done by two people. Taking notes was essential given the number of people and places we had to visit. In this project every place eventually gave us their approval, although along the way there were some interesting misunderstandings, all resolved. We tried to keep officials informed of our schedule and progress.

Towns varied in the form of their official endorsement. We always got written approval in the form of the town's seal and its authority's signatures on a copy of the INAH letter or a letter written by the authority, stamped and sealed. Some towns asked that an official accompany us in the field, which can be good; if an official did come with us, we offered to pay the person a daily wage. Wages were not always accepted. Every crew member and the two vehicles carried copies of permissions. These were sometimes useful at police or military roadblocks.

We spent more time training crew than we had on prior projects. Untrained crew members are less than inefficient. All our crew members were experienced archaeologists but we all had to learn this project's field and lab procedures. The training was worthwhile. Most people need several field seasons to learn a ceramic sequence but basic temporal diagnostics can be learned quickly. Learning how to map component boundaries on a multicomponent site is an essential skill that takes training and experience. Crew members had to learn a common system for sketching architectural plans. Toward the end of the field season we were helped in the field and lab by experienced students from the Escuela Nacional de Antropología e Historia.

Each crew member (Figure 1.8) usually had the following items: pack, hat, sunscreen, water, work boots, pocket knife, black ball-point pens, mechanical pencil, eraser, standard 11 by 16 cm notebook, copy of the database form, list of site num-

1.7 *The palacio municipal, San Agustín Tlacotepec.*

bers available, photocopy of a section of the 1:50,000 INEGI topo map, letters of permission, ID, clipboard, graph paper, millimeter/centimeter scale, compass, rain gear, first-aid kit, plastic bags for collections, tags, string, and food. Binoculars were sometimes useful. Each crew or vehicle had a camera, film, book of blank receipts, GPS, extra set of truck keys, tools, and a road emergency kit for the vehicle (never the right stuff). Two-way radios rarely worked; we will try cell phones next time. In the future we will carry more digital cameras.

"And Don't Come Back Until It's Done"

Regional survey never escapes the tension between two desirable goals—to go quickly and cover a lot of ground versus to go slowly and record as much intrasite detail as possible. That tension begins in the original research proposal and it is felt every day in the field.

Daily and weekly planning and logistics were essential. Each day's work was planned to cover a contiguous block of ground. We called these one-day trips *"vueltas."* Ideally every day a crew made a loop, going out by one route and coming back by another, surveying the way out, the way back, and everything in between, leaving no uncovered area. In other words we planned to cover tracts of land, not to go to sites. We tended to have two two-person crews per vehicle. The perfect vuelta had the vehicle parked in the center and the two crews each doing a loop to completely cover a block of territory, and of course returning to the truck at precisely the

1.8 Laura Stiver Walsh taking notes and Tom Pluckhahn orienting with the topo map at LET 2, a small artifact scatter.

same time. If the topography dictated a single linear pass instead of a loop, such as a long ridge crest, crews walked out and surveyed back. Another tactic was to arrange a drop-off in the morning and a pick-up at the end of the day. In a few situations it was possible for two crews and a vehicle to leap-frog along a road.

How much land does a vuelta cover? On the 1999 project we worked for five months, January to May, and tried to have the equivalent of four two-person crews in the field five days a week, totaling 800 person-days. The 1999 project surveyed 1,343 km² or 3.36 km² per two-person crew per workday. This would be far too much for survey in other circumstances, such as the Teotihuacan Valley or the U.S. Southwest, but in the Mixteca Alta much of the land surface is steep, uninhabited slope, and in those circumstances crews covered the ridge crests and not the uninhabitable slopes.

If average conditions always prevailed, planning a week's survey work would be easy, but conditions were rarely average. We did not know beforehand what archaeological, ethnographic, diplomatic, automotive, topographic, climatic, culinary, or canine events we would encounter. Local permissions came unglued, an accompanying *topil* (village policeman) did not show up, the vehicle did not start, someone came down the wrong ridge and was 2 km from where they were supposed to be, or you ran into a big complicated site at 8:00 A.M.—or worse at 3:30 P.M.—and 4 km from the truck.

There is a syndrome called "survey madness." It occurs late in the afternoon when surveyors are high up and a long way from the truck. They feel a compulsion to cover the remaining terrain in their vuelta; they know it would be inefficient to come back the next day and walk 4 km over ground already surveyed just to complete a piece they think is no more than one knob. But often it is not just one more knob—it is another big descent and climb plus a great Early Ramos site with terraces and mounds. They almost blindly plunge ahead, the sun sinks quickly, they succumb to the compulsion: survey madness. Typically the other crew waits anxiously and impatiently for hours at the agreed meeting place, wondering what happened.

The night before each field day crews laid out their plan of work, vuelta maps, and permission letters. There was always a back-up plan with its vuelta maps and permission letters so if we could not survey in one municipio, we could go to another the same day.

We had two different survey tactics, the choice of which depended on the topography. Gently sloping or flat land called for sweeping back and forth and was best done with three or four people. Mountains required walking all the ridge crests until the slopes were too steep for habitation and walking the toe slopes and the edges of larger streams. Mountain survey was best done with two-person crews. This project had a lot of mountain survey. Knowing when to switch from mountain to valley-floor tactics was important.

Crew members plotted where they surveyed and the direction of their travel on photocopies of the topographic map. Figure 1.9 is the aggregate vuelta map for the 1999 project showing where we surveyed. Vuelta maps were also used to plot archaeological site boundaries and their site numbers, lama-bordos (LB A, B, C . . .), and other points of interest such as *mojoneras* (modern boundary markers, Figure 1.10) or caves. Notebook entries were by site numbers or points marked on the vuelta map. Notebooks and each page were labeled by surveyor's initials, volume, and page number: VYH II:38. Crew members carried a copy of the database form as a reminder of things to record. We did not use printed site forms mostly because they are bulky and often redundant.

Archaeological survey is a mental activity. You think about the land, what it is like now and what it might have looked like in the past; about where to go and look next; about what pattern there might have been to ancient walls and terraces; about sherds and lithics; about dating and component boundaries; about whether tortillas hot off the comal might be begged at the house by the next knob; about the pattern of settlement; about where your crewmates will be in the next five minutes (you always stay in contact, never lose each other); about what you will say when somebody asks if you have permission from Bienes Comunales and you forgot your permission letters; or about why anybody would have lived up on this crag with the nearest water 250 m downhill. You talk and write about what you are thinking.

Experienced survey archaeologists visually attend to the horizon, the lay of the land 20 to 100 m away, the next likely place to see artifacts, where their crewmates are, the map, and the vicious dogs over on the right. Inexperienced surveyors have their heads down looking for artifacts. This bobbing attention, this looking at everything but your feet, means you fall a lot. We do not preach straight transects. A surveyor's actual path wiggles and zigzags back and forth to check the possibilities, following

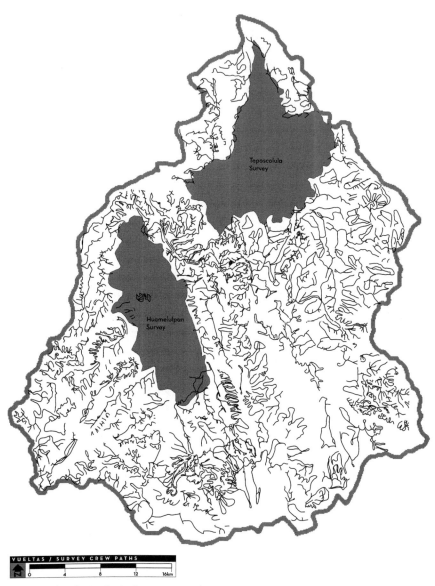

VUELTAS / SURVEY CREW PATHS

0   4   8   12   16km

1.9 General paths (vueltas) of survey crews during the 1999 project.

curiosity. If you are not quite sure where you are on the map or if you cannot figure out a site, resist the tendency to stop; instead keep moving and circle around.

Encountering a site means changing the scale of movement; it does not mean stopping. Typically a crew divides the tasks with one person taking notes and drawing architecture and the other circling about, taking measurements, tracing com-

1.10 Mojonera on Cordón la Corona, marking the boundary between San Miguel Achiutla and San Cristóbal Amoltepec.

ponent boundaries, communicating observations to the notetaker, and plotting site limits on the topo sheet. GPS units were used only occasionally, for example when the forest made it difficult to find a location on the map.

Site boundaries were determined by zigzagging from ground with artifacts or features to sterile ground and back again (how far depended on the terrain). Component boundaries were traced in the same way, which is why surveyors must know the ceramic sequence.

The main purpose of artifact collections was to date components; secondary aims were to gain a preliminary understanding of economic patterns and to amass reference collections for future investigations. Our collection method was opportunistic. Several regional surveys in Oaxaca (Kowalewski 1976; Finsten 1996) have experimented with controlled collection procedures but the results were disappointing in representativeness, information quality, and efficiency. Instead for regional-scale survey in highland Mesoamerica taking numerous opportunistic collections and gathering diagnostic artifacts judged to represent variability within specified proveniences seems to be the best strategy for purposes of dating and gathering basic economic information. We took small opportunistic collections of sherds and only enough lithics (Appendix 2) to represent raw materials, tool types, and PPKs (projectile points/knives). Surveyors regularly made note of many more sherds and stone artifacts than were collected.

Prime collection areas were public architectural complexes, clusters of adjoining residential terraces and other habitation loci, refuse areas below habitation or public construction, and other contexts affording opportunities for dating or gathering economic data. We made notes on each collection area including its size, purpose, and representativeness or target area. We also sought temporally diagnostic artifacts in exposed profiles of buried deposits and ancient construction.

Standard nomenclature and means of recording architecture were followed as best we could (see the Terminology section below). Wherever preservation permitted we made plan sketches of architectural and residential terrace complexes. These sketches were done on graph paper in pencil, usually at 1:1,000 scale, with compass orientation and contour lines impressionistically drawn using the topo maps as a base. We recorded toponyms for sites and other landscape features but not in the ethnographic depth that Byland and Pohl had done (1994). We took photographs with 35 mm film cameras. Each frame was recorded in the notebooks. Smith recorded several hours of fieldwork using a digital video camera.

Laboratory Procedures

The project's principal innovations had to do with data organization. Each of the big Oaxaca survey projects paid more attention to formal data procedures than its predecessor but the Central Mixteca Alta efforts were a giant step forward. John Chamblee built a relational database and geographic information system and everyone kept up with computer work and paperwork daily so there was little backlog.

The original database used the field-numbered site as the object to which all attributes were linked, including artifacts, architecture, photographs, and collections. In the field the three great advantages of the database were that it made us standardize information, it facilitated error checking, and it let us generate INAH site forms. Chamblee built an electronic version of the INAH site form so we were able to hand in all our completed forms before leaving Oaxaca in June 1999. In 2003 Chamblee restructured the database to make the component the central object instead of the field-numbered site. In data analysis the basic unit one tracks through time is the component, not the field-numbered site. Chamblee's revised database dramatically enhanced our ability to retrieve usable information quickly.

The GIS employed digital elevation data, our component shapes and locations, and database data. Chamblee constructed it in 1999 after the field season ended and digitized every component. The GIS topography comes from an Instituto Nacional de Estadística, Geografía, e Informática (INEGI) digital elevation model. The two main advantages of the GIS were that it gave us accurate regional settlement pattern maps (including measurements of component areas) within six months of leaving the field and it made analysis more efficient.

After each day in the field crew members entered their site, UTM, artifact, and architectural information in the database. They made photocopies of their field notes and vuelta maps. The master vuelta map was kept up. Three sets of the six 1:50,000 topo sheets were hung on the walls. One was a site map, another was for off-site features, and the last and psychologically most important showed the progress of the surveyed area—a red blob that grew steadily outward.

Each site had a file folder, filed alphanumerically. The first item in the folder was a page-size photocopied portion of the topo sheet showing the outline of the site. Each component's shape was shown in colored pencil: green for Cruz, blue for Ramos, orange for Las Flores, and red for Natividad, with different shades for phases of these periods. The color coding was not trivial because the same scheme was used in analysis and GIS work. The second page in the site folder was a site summary report from the database. Then followed copies of the field notebook pages and architectural sketches. Lithic and ceramic forms were added when those materials were tabulated. Updated forms were added to folders but the originals were kept.

Roberto Santos and Laura Stiver Walsh inked the architectural sketches to standard form. Later in Atlanta, Charlotte Smith stretched and jiggled the drawings to fit the INEGI air photos. Note that although the final drawings (as in Figures 2.10, 5.52, and similar figures) convey a good sense of the site and have a high-quality, finished appearance, they are based on rapid sketches made with compass and pacing, without the benefit of air photos in the field, and are sometimes incomplete because many architectural features are plowed or eroded away.

Artifact collections were all washed, tabulated, and repackaged for curation while we were in the field. Balkansky did the bulk of the ceramic classification but everyone participated; Stiver Walsh contributed greatly and Kowalewski looked at most of the collections. Collections were often reviewed and discussed. Field crews benefited from quick feedback on ceramics. Later Roberto Santos and Naoli Lona drew and Smith photographed selected sherds.

Projects must design procedures to catch and correct errors. Errors included missing data, bad data, duplicate numbers, failure to update information, data linked to site but not component, different entries in database and GIS, failure to use current version, and introduction of new errors when making corrections. The sooner errors are corrected the better because if they hang around they tend to multiply. Many persistent errors came from sites where there were problems with the original data recording in the field. Sites shared by two map sheets, two crews, two jurisdictions, or apparently any two entities seemed to breed errors. Survey of new areas should not be undertaken in the last few days of a field season, because the haste to finish too often leads to incomplete recording. The lesson is to catch problems the day they are born. At the lab in Athens, Georgia, we kept a lab log in an attempt to head off errors.

We went through three main bouts of error-checking in which every site was reviewed. The first was a check of the database during the fieldwork. This enforced standard entry, filled in missing information, and resolved inconsistencies at a time when all the crew was present. The second bout was in Tlaxiaco at the end of the field season. This focused on confirming that all component sizes and shapes were consistent on maps, on collection forms, in notes, and in the database. The third round of checking took place in Athens after the GIS was completed. In that phase we reviewed each site folder; assigned the intrasite population density levels for each component; reconciled component areas in field notes, database, and the GIS;

and checked all the GIS component shapes, locations, and labels. At this point the database was updated to calculate the population estimates.

Further improvements should be made. Analysis would benefit if more data were accessible by the database and GIS. We still rely on the paper folders for analysis. In the future, surveyors should type the full text of field notes each day (paper notes are still superior to digital notes while on site). Digital images should be linked to the database and GIS. We also need to define component dates and areas and assign attributes to components earlier in the process.

Population Estimates

The purposes of estimating the population of archaeological sites are to allow comparison and to permit quantitative analysis using best approximations of population sizes. We estimated past populations component by component using methods comparable to other systematic regional surveys in highland Mesoamerica (Sanders et al. 1979:38–39; Blanton et al. 1982:11; Kowalewski et al. 1989:35; Stiver 2001: 54–58). Population estimates were determined by two variables: component area and estimated habitation density. Densities were not based on sherds because surface-artifact densities are mostly determined by depositional and visibility factors. Instead we made judgments in the field based on a broad range of factors. Most sites (compact low-density villages) are assigned a density of 10 to 25 persons per ha; lowest-density scattered settlements are assigned 5 to 10 per ha. For isolated residences we use 5 to 10 persons.

Many modern villages in our study area are dispersed. We selected ten for a study of habitation density (Tidaá, Nejapilla, Nuñu, Diuxi, Anama, San Juan Achiutla, Atoyaquillo, San Miguel Achiutla, Tlatayapam, and Huendio). We measured their areas from air photos and obtained their 1970 populations from official INEGI censuses (which may be undercounted in these small places; Kowalewski 2003b). The range is 2.4 to 9.4 persons per ha with an average of 5.9. Although there may be problems with these data, it appears that modern dispersed villages in the Mixteca Alta are within the range of 5 to 10 persons per ha that is used by archaeologists for lowest-density scattered villages.

Residential terraces increased settlement densities dramatically. A sample of ten completely terraced sites from the Valley of Oaxaca where populations were estimated from house counts multiplied by 5 to 10 persons per house yields an average range of 69 to 138 persons per ha. A sample of six sites from Teposcolula has an average range of 50.25 to 100.50 persons per ha. A sample of four from the 1999 project area yields an average of 70 to 140 persons per ha. Three sites in the Valley of Oaxaca intensively mapped by Feinman and Nicholas (2004) have varying densities of terraces: El Palmillo and the Mitla Fortress were heavily terraced and have population estimates based on house counts of 46 to 92 and 54 to 107 persons per ha; Guirún, with much of its area unterraced, has a range of 24 to 49. In this report we use a range of 50 to 100 persons per ha for those portions of sites that were covered by residential terraces.

Sometimes different places within site components may have different densities. If so, we apportioned the total component area into fractions. These subareas were multiplied by one of three density ranges. The component population estimate is the sum of the high and low ranges for the subareas. For example, a settlement of 21 ha might have consisted of 3 ha with residential terraces, a compact low-density area of 8 ha, and a scattered lowest-density area of 10 ha. For the low end of the range the calculation would be (3 ha × 50 persons/ha) + (8 ha × 10 persons/ha) + (10 ha × 5 persons/ha) = 280 persons. The result for the high end would be 600 persons. The average estimate, a figure we often use for convenience in comparisons, is (280 + 600)/2 = 440 persons. We occasionally assigned other densities depending on specific circumstances.

Terminology

In this book "macroregion" refers to multiregional areas and their social systems up to the scale of Mesoamerica. We use "region" to refer to physical or social phenomena covering thousands of km^2, such as the Valley of Oaxaca or the Mixteca Alta. "Subregions" are smaller behavioral and physiographic regions. These subregions reflect the fragmented Mixteca Alta landscape. Most are small valleys partially enclosed by mountains and definable by watersheds or drainages. They are multicommunity places and the smallest unit that encompassed a potentially autonomous polity, the ñuu. They often correspond to today's municipios. Subregions are our descriptive units in Chapters 2–6. Our combined study area, the Central Mixteca Alta (Huamelulpan, Teposcolula, and the 1999 project area), is made up of twenty-six subregions (Figure 1.11).

"Localities" as physiographic places are small enough (a few km^2) to be fairly homogeneous environments such as a small tributary valley; socially they might be the places of a single nucleated settlement and its immediate catchment or a small cluster of dispersed settlement.

A "site" is a place that has evidence of past human use. A "component" is the phase-specific use of a site. In highland Mesoamerica sites are bounded. We use the 100-meter rule for separating sites and components: an unoccupied space of more than 100 m between contemporary prehispanic occupations means two components.

Site designations have letters indicating district, municipio, and agencia (see Table 1.1). These we call "field-numbered sites." (This scheme was mandated by INAH in the 1970s, and highland Oaxaca survey projects have followed it ever since.) Within each agencia, site numbers only roughly follow the order of their discovery as we often had several crews working independently in the same jurisdiction on the same day. There are unused numbers—this is meaningless. We made sure that the last three letters (the agencia prefixes) were unique with no duplicates. Sites can be referred to just by the agencia and number, so GPE 1 is the same as TLA-PMY-GPE 1. Lowercase Roman numerals, as in Late Ramos SAT 9ii, refer to components of the same phase separated by a distance of more than 100 m in the same field-numbered site.

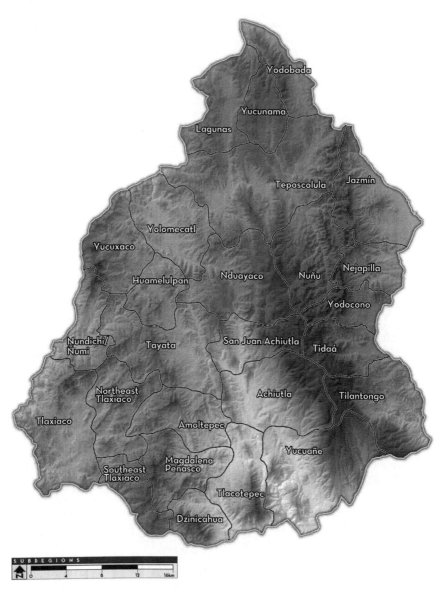

1.11 The subregions of the Central Mixteca Alta study area.

We use "hamlet" (roughly 10–100 inhabitants) and "small village" and "large village" (100–500, 500–1,000) as convenient terms to describe settlement size with no technical or culturally specific meaning implied. Likewise a "town" had more than 1,000 people and usually some diversity in central place functions. "*Ranchería*" is a good term for dispersed settlement, either multiple isolated residences or low-density hamlets or villages.

Certain architectural terms have meanings that must be made explicit. A "structure" (Str.) is a stone or earthen mound that was a platform for a building. A "stone foundation" (S.F.) is the remains of a building at or above ground level in the form of stone walls or floors. "Plazas" (P.) are architecturally defined, flat, open public spaces. A "terrace" (T.) is a flat or gently sloping space created on a slope by filling behind a retaining wall or cutting into the slope. We distinguish between these and agricultural terraces, which may be contour terraces on a hillside or terraces built across a drainage (lama-bordos).

In practice, keeping to these innocent definitions was not always straightforward. Terraces could blend into platforms or structures. Plazas were not always distinguishable from terraces and some open spaces no longer architecturally defined might have been plazas. Distinguishing rock piles, structures, and stone foundations with consistency could keep a tired sherd dog awake at night.

Limitations

This project is a regional surface survey and is subject to the advantages and the limitations of studies at that scale. The grain of the data is coarser than that of single-site studies or excavations but the aim is broad regional and broad temporal coverage, which other methods cannot provide.

Chronological precision is rougher than we would like. Most surveys and many excavations in Mesoamerica deal with change on the ca. 300-year scale. We have difficulty dividing the Postclassic period, which is perhaps 700 years long, into phases that can be distinguished with surface collections. Ceramic dating in more remote areas may not achieve chronological distinctions even to that scale because pottery in marginal areas tends to be undecorated and sometimes the sample sizes are small.

Our information does not cover all of culture. We are not in a position to write a full social history of the Mixteca Alta. Our contribution is based in settlement patterns, a fundamental starting point. We can add a few things about economy, political institutions, social organization, warfare, and ceremonial observances. The interpretations in this volume are often hypotheses that push the data to or beyond their limits. They require further testing with other kinds of information.

CHAPTER TWO

The Western Nochixtlán Valley

Today and in the past the well-watered hills and small valleys on the western side of the Nochixtlán Valley have been favored places for human settlement. The soils are quite fertile but they are easily eroded. Today and in the past farmers have terraced the slopes and drainages to capture and hold the soil and water. Subsequent abandonment of the terraces inevitably leads to further, accelerated erosion, so paradoxically a place that now looks utterly wasted was likely to have been very productive sometime in the past.

The western Nochixtlán Valley readily breaks into five physiographic and cultural subregions, each the valley of a tributary stream separated from its neighbor by volcanic hills and each home to separate sets of communities. From north to south these subregions are Jazmín, Nejapilla, Yodocono, Tidaá, and Tilantongo. Jazmín and Tilantongo, at the opposite ends of the mountain chain, were the dominant places; the three smaller valleys were sometimes independent and sometimes subordinate to one another of their bigger neighbors.

The area has a long history of occupation beginning in Archaic (Preceramic) times. The two larger valleys, Jazmín and Tilantongo, had major clusters of settlement in the Formative period. The three smaller valleys also had a few Formative villages that were probably parts of neighboring communities. This pattern lasted for nearly a thousand years but it was thoroughly disrupted around 300 BC at the beginning of the Ramos period.

The typical Ramos site was a defendable, often fortified hilltop. The most famous of these is Monte Negro in Tilantongo but Monte Negro actually had quite a few peers or rivals. The roots of urbanism in the Mixteca Alta are embedded in these and other Late Formative hilltowns.

The ñuu—the potentially autonomous polity and building block of the state—emerged here in the Classic and Postclassic. Already by the Early Classic the settlement pattern and civic-ceremonial hierarchy was quite like the cacicazgo of the sixteenth century. Each subregion might be considered a ñuu with Jazmín (Yanhuitlán) and Tilantongo being the major players. Yodocono in the Classic might have been an independent statelet. Nejapilla and Tidaá seem to have been subordinate to Jazmín and Tilantongo, respectively.

JAZMÍN

This is the western side of the Yanhuitlán Valley from its head at La Cieneguilla south 13 km to Santiago Tillo (Figure 2.1). Also included are the modern towns of San Pedro Añañe, Xacañi, and Santa María Tiltepec. Above about 2,300 to 2,400 m the bedrock is volcanic, a gray andesite. Below that are the heavily eroded hillsides composed of alternating beds of pink shale and sandstone of the Yanhuitlán Formation. West and south of Cerro Jazmín—the largest archaeological site—the Yanhuitlán beds are dominated by conglomerates. The whole Yanhuitlán Valley has some 80 km^2 of fertile soils derived from these sedimentary beds, one of the largest patches in the Central Mixteca Alta.

Early/Middle Cruz

The area was settled by Middle Cruz times (Figure 2.2, Table 2.1); we found no Archaic evidence. Sites are relatively low in elevation (2,150 to 2,375 m) compared to those of later times. We found no Early/Middle Cruz occupation on Cerro Jazmín itself. Instead Middle Cruz people chose the permanent water and fertile soils of the piedmont. Today these sites are all heavily eroded. One site, TIP 9, is situated at a higher elevation (2,400 m) on an important trail. It is a single-component isolated residence.

The Jazmín subregion had a relatively high population in Cruz times. The total settled area of about 90 ha implies a population of 1,000 to 2,000 people. Most lived on the piedmont ridges northwest of Cerro Jazmín; all the other settlements were small hamlets. We found no Cruz period public architecture. Artifact densities varied from heavy to light depending on local erosion. In some places there were mod-

2.1 The eroding slopes above San Pedro Añañe, seen from the north on the highway between Yanhuitlán and Teposcolula.

erate or heavier concentrations, perhaps indicating individual households. There was considerable continuity of occupation into Late Cruz.

Late Cruz

In the preference for lower elevations near permanent water, the pattern of large villages and hamlets, the overall population size, and in many cases the use of the same sites, Late Cruz was a continuation of the Middle Cruz pattern (Figure 2.3, Table 2.2). The pottery suggests continued occupation in the earlier and later phases of Late Cruz. All settlements were between 2,100 and 2,270 m in elevation on the red soils of the piedmont; the volcanic cap above 2,300 m was not yet used for habitation.

The total population may have been around a thousand people. This figure is a little lower than in the previous phase mainly because we did not find Late Cruz at the large XAC 4 site. As in Middle Cruz, no single site can be identified as preeminent. Population clustered on the hills at Xacañi and San Pedro Añañe. The southern flanks of Cerro Jazmín at Tillo and Tiltepec were only lightly occupied.

On top of a hill in the piedmont near Tillo is a 10 by 7 m low mound. This is the center of the TLO 7 site, a multicomponent occupation. Cruz pottery occurs around the mound but so does that of Las Flores and Natividad. This would be the only candidate for Cruz period mounded architecture here. However, further east in the Yanhuitlán Valley Spores (1972:83, 90–91) found platform mounds and Cruz pottery at Loma Taza and Dequedená.

2.2 Early/Middle Cruz sites in Jazmín.

Ramos

All of the Cruz settlements were abandoned at the beginning of Ramos (Figure 2.4, Table 2.3). We list only one Ramos site in the piedmont and that is based on one bridge spout at the Late Cruz site of SPA 6. Except for this and one small site on a mountain above Cieneguilla in Ramos everyone lived atop Cerro Jazmín, which had not been occupied earlier. The peak of Cerro Jazmín is 2,480 m; the average ele-

2.3 Late Cruz sites in Jazmín.

vation for the Ramos component is 2,380 m. Ramos period people lived above what had been their favored red soils; now they were on the cap of gray andesite. Water would have been available in springs within or just below the settlement. Six major lama-bordos radiate down from Cerro Jazmín. They may have begun in Ramos.

Cerro Jazmín was one of Oaxaca's major towns in the Late Formative. The occupation covers almost 80 ha including the top of the mountain, its broad and more gently sloping eastern and northeastern slopes, and the ridges descending to the west, northeast, and south. This whole area is covered by residential and public

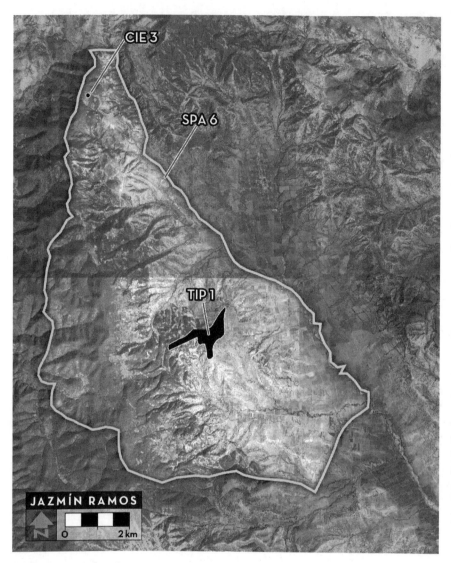

2.4 Ramos sites in Jazmín.

terraces. The top of the hill could have had long concentrically arranged terraces in the Late Formative mode but Las Flores and later construction may have modified the earlier configuration. The midslope terraces on the east and northeast sides may also be post-Ramos constructions in old Ramos residential areas. Population was undoubtedly quite high, between 4,000 and 8,000 people. Cerro Jazmín probably drew people from our Jazmín subregion, from the rest of the Yanhuitlán Valley, and perhaps from elsewhere.

The site had significant Ramos public architecture. There was also Las Flores and Natividad construction and use rendering the Ramos configurations difficult to interpret without excavations. Nevertheless, Ramos material was found on and around nine mounds. There are three distinct mound and plaza groups. Near the top of the site is a linear arrangement of a small structure, a plaza, and then a second mound on the narrow peak of the mountain. This was the most secluded part of the site. Down about 100 m to the east and well within the Ramos town is a second mound complex with two plazas. One plaza is flanked by platform mounds on three sides; the other has two mounds in an L arrangement, one of which is also the south mound of the first plaza. The third cluster of public buildings is about 500 m northeast of the top of the mountain. It consists of three mounds forming two plazas. These architectural elements (the linear string and two separate two-plaza groups with mounds in an L arrangement or enclosing three sides of plazas) are found at other Ramos-only sites in the Mixteca Alta. Cerro Jazmín's nine platform mounds in three groups place it in the top tier of Ramos civic-ceremonial places.

The pottery at Cerro Jazmín is consistent with an occupation limited to Early Ramos. Conceivably, a slight Late Ramos occupation could be hidden by the Early Ramos and Las Flores components but the site lacks the decorated and distinctive pottery one would expect of an important Late Ramos town.

Interestingly, the small site of CIE 3, situated high above the pass between the northern Yanhuitlán and Teposcolula valleys, is a Late (not Early) Ramos occupation. This is the only Late Ramos site in the Jazmín subregion, which must have been largely abandoned.

Las Flores

In the Early Classic, Cerro Jazmín became one of Oaxaca's leading cities. There was also rural settlement in the basin of the Barranca Cacalote just south of Cerro Jazmín (Figure 2.5, Table 2.4). The northern part of the subregion, which had seen substantial Cruz settlement, remained deserted. The abandonment of the northwestern Yanhuitlán Valley corresponds to a similar lack of rural settlement across the mountains in the northern Teposcolula Valley where the Las Flores population was consolidated into three large sites.

Rural settlement favored the piedmont, the soils of the Yanhuitlán beds, and the permanent water of small streams between the steep slopes to the west and the flat valley floor. Most rural people lived between 2,100 and 2,200 m. This rural non–Cerro Jazmín population was substantial, about 2,700 people according to our average estimate.

The urban population was much larger. The Las Flores size of Cerro Jazmín was 229 ha, all of which was high-density, terraced occupation, yielding an average estimate of 17,000 people (about the size of Early Classic Monte Albán and Jalieza in the Valley of Oaxaca). The better-preserved parts of the city are on the upper slopes above 2,300 m where the bedrock is andesite, not the easily eroded conglomerates. Here the terraces are grand in scale, long, broad, and high at the retaining

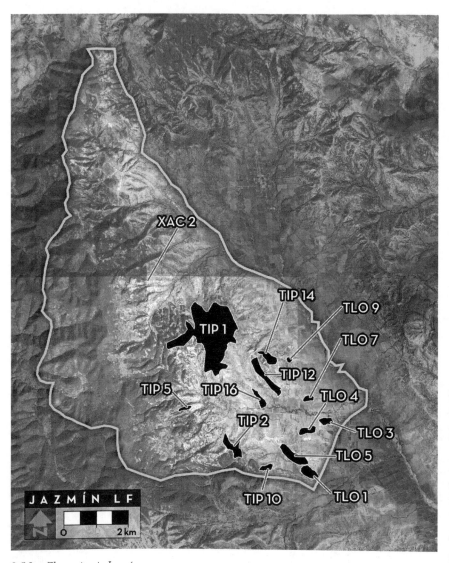

2.5 Las Flores sites in Jazmín.

wall (Figure 2.6). These terraces had multiple dwellings as at Monte Albán. Much of the site must have been planned.

A remarkable feature of Cerro Jazmín is its internal street network. Climbing from the east one encounters the lower end of the main ancient road at about 2,420 m, well within the site boundary. This ascends to the west straight up the slope and soon meets the two other roads, which branch off to the north and south. The north road follows the contour around through the residential areas on the north side of

2.6 Cerro Jazmín, north side, long residential terrace with high retaining walls in back and front and cut building stone on surface.

the mountain (Figure 2.7) and services the Str. 7–9 plaza group as well. The south road passes through terraced areas before dropping in elevation and heading down the south ridge toward Tiltepec. The main street continues straight up to the west between residential terraces. Small stairs give access from the street to adjoining residential terraces (Figure 2.8). The street passes by Plaza 3, the southern of the two mound-and-plaza groups. The street culminates in a stairway 20 m long and 5 m wide, with *alfardas* (side walls). The stairway leads up to Str. 2, which in turn gives access to Plaza 1 and Str. 1 at the very top of the mountain. All three roads are 2 to 3 m wide, are well defined by stone side walls, and often have stone paving and steps. Intra-urban roads are common at hilltop sites of the Classic period in Oaxaca but these have well-preserved detail and excellent associations with prehistoric urban neighborhoods. Dating is not certain because of the strong representation of Ramos and Natividad components.

Cerro Jazmín was in the top tier of Classic civic-ceremonial centers in the Mixteca Alta to judge from the number and size of mounds and the variety of arrangements. There was a linear string of mound-plaza-mound accessed only by the formal stairway and two separate two-plaza mound groups (Figure 2.9). Similar elements are found at other single-component Ramos and Las Flores centers. Cerro Jazmín is distinctive in the relatively large size of its mounds, their number, and especially its urban design.

TLO 7 has a single mound that could date to this period, and TLO 3, at the edge of Tillo, has a three-mound group plus two other mounds, all sharing a common

2.7 A section of the north road, Cerro Jazmín. Note the stone walls on both sides.

2.8 Cerro Jazmín, east side. Road is center-left, with broad residential terraces on both sides. Jackie Saindon, Verónica Pérez.

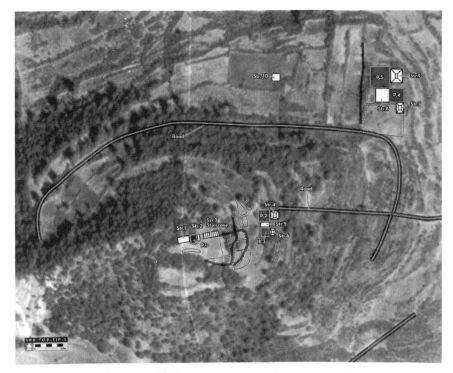

2.9 Roads and mound groups at Cerro Jazmín. Only a few of the terraces are shown.

platform (Figure 2.10). We do not know how much of this construction is Las Flores and how much is Natividad.

In Las Flores the Jazmín polity probably spread south to include the secondary center at Topiltepec (TOP 1) and nearby sites in the Nejapilla subregion. TOP 1 has six mounds, including two large L-shaped plaza groups and a mound 6 m high. An undated, fortified site, XAC 8, could go with the Classic occupation of Cerro Jazmín. It is described in the following section.

The ceramics point to an Early Classic occupation with only a few hints of lingering Late Classic settlement in a few places. Only a few sherds here and there, not whole collections, are similar to the shapes and finish of Monte Albán IIIB–IV. There is no ceramic transition into Natividad from this Early Las Flores complex. We think the Jazmín subregion was again mostly abandoned in the Late Classic/ Epiclassic (Late Las Flores).

Natividad

This was the time of greatest population and most extensive settlement. We recorded thirty-nine sites with a total occupied area of over 11 km², which is about

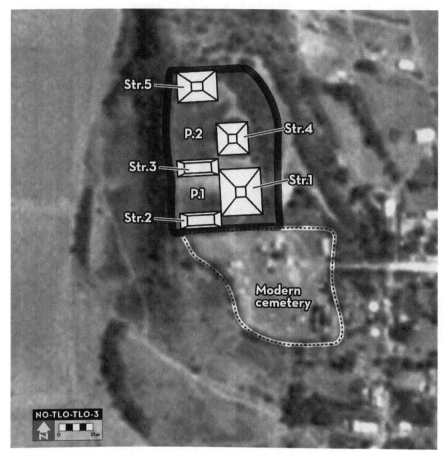

2.10 Focal architecture at TLO 3.

a fifth of the land area of this subregion (Figure 2.11, Table 2.5). Añañe, Xacañi, Tillo, and Tiltepec all had substantial settlements. This evenness of occupation did not occur in earlier periods.

All the large villages are between 2,100 and 2,300 m, the upper reaches of the Yanhuitlán beds where numerous lama-bordos begin. These sites extended along the ridge crests and upper slopes of piedmont hills, accounting for their long, linear form. In many cases Natividad artifacts are abundant and dense. For the most part this was fairly dense not dispersed settlement. Today these hills are so eroded that ridges are gnawed to narrow and precarious edges and exposed ground is often bare endeque. Sometimes the erosion sweeps everything away but the artifacts and building stones; in other cases the artifacts are washed down and found in improbable gullies. The site outlines we defined are where the Natividad people lived, not where their artifacts ended up.

2.11 *Natividad sites in Jazmín.*

Only a few small sites occur above 2,300 m. Some of these may have had special functions. There are accounts of hilltop special-use sites in the Inquisition proceedings against the *cacica* of Yanhuitlán (Sepúlveda y Herrera 1999:77–78, 83). CIE 3, at 2,560 m, is the same place that had an unusual Late Ramos occupation. SPA 4 had Natividad and Colonial occupation. SPA 5 has an unusual cream-colored chert not seen on other sites in this area and the cores and flakes suggest production.

2.12 Yanhuitlán from the top of Cerro Jazmín. The sixteenth-century Dominican monastery is in the center of the picture. Note bromeliad on the oak tree, left, and tree with large white flowers, right. Citing Spores, Byland and Pohl (1994:102–103) associate the name "Jazmín" with a tree with white flowers and place signs in Mixtec codices.

XAC 8 is a fortified site 3 km west of Cerro Jazmín on a high peak on the divide between Teposcolula and Yanhuitlán. It has a rock wall 3 m high blocking the saddle north of the peak where a main east-west trail crosses the divide. No artifacts were found so XAC 8 is undated. It might pertain to Las Flores or Natividad.

The urban center of the Yanhuitlán Valley during Natividad was Cerro Jazmín (Figure 2.12). The Natividad occupation is the largest component at this site, covering 5.8 km². Cerro Jazmín is not a case of casual, ephemeral, or special-use of an earlier Classic site—the Natividad occupation was dense. We estimate that two-thirds of the site was inhabited at urban, terraced densities. Natividad ceramics are found consistently over the old core of the site above 2,300 m. On the ridges descending to the piedmont on the north, east, and south, Natividad is the best-represented period. Occupation extended all the way down to the present-day villages of Río Grande on the north, Jazmín on the east, and Tiltepec on the south. Living on these slopes would have required terraces but we could not map terraces on the lower slopes because of erosion. Our mean estimate for the population of Cerro Jazmín is 32,000; even the lower estimate of 21,000 is surprisingly large. Again the reason we reach these large numbers is because of the areal extent of the site and the fact that this was a dense occupation (even a standard density of 10–25 people/ha gives a mean estimate of 10,000 people but this density is far too low for the quantity of artifacts and residential construction).

Cerro Jazmín had eleven mounds in use in Natividad. This puts the city into the second rank of civic-ceremonial places in the study area (the Pueblo Viejo at Teposcolula has much more public architecture). There was little new construction; almost all was reuse of platforms constructed in earlier periods. However, at least some of this reuse was quite substantial. The civic-ceremonial center of Cerro Jazmín was the two plazas and three mounds (Strs. 7–9) on the northeastern lobe of the mountain. This complex is well located on the ancient road system and it has broad, open, flat areas that may have been public spaces. Adjacent to Strs. 7–9 are abundant obsidian blades, some quite long, and Fine Cream brazier and censer fragments, indicating ritual activities. On the same ground there are also domestic wares and fancy and exotic bowls (Fondo Sellado, Polychrome, possibly Texcoco Red). One might speculate what relation this Strs. 7–9 complex had with the Colonial cacique's house in Yanhuitlán. Perhaps it was the earlier seat of power.

The group of five mounds at TLO 3 and the single mound at TLO 7 are the only other places with civic-ceremonial architecture in use in this period. The Jazmín subregion did not have much new mound construction in spite of the large increase in population.

NEJAPILLA

Nejapilla is our name for the basin of the Río Nejapilla and the Barranca Cayua on the eastern flank of the Sierra de Nochixtlán. The northern side of the basin is the Cerro Topiltepec, an andesite mass similar to Cerro Jazmín. The southern limit of this valley pocket is the limestone mountain Debueyuculuchi. The basin itself is formed from the sandstones and conglomerates of the Yanhuitlán beds. There are four municipios here: Santo Domingo Tlatayapam, San Pedro Topiltepec, Santo Domingo Tlachitongo, and Santiago Nejapilla, all of which pertain to the district of Teposcolula.

Archaic

Nejapilla has fair evidence for human presence in the Archaic. SDT 10 and 11 are on the northwestern flank of the Cerro Debueyuculuchi where there are two cliffs known as the Peña del Aguila and the Peña de la Virgen, ritually important in prehistoric and historic times. SDT 10 is a rock-art site. It consists of a red-painted human figure and higher up on the cliff another red-painted fragment. SDT 11 is a rockshelter that measures 10 by 15 m. The cave ceiling is blackened by smoke. Without excavation there is no way to tell if there are intact Archaic deposits.

We think two open sites may have Archaic remains. NEJ 15 is 3 km northwest of Nejapilla across the divide on a plateau (elevation 2,500 m) overlooking the upper reaches of the Río Negro. This would have been an excellent location for an Archaic hunting camp; it does not fit with later settlement patterns since the Río Negro gorge was hardly settled at all in ceramic times. It is a lithic scatter covering an area 200 by 100 m; there are no ceramics. Artifacts consist of large tertiary and

2.13 Early/Middle Cruz sites in Nejapilla.

secondary flakes and expedient tools. Materials are white and gray chert and a little quartz. The second possible Archaic site would be an extensive chert scatter within the large TGO 1 site on the hill just north of Tlachitongo. Further research is necessary to determine whether these four sites were in fact Archaic.

Early/Middle Cruz

The only Early/Middle Cruz site is SDT 1 near the Tlatayapam cemetery (Figure 2.13, Table 2.6). It was a small hamlet. The nearest head town would have been Etlatongo, 6 km east.

Late Cruz

There are five Middle Formative sites, all small hamlets. The favored situation was on low hills just above permanent water (Figure 2.14, Table 2.6). SDT 7 has at least one large mound (on which the village cemetery is situated). Spores had found the Cruz site in the middle of Topiltepec (his N070, our TOP 3) and we recovered more sherds. The total population of the Nejapilla subregion in Late Cruz was about 200 inhabitants.

Ramos

All the previously inhabited places were abandoned before the beginning of Ramos. People concentrated into two hilltop towns (Figure 2.15, Table 2.7), Cerro

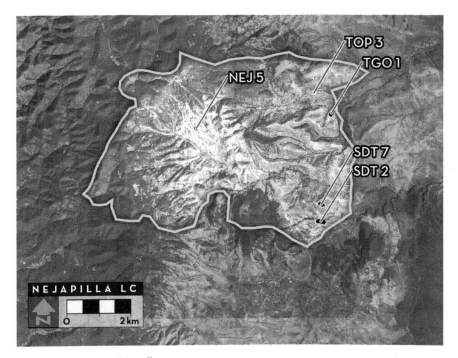

2.14 Late Cruz sites in Nejapilla.

Topiltepec and Loma Xatacahua (Loma del Baño), which are the hills defining the northern and southern edges of this valley. The sites are about 180 m above the local valley floor and at least 100 m higher than the Cruz settlements.

Loma Xatacahua is on a ridge and saddle north of the Cerro Debueyuculuchi. Unfortunately, it has been so plowed and modified by modern agriculture that its terraces and platform mounds can no longer be identified or mapped. There had been several platforms with mounds and there were terraces on both the east and west sides of the ridge. This layout is similar to that of the better-preserved sites SBY 3 and SPT 3. It must have been a substantial village. We estimate it covered 11 ha and had 800 people.

Cerro Topiltepec is better known for its Las Flores component but it began in Early Ramos. Early Ramos sherds are found around the top of the hill covering some 10 ha. The Ramos terracing was undoubtedly modified later. Topiltepec has two large plazas, each defined by two mounds in an L arrangement (as at Cerro Jazmín and several other Mixteca Alta sites of the Late Formative). There are two other mounds. Like Loma Xatacahua, Topiltepec had about 800 inhabitants.

The Ramos in Nejapilla is Early Ramos. The subregion was abandoned in Late Ramos. The notably higher population in Early Ramos is difficult to derive from the small hamlets of Late Cruz. A likely source would be the piedmont to the east—the Etlatongo area.

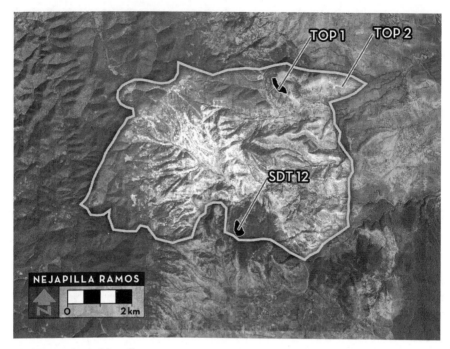

2.15 Ramos sites in Nejapilla.

Las Flores

After the Late Ramos abandonment, Nejapilla was re-inhabited in Early Las Flores (Figure 2.16, Table 2.8). Cerro Topiltepec was larger than it had been before, and Loma Xatacahua was reoccupied and was about the same size as it had been in Ramos. Six small villages and hamlets were founded at lower elevations, and three sites were placed atop the high divide of the Sierra de Nochixtlán, perhaps for defense.

The town of Cerro Topiltepec reached its maximum size at this time with perhaps 4,000 people living on residential terraces that covered 66 ha. Its six mounds and two large plazas (Figure 2.17) place it in the second tier of civic-ceremonial centers in the Mixteca Alta. In some sense Topiltepec must have been secondary to Cerro Jazmín, only 5 km away and clearly visible. Topiltepec in turn was the dominant civic-ceremonial center for the Nejapilla subregion. Loma Xatacahua (Loma del Baño) probably had public architecture too but it must have been smaller in scale. None of the smaller villages and hamlets had public architecture.

The Las Flores settlement pattern was similar to that of Early Ramos in Nejapilla in that the two main sites were on the high hills that define the sides of the basin. The differences are that in Las Flores, Cerro Topiltepec had a much larger population, there were smaller villages at lower elevations (in Ramos there was virtually no such settlement), and there were sites on Nejapilla's western boundary.

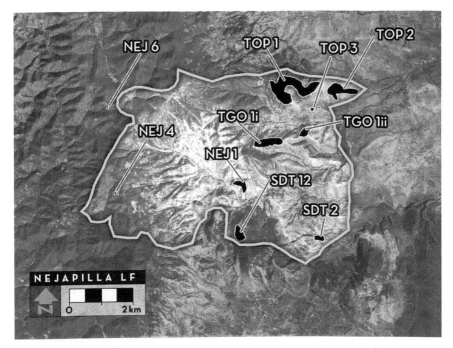

2.16 Las Flores sites in Nejapilla.

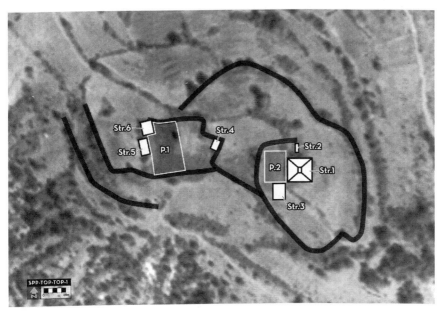

2.17 Focal architecture at TOP 1, Cerro Topiltepec.

Three small sites were established on the divide between 2,600 and 2,800 m in elevation. NEJ 2 is on top of a peak about 1 km north of the Cerro Cabano and 3 km west of the town of Nejapilla. It has a commanding view of the Nochixtlán Valley. The northern approach to the peak is fortified by a ditch and wall, a second ditch and wall, and possibly more terrace retaining walls. On top of the peak is a possible structure. The approach from the southeast is fortified by a ditch, a wall, and perhaps seven terrace retaining walls. The other approach is from the west but it is quite steep and near the top there are several terrace retaining walls. The ditches are 1 to 2 m deep. Terraces were small, for example 12 by 3 m, 9 by 2 m, and 10 by 3 m. The site is in oak forest and ground visibility is poor. No artifacts were found so the site is undated; however, there is a strong Las Flores presence at nearby NEJ 4.

NEJ 4 is 200 m down from the fortified peak of NEJ 2 on flatter ground. In the recent past it had been used for agriculture and is now covered by secondary growth, into which the survey crew ventured to find Las Flores domestic wares and white chert flakes. This is a single-component site.

NEJ 6 is situated on the same divide about 2.5 km to the north on the pass between Nejapilla and the Nuñu Valley to the west. It has both Las Flores and Natividad domestic wares. A lama-bordo heads at the edge of the site. The occupation extends from a peak, on which there is a looter's pit in a possible mound, down the slope and into a saddle. The saddle has retaining walls 1 m high on both sides. Other than its situation atop a high peak on the divide, NEJ 6 is not a special defensive site and it is not fortified. The whole site covers only 0.3 ha so the flat saddle is probably too small for a market plaza.

Nejapilla was largely abandoned again in Late Las Flores. Most of the ceramics fit only into Early Las Flores, but a few conical bowls with G-35 finish at Cerro Topiltepec and Loma Xatacahua could also date to the Late Classic.

Natividad

The heaviest occupation in Nejapilla was in Natividad. Almost all the sites ever occupied were inhabited in this period. All four modern towns have multiple Natividad sites in their territories and all had large villages. Settlements were spread over the entire basin with habitation sites ranging from 2,100 to 2,460 m (Figure 2.18, Table 2.9). The larger sites are at lower elevations; those on upper slopes are smaller. Residential sites were oriented toward farming the Yanhuitlán soil slopes and lama-bordos. Today the area is extremely eroded.

The largest settlements in extent and in population were not hilltop terraced sites as was the case earlier. In Natividad the largest sites were the sprawling settlements (TGO 1, 2) that covered the piedmont hills between Tlachitongo and Topiltepec. These hills rise only 130 m or so above the permanent streams at their base. Natividad remains are found on a total of 278 ha and we estimate a total of 5,000 people. The Cerro Topiltepec was the next-largest site with about 1,500 inhabitants. The other villages had between 50 and 500 inhabitants each. Our mean estimate for the total population of Nejapilla (if all the places were inhab-

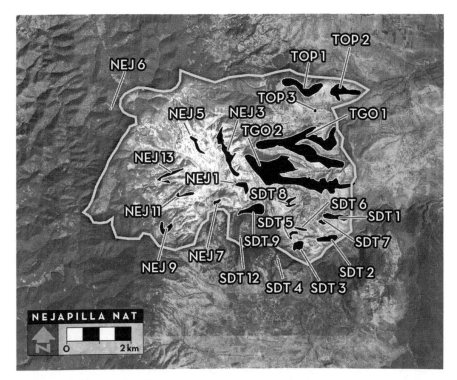

2.18 *Natividad sites in Nejapilla.*

ited at the same time of course) is 9,300, several times greater than the modern population.

Nejapilla in Natividad had little public architecture. There is a single mound at SDT 7 associated with this period. The tiny reoccupation at Loma Xatacahua is not enough to account for anything more than very occasional use of whatever mounds may have existed. There is no Natividad occupation around the Cerro Topiltepec mounds (the Natividad settlement is on the next hill to the east). In the absence of civic-ceremonial architecture it is difficult to identify a leading political center.

YODOCONO

Yodocono is a basin of some 25 km² on the eastern flank of the Sierra Nochixtlán. It is limited on the north by the limestone block of the Cerro Debueyuculuchi and on the south by Cerro Yucuayuxi, an andesite hill. This valley pocket has a narrow outlet to the northeast but the eastern side (outside our survey area boundary) is blocked by a ridge called La Cumbre. The flows of water from the mountainsides on the west are mostly captured in the alluvium of the valley floor. The valley floor of 4 km² is the largest patch of Quaternary alluvium outside of the main river bottoms in

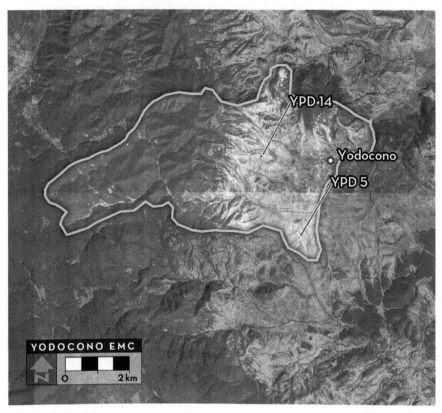

2.19 Early/Middle Cruz sites in Yodocono.

the Nochixtlán Valley. However, the floor of the basin is quite a bit higher (150 m) than the neighboring valleys to the north. We surveyed only the western two-thirds of the Yodocono basin.

Early/Middle Cruz

We found no Archaic sites. The earliest sites date to Middle Cruz. They are situated on low piedmont hills with access to perennial streams or are adjacent to the valley floor alluvium (Figure 2.19, Table 2.10). It is possible that older sites are buried by recent alluvium.

YPD 14 is a small single-component site on a heavily eroded piedmont hill at the edge of the mountains about 1 km away from the flat valley floor. There were many artifacts on the surface, perhaps dug out by a looter. At YPD 5 one of our collections had several sherds that probably indicate a Middle Cruz occupation but the Late Cruz component is much larger. Adjacent to YPD 5 but on the lands of San Pedro Tidaá is a larger (7.3 ha) Middle Cruz site, SPT 7. These three settlements

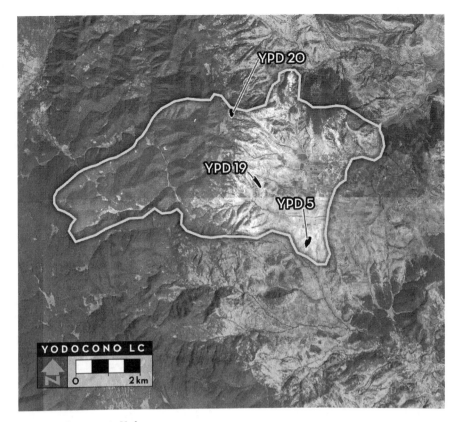

2.20 Late Cruz sites in Yodocono.

may have been outliers of Etlatongo or of Tilantongo, which is closer and more easily reached.

Late Cruz

Between Middle and Late Cruz two of the three settlements were abandoned and one, YPD 5, grew in size. Overall, slightly higher elevations on piedmont ridges back from the valley floor were favored in Late Cruz (Figure 2.20, Table 2.11). The total population grew to perhaps 500 people. Yodocono was a separate cluster of settlement by Late Cruz. Yet none of the sites have mounds and none stands out as a center.

We recorded five Late Cruz sites; all share similar pottery that suggests a date equivalent to Monte Albán Early I. Two sites, SPT 9 and 11, are on the lands of Tidaá but they are close to the Yodocono sites and clearly belong to the same cluster in Late Cruz. SPT 9 and 11 and YPD 19 are on fairly narrow upper piedmont ridges that have good arroyos on both sides.

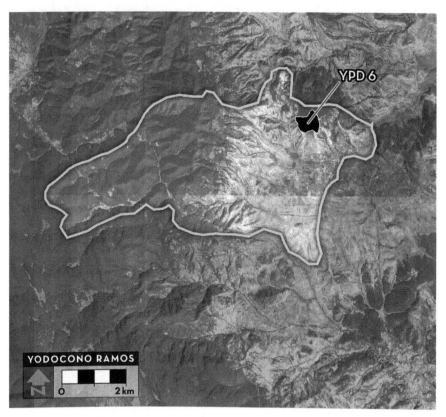

2.21 Ramos sites in Yodocono.

YPD 20 is in a very unusual location for a Cruz site. It is at 2,600 m at the base of the volcanic rock cliff that is the last ascent to the high divide. This is very rocky and eroded ground. YPD 20 is not a dubious Late Cruz site—it is a single-component occupation with domestic ceramic wares and white chert flakes. We saw no evidence of special activity.

Ramos

At the beginning of Ramos there was a total shift in settlement. Every Cruz site was abandoned. A new site (YPD 6) was founded on Cerro Debueyuculuchi on the north edge of the valley (Figure 2.21, Table 2.12). In effect, people moved away from the mountains to a pyramidal-shaped hill that is steep on all sides and rises 220 m above the valley floor. This new settlement may have been larger in population than the total combined size of the Late Cruz population in the area we surveyed.

Locally, the site is called La Coronita. Its top has an encircling wall, a dense artifact scatter, and a poorly preserved mound. Several other rises may have been mounds but it is now impossible to tell. Here and there are remains of residential terraces: toward the saddle to the east, on the south, and on the steep western slope. The sherd density suggests a major habitation site. The settlement may have been continuous with SDT 12 but there are several hundred meters of steep slope and dense vegetation between them. La Coronita with or without SDT 12 would have been a large settlement in Early Ramos. We think it had a high density of habitation, and given its size it would have had at least 1,000, perhaps 2,000 people.

At the beginning of Early Ramos in every subregion along the eastern front of the Sierra de Nochixtlán from Yanhuitlán to Tilantongo people abandoned their Cruz settlements in the piedmont and constructed fortified hilltowns. These were situated not backed up against the mountains but out several kilometers to the east on conical hills on the northern or southern edges of the valley pockets. Cerro Jazmín, Cerro Topiltepec, YPD 6/SPT 12 on Cerro Debueyuculuchi, and Cerro Yucuayuxi at Tidaá all fit this pattern. The next to the north was El Fortín at San Juan Teposcolula; the next to the south was Monte Negro. All of these had populations equal to or greater than their subregional populations of the prior Cruz phase.

Las Flores

We found no Late Ramos sites in Yodocono. Like its neighbors, this subregion was abandoned in the Terminal Formative and reoccupied in the Early Classic. The Las Flores settlements were diverse in their environmental situations. Two were on the edge of the valley floor, five were on hills in the piedmont, and two were in the mountains (Figure 2.22, Table 2.12). La Coronita (YPD 6), the Early Ramos hilltown, was reoccupied in Las Flores and it had the subregion's largest population.

The outstanding Las Flores site was Yucunee (YPD 1), built on a mountain peak at 2,820 m. YPD 1 is on the high divide overlooking the whole Yodocono Valley, the head of the Río Grande that flows northwest to Nuñu and Teposcolula, and trails running north-south and east-west (Figure 2.23). It is too high and the slopes are too steep for agriculture. Yucunee was the major civic-ceremonial center for Yodocono. Its ten mounds and large plazas put it in the same top rank as Cerro Jazmín but its residential area was small and it probably had only a couple hundred inhabitants. Yucunee's public architecture was built to impress. The site has a linear string of platforms, plazas, and mounds on the peaks of the ridgetop, surrounded by a tight oval of concentric terraces, retaining walls, and roads (Figure 2.24). The architecture is unusually well preserved. The lower north end of the complex has a platform with a mound at its end. The drop-off from the back of the structure was 4.5 m plus the slope below to Terrace 20. In the other direction, to the south, this platform drops to another platform or plaza, Str. 8. At the south end is Str. 7, a mound 2 m high. Continuing south the ridge slopes up over the bedrock to the front of a platform 5 m high that supports another plaza. At the opposite, south end of the plaza the next and highest platform, built on the peak of the mountain, steps up another 3.5 m. This platform supports an unusual configuration: two rectangular

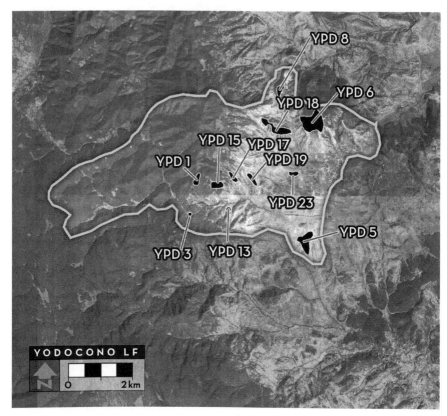

2.22 Las Flores sites in Yodocono.

enclosures that open on one side and two other mounds. This is the most secluded part of the site. The footprint of the whole public architectural complex extends for 250 m and is 50 m wide at its widest.

Yucunee was the leading center but other places had lesser civic-ceremonial functions. The low-elevation village at YPD 5 had a platform with an almost destroyed mound on top of it. Here we saw a disturbed burial with scattered human bone, two pieces of shell, green and gray obsidian blades, and a greenstone pendant. Las Flores is the predominate period in the ceramics at this mound but Natividad, Ramos, and Cruz are also present at the site. There was at least one mound at La Coronita and there may have been public architecture at SDT 12, the site on the same ridge north of La Coronita. YPD 8 had a Las Flores mound.

In all, this Yodocono cluster appears to be an integrated system of settlements with different functions. The inhabitants of several villages were probably involved in valley-floor agriculture; higher piedmont settlements may have practiced lama-bordo and contour terrace farming. The largest town was probably at La Coronita but the most important civic-ceremonial place was high up on the mountain at

2.23 Yucunee, looking north from the western slopes of Cerro Chiyuco. The photographer was at an elevation of about 2,600 m and the top of YPD 1 is at 2,820 m. Note the vertical erosion cut at the bottom of the picture.

Yucunee. YPD 3 may be a special-function site. It is in the mountains at 2,580 m on a flat spot with trails nearby. It has a little Las Flores and Natividad pottery and white chert.

Perhaps all of these sites were not occupied at the same time. Yucunee, perhaps La Coronita, and several of the other larger villages probably pertain to the earliest Early Las Flores (equivalent to Transición II–IIIA). The collection resembles that of the Cerro Encantado in Tlaxiaco, which is clearly Transición. La Coronita appears to be Early Las Flores as does YPD 8; YPD 15 seems to be Late Las Flores and YPD 5 may begin in Early Las Flores and continue into Late Las Flores.

The Las Flores population of Yodocono was probably somewhat larger than that of the Ramos period. Our estimates are a low of 2,200 and a high of 4,700. Given uncertainties about the density of La Coronita and the probable non-contemporaneity of settlements, the lower figure may be more accurate in this case.

Natividad

The Postclassic population was dispersed in several villages and numerous hamlets. There were no large centers. No places have evidence of mounded architecture in use in this period. There was a wide range of site settings from low hills near the valley floor to upper piedmont ridges; a few small sites were in the mountains (Figure 2.25, Table 2.13). Above 2,450 m all sites are small. The larger villages are situated between 2,300 and 2,400 m in the piedmont above the valley floor.

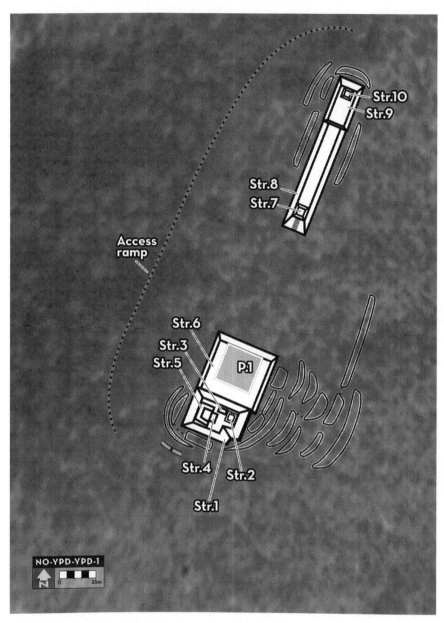

2.24 Architecture at Yucunee, YPD 1.

These sites were severely eroded. In some places artifacts that clearly had been on a ridgetop were found well downslope and the former settlement had been reduced to rock and endeque. The heavy erosion is attributed to the erodible soils

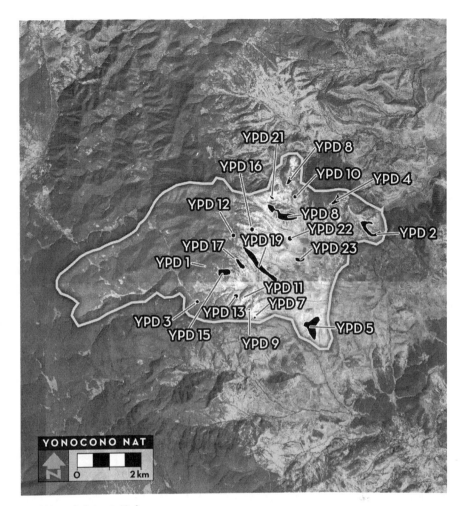

2.25 *Natividad sites in Yodocono.*

of the Yanhuitlán beds, intensive farming, the abandonment of terraces, grazing, and forest clearing.

The site known locally as the Pueblo Viejo is YPD 2 on the outskirts of the modern town of Yodocono de Porfirio Díaz. Natividad artifacts are found just downslope from the church and continue for 800 m up to the residential area of the modern town. YPD 22, a small hamlet on a hill 1 km west of Yodocono, still has portions of house foundations visible on the surface, scattered human bone, and fairly abundant artifacts.

The total population was around 1,800 people. Yodocono and its southern neighbor Tidaá were not as densely populated in Natividad as Tilantongo to the south or Nejapilla and Jazmín to the north. Today Yodocono's people live in four

2.26 San Pedro Tidaá, looking south-southwest from SPT 3.

clusters, or barrios, which are themselves dispersed. A pattern something like that seems to have been true in Natividad too, when there were four larger villages and numerous small hamlets.

TIDAÁ

Our Tidaá subregion is the valley of the Río Yuteluchi and the Río Yutecán. This is a small but distinctive pocket of 20 km^2 (Figure 2.26). The valley lies at 2,300 m. It is formed from the sandstones and conglomerates of the Yanhuitlán Formation. On the north Cerro Yucuayuxi, an andesite intrusion, separates this pocket from Yodocono. On the west and southwest Tidaá is bounded by the steep wall of the Sierra de Nochixtlán. On some maps this section of the Sierra Nochixtlán is labeled Cerro Negro, which should not be confused with Monte Negro, the archaeological site south of Tilantongo. To the west the slopes above 2,400 m are composed of igneous rock and to the southwest the high Cerro Negro is limestone. On the south side of the pocket a low ridge divides Tidaá from the northern lands of Tilantongo. Our survey boundary included most but not all of the Tidaá basin. Several square kilometers of the eastern edge were not surveyed.

Early/Middle Cruz

We found no candidates for Archaic sites in Tidaá. In the Yodocono section we described the substantial Middle Cruz settlement of SPT 7 on the northern edge of Tidaá.

2.27 Late Cruz sites in Tidaá.

Late Cruz

The two Late Cruz sites on the lands of San Pedro Tidaá, SPT 9 and 11 (Figure 2.27, Table 2.14), were described above in the Yodocono section. They and nearby Yodocono sites formed a single settlement cluster.

Ramos

Tidaá had an important town in Ramos. It was located on Cerro Yucuayuxi (SPT 3) just above San Pedro Tidaá (Figures 2.28 and 2.29, Table 2.15). With 20 ha of high-density occupation Yucuayuxi would have had 1,000 to 2,000 inhabitants. The residential terraces are on the south, valley-facing side. The top of Cerro Yucuayuxi is a long, thin ridgeline running east-west, which was modified to become an impressive civic-ceremonial complex (Figure 2.30). The west end of the ridge is a long terrace. Moving east one ascends to a second terrace (T.1) at the east end of which is Str. 3. This structure provided entry into the enclosed Plaza 1. At the east end of this plaza is Str. 2, built on a platform. The back side of Str. 2 is difficult to access. A second plaza comes next and on the east side of this small plaza is Str. 4. Moving east from Str. 4 is a long terrace. Finally at the opposite end of this terrace is Str. 5. The back (east) side of Str. 5 drops dramatically.

The directional flow in linear string architecture is a common feature of civic-ceremonial centers in the Mixteca Alta, well illustrated at this Tidaá site. Given the

2.28 Ramos sites in Tidaá.

2.29 SPT 3 (Cerro Yucuayuxi) and the Tidaá Valley pocket from the west.

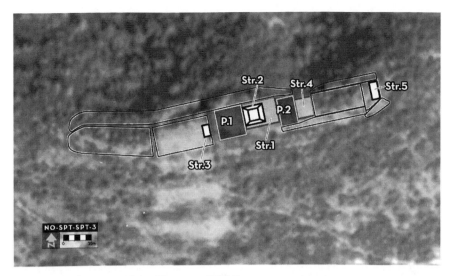

2.30 Focal architecture at Cerro Yucuayuxi (SPT 3).

steep slopes on the sides and east end of the complex it must have been designed for a west-to-east approach, from lower to higher levels, and up stairways and across platforms that increasingly restricted traffic. There was another way to move east-west along this axis, at the lower level of Terraces 6 and 7, which would have provided a 250 m avenue (if one could maneuver between the houses on these terraces).

This was an Early Ramos occupation as at Monte Negro. Ramos sherds are common enough to indicate that the residential terraces and the public architectural area had substantial occupation in this period. However, the full development of the platforms, plazas, and mounds as described here may not have been realized until Las Flores. Sherds from a looter's hole in Str. 2 indicate a Las Flores date for at least some of the construction.

Almost every valley in the Central Mixteca Alta has at least one Early Ramos fortified hilltown. It is interesting that Tidaá is no exception even though its earlier Cruz period occupation was minimal. (The only other Ramos site recorded in Tidaá is SPT 10 but this assignment is dubious, based on a single Red-on-Tan sherd.) As in many other places the hilltown and the whole Tidaá subregion were abandoned in Late Ramos.

Las Flores

Settlement in the Tidaá pocket consisted of the large hilltown at Yucuayuxi, an outlier of this site on the peak just to the northeast, two small villages and a hamlet on hills just west and south of (and extending into) the modern town, and rancherías on the high ridge below Cerro Chiyuco (Figure 2.31, Table 2.16). The total population was about 2,000 people.

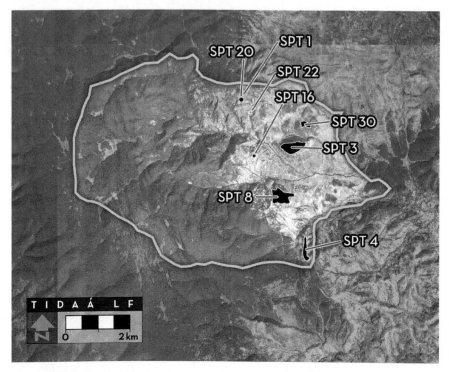

2.31 Las Flores sites in Tidaá.

Yucuayuxi and its civic-ceremonial complex of five mounds and two plazas reached its maximum size in Las Flores. In architectural scale and complexity it was a center of the second rank, below places such as Cerro Jazmín. Less than 1 km to the northeast was a satellite site, SPT 30. It had one mound 2 m in height (Figure 2.32) and on either side flat areas that may have been plazas. Slight rises on these plazas may have been structures but they have been planed away by farmers in recent times. None of the other settlements had mounded architecture. Most of the Las Flores in Tidaá appears to be Early.

Natividad

Settlement in Tidaá was dispersed, as it is today, with no large population or civic-ceremonial centers (Figure 2.33, Table 2.17). The average of our low and high population estimates is about 1,800 inhabitants. The largest village, SPT 8, had fewer than 400 people.

There are three clusters of settlement. The largest was on the slopes on the northern and western sides of the Yucuayuxi mountain extending up the ridge toward Cerro Chiyuco. At two sites in this cluster, SPT 24 and 26, we found stone foundations that could be Colonial in date. West and south of the modern town and

2.32 SPT 30, looking west to Str. 1, where Dmitri Beliaev found Early Las Flores and Natividad sherds.

extending into it is another cluster of Natividad settlement. The third cluster consists of four small sites on the slopes of Cerro Yucuavigüi west of San Pedro Tidaá. SPT 16 is covered by modern houses. SPT 18 is on the northeastern peak of this ridge. From below it looked like there was prehispanic architecture on this site but it turned out to have none and only sparse artifacts. The Las Flores mound at SPT 30 may have been used in Natividad. Str. 4 at Yucuayuxi might have been visited for ritual but there is no indication of new building or continuous use. As at Yodocono, Natividad in Tidaá had scattered settlement with no civic-ceremonial centers or large population centers.

TILANTONGO

This valley is composed of Yanhuitlán sandstones and conglomerates. The valley slopes downward to the east and south; the upper valley is over 2,400 m in elevation in the northwest but only 2,200 m in the southeast. The land is deeply dissected by four main and scores of small *barrancas* (ravines). These are deep—typically from the bottom of a main arroyo to the top of the adjacent ridge is a 150 m climb. The main arroyos carry water year-round and there are numerous springs. As everywhere else where Yanhuitlán bed soils have been intensively farmed, grazed, and abandoned, the Tilantongo area is terrifically eroded (Figure 2.34). Rimming the valley pocket on the west, south, and east are higher limestone ridges. The western and southern mountains are Tilantongo's watershed and source of wood and lime.

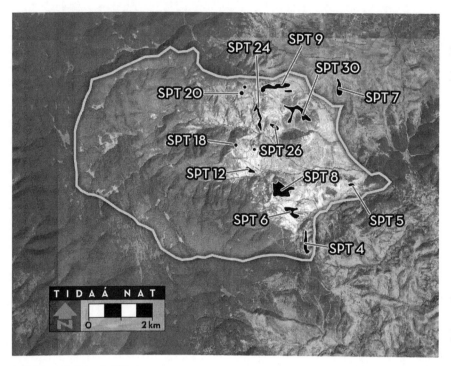

2.33 Natividad sites in Tidaá.

Today the valley is divided into two municipios. San Juan Diuxi is nestled into the head of the well-watered, lowest, and southernmost barranca. Santiago Tilantongo spreads over the ridge downstream from Diuxi. The rancherías of La Providencia and Buenavista are on hills north of the Tilantongo main center. Butterworth's 1974 ethnography of Santiago Tilantongo shows that only a fraction of this municipio's population lived in the cabecera. Most people lived in scattered rancherías (Butterworth 1975:59–63, 155–157). Diuxi is just as dispersed.

Byland and Pohl (1994) carried out a study in Tilantongo and Jaltepec, which adjoins Tilantongo on the east, to see how surface archaeology and the Mixtec codices could be brought together in detail in particular localities. Our survey area overlaps theirs west of the north-south trending ridge separating Tilantongo from Jaltepec (Loma Larga and Cerro Yucuyoco, which they identified as Hill of the Wasp).

Archaic

The lower slopes of the ridge overlooking the Río Grande Yutecán in the far southeastern corner of our survey area have lithic assemblages that deserve consideration as potentially Preceramic. The lower parts of three sites, TIL 13, 15, and 17, have lithics but not ceramics. No diagnostic points or tools were found. Materials

2.34 The Tilantongo Valley and Santiago Tilantongo.

were cherts in several colors and quartz. Flakes were common and there were a few large chert scrapers and bipolar and polyhedral cores. We noted several heat-treated cores of dark chert.

Whether this represents Archaic or later lithic use is untested. Three circumstances make an Archaic occupation interesting. One is the strategic position of the sites at a narrowing of the major river and east-west corridor. Second is the possibility of Archaic to Formative continuity. There was Early/Middle Cruz at TIL 11 and Late Cruz at TIL 13 and 15. Third, Byland and Pohl found an isolated Coxcatlán point of Late Archaic age near Jaltepec, 6 to 8 km from these sites.

Early/Middle Cruz

Tilantongo was home to major settlement in Olmec times. We recorded five Middle Cruz sites (Figure 2.35, Table 2.18). Given the amount of erosion and later occupation the solid and persistent ceramic evidence for this occupation is somewhat surprising. In other words there could have been more Cruz that we are no longer able to see. The occupied area we recorded is more than 60 ha. At standard densities of residential occupation this would mean a population of 1,000 people.

The largest site is SJD 7, at Diuxi. We picked up Middle Cruz ceramics in multiple collections and saw more sherds between our collection areas. This is, however, a multicomponent site with Late Cruz and later periods. SJD 9 had a leveled-off prehispanic mound with a modern shrine on top. Later phases are present but there is the possibility of a Middle Cruz construction stage. La Providencia (TIL 7), which

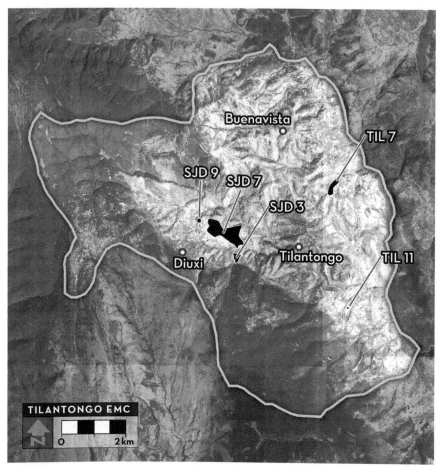

2.35 Early/Middle Cruz sites in Tilantongo.

became much larger in Late Cruz, has a small Middle Cruz component (along with almost every other component in the sequence). TIL 11, at the foot of the ridge, is near the possible Archaic lithic areas.

We have no good evidence of an Early Cruz occupation but further work might produce it. During Middle Cruz a cluster of a larger village and outlying hamlets had been established.

Late Cruz

In Late Cruz the orientation of sites shifted to the east (Figure 2.36, Table 2.19). Middle Cruz settlement had concentrated in the upper, Diuxi part of the basin. Diuxi had quite a few sites in Late Cruz, and perhaps it even had more inhabited area than we were able to record, but by Late Cruz the large villages and the centers with mounded architecture were on the Tilantongo ridge and on the slopes above the Río Grande Yutecán. One might ask if this shift to the east was associated with increased interaction with Mitlatongo, Jaltepec, or beyond.

For the most part Late Cruz sites were not on the highest ridges nor were they on the toe slopes next to the main rivers. Villages and hamlets were on side ridges and slopes above barrancas, a situation that put people's houses on or near contour and lama-bordo terraces, springs, and permanent water courses. Nine of the sixteen sites are on the lower slopes of the south rim of the basin, the best watershed. Today the whole area has lama-bordo chains and there are many scars of washed out lama-bordos.

The five SJD sites (apart from SJD 7, the Middle Cruz large village) were difficult to find and delimit. Late Cruz sherds occur among the houses and agricultural terraces of modern San Juan Diuxi. Modern sherds and refuse cover the same ground. Our Late Cruz site boundaries may be underestimated.

Tilantongo's population of 2,000 to 4,000 people lived in one town, a half-dozen small villages of 100 to 300 people, and some hamlets and isolated residences. The largest place was La Providencia (TIL 7). This is a sprawling multicomponent site, but the Late Cruz is all the way at the eastern end of the main ridge. This component occupies the high knolls at the end of the ridge and spills down the three ridges descending 180 m to the river (Figure 2.37). Much of the site is so eroded that in some sections there is no original ridgeline left and we could find Late Cruz material only where it had been washed downslope. At least two areas, on the north and the south ridges, had residential terraces but we do not know if they pertain to Late Cruz, Las Flores, or Natividad.

On the knoll atop the end of the south ridge at La Providencia is a complex of four structures and a plaza-like feature. The arrangement is a linear string. Las Flores is also present but there is considerable Late Cruz around the mounds. We think this was a Late Cruz civic-ceremonial area.

La Providencia had the largest mound complex but not the only one. TIL 13 had a single mound, although whether it dates to Late Cruz or a later period is unknown. At TIL 3 there were two mounds in an L arrangement on a plaza and another mound nearby (Figure 2.38). TIL 3 is on a distinctive landform, a conical knob overlooking the bottleneck of the Río Grande Yutecán. This was the ideal location for boundary maintenance on the eastern edge of Tilantongo. The top of the hill was circled by concentric rings of long terraces. Both the concentric arrangement of terraces and the plaza with mounds in an L arrangement are typical of the Early Ramos phase, but at TIL 3 we found no Early Ramos, but Late Cruz is well attested in good collections. TIL 3 has Las Flores so it could be that the final form of the terraces and mounds dates to that phase. Nevertheless, TIL 3 could be a precursor to the Early Ramos hilltowns and the southern knob at La Providencia is somewhat like it.

Taken as a whole the Late Cruz settlement probably dates to both earlier and later Late Cruz (Rosario and Monte Albán Early I) with more in the latter. We

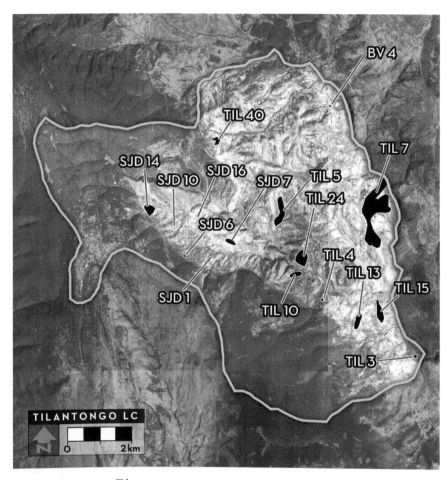

2.36 *Late Cruz sites in Tilantongo.*

found no Early Ramos indicators mixed with our Late Cruz sites. For the sites with public architecture—La Providencia and TIL 3—we cannot say how much Rosario-equivalent occupation there was, but at both sites the latter part of Late Cruz is well represented.

Ramos

Every Cruz site was abandoned by the beginning of Ramos (Figure 2.39, Table 2.20). In Early Ramos everyone lived on Monte Negro (Yucunoo, TIL 1). Before describing Monte Negro we will dispose of the other six sites recorded as Ramos.

All the other sites besides Monte Negro are very small or doubtful in date. On the western side of TIL 5, the Middle Cruz head village, we found one place with

2.37 Lama-bordo adjacent to the multicomponent site at La Providencia (TIL 7), looking northwest. Terraces are replenished from the eroding side slopes.

sherds that could be Early Ramos. This is not the same place as the Cruz components. There is one mound here. At TIL 7, La Providencia, on the western part of the site and apart from the Cruz component we found utility wares that again were similar to those of Early Ramos. The site at SJD 2 is ceramically quite uncertain. The three Buenavista sites are small; together their ceramics might suggest occupation at the very beginning of Ramos.

The results of the Caso and Acosta excavations at Monte Negro are well known (Acosta and Romero 1992). Byland and Pohl (1994:55) published an air photo tracing. Our recent article (Balkansky et al. 2004) places Monte Negro in an updated, broader context based on our survey.

Monte Negro covers the top of the mesa 2 km south of Santiago Tilantongo (Figure 2.40). Bedrock is limestone and the soils are derived from this material. Elevation at the summit is 2,680 m and the ancient occupation extended down to the north to an elevation of 2,560 m. It is 500 m above the main stream on the valley floor. The site is valley-facing in the sense that it is built on slopes nearest and with a view of the Tilantongo Valley. It might have been built on one of the higher peaks of the mountain a little further south but it was not.

Why here? What advantage did this place have over others? Monte Negro best satisfied three somewhat competing needs: enough room for 3,000 to 4,000 people, height and defendability, and nearness to the good farmland of the Tilantongo basin. The Cruz hilltown of TIL 3 failed the first test because it was not big enough.

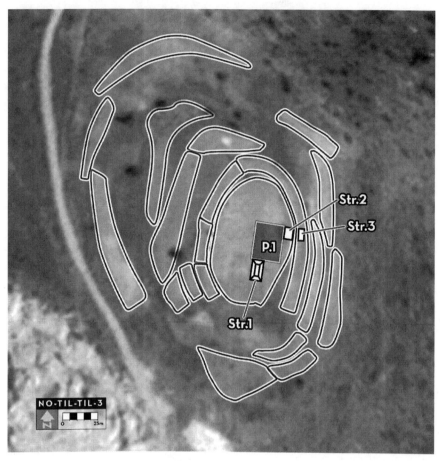

2.38 The architecture at TIL 3.

La Providencia failed the second test because it was too approachable. Any place on the north-south trending ridge between Tilantongo and Jaltepec failed the proximity criterion because it entailed crossing the main river. Mesas on the mountain anywhere to the west were too small and far removed from most of the Tilantongo Valley. The Monte Negro location was the highest, steepest-sided (though vulnerable from the south) place with the best (though not perfect) access to valley lands and was spacious enough for a large town.

The physical extent of the settled area is 77.8 ha, based on field judgments about the limits of in situ artifacts, building stone, and terrace remnants. Our site boundary is somewhat but not a great deal larger than the estimates of Acosta and Romero and also Byland and Pohl. Most of the site was terraced. There are terrace remnants but the ancient features are in poor condition. Monte Negro has an ancient trail leading from the valley into the site. It has six lama-bordo chains. Cut

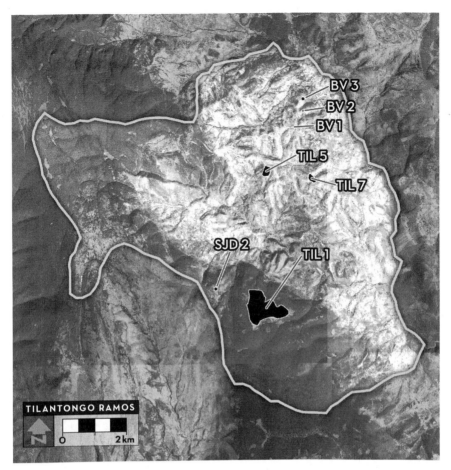

2.39 Ramos sites in Tilantongo.

stone used in building, including the kind of stones used in the circular column bases, is common on terraces.

The excavations and our survey point to a fairly high density of houses. Our survey mapped structures that had been cleared by the earlier excavation project but not put on the published map. We also mapped other structures that were not excavated. The area at the top of the ridge mapped in 1937–1940 plus our additions is about 4.5 ha. In that area we count 25 to 30 courtyards. Assuming these to be houses, at 5 to 10 persons per house the number of people here would range from 125 to 300, or 27 to 67 people per ha. Extending this to the rest of the site results in an estimate of 2,100 to 5,212, or using 25 to 75 people per ha, 1,945 to 5,835.

Monte Negro's architectural concept is unlike any other in Oaxaca (Balkansky et al. 2004:fig. 9). In its long series of abutting low mounds and patios it resembles

2.40 Monte Negro, from the north at Tilantongo. The church is in the center and the Late Cruz component at TIL 24 is just south of the church.

the linear strings found at other sites in the Mixteca Alta but the resemblance is superficial because Monte Negro has patio groups on both sides of avenues, it has no single focal point like the isolated temples on mountain peaks, and access to the complex is open. The complex spreads out in conformity with the breadth and shape of the hilltop. Certain individual elements have counterparts elsewhere, such as the narrow-room temples with round columns (Figures 2.41, 2.42), the patio group with large mound on the east like Winter's templo-patio-adoratorio mound groups (Winter 1986), or the almost generic house with four rooms around a patio. The individual elements are similar to buildings at other places but the whole is like no other place. There was no big plaza or obvious central focus around a structure larger than all others nor a node to which all traffic or attention was directed. Instead there were multiple temples, courtyards, houses, and avenues.

This is essentially a single-component site. There is a small and slight Natividad presence, possibly an isolated residence and minor ritual reuse of an earlier structure or two. Everything else dates to Early Ramos, as shown by the ceramics in the excavation report as well as our collections.

Las Flores

After a Late Ramos abandonment Tilantongo was resettled early in the Early Classic. The Early Las Flores extensive pattern was quite different from the Early

2.41 Monte Negro Temple X, looking north. Five of the six columns are visible.

Ramos concentration. In Early Las Flores people lived in a large town, a dozen large and small villages, and nine hamlets and isolated residences. Settlements were spread across the whole valley (Figure 2.43, Table 2.21). Most were on soils of the Yanhuitlán beds. Las Flores sites are strongly associated with past and present lama-bordos.

Our population estimates for Las Flores in Tilantongo have a wide range, from 6,600 to 15,500 people. It was sometimes difficult to tell if the dispersed and spotty artifact distributions were due to ancient settlement that was dispersed or to erosion. At SJD 18 and 20, for example, sherds were found everywhere there was soil but soil no longer existed on whole sections of the ridges that in the past would have been quite adequate for habitation. These two sites probably did have continuous but low-density dispersed settlement. TIL 5 on the ridge north of Tilantongo and BV 1 ("El Pulpo") on the ridge at Buenavista were large settlements but the artifact densities are lower than those of the Natividad period on the same sites. TIL 7 is such a large multicomponent site that the distance between its two separate Las Flores components is over a kilometer. Parts of TIL 24, at Tilantongo center, and the eastern part of TIL 7 had fairly dense occupation that is now quite disturbed or destroyed by modern land use. In short, Las Flores settlements seem to have had intrasite house densities that varied from relatively compact to dispersed.

The major center was TIL 24, referred to locally as the Pueblo Viejo. This is the hill of the Tilantongo church and the site extends to the ridge to the east. It has a strong Las Flores component. West of the church there had been a large platform. At least one Las Flores mound and perhaps others were built on top of the platform.

2.42 Monte Negro, Temple T.

There were more Las Flores sherds than Natividad around this structure; many were channel-rim bowls typical of Transición or Early Las Flores. Unfortunately, the complex is almost totally erased by modern agricultural terraces. The fields are full of cut stones from ancient structures.

The valley was ringed by seven villages that had one or a few small mounds. TIL 7 (the eastern component) was a reoccupation and expansion of the Late Cruz hilltop site. The architecture was a linear string of four mounds on the peak of the knob. TIL 3 was a reoccupation of the other Late Cruz hilltop site. It has two mounds in an L arrangement on a plaza plus another mound. Oddly, Monte Negro was not reoccupied. Instead a new site (SJD 2) was founded on the next lobe of the mountain to the west. It had two structures but whether they were built in Las Flores or Natividad is not clear. There is a single mound each at SJD 9, 18, and 20 and BV 1.

There was change in settlement during the Las Flores period. We cannot describe the change with precision or detail but it is clear that most of the occupation shown on the map is Early Las Flores. Possibly, there was Late Las Flores in addition to the Early phase at the core sites of SJD 7, the eastern component of TIL 7, and the Pueblo Viejo of Tilantongo (TIL 24) but we do not have whole assemblages showing Late Las Flores traits. Instead we have suggestive or possible Late sherds in a few collections. Tilantongo offers the possibility of population holding over into the Middle or Late Classic. But if there were many people living here for several centuries, we would expect to identify a whole ceramic complex, which we cannot do.

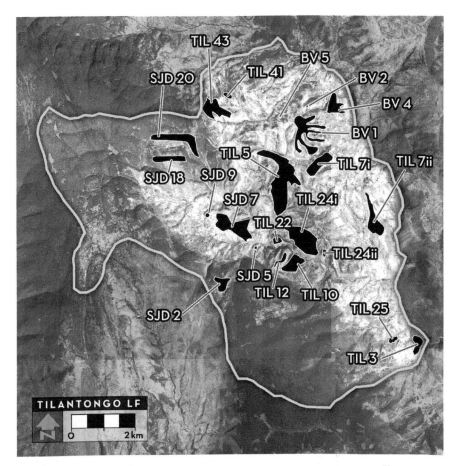

2.43 Las Flores sites in Tilantongo.

Natividad

In Natividad, Tilantongo took on the demographic size of its Oaxacan urban contemporaries such as Cuilapan and Mitla. It was not as large as Jazmín/Yanhuitlán or Teposcolula. The total habitation area was over 900 ha. The midpoint of the population estimate range is 18,000 people.

The major concentration of people was at the Tilantongo Pueblo Viejo, which was larger than modern Santiago Tilantongo; this settlement spread up the ridge north and northwest of town and along the La Providencia ridge (Figure 2.44, Table 2.22) and accounted for two-thirds of the subregional population. There were sixteen large and small villages and two dozen hamlets and isolated residences. The piedmont on the south side of the Río Tenu, below the mountain escarpment, was heavily settled. This zone has abundant water. Another notable cluster of settlement was on the piedmont ridge dividing Tidaá from Tilantongo (TIL 14, 40–43; SPT 4).

The core settlements (TIL 5, 7, 24) were heavily involved in agriculture. Almost every side-slope drainage has a lama-bordo. We observed close spatial associations between Natividad habitation areas and lama-bordos on all these sites including the Pueblo Viejo. Every site form and all the field notes say these sites and their immediate surroundings are severely eroded.

We found no firm evidence of Natividad construction of public buildings. One exception could be on the ancient platform on the hill of the church at Tilantongo but that area is now so modified by recent land use that one could tell only with many test excavations. In any case Tilantongo did not embark on a major building program in Natividad. Older mounds at six sites saw reuse in Natividad: the three core sites plus border sites TIL 3 and 13 and SJD 2.

As in other places the Late Postclassic settlement system here was heavily urban but at the same time it had strong rural development, with more small villages, hamlets, and isolated residences than in earlier periods. The agricultural emphasis is unmistakable. Tilantongo was one of the Postclassic cacicazgos that did not invest much in new public buildings. From the archaeology alone one would not guess its prominent place in the Mixtec codices; from the codices one would not comprehend the scale of its urban and rural settlement system.

SIERRA DE NOCHIXTLÁN

This is not a valley or a place with a settlement history at all but the opposite. The Sierra de Nochixtlán is the highest and longest mountain range in the Mixteca Alta. It is the largest systematically surveyed tract of land in Oaxaca without archaeological sites (actually there are a few, depending on how one defines the sierra). These mountains played a role as a place of resources, a place of mythological importance, a watershed, and a social divide.

The Mixtecs we met had no name for the Sierra Nochixtlán as a whole, despite its imposing place in the landscape, although they had many names for individual mountain tops and high, open plazas in the mountains. In the course of our months of walking up and down its many slopes and promontories we came to know the sierra affectionately as the "Green Monster," which any baseball fan will recognize as the nickname of the outfield wall at Fenway Park in Boston. Like its namesake, the Green Monster of the Mixteca Alta appears to have been a formidable barrier, as evidenced by the paucity of settlements that we encountered. However, modern-day people make extensive use of the network of trails that crisscross the Sierra Nochixtlán. In addition to those marked on topographic maps, we identified and recorded smaller trails, most running east to west across the range.

The roughly Y-shaped Sierra de Nochixtlán (Figure 2.45) begins in the northeastern portion of our survey area, where the modern highway takes advantage of a natural break in elevation as it passes from Santo Domingo Yanhuitlán to La

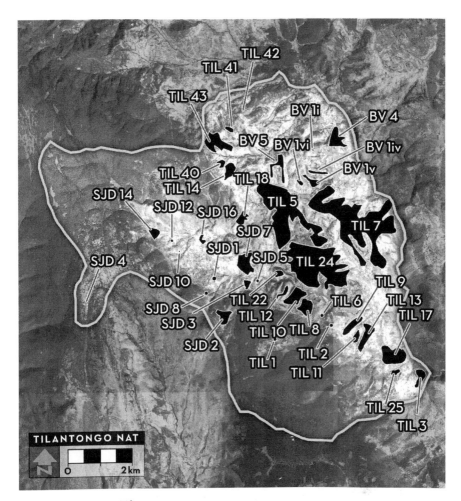

2.44 Natividad sites in Tilantongo.

Cieneguilla and thence to San Juan Teposcolula. South of the latter town the sierra is bifurcated by the valley drained by the Río Grande and its tributary the Río Negro. San Vicente Nuñu is located about midway between the two arms of the sierra. Farther south and reachable only by trail is the village of Anama. On the outside edge of the western arm of the mountain range is San José de Gracia. From here the mountains continue south to San Miguel Achiutla and San Bartolomé Yucuañe. Our survey ended in the south at Guadalupe Hidalgo but a more natural break in the mountain range is evident about another 8 km to the south where the elevations dip still further to the valley floor.

We noted pronounced changes in the physiography of the Sierra Nochixtlán over the course of the more than 40 km it stretches along our survey area. The

2.45 *The Sierra de Nochixtlán and modern towns at its edge.*

topography in the northern section from La Cieneguilla south to San José de Gracia and Nejapilla consists of long, narrow ridges. These ridges are commonly as little as 5 m wide and rarely exceed 30 m. The ridges descend relatively gradually to the west. To the east there is a sharp drop from the highest ridge tops (about 2,700 m) to the lower hills that slope more gradually into the Nochixtlán Valley. The ridge tops immediately above this steep slope afford commanding views of the valley below.

Small patches of pasture and milpas extend up the eastern and western flanks of the northern portion of the range; the ridgetops and barrancas in the interior are thickly wooded, generally with a mix of oaks and pines. Occasional rock outcrops were noted on the tops of these ridges.

Although the economic use of the northern portion of the Sierra Nochixtlán today is limited to scattered farms and pasture, municipal territories are strictly defended. Boundaries between political units are marked by well-maintained mojoneras and *rayas* (cleared lines) despite the challenges imposed to the construction of these landmarks by the steep and rugged terrain. The guides we hired to transport supplies via burros on our extended camping trips were careful to observe these boundaries and some spoke of conflicts between towns over water and other resources.

As the two arms of the Sierra Nochixtlán merge south of San José de Gracia and Nejapilla, the topography, vegetation, and land use begin to change. The narrow finger ridges that are characteristic of the northern portion of the Sierra Nochixtlán continue south, especially along the eastern edge of the mountains, but these gradually give way to broader ridgetops. The forests on these ridgetops are broken by large pastures, and great agave appear for the first time in the forests. The sierra reaches its highest elevation (3,200 m) between Tidaá and San Miguel Achiutla. Like many of the other high points in the middle section of the sierra, this consists of a rocky promontory that rises abruptly from the generally broad, level ridgetop.

The changes in vegetation and land use in this middle section of the sierra are evident in toponyms. Here our guides (from the towns of San Vicente Nuñu, Anama, and San Juan Achiutla) and informants (mostly shepherds who we met while surveying) often referred to the pastures or llanos on the ridgetops by specific names, including Plaza del Verano Grande, El Aguacate, Plaza del Lobo, Plaza del Venado Chico, Plaza del Elote, and Yudoo. The higher, rocky promontories were rarely if ever referred to by name. This stands in contrast to the northern section of the sierra where the toponyms we recorded were applied almost exclusively to the highest points on the ridgetops (e.g., La Muralla and El Cacahuate). The emphasis on the naming of llanos in the southern section of the sierra may reflect the economic importance of livestock grazing. Surprisingly, there appeared to us to be less boundary maintenance in this area. We saw fewer rayas and mojoneras and the people we encountered seemed less concerned about the territories of their municipios.

The top of this middle section of the sierra is more level but the flanks are steeper, particularly along the western margin above San Miguel Achiutla and San Bartolomé Yucuañe. Although the lower slopes are used for farms and grazing, the more rugged upper reaches often have a thick cover of trees and undergrowth. To the east the slopes of the mountain in the vicinity of Tidaá and Diuxi are generally more gradual or are broken up in smaller peaks.

From its high point east of San Miguel Achiutla the Sierra Nochixtlán slopes gradually to the southern edge of the project area. The ridgetop remains broad and relatively level in the south. Land use is a mix of woods and pasture with increasing amounts of cultivated land in isolated places. The ridge that continues southeast, which includes the site of Monte Negro, is mostly wooded. The ridge that continues south and southwest to the towns of La Paz and Guadalupe Hidalgo is more sparsely vegetated. Although it may have simply been a product of the timing of our survey (late in the dry season), this southern part of the sierra had more low scrub and fewer large trees, perhaps as result of less rainfall in general. The vegetation looks increasingly like the Mixteca Baja.

Using the rough boundaries outlined above, we have a total of sixty-three sites in the Sierra Nochixtlán (which are described in their respective subregions in this chapter and Chapters 3 and 5). However, even this relatively paltry total conveys a misleadingly high impression of the site density. Most of these sites are on the lower flanks and we identified only one (NO-YPD-YPD 1) above 2,700 m. The paucity of sites at the higher reaches of the sierra no doubt reflects the rugged nature of the terrain and the absence of reliable water. It undoubtedly is also the product of cultural choices—throughout history the sierra appears to have served as a buffer zone.

The use of the sierra varied through time, as the distribution of components suggests. The sixty-three sites include components dating to the Late Cruz (N=5), Ramos (1), Las Flores (22), and Natividad (35) periods. Three other sites were non-diagnostic. The relatively high proportions of Las Flores and Natividad sites reflect their abundance in the project area in general. Perhaps most surprising is the relative scarcity of components from Ramos, the single example consisting of Monte Negro on the lower flanks of the Green Monster in Tilantongo. The scarcity of Ramos sites in the sierra at a time when populations were generally moving to higher, defendable locations reflects a preference for isolated peaks at the edges of valleys rather than the high mountains of the Sierra Nochixtlán.

CHAPTER THREE

Greater Teposcolula

Greater Teposcolula is like a solar system: a Sun—the Teposcolula Valley itself—
and six planets held in its gravity. The subordinate ñuu (the planets) are Nuñu,
Yodobada, Yucunama, Lagunas, Yolomécatl, and Nduayaco. Here, even better than
with the area covered in the previous chapter, we can see how subregions were linked
together to form larger aggregations, *yuhuitaiyu* as they were known in the sixteenth
century. The leading position of Teposcolula was established with the first sedentary
villages in the Early Formative and it continued through the prehispanic sequence
and the Colonial era. Teposcolula is still the head town for a district that approxi-
mates the limits of its sixteenth-century cacicazgo. Teposcolula Valley centers were
larger and had more monumental and more complex civic-ceremonial architecture
than the centers in its outlying subregions. No urban center in the Central Mixteca
Alta was ever more imposing than the Natividad Pueblo Viejo of Teposcolula.

As in the western Nochixtlán Valley, the first densely occupied towns were
formed in the chaotic events of the Late Formative. Yet these hilltowns had little

organic relation to one another in stable systems of central places bound together by exchange. That transformation, meaning the emergence of complex, integrated hierarchies of settlements that had different functional mixes, did not occur until the Early Classic.

Just as we have seen along the western side of the Nochixtlán Valley, settlements were typically situated on and around pockets of soils well suited for farming, the major exception being the fortified hilltowns of Ramos and later periods. The settlement pattern suggests an economy strongly oriented to agriculture. Compared with other regions in highland Mesoamerica that have been surveyed with similar methods, the Central Mixteca Alta does not have much evidence for economic specializations other than in agriculture. Here, however, we found intensive use of chert at many sites in the subregions west of the Teposcolula Valley. This specialized production in the periphery may have fed into the urban core in Teposcolula.

Teposcolula and its subordinate subregions shared the same history of growth and decline as we saw in the western Nochixtlán Valley: slow and stable growth in the Early and Middle Formative, major disruption and warfare in the Late Formative, near abandonment in the Terminal Formative, growth in size and complexity in the Early Classic, another decline in the Late Classic/Epiclassic, and unprecedented growth again in the Late Postclassic.

TEPOSCOLULA

Picture four parallel north-south-trending geological blocks. The westernmost is igneous in origin, gray andesite that forms rugged mountains with broken relief. This is the western edge of the Teposcolula Valley. The second block is a series of limestone ridges. The Teposcolula Valley is an east-west fissure cut through this older limestone. Broad, high ridges of limestone running north-south occur elsewhere in Oaxaca; valleys that break through them are not common (Teposcolula is one such corridor, Tamazulapan is another; in a larger-scale and more complicated way so is the Valley of Oaxaca). This makes Teposcolula favorably situated on east-west and north-south travel routes.

The eastern half of the valley is the third major geological block, consisting of Yanhuitlán Formation shales, sandstones, and conglomerates. The two major drainages that are tributary to the Teposcolula Valley, San Juan Teposcolula and San Vicente Nuñu, are valley pockets of Yanhuitlán-derived soils. The fourth block forms the mountains on the eastern edge. These are volcanic like the hills on the western edge but higher.

The San Juan Teposcolula Valley is drained by the upper Río Teposcolula. At times during its history this branch had a somewhat separate history. We considered making it another small subregion peripheral to the Teposcolula core. But in Natividad times the San Juan branch was fully integrated as part of the core and in the early periods it may have been too small to have been independent.

Teposcolula is the largest subregion in the study area. Its 42 km² of valley constitutes the largest patch of flat land in the Central Mixteca Alta. The western

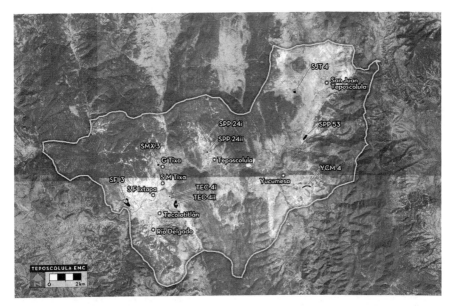

3.1 *Early/Middle Cruz sites in Teposcolula.*

half of the valley does not have many large lama-bordos. Nor are the limestone hills, today mostly covered with oak-pine forest, particularly inviting for intensive farming. Instead Teposcolula's considerable productive potential comes from the valley-floor alluvium and the potential for canal irrigation. The gentler slopes can be contour terraced. The San Juan Teposcolula arm has more lama-bordos and contour terraces. These agricultural resources help explain why Teposcolula had such a prominent place at several times in history. The Teposcolula Valley was thoroughly surveyed by Stiver Walsh (2001) and everything in this section is based on her work.

Early/Middle Cruz

Stiver Walsh's survey found no Archaic sites but she did find strong evidence of early sedentary villages (Figure 3.1, Table 3.1). Three sites have pottery belonging to Early Cruz. The sites are TEC 4 (Loma Mina), SPP 24, and SPP 53 (Yucuninde Lomas). They are located at low elevations not far above the valley floor. The total settlement area is probably only 8 ha or so. Little more can be said because there are only a few sherds and in every case they are mixed with later materials. All three sites have Middle and Late Cruz as well.

More is known about the Middle Cruz settlement pattern. With some 500 inhabitants Teposcolula was one of highland Oaxaca's more densely occupied places in Olmec-horizon times. There are seven sites with a total occupied area of 36 ha. Sites are generally not oriented to the limestone soils of the middle section of

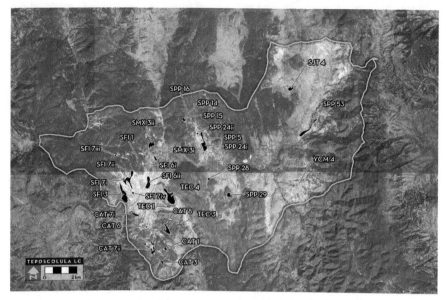

3.2 Late Cruz sites in Teposcolula.

the valley but to the San Juan Teposcolula and Ixtapa sectors (except for the small components at SPP 24). The eastern cluster has an average population estimate of about 180 and the western cluster has over 300. Loma Mina was the largest village at almost 12 ha. No public architecture can be securely dated to Middle Cruz but Loma Mina had become the head town by Late Cruz and it is possible that some of its six mounds were begun in Middle Cruz.

Late Cruz

By Late Cruz the inhabited area had increased fivefold to 186 ha. All the known Middle Cruz sites were still occupied and most had grown in size. Gentle rises and low slopes in the low piedmont were preferred as before. Most settlement was in one cluster in the western end of the valley but the eastern part of this cluster spilled up the valley beyond the first limestone ridge (Figure 3.2, Table 3.2). There were three sites in the San Juan Teposcolula Valley but this area was not heavily occupied.

Loma Mina, the largest site in Middle Cruz, now covered 27 ha. Its Late Cruz occupation was fairly dense and it had perhaps 500 inhabitants. This head village may have had two foci of public architecture. One was at the highest point of the site on the southern hill, the top of which was made into a level platform measuring 80 by 50 m. At the north end of this platform a slight rise and scattered building stone suggest a mound. At least five bell-shaped pits were seen on and around the possible structure. On the north hill at Loma Mina is a platform with three mounds

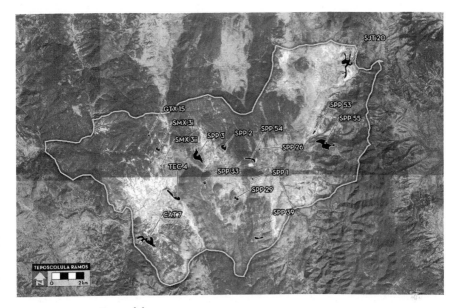

3.3 Ramos sites in Teposcolula.

arranged around a plaza. Late Cruz is found here, suggesting public construction in this period, but later phases are better represented.

There was a second tier of small subordinate villages. In the main cluster, SMX 3 has three possible Late Cruz mounds. SPP 29 has nine mounds but they may not pertain to this phase. The eastern cluster has Nicayuju (SJT 4) with two structures and Yucuninde Lomas with one structure that may date to this phase.

In all, Teposcolula had twenty-two small hamlets and isolated residences, seven small villages, and Loma Mina, the head town. Several of the settlements in the main cluster were extensive but low density (SFI 3, 7; CAT 7); all the sites in the eastern cluster were compact, a difference also seen in later periods.

Growth and continuity characterize Teposcolula's Cruz settlement. All the Early Cruz sites have Middle Cruz; all the Middle Cruz have Late Cruz. Within Late Cruz there is ceramic evidence for both an early and a late subphase. With a total population of 2,600 people Teposcolula, especially the western end of the valley, was one of the leading places in the Mixteca Alta. That the eastern arm of the valley had less population, mostly in two main villages, may have something to do with its larger neighbors to the east (Jazmín/Yanhuitlán) and the north (Tejupan).

Ramos

The two major settlement pattern changes following Late Cruz were nucleation into hilltowns at higher elevations and population increase (Figure 3.3, Table 3.3). Ramos was a break in the long continuity of settlement during the previous thousand years, yet the two long-standing clusters of settlements, one in the east and one in the west, did persist. These trends—the movement away from low piedmont sites to hilltowns, the great increase in population, and the continuity of the settlement clusters—apply only to Early Ramos. By Late Ramos, Teposcolula was essentially abandoned.

The movement to higher locations involved abandoning most (but not all) Late Cruz sites and making new settlements on hilltops. In the western cluster almost all of the Late Cruz valley floor and low piedmont sites were abandoned. The small sites in the piedmont around Santa Catarina Delgado were abandoned in favor of the new settlement on Yucuñunu 260 m above the valley floor. SPP 24 was no longer occupied but the nearby settlements on hilltops (SPP 2, 3) grew. In the San Juan Teposcolula arm SJT 4 was abandoned and most population was concentrated into the hilltowns of El Fortín de San Juan (SJT 20) and Yucuninde (SPP 55).

The settlement pattern shift in Teposcolula was emphatic but not as drastic as in many other subregions. Loma Mina, the prior head village, shrank in size by half but was not abandoned. SMX 3 had persistent Early Ramos occupation and SPP 29 continued, as did SPP 53, on the piedmont below Yucuninde. The settlements that continued might have been protected by being well within settlement clusters and near fortified hilltowns. Not all sites were large and nucleated. Teposcolula had ten sites whose average population estimate is about 100 or less.

The two clusters of settlement not only kept their integrity, they expanded. By building atop El Fortín de San Juan the inhabitants of the eastern cluster extended their boundary to the north. The western cluster maintained its western boundary and continued the gradual expansion upstream to the east. Could the expansion upstream mean increasing reliance on canal irrigation from the main river? This western cluster reorganized. The head town moved from Loma Mina 3 km away to Tres Arbolitos on a choke point above the valley and more central to the cluster. The two clusters were organized quite differently but their total population sizes were equivalent, about 4,000 people each.

Several of the new towns merit individual description. Tres Arbolitos (SPP 3) was built 160 m above the valley on the ridge just west of San Pedro y San Pablo Teposcolula. Its residential terraces were long and narrow and most of them were on the west side of the hill facing a small tributary valley. The focal architecture was a linear string of terraces that led upward to a small plaza that had two mounds facing each other (Figure 3.4). Almost all the building activity at Tres Arbolitos went into the residential terraces for the town's 1,500 inhabitants, not the civic-ceremonial architecture.

Near Tres Arbolitos was El Fortín (SPP 2), on the ridge northeast of San Pedro y San Pablo Teposcolula. It had five mounds in three separate groups. The upper slopes of the central spur were modified into long, broad terraces or platforms with massive and high retaining walls. Several stone walls that run perpendicular to the slope contour divide the site into sectors but these walls are probably later than Ramos.

On the southwestern frontier of the settlement cluster headed by Tres Arbolitos is Cerro Yucuñunu (CAT 7, Figure 3.5). Here the upper slopes of the rather steep

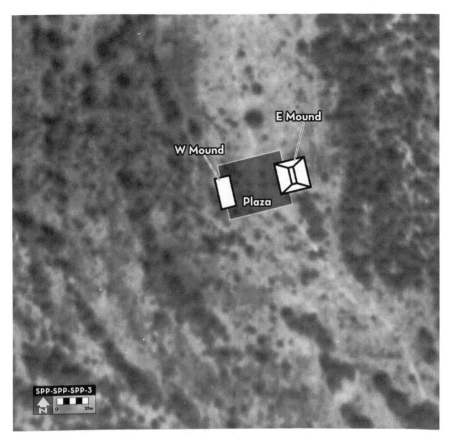

3.4 The south ridgetop at Tres Arbolitos, SPP 3.

peak had five tiers of long, concentric terraces. Residential terraces on the lower slope on the west side were situated just above a lama-bordo. The focal architecture was a string of terraces running up the spine of the ridge to an L-shaped platform with two mounds in an L arrangement. The site had three other mounds. The terraced area would have accommodated 900 people.

When people in the eastern sector relocated their main town, they chose one of the most strategic and defendable places in this subregion, Cerro Yucuninde. The valley floor here is at 2,260 m and the central peak, which has three platforms and a central mound, is at 2,560 m. The ascent is done in 1 km. A major trail connecting Teposcolula with Yanhuitlán runs just below the site. Over 2,000 people lived here in Ramos; it was the largest town in the subregion. Yucuninde needs to be described by someone who has walked it and returned:

> The slope plummets to the north; it cannot be scaled. The western arm of the site permits the only relatively gradual approach to the site center. Ascent from the

south is difficult but possible, requiring considerable effort and time. Along the ridge just to the east of the main summit, terraces climb the west slope of a small knob; on its top [a] mound stands on a platform. The narrow ridge spine continues to the east with sharp descents on either side. Less than 4 km outside of the site limits, the ridge descends to a saddle over which the . . . path crosses en route to the Nochixtlán Valley.

. . . In addition to its natural inaccessibility, the center's constructions further restrict entry. . . . Just below the principal summit, the eastern ridge becomes a 2 m wide passage over a narrow land bridge, cut by trenches and cordoned off by two defensive walls. Climbing up toward the summit, the steep slope is heavily modified to form residential terraces, some of them 4 or 5 m above the terrace below. One retention wall that effectively doubles as a defensive wall circles around the peak for some 180 m. From the east, and all around the south face to the west, terrace walls control access. On the western side, the more gradual route curves upward past 12 small mounds, some positioned on opposite sides of a pathway used today. Others block off all but a couple of meters of the narrow crest of the loma. . . . [B]etween the sheer cliff dropping off to the north and the residential terraces to the south, the approach is guarded carefully. (Stiver Walsh 2001:125–126)

The other major town in this upper arm of the valley was El Fortín de San Juan (SJT 20). It too is located above a trail between Yanhuitlán and Teposcolula at the head end of the Teposcolula Valley. The occupation at SJT 20 centers on the high summit and extends down several narrow ridges. There are mound groups with Ramos (and later) sherds in six different places. At the north end of the highest summit was a group of five mounds on a plaza; to the south is another structure. The northwest spur has a knob surrounded by concentric rings of long terraces. Atop this peak is a platform that has two small plazas separated by a central mound. The north plaza has two other mounds and the south plaza has another mound facing the central mound in an L arrangement similar to those at Cerro Jazmín and Topiltepec. A nearby knob has another mound group. On top of the southern ridge is a single plowed-down structure and there is another single mound near the southern limit of the site on the same ridge. In all there are eleven mounds in the Ramos settlement.

Of the sixteen Ramos sites in Teposcolula only two do not have mounds with Ramos sherds. However, virtually all of these are multicomponent situations and it will take excavation to demonstrate the construction histories. At many of the leading towns, including those just described, the survey found fancy varieties of Ramos ceramics in and around the mound groups.

The distribution of site sizes and mounded architecture suggests not an integrated civic-ceremonial hierarchy but instead various places that enjoyed differing degrees of power and wealth. The eastern cluster of settlements consisted of two towns almost equivalent in population and civic-ceremonial functions. Both places had multiple dispersed platform mounds instead of single, focal administrative precincts. In the western cluster Tres Arbolitos was the population center. The sizes of settlements approach a rank-size distribution. Yet there was more civic-ceremonial

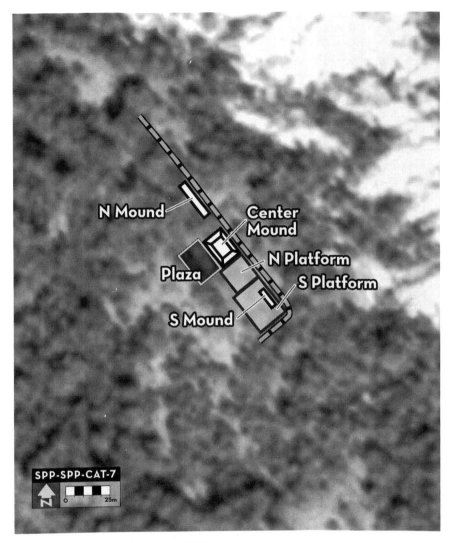

N Mound

Center Mound

N Platform

Plaza

S Platform

S Mound

SPP-SPP-CAT-7

N   0   25m

3.5 The summit of Cerro Yucuñunu, CAT 7.

architecture at outlying sites than there was in the center (although Las Flores reoccupation makes it difficult to assign mounds to phases). We suggest there was village and town autonomy in matters that involved plazas and platform mounds. Boundary maintenance and perhaps other matters may have held towns and clusters of settlements together. After a period of no more than two centuries, and perhaps considerably less, all this collapsed. While Huamelulpan and Yucuita grew to urban proportions, Teposcolula was left uninhabited.

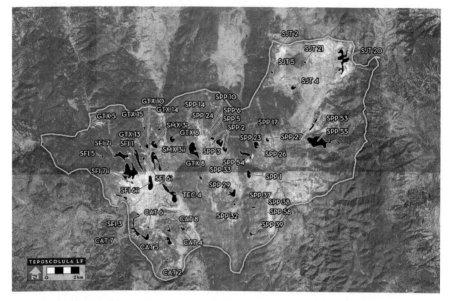

3.6 Las Flores sites in Teposcolula.

Las Flores

Population in Teposcolula was higher in the Early Classic than at any previous time. Differences in settlements suggest greater complexity and integration too. All the Ramos hilltop sites were occupied again and most were larger in Las Flores. New towns and villages were established near the valley floor; there were a few new sites at high elevations (Figure 3.6, Table 3.4).

The settlement pattern suggests two parallel orientations. One was a continued emphasis on defense and living in high, nucleated settlements with houses packed onto residential terraces. El Fortín de San Juan (SJT 20), Yucuninde (SPP 55), El Fortín (SPP 2), Tres Arbolitos (SPP 3), Tixa Viejo (SMX 3), and Yucuñunu (CAT 7) were major hilltop towns. These six were the largest population centers in Teposcolula and held two-thirds of the population. There were smaller terraced hilltop villages too, such as Yatitiñe (GTX 6) with its 150 people.

The second orientation, which makes Las Flores quite different from Ramos, was the spread of settlements in exposed locations on the low piedmont and edge of the valley floor. Over 5,000 people, almost a third of the total population, lived in places below 2,250 m. Most of these valley-floor sites were in the western settlement cluster. Las Flores also had many more small hamlets and isolated residences. Of the fifty-one sites, thirty were 5 ha or less in size.

The eastern cluster had the same nucleated structure it had in Ramos, with only a few small occupations at lower elevations. El Fortín de San Juan and Cerro Yucuninde (SPP 55) were even larger than they had been before. At Yucuninde the pattern of multiple groups of small mounds continued and three new structures were built, for a total of twenty-two structures in use. The site expanded up the ridge to the east (in the direction of Cerro Jazmín) and down the slope toward the valley floor in the main residential zone, for a total occupied area of 63 ha.

A western cluster of settlement was reestablished in Las Flores but it differed from that of Ramos in its territorial extent, locations of settlements, and internal structure. This settlement cluster spread farther in every direction with small villages and hamlets in the hills to the north and south and substantial occupation again (as in Cruz) in the Santa Catarina Delgado area to the southwest and significantly to the east beyond the last limestone ridge into the lower San Juan Teposcolula Valley. Both sides of the main river were occupied, the north somewhat more than the south. Quite a few settlements were spread out along the piedmont hills from the valley floor to high knobs (CAT 7, TEC 4, SMX 3, SFI 6, SFI 7). Several sites had low habitational density, such as SFI 7. Small hamlets and isolated residences were on the outer edges of the western cluster, higher up in the hills than the larger villages and towns.

The internal structure of the settlement system in western Teposcolula was also a departure from Ramos and Cruz. There were three large towns of 1,500 to 2,000 inhabitants: Tres Arbolitos (SPP 3), Tixa Viejo (SMX 3), and El Fortín (SPP 2). Of these, Tixa grew the most during Las Flores. The site consisted of two parts on long parallel ridges. The mounded architecture was distributed in multiple groups of small mounds, as at Yucuninde. The most impressive public architecture was the string of monumental platforms on the spine of the east ridge. Because only a few hundred meters separate them, a case could be made for combining all the sites between SMX 3 and SFI 7 into one aggregate town that would have had a population of 3,000.

Change within Las Flores can be documented. The Transición phase is found on at least fourteen sites including all the major hilltop fortified towns (SJT 4, 20; SPP 1, 2, 3, 29, 33, 53, 55, 58; SMX 3; TEC 4; SFI 6i; and CAT 7). The old hilltowns were the first to be reoccupied after the Late Ramos hiatus and they grew quickly. Tixa Viejo was still a small village whose rise to prominence occurred in the Early Classic after Transición, as did the further growth of population and the expansion to the valley floor. The population peak of over 16,000 was achieved in Early Las Flores after the Transición re-colonization. Late Las Flores is represented by only a few sherds at a few sites (Tixa Viejo, SMX 3; Colonia Rosario, SFI 1; Yucuninde, SPP 55; and El Fortín de San Juan, SJT 20). Teposcolula, like many other places in the Mixteca Alta, appears to have been virtually deserted in Late Classic/Epiclassic times.

Natividad

In the Postclassic, Teposcolula was one of the most populous, most urbanized, and economically most powerful places in the Mixteca Alta and highland Oaxaca. Its archaeology is spectacular, from the sheer abundance of archaeological sites, to

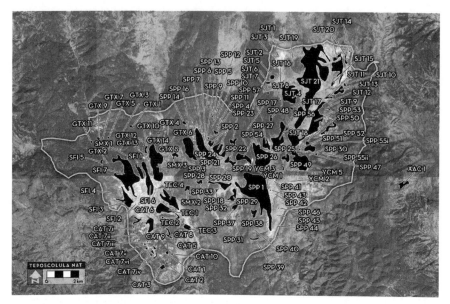

3.7 Natividad sites in Teposcolula.

the outlines of houses in sprawling residential areas of Diquino and Nicayuju, to the palaces of the urban capital Teposcolula Viejo.

If you stood in the Río Teposcolula at any point in the valley and raised your arms to the hills on either side, you would always be pointing to a Natividad settlement. They are on every single hill along the edge of the valley and on both sides of the river. The survey found 121 separate Natividad sites, twice the number of the next highest period, Las Flores. The total occupied area was 2,457 ha (Figure 3.7, Table 3.5).

Settlement was strongly oriented toward the valley floor and lower elevations. Some 7,000 people, 23 percent of the total, lived in sites with average elevations below 2,250 m. More than half of the population lived in settlements within 1 km of the main river. Residential sites were located on piedmont rises right up to the alluvium but not on it. Numerous arroyo banks and other profiles in the alluvium of the valley floor were examined and only in one place, where the river has cut back into piedmont soils, were Natividad deposits found (at Diquino, SJT 21, where the habitation area extended to the river). The flat valley floor was evidently left for farming.

The highlands were occupied too. Thirty-three sites were found above 2,375 m in elevation. All were small hamlets or isolated residences.

Natividad settlement patterns have strong urban and simultaneously strong rural components. Almost 40 percent of the people lived in the two largest places, Teposcolula Pueblo Viejo (SPP 1) and Diquino (SJT 21). On the rural side 87 of the subregion's 121 sites had estimated populations of less than 100 people. These hamlets and isolated residences account for about 2,000 people, 7 percent of the total. A little more than half of the total population lived in settlements that had between 100 and 1,700 inhabitants.

The Pueblo Viejo (Yucundaa, SPP 1) was a large, densely settled urban center (Figure 3.8). The site covered 289 ha. It had over 1,000 residential terraces; the survey was able to map 500. In a carefully mapped terraced area of 39.06 ha we calculated that there were 444 households, which would represent a density of 57 to 114 people per ha, comparable to other Mesoamerican cities. Additionally, about 201 ha of the site are thought to have had a standard density of 10 to 25 people per ha and another 49 ha may have had a light density, 5 to 10 people per ha. The conservatively estimated range for the population size of the Pueblo Viejo is 4,475 to 9,954.

The site has twenty-nine non-residential mounds, seven plazas, and at least seven monumental platforms. It has the internal functional differentiation of an urban center. We can try to convey some of this heterogeneity by describing five zones of the site, each of which has different public architecture.

Zone 1 is the north summit. Here there is a 2 ha area with some Early Las Flores occupation and construction but everything visible today pertains to Natividad. The focal architecture was built on massive stucco-covered platforms. There are two main plazas, rather closed and secluded. These are surrounded by mounds, two of which are 6 m high. The top of the largest mound, on the east side of Plaza 1, measures 28 by 10 m. This would have been the largest superstructure space; the other mounds have smaller and narrower tops. Surrounding these mound groups are platforms that have large houses with sunken patios. There are masonry walls still standing and several tombs and bell-shaped pits often used for burials. Access to this elite zone was restricted by walls, terrace retaining walls, high platforms, and several defensive walls, which in places are still 2 m high. About 75 m below the summit precinct is a main defensive wall that can be followed for almost 2 km from the north slope to the saddle south of Zone 1. The slopes below the top of the hill are covered with residential terraces. On the western side there are two separate stone walls that run straight up and down the slope, segmenting the residential area. The eastern and western routes up into Zone 1 are lined with patio groups, mounds, and stone buildings.

Zone 2 is the saddle south of the summit and Zone 1. It has a ball court and several terraces. Lama-bordo cascades begin here. Continuing south and up the next hill is Zone 3, an important civic-ceremonial area. Access to the Zone 3 buildings and plazas is easier than to the Zone 1 precinct but the platforms and mounds are nonetheless imposing. Str. 40 is 7 m tall and faces a 32 by 38 m plaza with an adoratorio in its center. Zone 3 also has patio groups and residential terraces.

Zone 4 is on a hilltop 350 m south of Zone 3, past residential terraces. On the peak is a small three-mound group on a small plaza with an adoratorio and another plaza in front. Zone 5 is at the base of the hill on the eastern side, within the modern settlement called La Campana. There are two mounds, several platforms, and two other buildings, all in a Natividad residential area.

The site's artifact patterns also suggest urban differentiation, as Stiver Walsh notes:

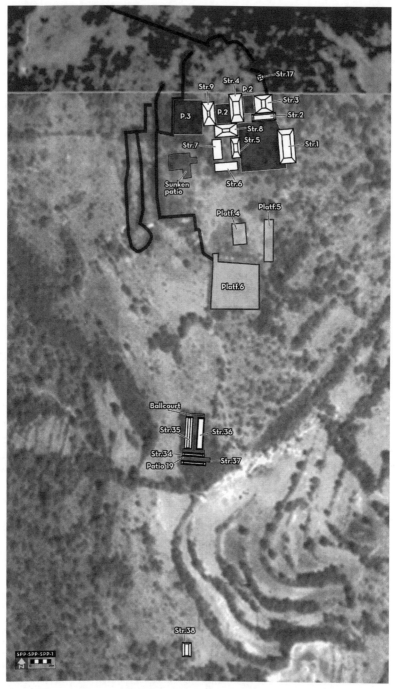

3.8 Major architecture at Teposcolula Pueblo Viejo, SPP 1.

In addition to the high-status residential area in Zone 1, architecture and artifacts distinguish four other elite domestic areas. Polychrome and other less common pottery types mark these areas, as do unusual ceramic figurines . . . and stamps or seals, greater quantities of obsidian. . . . Greater quantities of sahumador and censer cover fragments also correspond to such areas, suggesting greater participation in formal ritual activities. (Stiver Walsh 2001:197)

Diquino (SJT 21) was the major secondary center in the San Juan Teposcolula wing of the valley. Its Natividad area was 4.41 km². Part of this area was probably low density and about a third was more compact (10 to 25 people per ha). The mean of the population estimate range is 4,739. There are hundreds of walls, house foundations, terraces, and other features exposed on the surface. A single area of 75 by 75 m has forty-three houses and six patio groups. Such densities do not speak for the whole site because houses and clusters of houses like this were often interspersed with lama-bordo terraces and small contour terraces that were probably cultivated.

At nearby Nicayuju, Verónica Pérez used the regional survey to select likely places to study commoner-class households (Pérez 2003). Her excavations found substantial houses with patios surrounded by elevated rooms. Houses had some continuity in place and underwent several remodelings. She trenched narrow terraces (1.0 to 1.5 m wide) on the lower slopes and found that these had no structures and may have served for erosion control and cultivation of maguey or trees.

Diquino has four separate places with public architecture, most of which was built in Natividad. A small, single mound on the Diquino hilltop may have been a ritual place. But the three other mound groups are embedded in residential areas with large and well-built houses. Objects associated with rituals are common on the surface at these places. These may represent the centers of barrios or sections.

We suggest that the archaeological data show four levels of integration:

(1) The whole cacicazgo, the valley itself plus outlying subject towns, many of which we surveyed and report in this chapter. We address this level of state integration in Chapter 10.

(2) The Teposcolula Valley, highly integrated and administered by the Pueblo Viejo. The valley held a settlement cluster bounded by uninhabited terrain on all sides. Internally, there were no gaps between sites greater than 2 km. Given the short distances and large numbers of people, interaction must have been high throughout the whole valley. The distribution of site sizes for the top twenty sites is close to rank-size expectations for an integrated system of central places. Integration of the whole valley is new to Natividad; it did not happen in earlier periods. The San Juan Teposcolula and western clusters were joined by a strong mid-valley development. Cacique control of valley-bottom lands and the canal irrigation of those lands were important for valley-wide integration.

(3) Three settlement clusters corresponding to the main sixteenth-century towns in the valley: San Juan Teposcolula (Diquino), the cluster in the central part of the valley (San Pedro y San Pablo Teposcolula and the Pueblo Viejo), and the western cluster of settlements (Tixa and Ixtapa). The second-ranking centers after the Pueblo Viejo were Diquino (SJT 21) with seven mounds

and 4,200 people and Tixa Viejo (SMX 3) with ten mounds and 1,100 people. Combining Tixa Viejo with the nearby sites SFI 1, 6, and 7 would mean 3,100 people. The western and San Juan clusters have recognizable continuity from as long ago as Cruz times.

(4) Sections or barrios, which were quite local. Many of the single mounds or small mound groups built or reused in Natividad may have been shrines or temples for local, community-based rituals. Some of this architecture is in villages or towns, such as the multiple mound groups at TEC 4 and Nicayuju (SJT 4). Other mounds are at small sites on hilltops (the single mounds at SPP 46 and CAT 10). At several Ramos and Las Flores mound groups there is little Natividad domestic refuse but Natividad sahumadors and censer fragments are found and there are obsidian blades. In all, there may have been twenty or so of these places with a single mound or small group of mounds. The distribution of small mounds is quite even over the whole subregion. In the west where there already were platform mounds from earlier times, people reused them. In the San Juan Teposcolula arm, because earlier populations had concentrated into only two or three sites, new structures were built for the settlements on the valley floor.

To conclude, the Teposcolula subregion offers spectacular archaeological remains. It provides insight into each level of the Postclassic hierarchy. Houses and households are well represented in urban and town situations as at the Pueblo Viejo, Diquino, and Nicayuju. There is a wide range of variation among and between commoner and wealthy households, based on house size and artifacts. Evidence of barrio or section organization consists of numerous small mound groups embedded in residential areas or placed on hilltops above settlements. These mound groups were often places of ritual and several have higher-status residences and artifacts.

Above the level of the barrio were clusters of settlements, three in the case of this subregion. In some respects these correspond to the ñuu or the municipio of historic times. They were headed by towns that were secondary centers in the regional hierarchy. The Teposcolula Pueblo Viejo has more monumental public architecture than the other two towns and it was much larger. Economic and political ties must have been quite close among the three major towns in the Teposcolula Valley. This group formed the core of the greater Teposcolula cacicazgo. At the Pueblo Viejo we see a scale and complexity of architecture that was far greater than that expected for the cabecera of a couple of ñuu. The secluded residential, civic, and ceremonial precinct atop the hill in Zone 1, the monumental open-plaza architecture of Zone 3, and the ball court in between are features found only in the largest and most powerful cacicazgos. This was the architecture of the greater state, the Teposcolula Valley core plus its outlying subregions.

NUÑU

This pocket is situated on tributaries of the southern branch of the Río Teposcolula, which is called the Río Grande. The Nuñu Valley is similar in size, geology, soils, elevation, and topography to the San Juan Teposcolula branch.

3.9 San Vicente Nuñu, looking west from SVN 10. On the hills on the western side of the valley, from left to right, are SVN 32, SVN 22, and SVN 4.

The Río Grande rises in the high mountains 10 km south of San Vicente Nuñu and runs through a narrow, V-shaped gorge for most of its length. Around San Vicente the mountains open into a patch of lower, more gently sloping terrain (Figure 3.9). This is a 2.5 km wide swath of Yanhuitlán shale, sandstone, and conglomerates. On the east the pocket is bordered by volcanic mountains; on the west rises an equally high limestone range. Only 3 km downstream from the northern end of the Nuñu Valley the Río Grande joins the Río Teposcolula at the Teposcolula Pueblo Viejo.

Just south of San Vicente Nuñu the Yanhuitlán beds pinch out, there is a pass, and the trail drops into a narrow valley, the setting of San Pedro Anama at 2,530 m elevation. We include Anama in the Nuñu subregion because over time it has been subject to Nuñu Valley centers.

Late Cruz

The earliest occupation for which we have a record is Late Cruz (Figure 3.10, Table 3.6). Its principal site (SVN 4) is on the piedmont ridge just west of San Vicente overlooking the Arroyo Nuñu. There are several modern houses on the site, many fields, and slopes used for grazing. Parts of the site are eroded to endeque. The Late Cruz covers 21 ha and we estimate a village of perhaps 300 people. The pottery suggests earlier and later Late Cruz. It is a multicomponent site with the oldest components, and even the possibly older material within Late Cruz, at the northern, lower end.

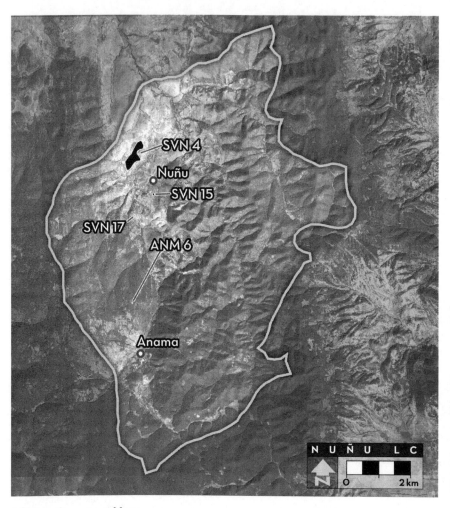

3.10 *Late Cruz sites in Nuñu.*

We found three sites the size of isolated residences upstream from SVN 4. One is on the end of a ridge at the southern edge of San Vicente around the modern houses and equally modern refuse. Farther up the drainage is SVN 17. On top of the Cerro Ticoteo 1 km north of Anama is the third small site. ANM 6 is in pine and secondary-growth forest on very eroded terrain among limestone outcrops. This site is anomalous because of its elevation, 2,720 m.

The occupation of Nuñu began by Late Cruz, in its early half (perhaps even earlier). The main site was a village on a piedmont hill in mid-valley. There were also several sites the size of isolated residences that perhaps date to the last half of Late Cruz.

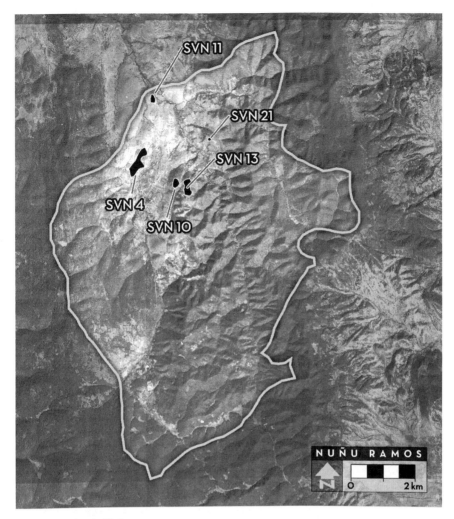

3.11 Ramos sites in Nuñu.

Ramos

Early Ramos began the movement upward to sites on conical hilltops (Figure 3.11, Table 3.7). But the movement was not total. SVN 4, the main Cruz village, was not abandoned until Late Ramos; it seems to have stayed about the same size as it had been. SVN 11 was a small residential site just above the Río Grande on the road between San Vicente and Teposcolula. Within the site boundary of SVN 11 is a small, steep hill, on the top of which is a mojonera marking the boundary between the two municipios. All the Late Cruz isolated residences higher up in the watershed and the Anama Late Cruz hilltop site were abandoned in Ramos.

3.12 The western slope of SVN 10 with its concentric tiers of long terraces.

The new and largest settlements were SVN 10 and 13, Ndicaynu and Ayodo. SVN 10 is better preserved (Figures 3.12–3.14). It is a steep hill just east of the modern town. The top is 100 m above the town. The site was begun in Early Ramos and expanded in Early Las Flores. The Early Ramos occupation covered 4.6 ha at the top and extended downslope two or three levels of terraces; on the north and east sides the occupation spread down to the long wall that almost encircles the site. Terraces and their retaining walls are long and form a doughnut of concentric rings. The top of the hill was modified into a broad terrace, on which there are two mounds facing each other across a plaza.

Across a saddle to the east of SVN 10 is Cerro Ayodo, probably part of the same community. Early Ramos extends from the top of this hill, down south to the saddle, and part way up the next ridge to the south. The higher crests farther to the south were heavily occupied in Las Flores but not in Ramos. Cerro Ayodo must have been terraced for people to have lived there but only scattered building stone and artifacts remain. Several lama-bordos take off from the saddles and barrancas of SVN 10 and 13.

A fifth site is an enigmatic Ramos component (SVN 21) on a ridgetop at 2,460 m on the northeast edge of Nuñu. It has five mounds arranged in a linear string but the Natividad component is better represented. It is possible that SVN 11 and 21 were sites with boundary functions.

SVN 10 and 13 together probably had over 1,100 people in Early Ramos. Nuñu's total population (midpoint of the range) was 1,600. This was a major popu-

3.13 The architecture at SVN 10.

lation increase. It is possible that there was a sequence involving the abandonment of SVN 4, and then the building of SVN 10 and (or) SVN 13, all within Early Ramos, but even that idea would still entail considerable population growth. There is no evidence of Late Ramos occupation in Nuñu.

3.14 SVN 10, looking west from Terrace 6 up the terraced slope toward the plaza.

Las Flores

This was a time of growth and expansion of settlement. There were twelve sites with a combined occupied area of 125 ha (Figure 3.15, Table 3.8). Four of these had the high residential densities found at terraced sites. The total population is estimated to have been between 4,000 and 8,000.

Las Flores settlement was generally at higher elevation than the Ramos. Most people lived above 2,400 m probably for defense. In Nuñu there were conical hills and long ridge crests suitable for defense and fortification east of the modern town. This is where most of the population clustered. These ridges are at the upper edge of the Yanhuitlán Formation and there are lama-bordos in most of the barrancas surrounding all the big Las Flores sites.

SVN 10 is Ndicaynu, the hilltown begun in Early Ramos just east of San Vicente Nuñu. It grew larger in Las Flores and had seventy-two terraces on the well-preserved upper slope. The terraces are long and accommodated multiple houses. Remains of houses—rises with foundation fragments and building stone—can often be seen on the back sides of terraces. For the well-preserved part of the site, if we assume that a household cluster took up about 300 m^2 of space, the residential terraces would have had space for 120 houses (54 single-house terraces plus 66 houses on multiple-house terraces). More of the site had been terraced but is now poorly preserved. Our estimate of the population of the whole site is about 1,200 people. The west and northwest sides are protected by defensive walls 5 m high and over 100 m long. The other sides of the hill are less vulnerable because they are steeper.

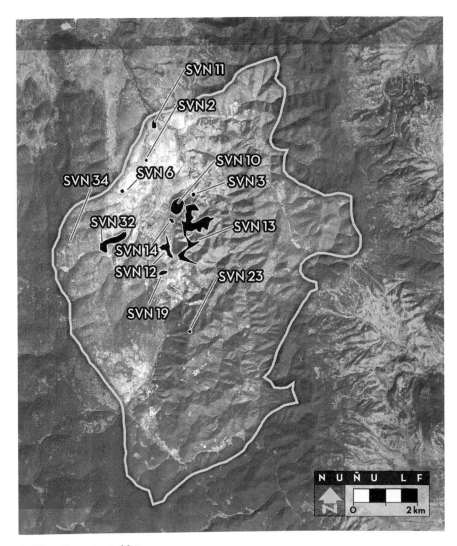

3.15 Las Flores sites in Nuñu.

On top there is the broad, flat terrace with two mounds facing each other across the plaza mentioned in the Ramos section.

Cerro Ayodo and the higher knob Cerro Yucuxato formed the largest center (SVN 13). This is the high ridge east of SVN 10 that runs south for 2 km. The crew claimed it was steep. The civic-ceremonial architecture is spread out with no central monumental focus. There is a structure and often a plaza on each of four peaks. Structure 5, also a single mound on a plaza, is in a saddle. Unfortunately, many archaeological features are plowed down and eroded away and the structures

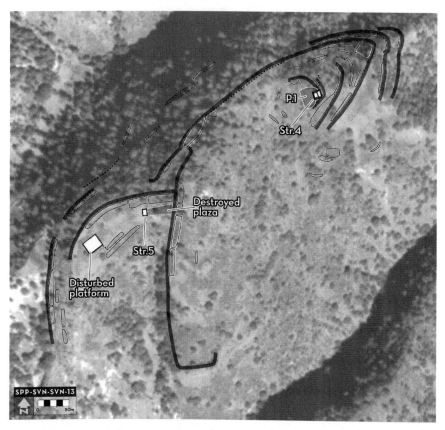

3.16 Architecture on the best-preserved part of SVN 13.

are looted. On the ridge crest we mapped fifty-two terraces, many retaining walls, ramps, stairways, and roads (Figure 3.16). Stone house foundations, stucco floors, and concentrations of building stone indicate domestic construction. This was a large town. The Las Flores component sprawls along for 62 ha and we estimate that two-thirds of the site was modified into residential terraces. Our average population estimate is 3,500 inhabitants. There are five lama-bordos sometimes obviously associated with Las Flores archaeological features. For example, residential Terrace 40 is 67 by 7 m and its retaining wall is connected to the wall of one of the uppermost fields of a lama-bordo. Unlike at SVN 10 the ceramic collections from SVN 13 do not have diagnostics of the Transición phase. SVN 10 was begun a little earlier and the expansion up the mountain to SVN 13 dates to the Early Classic after Transición.

SVN 3, 12, 14, and 19 are outliers of the Ndicaynu-Ayodo-Yucuxato community. There are quite a few lama-bordos associated with these sites. At SVN 14 there is another mound on a platform.

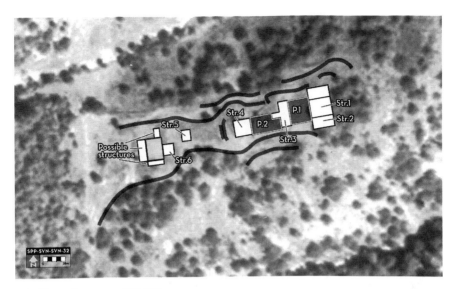

3.17 The architecture at SVN 32.

There was another Early Las Flores large village at Diquindiyi (or Nuutende, SVN 32) on the long ridge on the north side of the Barranca Xatixisno. It is a single-component site that in date should pair with SVN 10 as Transición. Erosion is severe and virtually every ancient wall and structure has been covered by rocks in modern times. Several lama-bordos were noted.

SVN 32 has the most impressive Las Flores civic-ceremonial complex in Nuñu. This is a linear string (Figure 3.17). Proceeding from lower to higher elevation we mapped a patio group that may have had four mounds and then a single mound that may have had a plaza. Uphill from the possible plaza were two retaining walls, and on the next level up a mound, a plaza, and then Str. 3, which probably had a stairway facing the plaza. The opposite side of Str. 3 faced another plaza and on the other side of that plaza on the top of the knob was Str. 1, built on a platform. As in other linear strings that stretch along ridge crests there are terraces paralleling the complex on a lower level off the side of the crest. The back of the focal mound, Str. 1, joins the steep natural slope of the peak, preventing access from that direction and increasing the dramatic effect of the structure's height.

The Nuñu settlement cluster was ringed by six small sites (SVN 11, 2, 6, 34, 23, and perhaps 25). This pattern of small sites on the boundaries of Las Flores local polities is something we have seen in other subregions, for example, at Teposcolula and Nejapilla. Where ceramics are sufficient to date more precisely, these boundary sites seem to be Transición. Anama was apparently not occupied in Las Flores. SVN 2, 6, and 11 are ordinary residential occupations except that SVN 11 is on the present-day boundary with San Pedro y San Pablo Teposcolula. SVN 34 is located on the western side of the divide in the mountains above SVN 32.

Another border site is the tiny SVN 23 on Cerro Tiandacoo, at 2,800 m. This was a fortified peak. Today it is covered in forest. Its local name is La Muralla (the wall) for good reason. On the north end the very steep slope was made more challenging by building seven successive stone walls, each 12 m long and 1 to 2 m high; the average width of the terraces formed by these is only 2 m. After ascending these walls there is more construction: two platforms rising to a mound on the peak. There were few surface artifacts but we saw Transición sherds on the south slope. There is another tall wall guarding the south approach. The location is strategic, overlooking the southern approaches to Nuñu.

A final candidate for a Las Flores border site would be the sherdless, undated fortification and mound SVN 25 located on a prominent hilltop on the opposite side of the Río Grande about 2.5 km from the main town of SVN 13. The site overlooks the junction of a stream that enters the river from the east, which is the Nejapilla subregion. The construction here consists of a defensive wall built across the ridge crest, a second one 30 m up the slope, and a structure on the peak of the hill. The closest dateable site is a Natividad isolated residence 800 m up the side canyon.

In sum, after the Late Ramos hiatus Nuñu was reoccupied in Transicíon initially at the SVN 10 fortified hilltown, the village at SVN 32, and many of the small sites that ring the valley. This was a substantial population of perhaps 2,000 people. The civic-ceremonial center in these times may have been at the new site, SVN 32, where there was a string of structures and platforms. There were a half dozen small hamlets. On its southern and perhaps eastern flanks the community was protected by forts. The major town of Ayodo-Yucuxato (SVN 13) seems to date after Transición, in Early Las Flores. It is uncertain how much of the Transición settlement was abandoned in favor of the cluster in the immediate vicinity of the major town. SVN 13 has a small, separate mound and plazas, not the concentration expected at a major administrative center.

Natividad

There is no evidence of Late Classic occupation in Nuñu. The Natividad was a reoccupation after a period of abandonment. In the Postclassic the population size was lower than it had been in the Early Classic, the opposite of the usual pattern.

People were dispersed in many small settlements (Figure 3.18, Table 3.9). SVN 1 on the low hill north of town was the largest single settlement, a village of some 700 people (Figure 3.19). There were six smaller villages, eight hamlets of less than a hundred people each, and sixteen possible isolated residences. All of these sites have Natividad components that are low density and dispersed; there are no dense concentrations of materials.

Settlement was oriented toward the Yanhuitlán Formation soils with the exception of a few small, perhaps special-purpose sites in the mountains. The field notes record intensive recent farming on and around most sites and of course severe erosion. Natividad sites in Nuñu are often closely associated with lama-bordos. For

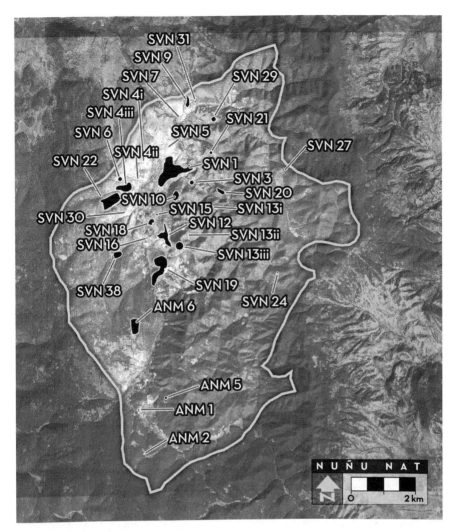

3.18 *Natividad sites in Nuñu.*

example, at SVN 1 there are four lama-bordos directly associated with the Natividad component (and see Figure 3.20). Generally, people in Nuñu lived in dispersed ranchería settlements interspersed with fields.

There were no high-ranking central places but almost everyone lived only 2 to 4 km from one of the Mixteca Alta's leading centers, Teposcolula Pueblo Viejo. At SVN 13, Nuñu's major center in the Classic period, we found Natividad artifacts at the single mounds on three separate peaks on the ridge crest. From the artifacts it seems that this was ritual visiting and not domestic use. There are single, poorly preserved mounds at SVN 1 and SVN 18, where we also found a censer cover. At

3.19 *San Vicente Nuñu, looking north to the hill of SVN 1, a mainly Natividad occupation.*

3.20 *Abandoned lama-bordo associated with SVN 19.*

SVN 5 and 9 we saw what may have been houses with sunken patios. The most interesting architecture is on two ridgetops (2,460 m elevation) near the eastern edge of the Yanhuitlán soils. These are SVN 20 and 21, about 1 km apart. SVN 20 has a small structure on a platform and possibly another structure at the end of the same platform. This group is a small version of the linear string at SVN 21, which has five or six mounds set transversely to the ridgeline. Both sites also had a few eroded residential terraces. What special activities took place at SVN 20 and 21 we do not know.

Anama saw some use in Natividad. Cerro Ticoteo (ANM 6) was the largest site, with about 200 people. There were three small sites south of the modern town, including one (ANM 1) on a trail.

YODOBADA

Yodobada, after the modern village of the same name, is the term we use for the watershed of the upper Río Tejupan. The Río Tejupan flows north but the landscape is very similar to that of the San Juan Teposcolula Valley, which is just across the divide to the south. Both valleys are only about 1 km wide and both are framed by the same limestone ridge to the west and the same igneous mountains to the east, with fertile but easily eroded beds at lower elevations. In Yodobada these beds are formed from mudstones and sandstones. The fall from the head end of the valley in the south to the end of our surveyed area in the north, a distance of 13 km, is from 2,350 m to 2,150 m.

The Yodobada subregion was never a core or autonomous polity but over time it showed subtle changes in the directions and boundaries of interaction. Historically, it belonged mostly to the cacicazgo and municipio of Tejupan; the upper (south) end, the lands of the village Refugio de Morelos, today is part of San Juan Teposcolula.

We covered about two-thirds (about 35 km²) of this valley, our intention being to make sure we had overlap between the Teposcolula survey area and Byland's (1980) survey of Tejupan. The descriptions here use both Byland's and our data for the areas of overlap and we refer to his results for the larger Tejupan area that we did not survey.

Early/Middle Cruz

The largest occupation was at YBA 2 on a hill 60 m above the valley floor just southeast of the modern village of Tierra Blanca (Figure 3.21, Table 3.10). This is a hilltop used in several phases beginning in Middle Cruz. Our site size of 7.5 ha is not based on many definite Middle Cruz sherds. There are ancient terraces and one mound, but given the light density of Middle Cruz ceramics relative to later phases, this architecture, at least in its present form, probably postdates Middle Cruz.

YBA 1 is a low hill with a strong Late Cruz occupation and later components as well. Some of the pottery could be earlier than Late Cruz, so we suggest a Middle

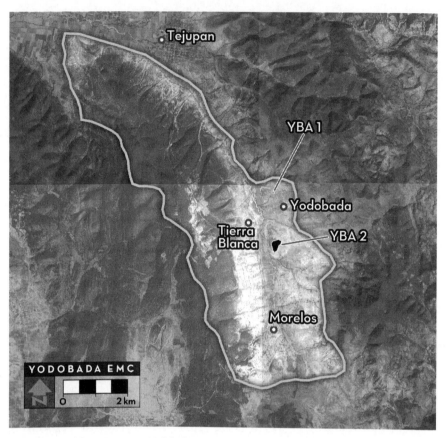

3.21 Early/Middle Cruz sites in Yodobada.

Cruz presence. Byland's survey in 1977 found an Early Cruz component here, equiv-alent to an isolated residence, and a 1.5 ha Middle Cruz occupation.

In addition to the two sites we located, the 1977 survey found Early Cruz at two other sites, our MOR 4 and another site on the eastern edge of the valley. Each component is based on one or two diagnostic sherds, which is common at many Early Formative sites as they are initially recognized on surface survey.

Drawing the data from the 1977 and 1999 surveys together, there are three pos-sible Early Cruz sites in the Yodobada subregion, each the equivalent of an isolated residence, spaced about 2.5 to 4.0 km apart. This is the pattern Byland reports for the Tamazulapan-Tejupan survey area as a whole. The Middle Cruz pattern may show a little growth but it is not much different: four sites in Yodobada have small Middle Cruz occupations, of which three were hamlets and one was a single resi-dence. There are mounds at the Middle Cruz sites YBA 1 and 2. Nothing in the surface evidence firmly ties mound construction to Middle Cruz but the continuity of occupation into later times on sites that have public architecture is noteworthy and is seen elsewhere in Oaxaca.

Early and Middle Cruz settlements in Yodobada are nearer to each other than they are to any contemporary sites to the south or west; they are close to similar isolated residences and hamlets in Tejupan and Tamazulapan. Interaction was probably more oriented to Tejupan-Tamazulapan than elsewhere.

Late Cruz

Late Cruz settlements grew, mostly in the same places occupied earlier (Figure 3.22, Table 3.11). Together, the 1977 project, the Teposcolula survey, and the 1999 project located eight Late Cruz sites. Generally, they are on low hills at the edge of the valley floor. Most have evidence of earlier occupation and most have Las Flores or Natividad components too.

The total occupied area, counting all eight sites, was about 64 ha. Byland's TA 20 covered almost 8 ha, YBA 2 was about the same size, and the two largest villages, YBA 1 and MOR 4, each had over 20 ha. The other sites were tiny hamlets and isolated residences. Most of these Late Cruz settlements had fairly low, dispersed intrasite house densities, one possible exception being YBA 1, the northernmost of our sites in Yodobada, where artifact densities are higher. Total population was between 500 and 1,500 people.

The YBA 1 site has two mounds that face each other across a plaza. They probably date to this phase. YBA 2 and MOR 7 have one mound each but later phases are better represented on and around the mounds and it is unclear whether they had Late Cruz construction stages.

Two other sites are distinctive. MOR 4 had its major occupation in this phase. Artifacts include quite a bit of groundstone, and on the upper, western part of the site, at the edge of the limestone formation, there is evidence of the reduction of locally available chert cobbles. TBA 2, at 2,570 m asl, is the highest Late Cruz settlement in Yodobada. This is an isolated residence on a saddle on top of the ridge between Yucunama and Yodobada. It may have pertained to the Yucunama settlement cluster since its nearest neighbor lies on that side of the divide.

Our ceramic evidence places the peak of Late Cruz settlement and population growth in the latter part of Late Cruz, equivalent to Monte Albán Early I. The earlier (Rosario-like) phase is also present. In the broader regional context the Late Cruz growth and differentiation of settlements in Yodobada was part of the same trend in the valleys north, west, and south. In Tejupan one village, Nuundaa, emerged as a leading center. Byland reports it had two mounds and covered almost 26 ha, about the size of MOR 4, YBA 1, YUC 21 (in Yucunama), and the largest villages in Teposcolula but twice as large as the next largest village in Tamazulapan-Tejupan. This rather even distribution of larger village sizes and the equally even distribution of public architecture among them suggest that subregions like Yodobada were not strongly centralized.

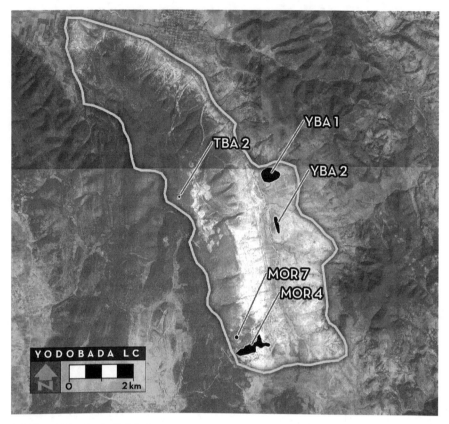

3.22 Late Cruz sites in Yodobada.

Ramos

Most settlements in Yodobada were abandoned in Early Ramos and there was even less occupation in Late Ramos. In the geopolitical climate of the Late Formative a small place such as Yodobada, on a major route north-south but near no protectors, may have stood little chance.

Byland's survey observed a general decline in settlement in Tamazulapan-Tejupan. In our survey there are two Ramos sites, one Early (YBA 2) and one Late (TBA 5, Byland's TA 23) (Figure 3.23, Table 3.12).

YBA 2 is a low hilltop at the edge of the valley floor. It has a Cruz occupation but no Las Flores, one mound, and residential terraces. Our field crew observed Early Ramos ceramics at the top of the hill and on the upper part of the south slope but the density was not great and the phase is not well represented in our collections. We list it as a small village of 400 people. We think the terraces were made either late in Late Cruz or early in Early Ramos but the site was not occupied long in Early Ramos.

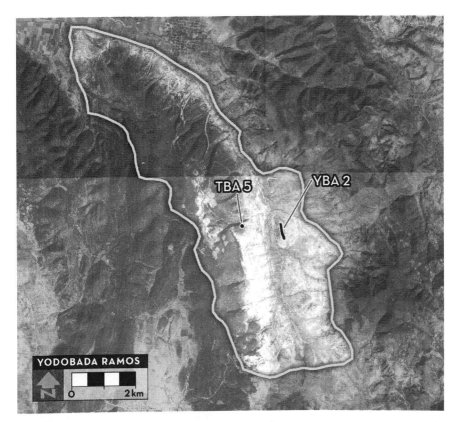

3.23 Ramos sites in Yodobada.

TBA 5 is on the western wall of the valley on a ridgetop at 2,420 m asl. Today this high piedmont is used for grazing but it was cleared in the past because some of the site is covered with secondary growth. Erosion is locally severe and we found sherds directly on calcrete. There is a small plaza with one mound on the east side and two mounds on the west. The site is larger in Las Flores but the Late Ramos materials come from the center around the mounds, which suggests there may have been Ramos mound construction.

Las Flores

After several centuries of decline population expanded again in Las Flores. We have nine sites with about 94 ha of total occupation (Figure 3.24, Table 3.13). Population was between 1,600 and 3,600.

Most people lived near the valley floor at some of the same sites founded in Cruz times and in several new places, at elevations of 2,300 m and below. Three sites with small numbers of inhabitants were situated around 2,450 m. This use

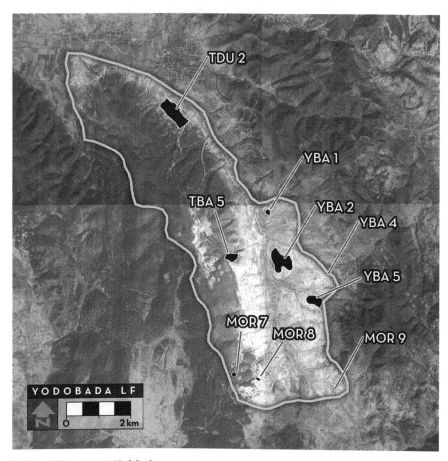

3.24 *Las Flores sites in Yodobada.*

of higher and lower situations is typical of Las Flores elsewhere in the Mixteca Alta.

The largest village (in population) was YBA 2, the hilltop terrace site that had been important in Cruz and Early Ramos. If almost half of the site area had been terraced, as we think, the average population estimate would be about 1,300 people. The second-largest settlement was TDU 2, an artifact scatter that extends across three lobes of the piedmont just above the valley floor near Tejupan.

Four sites have mounded architecture. In each case construction could have started earlier than Las Flores; there are no sites with mounds that are exclusively Las Flores. We think there were probably Las Flores construction stages on the mounds at YBA 1 and TBA 5. There may have been use of the single mounds at MOR 7 and YBA 2. In any case the Yodobada subregion had relatively little civic-ceremonial architecture in the Classic period. But the evidence does suggest continuity in use of traditional, locally important places, not just as shrines on the landscape but as centers of the larger villages.

There are ceramic grounds for suspecting settlement change during Las Flores. Four sites have enough diagnostics to assign Early and Late components (a Transición presence is not obvious). YBA 1 and TBA 5 have clear Early Las Flores. These were both locally important sites that were occupied in Ramos; at TBA 5 there was direct continuity from Late Ramos. Two sites have a clear Late Classic: YBA 1, which also had Early Las Flores, and TDU 2 across the stream from Tejupan and the northernmost site in our survey.

In Las Flores the Yodobada subregion was probably split politically. A southern fringe of small sites was close to Yucunama and the El Fortín de San Juan center. Between these and the rest of the Yodobada sites was a gap of 2.5 km. Most settlements were in the orbit of the large center at Tejupan only 6 km from YBA 2, the largest Yodobada site.

Natividad

This was the time of heaviest settlement and highest population. Every site we found has Natividad (although a few re-occupations are quite small) and there were many new sites that had never been settled previously. Settlements were located over the widest range of elevations of any period (Figure 3.25, Table 3.14).

The total occupied area was over 270 ha in twenty-five sites. Intrasite population density was not high. There are no sites with the closely spaced dwellings one finds on hilltop terraced sites. The total population may have been around 4,700.

There were three main clusters of population: the southern end of the valley, Yodobada, and around Tejupan. There was also a scatter of hamlets in the mountains on the western side of the valley.

The upper, southern end of the valley has numerous sites that are outliers of the sprawling town of Diquino (SJT 21) at the upper end of the San Juan Teposcolula Valley. In Yodobada all the MOR sites except MOR 6 belong in this cluster, by proximity and because there is a break in settlement between them and the group around Yodobada itself. Today the territory of Refugio de Morelos is part of the San Juan Teposcolula municipio. Settlements of this southern cluster are low in habitational density and dispersed. Almost all are on soils of the Yanhuitlán beds. In several cases sherds were mainly found in erosional gullies. At MOR 15 the site had clearly been on top of the hill but we found its artifacts in the barranca below. These sites tend to be fairly high in elevation because they are at the head end of the valley in the piedmont, well situated for lower-slope and lama-bordo farming. There are many lama-bordos (Figure 3.26). At MOR 2 there were two structures, a mound at the east side of the site and another at the west end. Both were small and now not in very good condition. MOR 7 has a small mound probably built earlier and used in Natividad.

The settlement cluster around Yodobada and Tierra Blanca consists of the six YBA sites plus MOR 6. This was the most populous cluster. It is linked by almost

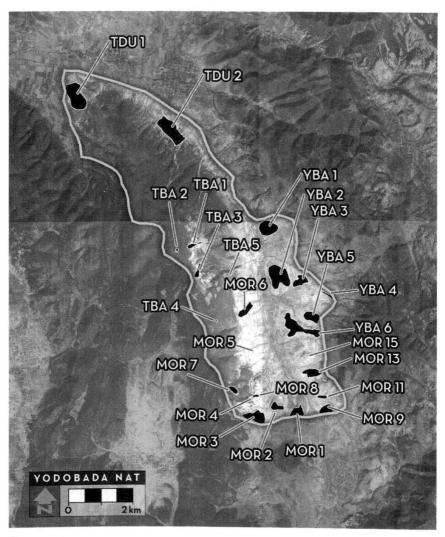

3.25 *Natividad sites in Yodobada.*

continuous settlement to Tejupan. Most of these sites were occupied earlier but the Natividad component was the largest. The within-site habitational density was not as compact as it had been in previous periods. YBA 6 was notably dispersed and patchy. The mounds at YBA 1 and 2, built earlier, were probably used in Natividad. There is no other evidence of new civic-ceremonial construction.

The TBA 1–5 sites on the mountain ridges on the west side of the valley are a type of settlement seen only rarely in prior phases. These are small hamlets. Elevations range from 2,410 to 2,580 m and the setting is the limestone mountain

3.26 A lama-bordo near MOR 3, in the process of eroding headward.

ridge dividing Yodobada from Yucunama. Today these places are used for grazing and woodcutting. TBA 5 is a small reuse of the Ramos and Las Flores three-mound group.

The other cluster of settlements has two sites, TDU 1 and 2, on piedmont slopes at the foot of the mountain just above the Río Tejupan. They are part of the very large and populous core of the Tejupan cacicazgo.

Yodobada illustrates the close and porous boundaries of Late Postclassic communities and polities. The southern end of the valley was part of the Diquino sphere, the mountain hamlets may have had as much to do with their Yucunama neighbors as they did with the valley-floor villages and Tejupan, and Yodobada itself was the southern extension of a very developed and autonomous center at Tejupan.

YUCUNAMA

North of the Teposcolula Valley there are three parallel, north-south running valleys: Yodobada on the east, Yucunama in the center, and Lagunas on the west. Of the three, Yucunama is the smallest, the highest, and the most enclosed. It is a perched 5 by 2 km patch of Yanhuitlán shale and sandstone surrounded by higher limestone ridges. The north end is internally draining and there are several dry lakes (we do not know if they were dry in prehispanic times). The Yanhuitlán beds are below about 2,500 m. The hilly floor of this valley is 2,460 m in the north and 2,400 m at the south end. Yucunama is colder than Teposcolula. Stiver Walsh surveyed

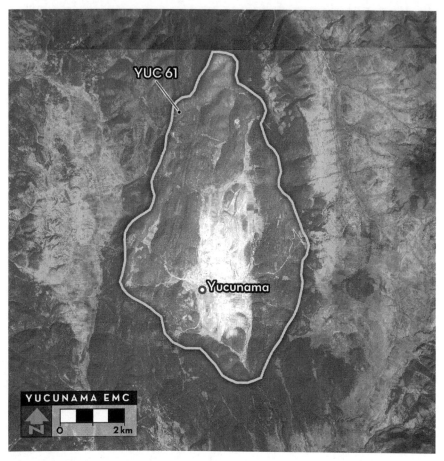

3.27 Early/Middle Cruz sites in Yucunama.

Yucunama as part of her Teposcolula project and this section is drawn from her work (2001).

The only modern town is the municipio of San Pedro Yucunama, which has always been part of the Teposcolula district. In earliest Colonial times Yucunama was subject to the cacique of Teposcolula 6 km to the south. A trail also leads 12 km north to Tejupan.

Early/Middle Cruz

There are no Archaic or Early Cruz sites known. The earliest is an odd, 1.0 ha Middle Cruz hamlet (YUC 61) not in the valley proper but north on the Barranca Nduandi, a fissure that drains to the west and to Lagunas (Figure 3.27, Table 3.15). At 2,460 m this is high for an Early or Middle Formative site. The barranca may

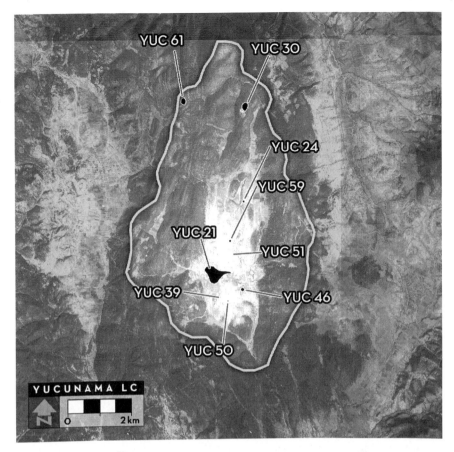

3.28 *Late Cruz sites in Yucunama.*

afford a sheltered microclimate. The site is also on the main north-south trail. YUC 61 was not ephemeral—it persisted into Late Cruz and Ramos times.

Late Cruz

This was the period when Yucunama was settled. Eight new sites appeared and YUC 61 continued (Figure 3.28, Table 3.15). Also two nearby sites, SIL 6 and TBA 2, which are only 1 km from Yucunama sites and much more distant to their closest neighbors in Lagunas and Yodobada, could be grouped in this cluster. Growth continued through Late Cruz so that by its end there may have been 500 people.

Yucunama Centro (YUC 21) was the main village with perhaps 400 people. It was on a low hill that constricts the Yucunama Valley and where there are several water sources. The village is under the modern town; in fact, the ancient site center was probably leveled during the construction of the Colonial church. Portions were excavated by Matadamas (1991–1992), who encountered part of a public, non-residential area with a platform and several superimposed floors, the last one of flag-stones. The area had been kept clean of domestic refuse. There were numerous burials with differences in treatments and offerings suggesting hereditary social ranking. The Yucunama head village would have had as peers other places such as Nuundaa in Tejupan, YBA 1 and MOR 4 in Yodobada, and XAC 6 near Cerro Jazmín. These were all somewhat smaller than Loma Mina, the Teposcolula head town.

All the other Yucunama settlements were small hamlets and single residences. There were five within 1 km of Yucunama Centro. By the latter half of Late Cruz, Yucunama had a hierarchically organized settlement cluster separate from Teposcolula, perhaps in some sense subject to its larger and older neighbor.

Ramos

The beginning of Ramos and the end of Cruz saw a major settlement shift. All Cruz settlements were abandoned except for the persistent YUC 61. Yucunama Centro, the head village, was abandoned. People consolidated into fewer sites (there were only five—Figure 3.29, Table 3.16). But two of these were larger in population than any Cruz settlement had been: Diquiyucu, the hill just west of the modern town, and Ñundito, on a hilltop 3 km to the east. These two places had 2,000 and 600 people, respectively. There was a significant movement to higher elevations. Three of the five Ramos sites were above 2,500 m; none had been before. There were no sites below 2,400 m.

People did not move even higher to one of the northern ridges (2,600 m), probably because none of the other ridges had the conical peaks favored for fortifications and none was as easy to defend. The mountains farther north in Yucunama were distant from farmland, whereas the hills chosen were near land that had been farmed since the initial colonization. Finally there may have been advantages in political ties and communication with Teposcolula. Relocating to higher places to the north would have taken people away from Teposcolula and possibly inserted them in Tejupan's sphere.

All five sites are situated directly overlooking trails: YUC 45 on the trail to Teposcolula (and on the municipio's boundary), YUC 61 on north-south and east-west trails (and on the municipio's boundary), the two large sites on the east-west route and on the axis of the valley itself, and YUC 56 more directly situated over the east-west route. Some of these (not YUC 61) are inter-visible.

The total Yucunama population increased fivefold, even more than the substantial growth in Teposcolula. The average estimate is 2,600 people. Given abrupt settlement change at the beginning of Early Ramos and the relatively short duration of this phase, people probably came here from elsewhere. One source could have been Yodobada, which lost population from Late Cruz to Ramos.

The largest settlement was Diquiyucu (YUC 16, Figure 3.30), a fortified hill-town with rings of high-walled terraces surrounding the top on three sides (the west side is quite steep). These were multi-house residential terraces. The site has six

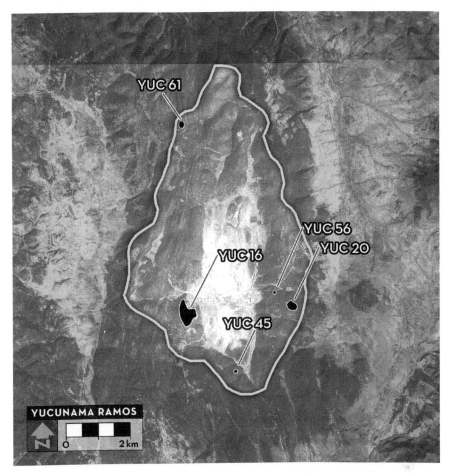

3.29 *Ramos sites in Yucunama.*

mounds and platforms on the top of the hill in an elaborate civic-ceremonial precinct. The form of this complex is a linear string. It has three platforms rising one above the next with a single mound on the second platform and two mounds facing each other on the third. Two of the mounds are 6 m tall. In population size and in monumental architecture Diquiyucu was the peer of other large hilltowns such as El Fortín de San Juan.

The other settlement of substantial size was Ñundito (YUC 20). It too was a fortified hilltown (Figure 3.31). Around its base is a 400 m long wall and ditch. It also had tiers of residential terraces with substantial retaining walls. Although its mounds were not as tall as those at Diquiyucu, the layout of the civic-ceremonial complex was grand, an alignment along the top of the north end of the hill. There were four monumental platform-terraces rising one after another toward the top. At

3.30 Diquiyucu, seen from San Pedro Yucunama.

the very top there were three mounds facing each other on a secluded court and just south of this group was another three-mound group, closed in such a way that it presented its back to the more public area on the platform-terrace below.

As in Teposcolula all this Early Ramos development disappeared within two centuries or less. There is no Late Ramos in Yucunama.

Las Flores

Re-population of Yucunama began in the Transición phase between the Terminal Formative and the Early Classic. The two hilltowns, Diquiyucu and Ñundito, were resettled in Transición. There are sixteen Las Flores sites (Figure 3.32, Table 3.17); Diquiyucu and Ñundito were the largest with 2,200 and 1,000 people, respectively, followed by YUC 24, a small village. The other places were small hamlets and a couple isolated residences. Total population was higher than in Ramos at about 3,700 people.

Settlements occupied a wide range of elevations from 2,350 to 2,525 m. The distribution of sites was compact—all fit within a 3 km radius. Three other sites probably belong in this cluster, by proximity. They are MOR 7, SJT 2, and SJT 5, on the eastern border.

Yucunama is notable for having more small hamlets and villages than its neighbors to the east and west. In San Juan Teposcolula, Yodobada, and Lagunas people were concentrated into just a few large settlements. In Yucunama there were large towns too but there were also many small settlements.

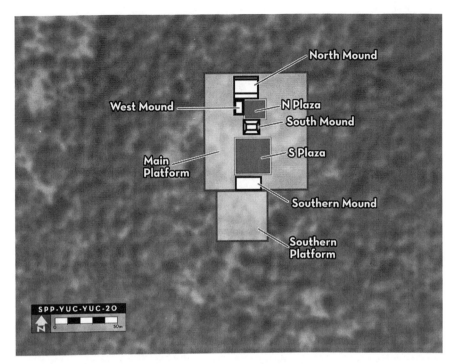

3.31 Ñundito (YUC 20) summit.

At the two large hilltowns the same public architecture described in the Ramos section above was still in use. These complexes were probably expanded to their final dimensions in Las Flores. Although impressive, neither complex is as large or differentiated as the major Las Flores centers in Teposcolula, which have two or three times as many mounds and platforms. We think Yucunama was subordinate to Teposcolula.

Yucunama had a third center with substantial public architecture. This was Cerro la Neblina (YUC 38) on a knob of the limestone ridge at the boundary with Lagunas overlooking the principal east-west route. La Neblina was a hamlet of less than fifty inhabitants. It had some residential terraces on the slopes and a notable architectural complex on top. This consisted of a substantial mound (3.5 m high) that faced a plaza with an adoratorio and two other mounds; all of this was built on a 100 by 40 m platform. Architecture this large probably had functions beyond the needs of the hamlet's inhabitants. On the opposite edge of the Yucunama subregion, MOR 7 had a single mound. No other settlements had mounds.

The Las Flores buildup began in Transición, it peaked in Early Las Flores, and it was over by Late Las Flores. The survey found no convincing Late Las Flores ceramics. The abandonment is another episode of history that Yucunama shared with Teposcolula.

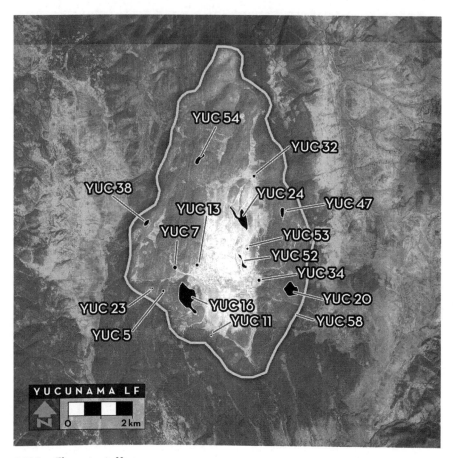

3.32 *Las Flores sites in Yucunama.*

Natividad

Ranchería settlement predominated as in no other period. We count fifty-six sites in Yucunama (Figure 3.33, Table 3.18). None was larger than 27 ha and none had an average population estimate greater than 419 people. Almost half of the total population of 1,900 lived in settlements of less than 100 people (there were fifty-one such hamlets and isolated residences). Only five sites had more than 100 inhabitants. In many cases the within-site habitational densities were of the lowest category, 5 to 10 persons per ha.

This was the time of the most even and widespread distribution of settlement in the whole sequence. All parts of the subregion had small settlements, from the mountain ridges at higher elevations to the edges of the barrancas below 2,400 m. Habitation sites were found out to the Yucunama boundaries in all directions except the ridge at the northern tip, which is terrain of steep ridges that was never used

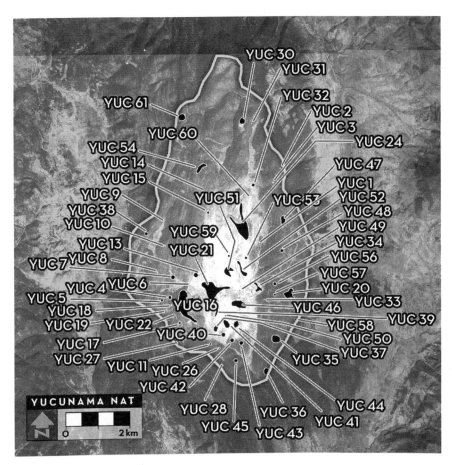

3.33 *Natividad sites in Yucunama.*

for settlement. As elsewhere in highland Oaxaca during the Postclassic, boundaries were fuzzy and porous and settlement clusters were not as delimited by uninhabited zones as they had been in earlier periods.

There was some concentration of settlement around the site of the modern town. Twenty sites are located within 1.5 km of YUC 21, the village on today's townsite. Over half the population lived in these twenty sites.

Diquiyucu (YUC 16) was the probable administrative center. It too was a more dispersed settlement than it had been earlier (we estimate 16 persons per ha compared to 75 per ha in Las Flores). No new civic-ceremonial architecture was built in Natividad. There was considerable reuse of the old mound complexes at Diquiyucu and Ñundito and minor use of the structures at YUC 38, Cerro la Neblina.

We see Yucunama as a prime example of ranchería development. It was economically tied to its neighbors, especially Teposcolula and Diquino and to a lesser

3.34 *The western side of the valley at San Andrés Lagunas. Note caliche on eroded parts of the slope, contour terraces on the hillsides, and the flat valley floor. Javier Hernández and Ezekiel Cristóbal, foreground.*

extent Yodobada and Lagunas. It was politically subordinate to the cacicazgo of Teposcolula. It had no defensive sites and no new public architecture.

LAGUNAS

This northwestern subregion is a long, narrow, flat-floored valley consisting of two internally draining basins. The valley floor lies at 2,300 m, not as high as Yucunama. The northern basin is less than 3 km long. It is separated from the southern basin by high ground where present-day San Isidro Lagunas sits. The southern basin is almost 6 km in length. Both are no more than 1 km wide. The name Lagunas is apt as local people say the valley used to have extensive wetlands.

The eastern wall of the valley is an abrupt, steep, hard limestone ridge. The western edge is composed of the sedimentary materials (shale, sandstone, and a softer limestone) of the Yanhuitlán beds; the western side today and in the past has the most settlement (including San Andrés Lagunas, the cabecera municipal—Figure 3.34). Today farmers on the lowest slopes make contour terraces to catch eroding soils. The higher slopes on this western side are deeply, precipitously, and fantastically cut by gullies. One can see the soil being mined away and transported during any rainstorm. According to local farmers some of the soils eroded down from the western slopes are infertile (perhaps too sandy and lacking in organics and minerals). The mountains forming the southwestern edge of the valley are an igneous (andesite) mass not especially favored for settlement.

Historically, Lagunas has been subject to Teposcolula, 11 km south as the crow flies. There is also an easy route northwest to Tamazulapan, which would be slightly closer for people at the northern end of the Lagunas subregion. This may be relevant because in several periods, including early on, northern Lagunas had the more important sites.

Early Occupations?

We have no definite Archaic sites. A single non-diagnostic artifact attracted our attention on a site (SAL 14) on the divide west of La Soledad. This was an unusual chert core, 12 by 8 by 3 cm, with large flake scars. The site is a 20 by 10 m scatter of Natividad Sandy Cream sherds and other lithics of the kind common on sites of ceramic times.

We found no Early or Middle Cruz sites. On the valley floor we surveyed all the possible places for exposures and all the rises, but if there were Early/Middle Cruz sites on little piedmont spurs, these are now covered by meters of alluvium. Given the likelihood of attractive wetlands and the massive alluviation, it is possible that earlier sites are buried.

Late Cruz

The main site we know about is the eastern spur descending from Cerro la Culebra (SIL 6) overlooking the northern Lagunas basin (Figure 3.35, Table 3.19). This is on the limestone ridge and the Late Cruz occupation is at 2,500 m asl. A mojonera for the Yucunama-Lagunas boundary stands near the site. YUC 61, which also has Late Cruz, is less than 1 km away. SIL 13 is a concentration of Late Cruz sherds in a tiny area within a much larger Natividad site 160 m above the valley floor, opposite SIL 6 on the western side of the valley. Aside from these two sites at high elevations in the northern end of Lagunas, we found no other Late Cruz. The possibility of buried sites should be kept in mind.

Ramos

Lagunas had substantial population, perhaps 1,200 people, in six settlements (Figure 3.36, Table 3.20). All were on hilltops 100 to 200 m above the valley floor. Four were villages of several hundred people each and two were small hamlets. Most of the sites are badly damaged by plowing and erosion and site sizes are only approximate.

The best-preserved is SAL 16 (Figure 3.37), Cerro Ñunducha or Cerro de Agua (there is a good spring on the site). The top of the hill has three or four tiers of terraces and retaining walls still in fairly good shape (Figure 3.38). Below that the slopes are heavily plowed but we did see ancient retaining wall fragments. The top

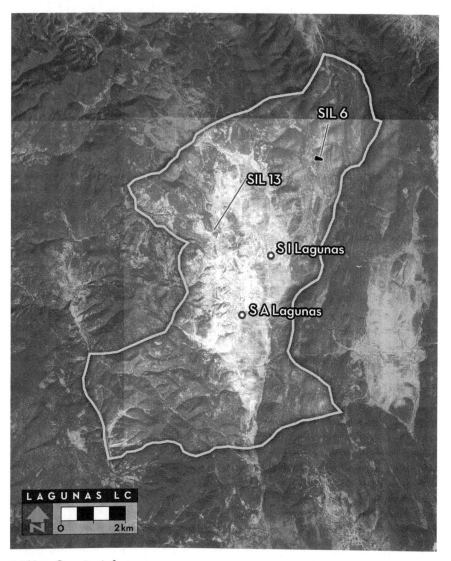

3.35 *Late Cruz sites in Lagunas.*

of the hill had been leveled to create a large plaza, on which are two mounds facing each other (Figure 3.39). Plowed-up building stone suggests other structures on this open area. The residential terraces, of which we mapped thirty, are long and narrow, for example, 36 by 5 m, 60 by 3.5 m, and 69 by 4 m. They are arranged in concentric rings. A lama-bordo begins at the outermost residential terraces.

Site-wide planning is evident. The wall-building and slope modifications affected more than just one household. A north-south axis can be traced from the

3.36 Ramos sites in Lagunas.

plaza to the outermost, lowest ring of terraces. In several places such as at Terraces 1, 2, 12, 13, 29, and 30, terrace ends, ramps, and stairways were coordinated across three tiers so that access ways coincided.

We can estimate the number of houses at Ñunducha from the field observations of foundations and from assumptions about the amount of space a domestic unit requires. Based on excavated house clusters in the Valley of Oaxaca (Winter 1976; Blanton 1978:30), domestic units occupied about 312 m². We used that figure

3.37 SAL 16 is at left and Cerro Verde (SIL 1) is on the distant ridge, far right.

to calculate how many houses a terrace would have had. Several very narrow ter-races were eliminated because we did not see how they could be residential. The estimated number of houses was thirty-three. This is conservative because a 60 m long, 3.5 m wide terrace is presumed to have had space for only one house. With thirty-three houses at 5 to 10 people per house the site estimate is 165 to 330 people. The house estimate for SAL 16 is better than for the other Lagunas sites, which are not as well preserved.

Cerro Culebra (SIL 6) and Cerro Verde (SIL 1) were also hilltowns with ter-races and public architecture. A lower ridge at Cerro Culebra had a Late Cruz occupation but in Early Ramos the settlement moved to the hilltop. There are two mounds built in an L arrangement on a plaza. The site is in terrible shape because of plowing and erosion. We saw several stone foundations.

Cerro Verde has a linear string of terraces on the ridge crest that rise one after another to a plaza on the summit, on which there are two structures in an L arrangement (Figure 3.40). The residential terraces are long and fairly narrow and form concentric rings or tiers. We began mapping them at the top but got only to Terrace 17, after which there was nothing original left. Ninety percent of the site is destroyed. Looting was evident all over Cerro Verde. We were able to take quite a few collections. Ramos is well represented; Early is stronger than Late but both are present.

Two other sites also have architecture but the Ramos component is quite small and other components are better represented. SIL 11 had several long, 0.5 m high retaining walls but little else can be said.

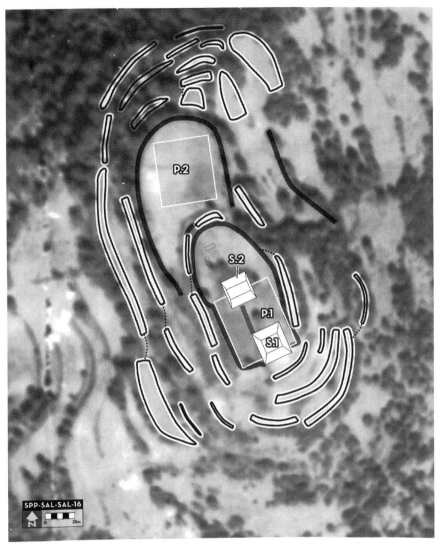

3.38 The architecture at SAL 16, Cerro Ñunducha.

SAL 28, at the southern end of the valley above the historic and modern hamlet of La Soledad, has a massive platform on the hilltop with a stone wall face that our crew thought might have served for defense. On the platform is—or rather was—a three-mound group. The site probably dates to Early Ramos. Little residential area could be found. However, the slopes west of the site are very heavily forested with dense secondary growth. The site of SAL 12, on the ridgetop, has stone construction that is probably prehispanic. We listed this as a Natividad site because we found

3.39 The plaza and Str. 2 at SAL 16, from Str. 1.

a couple Natividad diagnostic sherds but the form of the massive terrace walls suggests earlier times. Visibility was quite poor. There apparently was a platform on the top of the knob and five concentric rings of terraces. The terraces were roughly 7 m wide and had 1.5 m high retaining walls. Conceivably, SAL 28 and SAL 12 could be the (slightly) visible parts of a larger Ramos or Las Flores site now eroded and thoroughly hidden by vegetation.

Note that the Late Cruz and Ramos sites are generally at the northern end of Lagunas. SAL 28, with its civic-ceremonial group, stood alone at the southern boundary. We think that most of the Ramos occupation is Early. Late Ramos is present at Cerro Verde but it is not well represented and there is perhaps Late Ramos at Ñunducha. These are the two largest villages. If there was Late Ramos consolidation of population at these two villages, it probably did not last very long.

Las Flores

Lagunas settlement expanded in Las Flores, mostly in one tight cluster of sites around Cerro Verde at the northern end of the valley (Figure 3.41, Table 3.21). There are several locations never occupied before, nearer the valley floor and not as high as the old Ramos sites reoccupied in Las Flores. Las Flores settlement had a somewhat greater altitudinal range. The heavy erosion may prevent us from seeing the full extent of settlements. The whole Cerro Verde cluster had some 1,900 people.

Civic-ceremonial architecture was small in scale, not centralized, and dispersed in many sites. Cerro Verde was a terraced site with two mounds in an L arrangement;

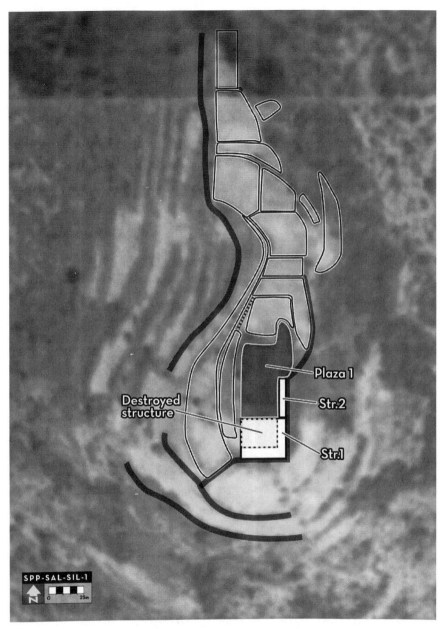

Plaza 1

Str.2

Destroyed
structure

Str.1

SPP-SAL-SIL-1

N 0   25m

3.40 The remaining architecture at Cerro Verde, SIL 1.

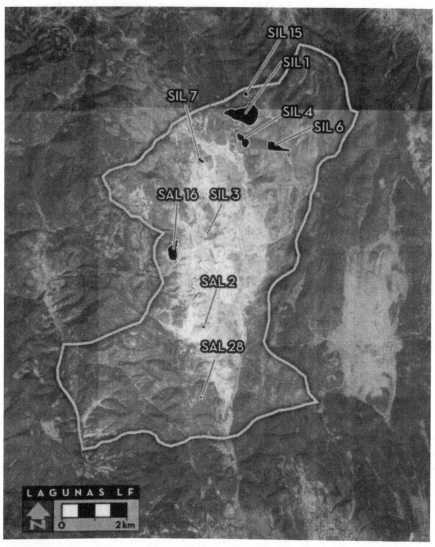

3.41 *Las Flores sites in Lagunas.*

nearby Culebra had two mounds in an L arrangement, SIL 4 had two mounds in an L arrangement, and SIL 15 had a single mound on a platform. Since most of the heavy work of slope modifications and terracing was already done in Ramos, in Las Flores the work was expansion and maintenance.

South of this main cluster the site of Ñunducha was occupied again; it has two mounds facing each other on a plaza. The three-mound group at the small site of SAL 28 also has ceramic evidence from Las Flores. SIL 3 and SAL 2 had small Las

Flores occupations. There is no mounded architecture associated with these two components.

All of these Las Flores sites are Early; it is not clear whether there is Transición. At SIL 1, Cerro Verde, there may be both Early and Late Las Flores. We list the Late Las Flores site size for SIL 1 as the same as in Early Las Flores but there is room for doubt.

Natividad

This was the demographic high point, with more settlement than any time before or since. The midpoint of our population estimates is about 8,000 people.

For the first time the southern part of the valley was heavily developed (Figure 3.42, Table 3.22). The piedmont and mountains above Soledad, San Andrés, and San Isidro had settlement on most ridges and hilltops. Settlements extended to and across the divide between Lagunas and the next valley to the west, Magdalena Cañadaltepec. Sites ranged in elevation from 2,300 to 2,600 m but all the large sites were below 2,430 m. As before, there were few sites on the east side except in the north around Cerro Verde.

Three sites had over 1,000 inhabitants (SIL 1, SAL 1 and 9), a dozen had between 100 and 600, and there were nineteen hamlets and isolated residences. Settlement is so extensive and continuous that these terms may have little behavioral meaning. Alternatively, we can point to three or four clusters of sites that are slightly separated by uninhabited space: the north around Cerro Verde, the heights west of San Isidro, and the hills and mountains west of San Andrés and Soledad (which could be divided into two).

These clusters were big villages rather than dense and differentiated urban communities. At eight (and perhaps one or two more) places there were mounds that were used in Natividad. No single place stands out as the top of the subregion's civic-ceremonial hierarchy but there are more sites with mounds at the north and south ends of the valley.

The long sites on opposite sides of the barranca in the southwestern part of the area are SAL 1 and 9. They are at 2,400 m on relatively broad ridgetops with limestone bedrock. This is today oak, pine, and juniper forest. A little winter wheat is grown but informants say there had been much more agriculture here a hundred years ago. A recently used *era*, or threshing floor, occurs on a high point at SAL 1, placed here to catch the breeze (this is why eras are often found on archaeological mounds). The barrancas just south of SAL 9 have very large lama-bordos.

Artifact densities are patchy. Building stone, fragments of stone foundations, and retaining walls are frequent but too fragmentary for meaningful measurements. Chert nodules occur locally and the evidence of chert reduction is abundant. At nearby SAL 5 there were stretches of the site that had hammerstones, cores, and primary reduction flakes (with a few sherds), then places with more houses and secondary and tertiary flakes, and then places with only lithics. None of these sites have many formal tools but we did see a unifacial scraper and several PPKs. SAL 9 was

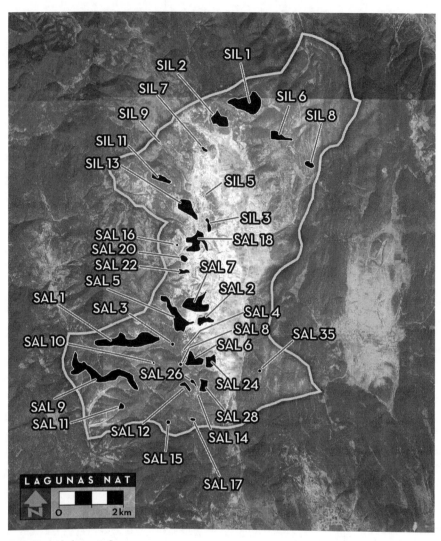

3.42 Natividad sites in Lagunas.

surveyed uphill from west to east and at a point about 1 km from the eastern end the crew observed an "extraordinary concentration" of obsidian flakes, blades, and a few cores. This obsidian scatter continued to the top of the ridge and the eastern end of the site. By Oaxaca standards this is an obsidian work area. It also had local chert and domestic debris.

At several sites in this southern area we saw good groundstone manos (sometimes rectangular in cross-section) and metates made on a hard, crystalline pink rock we called basalt. This does not occur locally; it had to have been traded in.

SAL 22, in the central cluster of settlement above San Isidro and San Andrés, offers an interesting case of the beneficial effects of sheet erosion in promoting archaeological visibility. This site is in oak and juniper forest with pines on the slopes. The top of the hill is eroded away, leaving limestone cobbles, building stone, fragments of house foundations, and artifacts.

SAL 18 sprawls over the main and side ridges, knobs, and saddles of the hill east of Cerro Ñunducha. Within this sprawl the knob on the southwestern end has a 50 by 50 m artifact concentration, including a 6 by 3 m cobble floor and foundation on the very top of the knob. At the foot of this knob an arroyo has cut down 2 to 3 m, exposing buried *camellones*, or berms, of agricultural fields. The camellones are no more than fifty years old but they had already been buried by soil washed from above and then exposed by down-cutting.

In the northern settlement cluster the principal site was Cerro Verde. This was a large site in Natividad but habitation was not as dense as it had been in earlier periods. The northern cluster of sites in general does not have unusual amounts of chert or obsidian working, but SIL 2 is an exception. Here the crew recorded a high density of chert cores, flakes, and expedient tools, and some chalcedony.

The ridge separating Lagunas from Yucunama usually was unoccupied, especially on the Lagunas side. But in Natividad there was SAL 35. This small site had two small mounds. About 500 m south on the next and highest knob on this ridge is a site (SIL 34) we left undated because we could find no ceramics. It has a bell-shaped pit with an opening 60 cm in diameter. It was looted and emptied. There are some possible terrace walls and white chert flakes. Surface visibility was nil because of vegetation but this seems like a Natividad site.

To conclude, Lagunas in Natividad was a populous place. Like Yucunama it had a substantial number of inhabitants spread out over the whole subregion but no urban or town central places. Lagunas was probably subject to the cacicazgo of Teposcolula. It had strong economic ties to Teposcolula. The strong orientation of Lagunas settlement toward the north in most periods and toward the west in Natividad may signal important interaction in those directions.

YOLOMÉCATL

This subregion is a distinct pocket formed by volcanic mountains surrounding eroded hills composed of the various materials of the Yanhuitlán Formation (softer limestone at the higher elevations, mudstones and sandstones to the west). It is drained by three streams: the Río Teposcolula, which enters from the east through a narrow constriction separating Yolomécatl from the Teposcolula Valley; the Río Cacalo, which has a large watershed in the mountains to the west; and the Río Negro, which heads in the mountains near Nduayaco and runs west through Santo Domingo Ticu before meeting the Cacalo in the Yolomécatl Valley (we include Ticu in the Nduayaco subregion). These streams join to form the Río Mixteco at the north edge of Yolomécatl by the volcanic hill Cerro Yucudavico. This land is the lowest in the northern part of our study area. At the eastern end where the valley opens out the elevation is 2,100 m. The lowest point, on the western side, is 2,040 m.

The subregion, roughly the municipio of Santiago Yolomécatl, is about 70 km², including the surrounding hills and mountains, but the valley where most settlement has been—the Yanhuitlán Formation soils between the rivers—covers just 25 km². The valley is hilly and cut by arroyos. It is cleared of vegetation and has been intensively farmed. Oak and pine are found at higher elevations.

Historically, Yolomécatl has been subject to Teposcolula 9 km to the northeast. To the west and north the land is mountainous and there are few villages and towns. To the southwest is Huamelulpan, also 9 km distant. Yolomécatl's position equidistant between these two centers has been important in its history.

Late Cruz

We found no Early or Middle Cruz sites. Perhaps they are eroded away or buried on the valley floor. We found seven Late Cruz sites (Figure 3.43, Table 3.23) and often Middle and Late Cruz settlements coincide. YOL 6, 9, 23, and 30 are on low hills overlooking the two main rivers. YOL 45 is on a low hill just above the arroyo Novadavi at the eastern edge of the valley. YOL 40 and 42 are back in the hills at somewhat higher elevations. These were small villages and hamlets. The largest were about 8 ha in area and the smallest was about 1 ha. Total population was between 400 and 900 people.

There are mounds at some of the sites but whether the mounds go with the Late Cruz components is uncertain. Yol 6, just west of modern Yolomécatl, includes the modern cemetery where there is one mound; there is another on the southwestern part of the site. At YOL 40 there is a 70 by 40 m platform with two former mounds facing each other on top. A farmer said he had leveled the mounds and saw human remains, axes, figurines, and bowls. If the mounds at these places had Late Cruz construction, it would place the sites in the lowest tier of the civic-ceremonial hierarchy. There is no clear center in Late Cruz Yolomécatl.

Yolomécatl was apparently not an independent development or separate entity in the Middle Formative. The data in hand are more consistent with these villages being an expansion of the Loma Mina polity of western Teposcolula. YOL 45 is less than 1 km from CAT 7, a Loma Mina neighbor, and the series YOL 42-40-30 is a string whose eastern end is in the Loma Mina cluster. The Ticu Late Cruz sites in the uplands to the southeast probably were part of the Loma Mina cluster too.

Ramos

All of the Cruz settlements were abandoned at the end of Late Cruz. Five Ramos sites were founded in new places (Figure 3.44, Table 3.24). The Early Ramos population was about 1,950 persons.

The most important site in the Yolomécatl Valley proper was on Cerro Yucuniñi (YOL 8). This is a strategic location on a choke point of the Río Teposcolula. The

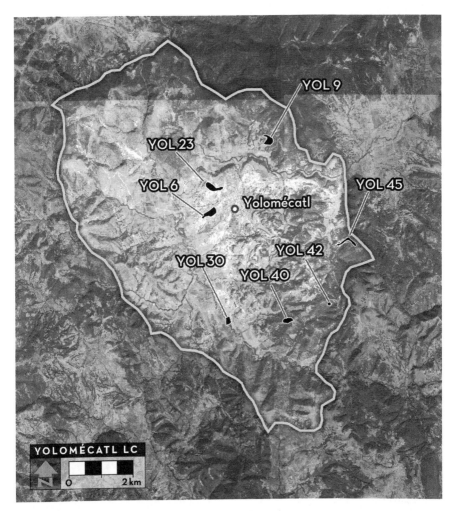

3.43 *Late Cruz sites in Yolomécatl.*

village spread from the top of this 200 m high hill down the south slope almost to the valley floor. We estimate conservatively that about 15 percent of the site's area had residential terraces and that the number of inhabitants was between 350 and 800 people. Much of the site is single-component Early Ramos. Lama-bordos are closely associated with this component. On top there is a linear string consisting of a mound that faces a small plaza on a platform, which is connected to another plaza on a platform, at the opposite end of which is a second mound. Behind this mound is a much smaller mound.

Two other sites in the valley are YOL 13, an isolated residence, and YOL 4, a hamlet, in the hills southeast of the modern town. YOL 4 may have had two

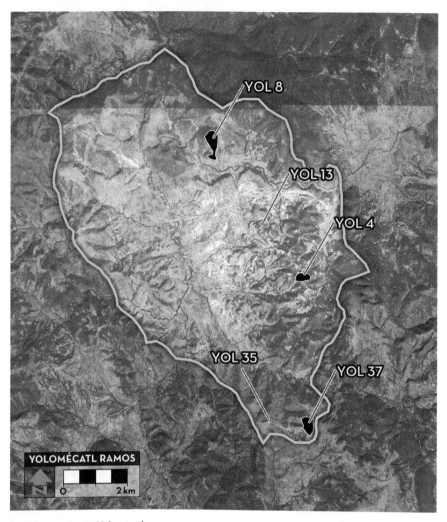

3.44 *Ramos sites in Yolomécatl.*

mounds. It is at the top of a long and gradually rising ridge but this is not a defensive location.

The largest settlement was at Cerro Cuate (YOL 37), called this because the top of the mountain consists of two similar peaks. The Early Ramos component is the southern of the two friends; the northern buddy was occupied in Las Flores. Virtually all of the Early Ramos site was taken up by residential terraces, which are on the southern and western slopes facing and just above the fertile farmland of the modern village of La Estancia, which today belongs to Santa Cruz Tayata. YOL 37 could have had 800 to 1,600 people. On the very top is a closed four-mound

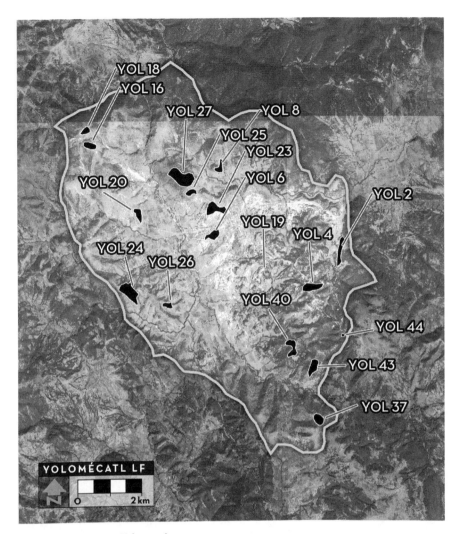

3.45 *Las Flores sites in Yolomécatl.*

group. It is uncertain whether Cerro Cuate was part of the Huamelulpan or the Teposcolula polity in Early Ramos. On the next hill to the west is a questionable Late Ramos component, but aside from this, Yolomécatl was virtually abandoned in Late Ramos.

Las Flores

The Early Classic was a time of population growth and settlement expansion. We count seventeen sites with a total habitation area of 158 ha (Figure 3.45, Table

3.25). The average estimate for the total population is 5,000 people. The valley center had the most people. There were also villages on ridges on Yolomécatl's western and southern edges.

Cerro Yucudavico (YOL 27) was the largest town. This is the steep hill at the confluence of the Río Teposcolula and the Río Cacalo, a strategic spot. Most of the occupation at Cerro Yucudavico pertains to this phase; it was not inhabited earlier. Intensive agriculture in historic times has destroyed much of the ancient town including its residential terraces. On the north and west sides there is still a stone encircling wall that can be traced. The eastern and southern slopes had terraces but whether there was also a wall is unknown. The site may have had 2,000 inhabitants, three times as many as the next largest village. On the summit are the remains of what had been this subregion's most important civic-ceremonial center. We could discern a three-mound group with another plaza flanked by the western mound of the group and a fourth mound on the west side of this plaza.

The north peak of Cerro Cuate (YOL 37) was reoccupied in Las Flores after the Late Ramos abandonment. The upper slopes were terraced, an encircling wall was constructed, and it became a village of some 600 people. The top of the peak has a patio group, perhaps residential. The site does not have a high artifact density and one wonders if this occupation lasted very long.

Apart from these two prominent sites all the other settlements were small villages and a few hamlets. For example, YOL 24, on the ridge beyond the western edge of the valley, covers 17 ha; in Las Flores it may have had residential terraces. YOL 16 and 18, at the northwestern corner of the subregion, were similar small villages with some residential terraces.

It is striking how many Las Flores sites in Yolomécatl had mounded architecture—twelve not counting the patio group at Cerro Cuate. Probably most or all of these had Las Flores construction and use. At YOL 24, for example, there are the remains of three mounds in a string. In a looter's backdirt pile by one of the mounds our crew found fragments of Las Flores urns, braziers, and domestic wares. YUC 20 has a structure on a platform. YOL 43, an otherwise nondescript small site, had poor visibility because of pine trees but we found three structures. Many villages and hamlets with mounds were on the subregion's edges but several were in the center of the valley. The small sites had one to three mounds and perhaps small plazas in front (YOL 4 may have had four in Las Flores). Invariably, these small complexes were situated on the highest knob with residential areas located on the slopes and ridges below. Mounds were typically central to their residential areas. They were not much smaller, if at all, than the mound and plaza complex at the leading town, Cerro Yucudavico. The civic-ceremonial architecture did not form much of a hierarchy.

Cerro Yucudavico is the only site with a strong Transición presence. It may have been the first substantial re-colonization in Yolomécatl after Late Ramos. All the other sites plus Yucudavico have solid Early Las Flores occupations. Teposcolula had quite a bit of growth in Transición but perhaps Yolomecatl was not extensively resettled until Early Las Flores proper, when Huamelulpan was declining. We have no good evidence of Late Las Flores anywhere in Yolomécatl.

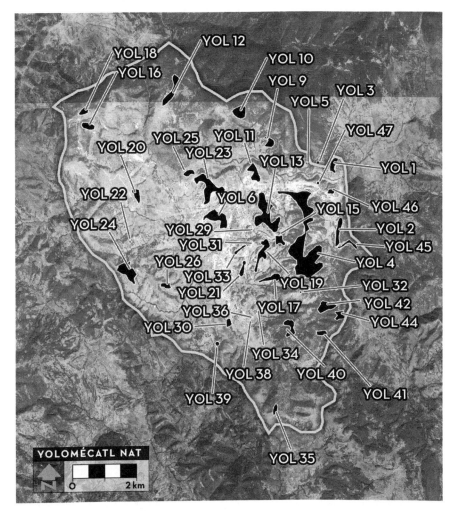

3.46 Natividad sites in Yolomécatl.

Natividad

This was the time of maximum population growth and settlement expansion. We mapped forty sites for a total habitation area of 427 ha, three times that of Las Flores. The average estimate for the total population is 7,500 people. The main cluster between YOL 25 and YOL 4 had two-thirds of the people. There were also villages on hills or ridges on Yolomécatl's northern, western, and southern edges (Figure 3.46, Table 3.26).

The Yolomécatl main cluster was similar in extent to the continuous settlements along the Teposcolula Valley. This dispersed town was far larger than modern

Santiago Yolomécatl. We found habitational debris all over the tops and side ridges of the hills around the modern town and for more than 3 km to the southeast, between 2,100 and 2,300 m asl. The gap between YOL 6, 23, and 13 is the modern town. Much of the town is paved and there must have been a site here too. All of this land was intensively farmed in historic and prior times. Almost every drainage has a lama-bordo. Clearing, plowing, making agricultural terraces, replanting in pine, and other activities have erased sections of the Natividad settlements around YOL 15, 17, and 19 at the lower elevations and close to town. At many sites we were picking out precolumbian refuse from the Colonial and the more copious modern garbage. The Natividad town must have been larger than we show it here.

YOL 4 is locally known as the Iglesia Vieja, where, it is said, the king lived. The site is a continuous spread of Natividad material extending for 2.5 km along the gradually sloping ridgetop and its side ridges. The Templo Viejo itself may be a single mound (Str. 4) on the highest point of YOL 4; just below this is a perhaps circular platform (Str. 3) supporting another mound, Str. 2 (there are earlier components here too).

YOL 6 at the southwest edge of Santiago Yolomécatl includes the modern cemetery. There are two mounds. It is said that a cacique used to live at the mound on the southwest side of the cemetery. YOL 4 or 6 or some place under the modern town could have been the political center but there is no outstanding civic-ceremonial complex or hierarchy of centers. Teposcolula, to which Yolomécatl was probably subject as it was in early Colonial times (Gerhard 1993:289), is about 10 km away.

A dozen sites have mounds but all except one have earlier components. There are fragmentary patio groups or ground-level houses from Natividad but no new mound construction. The one exception might be YOL 33, a site extending up a ridge east of the highway between Yolomécatl and Huamelulpan. This was part of the core settlement cluster. On the hilltop is a mound, perhaps with a small platform or plaza adjoining its front. It is less than 1 m high and hardly monumental. There were a few historic sherds and about 40 m away is an abandoned adobe and stone historic structure.

Yolomécatl offers possibilities for the study of Natividad, Colonial, and later historic relationships. Several sites have post-Natividad abandoned structures (the undated site YOL 28; YOL 25, 33, 41) and others have Colonial pottery.

Chert nodules and blocks occur in abundance in the limestone beds around Yolomécatl. The material was undoubtedly worked in all periods. Because there are so many single-component Natividad sites and because there are Natividad components at almost all sites, we limit our description of the industry and its context to this period. Our observations on lithics are superficial; further research is needed to test the hypothesis suggested here.

We have four types of chert-working sites in Yolomécatl: (1) quarries on or near habitation sites, with primary reduction; (2) work areas not on habitation sites, with secondary reduction; (3) secondary reduction areas on habitation sites; and (4) flake and tool occurrences on habitation sites with no specific evidence of special reduction areas.

Six sites are on or near quarries and have evidence of primary reduction. These are YOL 1, 3, 5, 9, and 10, all on the slopes north of the Río Teposcolula. YOL 1 is at a quarry of good quality, with white to light brown chert bordering on chalcedony in knapping characteristics at the toe of a ridge. There are many chert cobbles and much primary and secondary waste. YOL 5 is a Natividad isolated residence that also has primary reduction debris and large, blocky blades. At YOL 10 large chert blocks were extracted.

These four sites (YOL 14, 48, 49, and near YOL 22) are undated because we found no sherds; hence, they are non-habitation site work areas and they may or may not date to Natividad. All are on the slopes west and south of the hamlet of Nutiño. North of YOL 22 the hillsides have persistent lithic debris, sometimes in concentrations. One concentration of white chert was only about 5 by 7 m. YOL 14 has white chert bifacial reduction flakes, PPKs, and other bifacial tool fragments. YOL 48 and 49 have persistent light-density lithic debris and patches of heavy concentrations. At YOL 48 the concentration is 100 by 50 m; at YOL 49 it is 80 by 80 m. These are all or mainly white chert with flakes of various sizes and PPKs but not early-stage reduction debris. Perhaps a difference between the western and northern lithic sites is the size of the raw material.

The habitation sites with specific evidence of secondary and further reduction activity areas are YOL 4, 6, 12, 13, 20–22, 26, 32, 40, and 46. Most are in the major concentration of sites in the eastern part of the valley but three are at the foot of the hills on the west side and YOL 12 is perched atop the northern ridge. These sites range from isolated residences to YOL 4, the largest site in Yolomécatl, where we saw cores, chunks, flakes, a unifacial scraper, and PPKs; a black-and-white chert is the local color but there is also white, brown, and black chert. There is a concentration of reduction debris at the base of the highest knob on the site.

YOL 32 is an isolated residence. The total artifact scatter is 30 by 50 m, about half of which has abundant lithics. The crew described this as a place producing bifacial tools. YOL 46 has chert debris in a 30 by 30 m area consisting of flakes, PPKs, and other bifacial tool fragments. Chert colors were the black-and-white and white with pink or with brown. YOL 20 and 26 have lithic work areas in close association with mounds (two at YOL 26, Strs. 2 and 3).

Nine more Natividad habitation sites have chert flakes, tools, or other debris but we did not find special activity areas: YOL 4 (again), 17, 19, 29, 33–35, 38, and 39. These sites are all in the southern part of the subregion, mostly in an area that has been intensively farmed, which could explain why we did not see distinct chert concentrations. Alternatively, there may not have been special activity areas away from the sources and at the final ends of tool reduction sequences.

The chert activity and locational patterns suggest quarrying and nodule testing at or near outcrops. Further reduction either specifically to make chert tools or in the course of activities requiring tool refurbishing took place at habitation sites, sometimes in specific places where lithic debris accumulated. One common end product was the PPK. Chert of several colors was quarried. White and a black-and-white were the most common (no color is distinctive to Yolomécatl). How chert was exchanged we do not know.

In broader perspective, Yolomécatl in Natividad was the western end of an almost continuous spread of settlement that extended east through Teposcolula and north through Yodobada to Tejupan. A person walking these 30 km would have never been farther than a dog's bark from settlement. Yolomécatl in the sixteenth century was subject to Teposcolula and must have been linked to it economically as well. The chert procurement from the edges of the Yolomécatl subregion may be an indicator of other upland products moving from the fringes toward the urban core.

NDUAYACO

Nduayaco is the name we apply to a large and complex area south of Teposcolula. These are the mountainous upland watersheds of four drainages: the Río Yodonda, which flows north to the Teposcolula Valley; the Río Negro with its many branching tributaries, which becomes El Cacalo in Yolomécatl; the stream that heads at La Estancia (LET) and flows to the south; and the Río de las Lajas, which runs south to Achiutla.

The underlying rocks and their characteristic landforms and soils have been important to human use and settlement in Nduayaco. The eastern edge of this subregion is a high, steep ridge formed of crystalline limestone. It was never favored for settlement. On its western edge a long, north-south fault marks the contact of this limestone mass with three distinct formations. From north to south these are weathered and eroding sedimentary materials dominated by relatively soft limestone of the Yanhuitlán Formation, younger andesite, and a patch of Yanhuitlán sandstones. There are also several high ridges of crystalline limestone in the southwestern part of Nduayaco; these were not much settled. The upper part of the La Estancia drainage is a pocket of prized farmland derived from Yanhuitlán conglomerates, shale, and sandstone, extending back into the uplands to the modern ranchería of Unión Paz y Progreso (UPP). The areas with the heaviest settlement have been the north-south fault that makes the narrow valleys of the Yodonda and the Lajas where San José de Gracia and Santa María Nduayaco are today (SJG, NDU), the uplands of the Río Negro with their volcanic soils (TIC, NDU, and SJG), and the La Estancia pocket.

Nduayaco belongs to the Teposcolula district. It is closer to Teposcolula than to any other major center. But the mountainous terrain makes communication between Nduayaco and Teposcolula somewhat more difficult than it is between the cabecera and its other outlying subjects such as Nuñu or Yolomécatl. Nduayaco is also not far from Huamelulpan, the major Ramos center. Today La Estancia is an agencia of Santa Cruz Tayata in the district of Tlaxiaco. We might have included it in the Tayata subregion but the two are separated by a high mountain ridge and La Estancia's closest neighbors have been Nduayaco and Yolomécatl settlements. The settlement patterns suggest that Nduayaco was somewhat fragmented, that it had

3.47 *Dmitri Beliaev looking at lithic scatter at NDU 23.*

lesser hierarchical complexity than the leading subregions, and that it was usually subordinate to Teposcolula.

Archaic

There are two probable Archaic sites, both on broad saddles in the mountains east of the Nduayaco Valley not far from the main trail between the Nduayaco/San José de Gracia valleys and the Anama Valley to the east.

NDU 22 is at 2,740 m asl over 1 km away from the valley in pine forest with some grass cover. The area is used today for woodcutting and grazing. The site is a dispersed scatter of lithic artifacts that also has a 0.75 ha Las Flores ceramic scatter. We observed a wide variety of cherts: a gray-black amorphous core; a yellow core; secondary flakes of white, red, brown, and purple chert; two PPK fragments of white chert; and a unifacially worked piece of white, red, and brown chert. There was also a gray obsidian flake tool. There were no temporally diagnostic tools but the unusual location, the variety of raw materials carried in, and the bifacial industry are more consistent with Preceramic than later use.

NDU 23 is in a similar situation about 2 km south of NDU 22 and 2 km away from the valley at 2,680 m. A moderately dense scatter of lithic artifacts covers 0.5 ha (Figure 3.47). There are fairly large cores of white chert and brown chert, primary reduction flakes, and a broad, stemmed PPK (see Appendix 2) probably belonging to late Archaic times.

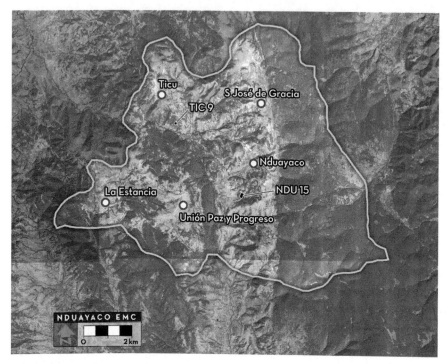

3.48 *Early/Middle Cruz sites in Nduayaco.*

Early/Middle Cruz

There were no Early Cruz sites but there were two small Middle Cruz hamlets (Figure 3.48, Table 3.27). They were equidistant from the Tayata and Teposcolula settlement clusters, but given the locations, travel to Teposcolula would have been easier.

TIC 9 is on a hilltop 60 m above the Río Negro 1 km south of the modern village of Santo Domingo Ticu. Today this is heavily eroded farmland. It is a single-component site. NDU 15 is about 40 m above the valley floor 1 km south of Santa María Nduayaco on the shale-and-sandstone-derived Yanhuitlán Formation soils. The hill where the site is situated is quite cut up by gully erosion. In places there is no soil on the endeque but the washing has left concentrations of sherds. A lama-bordo heads within the Middle Cruz settlement but it may not be associated with this component.

Late Cruz

There were seven small occupations (Figure 3.49, Table 3.28) but several may have dwindled in size due to erosion. The two Middle Cruz sites did not continue into this period. NDU 17 and TIC 6 were within 1 to 2 km of predecessor Middle

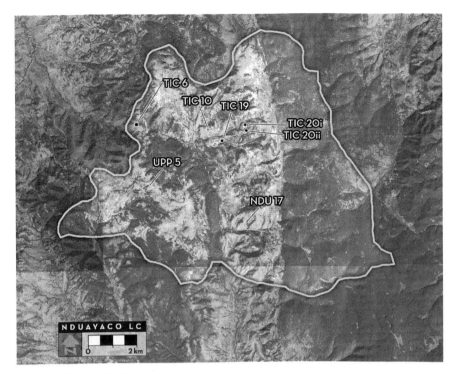

3.49 *Late Cruz sites in Nduayaco.*

Cruz hamlets. UPP 5 was on a hill up the arroyo from La Estancia. The other settle-ments (TIC 10, 19, 20i, 20 ii) formed a cluster on ridges at the head of one of the main Río Negro tributaries. TIC 10 may have been inhabited early in the phase; UPP 5 was probably occupied late in Late Cruz.

Nduayaco in Late Cruz had no central places and a population that might have been only 100 people. The nearest neighbors were to the north in Yolomécatl and Teposcolula. Continuity is suggested by there being both Middle and Late Cruz hamlets and earlier and later Late Cruz but the particular sites were not the same. Of the seven Late Cruz components only TIC 6 continued in Ramos.

Ramos

We found ten sites, nine most likely Early Ramos and one Late Ramos. The Early Ramos settlements consisted of two large terraced hilltop villages (UPP 2 and SJG 11) and seven hamlets (Figure 3.50, Table 3.29). The total Early Ramos popu-lation was about 955 people.

SJG 11 is a gem of a site (Figure 3.51), special because it is so well preserved. It may be preserved because its prehispanic inhabitants built it massively and well. The site is a fortified hilltown on a conical knob along a ridge 1 km west of San José

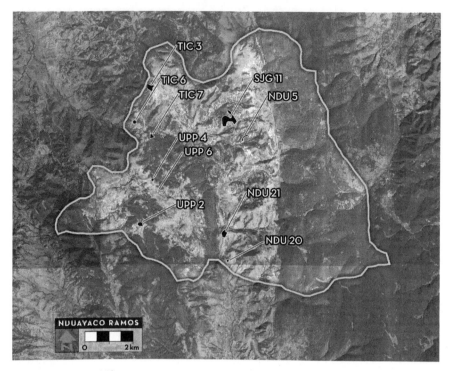

3.50 Ramos sites in Nduayaco.

de Gracia overlooking upper tributaries of the Río Negro. The elevation difference between the summit and the ridge crest is 50 m, and from the summit to the river below it is 160 m. Today the site is forested and some of the terraces are used as fields. Three lama-bordos originate on the site.

We mapped fifty-five terraces, virtually all that had been built. The terraces and other stone retaining walls form concentric rings on the north, east, and south sides. The knob itself is steep—the slope is as much as 36 percent on the sides that are terraced and the west, unterraced side is even steeper. As a consequence the retaining walls are high, impressively engineered, and formidable barriers. These walls still hold the site together. They average 2 m in height. The terraces are long but they are not as narrow as is often the case with long terraces, and their breadth added to the requirements for fill and retaining-wall height.

Our population estimate for SJG 11 is based on house mounds mapped by the crew; where no house mounds could be seen we assume one house per terrace. There were at least sixty houses in all, which at 5 to 10 persons per house gives 300–600 people on the terraced part of the site plus some 250 people living at much lower densities along the ridge to the east. The civic-ceremonial focus was a large plaza created by leveling off the top of the knob. On it were two mounds in an L arrangement. The eastern mound was elevated on a platform.

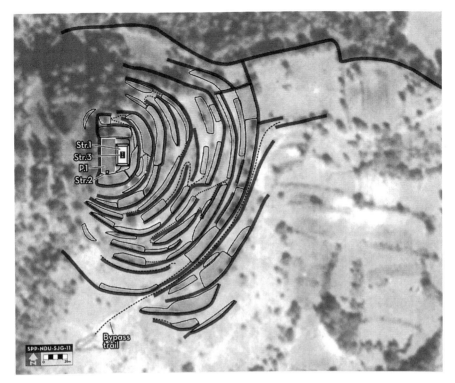

Str.1
Str.3
P.1
Str.2

Bypass
trail

SPP-NDU-SJG-11

3.51 SJG 11, an unusually well-preserved hilltown.

UPP 2 is a hill in the upper reaches of the arroyos that wash down to La Estancia. It probably was a densely occupied, terraced village, but being on a hill composed of Yanhuitlán Formation sedimentary deposits, the terraces and rock work are all eroded away.

The Late Ramos population of about 400 was concentrated at a single hilltop terraced village, NDU 21. This site covers two knobs. It is such a strategic place that today the north-south motor vehicle road passes through the saddle between the two knobs. The Ramos occupation was just the eastern knob; the other was occupied in Las Flores. On top a modern house sits on what had been the southern mound of a four-mound group with a 25 by 25 m plaza. The terraces are ruined and not mappable.

The Early Ramos in Nduayaco continued the older orientation toward the upper Río Negro and the upper reaches of the arroyos east of La Estancia, specifically the UPP and TIC sites plus SJG 11 and NDU 5 on the Río Negro drainage. There was little interest in the north-south valley or its choke points. The orientation changed in Late Ramos when all the Early Ramos sites were abandoned and NDU 21 was built at a constriction of the Río Las Lajas Valley. Also in Late Ramos another hill just inside the San Juan Achiutla Valley to the south was occupied by

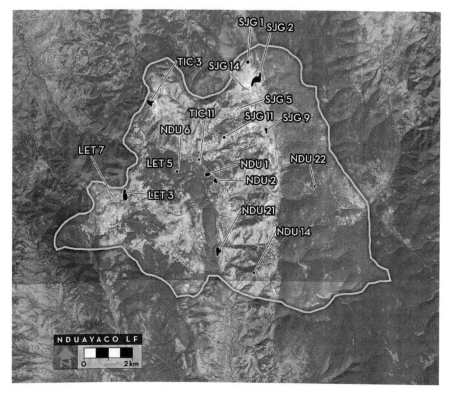

3.52 Las Flores sites in Nduayaco.

a similar fortified town. A 48 ha Late Ramos settlement with civic-ceremonial architecture grew up just south of La Estancia; this was a satellite of Huamelulpan.

In sum, rural, upland Nduayaco persisted and grew in population in Early Ramos. Although many people were gathered together at SJG 11, the Nduayaco upcountry still had some small unprotected settlements. But by Late Ramos all this was gone. The only settlements were the Huamelulpan administrative center south of La Estancia and a hilltown in the Nduayaco Valley, which may have had regional strategic significance in Ramos but was unimportant in earlier times.

Las Flores

Compared to neighboring subregions, Nduayaco had relatively light settlement and no major centers. Clusters of sites appeared in Early Las Flores in the valley of the Río Yodonda, on the upper reaches of the Río Negro west of Santa María Nduayaco, at the constriction of the Río de las Lajas Valley at the border with San Juan Achiutla, and on the southern flanks of Cerro Cuate in La Estancia (Figure 3.52, Table 3.30).

Overlooking the Río Yodonda were SJG 1, 2, 5, 9, 11, and 14. There were ancient lama-bordos at SJG 1, 2, and 11. SJG 2 was the largest settlement with between 400 and 800 inhabitants. It is a low hill that had been terraced. The top had a plaza and two small structures. The other five sites in this cluster were small sherd scatters except for SJG 11, which was a reoccupation of the top and eastern slope of the Early Ramos center. The pottery indicates that this cluster dates to early Las Flores.

The hills west of Santa María Nduayaco had four small hamlets, NDU 1, 2, 6, and TIC 11, probably from Early Las Flores, with nearby lama-bordos.

NDU 14 and 21 are at the southern end of the Nduayaco Valley and were part of a cluster of sites that included three San Juan Achiutla sites (SJA 2, 5, and 6). This cluster occupied both sides of the constriction of the Río Las Lajas Valley, a strategic place on the major north-south route. NDU 21 is the knob on the western side of the saddle through which the modern road cuts. The Las Flores hill was also terraced, but when we surveyed it, the secondary vegetation was so dense that we could not map the terraces. Our population estimate of 300 to 600 people is based on a site area of 6.3 ha and the density of 50 to 100 persons per ha expected of terraced sites. The summit has a plaza with two mounds in an L arrangement. NDU 21 is Early Las Flores. The other site, NDU 14, is a single-component mountaintop occupation with a structure on a platform and some terraces. This was definitely a defensible site. The ridgeline runs east-west. The mound is on the top of the knob. It stands 1 m in height from the plaza and an imposing 7 m high when viewed up the steep slope from the east. The east and west approaches along the ridge are blocked by high retaining walls; the north and south slopes are very steep.

There is a trickle of settlement in La Estancia (LET 3, 5, 7), perhaps associated with the Las Flores site on Cerro Cuate (YOL 37). These are sherd scatters on grazing land and milpas.

In wider geographical perspective the Early Las Flores settlement clusters in Nduayaco appear to have been small and the centers were at the bottom rank of civic-ceremonial places. Neighboring subregions had larger populations and centers with more mounded architecture. The prime places for agriculture had some settlement and the cluster at the edge of San Juan Achiutla and Nduayaco seems to be strategically placed. We found no Late Las Flores occupation in these uplands.

Natividad

This was the time of greatest settlement expansion and population. The biggest development was in the San José de Gracia area in the valley and on the ridges of the headwaters of the Río Negro. There were also clusters of settlement at Ticu, in the valley south of Santa María Nduayaco, and at La Estancia (Figure 3.53, Table 3.31). All together there may have been 4,000 people. We recorded sixty-one sites, most of which are small, including fifteen isolated residences and forty-one hamlets of less than 200 people. This was a rural area.

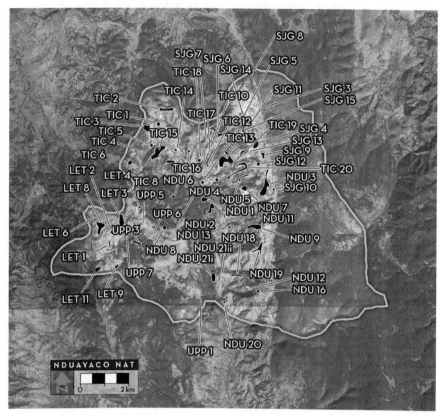

3.53 Natividad sites in Nduayaco.

The major concentration of settlement and the cluster with the largest village is at San José de Gracia (the modern boundaries with Ticu and Santa María Nduayaco are quite near San José, as reflected in our TIC, NDU, and SJG site numbers in this cluster). The twenty-seven sites involved are NDU 1–3, 5–7; SJG 3–15; and TIC 10, 12, 13, and 16–20, for a total population of about 2,500. Sites are in two situations: the hills above the upper Río Negro and the valleys of the Río Las Lajas and the Río Yodonda. There is a break in settlement between Ixtapa in the Teposcolula Valley and this cluster. The western and southern limits are not as clear. Sites at higher elevations are on land that had been farmed and eroded in the past but much of the area has been reforested in pine and is used mostly for grazing now. The hills above the main north-south valley are heavily farmed and were also intensively used in the past. Notable lama-bordos are at SJG 10 and 11, NDU 2 and 3, and TIC 10.

NDU 3, on a low ridge overlooking the valley, midway between San José and Santa María, is the largest site and may be the "Pueblo Viejo." Occupation was fairly dense. There are ruined ancient terrace walls and we were able to observe five structures, which were all small and probably high-status residences rather than public buildings. At Structure 1 we found a green obsidian blade and fragments of bowls, a ladle, and a censer. SJG 4 is on the western side of San José and it includes a Natividad mound in the modern cemetery where we found a green obsidian blade, chert, and a brazier fragment. SJG 6 is also notable—it has numerous stone house foundations and several house mounds and patio groups. One residential mound group on the hilltop is within a space defined by substantial retaining walls. This site produced green obsidian blades, white chert unifacial tools, a Fine Cream figurine of a woman wearing a huipil, and a censer cover.

SJG 11 is a fairly substantial reoccupation of the old Ramos site. The Natividad artifacts included a Fine Cream spoon or ladle with a distinctively greenish paste that is also found throughout the Teposcolula survey area. TIC 17 might have been a shrine rather than a habitation site.

The cluster south of Nduayaco (NDU 9, 11–13, 16, 18–21; UPP 1) extends to the edge of San Juan Achiutla. The habitation sites are all hamlets and isolated residences and the total population probably did not exceed 500. One of the two larger settlements was Cerro Dicatijui (NDU 19), a mountaintop site that has one mound. The other larger settlement is NDU 9, which also has a single structure at the highest point, a sunken patio residence, and several destroyed house mounds. NDU 12 at 2,600 m is the highest and most unusual site in this cluster. It has a ball court on its peak, four terraces not considered residential, and not many artifacts. It is probably significant that this isolated ball court is situated at the southern edge of the Nduayaco subregion on what is also today the district and municipal boundary.

The beginnings of modern Ticu can be traced to its Natividad settlement cluster (TIC 1–6, 8, 14, 15). The total estimated population is between 400 and 900 people. TIC 4 and 5 are near the modern cemetery (TIC 4 has one structure on the top of the hill) but the main settlement was just south of the modern town (TIC 15). Among the modern houses and agricultural features on this low hill we found persistent Natividad artifacts.

The La Estancia pocket also had its most settlement ever in Natividad—about 600 inhabitants dispersed in fourteen small, low-density hamlets and isolated residences (NDU 4, 8; UPP 3, 5–7; LET 1–4, 6, 8, 9, 11; and SZT 1, 3, 5 could be included). LET 11, near the modern cemetery, has a single mound on a platform and NDU 8 has a sunken patio but there are no obvious central places. We recorded censer or brazier fragments at four sites: NDU 4 and 8, UPP 5, and LET 11. A well-built stone structure, possibly the historical estancia, is at LET 1.

La Estancia sites have notably more evidence of chert working than sites in the rest of Nduayaco. Eleven of the fourteen sites have at least some chert and six of these have moderate or heavy densities of cores, chunks, flakes, and unifacial and bifacial tools. White chert is the most common but pink and other colors also are found.

To recapitulate, Nduayaco had substantial population in the Nduayaco–San José de Gracia–Ticu area along the Río Negro and the north-south valleys. The architecture in this subregion was small in scale and there is nothing suggesting administration other than that which could have been carried out from the residences of local, low-ranking nobility. Although topographically distinct and removed from major centers in Teposcolula, people seemed to have had access to pottery and obsidian, for the amounts of decorated wares and elaborate forms do not suggest impoverishment. Nduayaco was the southern limit of the Teposcolula cacicazgo. Perhaps the ball court at NDU 12 marked the boundary with Achiutla to the south. People in La Estancia were on a frontier equidistant from Huamelulpan and Yolomécatl.

CHAPTER FOUR

Greater Huamelulpan

The three valleys described in this chapter—Yucuxaco, Huamelulpan, and Tayata—are crucial to understanding the rise of urbanism and the state in the Mixteca Alta. A large part of this area was surveyed in 1994–1995 (Balkansky 1998b) and we did more in 1999. All of these results are drawn together in this chapter. Balkansky has begun a more intensive investigation of Tayata that will add much more to what is reported here. Tayata was the seat of a large Formative head town, peer to Oaxaca's other Olmec period centers. But to judge from the settlement pattern there was no continuity between the Early/Middle Formative polity and the hilltowns that arose subsequently in the Late Formative. The disruption was too complete.

Many places in the Mixteca Alta were abandoned during the Late Formative and unoccupied in the Terminal Formative, but in Huamelulpan people congregated to form the first truly urban center in the Central Mixteca Alta. Terminal Formative (Late Ramos) Huamelulpan was a large, densely settled, differentiated, and dominant city whose counterparts were places like Monte Albán in the Valley of Oaxaca.

This area never regained the regional prominence it had when Huamelulpan was at its height. Although the size of its population, especially in the Postclassic, was not much less than that of most of its neighbors, Huamelulpan had rivals with greater agricultural, demographic, and trade clout in Teposcolula and Tlaxiaco. Little is said about the ñuu of Yucuxaco, Tayata, and Huamelulpan in the sixteenth-century sources; they were subject to Tlaxiaco.

YUCUXACO

This subregion is the municipio of San Pedro Mártir Yucuxaco, lying north of Huamelulpan and west of Yolomécatl. The Río la Rana (Poblano) is the western and northern limit of the subregion. The western side of Yucuxaco takes in a mountain ridge of igneous origin that has peaks up to 2,800 m. Another volcanic ridge, lower in elevation, frames the eastern side of Yucuxaco. The heart of the area and the zone most favored for settlement is an eastward-tilting, hilly upland of the Yanhuitlán Formation, with mainly sandstones and conglomerates on the west and sandstone and shale to the east.

Much of this subregion from Huamelulpan north to Cerro la Calentura was surveyed in 1994–1995 (Balkansky 1998b); in 1999 we extended the survey north and west.

Late Cruz

The area was apparently not settled until Late Cruz. We found no Archaic or Early/Middle Cruz sites. There are quite a few aceramic lithic sites but these are probably associated with ceramic-era chert procurement and do not have evidence of preceramic use.

We found nine Late Cruz components (Figure 4.1, Table 4.1). Most are situated around 2,200 m asl on soils of the Yanhuitlán Formation. However, there is a small occupation at La Calentura, the prominent volcanic peak. All sites except one were isolated residences and tiny hamlets of no more than 2 ha. The exception is PMY 14 at the modern town of San Pedro Mártir Yucuxaco. This is a distinctive place, a low, broad, now bald rise at 2,220 m, where at least seven arroyos have their heads. The Late Cruz site covers over 13 ha.

Yucuxaco was perhaps a northern colonization by the Tayata polity in the Middle Formative, just as Yolomécatl might have been a western expansion of Teposcolula. Yucuxaco's nearest major town was Tayata. Totonundo, another large village in the Tayata sphere, was only 3 km away.

Ramos

The Late Cruz settlement pattern was completely replaced by a different one at the outset of Ramos. All the lower more exposed settlements were abandoned. All the Ramos settlements were at higher elevations on steep-sided knobs (Figure

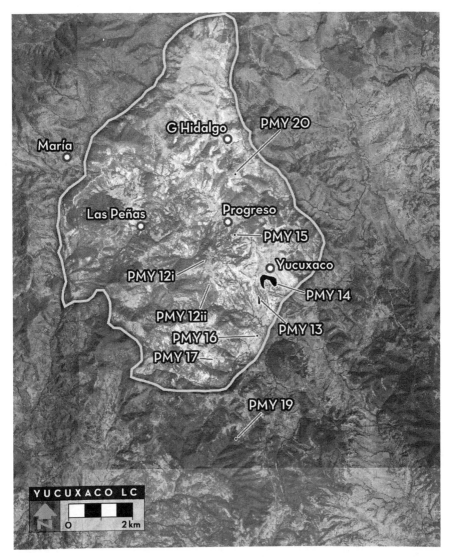

4.1 *Late Cruz sites in Yucuxaco.*

4.2, Table 4.2). For example, the two largest settlements were on the top of La Calentura at over 2,380 m and on La Cumbre at 2,400 m. The orientation to Yanhuitlán Formation soils continued, since people did not repair to the highest and most remote ridges but instead selected all the easily defended peaks nearest their fields. There were fewer sites in Ramos than in Late Cruz but they were larger, more nucleated, and more densely settled.

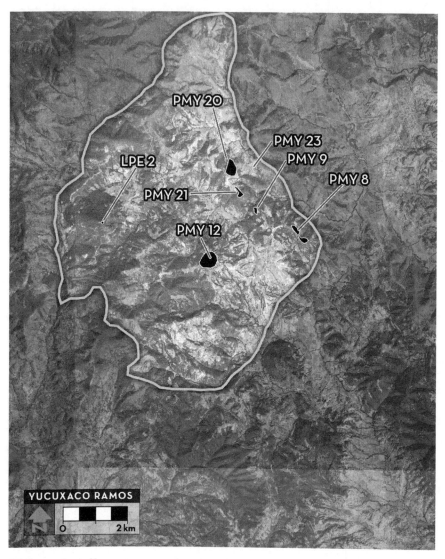

4.2 Ramos sites in Yucuxaco.

Yucuxaco is one area where there was growth from Early to Late Ramos. Most of the sites have both Early and Late Ramos but the Late Ramos tends to be more extensive and better represented. Our average estimate is 2,500 people by Late Ramos.

La Calentura (PMY 20) was a fortified hilltown with residential terraces and defensive walls. It was the Early Ramos center for the Yucuxaco subregion. La Calentura had a total of five mounds and a plaza. La Cumbre, near the modern rancheria of La Unión, was the primary center for this subregion in Late Ramos. PMY 8, on the crest of the mountain east of the modern town of Yucuxaco, had one mound. These three sites effectively surround on three sides Yucuxaco's pocket of good farmland. The south faced Cerro Volado, the region's major center, only 4 km away.

Las Peñas, the appropriately named peak due west of the Yucuxaco Valley, had a small Ramos occupation. The Ramos component is on the summit but most of the site is an impressive chert-working scatter that spills down the northeast ridge to the valley below, where there is a larger Natividad component. It is possible that some of the chert working dates to Ramos but alternatively the peak may have been used for strategic reasons in Ramos and the lithic working could pertain to Natividad.

As elsewhere in the Mixteca Alta, Early Ramos in Yucuxaco saw a drastic shift in settlement to higher, more defensible locations. Population grew over the length of the period. Unlike some other places Yucuxaco was not abandoned in Late Ramos. Instead this subregion participated in the rise of Huamelulpan and was the northern sector of this urban regional system.

Las Flores

Population may have declined somewhat from Late Ramos to Early Las Flores, but not a great deal. Sites were varied in size and situation (Figure 4.3, Table 4.3). The strong Ramos period emphasis on defense seems to have been relaxed. La Calentura (PMY 20) and La Cumbre (PMY 12) continued to be occupied although they were smaller than before. Yucuxaco also had two farming settlements west of Cerro Volado (PMY 17, 18), two isolated residences, and a hamlet or small village on a broad hilltop on the north side of the Río Cacalo (GPE 17).

La Cumbre was the most populous settlement. Most of the site had residential terraces. Seven mounds and two plazas make this the leading civic-ceremonial center. PMY 17 has three mounds and a plaza that date to this phase.

In the Transición phase and into the Early Classic proper, Huamelulpan was still the largest center in the northwestern part of our study area and the nearest large center for Yucuxaco. Yucuxaco was probably affiliated with Huamelulpan. However, as Huamelulpan declined in Las Flores, Teposcolula grew and so did its dependency Yolomécatl, Yucuxaco's eastern neighbor. Yolomécatl had 5,000 inhabitants in Las Flores, far more than Yucuxaco. The boundary between the two subregions had several new villages (YOL 16, 18, 20, 24, 26).

Natividad

This was the time of maximum settlement and population. We mapped twenty-nine sites totaling 209 ha of inhabited area (Figure 4.4, Table 4.4). All parts of the subregion were occupied, from the high mountains on the west and north to the gently sloping hills around San Pedro Mártir Yucuxaco. The valley of the Río

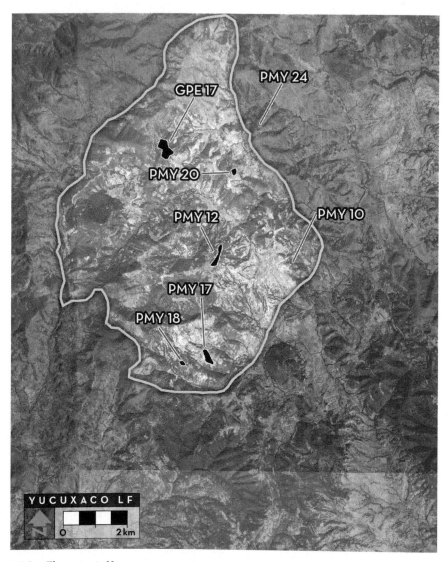

4.3 *Las Flores sites in Yucuxaco.*

Yuteyoco was heavily settled, the first time that area had any substantial occupation. Chert working was an important activity at sites all along the Yuteyoco and elsewhere on the outer fringe of Yucuxaco.

The largest town was at La Cumbre where the Natividad component covered 46 ha. The hillsides are quite eroded, but if 90 percent of the site area had residential terraces, which seems likely, then the population would have been between 2,100 and 4,300 inhabitants. Two mounds have evidence of Natividad use, the only

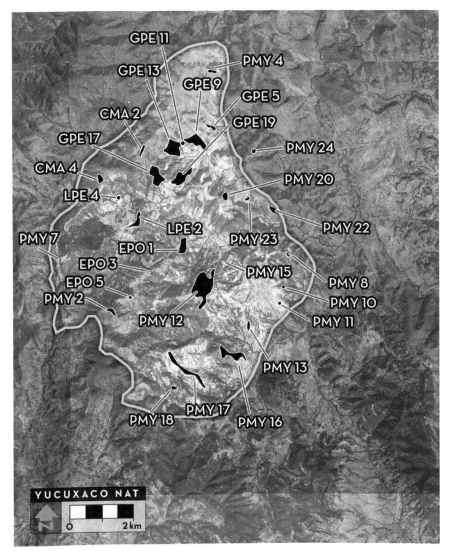

4.4 Natividad sites in Yucuxaco.

such structures in Yucuxaco. PMY 16 and 17 were the next largest sites. They had some fairly densely occupied areas and populations of roughly 800 to 1,000.

All the other settlements were small and dispersed: seven small villages, thirteen hamlets, and six isolated residences. Low densities and wide dispersal of sherds characterize these sites. About a third of the population lived in these small settlements.

CMA 2 is notable for its very well-preserved residential architecture. This site is high (2,470 m) on the mountain ridge at the northern edge of Yucuxaco in the pine-oak forest. The occupation extends along a narrow ridge. Artifacts are relatively few but there are numerous stone foundations of houses and intact patios with surrounding structures.

PMY 2 is atop the Cerro Montezacate at 2,760 m. This is a defensive site. The western slope of the peak, facing the saddle, has three or four parallel ditches, one of which has an intact stone wall. A ramp or access way leads across the ditches.

Yucuxaco had more intensive and widespread chert working than any other subregion. The Yolomécatl chert workings (Chapter 3) are probably part of the same industry. Chert working at Yucuxaco certainly dates to Natividad times. Virtually every Natividad site on the northern and western edges of Yucuxaco (almost every site with a CMA, EPO, GPE, or LPE prefix) was involved in chert working. The raw material was a good-quality chert, most frequently white in color but sometimes red or pink, brown, or translucent white. We did not see quarries where large blocks were removed; small boulders or cobbles may be how the material usually occurs.

Sites have abundant secondary and tertiary flakes, cores and core fragments, and less frequently unifacial and bifacial tools and tool fragments, including broken or incomplete PPKs. Most tools that are not PPKs are expedient rather than formal.

Most (but not all) sites have chert debris much denser and more widespread than the distribution of sherds. LPE 2, on the Cerro Las Peñas, is a spectacular example. The chert scatter runs from the peak of the mountain at 2,720 m, down the northeast ridge for 2 km, to a hilltop overlooking the Cacalo—an elevation drop of 380 m. There is a tiny Ramos occupation at the top, the Natividad habitation site is at the bottom, and the whole ridge between has chert flakes, cores, and tool fragments.

The total extent of the chert-working debris at these Natividad sites is 98 ha. We also have six sites that have lithics but no ceramics and are therefore undated: PMY 6 and GPE 1, 3, 7, 15, and 21. These are chert-working areas with no domestic debris. They are located along the upper Río Yuteyoco. PMY 6 and GPE 1 and 3 are farther up the ridge from the habitation sites in this area but the others are interspersed between the residential sites GPE 9 and 19. All except GPE 21 have high densities of chert. The reduction products are the same as at the habitation sites, that is, white chert cores, flakes, bifaces, and expedient tools. These undated sites are small (from 60 by 30 m to 450 by 150 m) compared to habitation sites, but nevertheless, the total of 14.5 ha in the undated sites represents considerable activity.

With its comparatively small, dispersed population and no major centers, Yucuxaco appears to have been a subordinate polity. But subordinate to whom? In Colonial times it was not subject to Teposcolula. The closest large Natividad center was Huamelulpan, which in Colonial (and recent) times was a dependency of Tlaxiaco, more than 20 km south of Yucuxaco.

The Spanish reorganization must have had a major impact on Yucuxaco. The modern town was a congregación (perhaps from La Cumbre and other rancherías). Note also that the names of the modern settled places are twentieth-century

Mexican (e.g., Guadalupe Hidalgo, La Unión, Progreso), not Mixtec place-names, suggesting a post-Colonial origin.

HUAMELULPAN

This subregion coincides with the municipio of San Martín Huamelulpan, including its dependencies Totonundo, Plan de Guadalupe, and Morelos. Excavations by Gaxiola (1984) and Winter and colleagues (1991) and the survey of 1994–1995 (Balkansky 1998b) have shown that in the Terminal Formative Huamelulpan was one of Oaxaca's leading urban centers. We resurveyed parts of the urban center in 1999.

The landmark and archaeologically important Cerro Volado stands at the center of this subregion. It is an Oligocene-Miocene volcanic cone composed of gray andesite. The hill is about 200 m high and covers a little more than 1 km^2. Mountains just to the south are formed of the same material; the southmost and highest of these is Cerro Yucusavi. At lower elevations soils are derived from the older Paleocene-Eocene shale and sandstone of the Yanhuitlán Formation. The higher mountains forming the southwestern edge of the valley are composed of volcanic-sedimentary tuffs and sandstones of younger Miocene-Pliocene age. The valley's lowest elevations are about 2,140 m and the volcanic peaks rise to 2,400 m.

The old volcanoes form the divide between northern and southern drainages, the northern arroyos flowing toward Yolomécatl and the southern toward Tayata. Huamelulpan is the head of westward flowing streams too (the modern highway to Tlaxiaco runs along this divide).

Cerro Volado, on the divide between three watersheds, may have had regional strategic value in Late and Terminal Formative times. Huamelulpan also had potential for agricultural intensification. It had 10 km^2 of fertile Yanhuitlán Formation soils at the upper reaches of many arroyos, an ideal situation for lama-bordos.

Early/Middle Cruz

The earliest known site is MRS 1, an isolated residence at Morelos on the valley floor (Figure 4.5, Table 4.5). The location is interesting as it is on the low divide between the north-flowing and south-flowing streams. This is the only Early/Middle Cruz site in Huamelulpan. By this time Tayata was already the region's major town. MRS 1 is only 5 km from Tayata and must have been part of the Tayata polity.

Late Cruz

This was when the subregion was really colonized. From almost no occupation in the preceding phase Huamelulpan added thirteen new settlements totaling 47 ha of habitation area. We estimate the Late Cruz population in Huamelulpan to have been between 700 and 1,500 people. Many of the places used for settlements were on hills or the flanks of higher ridges but these were generally exposed and not defensive positions (Figure 4.6, Table 4.5).

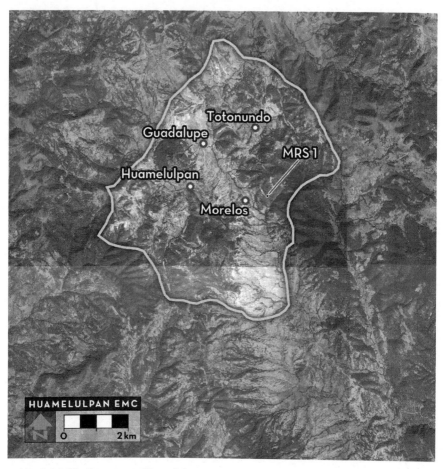

4.5 *Early/Middle Cruz sites in Huamelulpan.*

The largest settlement was the large village at Totonundo (TTN 1). The site was on a hill 100 m high with ready access to arroyos and Yanhuitlán Formation soils. Some of the site may have had residential terraces as early as this phase. If Huamelulpan had its own local center at this time, it was probably Totonundo.

The tiny initial settlement at MRS 1 grew to 3 ha. Two places on the lower slopes of Cerro Volado (SMH 1i, 1ii) had small Late Cruz occupations. A 3 ha village (SMH 4) was built on the top of the ridge just south of the modern town, 100 m above the valley floor. Another village (SMH 26) was dispersed along 1.6 km of a ridge on the eastern flank of Cerro Yucusavi.

Huamelulpan's Late Cruz settlement was an extension of Tayata. Yucuxaco, just to the north, was also part of this expansion. Tayata remained the head town for this enlarging settlement cluster.

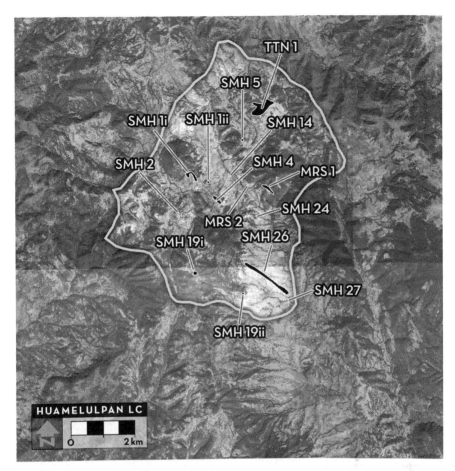

4.6 Late Cruz sites in Huamelulpan.

Ramos

In this Late and Terminal Formative period Huamelulpan urbanized and became the seat of one of Oaxaca's leading cities. By Late Ramos most of the northern (Yucuxaco) and southern (Tayata) subregions that had been part of the Cruz polity were largely abandoned and population was consolidated around Huamelulpan. There are twenty-five Ramos archaeological sites with a total occupied area of 270 ha and a mean Late Ramos population estimate of 16,800. The sites form two parallel lines on the volcanic ridges and hills east and west of the valley floor (Figure 4.7, Table 4.6). This arrangement brought the most labor to the best agricultural land.

Beginning with the smallest sites, we found thirteen that are small enough to be isolated residences. Six are spaced along the floor of the valley around Plan de

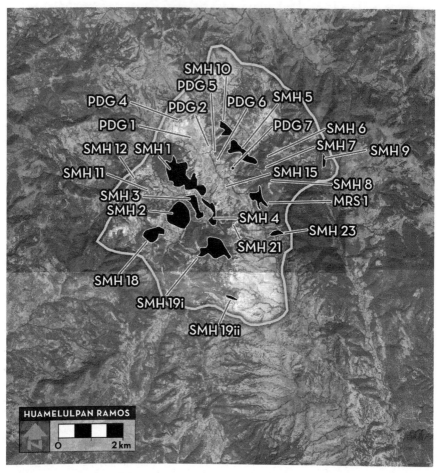

4.7 *Ramos sites in Huamelulpan.*

Guadalupe. All are in the shadow of the urban center. In the rest of the Central Mixteca Alta it is rare to find Ramos isolated residences.

There were four hamlets and small villages (SMH 9, 10, 19ii, and 23). SMH 9 on the eastern edge of the Huamelulpan subregion had two mounds and SMH 10 on the northern edge had one mound.

Two settlements on the eastern side of the valley had estimated populations of about 1,100. MRS 1, the oldest site, grew in Ramos to cover 16 ha. Most of the settlement was densely occupied and there were three mounds. Loma del Aguila (SMH 5), 1 km north of the Morelos site, was even larger, at almost 25 ha. It has three mounds and defensive walls as well.

The big sites on the western side of the valley (SMH 1–4, 18, 19i), including Cerro Volado (SMH 1) and Cerro Yucusavi (SMH 19i), formed a single urban com-

4.8 The south face of Cerro Volado. Note the terraces.

plex. We recorded them as distinct archaeological sites by our normal field procedures but they are separated only by lama-bordos. The maximum distance between them is 500 m and usually much less. These sites are akin to Monte Albán's spatially separate site subdivisions El Gallo and Atzompa. SMH 18 and 19i each have three mounds. Together these site subdivisions cover 205 ha and the combined population estimate is 8,000 to 17,000. By comparison, Monte Albán in Monte Albán II covered 416 ha and its population estimate range is 9,650 to 19,300 (Blanton 1978:44).

SMH 1 (Figure 4.8) was the monumental center of the city. The architecture suggests multiple functional areas. The SMH 1 sector had twenty mounds, seven plazas, and, rising from the saddle above the modern town, a series of long, massive platforms where there are carved stone monuments (Figure 4.9). The main administrative precinct was probably the area that has been partially reconstructed. It has a closed four-mound group with two more mounds on the north side forming a second courtyard. Just west of this complex is an I-shaped ball court.

The lower slopes of Cerro Volado have two two-mound groups, one of which has two mounds in an L arrangement. Atop Cerro Volado is a 100 m long plaza with huge mounds at the east and west ends and a smaller structure in the center (Figure 4.10). This group may have been the major ceremonial precinct. It was separated from surrounding residential terraces by high retaining walls that could have served for defense.

Residential areas of the city were terraced. Terrace sizes, shapes, and habitation density were variable. On Cerro Volado there were broad terraces that may have

4.9 Prehispanic architecture and the historic church at Huamelulpan. The series of massive platforms is characteristic of monumental architecture in the Mixteca Alta.

4.10 Structures 1 and 2 on Cerro Volado.

had space for both domestic and agricultural activities or, alternatively, multiple houses. At SMH 3 terraces were long and narrow (e.g., 28 by 5 m and 63 by 4 m).

Virtually every barranca originating within and between the site subdivisions has a lama-bordo. There is no doubt that intensive agriculture was carried out within the city (our site boundaries delimit only the habitation area, not lama-bordos).

There was considerable growth and change during the Ramos period. Cerro Volado, Cerro Yucusavi, MRS 1, SMH 5, and SMH 10 were all occupied in Early Ramos. These settlements may have looked a lot like other Early Ramos hilltowns—conical peaks, concentric rings of long terraces, and a plaza with a small mound group on top. In each case the Early Ramos occupation was smaller than in Late Ramos. No large Early Ramos sites were abandoned. New ones, including many of the isolated residences and small sites, were founded in Late Ramos.

Huamelulpan was already different from many other places in the Mixteca Alta in Early Ramos times. It had a greater density of sites. It had relatively more small sites. In Late Ramos this subregion developed an urbanized system, something new in scale, complexity, and organization. Its peers at that time were Yucuita and Monte Albán.

Las Flores

Twenty-three sites have Las Flores components ranging in size from Cerro Volado's 67 ha to eleven small sites that were isolated residences or the tiniest hamlets (Figure 4.11, Table 4.7). The total occupied area (114 ha) and the estimated population (3,500 to 8,300) declined from Late Ramos; nevertheless, Huamelulpan still was an important place after Late Ramos.

Cerro Volado itself did not retain its Late Ramos size. Our collections show that it declined during Transición. The large number of mounds and plazas place Huamelulpan in the top tier of Early Las Flores places, but how long into the Early Classic Cerro Volado's prominence lasted is in doubt.

The city's other Late Ramos subdivisions—SMH 2–4, 18, 19i—all shrank in size and population. So did the large settlements on the eastern side of the valley; SMH 10 disappeared completely.

Some neighboring subregions had had no settlement in Late Ramos, whereas Huamelulpan attracted people and flourished. When (in Transición and Early Las Flores) the resettlement of previously abandoned places was in progress, Huamelulpan declined from its previous demographic peak and its position as leading urban center. Huamelulpan became for a time a peer to major centers in Teposcolula and elsewhere. By Late Las Flores, Huamelulpan, along with many of its neighboring subregions, was deserted only to rise again in the Postclassic.

Natividad

This was a time of settlement expansion equal to that of Late Ramos. We mapped twenty-nine Natividad components that cover a total area of 277.5 ha

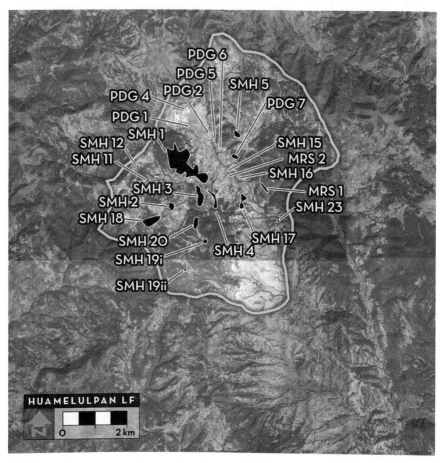

4.11 Las Flores sites in Huamelulpan.

(Figure 4.12, Table 4.8). Whereas in other subregions, including Yucuxaco just to the north, people resided in every locale fairly evenly, in Huamelulpan settlement strongly favored one area and eschewed another that had been important in earlier phases. Almost everyone lived on the hills and ridges on the west side of the valley where settlement was almost continuous and broken only by the numerous lama-bordos. There were very few and only small sites on the east side. On the east side only Totonundo at the northern end had a modest-size village.

The largest site was SMH 19. The Natividad occupation extends from the southern end of Cerro Yucusavi, southwest along the ridgetop, and then south and southeast on a ridge that slopes toward the valley. SMH 19 is not on the high divide but on the next ridge to the east, separated from the divide (where the modern highway to Tlaxiaco runs) by a deep valley that probably had lama-bordo terraces. The Yucusavi part of the site is on the andesite bedrock of the Volado-Yucusavi

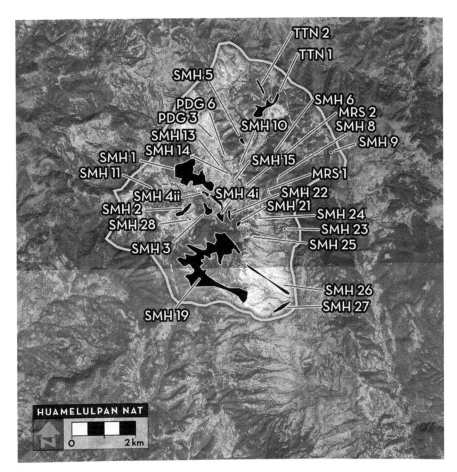

4.12 Natividad sites in Huamelulpan.

hills but the southern half is on the volcanic-sedimentary tuff formation. Today the slopes are in oak-pine forest and some of the ridgetops are cleared and used for milpas. SMH 19 has a total of three Natividad mounds—no major public construction here.

The Cerro Volado complex was again an important site. Most of Cerro Volado proper has Natividad occupation and the nearby ridges to the south do too. There is no evidence of new Natividad civic-ceremonial construction. Cerro Volado's twenty mounds and plazas may have had importance in Postclassic times. Perhaps the ball court was used in Natividad.

It is interesting how concentrated the population was. Almost 90 percent of the subregion's inhabitants lived in the two large centers, SMH 1–4 and SMH 19. Totonundo (TTN 1, 2) accounted for another 5 percent. In Natividad no other subregion had such a high degree of concentration in so few large sites. If we add SMR 2, less than 500 m south of SMH 19 in our Tayata subregion, this whole complex had about 19,400 people (using the midpoints of our population ranges). An aggregation of this size would be comparable to important cacicazgos of the early Spanish contact era. Yet neither Huamelulpan nor Tayata is outstanding in sixteenth-century history. Perhaps its population or political zenith came earlier in Natividad.

Huamelulpan was near the edges of two or three spheres of influence in the Postclassic. To the northeast was Teposcolula, to the south was Tlaxiaco, and Achiutla was 12 km to the southeast. Yucuxaco's ties had always been strongest to the south and its main settlements were much closer to Huamelulpan than to Yolomécatl or Teposcolula. One explanation for the lack of settlement on the east side of the Huamelulpan Valley and the fact that settlement clung to the heights on the west side could be friction with Teposcolula.

TAYATA

This is the southern reach of the valley that heads at Huamelulpan. The valley has soil and water resources that have attracted people for 3,000 years. It is a comparatively large patch of Yanhuitlán Formation soils (shale and sandstone in the west and conglomerates and sandstones in the east) sandwiched between mountains composed of andesite. The heights on the northern end of the west side are formed of volcanic tuffs and sandstones. The southeastern side of the valley is a high limestone ridge.

The Yanhuitlán sedimentary material is fantastically eroded into narrow, parallel ridges that are in turn being narrowed further by gullying on their side slopes. Tayata is drained by many gullies and barrancas that flow eastward and then through a single gap in the limestone ridge to leave the valley and flow into Achiutla. A branch of this river comes down the crease from La Estancia and joins the main stream at a gap in the ridge. The modern road between Tayata and Achiutla clings to the side of this same gap.

Today this valley has three municipios: Santa Cruz Tayata, Santa Catarina Tayata, and Santa María del Rosario. The two Tayata cabeceras are in mid-valley on the lower hills of the eastern side; Santa María is situated on a shelf of the western mountain wall. Santa Catarina has a dependency, Cuauhtemoc, in the southern valley. Santa María includes the ranchería settlement of La Unión Vista Hermosa, which is above the valley on the divide near the broad pass called Boca del Perro. All three municipios pertain to the district of Tlaxiaco. Tayata was part of the 1994–1995 Huamelulpan survey (Balkansky 1998b). We surveyed the rest of the valley in 1999.

Early/Middle Cruz

Tayata was occupied early in the Formative period. It had one of the important Early and Middle Formative settlement clusters in the Mixteca Alta. Six sites

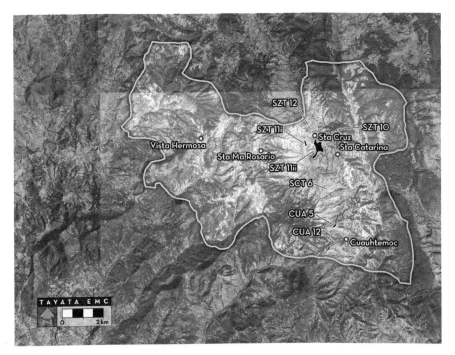

4.13 Early/Middle Cruz sites in Tayata.

have Early/Middle Cruz ceramics (Figure 4.13, Table 4.9). Two more, MRS 1 in Huamelulpan and SCA 1 in Amoltepec, lie just outside the subregion but were part of this settlement cluster. All are on low rises above the valley floor. The elevations of these sites are telling: all are around 2,150 m; the valley floor lies at about 2,100 m. MRS 1 is at 2,250 m but the base of the Huamelulpan Valley is higher, and in fact MRS 1 is also just above the local valley floor.

The Tayata settlement cluster is comparable to others in Early Formative Oaxaca in that it had a head village surrounded by smaller satellite settlements. The largest settlement—more than 20 ha—was SZT 11, 12, on the low hill just south of Santa Cruz Tayata. The other sites are small, 0.5 ha or less. This is a large and complex multicomponent site. It has both Early and Middle Cruz.

The head village has mounded construction, but according to the preliminary results of the excavation project, there is no evidence of mound construction stages prior to Late Cruz. CUA 12 may have had one mound.

Late Cruz

The total habitation area, number of sites, and population grew substantially during this period. Habitation area increased to 215 ha. There were now twenty-nine components (Figure 4.14, Table 4.10). All parts of the subregion were settled

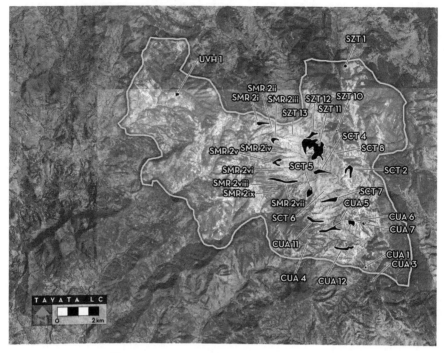

4.14 Late Cruz sites in Tayata.

and by this time the Tayata cluster had expanded to the north into Huamelulpan and Yucuxaco. With an average population estimate of 4,200, Tayata was one of Oaxaca's more densely settled places in the Middle Formative.

In the low-elevation settings that had been favored since Early Cruz the number of villages and their sizes grew. A half-dozen villages just above the valley floor had sizes of 10 ha or more. There was also expansion of settlement on slightly higher hills and on the many narrow ridges that descend from the mountains on the western side of the valley. Elevations are only 100 m or so above the older settlements but this was a new niche. In this setting one could not do floodwater farming, but dry farming, contour terracing, and lama-bordo terracing would have been possible. Small-scale canal irrigation and use of springs may also have been feasible. No similar opportunity existed on the steeper volcanic and hard limestone crags on the eastern side of the valley where no settlements were founded.

The Tayata head town (SZT 11, 12) spread over almost 77 ha. It was one of the Mixteca Alta's and Oaxaca's major towns in the Middle Formative. There are two mounds, one of which is actually a mound atop a large platform. The site is on a ridge about 1 km wide between two major branches of the valley's river. On both the north and south sides the valley bottom is at its broadest. The highest point on the site is only 100 m above the valley floor and most people resided much closer

4.15 Ramos sites in Tayata.

to the valley than that. The local setting is perhaps the best place in the subregion for valley-floor or low piedmont farming. Gullies, seeps, and arroyos here provide fertile pockets for trees and small cultivated fields. At least one lama-bordo has its origin in the site.

Four other sites have evidence for Late Cruz mounded construction. In addition to the head town (SZT 11, 12) there are single mounds at SCT 4, CUA 11 and 12, and SZT 1. The latter is a boundary site on the La Estancia drainage. UVH 1, on a hill overlooking the Río Yutecano west of Boca del Perro, is another site on an important path or boundary.

Occupation of Tayata appears to have been continuous from Early through Middle Cruz and both early and late Late Cruz. Collections from some of the outlying sites lack early Late Cruz and we suspect that more sites were founded and the system reached its maximum extent in the latter half.

Ramos

What happened to the Late Cruz settlement system is remarkable. This valley, in the prior phase one of the leading polities in highland Oaxaca, was deserted by Ramos times. Only one settlement was left in the heart of the Tayata Valley. A handful of sites on ridges in the north were Huamelulpan border settlements (Figure 4.15, Table 4.11). Three small sites were on top of the steep ridge between SZT 1 and Huamelulpan (SZT 2, 4, 8). SZT 10, a small village, was all that remained of the Tayata head town.

SZT 1 is in an unusual situation on a high limestone hill along the east side of the La Estancia drainage. There had been residential terraces and we noted several house mounds. Approaching the top of the hill from the south one has to climb a series of artificial terraces. On one of these, 100 m from the top, is a group of three mounds around a courtyard on a platform with another mound a few meters away. Ascending, one passes a single mound at the edge of a terrace before coming to the main group on the summit. This was probably a four-mound group with the largest mound on the east. SZT 1 has a small Late Cruz occupation, it continued as a small site in Early Ramos, and it was expanded to its full extent in Late Ramos. The site may have had boundary maintenance functions for the Huamelulpan urban core.

Over the divide to the west are two somewhat isolated Ramos sites. UVH 2 is on an east-west trail near the modern village of La Unión Vista Hermosa. It has two mounds facing each other on a small platform and some ruined residential terraces. It dates to Late Ramos. SMR 3 is Early Ramos. It is on top of a high knob overlooking the trails to the southwest (Tlaxiaco). On the top of the peak is a 15 by 15 m platform with a 3 by 3 m mound built on it. There are several ancient terrace retaining walls.

Las Flores

Tayata was repopulated in Las Flores. The settlement pattern was more like the present day than that of any prehispanic period. There were four villages of several hundred or a thousand people situated roughly where the four modern villages are (Figure 4.16, Table 4.12). The pattern goes back to the Late Cruz, when farmers' interests were in the valley floor and in arroyos and hills slightly upslope.

SCT 8 and 10 are near the old Tayata head town just above the valley floor (corresponding to Santa Catarina and Santa Cruz today). Together they covered 45 ha and may have had 1,200 inhabitants. SMR 2, near modern Santa María del Rosario on the western slopes, was a comparatively small site in area but it had been terraced and supported a dense population. SCT 6 is spread along a low hill between Santa Catarina and modern Cuauhtemoc.

In Las Flores there was also a small settlement atop the steep ridge on the west side of the La Estancia defile (this had been occupied in Ramos). The UVH 1 site west of Boca del Perro also had a small occupation.

As Huamelulpan grew in Ramos and took in population, Tayata emptied out. In Las Flores the opposite happened: Huamelulpan declined somewhat and Tayata was reestablished. Its Las Flores settlement was not as extensive as it had been in Late Cruz and Tayata must have remained subordinate to Huamelulpan. We found very little indication of Late Las Flores—Tayata was again abandoned.

4.16 *Las Flores sites in Tayata.*

Natividad

More people lived in Tayata in Natividad than at any other time in history. We mapped thirty-nine sites with over 330 ha of occupied area and an estimated population between 8,000 and 16,600. All parts of the valley were settled, from the north to the south, and from the upper slopes of the western side of the valley to the low hills above the valley floor (Figure 4.17, Table 4.13). Tayata was part of a larger spread of Natividad settlement that included Huamelulpan. This greater cluster was one of the Central Mixteca Alta's demographic hot spots.

The biggest and most distinctive site was SMR 2. On our maps this is the nine-pronged rake on the western side of the Tayata Valley. The top of the site extends for 3.5 km along the steep shelf at 2,350 m, at the upper limit of the Yanhuitlán Formation where this is overlain with volcanic tuffs. All the steep-sided, narrow ridges descending from this level toward the valley had Natividad occupation. To live here people must have built many terraces and we did note some terrace remnants. Today there are many agricultural contour terraces; the drainages have lama-bordos. We estimate that the site had between 5,000 and 10,000 people. SMR 2 has three mounds. SMR 2 is only a few hundred meters from SMH 19, which in turn is near Cerro Volado. These sites make up a multicentric urban area.

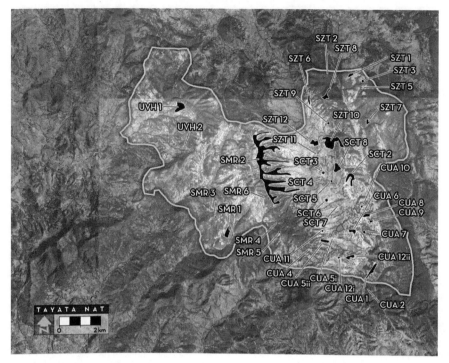

4.17 Natividad sites in Tayata.

In addition to SMR 2, Tayata had several other settlement clusters with numerous sites and dispersed, small mound groups. In each of these settlement clusters, nearest neighbor distances between sites within the cluster are smaller than the 0.5 km or more that separates nearest members of different clusters.

The next largest cluster of settlement was that formed by SZT 10, 12 and SCT 2, 8—the site of the old Formative head town just above the valley floor. Roughly 3,000 people lived on the hill between Santa Catarina and Santa Cruz.

All the other sites were quite small. There were thirty-two sites with average population estimates less than 100. Most were on the low hills above the valley floor and were within a few hundred meters of their nearest neighbors.

At the outer edges of the subregion were small settlements that might have pertained to Tayata or to one of the neighboring subregions; in other words, boundaries were not always clear. Some of the outer settlements had mounds, which were probably built in earlier periods and used in Natividad for ritual (inferring from the artifacts). SZT 1, 3, 5, and perhaps 7 might have been associated with La Estancia and Nduayaco or with Tayata. SZT 1 has mounds but the Natividad component is south of the mounds. The other sites in this group have no structures. SCA 1, 5, 7, and 11, south of Cuauhtemoc, are much closer to Tayata sites than they are to Amoltepec. None has mounded architecture.

There is a cluster of sites west of the Santa María del Rosario divide along the present-day boundary between Tlaxiaco, Santa María, and Amoltepec. The Natividad territorial affiliation is not clear. SMR 5 is on the summit of Cerro Yucusaito and it has three mounds. SMR 1, on two hills overlooking the Río Curtidor, has no mounds. SMR 3 is a reoccupation of a Ramos site on a hilltop. It has a mound on a platform and an Aztec-style Black-on-Orange bowl. UVH 1 has one structure and UVH 2 has two mounds on a platform; in both cases the mounds were built in earlier periods.

A case can be made for continuity between the Natividad settlement and present-day jurisdictions and settlements. The huge MRS 2 town is on top of the much smaller modern municipio of Santa María del Rosario. SZT 10 and 12 are next to Santa Cruz Tayata and SCT 2 and 8 are next to Santa Catarina Tayata. Santa Catarina's agencia Cuauhtemoc is in the center of the numerous small CUA sites. The little cluster of TLA and SMR sites on the southwestern edge of the subregion could correspond to the modern ranchería called San Isidro del Rosario. UVH 1 and 2 are at La Unión Vista Hermosa. Finally, SZT 1, 3, 5, and perhaps 7 could have been part of La Estancia, which today pertains to Santa Cruz. In Natividad these settlement clusters, with their ritual places and petty nobility, may have corresponded to the siqui or barrio.

CHAPTER FIVE

The Inner Basin

Between the Sierra de Nochixtlán and the next big mountain range to the west are seven little valleys, each of which had at one time or another a recognizable polity, or ñuu. No one subregion dominated this inner basin. It supported an important Early/Middle Formative cluster of villages. Every one of its subregions had one or more fortified hilltop sites in the Late Formative, but of these only the one spectacular site of Dzinicahua, plus a few outposts of Huamelulpan, survived or flourished in the Terminal Formative. Some of these subregions had significant Early Classic (Las Flores) development but others had little. Those subregions with sufficient occupation display the complex and differentiated settlement hierarchies we have also seen in Teposcolula and other places in the Early Classic.

In the Postclassic the inner basin was one of the most densely settled, intensively farmed regions in the Mixteca Alta. Populations were higher then than they were in the twentieth century. Today's incredibly eroded land can testify to its earlier intensive use and subsequent abandonment. We found little evidence of non-agricultural economic specialization here. Yet there were quite a few large and densely settled towns and cities.

In the sixteenth century, of these seven ñuu, only Achiutla seems to have been an independent cacicazgo. A few of its neighbors (e.g., San Juan Achiutla) were subordinate to it. The rest were probably part of a much larger alliance, or yuhuitaiyu, whose center was in Tlaxiaco across the mountain to the west (Chapter 6). The inner basin was thus Tlaxiaco's demographic heart and its great milpa.

SAN JUAN ACHIUTLA

This small valley is a link in a chain along the fault that runs from Achiutla in the south to Ixtapa in the Teposcolula Valley. It is a patch of sandstone-dominated Yanhuitlán beds rimmed on the east and west by less erodible crystalline limestone. San Juan Achiutla is separated from its northern neighbor Nduayaco by a pass through a tight constriction and it is separated from San Miguel Achiutla by a narrow gap in a limestone ridge. San Juan Achiutla is compact, less than 6 km long and only 1 km wide, and all of that sloping inward. Flat land is scarce but people today and in the past have made contour terraces. Modern San Juan is a dispersed town. Houses are scattered from one end of the valley to the other. Houselots, fields, and orchards are interspersed and are often on wide contour terraces with long retaining walls of stone, trees, and maguey.

The main valley is drained by the Río de las Lajas, which over its course here falls from 2,140 m in the north to 1,960 m at the south end. The side slopes have plenty of pitch too—on the gentler west side at the modern town the fall in elevation from the hillside across 1 km to the river is 140 m.

San Juan Achiutla also includes a segment of the valley of the Río Achiutla from where this river comes through the gap from Tayata to Atoyaquillo, a barrio of San Miguel Achiutla. A small ranchería here is called La Cieneguilla.

Today this is a single independent municipio. We have made it a separate subregion because it is a compact unit but it is closely associated with San Miguel Achiutla (which we refer to simply as "Achiutla").

Late Cruz

We could find sites no earlier than Late Cruz. There are two of these, perhaps part of the cluster of sites in San Miguel Achiutla (Figure 5.1, Table 5.1). Erosion left us with few remains in poor condition.

SJA 25 covers almost 13 ha on two mountain ridges. The ground is eroded to endeque and partly covered in pine forest. Site size and even dating are somewhat uncertain because the surface sherds are themselves quite eroded. Our best determination is Late Cruz (if not, then Early Ramos). It seems to be a single-component site. SJA 14 is a small concentration of sherds at the nose of the ridge at the southern end of the valley.

5.1 Late Cruz sites in San Juan Achiutla.

Ramos

We have three sites, two from Early Ramos and one from Late Ramos (Figure 5.2, Table 5.2). The occupations shifted several times during Ramos but overall the subregion seems to have been a buffer or route between other places.

SJA 10 was a minor center, a 3 ha site on a knob on the eastern wall of the valley. It is relatively well preserved in spite of some modern agriculture and re-piling of the stones from ancient retaining walls. On the summit is a three-mound group, a string of a structure, terrace, largest mound, plaza, and third mound (Figure 5.3). Residential terraces spill down the ridges away from the site center. There is a lamabordo directly associated with the ancient features. We recorded several probable houses and stone foundations. Sherds were scarce. The occupation could be early in Early Ramos.

SJA 18 is in the saddle north of the Cerro Yucuyoo, a place with a good view of the valley and the Cieneguilla gap. It has two small mounds built only 3 m apart and it probably dates to Early Ramos.

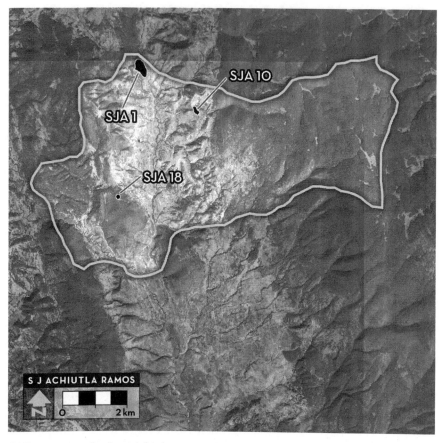

5.2 *Ramos sites in San Juan Achiutla.*

These two sites were abandoned by Late Ramos and were replaced in earliest Late Ramos by SJA 1. This is a terraced site on a hill 120 m high that blocks the northern end of the valley. It is only 1 km from NDU 21, another Late Ramos hilltop terraced site on a strategic point. On the summit is a single mound on a 56 by 20 m platform defined by a well-preserved stone wall 1 m high. A lama-bordo is associated. Most of the residential terraces are not preserved. Given the site's size and habitation density we think that 300 to 600 people lived here.

There was considerable change within Ramos along the corridor between Nduayaco and Achiutla. The site just next to SJA 1, NDU 20, dates to Early Ramos and was probably not contemporary. On the northern edge of Achiutla there are two Ramos hilltop villages, one Early (SMA 31) and the other Late (SMA 3). We suspect that these histories have more to do with larger events such as the general militaristic climate of Early Ramos and the rise of Huamelulpan in Late Ramos than with indigenous local development.

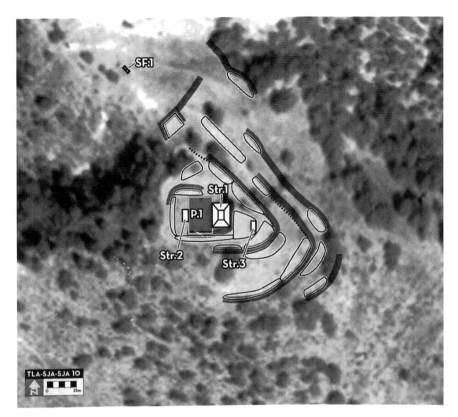

5.3 Plan of SJA 10.

Las Flores

In contrast to some other places in the study area, in San Juan Achiutla the Classic was not a time of expansion and development. It remained a place of outposts, not an area of robust internal development.

We found eight sites, none larger than 9 ha (Figure 5.4, Table 5.3); none was densely inhabited and artifacts were sparse. Only one site (SJA 31) had civic-ceremonial architecture and that was a single mound. SJA 31 is less than 1 km from the Achiutla sites SMA 3 and SMA 31 and it was probably part of that important cluster. An unusually high proportion of San Juan Achiutla Las Flores sites had no other component present. The total population was no more than it had been at any time during the Ramos period, not more than 500 people. Of the pottery assemblages large enough to make a determination, all fall into Early Las Flores.

Although San Juan Achiutla's agricultural resources were not equal to those of Tayata or places in the Nochixtlán Valley, it could have been developed more than it had been. This was a buffer zone where regional competition suppressed local development. Perhaps neighboring subregions kept attracting its potential population.

5.4 *Las Flores sites in San Juan Achiutla.*

Natividad

The settlement pattern of this time period was most like that of today, with dispersed habitation all along the western flank of the valley (Figure 5.5, Table 5.4). Natividad sites here are patchy and diffuse and have low to moderate artifact densities. Our average population estimate is 1,150 persons distributed among eighteen sites. This was the highest population ever for San Juan Achiutla.

SJA 12, on the lower slopes of the Cerro Yucuyoo, is the largest single site. The artifact scatter is diffuse and secondary growth vegetation makes surface visibility poor in places. There are remnants of ancient walls and terraces amid recent agricultural terraces. A ruined structure with mortared stones dates to the Colonial period.

On top of the ridge above the modern town center is a long, discontinuous scatter of Natividad domestic debris, SJA 9. It has a single mound with an accumulation of modern broken glass. There are a few poorly preserved terrace remnants.

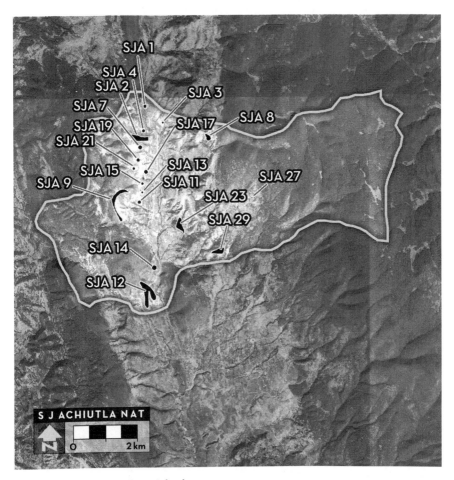

5.5 *Natividad sites in San Juan Achiutla.*

Next to the modern cemetery is SJA 23, which is the most artifact-rich site. This hill has modern agricultural terraces, houses, and garbage. Mixed with the recent refuse we found a chert production area, white chert blades and flakes, and green and gray obsidian. To each side there are lama-bordos in use today.

Another site in the mountains on the east side of the valley is SJA 8. This small settlement was situated in a saddle and it has unusual features. Built across the saddle is a wall that joins a structure on one side of the saddle. The structure measures 9 by 4 m at the base and is 0.5 m high. The pottery is that of normal domestic activities.

Survey archaeologists do not relish the claustrophobic tension of working the infields, houselots, fences, furious dogs, and garbage in modern towns. Citizens are of course curious about one's odd behavior. The archaeology is not easy either because the ancient settlement has to be picked out and reconstructed through a mesh of historic disturbance. SJA 2–4, 7, 11, 13, 15, 17, 19, and 21 represent our interpretation of the Natividad settlements that preceded modern San Juan Achiutla. Perhaps the inhabited area covered a little more ground than we show here.

At SJA 2 we found a Yanhuitlán Fine Cream sherd with an eccentric, misfired rim—kiln wasters or even slightly misfired vessel are rare in our study area. SJA 13 was littered with green obsidian tertiary flakes, indicating pressure-flaking for the final stages of toolmaking.

San Juan Achiutla was part of the Postclassic and Colonial Achiutla cacicazgo. Natividad was the first time in the sequence when the regional political climate seems to have allowed a San Juan Achiutla settlement system to develop an adaptation optimally suited to local resources. The dispersed distribution of a fairly large population, covering the whole valley and using numerous lama-bordos and contour farming terraces interspersed with residences, was certainly a departure from prior settlement patterns.

ACHIUTLA

This is the municipio of San Miguel Achiutla and its agencia San Sebastián Atoyaquillo. Achiutla is not as large a valley as Teposcolula or Yanhuitlán but it has more flat land than most other places in the Mixteca Alta. The valley is 6 km from north to south; including the piedmont up to the upper limits of most farming, it is roughly 5 km wide (Figures 5.6, 5.7).

In cross-section, Achiutla is an asymmetrical basin. The western rim is a formidable limestone ridge called Cordón la Corona. It remains in pine and oak forest. The lower slopes from about 2,060 m to the valley floor at 1,900 m are composed of an older, more weathered formation of limestone, mudstone, and sandstone. The soils derived from this formation are fertile. The valley floor boasts two patches of flat alluvium, one at the northwestern end (Figure 5.8) and another south of the Convento, which is prominently ensconced in the center of the basin. The eastern piedmont is broader and not as steep as the western side. These eastern slopes are formed of Yanhuitlán sandstones and conglomerates. The Yanhuitlán Formation materials in Achiutla extend over 7 by 2.5 km up to about 2,200 m. Above this elevation rise the imposing slopes of the Sierra de Nochixtlán with open oak forest giving way to pine forest at higher elevations.

The prominent ridge in the center of the valley, on which the Convento, the Pueblo Viejo, and earlier civic-ceremonial centers were situated, is limestone. The hill at the southeastern limit of Achiutla and the beginning of Yucuañe is a distinctive andesite tuff.

The Río de las Lajas, coming down from Nduayaco, and the Río Achiutla, which flows through the gap from Tayata, join in the northwestern end of the valley in front of Atoyaquillo and west of the Pueblo Viejo. Then the river flows south, falling 100 m before it leaves Achiutla through a narrow canyon below Huendio. Both sides of the valley have springs and are drained by many barrancas.

5.6 The Achiutla Valley and the sixteenth-century Dominican Convento, looking south from the Pueblo Viejo (SMA 4). From left to right the five peaks, all with sites, are Cerros Yucuañe, Tlacotepec, Yucuñushiño, Yucuñucu, and Gachupín (above Magdalena Peñasco).

5.7 The Achiutla Valley from the south. The Convento is in the center and San Miguel Achiutla is at the right.

5.8 The valley floor at Atoyaquillo, ATY 2 on the piedmont ridge, and the high Cordón la Corona.

San Miguel Achiutla and Atoyaquillo are dispersed, low-density settlements (Figure 5.9). Houses are often on broad contour terraces with orchards, magueys, and milpas interspersed.

Archaic?

We can identify no Archaic sites with certainty but one place merits revisiting. This is a rockshelter and nearby aceramic lithic scatter west of the high knob at ATY 6, a Natividad site above the cemetery at Atoyaquillo. We found only one tool, a chert scraper.

Late Cruz

We could find no Early/Middle Cruz but perhaps it is here and as yet undiscovered in one or more of Achiutla's multicomponent sites. Late Cruz is well represented. We found eight isolated residences and hamlets, the largest of which is 6.5 ha (Figure 5.10, Table 5.5). To the eight Achiutla sites one could add the nearby SJA 14 and SDH 16 and perhaps two northern Yucuañe sites to complete a settlement cluster. The eight Achiutla sites are all places with Late Cruz ceramics embedded in much larger sites with later components. Sites are evenly dispersed on both sides of the valley. The total population was in the range of 150 to 350 people. No site stands out as a center and there is no associated mounded architecture.

5.9 San Miguel Achiutla, a dispersed town at 1,940 m asl, from the west. Behind the town the Sierra Nochixtlán, which we knew as the Green Monster, rises to 3,200 m.

The sites on the western side of the valley occur on land that has been intensively farmed and remodeled by agricultural terraces. All the sites on the east side have modern houses and terraces as well. The collections generally could fit into the latter part of Late Cruz but two sherds from SMA 41 suggest a beginning in the early half of Late Cruz.

Perhaps the small and acephalous Achiutla cluster was an expansion of the Tayata polity whose head town was a 9 km journey through the Río Achiutla gap. The distance to the next closest head town, Yosojica, is a little longer (12 km) across a mostly vacant buffer zone.

Ramos

There was substantial population growth in Early Ramos then a steep decline in Late Ramos. Our mean estimate is 2,600 people for Early Ramos. The places inhabited in Ramos were not the same ones where people were living in Cruz. In Ramos four of the ten components were on high hills or mountains, a setting not used in Cruz. Settlements consisted of two large villages (ATY 1ii and SMA 31), four small villages (ATY 1i and SMA 1–3), and four hamlets (Figure 5.11, Table 5.6). For the first time there was mounded architecture, which occurs at many of the sites.

ATY 1ii is situated on an isolated lobe of the hills above Atoyaquillo. It was a densely occupied village of residential terraces but more recent agricultural terracing

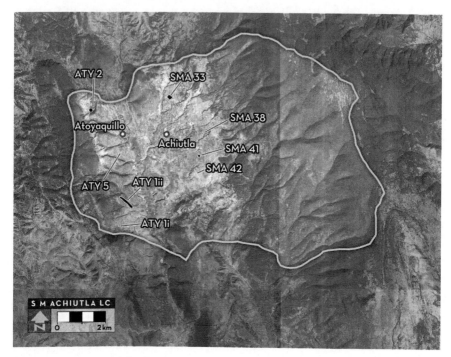

5.10 *Late Cruz sites in Achiutla.*

has obscured the ancient rock work. There are three mounds in no formal arrangement. SMA 31 occupies a 140 m high hill. It was also a terraced site. On the summit is a single mound on a plaza.

The four small villages were in high-elevation settings. SMA 2 is on the crest of the very steep Cordón la Corona. Although there is also Natividad here, the Early Ramos is well represented with various vessel forms indicating domestic use. There were residential terraces and on the north side are two defensive walls with a ditch between. The south side of the ridge is protected by a 200 m long, 1.5 to 2.5 m high wall. On the peak are two mounds in an L arrangement on a plaza. SMA 1 is also on the Cordón la Corona ridge but south of the larger site. ATY 1i is upslope from ATY 1ii. It has five structures; however, ATY 1 is a multicomponent site and we cannot be sure when the mounds were in use.

SMA 3 is on the mountain above the Convento and the Pueblo Viejo. In Early Ramos the occupation was quite small. There was a small mound at the north end of the site. The settlement grew in Late Ramos. We think the principal mound group and the ball court date to Classic times.

Of the hamlets ATY 4 may have had a mound but its stones were removed for recent constructions. SMA 40 also has an ex-mound, plowed away and not measurable. SMA 40 dates only to Late Ramos. Cerro El Moral, the southern limit of

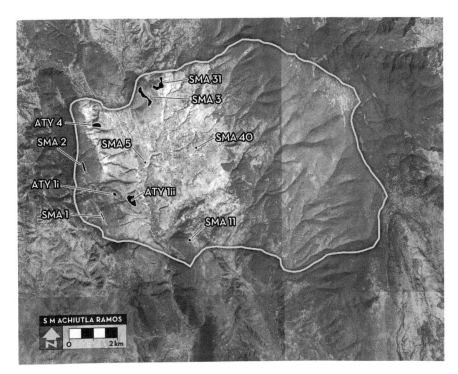

5.11 *Ramos sites in Achiutla.*

Achiutla, has an Early Ramos sherd scatter (SMA 11) and there was an Early Ramos occupation of unknown small size south of the Convento at SMA 5.

ATY 1ii and SMA 31 stand out as the leading settlements. Although no Achiutla site had monumental-scale mound groups, it is interesting that so many had at least one mound, which suggests a widespread distribution of civic-ceremonial functions. All the Early Ramos sites were abandoned by Late Ramos except SMA 3, which became the subregional center. The history of the Achiutla Ramos settlements is related to that of their neighbors in Huendio just to the south in the Tlacotepec subregion (Figure 5.12).

Las Flores

The area was resettled in Early Las Flores. The reoccupation was not complete or uniform over the valley but clustered mainly in several sites around the Late Ramos village at SMA 3. There was a cluster of small sites at the southwestern edge of the valley and a village above Atoyaquillo (Figure 5.13, Table 5.7). But compared to Natividad in Achiutla and compared to the extensive Las Flores settlement in other subregions such as Teposcolula and Tilantongo, this resettlement appears tentative.

5.12 From Cordón la Corona looking south to the Ramos sites of SDH 1 and 2 (the two coni-cal hills in the center), beyond to Cerro Yucuañe (the higher ridge, center) and the range above Tlacotepec on the right.

We mapped nine sites and estimate a total population between 940 and 2,070 people. The cluster of SMA 3–5, 30–32, plus SJA 31 accounts for most of the population. The largest site is SMA 31, the Early Ramos terraced hilltop reoccupied in Las Flores. But the civic-ceremonial center may have been SMA 3 on the ridge above the later Pueblo Viejo. This has two mounds facing each other across a closed plaza (Figure 5.14). Just behind the larger mound is a 36 by 8 m ball court. Las Flores is well represented around the mound group and the ball court; we found no Natividad here. We noted a fair amount of black obsidian.

SMA 3 dates from Transición and the collection from SMA 5 also has Transición markers. The other sites where a determination could be made were Early Las Flores. There is no Late Las Flores—Achiutla was uninhabited during that time.

Natividad

Achiutla was a prominent cacicazgo at the time of the Spanish invasion. Our survey shows that it had demographic clout. The average of our low and high population estimates is 11,700. We mapped 779 ha of settlement area.

Residential areas lined the east and west flanks of the valley as if it were a ball court (Figure 5.15, Table 5.8). The place Achiutleños recognize as the Pueblo Viejo, the seat of the cacique, was on the prominent ridge in the center of the valley above the flat alluvium. This is where the Dominican monastery was built in the sixteenth

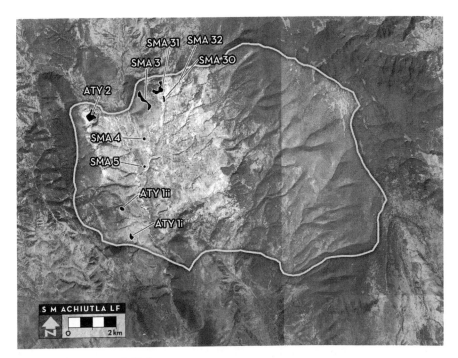

5.13 Las Flores sites in Achiutla.

century. Just as this building is visible from the whole Achiutla Valley, the cacique standing at his palace could see his domain; in turn his house was seen by his subjects (Figures 5.6, 5.7).

The slopes above Atoyaquillo on the west side of the valley (ATY 1–6) had extensive settlement. Today this land has been sculpted into agricultural terraces running along the contours (Figure 5.16). The Natividad town had similar features but the ancient terraces were reworked by more recent farmers. Artifact densities are quite patchy, ranging from moderate concentrations to ridges where all the soil and artifacts have washed away. The Natividad settlement consisted of houses on terraces, farming terraces on the slopes, and lama-bordos in the barrancas.

At ATY 1 there are thirteen mounds, most built in earlier times, scattered in five separate places. ATY 3 has two structures, probably house mounds. ATY 5 has a large platform, 40 by 20 m on top, supporting a patio group of three stone foundations arranged around a courtyard. The western edge of the platform has a profile revealing 2.5 m of a floor. This site also has two bell-shaped pits (locally called *sótanos*). ATY 6 has a platform with a sunken patio on top.

ATY 1–6 have considerable lithic debris but because much of the area is multicomponent we cannot assign it all to Natividad. At ATY 4 we found a gold-green obsidian blade core that is probably Natividad.

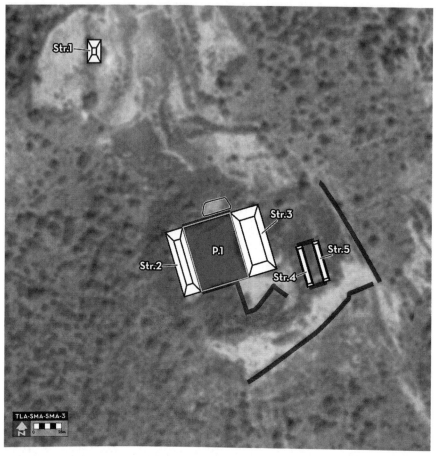

5.14 Plan of the closed mound group and ball court at SMA 3.

The cluster of SMA 30, 32–35 is at the north end of the modern town of San Miguel Achiutla along the arroyo Yutecabaxi. Except in a few places almost all of this is single-component Natividad. Artifact density is variable and patchy. Consistently there are white chert flakes. At SMA 30, which also has Las Flores, white chert was quarried and there are many primary flakes. Later-stage reduction took place at the other sites in this cluster where we found secondary flakes, cores, blades, and bifacially retouched pieces. Gray, green, and black obsidian was also worked at these sites; gray is more frequent and black is rare. We found both flakes and blades. SMA 42 is also a large site covering 50 ha. It has white chert flakes, cores, and a few blades.

We mapped single mounds at SMA 6, 40, and 43 on the eastern side of the valley. Whether these were house mounds or civic-ceremonial places is not known. We found no mounds at the large cluster SMA 30, 32–35.

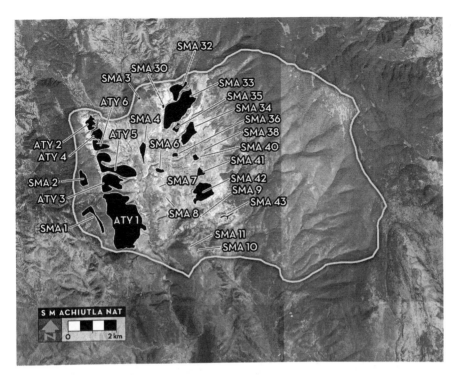

5.15 Natividad sites in Achiutla.

There are two special sites on the Cordón la Corona crest. These probably had boundary significance. SMA 1 is on the lower southern stretch of the ridge. On top of a knob there is a series of house mounds and patios and on the adjacent slopes there are residential terraces. South of this peak is a cave. The site continues onto a knob west of the peak where we found a 15 by 12 m area described in the field notes as "a carpet of obsidian," which sounds like a fine idea. This concentration had more green than gray obsidian and more flakes than blades.

The highest peak on the Cordón is SMA 2, which was a Ramos site reoccupied in Natividad. It has defensive walls. We saw gray and some black obsidian flakes perhaps indicating obsidian working.

The Pueblo Viejo is SMA 4 (Figures 5.17–5.19), an impressive site but unfortunately in only poor to fair condition because of recent agriculture and other use. The site occupies the spine and upper side slopes of the ridge from just south of the Convento up to and including the first plateau on the ridge, which is about 50 m in elevation above the modern road. The Classic site called Puerta del Sol is higher up on this same ridge. The whole length of the ridge from the southern end of the plateau to below the Convento was modified into a series of broad, rectangular platforms or terraces (the monastery was built on one of these). Much earth and stone were moved to make these terraces, as they measure 63 by 34 m and have retaining

5.16 ATY 1 and 2 and Cordón la Corona, looking west-southwest.

5.17 The early Colonial chapel, built at the Pueblo Viejo (SMA 4), looking north from the Convento. Some of the Natividad platforms are visible behind the chapel. The lowest is the site of the cemetery. A crew member is sitting in the truck, in the shade.

5.18 Massive terrace at the Pueblo Viejo (SMA 4), looking upslope to the north.

walls 3 m high. Two of the platforms are used today for the town cemetery. One platform north of the cemetery has a mound and several standing walls. On the side slopes there were residential terraces.

Achiutla's Pueblo Viejo does not have standing palaces or large mounds like Mitla or Teposcolula. Instead, its monumentality lies in the massive platforms stepping up the hill. What was built on these cannot be known without excavation. We speculate that some had palaces and others, perhaps where the Convento is, were open plazas.

Natividad sites have relatively abundant artifacts. Braziers and censers are widespread and occur in residential areas. We noted Polychrome only at the Pueblo Viejo. Collections from ATY 1 and the two sites on Cordón la Corona may suggest Early Natividad. The Pueblo Viejo seems to be Late. All the other material appears to be uniform and presumably of the same Late (?) date.

Historically, Achiutla was an independent cacicazgo famous for its oracle and as a religious center (Burgoa 1989:1:276–277). The survey shows that it was a major population center. People must have practiced intensive infield agriculture on lama-bordos and contour terraces near their houses and they probably cultivated fields on the valley alluvium. Political control was exercised through a single center, the Pueblo Viejo. There are mounds in outlying settlements but they are small, often single, and scattered rather than in formal groups. Some may be residences of local petty nobility or the well-to-do; others are older structures reused for ritual. It is possible that single mounds were ceremonial structures pertaining to supra-household groups such as barrios. In any case we see no evidence of an architectural investment

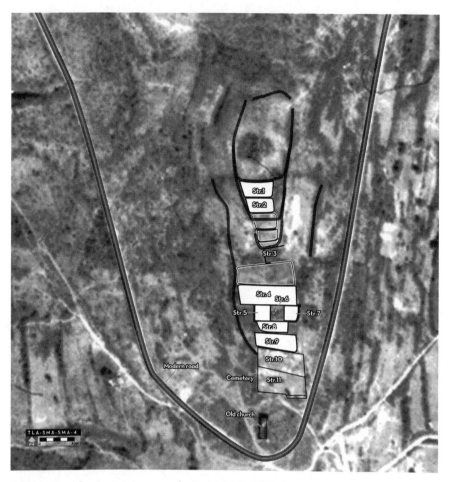

5.19 Sketch of the massive terraces at the Pueblo Viejo, SMA 4.

in bureaucracy or specialized administration below the level of the cacique and his center.

YUCUAÑE

To the municipio of San Bartolomé Yucuañe, we add lands of La Paz, Las Palmas, and Guadalupe Hidalgo, three agencias of Santiago Tilantongo. This is periphery or backcountry, a land of steep mountains, narrow canyons, and small and isolated settlements. San Bartolomé is reached today by road from Achiutla. To get to Guadalupe Hidalgo, La Paz, and Las Palmas by road one has to go through San Bartolomé. Las Palmas though is only 5 km southwest of the archaeological site of Monte Negro in Tilantongo.

5.20 Modern agricultural terraces south of San Bartolomé Yucuañe. Note cazahuate and guaje trees on edges.

Yucuañe is lower, warmer, and drier than other places in our study area. It is drained by streams that flow north to south. In a narrow canyon on the west is the Río Los Sabinos, which is the Achiutla River. The San Bartolomé Valley is tributary to the Sabinos. An important stream from San Mateo Peñasco—the Río Yuteyucui—joins the Sabinos after coming through a dramatic gap. Guadalupe Hidalgo and La Paz/Las Palmas are on south-flowing arroyos. In places there are springs on the mountain slopes.

The subregion is mostly mountains—north-south trending, high, steep, limestone ridges. Good farm land is scarce (Figure 5.20). Patches of fertile soil at lower elevations coincide well with modern and ancient settlement. San Bartolomé occupies a pocket of Yanhuitlán Formation sandstones and conglomerates but here the valley is steep and narrow. The whole eastern side of the valley is contour terraced for fields, orchards, and the houselots of the modern town.

South of San Bartolomé is a 1 km² basin of residual clay soils, and near this little basin is the ranchería Guadalupe Hidalgo and a cluster of prehispanic sites. North of Guadalupe Hidalgo and east and across the Sierra de Nochixtlán from San Bartolomé is another break in the high limestone ridges, a small outcropping of older, more weathered limestone, sandstone, and mudstone. Here is La Paz, at 2,540 m asl. Less than 2 km in distance and 250 m in elevation below La Paz is Las Palmas, which apparently owes its livelihood to the only other island of good soil, a narrow and steep crease of Yanhuitlán sandstones and conglomerates.

In sum, in this somewhat forbidding landscape of high mountains, there are only four places with better soils. There are only four modern villages. The soils and the villages coincide.

We have a high number of undated sites (LPZ 3; SBY 9, 12, 30). All had sherds but they were eroded, small, and undiagnostic. Three even had mounds. LPZ 3 might have had at least three, SBY 9 had one, and SBY 12 had a feature that may have been a mound.

Late Cruz

We found three small sites, two on the slopes above San Bartolomé and one overlooking the little valley to the south (Figure 5.21, Table 5.9). At all three the ground was covered with secondary growth, there were recent agricultural terraces, and there were sections of older retaining walls of unknown date. The sites and the sherds themselves were eroded but we saw enough to assign a Late Cruz date. In Late Cruz, Yucuañe must have been peripheral to more developed neighbors— Achiutla, Tilantongo, and Peñasco.

Ramos

Again there were three sites, probably two small villages and a hamlet. None is a Cruz site; all are in new places on ridgetops (Figure 5.22, Table 5.10). All three date to Early Ramos, when the population may have been about 900 people. We found no evidence of anyone living in Yucuañe in Late Ramos.

Cerro Yucuañe is an impressive mountaintop with excellent views. It has an Early Ramos occupation (SBY 3) of indeterminate small size. This was a terraced and fortified settlement. The narrow crest of the ridge has a linear string of well-preserved platforms, terraces, and mounds. The side slopes have enough remnants of retaining walls to say that there were residential terraces. The northern approach is blocked by a massive defensive wall. How much of this dates to Ramos is unknown. Artifacts are scarce. Caution suggests using the lower end of our population estimate range.

A second hilltop terraced site is SBY 11. Unfortunately, it is in a poor state of preservation. The top of the knob has two or three structures. The site has some retaining wall and terrace remnants and other stone walls that may have been defensive. SBY 8 is an open site of which there is not much left.

We interpret the Early Ramos settlement as short-lived. This was the time of much larger consolidations of people in Tilantongo, Huamelulpan, and Peñasco. Yucuañe was not in a position to develop a stable settlement system in that competitive environment.

Las Flores

Las Flores was a big period in this area. We found sixteen sites (Figure 5.23, Table 5.11), half of them single component. The total occupied area was over 150

5.21 Late Cruz sites in Yucuañe.

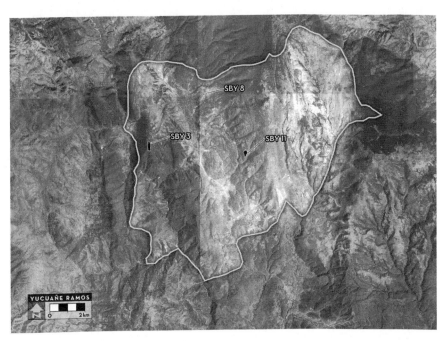

5.22 Ramos sites in Yucuañe.

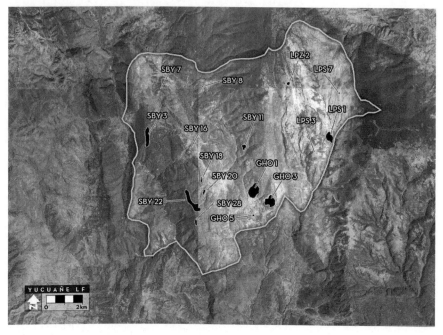

5.23 Las Flores sites in Yucuañe.

ha. Many of the sites had residential terraces. However, these sites are not as well studied as we would like. In several cases (GHO 1, 3, 5) there is a confounding mix of recent agricultural terracing and remnants of old rock work. Farmers have moved stones to make new retaining walls and new piles, frustrating the most experienced sherd dog's ability to pick out the ancient from the modern features. At the two largest sites (SBY 3 and 22) a combination of dense vegetation and prior agricultural use made mapping very difficult. With more time and some test excavations it might be shown that these sites were more dense and more complex than described here. As it is, our population estimate range for Yucuañe is 3,900 to 8,300 people.

Western Yucuañe has two prominent mountain peaks, Cerro Yucuañe and Cerro Yucunuviso. Between them flows the tributary stream coming out of the San Bartolomé Valley; at the base of their western slopes is the canyon of the Río Los Sabinos. In Las Flores, people built towns on both mountains.

Cerro Yucuañe (SBY 3, Figure 5.24) had been occupied in Early Ramos but the Las Flores is more extensive and we think the full architectural complex was completed in the Classic. The civic-ceremonial center is a linear string of terraces, platforms, and mounds that occupies the north-south crest of the ridge. There is a defensive wall on the northern approach and quite a few residential terraces. No other Yucuañe site has as many civic-ceremonial structures. Compared to other Las Flores centers this site ranks high in the third tier of a regional civic-ceremonial hierarchy.

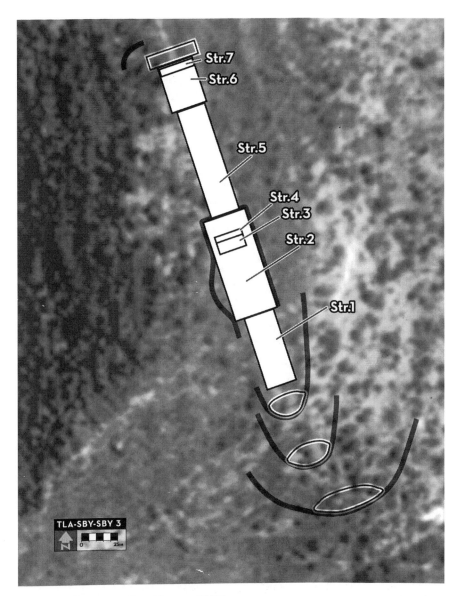

5.24 The architecture at Cerro Yucuañe, SBY 3.

Cerro Yucunuviso (SBY 22) was the largest site in population with 1,600 to 3,200 people. The site covers 32 ha, all of which must have been terraced to create flat habitation space. Most of the terraces and some of the civic-ceremonial architecture have been plowed, eroded, and reformed (Figure 5.25). In several places ancient residential terrace walls turn into lama-bordo retaining walls (an association

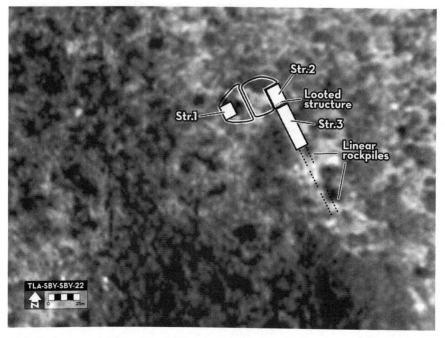

5.25 The remaining architecture at SBY 22, Cerro Yucunuviso.

also found at nearby SBY 20). Artifacts have locally heavy densities. We saw one possible carved stone. The top of the ridge has an unusual modification: a 90 m long access way consisting of parallel stone walls 6 m apart. This ascends directly to Str. 2, which has a building on top facing the access way (like Cerro Jazmín). Another mound is on a terrace adjacent to the terrace of Str. 2. SBY 22, an outlier on the knob to the south, has a platform with a structure as well.

GHO 1, 3, and 5 form a cluster of Las Flores settlement at the southern edge of our study area. We do not know if there are related sites to the south. These are hillsides and hilltops used for agriculture. We mapped the site boundaries and found enough ceramics to firmly date the sites to Las Flores. The cluster has five mounds.

Another cluster of sites is at Las Palmas/La Paz, on the edge of the study area. LPS 1 is the hill just south of Las Palmas. On top of the hill is a very visible tall mound. It was built on a large platform and faces another mound also built on the platform. We found an urn fragment here. There had been some residential terraces off the sides of the platform. A hilltop (LPZ 3) on the ridge southeast of here has at least three destroyed mounds but the entire site is eroded to bedrock and no diagnostic sherds were found. The crew thought it might be like LPS 1 but we list LPZ 3 as undated. The other Early Ramos hilltop fortified site, SBY 11, also has Las Flores occupation. It had a civic-ceremonial zone on the hilltop.

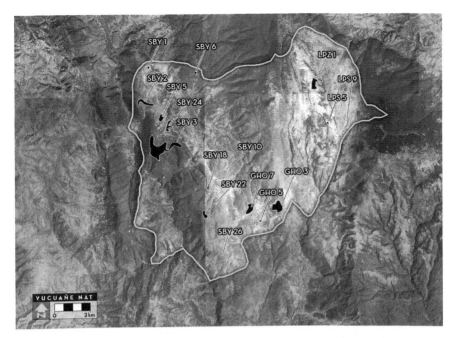

5.26 *Natividad sites in Yucuañe.*

Our interpretation of the settlement system is limited because nothing is known about the area outside our survey boundary and because disturbance, dense vegetation, and lack of time limited our observation on key sites. Las Flores was the peak time for population. The strategic mountain peaks above the Río Sabinos had towns. The Guadalupe Hidalgo and Las Palmas localities were occupied for the first time and rather heavily. We infer intensive lama-bordo construction and contour terrace farming similar to recent practice in the same places. Civic-ceremonial architecture is found in all the settlement clusters. Pottery from these sites is Early Las Flores. At LPS 1 the Las Flores occupation began in Transición. No sites have Late Las Flores. In the larger regional Las Flores picture the major Yucuañe sites were well situated astride north-south and Peñasco-Tilantongo corridors.

Natividad

There was a large population in Natividad, between 5,000 and 11,000 people. All the small valleys occupied in Las Flores and today were settled in Natividad (Figure 5.26, Table 5.12). Three-fourths of the people lived at one site, Cerro Yucuañe, which spread to become more extensive than ever. Looking beyond this town to the rest of the subregion the occupation is not as impressive. Settlement density away from Cerro Yucuañe was no more than it had been in Las Flores. There was little or no new civic-ceremonial construction.

5.27 *San Agustín Tlacotepec from SAT 9. The peak to the west is El Gachupín. Note the heavy erosion.*

Cerro Yucuañe sprawled over 80 ha. Houses were built on the old residential terraces around the top of the mountain and the town expanded to cover the eastern ridges. Outlying settlements (SBY 2, 4, 5, 24) were built on the lower slopes. There are several lama-bordos. The old lama-bordo next to SBY 2 has been cut through by a gully, revealing stone retaining walls 2 m high. SBY 2 also has free-standing stone walls and ditches fortifying the hilltop.

SBY 22, Cerro Yucunuviso, was reoccupied not on the top of the hill but on the eastern slope. The Guadalupe Hidalgo hills also had Natividad settlement and there were small sites around La Paz/Las Palmas.

The Cerro Yucuañe cluster must have been closely associated with Tlacotepec and Huendio, which were quite large and just across the river. The La Paz and Las Palmas villages were probably associated with Tilantongo as they are today.

TLACOTEPEC

Tlacotepec (Figure 5.27) is a 10 km section of the long trough of Yanhuitlán Formation soils that extends from north of Yucuxaco to south of the Peñasco. It shares the same geological units seen in Tayata and Huamelulpan. The trough of Yanhuitlán sandstones and conglomerates is no more than 4 km wide, enclosed on the west by craggy mountains of andesite and on the east by the continuation of Tayata's limestone ridge and Achiutla's Cordón la Corona. The elevation of the val-

5.28 The Río Magdalena between Huendio and Totojaha.

ley in front of San Agustín Tlacotepec is 1,860 m. The upper edge of the Yanhuitlán beds is between 2,200 and 2,300 m.

The gully erosion of the Tlacotepec Valley is spectacular. Gullies are multiple and repetitive. The side slopes of the ridges above San Agustín have a deep gully every 30 m. Deep barrancas have gouged laterally into the slopes, forming long, pinnacled ridges. The sides of these ridges are in turn slashed by even steeper gullies. The pattern is fractal to the point where there is nothing left of a hill. However, on this same land that is washing away before one's eyes, agriculture flourished as late as the twentieth century and it could today if people had not emigrated to find employment elsewhere. The eastern wall of the valley has multiple springs and the barrancas are moist.

Our subregion is not the same as the modern municipio, for reasons of settlement history. San Agustín is the center of our Tlacotepec but we extend our area north to include Santo Domingo Huendio, formerly an agencia of Tlaxiaco and since 1990 an agencia of Magdalena Peñasco. Yosojica today is subject to San Agustín Tlacotepec but we include it with Dzinicahua because of its shared history with other settlements on the flanks of the Peñasco Grande.

Tlacotepec's arroyos run east toward the Río Sabinos, which is on the east side of the chain of limestone mountains. The Río Yuteyucui squeezes through a narrow gap at the southern end of the valley. The Río Magdalena (Figure 5.28) has broken through between Tlacotepec's Cerro Yucuñoo and Huendio's Cerro Yucuñushiño.

Settlements of the historic era favor the drainage divides because of the spring heads, the possibilities for multiple lama-bordos, and easier transportation. San

Agustín is up against the eastern wall of the valley on the divide between north- and south-flowing arroyo branches. Huendio is on another divide, a saddle between the Cerro Yucuñushiño and the Cerro Yucuñucu. There are also two valley-bottom rancherías: Totojaha, at the base of the ridges north of San Agustín, and Junta del Río, where the Magdalena meets the Sabinos (Figure 5.29) on the other side of the mountain. Junta del Río is an unusual place because it has flat alluvial land (less than 1 km²). It is also a tiny pocket of Yanhuitlán bed soils surrounded by limestone mountain slopes.

Archaic?

We have no certain Preceramic sites. But overlooking the gap where the Río Magdalena flows through the mountains, on the same ridge but below the ceramic and lithic scatter of the Natividad component SAT 11, we found a 30 by 25 m concentration of approximately fifty flakes. These were of a variety of chert materials. Perhaps 15 to 20 percent were fairly heavily patinated. All the artifacts were flakes—there were no tools or cores. It is possible that this concentration is a Natividad activity area but any future project on the Archaic of the Mixteca Alta should revisit this site.

Early/Middle Cruz

The earliest ceramic sites we found are from Middle Cruz. There are five (Figure 5.30, Table 5.13) in two clusters, one on the east side of the valley south of San Agustín and one on the opposite side of the valley 2 km away. Note the situation: low hills, low elevations, and near the upper end of the valley's main drainage. Today there are lama-bordos on all sides. All the sites are small. Because of erosion and farming there may have been more settlement than we were able to see.

SAT 2 appears to have Cruz (Middle and Late) and no other phases. There are two mounds, facing each other across a small plaza. Unfortunately, the mound group is highly disturbed by plowing and looting. Late Cruz is a little better represented. SAT 6 is mostly destroyed but we found a good ceramic collection concentrated in an erosion cut. Most of these sites are not in good shape. There seems to have been continuity from Middle to Late Cruz, as some of the sites have both phases.

Tlacotepec was part of and geographically central to a larger cluster of Middle Cruz settlement that included Yosojica and San Mateo Peñasco sites. This was equivalent to the Tayata settlement cluster to the north. It is not clear if this greater Tlacotepec cluster had a head village in Middle Cruz.

Late Cruz

This was a time of growth and expansion of the settlement cluster of Tlacotepec and its neighbors (Figure 5.31, Table 5.14). The demographic and civic-ceremonial

5.29 The Río Sabinos, near SDH 20, looking south.

5.30 Early/Middle Cruz sites in Tlacotepec.

center shifted to the lower slopes of the Peñasco Grande extending from Yosojica to San Mateo Peñasco (modern jurisdictional boundaries split this area). There were small sites in Tlacotepec proper, and the small valley of Junta del Río was colonized for the first time. The preference for open sites at low elevations was the same as in Middle Cruz. Some of the same sites continued to be occupied. We think there was continuity from Middle Cruz through Late Cruz with the greatest expansion of settlement occurring at the end of Late Cruz.

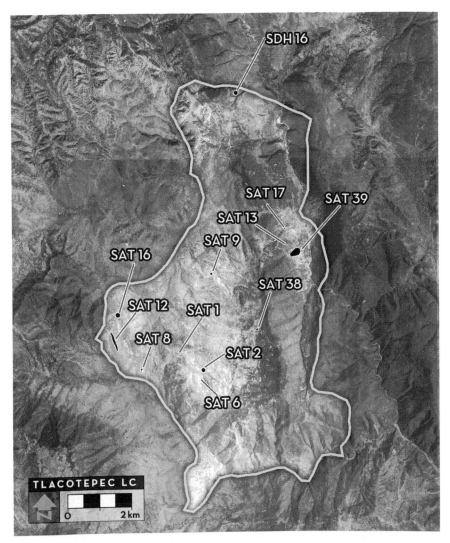

5.31 *Late Cruz sites in Tlacotepec.*

In the San Agustín area SAT 2 has two mounds facing each other on a small plaza. There is a single mound at SAT 9 that could have a Late Cruz construction stage. There were now three sites overlooking the alluvium at Junta del Río and one of them, SAT 39, has a formal mound group. SAT 39 also has a Natividad occupation so we cannot be sure of a Late Cruz attribution for mound construction. The arrangement is a linear string consisting of Str. 1 with a formal stairway with alfardas (side walls) built on a platform at the high point and then another platform, on which there was a group of three structures around a courtyard.

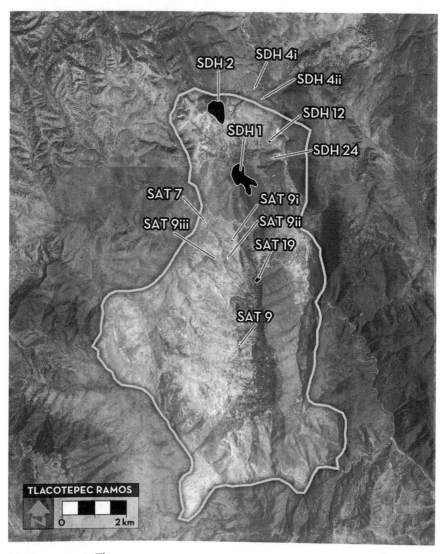

5.32 Ramos sites in Tlacotepec.

Ramos

Four radical changes happened in Ramos: the abandonment of almost all the Cruz sites, the Early Ramos founding of a community that centered on Cerro Yucuñucu, the abandonment of that community, and the establishment of another one centered on Cerro Yucuñushiño. Tlacotepec population increased from Cruz to Early Ramos (1,600 to 2,600 people) and by Late Ramos it was perhaps 2,800 (Figure 5.32, Table 5.15).

5.33 SDH 1, Cerro Yucuñushiño. The milpa in the foreground has Ramos, Las Flores, and Natividad sherds. The site's southernmost mound is in the trees in the center. Beyond, the slope plunges to the gap where the Río Magdalena flows to Junta del Río. The mountain at upper right is the ridge east of San Agustín Tlacotepec.

None of the Late Cruz components continued into Ramos. The whole southern end of Tlacotepec and the Yosojica area were abandoned. The Junta del Río occupation ended. In Early Ramos there was only one small site in Tlacotepec south of the Huendio area, SAT 9, high on the flanks of the mountain above San Agustín.

The new Early Ramos community on and around Cerro Yucuñucu consisted of the hilltown itself (SDH 2) plus small, open sites nearby (SDH 4 i, ii) and a small occupation on Cerro Yucuñushiño. The nearby Achiutla sites are also Early Ramos. Cerro Yucuñucu rises 220 m above the saddle at Huendio. It has little public architecture, only a single platform on the summit of the hill. At one time it had multiple concentric rings of terraces. There are several lama-bordos below but these may be associated with Natividad settlement.

None of these sites persist into Late Ramos except SDH 1, Cerro Yucuñushiño, which became the leading center in that phase. This is an interesting but challenging multicomponent hilltown. It has an impressive amount of rock work in retaining walls, freestanding walls, platforms, and mounds, but unfortunately, recent farmers have made their own additions and subtractions. We mapped several broad terraces on the top of the hill. There is one large platform (Str. 1) surrounded by several terraces. Terrace 3 has an exposed bell-shaped pit. Farther south along the ridgeline across several terraces is a second structure (Figure 5.33). The latter had ritual use from Las Flores, Natividad, and modern times. Plowed house remains (rises with faced-stone debris) were seen on many terraces. Late Ramos outliers of SDH 1 are

SAT 7, SAT 9 LR i–iii, and SAT 19 near Totojaha, and SAT 12 on the northeastern flank of Cerro Yucuñushiño. SAT 19 has plowed and ruined residential terraces; a lama-bordo is directly associated with this component. SDH 24 we listed only as General Ramos; it is eroded to bedrock and has two obvious house foundations.

Las Flores

We mapped 61 ha of habitation area in the valley settlements clustered on the western side. There was little occupation on the lower slopes of the eastern side. The largest town was on the crest of the mountain above the eastern side of the valley. Cerro Yucuñushiño had a Las Flores occupation and there were several hamlets in the Huendio vicinity (Figure 5.34, Table 5.16).

The leading town was on the ridge of the Cerro Yucuñoo (SAT 21), not on the very highest peak but still at 2,500 m, 600 m above the valley floor. This is oak and pine forest. The ridge crest is narrow, in places only 15 m wide. Terraces built up and reinforced the sides. The architecture on the crest is well preserved but the terraces on the side slopes are not. From the north there is a defensive wall usually 2 m and sometimes 3 m high. Inside the wall is a ditch. A break in the wall and ditch allows passage. Ascending the ridgeline is a series of four residential terraces. Then comes a linear string of structures and platforms beginning with Str. 1, followed by Str. 2. Str. 3 is a platform for three other mounds. A pile of stone in front of Strs. 5 and 6 could have been an adoratorio. Descending the platform toward the south are two more terraces and the defensive wall, which circles the site. If the whole site of 13 ha had residential terraces, the population would have been between 650 and 1,300 people. There is at least one lama-bordo that shares a common retaining wall with a residential terrace (T. 12). The pottery from SAT 21 indicates Transición and Early Las Flores. A modern shrine is maintained on the site.

SAT 11, north and below SAT 21, has one mound on the hilltop and several ruined residential terraces below. There are lama-bordos, several ancient stone foundations, and modern agricultural terraces.

The occupation at Yucuñushiño (SDH 1) seems to have been Early Las Flores, likewise most of the other sites. Only at SAT 8 and 14 did we think there was a possibility of Late Las Flores.

SAT 21 is similar in scale and layout to SBY 3 and SBY 22, on the tops of the mountains on the other side of the Río Los Sabinos. The three are of course inter-visible and would have been contemporary in Early Las Flores. Dzinicahua was another large site in the inner basin in Las Flores. Villages in southern Tlacotepec may have been affiliated with that town.

Natividad

Every part of the subregion was occupied (Figure 5.35, Table 5.17). Our median population estimate is 7,300 persons. The largest town ever, SAT 9, had over 4,000 inhabitants. All of today's outlying villages and hamlets (Huendio, Junta del Río,

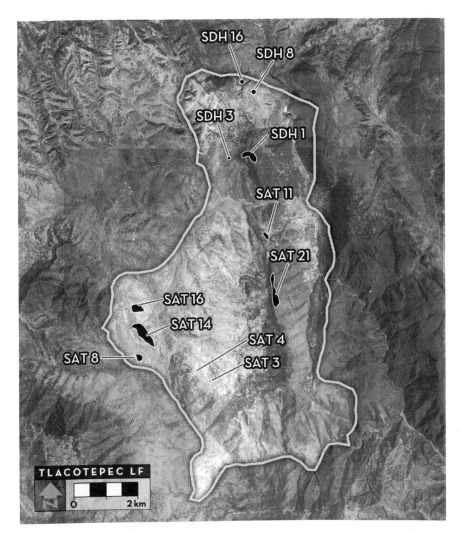

5.34 *Las Flores sites in Tlacotepec.*

Yosojica) were settled in Natividad and had larger populations than they do today. Although high hilltops were occupied, most people lived at lower elevations on the flanks of the valley. Of the thirty sites twenty-six are below 2,100 m.

The major center and the most intensively settled and farmed place was the northwestern slope of the Cerro Yucuñoo ridge. SAT 9 spread over every ridge from modern San Agustín to Totojaha, a distance of more than 3 km, and from 1,900 m uphill for 0.6 to 1.6 km to 2,100 m. Today these super-dissected slopes are all cleared for agriculture, although some land has reverted to secondary growth and grazing. Virtually every drainage has a lama-bordo, some of which are well associated with

5.35 Natividad sites in Tlacotepec.

the Natividad settlement. The functioning lama-bordos often have springs at their heads. Farmers collect water in cisterns and ponds on the upper lama-bordo terraces. Irrigation hose is the favored way of tapping these spring-fed pools. Contour terraces bordered by trees and magueys trap soil and water. The patchy—in places dense, in other places light—artifact distribution is consistent with residences interspersed among household agriculture features such as these. Everything is eroded and eroding. We saw remnants of what may have been prehispanic residential or contour agricultural terraces but not enough to map.

5.36 Chert boulder showing flake scars at SAT 28.

On the high ridge above SAT 9 there were two sites, a small reoccupation at the Las Flores town at SAT 21 and a large village even higher up at SAT 23. The latter has residential terraces, a mound and a plaza, and a lama-bordo on the east side. We found few artifacts because of the oak leaves and pine needles but the ubiquitous white chert flakes are here.

The cluster of small sites made up of SAT 1, 3–5 is on the ridge just south of San Agustín. One informant said this was the Pueblo Viejo. Not a lot is left, neither soil nor archaeological remains. There are lama-bordos on all sides, modern houses, and some fields. Another area with significant settlement was the valley slope west of San Agustín (SAT 16, 28) (Figure 5.36).

The small Junta del Río Valley has Natividad settlement on all sides—Huendio, Tlacotepec, and Yucuañe. The Tlacotepec sites SAT 15, 17, and 39 cover 20 ha. Chains of lama-bordos descend from the mountain flanks past these settlements.

The Huendio cluster is impressive. It consists of all the SDH Natividad components (sixteen sites), which together make over 1 km² of occupied area representing approximately 1,500 people. The sites are spread along the lower slopes of the two former hilltowns Yucuñucu and Yucuñushiño. Our crews found variable and spotty densities of Natividad artifacts and rock work on virtually every ridge around these two hills and lama-bordos in the drainages. SDH 19 has at least two residential terraces, stone foundations, and faced local and manuported stone for building.

These Huendio sites are not all alike. SDH 9 had very low artifact densities spread over 450 m with three concentrations, and in one concentration of 20 by 20 m several hundred green obsidian flakes. At SDH 17 we mapped three stone

5.37 Scenes from prehispanic life at Tlacotepec, depicted in the mural at the palacio municipal.

foundations on the ridgetop and recorded a fairly dense distribution of artifacts. A man who lived on the site showed us his collection of Postclassic figurines. SDH 18, the site in this cluster closest to Junta del Río, has lama-bordos and ancient agricultural terraces and check dams directly associated with Natividad residential areas.

The major center, SAT 9, has four mounded structures within its boundaries. They are on hilltops where there are earlier components but similar landforms with only Natividad do not have mounds. Certainly there was no major public building program. SAT 3 is what was said to be the Pueblo Viejo. It has a single mound, but Las Flores is present at the mound too. On Cerro Yucuñoo there could have been ritual reuse of SAT 21. There is a small mound and plaza, presumably Natividad, at SAT 23.

The Junta del Río sites are potentially interesting for their public architecture. The field crew described SAT 17 as having Natividad architecture (standing walls) built on top of a Late Cruz site. This is an intriguing complex of terraces, plazas or courtyards, structures, and patios. Nearby at SAT 39 there are six mounds and also Late Cruz.

SDH 4 has two mounds facing each other on a plaza (Ramos is present too). SAT 21 is a better candidate for Natividad public building. It is a single component site with seven mounds dispersed along the ridgetop.

We feel confident that Tlacotepec did not have monumental public buildings. The examples just described are rather small in scale and presumably local in their intended functions. But we also think that there must have been more building complexes such as those at SAT 17 and SDH 21 because there are other sites with remnants now too disturbed to be interpreted.

For now we provide a minimal reconstruction in which the subregion had a leading population center, SAT 9, which was probably also the administrative center. Huendio, Junta del Río, and perhaps other places had local nobles who resided in large houses. There were also special ceremonial places, including mounds at older archaeological sites (e.g., SDH 4, where there are Natividad braziers on Ramos mounds) and perhaps new places like atop Cerro Yucuñoo (SAT 23). Tlacotepec was a potentially autonomous polity (Figure 5.37). It probably had close economic and political ties to its neighbors Dzinicahua, Achiutla, Amoltepec, Tayata, and San Mateo Peñasco.

AMOLTEPEC

San Cristóbal Amoltepec, the modern cabecera, is tucked up with its back to the base of an ancient volcano, Cerro Yucunuchi. It looks out to the south and east down a dozen deep barrancas and eroded ridges, its municipal domain. This is our Amoltepec subregion. We have appended Zaragoza, an agencia of Magdalena Peñasco, because it lies at the base of several of the ridges that descend from San Cristóbal.

Amoltepec is part of the familiar Huamelulpan-Tayata geological terrain. All the ridges that meet at San Cristóbal are composed of Yanhuitlán sedimentaries (more conglomerates in the uplands on the west, more mudstones and sandstones on the east). Of the dozen or so ridges the east, south, and west each have one ridge that is longer and higher and these three ridges have most of the prehispanic settlements. The western ridge is mostly forested, especially on the slopes, but everywhere else the land is cleared for farming or so actively eroding that nothing will grow.

The old volcano Yucunuchi is steep, barren of settlement, and heavily forested. In the saddle between its two peaks, at the base of the eastern one, is an undated archaeological site, SCA 8. It consists of two rock mounds that face each other across a plaza. The western mound is cleaved by a looter's hole. We could find no artifacts. Here at 300 m above the modern town is the shrine visited on the day of San Cristóbal.

Early/Middle Cruz

SCA 5 is a small site on a low hill above the valley floor south of Cuauhtémoc (Figure 5.38, Table 5.18). It has been cleared for agriculture and contour terraced but we did find a multicomponent site nonetheless. It has Late Cruz, Ramos, and Middle Cruz. The site would have been part of the Tayata cluster.

Late Cruz

We found three small Late Cruz settlements (Figure 5.39, Table 5.18). These were on the southern fringe of the Tayata polity. SCA 5, the Middle Cruz site, grew a bit in Late Cruz, which is well represented in sherd collections. That SCA 2 and

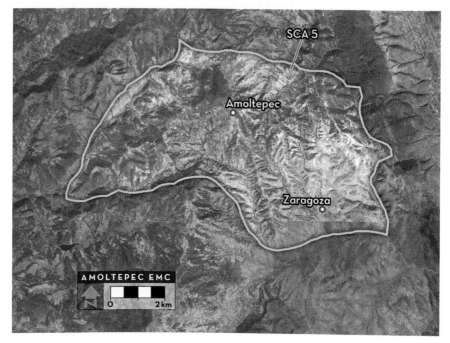

5.38 *Early/Middle Cruz sites in Amoltepec.*

ZAR 2 were occupied at this time is certain but little else is known about these places because the sites and their artifacts are scrubbed and worn down by erosion.

Ramos

This time sees the first major change. The settlement patterns also lead us to suggest hypotheses about Ramos political boundaries and continuity between the present-day and these 2,000-year-old boundaries. In Early Ramos there were many more people, more sites, and larger sites. We found seven sites (Figure 5.40, Table 5.19). All of these but one were small. The exception is SCA 2ii, which covers 37 ha. The midpoint of the population estimate range is 1,200 persons, an increase from Cruz times that would be difficult to achieve by local natural increase alone. Each of Amoltepec's main east, south, and west ridges was settled. Hilltops were favored, although not necessarily the highest or steepest.

SCA 2ii resembles other Early Ramos large settlements in some ways and differs in others. Like sites in Huamelulpan or SDH 1 and 2, SCA 2ii is in a sense a hilltop place: it is on the western flank of the north-south trending chain of valleys, it has residential terraces and two mounds facing each other on a plaza (all on an oval platform), and it had a population of about 1,000. However, SCA 2ii was not built on an isolated conical hilltop. Instead it extends for 1.4 km along the main ridge

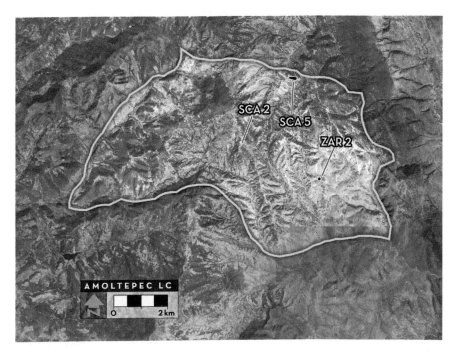

5.39 Late Cruz sites in Amoltepec.

that descends from San Cristóbal. Apparently, only part of the settlement was ter-raced—the upper prong about halfway along the length of the main ridge. We took five separate collections and most have a high proportion of well-made, decorated Nochixtlán Gray vessels, which is unusual for sites in this part of our study area. Amoltepec may be somewhat off the main routes today but it was well connected in the Early Ramos world.

This subregion differs from many in its high frequency of small Early Ramos sites. Three of the small sites are on present-day municipio boundaries with mojon-eras or rayas on the site (SCA 3, 5, 14). Another, SCA 16, is potentially near a boundary position. At SCA 2ii there is a mojonera on Str. 1. All these places have Ramos domestic refuse—they were not single-purpose sites. SCA 14 and 16 are Las Flores hilltop terraced sites with a little Early Ramos.

Farther afield from Amoltepec are other small Ramos sites that may be in boundary positions. SMR 3 was a hilltop Early Ramos site with one mound, also used for Natividad rituals. TLA 15 is a hilltop Late Ramos site with three mounds. UVH 2 has a structure on a platform dating to Late Ramos. It is near the divide west of Huamelulpan but we do not have the modern boundaries in this area. SMP 12 is probably not on a modern boundary. SMP 13 has no mojonera or raya but it has two shrines. SMA 1 and 2 both have modern mojoneras. Not all small Ramos sites can be associated with modern boundaries, but some are.

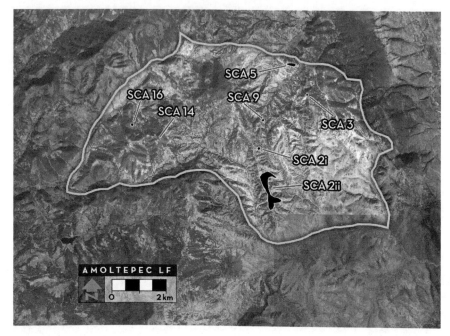

5.40 *Ramos sites in Amoltepec.*

In Oaxaca an association between Late Postclassic settlement patterns and seg-
ments of modern municipal boundaries has been known for some time (see, e.g.,
Flannery and Marcus 1983; Byland and Pohl 1994). It has also been suggested for
the Late Classic in the Valley of Oaxaca (Kowalewski et al. 1989:263–270).

Several alternatives need to be examined before a proposition about Ramos
boundaries and their historical continuity can be accepted. Because Early Ramos
sites tend to be on hilltops and modern municipal limits tend to run along high
divides, the association could be coincidental, vague, or trivial. A more detailed
study of modern and historical boundaries is needed. If some of Amoltepec's Early
Ramos sites were located on a polity limit, was this local, regional, or both? Were
SCA 14, 16, 2ii, 3, and 5 arrayed around a specific Amoltepec unit, or were they
part of a larger chain around a greater regional polity such as Huamelulpan? What
happened with these hypothesized boundary sites in Late Ramos when Amoltepec
had little or no occupation?

Las Flores

Again there was a major change in settlement pattern. When Amoltepec was
reoccupied at the beginning of Las Flores, people favored a different area, the higher
ridge that runs west from San Cristóbal. Only the flanks of the Cerro Yucunuchi
here have soils derived from volcanic rock; most of the ridge is formed of Yanhuitlán

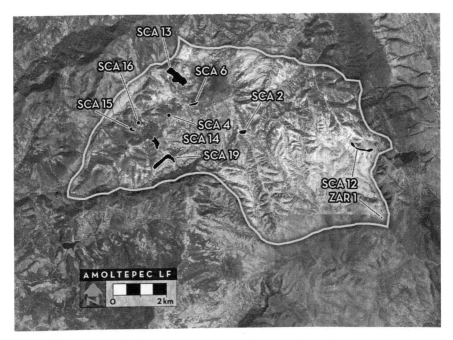

5.41 Las Flores sites in Amoltepec.

Formation conglomerates. Generally, settlements were at higher elevations. Several were compact and defensible. The total population was about 1,750 persons in five small villages, four hamlets, and an isolated residence (Figure 5.41, Table 5.20).

The village with the most inhabitants was probably Yucuñucoo (SCA 14). The summit of this pine-covered hilltop has three mounds, two of which are in an L arrangement on a plaza (Figure 5.42). Residential terraces ring the upper slopes. A section of an old (Colonial?) road can be seen running east-west on the north slope.

Other sites in the same cluster include SCA 4, which has two mounds facing each other on a plaza, all built on a platform, and ruined residential terraces. SCA 16 is also a fairly compact site. In contrast, SCA 2, 6, 13, and 19 were dispersed villages and hamlets with no public architecture. There are lama-bordos near SCA 16 and 19.

Two sites (SCA 12 and ZAR 1) probably belonged to the Huendio settlement cluster. SCA 12 has three structures and a mojonera perhaps marking the Amoltepec, Huendio, and Achiutla boundaries. Aside from these two there were no other sites in the hills east and south of Amoltepec.

The main cluster of sites was probably part of the same polity that included the large towns at SMP 32 and 35 on the same divide as the Amoltepec villages. These heights separate the Tlaxiaco drainages from the Río Sabinos side. Like many Las Flores settlements in the inner basin, all of these are on hilltops at high elevations.

5.42 Verónica Pérez on SCA 14 Str. 1. Photograph taken looking northeast from Plaza 2.

There are indications of change within the Las Flores period but we are dealing with small samples of pottery. Transición markers appear at SCA 12 near Huendio and perhaps SCA 16 and 19. Almost all assemblages look solidly Early Las Flores. A spiked brazier from SCA 14 and a few attributes from SCA 15 raise Late Las Flores possibilities, but the evidence for Late Las Flores is unconvincing.

Natividad

We found eighteen sites: fifteen hamlets and isolated residences, two small villages, and SCA 2, the large town that accounted for 85 percent of Amoltepec's population. The small sites are widely distributed on the west, east, and southeast ridges but none are within 1.4 km of SCA 2 (Figure 5.43, Table 5.21). Twelve sites have lama-bordos originating within the settlement or nearby.

SCA 2 had between 2,400 and 6,000 inhabitants. It was a peer of other large towns such as Huamelulpan, Santa María del Rosario, Tlacotepec, and Achiutla but the setting is somewhat different. SCA 2 occupies almost the entire ridge that runs down to Magdalena Peñasco from San Cristóbal (Figure 5.44). This ridge is, or was, relatively wide and it has numerous broad-topped side ridges on the eastern side. It drops gradually from 2,220 m to 2,100 m over the 4 km length of the Natividad town. Parts have pine forest but everything has been intensively farmed. A passage from the field notes says, "[T]he severity of the erosion on the west slope and the steepness of the erosional surfaces make it impossible to define the west boundary,

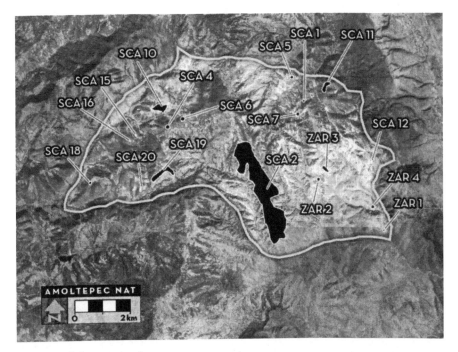

5.43 Natividad sites in Amoltepec.

5.44 In the center, the long, north-south ridge of SCA 2. San Agustín Tlacotepec is the town in the center, beyond the ridge, and the tall mountain left of Tlacotepec is the Cerro Yucuñoo.

and too dangerous." In places the ridge crest is scoured clean to bedrock and good ceramic concentrations are found in the washes. Basalt manos and flakes suggest some working of this material.

Amoltepec had no new civic-ceremonial construction in Natividad, not at SCA 2 nor at the smaller sites. We did find evidence of reuse of older mounds, but whether any new buildings were placed on older mounds is not known.

Amoltepec seems to have had wide distribution of decorated ceramics of various wares, consistent with good market access, perhaps access to multiple markets. There is obsidian but the amounts are small compared to some other subregions. Chert and basalt toolmaking seems to have been done but not intensively. By proximity, Amoltepec probably was most closely associated with Magdalena Peñasco and Tlacotepec.

MAGDALENA PEÑASCO

Geologically, this subregion is a pocket of Yanhuitlán Formation shale and sandstone flanked at its upper end by high and craggy escarpments formed of andesite. The upper end is a C-shaped basin. The ends of the C are volcanic but the middle is a narrow ridge of sedimentary material. In Natividad this narrow divide was the civic-ceremonial seat locally known as the Pueblo Viejo. The other (south) side of the ridge is the upper Yosojica basin. The ridge is eroding from both sides and stream capture will happen eventually.

The subregion is drained by the Río Magdalena, which heads beneath the volcanic cliffs and the Pueblo Viejo and flows out northeast past Magdalena Peñasco to join arroyos from Huendio and Tlacotepec. Then the stream runs through the gap to the Río Sabinos at Junta del Río. Our subregion extends 10 km east-west, over which the elevation drops from 2,600 m to 1,850 m.

The modern town of Magdalena Peñasco is strung along the remaining knife-edge crest of a long ridge (Figure 5.45). The paved highway from Tlaxiaco to Tlacotepec and Chalcatongo passes through. Our crews placed imaginary wagers on how much longer the town would last before the tremendous erosion of the side slopes would carry it away—no one gave it more than a few decades. Magdalena Peñasco (our SMP) has several dependencies important for the archaeological past. San Isidro Peñasco (SIP) is in the upper basin. Cabacoa is a ranchería near the western divide and the border with Tlaxiaco. Yosocahua is a ranchería in the basin south of the Pueblo Viejo ridge.

Early/Middle Cruz

We found nothing earlier than Middle Cruz but this phase has a strong presence. There are four sites totaling 7 ha, all at the upper reaches of Río Magdalena tributary arroyos just south and east of Magdalena Peñasco (Figure 5.46, Table 5.22). These are hilltop situations at 2,050 to 2,150 m (for comparison, the modern town is at 1,960 m). The situation is similar to the nearest neighbors SAT 16 and

5.45 *Erosion of the Yanhuitlán beds around Magdalena Peñasco. The church is visible on the right. From near SMP 9.*

28. Today these hills are heavily dissected. The land has been cleared for agriculture and for modern houses but there is some reforestation.

Late Cruz

Settlement and population modestly expanded from Middle to Late Cruz in the same area around Magdalena Peñasco. We mapped ten sites with a combined occupied area of 13 ha (Figure 5.47, Table 5.23). The largest sites cover 4 ha and six are 0.5 ha or less. The average population estimate is 250 persons.

These figures could be somewhat low because of site area lost to erosion. Intensive farming over many centuries has caused rather spectacular loss of hilltops. At several places our site boundaries coincided with a vertical drop into a deep gully. However, surviving crew members were able to recover good Late Cruz collections, especially from SMP 7. At SMP 2 a rock-filled pit containing Late Cruz was exposed in the side of a wash (Figure 5.48). About 6 m from the pit was a deposit of human bone.

Apart from the old and continuing settlement cluster around Magdalena Peñasco there were two sites in anomalous situations. One was a single-component site on a ridge southeast of the Cabacoa agencia building at 2,460 m. SMP 32 also had good Late Cruz markers. This site is on the high ridge that divides Magdalena Peñasco from Tlaxiaco, overlooking the narrow valley and pass of Río El Boquerón.

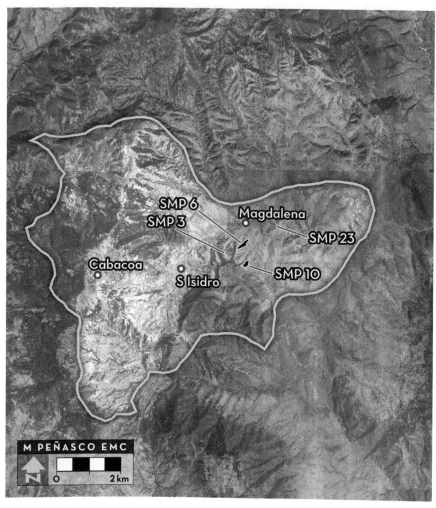

5.46 *Early/Middle Cruz sites in Magdalena Peñasco.*

The Cruz settlement cluster has no obvious head village nor any remaining public architecture. It is spatially separate from the much larger Cruz cluster at Yosojica and the base of Dzinicahua but may have been subordinate to it.

Ramos

At the beginning of this period the long-standing Cruz settlement pattern was completely discarded and a new one adopted. Virtually all Cruz settlement was abandoned. People congregated mainly into one nucleated village atop a steep and very defensible hill, Cerro Yucuñucuiñe (Hill of the Tiger). There was also a small

5.47 Late Cruz sites in Magdalena Peñasco.

occupation on the top of the Cerro Gachupín, the cliff that is Magdalena Peñasco's major landmark (Figure 5.49, Table 5.24).

Cerro Yucuñucuiñe (SMP 13) is a conical, steep-sided knob 220 m above the local valley floor. The site here is a single-component Early Ramos occupation. One might conclude that no one wanted to live there before or since. Perhaps they did not inhabit this place very long for we did not see many sherds or lithic artifacts. On the peak are two mounds that face each other on a plaza. There is a modern shrine on the same plaza. Around the slopes below the peak are preserved and destroyed residential terraces, not the long terraces seen at other Ramos sites but half-moon-shaped terraces, measuring, for example, 9 by 8 m and 16 by 5 m. Along the ridge

5.48 SMP 2, rock-filled pit containing Late Cruz sherds (Yucuita Tan and Polished Brown). Erosional profiles here revealed possible structures and human burials.

down to the saddle on the west is a string of residential terraces. As we have often seen, this saddle is protected by retaining walls. Lama-bordos head in both directions from the saddle.

El Gachupín (SMP 14) was occupied for the first time in Early Ramos. Its Las Flores and Natividad components are better represented and we think most of the architecture dates to the Classic or later. Nevertheless, sufficient Early Ramos utilitarian vessel sherds were found to posit permanent habitation. Perhaps public architectural construction began in Ramos too. Today the narrow crest has the remains of a string of mounds, platforms, and plazas (described in the Las Flores section). The site at Cerro Gachupín has no residential terraces aside from houses that might have been part of the string on the crest.

The other two sites listed (SMP 11 and 12) are on lower hills on the same ridges as SMP 13 and 14. The Early Ramos assignments are based on a few utilitarian sherds and there is little indication that the public architecture has a Ramos component.

What happened between Cruz and Ramos in Magdalena Peñasco is similar to the abandonment of open Middle Formative settlements and the move to high, defensible places in Achiutla, Huamelulpan, and across the divide in Tlaxiaco. Unlike Huamelulpan and Dzinicahua, Magdalena Peñasco has no Late Ramos occupation.

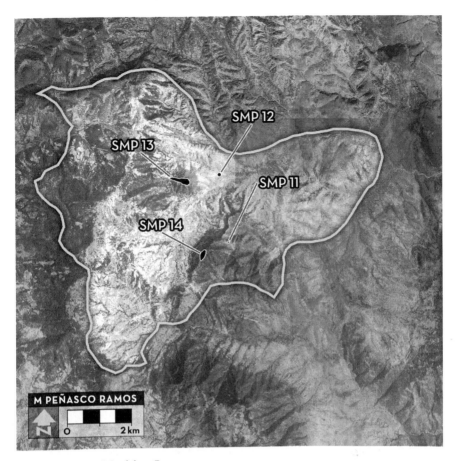

5.49 *Ramos sites in Magdalena Peñasco.*

Las Flores

The reoccupation of Magdalena Peñasco in Early Las Flores came with more people than ever and a new pattern of settlement different from both the Cruz and the Ramos. We have fourteen sites (Figure 5.50, Table 5.25) and our estimates suggest there may have been 3,000 people. There were three large villages; the rest of the settlements were small. Sites are found over the full range of elevations from 1,900 m up to the highest peaks on Cerro Gachupín (2,400 m) and on the Tlaxiaco divide (2,600 m). However, not all of the subregion had settlement or intensive use. The upper basin around San Isidro and the hills previously used in Cruz had little Las Flores settlement.

Eight sites, including all the larger ones and all those with public architecture, form a ring around the upper rim of the basin from Cerro Gachupín across the ridge of the later Pueblo Viejo and up the divide above Cabacoa. In fact this string of sites

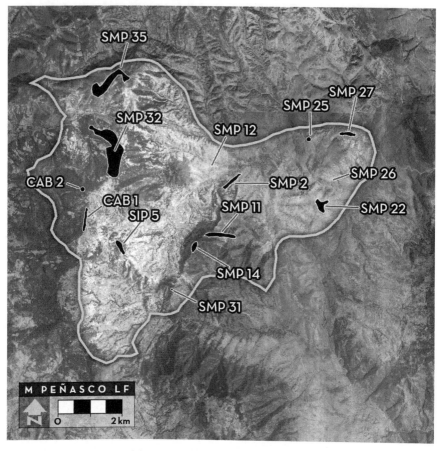

5.50 Las Flores sites in Magdalena Peñasco.

continues to the north where the Amoltepec Las Flores settlements have the same pattern. Magdalena Peñasco and Amoltepec could have been closely associated in this period.

We describe these sites on the rim from north to south. Yucudzanini, or Cerro de la Colmena (Beehive, SMP 35—Figure 5.51), has good Early Las Flores pottery and ruined residential terraces. On the ridge crest there is a linear string of public architecture, beginning with a platform that has two structures facing each other, then a slope up to Plaza 1, across which is Str. 1.

Apparently the site with the largest area is SMP 32, on the divide between Magdalena Peñasco and Tlaxiaco above El Boquerón. This is a dispersed scatter of good Early Las Flores material. Parts of the site are in pine forest and pine needles cover the ground. Our time on the site was cut short by rain and lightning. Site boundaries are therefore not as sure as we would like.

5.51 *Yucudzanini (SMP 35), the west end of the site.*

On the peak of Cerro Tucutinuno (CAB 2) are two looted mounds that face each other across a plaza, all on a platform. There are Early Las Flores sherds and no other component. CAB 1 has at least two small mounds, several terraces, stone foundations, and scatters of building stone, but the ground is covered in pine needles.

SIP 5 is the highest knob on the ridge that was to become the Natividad Pueblo Viejo. This is the only point on the site with Las Flores material. The knob and the ridge had at one time been terraced but the retaining walls, the terrace fill, and all the rest of the soil and artifacts have since been removed by erosion. On the top of the knob remains a raised rectangular block of endeque that may have been the base of a mound or platform. The ceramics are typical Early Las Flores.

Cerro Yucuyuyu (SMP 31) is another ceremonial site, like CAB 2. It has no residential terraces or lama-bordos but on the summit there are two structures facing each other on a plaza. Structure 1 was built to take advantage of the steep slope—the vertical drop from the back of the mound is 10 m.

The most impressive public architecture is at SMP 14, the top of El Gachupín (Figure 5.52). There are no terraces on the sides of this ridge—everything is on the crest for the good reason that the slope angle is 90 degrees. At the northeast end are a small mound, Str. 1, and then two structures forming a closed right angle, partially enclosed in a courtyard by a stone wall 0.5 m in height. Another construction lies just to the west. Following the ridgeline to the west, the next knob is the highest point, on which there is a plaza 25 m long with two mounds at the opposite ends. Descending the knob are three platforms with retaining walls 1 m high. This leads to Plaza 2, which may have had (residential?) structures. One ascends another slope

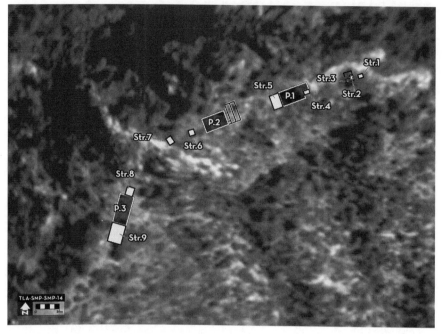

5.52 Architecture at El Gachupín, SMP 14.

to Str. 6 on a bedrock outcrop and then descends again across the bedrock to Str. 7. After another stretch of bedrock is Str. 8, Plaza 3, and, on the far side of the plaza, Str. 9. A wall stands behind Str. 9 and a break in the wall provides access to a ramp that runs along the side of Plaza 3. The complex is about 400 m long and perhaps 20 m wide. Our map may be too generous for the site's true width.

Architecture like the Gachupín's is usually treated as civic-ceremonial and public because of the labor involved and because the architectural effects are greater than in household construction. Yet the pottery includes the full range of domestic forms—bowls, jars, and comals similar to assemblages found at residential sites. Gachupín was inhabited, probably permanently. In its civic-ceremonial architecture it was comparable to Cerro Yucuañe and YPD 1.

Finally, SMP 11, below the cliff but on the same ridge, has some public architecture in poor condition and plenty of evidence for domestic and agricultural activities. One plaza could have had a mound on its east side and a second plaza has two mounds facing each other. There were residential terraces associated with lama-bordos.

Below the high rim of the basin were two clusters of small settlements. One was around the modern town of Magdalena Peñasco. Whole chunks of land, and with them possible Las Flores sites, have departed downstream. The true size could have been a bit larger. SMP 22, 25–27 (and ZAR 1) form another cluster on the low hills above the Río Magdalena. This is another area that has been intensively eroded. There is no civic-ceremonial architecture unless there had been something on the ex-hilltop at SMP 25.

Las Flores in Magdalena Peñasco shares a settlement pattern common in many subregions. It was Early and not Late Las Flores. Hilltops and mountains even higher and more defendable than those chosen in Early Ramos were used for settlements. But there were also open sites at low elevations. Some site locations appear to have been strategic. Other places that had good resources were not intensively used.

Magdalena Peñasco provides outstanding information on the distribution of public architecture. The association with a boundary is obvious and likewise the predilection for high places. Seven of the eight sites on the basin rim have at least some indication of plazas or mounds and El Gachupín had an impressive complex. Public architecture was not centralized in one site. Even at Gachupín, which has nine mounds to the next-ranking site's four mounds, the architectural plan was not centrally focused. There were four or five separate mound and plaza groups. At this subregional scale civic-ceremonial functions were multiple and widely distributed.

Most of these archaeological mounds are also places that have modern shrines where people come periodically to pray and make sacrifices for rain and for curing. The special importance of these places has not prevented rampant and severe looting.

Natividad

The Late Postclassic was the time of the maximum expansion of settlement, population, and production. According to our estimates, over 10,000 people lived here. We recorded thirty-eight sites (Figure 5.53, Table 5.26); however, in many cases separate sites were probably parts of the same local communities. Broadly, there were three main clusters, which correspond to three of the principal local communities today: one around Magdalena Peñasco, one in the upper basin (San Isidro Peñasco), and a third on the divide at Cabacoa. There were also four special sites at the cardinal points on the subregion's boundaries.

All parts of the valley were intensively settled and farmed, from the head of the basin and the divide with Tlaxiaco, down along the Río Magdalena, to the lower valley at 1,900 m asl. Lama-bordos are frequently associated with Natividad sites. The same places have been intensively farmed with contour terraces and other modifications in historic times. Many sites are occupied by houses today.

Magdalena Peñasco's population was divided between urban and more dispersed settlement. Of our thirty-eight sites twenty-seven are the size of hamlets and isolated residences. They account for 10 percent of the population. Thirty percent of the population lived in villages. Fully 60 percent lived at the Pueblo Viejo, SIP 5.

What people from San Isidro call the Pueblo Viejo is the civic-ceremonial center of a sprawling, terraced town that covers 129 ha (SIP 5). There are many lama-bordos. Almost the entire north slope of the basin rim has Natividad residential remains. Subsequent use has destroyed most of the terraces but building stone

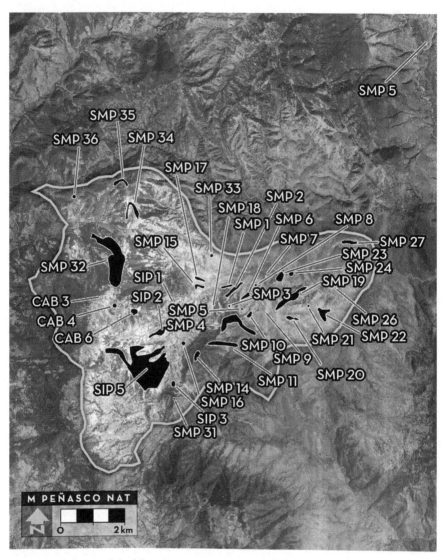

The following labels appear on the map:

SMP 5
SMP 35
SMP 36 SMP 34
SMP 17
SMP 33 SMP 2
SMP 18
SMP 1 SMP 6 SMP 8
SMP 15 SMP 7 SMP 27
SMP 23
SMP 32 SMP 24
SIP 1 SMP 19
CAB 3 SIP 2 SMP 3
CAB 4 SMP 5 SMP 26
CAB 6 SMP 4 SMP 21 SMP 22
SMP 10
SMP 9
SIP 5 SMP 11 SMP 20
SMP 14
SMP 16
SIP 3
SMP 31

M PEÑASCO NAT
N   0   2 km

5.53 Natividad sites in Magdalena Peñasco.

and artifacts indicate the extent. We estimate that half the site had high-density settlement.

The ridgetop (Figure 5.54), a narrow saddle between San Isidro and the upper basin of the stream that flows through Yosocahua and Yosojica, is composed of Yanhuitlán Formation sedimentary materials. It was the civic-ceremonial center of the town. Today this ridgetop is occupied by ranchería settlement. One of the mounds, for example, has a modern latrine. Some of the civic-ceremonial archi-

5.54 *The civic-ceremonial center of the Pueblo Viejo (SIP 5), looking southeast along the ridgeline of the saddle.*

tecture has been destroyed but there are still two major complexes (Figure 5.55). One is a ball court and a platform 110 m long (Figure 5.56). The other is a linear arrangement of several long, impressive platforms, three plazas, and two pyramids that would have supported long, narrow structures. We saw stucco floors, in one instance painted red. All of this was new Natividad construction, not reused older mounds.

Another site with significant public architecture is SMP 4, on a ridge overlooking the Magdalena cluster. It had at least two large plazas, each with a structure. SMP 4 is a single-component Natividad site. Perhaps it had market or other functions for the Magdalena cluster the way SIP 5 did for the sites at the head of the basin.

This subregion seems to have been fairly well placed for access to diverse goods. Obsidian is widespread; at the leading center and SMP 4 it is rather abundant. We recorded gray and green obsidian blades and flakes at both of these centers and at the Pueblo Viejo several cores, one of which was not a prismatic blade core. Dark gray and pink basalt tools were probably made here from raw materials either obtained locally or from a place such as Huendio. Chipped stone is widespread but we did not find many reduction areas here as we did in Yucuxaco.

Four sites seem to have had special boundary functions. On the east is SMP 30, a 0.8 ha undated site (we found no sherds). It is situated on top of the easternmost high peak of the Gachupín range. There is a small plaza, a scatter of chert and chalcedony flakes, a scraper, and a modern mojonera. The southern point is SMP 31, Yucuyuyu. It is a reused Las Flores site that has a plaza and two mounds and no

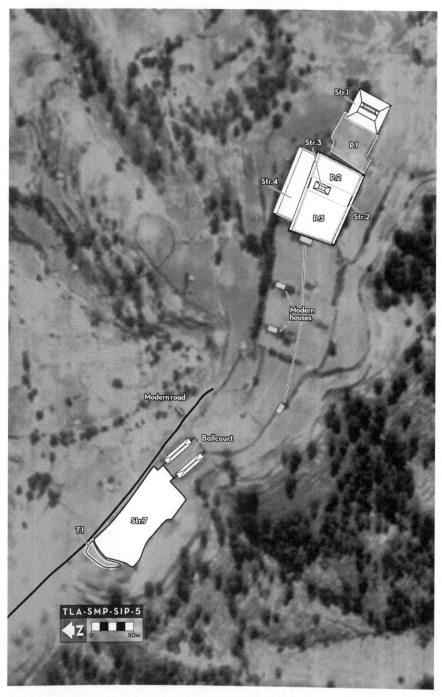

5.55 *The two better-preserved architectural groups at the Pueblo Viejo.*

5.56 *Ball court at the Pueblo Viejo, looking northwest.*

terraces. LLG 1, at 1.8 ha, sits on top of the high divide between the Pueblo Viejo and the Ojo de Agua ridge. This is the western point. It has a small structure. The northern limit may have been marked by SMP 35, Yucuzanini. This site has a linear string of public Las Flores architecture and Natividad debris. In addition to these four possible boundary points Natividad people also made use of Cerro Gachupín and SMP 11 (on the ridge below the highest cliffs at El Gachupín) for rituals.

Following these interpretations, the civic-ceremonial architecture pattern is as follows: (1) Pueblo Viejo, monumental platforms, large plazas, ball court; (2) large plazas and several mounds at SMP 4, the Magdalena cluster's central place; (3) ritual places—four boundary sites and the two spectacular and venerable places on the Gachupín.

We have stressed Magdalena Peñasco's local organization and economy. In the broader context it was one several subregions west of the Sierra de Nochixtlán that developed quite strongly in the Postclassic. Magdalena Peñasco's basis in wealth must have been its agricultural resources and labor. It has several public facilities that are unusual—the ball court and the large plazas at two centers. The latter we think served as market places. The Pueblo Viejo complex in particular would have been very well situated for interchange with the west and south.

DZINICAHUA

Before our surveys little was known about Dzinicahua's archaeology. Now it is apparent that it was an important center in Late Cruz, Ramos, Early Las Flores, and

Natividad. Dzinicahua is a Mixtec name meaning "head of the cliff" or "head of the mountain" according to residents, or "cave" (Alavez Chávez 1988:110). It refers to one of the most prominent features of the landscape in the Mixteca Alta, the Cerro de la Peña Grande (or Peñasco Grande) that rises above San Mateo Peñasco. We use "Dzinicahua" as the name of a subregion centered on this Peñasco. The Peñasco is a block of andesite, part of the same unit that makes the cliffs at Magdalena Peñasco. It rests on Yanhuitlán Formation sedimentaries (the contact is at roughly 2,000 m asl). The mountain rises 650 m from the modern town to the peak, which is over 2,600 m, in just 2 km. In many places the sides are tall, vertical cliffs. The mountain is a good watershed. Several permanent springs feed the barrancas.

Dzinicahua is almost surrounded by two drainages, a branch north of the mountain that flows by Yosojica and a branch on the south flank that flows past San Antonio Sinicahua. These two head on opposite sides of the narrow ridge that bridges the Peñasco to the Tlaxiaco divide. After picking up water from the north and south sides of the Peñasco the two arroyos meet and then join the Río Sabinos. The canyon of these rivers is the major east-west corridor linking Tilantongo and Tlaxiaco. Dzinicahua is also well situated on a main north-south route.

Our subregion is divided among three municipios. Yosojica, in the stream valley on the north flank, belongs to San Agustín Tlacotepec. The main archaeological site belongs to San Mateo Peñasco. San Antonio Sinicahua, upstream from San Mateo on the south, has lands to the west and south. The Dzinicahua subregion is at the edge of our 1999 survey area and is not complete since we know little about the land to the south. In 1999 we did not reach Cerro de la Peña Grande until the last days of the project and we could not give it the attention it deserved.

In 2003 Heredia returned to begin mapping and making controlled surface collections on the Cerro de la Peña Grande (Heredia 2003). The map of the public architecture included here is one result of her fieldwork; she also mapped 281 terraces on the summit and 338 on the flanks of the mountain. As of this writing, completion of her project requires one more field season. What is already clear from Heredia's work is that this was one of the Mixteca Alta's premier sites. The following sections are based on the 1999 regional survey and preliminary results from Heredia's project.

Archaic

We found no conclusive evidence of a Preceramic occupation, but during the intensive study carried out by Heredia (2003) several rock paintings and petroglyphs were discovered at the base of the Peña Grande. It is possible that these features pertain to the Archaic.

Early/Middle Cruz

The northern Yosojica stream valley was occupied in Middle Cruz. There are two small sites on Yanhuitlán Formation soils at the edge of the valley (Figure 5.57,

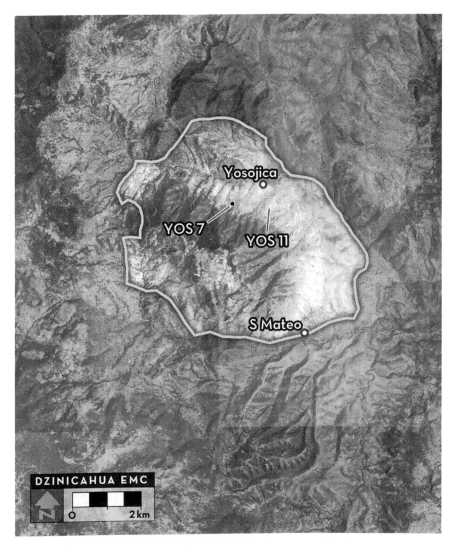

5.57 Early/Middle Cruz sites in Dzinicahua.

Table 5.27). These Dzinicahua hamlets belonged to a cluster of settlements 6 km in diameter that included Tlacotepec and Magdalena Peñasco.

Late Cruz

Population growth and expansion of settlement was very impressive. Dzinicahua was one of the most densely populated places in Oaxaca. In a 6 km stretch along the Yosojica stream we mapped 168 ha of occupied area in the YOS and SMO sites plus

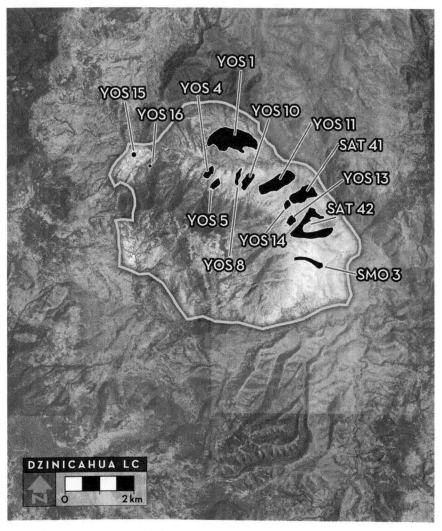

5.58 *Late Cruz sites in Dzinicahua.*

more at SAT 41 and 42 for a total of 242 ha (Figure 5.58, Table 5.28). At 10 to 25 persons per ha the average population estimate is 4,600.

This settlement expansion took place in open sites at low elevations. Most people lived between 1,900 and 2,000 m asl. The sites are on the gently sloping ridges at the base of the Peñasco. Today some of this land has been lost to erosion. At YOS 4, for example, we found Late Cruz artifacts wherever there was soil but some places that were probably occupied had no soil left and no artifacts. At YOS 10 much of the hill has disappeared and we found several exposed human burials. SMO 3 had residential terraces on the upper slope of the Late Cruz component but they are now mostly destroyed by modern agricultural terraces. At YOS 11 in a Late Cruz–only part of the site we saw a house foundation with Late Cruz sherds. There are quartz outcrops (and artifacts) at YOS 1 and chert outcrops (and artifacts) at YOS 8 that could have been used in Late Cruz.

The two large SAT sites are part of a Natividad-like sprawl that extends over 5 km on every ridge on the flanks of the Peñasco Grande. The separately numbered sites are divided only by barrancas. SAT 41 is next to the paved highway. It has a wide dispersal of Late Cruz and several stone foundations. SAT 42 is an even more impressive site. It seems to be single-component Late Cruz. Artifact density varies from low to high. Edges of the hill are extremely eroded, there is a lot of disturbance from plowing, and some places are covered in secondary-growth forest. The center of the site has four mounds, scattered and in no formal arrangement. There is another mound at the eastern tip of the south ridge. More small mounds might have existed, as suggested by slight rises in plowed fields. There are single mounds with Late Cruz association at YOS 1 and 8 and also at YOS 15, the site at the western end of the cluster.

Heredia (2003) found more Late Cruz ceramics in the piedmont on one of the ridges that extends down to the north from the Peñasco Grande. She has suggested that there may be more Late Cruz that could be detected by intensive survey and collecting. We think that this occupation would have been an extension of the Yosojica site.

As at Tlacotepec, the continuity from Middle Cruz to Late Cruz and the strong late Late Cruz suggest that the area was developing through the early half of Late Cruz and that this growth culminated in the latter half, at the time of Monte Albán Early I.

Ramos

The entire cluster of settlement at the base of the mountain was abandoned by the beginning of Ramos. In the Yosojica Valley where there had been over 4,000 people now there was no one (Figure 5.59, Table 5.29). During Ramos, people occupied the top of the Peña Grande, a more easily defended place (Figure 5.60) (sometime during this site's long history, perhaps in Ramos, people built a formidable defensive wall).

Our information on Dzinicahua's extent and occupation history is tentative. Heredia suggests that the Ramos occupation dates to Late—not Early—Ramos. It extends for at least 24 ha on the top of the hill (not the lower flanks). Late Ramos artifacts are found around most of the mounds described in the Las Flores section. The Late Ramos artifacts are exceptionally impressive. Heredia found sherds from vessels of high-quality manufacture that could easily provide illustrations for Monte Albán II pottery in *La Cerámica de Monte Albán* (Caso et al. 1967).

LLG 4 was a small outlier of Dzinicahua situated on the ridge bridging the divide to Tlaxiaco. It has one badly preserved structure. We list it as Early Ramos

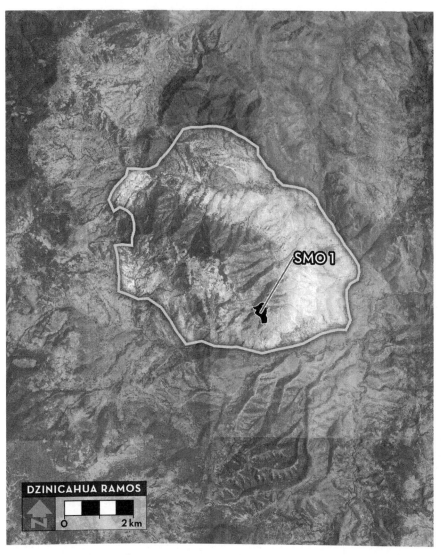

5.59 Ramos sites in Dzinicahua.

mainly on the basis of a single diagnostic sherd. On the high peak on the divide to the west is LLG 3, a small Late Ramos fortified habitation site with some public architecture (see Chapter 6). This too could be a Dzinicahua outlier.

In Late Ramos, Cerro de la Peña Grande was one of the more important centers in the Mixteca Alta, not as large as Huamelulpan and Yucuita but still a major town at a time when most subregions were abandoned. It would be premature to discuss Dzinicahua's role in the larger regional system. Important areas south of our study

5.60 The church at San Mateo Peñasco with the Peñasco Grande looming overhead.

limit have yet to be surveyed and the detailed Peñasco Grande site mapping needs to be completed.

Las Flores

Cerro de la Peña Grande (SMO 1) continued to be occupied. In Early Las Flores it had between 375 and 800 inhabitants (Figure 5.61, Table 5.29). Keeping in mind that the area to the south is still unknown we can still say that this was among the more important civic-ceremonial and population centers in the inner basin.

Population was concentrated on the mountaintop and not on the valley floor. Here in the Yosojica Valley where we had found so many Cruz sites, we found only SAT 41 and SMO 3. The latter site is small but it has considerable public architecture that probably dates to Las Flores—sherds from this phase were found in the mound fill and there are no later phases present. There is a plaza that has two principal mounds facing each other (possibly the other two sides of the plaza had small structures). Next to one of the principal mounds is another platform that has a closed four-mound patio group with the largest mound on the east.

El Cerro de la Peña Grande is large, complex, and visually one of Oaxaca's most spectacular sites. It has hundreds of terraces, fourteen structures, a ball court, two defensive walls, gates, stairways, four lama-bordos, and an unusual greater-than-life-size "human head" (?) sculpted in a cliff face at a major access point. The site consists of the mountain's summit (which at 2,500 m is 600 m above the valley floor)

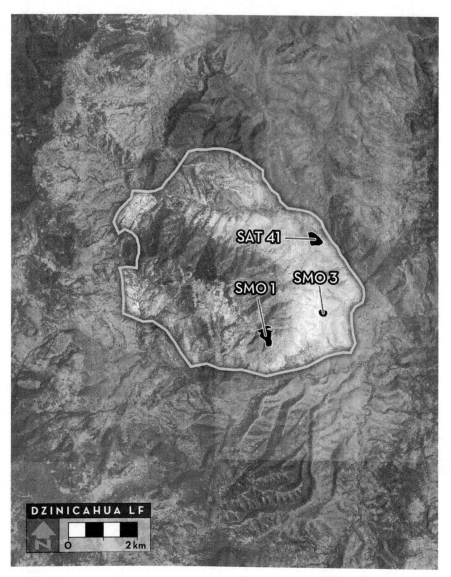

5.61 Las Flores sites in Dzinicahua.

and its lower flanks or pediment, which is dramatically separated from the summit by a 300 m high cliff.

All the civic-ceremonial architecture is on the summit (Figure 5.62). The main focus has a plaza enclosed by four structures, all on a platform. There is a sunken patio and a large ball court. There are four lone structures, several of which are in spectacular situations with their backs at the edge of the precipice, facing open

5.62 *From a possible plaza west to Str. 2, highest point on Cerro de la Peña Grande (SMO 1).*

5.63 *Possible plazas and the upper part of the civic-ceremonial area at SMO 1, from Str. 2 looking east.*

5.64 *From SMO 1 Str. 2 (visible at bottom left) toward the west.*

plazas. Str. 2 is at the highest point of the site and can only be accessed by passing through the main architectural group (Figures 5.63–5.64). Str. 1 is at the eastern-most point on the summit. There is also a lone structure south of the main civic-ceremonial focus and another to the southeast. The artifacts found in the main architectural complex date to Late Ramos, Early Las Flores, and Natividad. We think that most of the construction seen today probably was built during the Classic or Terminal Formative but the two lone mounds (Strs. 13 and 14) south of the main architectural group may have had Natividad buildings.

East of Str. 13 is a lama-bordo with long, wide milpas. A spring supplies plenty of water to this part of the summit. South of the lama-bordo stands Str. 14, built at the edge of a cliff overlooking the valley. Two tombs in terrace walls were observed on the hilltop. The tombs appear to be in good condition. People who have milpas on the Peñasco use these cavities to store tools and dishes.

Natividad

Dzinicahua was a major center of regional importance. Remains of Natividad settlement are found in every part of the surveyed area, including the modern town, the Yosojica Valley, and the summit and slopes of Cerro de la Peña Grande (Figure 5.65, Table 5.30). Even though the Cerro de la Peña Grande is not mapped in its entirety, Heredia did map 69 ha and estimated a mean population of 1,818 inhabit-ants. The site size is still not established; it may have been as much as twice this 69 ha

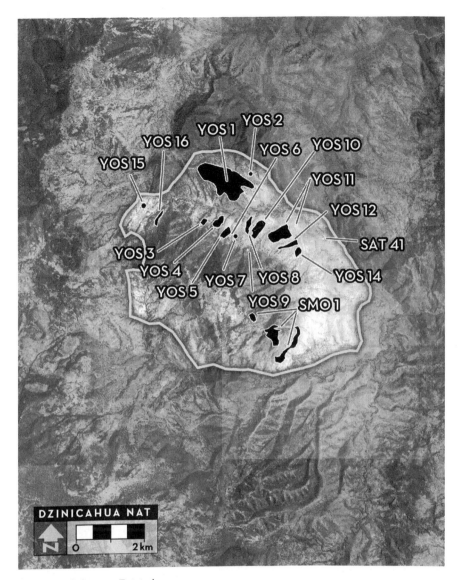

5.65 *Natividad sites in Dzinicahua.*

figure. Heredia mapped three of the ridges that form the skirt of the Peñasco Grande and reports that the most abundant and ubiquitous material dates to Natividad. The occupation on the southern flanks extends into what is now the town of San Mateo Peñasco (Figure 5.66). The Natividad pottery on the summit and around the mounds (described in the Las Flores section) suggests that this was the ceremonial center of Dzinicahua in the Postclassic.

5.66 Terraces on the northeast flank of Cerro de la Peña Grande, and the Yosojica Valley.

The Yosojica Valley alone had 163 ha of occupied area in fifteen separate site components. The largest single concentration was at YOS 1, above Yosojica. Lithic artifacts are common and often quite dense but they cannot be assigned only to Natividad with certainty. Chert outcrops in several places, especially white chert at YOS 8 and red chert at the single-component YOS 12 site. Human burials were seen exposed at YOS 5 and 10. With the intensive agriculture practiced here in three periods (Late Cruz, Natividad, and recent times) it is not surprising that the area and its sites are severely eroded.

CHAPTER SIX

Greater Tlaxiaco

The Tlaxiaco Valley is an important place: head of a Mixtec yuhuitaiyu, center of an Aztec tributary province, and Colonial and recent commercial, political, and ecclesiastical seat. It has somewhat limited land for agriculture but it is well watered and it lies at the juncture of major corridors for interregional exchange. The first section of this chapter describes the Tlaxiaco core (the valley itself) and the following sections explore its extensive and mountainous adjacent peripheries. The real economic power of this yuhuitaiyu in Natividad times resided beyond these peripheries in the prosperous ñuu of the inner basin (Chapter 5).

This whole area was colonized by sedentary villagers rather late. It has only a couple Cruz villages, a few Early Ramos hilltowns, and virtually no Late Ramos occupation. It was in the Early Classic that Tlaxiaco rose to a prominent place in highland Oaxaca. Then the region suffered the same Late Classic/Epiclassic decline seen elsewhere.

Tlaxiaco's peripheries to the north, east, and southeast are fragmented and not as favorable for agriculture as most of the subregions in the Central Mixteca Alta.

Only Nundichi/Ñumi was an autonomous ñuu. The northeastern and southeastern peripheries had villages but not distinct central place systems.

In this chapter we address a fundamental question raised by Spores (1967:55–56): "[T]he community . . . extended beyond the valley in the case of Tlaxiaco. . . . Archaeologists working here in the future should not only test the integrity of the valley as a comprehensible cultural-geographic unit but should also watch for a probably close relationship of the unit to the expanded area." In brief, yes, the Tlaxiaco Valley had an integrity and, yes, it looks like close relationships were cemented with the rich agricultural lands east of the divide in the inner basin. Archaeology suggests this larger structure of the yuhuitaiyu but only the documentary history could tell us how the Tlaxiaco Valley came to be the political center of this greater domain.

TLAXIACO VALLEY

Tlaxiaco is today a large municipio, the cabecera of the district of the same name, and the Mixteca Alta's most important commercial center. We covered a large part of the municipio but Tlaxiaco's land west of El Vergel remains unsurveyed (Spores's [1996] reconnaissance found important sites including a center at Cuquila).

The Tlaxiaco Valley subregion consists of the valley, the hills immediately surrounding it, and the hills to the west as far as the Río Ñumi, a total area of about 90 km². The site prefixes and numbers are SLC, CAL, and TLA 1, 24–44, 48.

The Tlaxiaco Valley has more gently sloping land (10 to 15 km²) than most other places west of the Sierra de Nochixtlán. Tlaxiaco is well watered, being at the juncture of six streams with substantial watersheds to the north and east. These form the Río Tlaxiaco, which exits the southwestern end of the valley through a narrow gorge. The elevation is 2,080 m at the modern town, slightly lower than Teposcolula but not as low as San Mateo Peñasco.

Tlaxiaco differs from other places in the Mixteca Alta in not having as much soil derived from the Yanhuitlán beds. The geology is more varied. There are older Jurassic sedimentary materials (limestones, mudstones, and sandstones) on the west and southeast and steep ridges and cliffs formed of andesite on the north and east. Yanhuitlán Formation materials (broadly defined, these are mostly conglomerates) appear in three small patches: just south of the modern town, at El Vergel, and east of the Cerro de la Virgen. Large settlements were attracted to these patches. The three total 10 km², only slightly more than in the small Yucunama Valley (8 km²) and much less than Yolomécatl's 20 km². Inasmuch as Yanhuitlán soils were a major intensifiable resource in other places, their scarcity in Tlaxiaco may be relevant to this subregion's development.

Historically, Tlaxiaco has been known for its preeminence in commerce, culture ("the Paris of Oaxaca"), and political clout. It is the central node in the regional peasant market system and the key link in trade between highlands and lowlands. Tlaxiaco was the seat of the Aztec tributary province of the same name.

Surveying Tlaxiaco meant a lot of walking through neighborhoods, *solares* (house yards), infields, alleys, and garbage. The town has recently and quickly sprawled outward. Our crews were able to find quite a few prehistoric sites amidst the modern houses. Many of these sites are being destroyed. They are important for understanding Tlaxiaco's history, especially in the fifteenth and sixteenth centuries. A project to retrieve information before it is destroyed would be highly desirable.

Late Cruz

We found nothing earlier than Late Cruz, perhaps owing to erosion, alluviation, and the modern town. There are two Late Cruz sites, both several kilometers away from the valley floor (Figure 6.1, Table 6.1). Another, TLA 17, is nearby in the Tlaxiaco northeastern periphery.

TLA 43 is on a low hill on an outcrop of the Yanhuitlán Formation. We found a single good Late Cruz sherd at a site with later components and two mounds and a platform. CAL 2 likewise was identified on the basis of one or two sherds. It is at the upper end of the drainage that heads west away from Tlaxiaco. Both sites have lama-bordos nearby. Although we may be missing some Cruz sites, Tlaxiaco clearly was not home to a large settlement cluster.

Ramos

Tlaxiaco had little settlement in Ramos compared to other subregions, suggesting that the lack of Cruz is not entirely due to the invisibility of sites. There are two small Ramos sites: Cerro Encantado (TLA 1), which was an important Las Flores town, and CAL 6 at the western edge of our study area (Figure 6.2, Table 6.2).

Cerro Encantado is a hilltop terraced site overlooking the valley. There had been a small Late Cruz site (TLA 17) about 2 km up the ridge to the northeast. Ramos is confined to the top of the ridge in the same area as the public architecture and one or two levels of terraces down the slope. We found diagnostic pottery of both Early and Late Ramos but the Las Flores is much better represented. Our interpretation is that Cerro Encantado was begun in Early Ramos as a small fortified village with long, narrow residential terraces and probably some public architecture. It continued to be occupied through Late Ramos. The lama-bordos that originate in the saddle below the hilltop could have been started in Ramos or later times.

CAL 6 is similar. It is a compact, hilltop terraced site with long, narrow terraces; lama-bordos; a linear string of public architecture; and evidence of Early and Late Ramos (Figure 6.3). As at Cerro Encantado, Las Flores is more widespread and much better represented. In sum, Tlaxiaco in Ramos and Cruz was small and peripheral to Huamelulpan and the inner basin. We do not know about the unsurveyed land west and south of the Tlaxiaco Valley.

Las Flores

Tlaxiaco grew in population and regional prominence in Early Las Flores. Our population estimate is a low of 7,500 and a high of 15,000. Five clusters of settlements

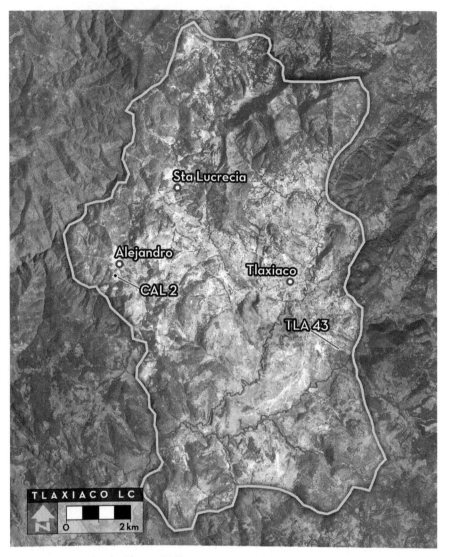

6.1 *Late Cruz sites in the Tlaxiaco Valley.*

on hilltops ringed the valley on all sides (Figure 6.4, Table 6.3). The two largest sites, Cerro de la Virgen (TLA 42) and Cerro Encantado (TLA 1), each may have had 3,000 to 4,000 inhabitants.

The settlement at Cerro Encantado spread over two hills and the saddle between. Lama-bordos began in the saddle. The whole site probably had residential terraces but they are preserved only on the higher, northern hill (Figure 6.5). The public architecture was a linear string with a single mound (Str. 5) on a terrace, a

6.2 Ramos sites in the Tlaxiaco Valley.

four-mound group enclosing a plaza, and a second plaza. The residential terraces were long and narrow. Below these were long walls that form even narrower terraces (1 to 1.5 m wide) that serve to stabilize the slope. The major occupation at Cerro Encantado dates to Transición and Early Las Flores.

Cerro de la Virgen extends over 60 ha in Las Flores and covers the main volcanic, cone-shaped hill and the saddle and ridge to the west. There is Natividad on the western ridge too, but the eastern hill is only Las Flores. The slopes must have borne

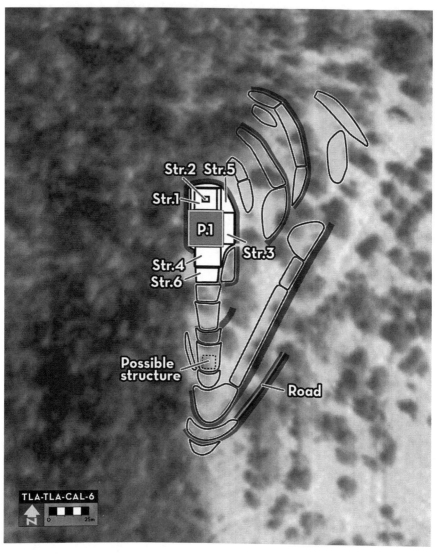

6.3 *The architecture at CAL 6.*

many residential terraces. Unfortunately, La Virgen has not been untouched—cultivation and erosion have destroyed much of it. The focal architecture is only one mound with two plazas, but the mound is 4 m tall. There are lama-bordos associated with the Las Flores occupation. Inhabitants probably exploited the Yanhuitlán Formation soils north and east of the site. This seems to be a solid Early Las Flores occupation, without the Transición that occurs at Cerro Encantado. Nearby is TLA 41, a single-component hilltop site with one or possibly two structures.

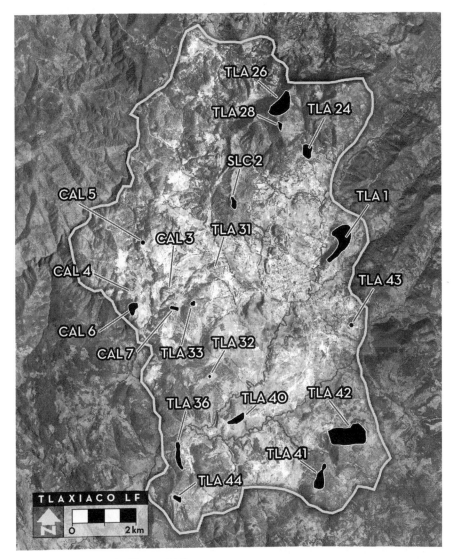

6.4 *Las Flores sites in the Tlaxiaco Valley.*

El Vergel (TLA 36) is the largest settlement in a cluster of sites at the southern end of the valley. Bedrock on the hill is limestone but just to the east is a good bottomland and a stretch of Yanhuitlán Formation soils. The north end of the hill ends at a precipice overlooking the narrow gorge of the Río Tlaxiaco—it is a spectacular location. The hillsides were terraced for houses and lama-bordos originate in the saddle. In addition to Las Flores there is a strong Natividad occupation, which makes dating the public architecture from surface remains uncertain. On top of the

6.5 *Cerro Encantado (TLA 1) and the north end of the Tlaxiaco Valley, from the west. Five or six tiers of long terraces can be seen on the site.*

northern knob is a group of three (perhaps four) mounds. On top of the southern knob are two mounds facing each other across a small plaza, plus two other mounds. These two-mound groups on the northern and southern knobs have the size and arrangement of Las Flores public architecture. Between these two groups, on the southern hill between the knob and the saddle, is a series of terraces with patio groups, a ball court, and an access way on the west side.

Also in this cluster with El Vergel is the single-component site TLA 40, on the hill just east of the modern village of El Vergel. This had few artifacts. The site has one structure and there could have been one more, now destroyed.

CAL 3–7 and TLA 31 and 33 form a cluster of small sites on the hills west of the valley. There had been a small Ramos village here, CAL 6, which was also occupied in Las Flores. CAL 6 has three structures on three sides of a plaza, a string of terraces along the ridgeline, and long terraces tightly packed along the slope below the crest. TLA 33, close to the valley, has a linear string of buildings including a closed group of three or four mounds, two plazas, two large terraces that also might have been plazas, and surrounding residential terraces. The architectural arrangement is very similar to that at Cerro Encantado. Except for CAL 6, artifact densities on these sites are low, suggesting short occupation during Early Las Flores.

Four sites cluster on and around Cerro Tambor, a volcanic crater overlooking the north end of the valley. SLC 2 is on Cerro Jabalí. It is a single-component site with three small dispersed structures. TLA 24 was a settlement with residential terraces at the base of the mountain in the Colonia Adolfo López Mateos. It has a structure on a platform; perhaps there was another platform. The largest site, TLA 26, extends over the saddle between Cerro Tambor and Cerro Yucushito. There are two structures facing each other. Finally, TLA 28 occupies the eastern peak of Cerro Tambor at 2,620 m, 500 m above the valley floor. It has both Las Flores and Natividad. There is a large plaza with substantial mounds on the north and south sides, some terraces (not mapped), and, on the northwest slope, three defensive walls, each 2 m high and 6 m wide and separated from each other by about 30 m.

Of the nineteen sites in the subregion all but two have mounded architecture. It is not possible without excavation to be certain about construction dates because most sites also have Natividad but we believe that most mounds were at least begun in Las Flores. For now we assume that El Vergel's figure of twenty mounds is inflated because of patio groups built in Natividad. If so, then no one site stands out in number of mounds and plazas. Cerro Encantado and Cerro de la Virgen, the largest, have mounded architecture not much different from that at the small sites CAL 6, TLA 33, and SLC 2. Within the settlement clusters there are several sites with mounds and plazas. Plazas may distinguish some places—El Vergel, TLA 33, Cerro Encantado, and Cerro de la Virgen have two plazas each.

Population began growing after Ramos in the Transición phase and picked up considerably in Early Las Flores. Relative to other subregions Tlaxiaco had major demographic growth in Las Flores. The western cluster of settlement may have lasted the shortest period of time. By Late Las Flores, Tlaxiaco may have been abandoned for we have no indication of sites dating to that time.

Natividad

We mapped twenty-four Postclassic sites—six isolated residences, seven hamlets, seven small villages, three large villages, and Cerro de la Virgen, the largest place at 3,200 to 6,500 inhabitants (Figure 6.6, Table 6.4). The total population was between 5,400 and 11,400. Tlaxiaco's political importance in the sixteenth century outstripped its relatively modest demographic rank.

Cerro de la Virgen (TLA 42, Figure 6.7) was the central town. The main Natividad occupation was on the western ridge, not the handsomely terraced hill that was the Las Flores component. The site is well situated between the three patches of Yanhuitlán Formation soils. We saw several lama-bordos. There are remnants of residential terraces. On the summit are two large platform mounds, one with a single mounded structure on top and the other with two. There is a clearly defined plaza between the two platform mounds.

Understanding Tlaxiaco in the Postclassic depends on how La Virgen is interpreted. We show the site covering 65.1 ha with a population density of 50 to 100 per ha, assuming that the entire hill had residential terraces. We interpret the mound group as new Natividad construction. A more detailed study should be carried out before the rest of the site is destroyed.

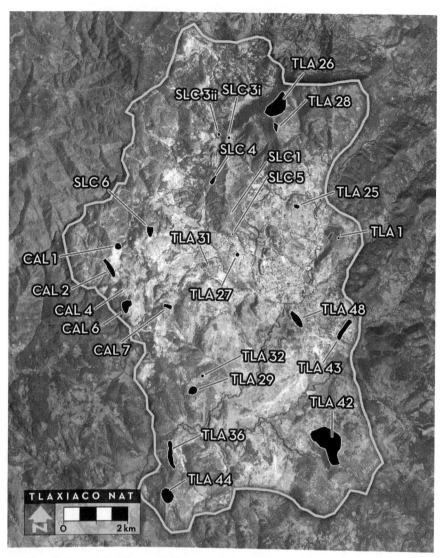

6.6 *Natividad sites in the Tlaxiaco Valley.*

El Vergel (TLA 36) was the second-largest settlement. It was a Las Flores settlement but it also has a strong Natividad component covering the whole site. El
Vergel is a promontory above the gorge where the Río Tlaxiaco leaves the valley;
it is also just west of good, flat farmland. Lama-bordos originate in the site. Some
of the focal architecture is probably Las Flores but some may have Natividad construction. The ball court at El Vergel (Figure 6.8) may be the feature from which
Tlaxiaco gets its Nahuatl name "Tlachquiauhco" (*lugar de lluvia del juego de pelota,*

6.7 Cerro de la Virgen (TLA 42).

"place of rain of the ball court") (Alavez Chávez 1988:104). The structures on the terraces ascending the south ridge appear to be wealthy residences not public architecture so our figure of twenty mounds for the site may be misleading.

There are six outlier sites and they all have public architecture. On two hills east of El Vergel are two sites we could not date for lack of sherds, TLA 38 and 39. TLA 38 has a single structure and TLA 39 has three structures around a plaza. South of El Vergel is TLA 44 with two structures facing each other across a plaza. TLA 44 has both Las Flores and Natividad. North of El Vergel is TLA 29 with a four-mound group on a plaza and TLA 32 with two structures facing each other on a plaza on an artificial platform. TLA 34, nearby, is another undated site. It has a single structure. We suspect that people in Natividad times used the mounds and plazas at these outlier sites and perhaps some of the construction dates to Natividad.

On the western edge of the survey area is a cluster of six small Natividad sites, SLC 6 and CAL 1, 2, 4, 6, and 7. CAL 6 was a reoccupation of an earlier hilltop terraced site with public architecture. CAL 2 and 4 have single mounds. SLC 6 has a single mound and well-preserved foundations of residential architecture. It has the look of a Ramos hilltop site but there were few artifacts, all Natividad in date. There are several lama-bordos in the area of this western site cluster. There is also a source of white chert at CAL 2 where we saw many cores and flakes.

Cerro Tambor must have been an important place for there are two large Natividad sites on the mountain plus another where we could find no sherds. As in the El Vergel area, all the sites have public architecture and there are both Las

6.8 *Roberto Santos stands in the ball court at El Vergel (TLA 36). Looking west.*

Flores and Natividad occupations. TLA 26 is in the saddle between Cerro Tambor and Cerro Yucushito. It has the largest residential area and two mounds that face each other across a plaza. TLA 28 (described in the Las Flores section) is on the eastern peak of the ancient crater; it has a four-mound group. TLA 30 is a small undated site on the western rim of the crater. It has a four-mound group with an open side on a plaza.

SLC 1, 3–5 are on the ridge that leads up to Cerro Jabalí above the modern Barrio Santa Lucrecia. We found five sites in barrios of modern Tlaxiaco. They are at lower elevations than the other Natividad sites. These sites are looted and in poor condition but they are important in Tlaxiaco's latest Postclassic and early Colonial history. TLA 25 is on a hill in the Barrio San Diego. There were residential terraces and probably three structures around a courtyard that measures 20 m on a side. TLA 27 is in the Barrio San Nicolás. TLA 31 is a small site with a single mound in the Barrio San Sebastián. In Barrio San Pedro are TLA 43 and TLA 48, which has two plazas formed by perhaps five structures.

In sum, the population was distributed in four clusters on the northern, western, and southern sides of the valley, plus the major town at Cerro de la Virgen. In round figures Cerro Tambor had 500 people, Santa Lucrecia had 100, the western cluster had 1,100, El Vergel had 1,100, and Cerro de la Virgen had 4,900. The sites in the Barrios San Nicolás, San Pedro, San Sebastián, and San Diego (totaling at least 600 people) are a very late phenomenon perhaps associated with the Aztec presence—these sites and Cerro de la Virgen have all the Aztec pottery we found in

Tlaxiaco. The northeastern and southeastern peripheries described in the next sections had additional settlement clusters that may have been part of Tlaxiaco.

At least half of all settlements had mounded architecture, it being uncertain whether these were built in Las Flores, Natividad, or both. At least use in Natividad is strongly indicated. A centralized civic-ceremonial hierarchy for the Tlaxiaco Valley is not obvious in the architecture. Instead, civic-ceremonial functions seem to have been widely distributed and carried out at the local level.

In our systematic surveying we found sites in the barrios and in the recent suburbs of Tlaxiaco but not in the old core of the town, which is paved and built up. In all our walking in Tlaxiaco (where we lived) we saw no prehispanic artifacts. However, we have been told that recent excavations for new construction in the center of town turned up late Natividad or early Colonial materials. Still, we think it unlikely that the largest Natividad site was any other than Cerro de la Virgen. It would be interesting to know if Colonial Tlaxiaco had been built on top of the seat (palace?) of the late prehispanic cacicazgo.

THE NORTHEASTERN PERIPHERY OF TLAXIACO

This is a terrain of four ridges and five arroyos that head on the divide at Santa María del Rosario (Tayata) and Amoltepec and descend to the Tlaxiaco Valley. Soils are derived from volcanic andesite bedrock. At Nueva Reforma there is limestone of Jurassic age, historically mined for cal. The subregion covers about 60 km². There is not much flat land. Except for rancherías along a corridor running east-west through the narrow valley of Río El Boquerón it is not much inhabited now nor was it any time in the past. Place names are Spanish and Catholic: Los Blancos and the three Cañadas—María, Santa María, and Purísima. This area pertains to the municipio of Tlaxiaco today.

Archaeologically, the area does not have much continuity of occupation from period to period. There is some overlap between Las Flores and Natividad occupations but this subregion has a high proportion of single-component sites.

Late Cruz

The earliest evidence of settlement is a small site on the ridge above Cerro Encantado, TLA 17 (Figure 6.9, Table 6.5).

Ramos

There are two sites at opposite ends of the area and the time span (Figure 6.10, Table 6.5). TLA 6 is a small, low-density, dispersed artifact scatter in the valley 3 km east of the town of Tlaxiaco. The sherds suggest a date very early in Ramos.

TLA 15 has been mentioned before in the Amoltepec section as a potential Late Ramos boundary site. It is on a steep-sided hilltop overlooking the canyon of the modern Tlaxiaco-Teposcolula highway. It has a 4 by 4 m mound atop a series

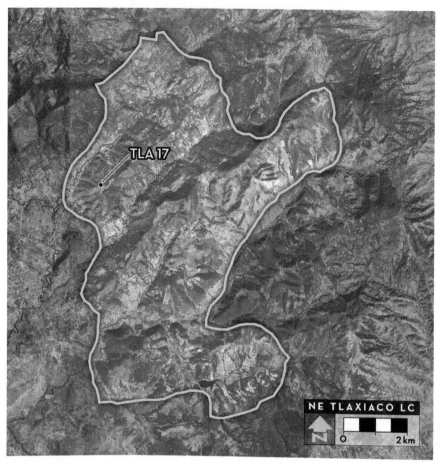

6.9 *Late Cruz sites in the northeastern periphery of Tlaxiaco.*

of three artificial platforms built on the most gently sloping side of the conical hill. There is another mound to the west. TLA 15 undoubtedly had more to do with the Huamelulpan polity than with Tlaxiaco.

Las Flores

We mapped ten sites, all small and extremely eroded. TLA 7, for example, is almost gone. Nevertheless there is a pattern: a series of settlements along the narrow valley and pass of the Río Boquerón linking Tlaxiaco with the major towns of Magdalena Peñasco (Figure 6.11, Table 6.6).

Three sites were found on the top and flanks of the mountain above Cañada Santa María. This is the western, Tlaxiaco end of the chain of sites. TLA 47, dat-

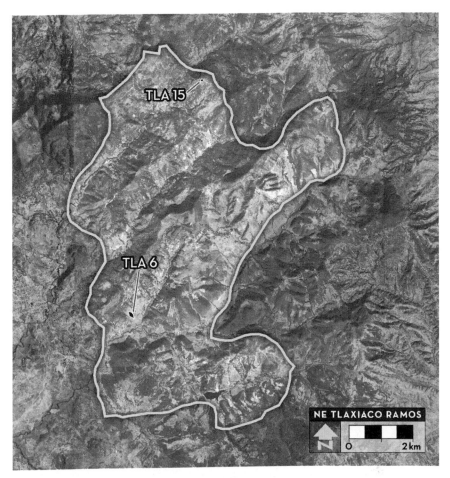

6.10 *Ramos sites in the northeastern periphery of Tlaxiaco.*

ing to Early Las Flores, was a fortified mountaintop village. On the summit are two mounds in an L arrangement on a plaza. This group is surrounded by terraces. Another mound was found 90 m to the northwest. The main knob has a defensive wall 210 m long.

TLA 45 and 46 have remains of platforms or terraces but removal of stone for modern fields makes tracing the ancient remains very difficult. TLA 45 seems to have had a platform or terrace and TLA 46 had a platform on which there may have been two mounds in an L arrangement. At TLA 45 we found an exposed red-painted floor.

To the east along the route to Magdalena Peñasco is TLA 14, located on a hilltop overlooking the narrow valley at the ranchería Cañada María; it has a low-density, dispersed artifact scatter. TLA 11 is at the ranchería El Boquerón in a similar

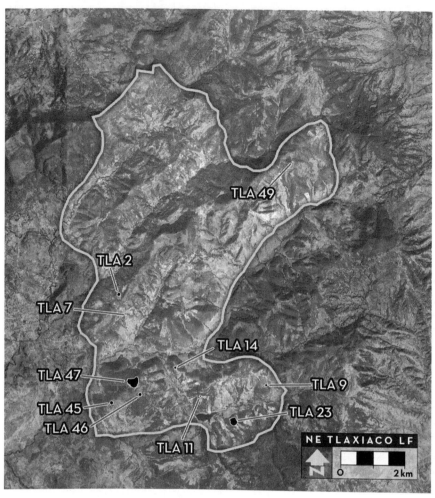

6.11 *Las Flores sites in the northeastern periphery of Tlaxiaco.*

situation overlooking the narrow valley. It has two structures in an L arrangement. Sherds from TLA 11 indicate a Transición–Early Las Flores date. TLA 23 is on a hill opposite Nueva Reforma. It has a platform with a mound and several residential terraces. TLA 9 is east of Nueva Reforma. From TLA 9 it is only 1.5 km to the large settlements (SMP 32 and 35) on the divide.

We found two tiny sites on the ridge east of Cerro Encantado, TLA 2 and 7. The former is near lama-bordos. TLA 49 is in a mountain saddle almost at the Tayata divide. Little is left of the site.

Adding up the estimated population from these sites we have almost 1,000 persons. Most were living at TLA 47. The series of small sites overlooking the obvious

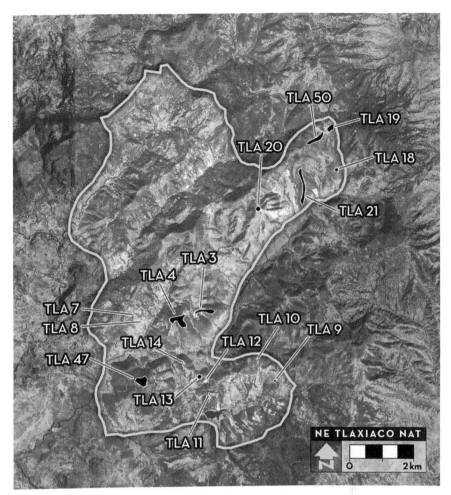

6.12 Natividad sites in the northeastern periphery of Tlaxiaco.

route between Tlaxiaco and Magdalena Peñasco/Amoltepec suggests interaction between these subregions. Five of the seven sites had mounds or plazas. TLA 47 was fortified. All of this dates to Early Las Flores and it probably began in Transición. There is no Late Las Flores at all.

Natividad

There were more sites and more people than at any other time. We mapped sixteen sites; the average population estimate is almost 1,400 persons (Figure 6.12, Table 6.7). However, only two zones were occupied, the corridor along the narrow valley between Magdalena Peñasco/Amoltepec and Tlaxiaco and the divide near

Santa María del Rosario. Sites in the latter cluster are nearest to Amoltepec or Santa María del Rosario and probably pertained to the Amoltepec or Tayata polities rather than Tlaxiaco.

Eleven small settlements were strung along the route to the Magdalena Peñasco pass. These were typically on hills above the narrow valley. The most populous village was the reoccupation of the Las Flores fortified hilltop at TLA 47. Nearby is TLA 4, the second-largest village, at the ranchería Cañada la Purísima. This is a single-component site. It had a four-mound group enclosing a courtyard 20 m on a side. A lama-bordo originates within the site. The other site with mounded architecture is TLA 11, which has two mounds probably constructed in Las Flores. These sites are not rich in artifacts.

TLA 18–21 and 50 are at the head of the ridge joining the high divide south of Santa María del Rosario. These are low-density artifact scatters without mounded architecture. Compared to the string of sites along the Boquerón corridor these seem to have at least as much artifactual variety, especially considering their small total occupied area and low artifact density.

THE SOUTHEASTERN PERIPHERY OF TLAXIACO

This subregion is essentially a long ridge that descends from the divide above Magdalena Peñasco, Yosojica, and Dzinicahua and runs to Cerro de la Virgen. The ridgetop for much of its length is about 2,350 m asl, 150 m above the streams along its sides. The stream at the foot of the ridge on its south side is the Río Tablas, our survey area's boundary. This is a mountainous place of many geological pieces. Much of the ridge is volcanic in origin, including the high divide on the east and the Cerro de la Virgen in Tlaxiaco. Next to La Virgen is a small piece of Yanhuitlán Formation conglomerates. Some of the central and southern parts are weathered, old limestones.

Today the area is covered in pine forest or cleared for agriculture. It pertains to two villages, Ojo de Agua in the valley east of Cerro de la Virgen and Llano Grande, a ranchería just south of our survey area. Both are dependencies of Tlaxiaco. The gravel road from Tlaxiaco to San Miguel el Grande and Chalcatongo passes through Ojo de Agua and along the top of this ridge.

Late Cruz

We found nothing earlier than Late Cruz, as was the case in the other subregions around Tlaxiaco. Indeed, we recognized no Early or Middle Cruz sites anywhere in our study area west of the Huamelulpan–Llano Grande divide.

For Late Cruz we have two occurrences, ODA 5 and 10 (Figure 6.13, Table 6.8). ODA 10 is an Early Ramos (and later) hilltop terraced site with public architecture. ODA 5 is a single-component, low-density artifact scatter on a hill at the base of the ridge overlooking the Río Tablas. This seems to have been an isolated residence.

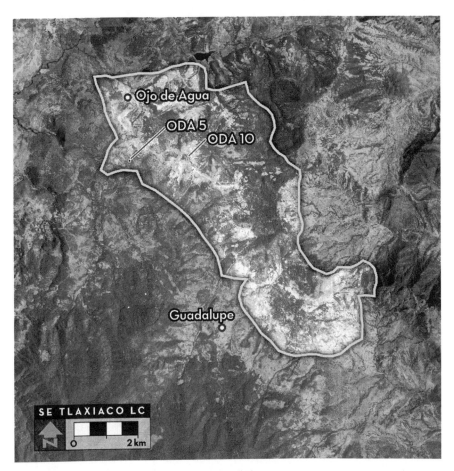

6.13 Late Cruz sites in the southeastern periphery of Tlaxiaco.

Ramos

This area had a fairly strong and quite nucleated Ramos presence (Figure 6.14, Table 6.9). ODA 10 was a hilltop terraced site with three lama-bordos originating in the settlement (Figure 6.15) and a six-mound architectural complex (where there had been a little Late Cruz). Several sherds on and around the mounds could be Early Ramos. Unfortunately, two-thirds of the site has been destroyed by agriculture. The other third is in pine forest and has well-preserved ancient residential terraces but null surface visibility (Figure 6.16). Just south of the main hill is another promontory that had fine surface visibility; our collection from here has good Early Ramos. Despite the paucity of Early Ramos at the mound complex and surrounding terraces we think this place was settled and that terracing and mound construction was undertaken in this phase.

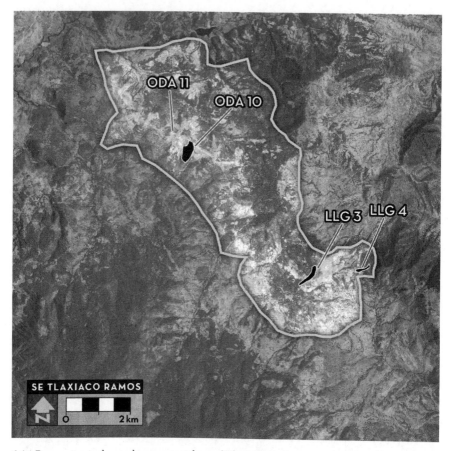

6.14 *Ramos sites in the southeastern periphery of Tlaxiaco.*

To the west the next hilltop is ODA 11. It too has a mound group on top, residential terraces, and lama-bordos. On the summit is a structure and plaza and perhaps there had been a second mound at a right angle to the main mound. The ceramics are predominantly Natividad but there is a small Early Ramos presence.

The two LLG sites have been mentioned in the Dzinicahua section. LLG 4 was an Early Ramos outlier of Dzinicahua situated on a saddle of the ridge ascending the divide. It has one badly preserved structure. The site is dispersed and extremely eroded.

LLG 3 is at 2,620 m on the high peak on the divide itself. This is a nucleated and compact Late Ramos fortified site with public architecture and some residential terraces. The site is entirely covered in nasty secondary vegetation. It has two structures in an L arrangement on top of a platform and, one level below this, a courtyard formed by this platform and two other mounds. There are defensive walls that rise to 1 m above the ground and elaborate gates in the walls.

6.15 Lama-bordo originating in ODA 10 (top right). Note trees and magueys planted along retaining walls.

6.16 Long terraces at ODA 10. Note the cut stone, especially on the back of the terraces.

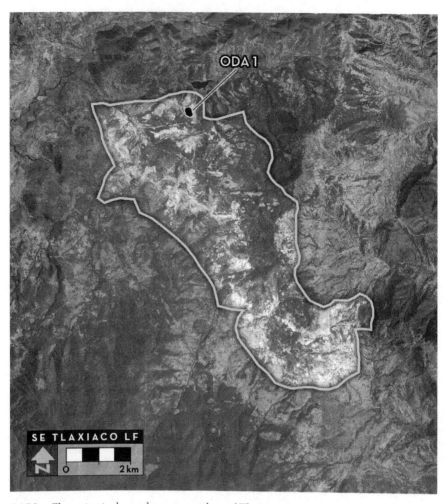

6.17 *Las Flores sites in the southeastern periphery of Tlaxiaco.*

LLG 3 is more likely to be a Dzinicahua than a Tlaxiaco outlier. Given the low population levels in Late Cruz in the Tlaxiaco core and peripheries it might be suggested that the Early Ramos settlements were colonizations from the east.

Las Flores

This area was virtually abandoned during the entire Classic period (Figure 6.17, Table 6.10). Along the whole southern strip of the study area between Cerro de la Virgen and Dzinicahua there were no settlements. Farther east, from Dzinicahua to Yucuañe, people were concentrated into a few nucleated hilltop sites.

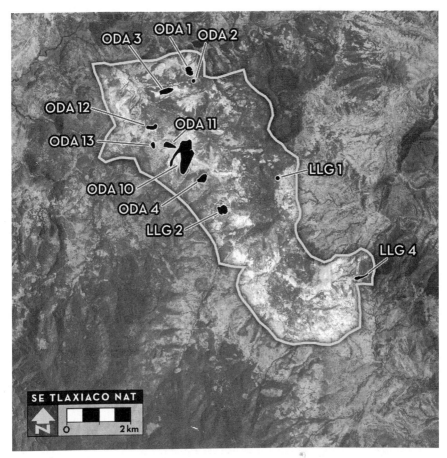

6.18 Natividad sites in the southeastern periphery of Tlaxiaco.

ODA 1 is the only Las Flores site. It was not on the main ridge but on the flank of the next ridge to the north, closer to the chain of settlements that extended between Tlaxiaco and Magdalena Peñasco. It is on a hill totally covered and modified by modern agricultural terraces and houses. On top there are the remains of a single mound and plaza. This was a village of 300 to 600 inhabitants.

Natividad

This was by far the period of biggest development. There are eleven sites totaling almost 90 ha of occupation, with population estimated between 1,700 and 3,800 persons. Most people lived on hilltops along the main ridge. There was also a cluster on the ridge to the north around modern Ojo de Agua (Figure 6.18, Table 6.10).

6.19 ODA 10, the western mound in the plaza group. A little Late Cruz material, along with Natividad, was found here.

ODA 4, 10–13, and LLG 2 form the largest cluster of settlement and ODA 10 was the largest single site. This was the old Ramos hilltop settlement. It was expanded in Natividad to form a U shape with a lama-bordo between the ridges. Two other lama-bordos head in the terraced area of the hilltop. There is a spring and holding pond on one of the upper lama-bordo terraces on the north slope. This is the site with the six-mound group (Figure 6.19). Given all the Natividad sherds around the mounds and on the terraced slopes these features should pertain to this period (with Ramos construction too).

ODA 11 is close by, another terraced hilltop with a structure or perhaps two in an L arrangement on a plaza with lama-bordos nearby. At ODA 4 there are two structures in an L arrangement on a plaza surrounded by remnants of terraces. Structure 2 at ODA 4 has an open tomb. LLG 2 has a structure, plaza, and residential terraces.

The Ojo de Agua sites (ODA 1–3) are on hilltops within the dispersed modern community. The archaeological sites have been substantially modified by recent agricultural terracing and modern houses. Even so, we recovered basic information. The total occupied area is about 20 ha. There are lama-bordos nearby. ODA 2 has a possible structure and a fair amount and variety of obsidian.

LLG 1 is situated on the top of the mountain above Yosocahua. The west side is all forested; the east side is all cultivated. There is one mound. LLG 1 overlooks the path between the ODA sites and the Pueblo Viejo at San Isidro Peñasco. LLG

4 is in the highly eroded saddle on the east side of the divide leading to Dzinicahua. Natividad is present but in low density.

In Natividad this subregion was home to a barrio (or two) that may have been equivalent to others in Tlaxiaco. Further interpretation should await survey south of our project area.

NUNDICHI/ÑUMI

The western edge of our study area north of Tlaxiaco is the Río Ñumi. We surveyed the left bank of this south-flowing stream. We covered almost all of the municipio of Santiago Nundichi and the southeastern corner of the municipio of San Juan Ñumi. On the north and south this subregion is bounded by the igneous ridges of Cerro Montezacate and Cerro Tambor. The low hills and valleys are composed of alternating beds of sandstones and volcanic tuff. The valley lies between 2,000 and 2,200 m asl. A large part of the valley remains unsurveyed so our conclusions are limited.

Archaic?

We found one biface resembling a Trinidad point in a lithic scatter, NUN 1. The site is just below the high ridge separating Nundichi from Tlaxiaco. Other artifacts include green and gray obsidian and white chert. It is likely that most of them pertain to later periods but the site is otherwise undated.

Late Cruz

As elsewhere west of the Huamelulpan divide, there are no Early/Middle Cruz sites. We found four small Late Cruz sites at low elevations just above arroyos (Figure 6.20, Table 6.11). SPN 32 is the largest. It is on a little hilltop at San Pedro Ñumi and it has a mound on top of a platform facing a plaza, all on a lower platform. The present form of the mound group probably postdates Cruz but there may have been a Late Cruz building of some sort on the spot. NUN 2 is on a piece of shrinking land at the junction of two arroyos 1 km west of Santiago Nundichi. It is a single-component site, probably an isolated residence. These sites may have been part of a larger cluster but the remainder of the valley needs to be surveyed.

Ramos

HID 2 is a small artifact scatter northwest of the second section of Hidalgo (Figure 6.21, Table 6.12). This is a hilltop overlooking the upper part of a west-flowing stream valley. There is no indication of mounds or defensive works. It probably dates to Late Ramos. SPN 36 is a low hill between San Pedro Ñumi and El Río Ñumi. This site dates to Early Ramos. There seems to have been less going on in this part of Nundichi/Ñumi than there had been in Late Cruz. Again there may have been more settlement west of the river.

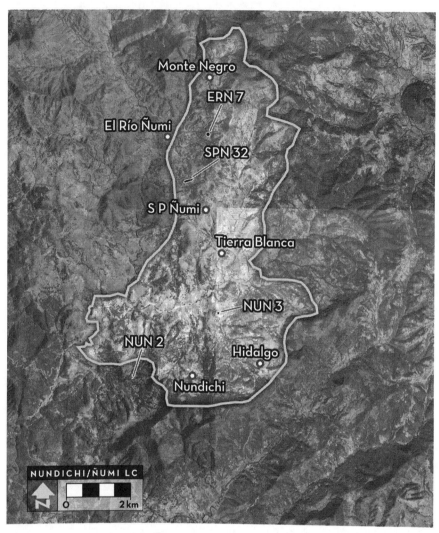

6.20 Late Cruz sites in Nundichi/Ñumi.

Las Flores

A major reoccupation of Nundichi/Ñumi took place in Early Las Flores. In the part of the valley we surveyed there are five sites with a total of 37 ha of occupied area and an average population estimate of 850 people. All the sites are clustered at the northern end of the subregion between El Río Ñumi and San Pedro Ñumi (Figure 6.22, Table 6.13). Sites are generally on hills at low elevations except for ERN 2, which is on a saddle and narrow ridge north of Cerro Yucunu.

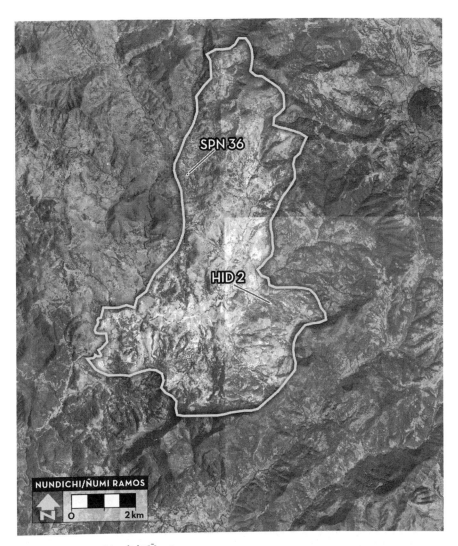

6.21 *Ramos sites in Nundichi/Ñumi.*

SPN 34 is a terraced hilltop with an elaborate civic-ceremonial and elite residential precinct on the summit (Figure 6.23). The precinct consists of an elevated platform on which there is a principal mound, a plaza, and three residences with sunken patios. The terraces were too altered to map but we saw many artifacts. Early and perhaps Late Las Flores is indicated. The clustering of settlement is striking. Note that there are no sites in most of the valley we surveyed and none between Cerro Tambor in Tlaxiaco and this cluster.

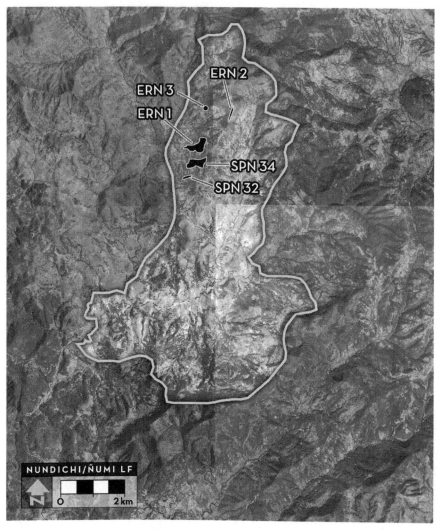

6.22 Las Flores sites in Nundichi/Ñumi.

Natividad

Most sites ever occupied have Natividad components. There are eighteen, covering 86 ha. The population was higher than at any previous time. The main concentration of settlement was around San Pedro Ñumi, extending up to El Río Ñumi, but there was also settlement in the lower valley around Santiago Nundichi and on the flanks of the southern ridge (Figure 6.24, Table 6.14). The pattern is like today's settlements: small, dispersed villages and rancherías, no large concentration. Some of these sites could have been larger than we recorded. Around Cañada de Tierra

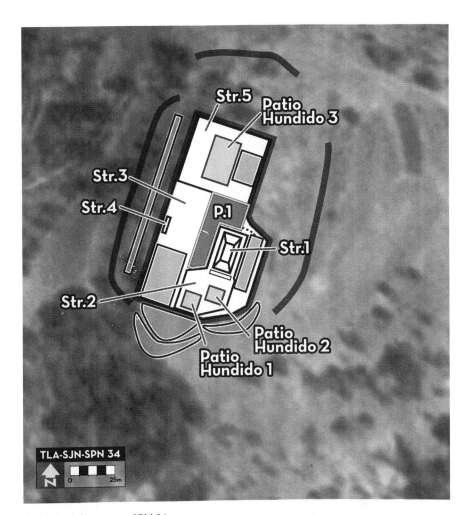

6.23 The architecture at SPN 34.

Blanca (CTB) crews were walking on calcrete and pine needles, and site appeared only where there was soil.

White chert flakes are ubiquitous; sites have one or two PPKs each. At HID 1, a hilltop west of the second section of Hidalgo, the site contained a 15 by 20 m concentration of white chert flakes and biface fragments, interpreted as a lithic work area.

Little public architecture is associated with Natividad components and what we did record was probably of local or barrio civic-ceremonial importance. SPN 32, occupied in Late Cruz and Las Flores, has a platform with a plaza, a structure facing the plaza, and a superstructure. A few sherds on the plaza and Terrace 2 at the Las Flores civic-ceremonial center SPN 34 indicate a bit of Natividad reuse. At CTB 2 there is a poorly preserved courtyard enclosed by walls and two mounds.

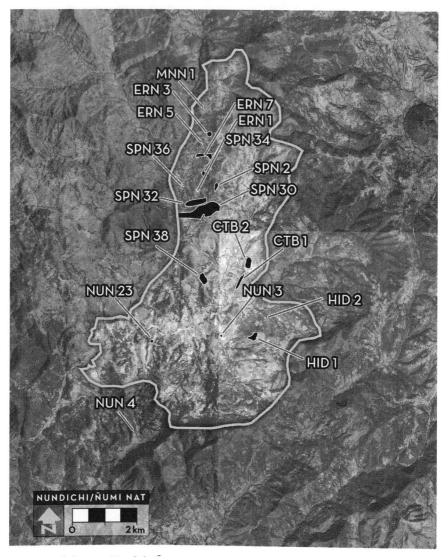

6.24 *Natividad sites in Nundichi/Ñumi.*

Our survey suggests a cluster of population in the Nundichi/Ñumi Valley but we probably do not have its center. The ceramic artifacts and lack of obsidian do not show great wealth or favorable market access yet the ceramics are of the same general types as those seen in Tlaxiaco and Huamelulpan. There may be gradual changes in ceramic complexes as one moves across the Mixteca Alta but the pottery in this westernmost subregion is not qualitatively distinct from that of its eastern neighbors.

CHAPTER SEVEN

The Polities of the Early and Middle Formative

The evidence for Archaic period populations in the Mixteca Alta is intriguing but too fragmentary for us to put together a picture of social life. Little is known about the transition between Archaic and sedentary social systems, and the question of continuity between Archaic and Early Cruz remains completely open. For the Early and Middle Formative our survey found settlement clusters made up of large villages and their smaller satellites. The larger, better endowed valleys were settled first and the smaller subregions were colonized later. Each settlement cluster probably was a distinct social and political group. The variations in settlement help us understand this organization and the larger-scale patterning.

ARCHAIC

Evidence of Archaic culture is difficult to find. It is deeply buried in valley sediments, washed away by erosion, or undetected amidst later material. Nevertheless

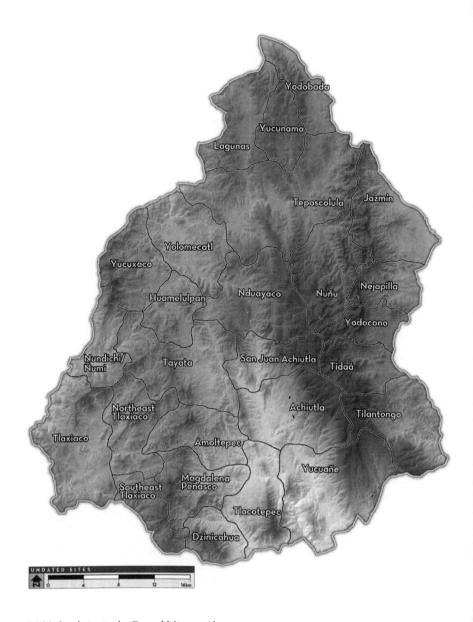

7.1 Undated sites in the Central Mixteca Alta.

we found a dozen sites where future investigations into Preceramic times might begin. Figure 7.1 shows all undated sites, including the possible Archaic sites; lithic scatters that could pertain to ceramic times; and even some sites with ceramics and architecture of unknown date.

The best indications of Archaic sites come from Nejapilla, Tilantongo, and Nduayaco. SDT 10 is a rockshelter and SDT 11 is a rock-art site, a cliff face with red-painted figures. Two open sites in Nejapilla (NEJ 15, TGO 1) have lithic assemblages that in their variety of raw materials and reduction debris differ suspiciously from the specialized chert works of ceramic times.

In Tilantongo three open sites with chert debris drew our attention because of the lack of ceramics and a suggestion that the reduction strategies involved more than the usual small biface and expedient industries of later times. These sites are TIL 13, 15, and 17. Here is the best possibility for investigating continuity from late Archaic camps to Early Cruz sedentary villages.

In Nduayaco, NDU 23 produced an Archaic PPK along with cores and flakes of various materials. NDU 22 had a similar assemblage but no formal tools.

Several other places deserve another look. In Achiutla the rockshelter and lithic scatter above ATY 6 merit attention. So does a lithic scatter near SAT 11 in Tlacotepec where we noted quite a few flakes of different raw materials, some of which were patinated. There are unexplored limestone caves in the vicinity including one about 3 km north of the site. SAL 14, in Lagunas, which caught our attention only because of a single core of unusual size and form, ought to be revisited; likewise NUN 1.

The potential Archaic open sites found in this survey resemble similar ones from the Peñoles study area (Garvin 1994:250–252). Archaic sites have a greater variety of lithic raw materials than later sites; they tend to have evidence of primary reduction from cores as well as later-stage reduction; and they are located in strategic places high on mountain saddles with a view or immediately overlooking places where valleys and streams narrow. One hypothesis is that these were hunting camps; more permanent camps having a broader range of activities were located in valleys where there were better plant food resources. Another possibility is that some of these sites were stops on long-distance routes. On the face of it the rather thin archaeological remains would say that the people of the Mixteca Alta prior to the second millennium BC were nomadic gatherers and hunters and that there were not many of them. Such a conclusion may be premature because some Archaic sites may be invisible to us because of erosion or deposition and because there has never been a full-scale project in the Mixteca Alta specifically aimed at finding Archaic deposits.

EARLY/MIDDLE CRUZ

By Middle Cruz, equivalent in time to the San José phase in the Valley of Oaxaca, there were roughly 4,000 people in the Central Mixteca Alta (Figure 7.2, Table 7.1). Six settlement clusters had been established. From north to south these were Tejupan (outside our study area but including our Yodobada), Jazmín, Teposcolula, Tayata, Tilantongo, and Tlacotepec (including Magdalena Peñasco and Dzinicahua). These settlement clusters consisted of six to twelve isolated residences, hamlets, and villages spread over a linear distance of 6 to 12 km. The clusters were separated from each other by mountain ranges and straight-line distances of 6 to 10 km.

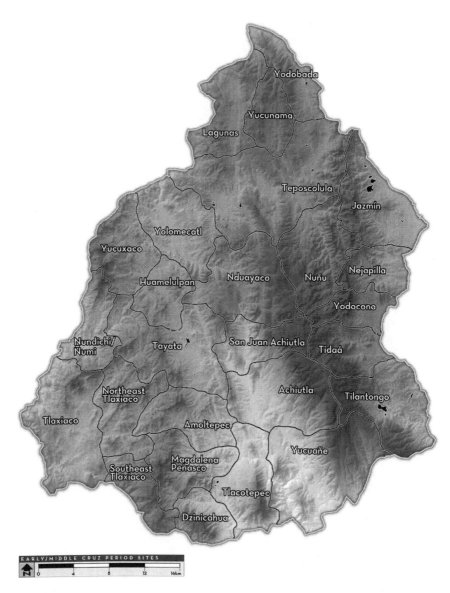

7.2 *Early/Middle Cruz sites in the Central Mixteca Alta.*

Only four of the fifty-one Middle Cruz sites did not fall readily into one of the clusters. They are all small. Three do not survive into Late Cruz. The sites within clusters had better chances of lasting into the next phase.

The valleys of the Mixteca Alta were favorable places for early sedentary farmers. Groundwater was plentiful and soils were fertile. Rainfall was generally higher than in Tehuacan or the Valley of Oaxaca. Sites were usually on low hills just above valley floors, where there were good soil and water resources for agriculture. Middle Cruz settlement clusters are found in larger rather than smaller valleys, Teposcolula rather than Yolomécatl, Tayata rather than Achiutla, Tlacotepec rather than Yucuañe. There was no settlement west of the Huamelulpan/Llano Grande divide.

The earliest sedentary farmers built their villages on the most fertile soils. The best agricultural soils are derived from sedimentary deposits of Tertiary age. These are the sandstones, siltstones, and conglomerates of the Jaltepec and especially the less acidic Yanhuitlán formations (Spores 1969; Kirkby 1972:3–24). Almost 80 percent of Early/Middle Cruz sites are found on the soils of these Tertiary sedimentary rocks (Table 7.2).

Settlement clusters had total populations that ranged between 250 and 1,500 people, using conventional densities of 10 to 25 persons per ha. Jazmín was the largest in population, followed by Tilantongo, Teposcolula, Tayata, and Tlacotepec. It is conceivable that Cruz settlements had lower internal densities, perhaps 5 to 10 persons per ha, if houses were interspersed among terraced fields as they are today in many villages in the Mixteca Alta.

In most clusters one head village was centrally located and larger. XAC 4, SJD 7, Tayata, and Loma Mina stand out as head villages. No clear central village has been identified in the Tlacotepec cluster. Head villages may have had public buildings but we cannot be sure in every case. Head villages were not as strongly developed or differentiated from other settlements as they would be in the following phase, Late Cruz.

In addition to the six head and satellite village clusters in the Central Mixteca Alta, in the neighboring Nochixtlán Valley there was one centered on Etlatongo (Blomster 1998) and another at Yucuita (Plunket 1983). Our Jazmín cluster should include sites in the Yanhuitlán Valley outside our study area (Spores 1972). Several sites on the eastern edge of our area were probably members of the Etlatongo cluster. The Tilantongo cluster extended farther east (Byland and Pohl 1994). A conservative total population estimate for these eight known settlement clusters in the Mixteca Alta is 5,000 people.

The pattern described is for Middle Cruz. In our project area there are several places with evidence of Early Cruz. These include SZT 11 in Tayata, possibly three sites in Yodobada, and three in the Teposcolula Valley. The most convincing and largest is Yucuninde Lomas, SPP 53. As in the Valley of Oaxaca, where the oldest evidence of sedentary life comes from the head village, San José Mogote, the older occupations in Tayata and Teposcolula are at sites that became substantial Middle Cruz villages or head towns.

The pattern of discrete settlement clusters of head villages and satellites holds for other regions in highland Mesoamerica, including Chalcatzingo, the Valley of Oaxaca, and Chiapas. It suggests a similar social system operating across different linguistic groups. Middle Cruz ceramics in the Mixteca Alta are local variants of widespread styles too. These similarities in cultural systems imply continuous interaction and integration between populations and across settlement cluster and linguistic boundaries.

LATE CRUZ

This is the Middle Formative period spanning from approximately 700 to 300 BC. We found 237 Late Cruz sites (Figure 7.3, Table 7.3). Most were at the edges of valley floors and at low elevations, the same setting that was preferred in Early/Middle Cruz. Site locations had the advantage of permanent water from streams and springs fed by watersheds in the high mountains.

Two-thirds of Late Cruz sites are on soils derived from Tertiary sedimentary formations, a preference for the most fertile land almost as strong as in the pioneering Early/Middle Cruz phases (Table 7.2). Late Cruz is the first phase for which we have indication of lama-bordos, the cross-drainage agricultural terraces. We counted thirty lama-bordos directly adjacent to Late Cruz sites (Table 7.4). In eight of these cases Late Cruz was the only component present. One can imagine that lama-bordo chains would have begun as a consequence of village life in hilly country where soils were both fertile and easily eroded. Clearing and foot traffic around villages would have accelerated erosion. Soil and water run-off could easily have been retained behind brush and stone retaining walls. It is likely that contour terraces on hillsides were also in use.

In Late Cruz, farmers expanded their attention to new niches. For example, in Tayata Middle Cruz settlements were on hills just above the valley floor. In Late Cruz the same places were used but people established new settlements about 100 m higher on the tops of long ridges above barrancas. In Tilantongo many settlements were on the lower slopes of the basin rim, which was the best watershed as well as a good situation for contour and lama-bordo terracing.

Although perhaps 90 percent of sites were in the low-elevation situations just described, a few isolated residences and hamlets were situated high in the mountains. For example, we found Late Cruz on the high divide between Magdalena Peñasco and Tlaxiaco, at 2,600 m in the mountains above Yodocono, and in the mountains north of the Lagunas Valley. These places could have had special economic or other roles but we found no evidence in the surface artifacts.

Late Cruz settlement systems expanded in population scale. The midpoint of our population estimates is 21,500, compared to 4,000 for the prior phase. Individual Middle Cruz settlement clusters grew in population in Late Cruz. Teposcolula increased in population from 500 to 2,600, Tilantongo from 1,050 to 3,000, Tayata from 250 to 4,200, and Tlacotepec from 300 to 1,625. Only Jazmín showed an apparent decrease, but Late Cruz sites found by Spores (1972) just outside our study area could make up the loss.

There was also territorial expansion. The Teposcolula, Tayata, and Tlacotepec settlement clusters grew in scale not only by adding more and larger sites to the original cluster, but they also expanded by founding new settlement clusters in previously unoccupied adjacent valleys. New settlement clusters were established on

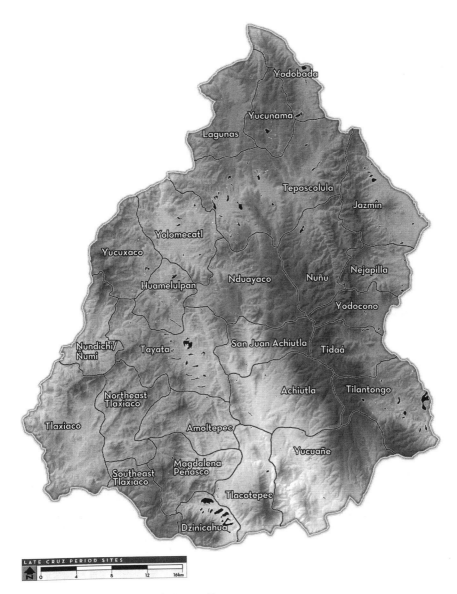

7.3 Late Cruz sites in the Central Mixteca Alta.

the Nochixtlán Valley edge of our survey area at Nejapilla and Yodocono but we are not sure of their affiliation in a larger cluster.

The territorial expansion occurred in a specific manner. Smaller valleys adjacent to the original cluster were settled not with single sites but by settlement clusters—sets of villages, hamlets, and isolated residences. These new settlement clusters were smaller than the cluster in the first valley settled, in part because the newly colonized valleys were smaller. The new settlement clusters were also less centralized and the head village, if one can be distinguished, was smaller and had less public architecture than the older head town. In other words, the Middle Cruz settlement clusters expanded by adding new settlement clusters, creating larger, more complex "super-clusters." Within these new territorial units there was a hierarchical relationship between older and newer settlement clusters. The following paragraphs describe three super-clusters.

Teposcolula expanded in all directions. The core consisted of two clusters, nucleated villages in the east and open sites around the head village of Loma Mina in the west. In Late Cruz six adjacent subregions were added. Nuñu had a population of 325 (using the average of the low and high ends of the range) in one village and three isolated residences. Yodobada is uncertain; it may have been divided between Teposcolula and Tejupan. It had several fairly large villages like the settlements nearest it in San Juan Teposcolula. YBA 1 covered more than 20 ha as did the Tejupan head village, Nuundaa. Yucunama, a small valley fairly high in elevation, had about 500 people and a head village of 23 ha. Lagunas had only two sites, perhaps part of the Yucunama cluster. Yolomécatl had 650 people in eight sites with no clear center but this cluster is quite close to Loma Mina, the Teposcolula head town. Nduayaco, the upland zone bordering the Tayata super-cluster, had only 100 people and its settlements were close to Loma Mina and Yolomécatl.

The Tayata super-cluster grew by expanding into the physically similar valleys to the north, to Achiutla to the east, and to nearby Amoltepec but not to the northeast or further south where Teposcolula and the southern Dzinicahua super-cluster were already established. Tayata was the hub for four subregions: Huamelulpan had 1,100 people with Totonundo as leading village; Yucuxaco had 315 people with one head village, PMY 14, at 13 ha; San Juan Achiutla, Achiutla, and Yucuañe together formed a settlement cluster of 550 persons in which no one village stood out.

The Dzinicahua super-cluster took in Magdalena Peñasco, Tlacotepec, Dzinicahua, and the southeastern periphery of Tlaxiaco. The core was in the Yosojica Valley and the flanks of the Peñasco Grande. There was an outlying settlement cluster of 250 people at Magdalena Peñasco, with no obvious head village. There was also a small cluster at Junta del Río.

Adding together all the components for each super-cluster, the Tayata super-cluster was the largest in population at 6,225, followed by Dzinicahua at 5,190, Teposcolula at 4,245, and Tilantongo at 3,000.

Garvin (1994) proposed that high elevations in places like Peñoles could not be productively exploited by early agriculturalists due to the relatively low yields of Formative period maize—unless regular exchange could be relied on to buffer agricultural risk. The idea gains support from the pattern of Cruz colonization and expansion in the Central Mixteca Alta. Initial farming settlements were at low elevations in large, well-watered valley pockets. Further expansion into smaller and higher valley pockets was carried out by social groups organized somewhat like the original groups, and these super-clusters probably maintained links of exchange and interdependence. We have no information on the part of Garvin's hypothesis having to do with maize yields.

Clusters and super-clusters were bounded by uninhabited areas and mountain ranges. These buffer zones contracted as super-clusters grew. Sites with Late Cruz mounded architecture located on the edges of super-clusters might have been boundary-related functions but further study is needed.

The public architecture is very suggestive of a hierarchy similar to the settlement-size hierarchy. However, Late Cruz public architecture is often lost, hidden by later construction, and small in scale. Our interpretation awaits more detailed investigation. The head towns had more mounds than other sites but even the most elaborate complexes fit within an area of 60 by 40 m. Public buildings were relatively open and accessible compared to some of the architectural complexes of later times. Loma Mina had mound groups at two different places. La Providencia, the head town of Tilantongo, had four mounds and a plaza. Tayata had two mounds. SAT 42, head town at Dzinicahua, had five scattered mounds. Within the core settlement clusters a second tier of places had mounds, often just a single mound (in many cases it is difficult to tell because of later construction). Teposcolula's second tier consisted of four sites, Dzinicahua's had three single-mound sites (and a possible boundary site with mounded architecture at ODA 10), and Tayata had four single-mound sites including one on the edge of the territory.

Subordinate settlement clusters most often did not have mounds. We found no Late Cruz mounds for the clusters in Yodocono, Nuñu, Lagunas, Nduayaco, Yucuxaco, Huamelulpan, Achiutla, and Magdalena Peñasco. The subordinate clusters with some public architecture are Jazmín, Nejapilla, Yodobada, and Yolomécatl. Excavations by Matadamas (1991–1992) at the Yucunama head village uncovered platforms and stone paving under the modern town that represent Late Cruz public architecture. A regional survey would not have recovered that information.

The original settlement clusters of head and satellite villages, the colonization of adjacent areas by smaller, less centralized clusters, and the two-tiered hierarchy in mounded architecture are consistent with an interpretation that the settlement clusters were political units and that they formed larger polities, the super-clusters. Note that the basal political unit is the settlement cluster, not the single settlement or village.

Our model has political authority over core and subordinate clusters derived from precedence, not conquest. Valley size may have been a factor. Super-cluster head towns were in the oldest settlement clusters; subordinate clusters were newer colonizations. An exception was Tilantongo, where the center shifted internally from SJD 7 in Middle Cruz to La Providencia in Late Cruz. Nevertheless, there is no evidence that complexity was achieved by amalgamating previously independent polities under a paramount chief.

We found no pattern of evidence for economic differentiation or specialization. There was little evidence in site locations or artifacts to indicate special production. Few lithic work areas can be attributed to this phase alone. Head towns and larger villages may have had greater variety in ceramic assemblages and some more costly pottery vessels but better samples are needed to test and specify this impression.

How long did these settlement systems endure and what was the timing of expansion and growth? First, Late Cruz settlement systems were a continuation and expansion of those of Early/Middle Cruz. Many sites have Middle and Late Cruz components. In Teposcolula, for example, all the Early Cruz sites continued into Middle Cruz and all the Middle Cruz sites had Late Cruz occupations. This degree of continuity did not hold everywhere. In upland border-zone Nduayaco, Middle Cruz sites were abandoned and different places were used in Late Cruz. Even if individual sites did not continue, settlement clusters did for not one was abandoned in Middle and Late Cruz.

The early and late halves of Late Cruz can be distinguished given sufficiently large sherd collections. The early half corresponds to the Rosario phase and the latter half to Monte Albán Early I in the Valley of Oaxaca. Our survey did not always have assemblages large enough to assign sites to early or late phases. Nevertheless, Rosario-equivalent components in Yodobada, Teposcolula, Tilantongo, Yolomécatl, Nduayaco, Achiutla, and Dzinicahua strongly indicate that the population and territorial expansion was underway in the early part of Late Cruz. The peak of growth and expansion occurred in Late Cruz.

Already in Late Cruz there were hints of changes to come in the succeeding Ramos period. In Tilantongo the Middle Cruz head village was at SJD 7. In Late Cruz the center moved to La Providencia, TIL 7. The earlier place was at 2,220 m asl; La Providencia was almost 100 m higher and was less approachable because of steep slopes. TIL 7 may have had Late Cruz residential terracing. Another Cruz village, TIL 3, looks even more like an Early Ramos site. It is on a conical hill overlooking the choke point on the eastern edge of Tilantongo. It has concentric rings of terraces and two mounds in an L arrangement on the summit. Fortified hill villages became the dominant settlement type in Early Ramos.

Settlement clusters similar to these have been documented elsewhere in highland Oaxaca in Middle Formative times. Plunket (1983:341–359) estimated the Late Cruz cluster of a head village and surrounding settlements at Yucuita to have had about 1,100 people. Spencer and Redmond (1997:301, 599–600) describe two Perdido phase clusters in the Cuicatlán Cañada. In the Valley of Oaxaca in the Rosario phase there were three clusters of roughly 1,000, 400, and 350 people according to regional survey estimates (Kowalewski et al. 1989:73).

However, events in the Valley of Oaxaca took a different course in Monte Albán Early I during the latter half of Late Cruz. The Valley of Oaxaca was also growing in scale but it had began to depart from the settlement cluster system when Monte Albán was founded in Early I. This entailed greater regional economic interdependency, specialization, hierarchical complexity, investment in governance and ideology, and centralization (Blanton et al. 1999).

A comparison of Valley of Oaxaca and its contemporary Mixteca Alta polities is instructive (Table 7.5). Polities in the Mixteca Alta and the Valley of Oaxaca were keeping pace with each other in population scale. Four Mixteca Alta simple settlement clusters were as populous as the valley-arm settlement clusters in the Valley of Oaxaca. Monte Albán was larger than any Mixteca Alta simple cluster. But the Tayata, Dzinicahua, and Teposcolula super-clusters each had about as many people as Monte Albán. If this were a competitive world, integration of larger numbers of people would have been advantageous. Larger-scale integration was the key structural way in which the Valley of Oaxaca differed from the Mixteca Alta between 500 BC and AD 200. The Valley of Oaxaca united its three clusters of settlement into a single state during Monte Albán I. In Table 7.5 note that a combined Valley of Oaxaca population of 15,000 eclipsed any Mixteca Alta super-cluster. The Mixteca Alta as a whole had more people but they were organized as multiple subregional systems, not as a centrally organized regional polity like the Valley of Oaxaca.

Late Cruz had a somewhat higher density of mound sites and about the same number of mounds per unit area as the Valley of Oaxaca in the Rosario phase (Kowalewski et al. 1989:76–77). By Early Monte Albán I in the latter part of Late Cruz, Valley of Oaxaca mound construction leaped ahead in number of mound sites and number of mounds per square kilometer (Kowalewski et al. 1989:104–107). Up until the founding of Monte Albán and the accompanying hierarchical growth in the Valley of Oaxaca, the Mixteca Alta was equal to the valley in public construction. A Mixteca Alta Late Cruz site with five to seven mounds would have been a top-ranking center, but in the Valley of Oaxaca in Early I it would have been only in the third-highest of four ranks. An important question that we cannot answer here is whether the disparity in mound-building indicates real difference between the two regions in the density of governance and ceremonial activity.

In sum, we have postulated settlement systems of a head town and satellite villages occupying a single valley, with occasional border sites, and larger units composed of these core settlement clusters plus smaller settlement clusters in surrounding smaller valleys. This was the pattern in site size and spacing. The same pattern was mirrored in the distribution of civic-ceremonial architecture. The structure of the Late Ramos, Las Flores, and Natividad polities in the Mixteca Alta was in some ways similar to those of Late Cruz, although the scale was vastly different.

CHAPTER EIGHT

The Emergence of Urbanism and the State

The first cities in the Mixteca Alta arose during Ramos, the Late and Terminal Formative. We think that the complex, hierarchical institution of the state was in place by the end of the period. The Middle Formative polities (Chapter 7) did not simply grow larger and become the ñuu of Classic times. The transition from the head-and-satellite-village polities to urbanism and the state was not smooth, for these were tumultuous times. The birth of the ñuu was a destructive and a creative process. There were three successive episodes: the abandonment of virtually all the earlier Formative settlements, the move to fortified hilltowns, and then the winnowing of these until only a few large aggregates were left. The survivors were the first cities and states of the Mixteca Alta.

EARLY RAMOS

At the largest perspective and at a quick glance, the Early Ramos settlement pattern

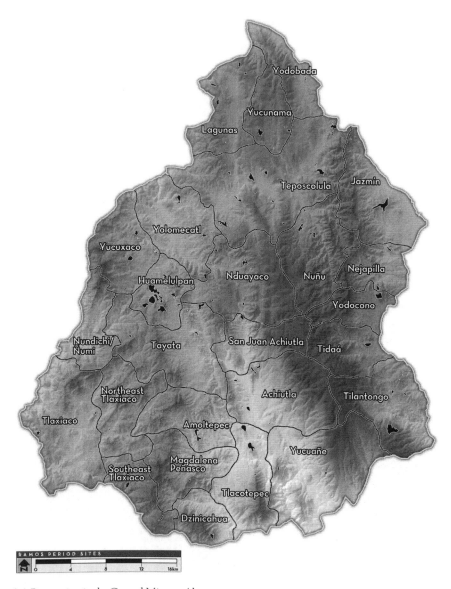

8.1 Ramos sites in the Central Mixteca Alta.

(Figure 8.1, Table 8.1) may not seem very different from that of Late Cruz. Most of the same subregions were occupied, the far western part of the study area had few sites, and some of the same subregions that had the most sites in Late Cruz continued to be important in Early Ramos. In Late Cruz the leading subregions in population were Dzinicahua, Tayata, Tilantongo, and Teposcolula. In Early Ramos the top subregions were Dzinicahua, Huamelulpan (Tayata's successor), Tilantongo, Teposcolula, and Jazmín.

Now that these few and unspecific continuities are mentioned we can get to the revolution. Early Ramos was the first major transformation in Mixteca Alta settlement systems since the transition to sedentary villages a millennium earlier.

The Early Ramos revolution occurred everywhere and at the local scale. There were several significant changes glossed over in our introductory statement about broad-scale continuities. Most subregions did continue and the most important tended to remain important. But Tayata, the largest Late Cruz cluster, almost completely disappeared in Early Ramos. The other pattern detectable even at a wide perspective is the general population growth. Early Ramos had more than twice the number of people as Late Cruz (21,500 to 48,100). The loss of Tayata and the population growth might be dismissed, the one as an historical quirk (it was not; it fit a pattern) and the other as an increase in quantity not organization (it was not; peoples' lives and the demographic regime fundamentally changed).

Almost all Late Cruz sites were abandoned. In all subregions but Teposcolula there was virtually no continuity between Late Cruz and Early Ramos locations. No new settlements were built in the low-elevation, valley-floor settings preferred during Cruz. For example, every one of the extensive Late Cruz villages in the Yosojica Valley and the flanks of the Cerro de la Peña Grande at Dzinicahua was abandoned and there was not a single new Early Ramos site—this in what had been one of the most densely occupied places in Oaxaca.

In Early Ramos, people built fortified hilltop villages and towns. These were on conical, steep-sided hills or knobs 100 m or more in elevation above the low hills favored in Late Cruz. Long ridges, plateaus, or remote mountain locations were not used. Conical hills, often volcanic in origin, were favored because their steep sides made access easier to control. The places chosen for these villages were not deep within the mountains but at the edge of valleys, perhaps within sight of peoples' cultivated fields. Often these places were locally strategic points overlooking routes in and out of valley pockets. Steep slopes were made more difficult for unfriendly access, at some sites by freestanding stone walls, ditches, and elaborate gates and everywhere by multiple high terrace walls interrupted by strategically placed ramps or stairs. People must have taken advantage of hillside springs and barranca heads for water.

About fifty to fifty-five Early Ramos sites are fortified hilltop villages or towns as just defined. There were other types of sites but they were small and demographically unimportant. The fortified, terraced hilltop village, which had less than a handful of precedents in Cruz, became the dominant settlement type. Most people—by far—lived in this kind of settlement.

Fortified hill villages were still valley oriented. They literally were valley facing in that the slopes chosen for most of a settlement's residential terraces faced the valley, not the mountains. People often had nearby access to the soils of the Yanhuitlán Formation. Less than 40 percent of the sites are on Yanhuitlán Formation soils; over half are on limestone or volcanic hills (Table 7.2). In most cases the distance from village to farmland was only a few hundred meters; in many sites lama-bordos originated within the residential area. Within settlements, clearing, construction, traffic, and use would have set loose the soil on side slopes. Extending the length of residential terrace retaining walls or building new ones to slow the process and catch the soil would have been easy to do. In this way lama-bordos and contour terraces for fields on lower slopes would be almost a natural outgrowth of hillside settlement. We mapped thirty-five lama-bordos directly adjacent to Ramos settlements, and of these, fifteen have only Ramos associations and no other period (Table 7.4). Most Early Ramos sites were near lama-bordos. It was in Early Ramos that this form of intensive agriculture expanded.

Fortified hilltop villages and towns represented a cooperative form of labor and organization at the community level for which we have no materialized precedent in the Mixteca Alta (Kowalewski, Feinman et al. 2006). The shift from valley floor settlements to hilltops was universal, complete, and in most places without transitional stages. It might have taken place in a just a few generations. The proper and timely initial clearing of pine and oak trees was no minor task. Because so much hillside was modified at each new site, the labor of residential terrace construction had to have been coordinated at a supra-household, probably community scale. Instead of growing accretionally, most of these new Ramos sites may have been designed and built mainly in one episode. Terraces were closely packed so changes at one spot would have affected slope stability above and below. Typically, Early Ramos sites have multiple levels of terraces and walls arranged in concentric rings like the layers of a wedding cake. Terraces were built to support multiple houses. Retaining walls could be 40 to 80 m long and 1 to 4 m high. Terraces were constructed mainly as fill operations. The sources of fill had to be coordinated. These sites have civic-ceremonial architecture on their summits that also required labor (including some very substantial platforms and platform-like terraces) but by far most of the work went into the residential terraces.

Ramos fortified hilltop settlements were more compact and densely occupied than Cruz sites. At well-preserved sites we could see and count house foundations. If we could not see individual houses, often we could measure terraces and estimate the number of houses per terrace. These house counts and estimates demonstrate that Ramos villages had house densities like those at Mesoamerican urban centers.

The Early Ramos revolution was broad in scale. It took place in every populated subregion. But local communities carried it out. Generally, subregional groups remained intact. For example, along the eastern side of the Sierra de Nochixtlán in each valley that had Late Cruz settlements, these were abandoned and hill villages established. All the valley groups continued, but with the new type of settlement. The same continuity is seen west of the Sierra de Nochixtlán where each subregion that had Late Cruz continued but people congregated into a few nucleated settlements. Even Teposcolula's two internal clusters continued from Late Cruz to Early Ramos, but not as valley floor settlements. Tayata lost population, but its people probably moved no farther than many others, just up the valley to Huamelulpan.

During the Early Ramos phase it appears that population grew overall. The Early Ramos estimates are higher than those of the preceding period. The militarization of the Mixteca Alta (to the extent that the fortified hilltop settlements tell us of warfare) did not halt population growth. Indeed, population seems to have more than doubled in the two centuries of Early Ramos. We conclude that the disruption and revolution were not sufficient to break long-standing subregional-scale social groups or their productive adaptations. That rupture would occur, but in Late Ramos.

The Late Cruz to Early Ramos transition could have been so rapid and uncertain that fortified hill villages could have been abandoned and others built nearby within a couple generations. In other words, not all these sites were exactly contemporary. On the basis of the ceramics from Nuñu sites we speculated that the earliest Ramos people continued to live for a time at the Late Cruz center (SVN 4), then abandoned that for the hill at SVN 10, and perhaps then expanded to SVN 13, adjacent to SVN 10 but farther back in the uplands. Even allowing for this non-contemporaneity of sites, Nuñu's population increased nevertheless.

Subregions varied in total population size from Teposcolula's 8,000 people to Magdalena Peñasco's 700; most had between 900 and 4,700 persons. Four subregions were undeveloped frontiers that had only small outposts: Yodobada, San Juan Achiutla, Tlaxiaco, and Tlaxiaco's northeastern periphery.

The subregions with the largest absolute population increases from Late Cruz to Early Ramos were those with large hilltop terraced sites—Teposcolula (which had six), Jazmín (Cerro Jazmín), and Huamelulpan (Cerro Volado and the immediately adjacent hilltops, nine in the subregion).

Some subregions had no sites other than fortified hill settlements. In subregions such as Tilantongo we recorded a handful of open sites that were all small and either doubtful in date or dated to the earliest Early Ramos. Other subregions definitely had small sites that were not fortified hill villages. Teposcolula and Huamelulpan had small sites probably protected by hilltowns nearby. In Nduayaco and Amoltepec, which are upland subregions, hamlets persisted.

We also identified border or boundary sites. These were small sites that had domestic debris and often a small mound or mound group. These sites were located on the edges of subregions or perhaps on the boundaries of larger regional polities. Nuñu, Yucunama, Tayata, Dzinicahua, Magdalena Peñasco, and Amoltepec had possible border sites, and other subregions may have had them too. We raised the hypothesis of long-term continuity of socially defined boundaries but there may be alternative explanations; modern municipio boundaries cannot be assumed to be ancient. Territorial and social group continuity is a significant topic for future investigation and it is made more problematic by the large-scale abandonments and disruptions in this sequence.

Nearly sixty sites had mounded architecture in apparent association with Ramos occupation. This was twice as many sites with public architecture as in Late Cruz. The mound arrangements generally exhibit open access but there is a trend to more restricted access at a few sites, notably Monte Negro, Huamelulpan, and TLA 15.

At many sites mounds and plazas have both Ramos and Las Flores ceramics represented. Although the preservation may be better than for Late Cruz public architecture, often it is not possible to distinguish Ramos and Las Flores construction layouts. A good case can be made for continuity in civic-ceremonial architectural arrangements from Cruz all the way into Las Flores.

Keeping in mind the problem of later construction, we propose a preliminary classification of civic-ceremonial sites to describe the range of variation. We have divided Early Ramos sites with mounds into four levels: (I) Monte Negro, which is unique; (II) eight sites with six to twelve or so mounds; (III) twenty-three sites with three to five mounds; and (IV) twenty-five sites with one or two mounds. Since there are issues of dating, preservation, and definition, these counts are only approximate.

Monte Negro (Caso 1938; Acosta and Romero 1992; Byland and Pohl 1994:54–55; Balkansky et al. 2004) was in a class by itself. As Byland and Pohl wrote, Monte Negro "is categorically different from any other Ramos phase site known anywhere in the Mixteca" (1994:54). No other known center in Oaxaca had architecture like Monte Negro's. The public architecture consisted of several strings of courtyards surrounded by elevated buildings along a long access way. The earlier excavations showed that some mounds were temples and others were houses. The buildings were numerous but not massive, as only one mound was as high as 3 m.

At all other sites civic-ceremonial architecture had simpler formal arrangements. The most basic arrangement was a single mound usually facing a plaza. Sometimes both mound and plaza were elevated on a common platform. A second mound was sometimes added either facing or in an L arrangement. Less frequent were groups of three or four mounds. The more elaborate arrangement was a linear string of platforms, plazas, and structures that rose to a highest mound, all on a narrow ridge crest. Linear strings had large areas or footprints, for example, 170 by 20 m, 150 by 40 m.

We identify eight Level II sites with notable architectural complexity: Cerro Jazmín (TIP 1), Fortín de San Juan (SJT 20), Yucuninde (SPP 55), SMX 3, YUC 16 and 20, probably Cerro Volado at Huamelulpan (SMH 1), and perhaps Topiltepec (TOP 1). What these sites had that others did not was more mounds and several architectural foci at different places on the site. Cerro Jazmín, for instance, had two mounds on the summit; a group on the hillside below with two plazas, each with structures in an L arrangement; and another four-mound group. Topiltepec and El Fortín had arrangements rather like the two-mound groups at Jazmín. These centers probably had more civic-ceremonial activities than the simpler and smaller sites.

Sites with three to five mounds (Level III) had compact mound groups or the linear string arrangement. Some had two separate architectural foci, for example, structures on different hilltops.

Level IV sites had one or two mounds in a single architectural focus and little investment of labor or space in public architecture. Their function must have been quite local. Some were border sites. Together the two simplest categories had forty-eight sites.

All the leading subregions in terms of population had Level I or II centers. But Teposcolula and Yucunama had five of the nine and two others were nearby. The lopsided distribution may mean some competitive civic-ceremonial investment in the Teposcolula-Yanhuitlán area. The largest centers in the smaller subregions were Level III or even Level IV.

Civic-ceremonial activities were not centralized; instead they were distributed in several places in the largest sites and in multiple places within subregions. Towns with large populations tended to have more mounds and plazas but these buildings were not concentrated in a single administrative focus. Not until Late Ramos was there architectural indication of segregated or specialized governing institutions much different from those commonly found in any of the large villages and towns.

At first glance the Valley of Oaxaca had more civic-ceremonial architecture in the Late Formative. Mixteca Alta mounds were smaller and there were almost half the number of mounds per unit area as in the Valley of Oaxaca. The Valley of Oaxaca had new monumental architecture representing the development of regional political and ceremonial institutions and a pan-regional hierarchy of four or five levels (Kowalewski et al. 1989:130–134).

However, monumental architecture in the Mixteca Alta had a different look from Cruz times through Natividad. Instead of pyramidal mounds, the largest public constructions were platforms or terraces. These were flat spaces created by filling in behind retaining walls, typically on the crest or sides of a ridge. Such platforms were three-sided terraces on sloping ground rather than four-sided mounds rising from a level surface. In some respects the long, tall, massive terrace walls that ringed and protected hilltop towns and villages were monumental public architecture too. Mixteca Alta hillforts were a strong development of community-scale collectivity.

The part of the Mixteca Alta we surveyed had some 48,000 people in Early Ramos. At the same time, due to its demographic surge in this period, the Valley of Oaxaca had 51,000. In other words, our part of the Mixteca Alta had a greater population than the Valley of Oaxaca in Late Cruz but in Early Ramos it was no longer leading. Also as the Valley of Oaxaca became increasingly integrated as a regional system, the Mixteca Alta was not so integrated. The largest territorial and demographic block in our study area was greater Teposcolula, consisting of the valley and its immediate neighbors, a total of 15,000 people. Monte Albán and its immediate hinterland, a comparable unit, had 23,000. Huamelulpan and the portions of Jazmín and Tilantongo we surveyed had only 4,000 to 6,000 people each. In a competitive environment these scale differences would have been important. Indeed, many Central Mixteca Alta subregions were abandoned by the end of Early Ramos. The Monte Albán state's greater integration changed the balance of macroregional relations. The balance was restored in Late Ramos when the Mixteca Alta reorganized.

LATE RAMOS

Most subregions in the Central Mixteca Alta were abandoned in Late Ramos. The only places with significant Late Ramos were around Huamelulpan and Dzinicahua.

In Huamelulpan and Dzinicahua the Late Ramos is strong and archaeologically unmistakable. Overall, the population of the Central Mixteca Alta fell by almost half. The western edge of the Nochixtlán Valley was abandoned from Monte Negro to Cerro Jazmín. This does not mean that the Nochixtlán Valley was abandoned, for there was a major buildup of population around Yucuita in northern Nochixtlán (Spores 1972; Plunket 1983). All of greater Teposcolula appears to have been vacant. Teposcolula had extensive Early Ramos occupation. It is possible that some Late Ramos in large Early Ramos sites went undetected because it was swamped by the earlier material, but such occupations, if they existed, must have been small and light.

Huamelulpan grew to its maximum extent in Late Ramos. Its greater hinterland included Tayata and Yucuxaco for a combined total of 20,300 people, the largest integrated polity in our study area to date. The Yucuita area had (conservatively) 5,900 (Plunket 1983:341) and Dzinicahua had about 3,000. Sandage is a similar site 18 km north of Yucuita in the Coixtlahuaca Valley.

Huamelulpan's Cerro Volado and the adjacent mountaintops formed a center of urban scale and complexity. It had several separate precincts with plazas, monumental platforms, and mounds. It had a ball court and a display of carved stone monuments. It must have been the economic as well as the political capital of the Mixteca Alta. The Huamelulpan polity was centralized. The Cerro Volado site had most of the civic-ceremonial architecture and there was some in the city's subdivisions, but outlying settlements had little. Only one other site, SZT 1, had notable buildings: a small set of courtyards that of all Ramos architecture most resembles that at Monte Negro.

The Huamelulpan polity was compact. It covered a linear distance of just 14 km. The Tayata subregion just south of Huamelulpan had little settlement. On the mountain ridges to the east and west were border sites, including SZT 1 and UVH 2, which had public architecture and resident populations.

A string of four Late Ramos fortified hilltop villages was located along the northsouth corridor between Nduayaco and Tlacotepec. These replaced Early Ramos sites, which may have traced their roots to local groups. The Late Ramos sites had a more regional, strategic orientation. Their affiliation is uncertain. The northern three were closest to Huamelulpan; the southern, to Dzinicahua.

In sum, Late Ramos was a time of abandonment and consolidation, but on a regional not just a local scale. Whole subregions, including places that had been leading centers, were abandoned. The places that continued—Huamelulpan, Yucuita, and Dzinicahua—grew in population and organizational complexity.

This regional abandonment, consolidation, and centralization were part of a larger macroregional process in Oaxaca and beyond. After centuries of increasing population scale this was a time of demographic stasis in the Valley of Oaxaca and the Central Mixteca Alta. The Terminal Formative was a demographic pause, but during this pause there was reorganization, urbanization, and state formation. Huamelulpan—large in population, urban, compact, and centralized—was the Central Mixteca Alta's organizational response and its entry into the macroregional arena.

CHAPTER NINE

The Classic Ñuu

After the time of regional abandonment, consolidation, and organizational development, Las Flores was the time of the "break out," the re-population of the abandoned areas, expansion into new places, and demographic growth (Figure 9.1, Table 9.1). The expansion took place with the organizational framework developed in Late Ramos. Compared to Late Cruz and Early Ramos, Las Flores society was more urban, more complex and differentiated, and more integrated. And it was not as compact and centralized as Huamelulpan had been in Late Ramos.

We mapped 341 Las Flores sites, a total occupied area of 3,468 ha. By comparison, the Valley of Oaxaca surveys found 1,077 Monte Albán IIIA sites with a total occupied area of 3,994 ha (Kowalewski et al. 1989:755, 757). The site area totals are more similar than the numbers of sites because the average site size was larger in the Mixteca Alta. The two areas had about the same number of large sites but the Valley of Oaxaca had many more small sites (90 percent of its IIIA sites were less than 6 ha).

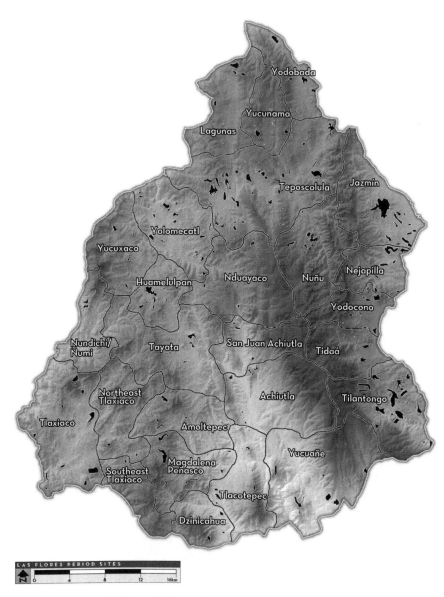

9.1 *Las Flores sites in the Central Mixteca Alta.*

As in Ramos, people in Las Flores were not distributed ideally on the best agricultural land. A little less than half the sites were on the sedimentary formations that have the best soils, down from almost 80 percent in Late Cruz (Table 7.2). Many people lived in defensible towns at high elevations—in some cases even higher than in Ramos. Their adjustment in part was to use lama-bordos. We found sixty-one lama-bordos directly adjacent to Las Flores sites (Table 7.4). Exchange with people in settlements at lower elevations was probably another response.

The estimated population for our whole study area was a low of 88,800 and a high of 167,200, the midpoint being 128,000. This was more than double the Early Ramos population and five times the Late Ramos. This growth started in Transición and culminated at the end of the Early Classic, a duration of perhaps three centuries.

A comparison of population figures with the Valley of Oaxaca provides perspective. The average estimate for the whole Valley of Oaxaca was 115,000. In the Central Mixteca Alta there were proportionally fewer sites and somewhat less occupied area. But the Central Mixteca Alta had a higher population because it had fewer small sites with low or moderate densities and more large ones with high densities. The Valley of Oaxaca had more rancherías and the two areas had about the same numbers (but different proportions) of hilltop terraced sites.

In our study area the Early Classic population was more evenly dispersed over the land than it had been at any prior time. Every subregion had substantial occupation. The subregions that were the least settled, the southeastern Tlaxiaco periphery and San Juan Achiutla, still had over 400 people each. Places west of the Huamelulpan/Llano Grande divide that had never before been densely settled had large Las Flores populations. For example, Tlaxiaco, which had never had more than 400 people, had over 11,000. Population was more evenly distributed than before on the regional scale, but within subregions there was uneven clustering.

This part of the Mixteca Alta had a lower Early Classic site density than the Valley of Oaxaca. On average in the Valley of Oaxaca there was a site every 2.0 km²; in our study area there was one site every 4.8 km². In the Mixteca Alta, sites tended to clump, creating dense clusters of settlement but leaving uninhabited areas between clumps. The Valley of Oaxaca distribution, somewhat agglutinated as one would expect in an urban system, still had a more even distribution of sites than the Mixteca Alta. The difference is due to two factors: the valley and mountain range topography of the Mixteca and the clustering within Mixteca Alta subregions.

The subregions with the most settlement were Jazmín (almost all at one site, Cerro Jazmín), Teposcolula, Tilantongo, and Tlaxiaco. No one of these dominated in size. Dzinicahua and Huamelulpan, important in Late Ramos, retained large populations too. Several small subregions were densely settled, including Nejapilla on the eastern flank of the Sierra Nochixtlán and Nuñu and Yolomécatl, dependencies of Teposcolula. Yucunama, usually not in the mainstream, had some 6,200 inhabitants.

The uneven clustering mentioned above left some places underused that had had important settlements earlier. These were Achiutla and Yucuxaco on the fringes of the Huamelulpan Late Ramos polity and the southeastern periphery of Tlaxiaco.

Larger demographic-economic groupings may correspond to the sixteenth-century yuhuitaiyu. A greater Teposcolula consisted of the core valley plus Yolomécatl, Nduayaco, Nuñu, part of Yodobada, and Yucunama, a total of roughly 33,000 people (using the midpoints of the estimate ranges). Jazmín's sphere undoubtedly extended over at least the Yanhuitlán Valley, for which we do not have estimates, but aggregating to it only Nejapilla and Yodocono would result in 28,000 people. Tilantongo is likewise truncated to the east but with its Tidaá neighbor it had 13,000 and Byland and Pohl's survey (1994) found more Las Flores in neighboring Jaltepec. In the inner basin, Dzinicahua might have been allied with Amoltepec, Magdalena Peñasco, and Tlacotepec for 14,000 people. Tlaxiaco headed another aggregation. Yucuañe's affiliation is uncertain; if it was in the Dzinicahua sphere, the total would rise to 20,000, not counting people outside our survey area. Blocks of this territorial and demographic scale were roughly comparable to or only a bit smaller than similar ones in the Valley of Oaxaca: Etla–Central–Monte Albán 26,000, Valle Grande–Ocotlán 48,000, and Tlacolula 41,000.

We now turn to a closer look at settlement systems at the subregional scale. In general, Las Flores settlement and civic-ceremonial hierarchies were more differentiated and complex than in Cruz or Early Ramos. Of the twenty-six subregions fifteen had site-size hierarchies in which one leading place was at least twice the size of the next largest settlement. This includes Tilantongo, where the two top archaeological sites, TIL 5 and TIL 24, practically ran into each other and could be combined. One major town with villages was the most frequent form of settlement hierarchy.

The exceptions to the pattern of major town with villages and hamlets are informative. Teposcolula had eastern and western site clusters, with Yucuninde (SPP 55) primate in the east and the cluster of sites around SMX 3 dominating the west. Yucuxaco and Tayata were still subordinate to their Late Ramos primate center of Huamelulpan. Nduayaco was in the same subordinate position vis-à-vis Teposcolula, and San Juan Achiutla was a small border community. The rest of the exceptions are in the southwestern part of the study area. Amoltepec, Magdalena Peñasco, and Tlacotepec each had two top places. So did Tlaxiaco and Yucuañe.

In general, the economically and demographically more developed areas had larger cities and towns and tended to have primate subregional organization (counting Teposcolula in this category). Lesser developed, subordinate, or marginal areas tended not to be as centralized in settlement hierarchy.

The size of the leading population centers ranged from Cerro Jazmin's 17,000 people to about 1,200 people, but most had several thousand. Middle-ranking places were well represented. Hamlets and isolated residences were underrepresented except in Teposcolula (and Tejupan; Byland 1980).

The scale of mounded architecture was greater than in Ramos, but most of the formal characteristics of mound and plaza arrangements had been developed earlier, at least by Ramos times. Las Flores does not show a distinct break in the style of civic-ceremonial architecture.

On the whole, Las Flores mounds were taller than their Ramos counterparts (more than a few were begun in Ramos). Platforms, the level fill-foundations for other mounds or plazas, reached rather massive proportions: for example, 68 by 44 by 5 m, 75 by 20 by 1.5 m, and 60 by 60 by 2 m (many on mountaintops where finding and hauling fill is by no means easy). The areal extent of public architectural complexes was larger, as several of the top-ranked centers equaled Monte Negro in size of civic-ceremonial area (for example, 230 to 270 m long by 30 to 60 m wide).

Most mound sites, complex or simple, were located on high promontories overlooking the drainage heads that feed lama-bordos and pockets of valley-piedmont agricultural land. Valley floors were eschewed as locations for civic-ceremonial centers.

We are impressed by how widely distributed civic-ceremonial architecture was within subregions. A third (116) of our sites had mounded architecture. The distribution was such that virtually no habitation site was more than 3 km from a place with at least one mound, and most either had their own or were within 2 km of a mound center.

Teposcolula, Tlaxiaco, Huamelulpan, Yucuañe, Yolomécatl, and Magdalena Peñasco were the subregions with the most mounds. Those with relatively few mounds and mound sites were the less developed subregions of the time: Achiutla, Tayata, Nduayaco, and the northeastern periphery of Tlaxiaco.

In ten subregions the site with the greatest number of mounds was also the largest in population. This included the leading centers of Cerro Jazmín, both clusters in Teposcolula, Huamelulpan, and Dzinicahua. In ten other subregions, however, the site with the most mounds was not the most populous. Yodocono, Yucuañe, and Magdalena Peñasco had ambitious and spectacular linear arrangements of mounds, plazas, and platforms on mountain crests but their largest settlements were elsewhere. In six subregions two or more sites had an equal number of mounds, and probably more subregions should be considered as not having one dominant civic-ceremonial center. These systems with no outstanding center include many of Teposcolula's satellites. Tilantongo and Tlaxiaco, although they each had quite a few sites with mounds, did not have single dominant places that we can discern from the public architecture.

We describe four levels of civic-ceremonial centers based on their architectural scale and complexity. These groupings are preliminary because without excavations all we have to go on are the numbers, sizes, and arrangements of the substructure platforms, not the structures themselves.

Level I. The top-ranked centers had nine or more mounds, some at least 3 m high, and at least two plazas. Cerro Jazmín had a linear arrangement of buildings on mounds reached by a monumental stairway, two plazas flanked by two mounds in an L shape, and a three-mound group. Huamelulpan, Dzinicahua, Yucuninde (SPP 55), and SMX 3 also had multiple groups of mounds, implying functionally (or factionally) distinct areas. In terms of numbers of mounds, SMP 14 and YPD 1, high on mountain crests, would have been in the same class but they have all their public architecture in a single linear string and were small settlements.

Level II. The second class of centers consists of sites having from four to seven mounds either arranged in linear strings of mounds, platforms, and plazas or consisting of a three- or four-mound group plus adjacent platforms, plazas, or other mounds. In places such as Yucunama, Nuñu, Nejapilla, Tidaá, Yucuañe, Tlacotepec, and Achiutla, sites of this order are the likely subregional centers or co-centers. Others in this class are satellite sites only 4 to 5 km from major regional centers; for example, SPN 34, SMO 3, TLO 3, SJT 20, TEC 4, and CAT 7.

Levels III and IV. A third class consists of the numerous sites with two or three mounds. A fourth comprises the single-mound sites. Single mounds typically had plazas. Two or three mounds allow more functions and can define additional plaza spaces. Levels III and IV sites are widespread and would have been of subregional or local importance. Their proliferation suggests the importance of local community and barrio functions in every valley.

Compared to prior periods there were more sites with closed-access public-building complexes, although as always most were fairly open. Major capitals had closed private spaces, such as the summit of Cerro Jazmín. But it is interesting that some smaller subregional polities, including Yodocono, Nuñu, Tlacotepec, and Ñumi/Nundichi, also had closed-access civic-ceremonial architecture.

In terms of the density of mounds and mound centers per unit area, the Central Mixteca Alta and the Valley of Oaxaca were about equal in the Early Classic (Kowalewski et al. 1989:236 240). The Valley of Oaxaca continued to have more hierarchical distinction, both in vertical and horizontal complexity, and it had Monte Albán, Oaxaca's most monumental center. The Valley of Oaxaca centers exhibited more vertical spread and more variety in architectural forms than their counterparts in the Mixteca Alta. Another aspect of collective activity in the Mixteca Alta was the construction of hilltop fortified towns. But in this too, the Valley of Oaxaca was carrying out a construction spree in the Early Classic, when many hilltop terraced sites were built or expanded.

We conclude from the distribution of mounds and plazas that activities related to them were widely dispersed and not centralized. Variation in location, arrangements, scale, and number of mounds and plazas indicates vertical or hierarchical differentiation and complexity. Sites with mounds were hierarchically ordered in three (or four) levels corresponding to regional, subregional, and local spheres.

Boundary maintenance was a concern. Many people lived high on hilltops in compact settlements with massive retaining walls. Defensible hillforts were practically everywhere. We recorded seventeen sites with fortification walls, ditches, or other features. These are clustered on the border between Teposcolula and Tamazulapan, in the Lagunas subregion, on Nuñu's outer edge, surrounding Yodocono (which borders Nuñu), around the edges of the Tlaxiaco Valley, and on the mountain crags of the inner basin from the Peñascos to Yucuañe. We occasionally found small border sites at the edges of subregions, as in Ramos; for example, the small sites in the uplands above western Teposcolula.

Several other arrays and distributions of sites suggest boundary maintenance. One is the chain of residential sites on the divide between Tlaxiaco and Magdalena Peñasco/Amoltepec. Another suggestive pattern is that of the three large nucleated sites in Jazmín and northeastern Teposcolula, where there are virtually no small or open sites in between.

Taken together the boundary evidence suggests the threat of hostilities, but not involving every subregion equally. Friction seems likely in the south involving Tlaxiaco, Dzinicahua, and Yucuañe. In the north, greater Teposcolula was running up against Jazmín and perhaps Tamazulapan.

Internally, Las Flores subregions were more integrated than in previous periods, meaning that there was more interdependence among settlements having different roles. In many subregions, sites were spread across a wide range of elevations and ecological situations. Settlements varied in size, density, and civic-ceremonial importance. To illustrate we review two places, the western half of the Teposcolula Valley and Yodocono on the western flank of the Nochixtlán Valley.

The western Teposcolula cluster involved fifteen sites, all within a 3 km radius centered on the valley floor. It had perhaps 5,000 people. Settlements were at all elevations, from 2,500 m to the valley floor at 2,150 m, including mountain ridges, hilltops, and low piedmont spurs. Suitable farming practices included canal irrigation on the valley floor, floodwater farming on the alluvium, lama-bordo terracing in the barrancas, contour terracing on hill flanks, and dry farming on ridgetops. Many of the hamlets and villages were low-density settlements. Others, like the upper parts of SMX 3, CAT 7, and TEC 4, were more densely packed hilltop towns. GTX 14 and 15 and CAT 5 were small sites on the mountain ridges separating Teposcolula from its neighbors Yucunama and Nduayaco. SMX 3 was the civic-ceremonial center and TEC 4 and CAT 7 were secondary civic-ceremonial places. CAT 5 and GTX 15 had single mounds.

Yodocono was a compact local system of about 3,400 people in eleven settlements, all centered within 2 km of the valley floor. The largest place was a fairly densely packed town on a hill overlooking the valley floor. The other sites were small villages and hamlets. Most settlement was at about 2,400 m in elevation, the point where flowing water could be controlled and a prime place for lama-bordos. There were sites on low hills in the valley and sites on the narrow tops of steep ridges descending from the mountains. One site, YPD 3, looked to us like a *llano de plaza*, a marketplace (boundary market, trail market) like those described by Pohl and colleagues (1996) and Stiver (1997). It is a broad, flat space in otherwise steep terrain, near major north-south and east-west trails. Yodocono's most spectacular site was YPD 1, its major civic-ceremonial center on the crest of a mountain overlooking the whole valley. At 2,820 m, it was the highest site. There were also smaller civic-ceremonial facilities at three sites on the northern and southern edges of the pocket.

Compared to Cruz or Early Ramos subregional systems, Las Flores systems, like western Teposcolula and Yodocono, had a greater variety of site types in a greater variety of environmental settings. Cruz villages were mostly at low elevations and contained less material evidence of administration and hierarchy. Early Ramos sites were most often fortified hill villages, alike except for their size and without much evidence of mutual interdependence. Many Las Flores subregions were like western

Teposcolula and Yodocono—systems with differentiated components, hierarchically organized, and interdependent. Late Ramos was the transition, the time when these organizational features were put in practice in Huamelulpan and Yucuita. Lithic artifacts can provide evidence of economic production and exchange, but unfortunately many Las Flores sites also have other components, making it difficult to assign non-ceramic artifacts to this period alone. Excavations of residences could test for varying economic functions at different sites.

The integrated, hierarchically organized systems at the subregional scale were the building blocks of the state. Based on civic-ceremonial architecture, we see two types of fundamental polities. One had a prominent leading center, subordinate barrios, and border sites or shrines. Examples include Achiutla, Yucuañe, Tlacotepec, Tidaá, Tilantongo, and Yodocono. The other type of subregion had no one outstanding center, but instead multiple barrios and border sites. Tlaxiaco and Yolomécatl are examples.

Not every subregion was its own state. Some were subject to and dependent on others. States in the Classic period in the Mixteca Alta consisted of core subregions and their allies and dependencies. In our study area these were Teposcolula, Jazmín/Yanhuitlán, Huamelulpan, probably Tilantongo, and perhaps a Dzinicahua alliance. These were the core subregions and the seats of yuhuitaiyu. These states had civic-ceremonial centers with complex and relatively large-scale public architecture. They had secondary centers in the home territory and in dependent subregions, and they also had elementary civic-ceremonial places (Levels III and IV) at the local level.

In terms of settlement-size hierarchy, Las Flores had the depth and vertical complexity expected of states. They also had demographic clout. Cerro Jazmín had about 17,000 inhabitants; the other leading political centers had 2,000 to 5,000 but their immediate hinterland settlements contributed more people. Smaller towns, large and small villages, and hamlets completed the settlement hierarchy.

Heredia (2005) carried out a study of wealth stratification at four Las Flores sites initially mapped by the 1999 survey: Cerro de la Cantera (TOP 1) in Nejapilla, Cerro Yucuayuxi (SPT 3) in Tidaá, Cerro Encantado (TLA 1) in Tlaxiaco, and El Vergel (TLA 36) in Tlaxiaco. She chose these sites because they were not the major regional capitals but were secondary centers more reflective of the internal social order. She made 614 controlled surface collections drawn randomly within 50 m grid cells that extend over the whole area of each site. Compared to other Mesoamerican sites sampled in similar ways these towns had plain, common, and not very costly artifacts. Exotic, luxury, and even ritual items were almost entirely absent. There were some differences between sites in the frequencies of bowls, jars, and comals, which might mean that the sites were different from one another in the mix of activities or functions. Another interesting difference is that the two Nochixtlán Valley sites (Cantera and Yucuayuxi) had a wider spread in the costliness of their pottery assemblages (indicated by larger standard deviations in pottery-production-step measures); the two Tlaxiaco centers showed much less internal differentiation.

Heredia's findings show the variation in wealth stratification within and between the ñuu of Classic times. Perhaps the Tlaxiaco towns were less stratified because they were in a political-economic periphery, whereas Cantera and Yucuayuxi were part of core-zone production and exchange. The overall pattern of plainness and sameness suggests collectivism at this level of secondary centers.

The Classic state in the Mixteca Alta was not territorially extensive. Teposcolula with its dependent subregions measured about 22 km across, for example. Total populations were from 15,000 to over 30,000 people. These were not vast regional states of Teotihuacan proportions. "City-state" might be a cross-culturally comparable term. But if the concept of city-state is used, one should note that these polities were territorially based in local agricultural production (they were not trading entrepôts) and hinterland settlements away from the leading center were important components.

Mixteca Alta states did not develop large bureaucracies requiring major administrative architecture or technology. Although there was variation among them, generally they were not strongly centralized. On the time scales shorter than the centuries we can now measure, competition, alliance building, and changes in rulership could have caused seats of power to move from one primary or secondary center to another. Thus, the size of states at any one moment might not be reflected in longer-term accumulations of settlements and mounded architecture.

We suggest that relatively small, not especially centralized states were the rule rather than the exception across highland Oaxaca and probably in many other places in Mesoamerica during the Early Classic (Kowalewski et al. 2004). To the extent that Monte Albán integrated the Valley of Oaxaca, it was the largest of highland Oaxaca states at that time. Partly because of its legacy of monumental architecture and carved stone monuments and the new works erected in the Early Classic, Monte Albán is thought to have maintained regional leadership. No one has found another site in Oaxaca that comes close to matching Monte Albán's grand architecture. Yet Monte Albán and its immediate hinterland were no greater in population size than Cerro Jazmín or two other contemporary centers in the Valley of Oaxaca, Jalieza and Dainzu-Macuilxochitl-Tlacochahuaya. Instead of large, centralized regional states with primate-center capitals we see a landscape of jostling small states, often allied in blocks, but not building a permanent, centralized administrative structure. Monte Albán may have had a special macroregional role.

In our survey area the Las Flores florescence lasted perhaps 400 years, beginning about AD 200 and probably ending by AD 600. This was a two-step process. The re-population of areas vacant in the Terminal Formative began in Transición Late Ramos–Las Flores, ca. AD 200–300. Transición ceramics occurred in almost every subregion in the study area. Typically, the large centers, especially the hilltop towns, had the earliest pottery. For example, TLA 1 in Tlaxiaco, the Yucuañe hilltop sites, many of the Teposcolula centers, the Yodocono civic-ceremonial center YPD 1, SVN 10 in Nuñu, and the mountaintop SAT 21 in Tlacotepec all had Transición occupations. Full Early Las Flores saw the further spread and maximum expansion of settlement in all subregions.

This survey found little Late Las Flores. Yucuita and Yucuñudahui in the Nochixtlán Valley are known to have had Late Las Flores occupations (Spores

1972; Plunket 1983). Some sites in the western Nochixtlán Valley also had Late Las Flores, including YPD 5 and 15 and places in Nejapilla. SIL 1 in Lagunas and several collections from Yodobada sites in the north also appear to date to Late Las Flores. At Cerro Jazmín, Tilantongo, and Teposcolula, we found just a few sherds among the masses of Early Las Flores that could date to the Late half but we never were able to identify whole assemblages. Elsewhere, west of the Sierra de Nochixtlán we identified no Late Las Flores sites or assemblages; we have no collections that bridge the ceramic gap between the orange wares and shapes of Early Classic times and the characteristic cream wares and distinctive shapes of the Postclassic. There are no new ceramic complexes like that originating in Epiclassic Xochicalco.

We conclude that the area west of the Sierra de Nochixtlán was largely abandoned during the Late Classic and Epiclassic. How long this lasted is uncertain because the beginning date for the Postclassic is uncertain. The abandonment would be similar to that which occurred in Late Ramos except that in Late Ramos several major centers flourished in our study area. In Late Las Flores none flourished but there were centers just to the east in the Nochixtlán Valley. Late Las Flores appears to have been another reorganizational spasm in Mixteca Alta cultural evolution.

CHAPTER TEN

The Postclassic Ñuu

In the Late Postclassic the Mixteca Alta was one of Mesoamerica's largest, wealthiest economies. Settlement and population increased to levels not seen before or since. The patterns of hierarchy and integration reconstructed from the archaeological data are similar to the cacicazgos described in the sixteenth century.

This study mapped 843 Natividad archaeological sites (Figure 10.1, Table 10.1). In many subregions almost every archaeological site ever inhabited has a Natividad component. The number of sites is more than twice that of Las Flores. The large proportion of Postclassic sites is characteristic of other areas in Mesoamerica.

The total occupied area was 10,260 ha, or 103 km²—almost three times that of Las Flores. The Valley of Oaxaca in Monte Albán V had 7,880 ha of occupied area. Our Mixteca Alta figure is especially remarkable when one realizes that the Valley of Oaxaca survey area is larger and our study area is made effectively smaller because of the uninhabited Sierra de Nochixtlán. In our survey area, where settlement occurred

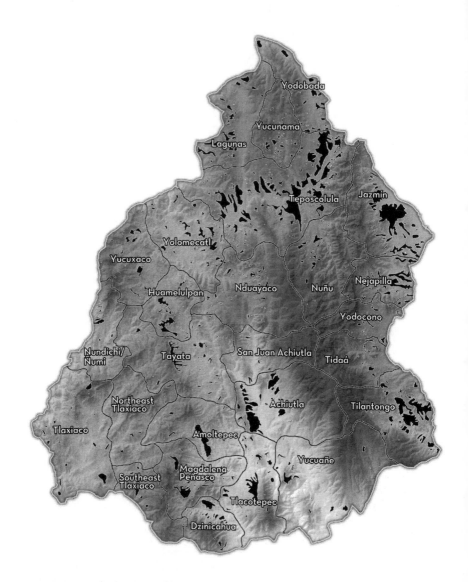

10.1 *Natividad sites in the Central Mixteca Alta.*

it was thick. Postclassic sites sprawled out continuously to cover much of the land in each valley pocket.

Two objections might be raised, one facile and the other more problematic. First, could we have mapped erosional spread instead of real habitation areas? The answer is plainly no. Survey crews drew site boundaries based on evidence for habitation, not on sherd occurrences. There may be a few instances of inflation by misjudgment of this sort but there are many more cases in which our boundaries probably underestimate site size because whole chunks of landforms have eroded away.

The second objection to such a large total site area is more serious. Natividad is an embarrassingly long period, running from perhaps the AD 800s to the 1500s. The ceramic chronology still does not allow routine field and lab assignment even to Early and Late with surface assemblages of commonly occurring wares. Our Natividad sites may conflate distinct occupations that may be centuries removed from each other. To some extent this is true and it should be kept in mind. Below we describe trends within the period on the basis of our present evidence. For purposes of comparison we point out that other places in highland Oaxaca are in the same chronological b(l)oat. Monte Albán V is equivalent in duration. As seems to be the case in the Valley of Oaxaca, we think that most of the Natividad remains fall into the Late Postclassic, perhaps after AD 1200–1300.

Our population estimates are derived from the occupied area and assessments of intrasite density. Natividad sites vary from dispersed rancherías (5 to 10 people per ha) to the great majority at 10 to 25 people per ha to those sixty sites at which all or part of the settlement had residential terraces and the density was 50 to 100 people per ha. When the usual calculations are done, the estimates for the whole study area are a low of 153,000 and a high of 303,000. The midpoint is 228,000. Because Natividad is a long period one might use the lower figure; for comparisons with areas where similar estimating procedures were used we take the midpoint.

The Valley of Oaxaca's midpoint estimate for Monte Albán V is 163,000 people. What components of the estimate make the population of the Central Mixteca Alta more dense than that of the Valley of Oaxaca? The total occupied area was one. There was 30 percent more habitation area in the Central Mixteca Alta than in the Valley of Oaxaca. The other major difference was that in the Mixteca Alta people continued to live in dense, residentially terraced hilltowns. We list sixty sites as having all or part of the settlement in residential terraces. In the Valley of Oaxaca at most hilltop terraced sites used in Monte Albán V the occupation was a dispersed reuse of a Classic or earlier site. In the Mixteca Alta there are some cases of dispersed reuse of terraced sites but many more instances of new Postclassic construction of terraced sites and also many cases in which reoccupation of older sites was intensive, often involving more area than the earlier settlement. Sites that had some proportion of their area given over to residential terraces account for 113,000 people—more than half the total population. These sites include some of the most important centers, including the cacicazgo capitals of Tilantongo, Cerro Jazmín, Teposcolula, Achiutla, and Tlaxiaco. Hilltop terraced towns and cities were a major component of Postclassic settlement systems in the Mixteca Alta.

Compared to other highland Mesoamerican regions the Mixteca Alta has an unusual proclivity for settlements to be found on particular soil types, an association not noted before in places such as the Basin of Mexico or the Valley of Oaxaca. People in the Mixteca Alta generally but not at all times favored soils of the Yanhuitlán Formation, which are easily worked, fertile because of their non-acidic chemistry, and highly erodible and mobile. Table 10.2 summarizes the links among agriculturally favorable soils, population, and urbanism (the key soil types are defined conservatively in this table). We use the proportion of the subregions' populations living in sites with more than 1,000 inhabitants as an urbanization index (population size alone does not define a city, of course). The population size of valleys was often related to the amount of fertile soil, especially at the onset of the farming way of life in the Early Formative and in the Postclassic. The association weakened in the middle of the sequence when many people were living on fortified mountaintops. In the Classic a subregion's degree of urban concentration was not associated with how much fertile land it had, perhaps again for reasons of warfare. But in the Postclassic, urbanization was strongly tied to the best agricultural land.

In Natividad over half the sites are on the sedimentary formations of the Tertiary (Table 7.2). Generally, the larger the patch of Yanhuitlán Formation soils the larger the population. All patches had Natividad settlement. Jazmín had the largest population and it was next to the largest single expanse of these soils—the Yanhuitlán Valley. Teposcolula had the next largest population, and although its Yanhuitlán Formation materials are all in the eastern valley, it had excellent canal irrigation potential on the Quaternary alluvial deposits of the western valley floor.

Tlaxiaco has small patches of Yanhuitlán Formation soils and a little Quaternary alluvium. Its Natividad population of 8,000 was likewise relatively modest. The demographic heart of the greater Tlaxiaco area was east across the divide, in the long stretch of Yanhuitlán Formation soils from Dzinicahua to Amoltepec and Huamelulpan. This speaks to Tlaxiaco's scale of economic integration.

Natividad farmers made intensive use of the land. There are close associations between Natividad settlements and lama-bordos. We counted 151 lama-bordo chains directly adjacent to sites with Natividad occupations; of these, 90 lama-bordos are in places that have only Natividad and no other period (Table 7.4). Natividad residential terrace retaining walls are often continuous with lama-bordo retaining walls. Ancient hillside contour terraces made for agriculture often have not lasted because of neglect, erosion, reuse of stone, and constant modification in historic times. Yet in the northern Teposcolula Valley many remnants of ancient contour terraces are still visible. The close association between ancient settlement and recent agricultural terracing on hillsides strongly suggests that Natividad people did the same thing.

Our settlement pattern maps display sites heavily clustered or lined up in parallel, often favoring one side of a valley or mountain range rather than the other. This patterning has to do with the distribution of Yanhuitlán Formation soils and probably with the availability of water in springs and arroyos. One especially favored setting for agricultural settlements in Natividad and at other times when people could live in close proximity to their fields was on hills of the Yanhuitlán Formation on divides where multiple springs and arroyos headed. Yucuxaco, Huamelulpan, Tayata, Tlacotepec, Magdalena Peñasco, and other places had important settlements on low divides. Another favored setting was higher, at the upper reaches of the Yanhuitlán Formation, especially on the side of a valley that had the most reliable watershed. Yodobada, all the small valleys on the western side of the Nochixtlán Valley, Lagunas, Huamelulpan, Achiutla, and Dzinicahua had extensive settlements in this situation.

Yanhuitlán Formation soils, Natividad agricultural terracing, and Natividad settlement were all closely associated and related to another physical fact: severe, extensive, often amazing erosion. This relationship has been observed by all students of the Mixteca Alta. Our results confirm it for areas of the Mixteca Alta not seen by earlier scholars and we also tie lama-bordo construction to specific episodes of prehispanic settlement. Contour and lama-bordo terracing were techniques by which people created a luxuriant land and great wealth. Cessation of maintenance on terraces, abandonment, livestock grazing, and re-clearing led to spectacular erosion: hillside gullying, slope failures, wholesale soil removal, and blown-out lama-bordos. Not all lama-bordos failed on abandonment—perhaps vegetation re-growth, sporadic maintenance, and other factors preserved many that are more or less intact today. Generally, the most eroded places in the Mixteca Alta today are the same places that had the most people and the most wealth in Natividad times.

Compared to Las Flores settlement, that of Natividad had even greater altitudinal range. Natividad sites were spread from valley floors to mountain crests. In many subregions, upland locations never or only sparsely settled before had some settlement in Natividad. Yet the emphasis was on valley-floor situations. Natividad had more low-elevation sites than Las Flores. The Nuñu subregion is a good example. It had Natividad sites from 2,650 m to 2,090 m, including quite a few small ones on low hills on the basin floor. Settlement also extended back into the mountains on the Anama drainage.

Compared to Las Flores, in Natividad there was more evenness in site distribution with fewer gaps and uninhabited areas. For example, in Nundichi/Ñumi, sites were more evenly spread over all parts of the valley—less unevenly clustered than in Las Flores. In Teposcolula the two clusters in the eastern and western valleys grew together, leaving no gap.

No modern Mixteca Alta town resembles the large ancient towns and cities but in many places the modern rural settlement pattern has its historical roots in Natividad. Today's villages and small towns—apart from the big, paved centers such as Tlaxiaco, San Pedro y San Pablo Teposcolula, and Yolomécatl—are dispersed settlements, smaller versions of some Natividad sites. Irrigated fields, agricultural terraces, orchards, and agave plantings are interspersed with houses as we think they were in the past. Mixteca Alta villages and small towns are green and moist oases. Places like these represent the accumulated investment of several generations of household labor.

Today's municipal head towns, dependent villages, barrios, and rancherías often correspond specifically to Natividad settlement clusters. For example, modern San Agustín Tlacotepec replaced the mountaintop SAT 9, and the nearby agencias Junta del Río and Huendio are at the centers of small Natividad settlement clusters. San Juan Achiutla is a dispersed village spread over the western side of its small valley and that was the Natividad settlement pattern too. In Yodocono today people live in four clusters or barrios, each internally dispersed; in Natividad there were four large villages near the same places and numerous hamlets. Tayata has the same pattern of local Natividad settlement clusters mapping onto the modern municipios and agencias. The Teposcolula Valley's three main towns (San Juan, San Pedro y San Pablo, and Tixa/Ixtapa) are identifiable as the three main Natividad centers. Similar correspondences can be made in most subregions. Smith (1993) concluded that the best historical or ethnographic model for the Late Postclassic settlement pattern in the Peñoles area between Nochixtlán and the Valley of Oaxaca was its twentieth-century organization of municipio center, agencia, and *sección*. More specifically, Colonial churches often were built over precolumbian constructions, as at the well-known town of Mitla in the Valley of Oaxaca. In the Central Mixteca Alta area this happened at nine places, including Tilantongo, Teposcolula's Pueblo Viejo, Achiutla, and perhaps Tlaxiaco.

In Natividad the subregions with the largest populations were Jazmín, Teposcolula, Tilantongo, Huamelulpan, Tayata, Achiutla, Magdalena Peñasco, and Dzinicahua. Those with the smallest populations include the peripheries of Tlaxiaco. Small subregions between or on the fringes of major urban centers also had fairly low populations. Yodocono and Tidaá were between Tilantongo and Jazmín; Nduayaco, Yucuñama, and Nuñu were peripheral to Teposcolula; San Juan Achiutla was between Teposcolula and Achiutla. Interestingly, these peripheral, low-population subregions all had dispersed ranchería settlement patterns and no large centers. Most had more population in Las Flores. Apparently, the large urban centers such as Teposcolula drew people away from their rural subregions.

Larger blocks of subregions led by an urban core are shown by the attraction of settlements and the urban-rural differences in settlement pattern just mentioned. For example, Jazmín and Nejapilla formed part of a larger Yanhuitlán block of over 50,000 people. Teposcolula and its immediate neighbors would have been about the same size. These two close neighbors had over 100,000 people. Another block centered on Huamelulpan would have had over 30,000 people. Tilantongo was the center of another with more than 20,000. The sites in the inner basin are so close to one another that they too could have been another block (at contact this area was not unified politically). This block would involve Dzinicahua, Magdalena Peñasco, Amoltepec, Tlacotepec, Achiutla, and Yucuañe for a total in the same league as Teposcolula or Jazmín. There was a high potential for interaction in these urban-led blocks (Chamblee 2000).

These large agglomerations in the Mixteca Alta were matched by similar ones in the Valley of Oaxaca. Etla had 19,000, the Central area had 23,000, and Tlacolula, divided between Mitla, Teotitlán, and Teitipac cacicazgos (if not others, too), had 76,000.

Natividad people tended to live in town or urban settlements. Sixty percent of the population lived in sites of over 1,000 people. This figure is similar to that of Las Flores. Two-thirds of the archaeological sites were settlements of less than 100 people but the total population of the hamlets and isolated residences was only

15,000 people, 7 percent of the total. The Valley of Oaxaca had proportionally and absolutely more small sites and more people living in small sites. It also had a lower urbanization index: 40 percent of the Valley of Oaxaca population in Monte Albán V lived in settlements of more than 1,000 people compared to 60 percent in the Central Mixteca Alta.

Most subregions had an outstanding (often primate) urban center or town, smaller towns or villages, and a few small sites. Eight other subregions had only villages and small sites, usually with no outstanding center. These were the subregions with ranchería settlement patterns that were the peripheries of the larger urbanized blocks.

Civic-ceremonial architecture exhibited a diversity of form and function, suggesting horizontal complexity, regional diversity, and vertical differentiation. Interpreting Natividad civic-ceremonial architecture is not straightforward. Future study is deserved. Site destruction is one factor. Even though Natividad buildings are the youngest, sometimes they were situated in places that soon became heavily eroded. Many mounds are heavily looted. In many (but not all) places there was a decline in the amount and volume of new mounded construction. There were also various kinds of reuse of earlier mounds. Reuse included minor construction on mound tops or ritual offerings at older mounds, with or without Natividad residential occupation of the immediately surrounding site. As in earlier periods there are cases in which making judgments on periodization is difficult because of a dearth of associated sherds. A further complication is deciding what may be public versus residential architecture when the functions may have been mixed and the scale of construction was not monumental—excavations are needed.

All of these factors render exact counts or measurements disputable. At face value we have 436 mounds at 144 sites. These numbers are slightly higher than for Las Flores but the comparison suggests fewer mounds and mound sites per capita. Many of these mounds were obviously ritual or other reuse of older mounds, not new construction; others were elaborate residences.

Yet it would be imprudent to ignore the new Natividad construction. Mounds where only Natividad ceramics are found constituted over half the total. Quite a few of the Natividad-only mounds were substantial in volume. For example, at San Isidro Peñasco there were Natividad mounds 7 m and 5 m high, platforms measuring 94 by 58 by 3 m and 87 by 25 by 2 m, and three other mounds. The Pueblo Viejo at Achiutla is a string of eleven impressive platforms that undoubtedly supported at least the ruler's palace. The Pueblo Viejo of Teposcolula had earlier components but the bulk of the construction was Natividad—and monumental. Natividad-only mounds at lesser centers were often no less substantial than their counterparts of Classic times.

Only a handful of sites had very closed, private civic-ceremonial architecture. Almost all the public buildings are relatively open. The places with the most restricted access included the center of the Pueblo Viejo of Teposcolula, which was set apart by tall and imposing platform façades. The palaces at Achiutla's Pueblo Viejo may have had secluded spaces like those at Mitla and Yagul.

Teposcolula was a first-order capital, the most monumental, most elaborate civic-ceremonial place in this study area and certainly one of the leading capitals in the Mixteca Alta. Achiutla and San Isidro Peñasco were the other two capitals with new public construction of monumental scale. Tilantongo was historically important but had only a comparatively modest civic-ceremonial area. Cerro Jazmín was a large population center with a reoccupied civic-ceremonial center. Perhaps sometime during Natividad or the earliest Colonial period the seat of power shifted to Yanhuitlán in the valley below.

Below the level of the first- and second-order capitals were small centers with groups of two to four mounds, often with plazas or platform arrangements that suggest non-residential function and a degree of elaboration greater than that at single mounds. Newly built two- to four-mound centers were mainly in Tlaxiaco, the Achiutla area, and in the eastern Teposcolula Valley. Elsewhere, especially in areas that had Las Flores construction, small mound groups show Natividad reuse and not new construction. Four-mound groups are not exclusive to the Natividad period but several were newly constructed, and the Postclassic form might eventually be shown to be distinctive. There were six four-mound groups within 8 km of Tlaxiaco, a notable geographical pattern. Single-mound sites tended to be located not in the centers of local population clusters but on their edges. There are many Natividad-only examples of these.

We found seven ball courts in this study area. Ball courts dating to Natividad were located at the Pueblo Viejo of Teposcolula, the Pueblo Viejo in Magdalena Peñasco, and Nduayaco, where there is an isolated court at the southern edge of the Teposcolula cacicazgo. In Huamelulpan the ball court at Cerro Volado could have been used; likewise the one at Dzinicahua. At the ball court above the Pueblo Viejo of Achiutla we found only Las Flores pottery, but because the other major capitals had ball courts it would make sense if it had been in use in Natividad. Tlaxiaco's ball court at El Vergel, the entrance to the Tlaxiaco Valley from the southwest, could date to Las Flores or Natividad. Just outside our survey area east of Tilantongo the Mogote del Cacique site has a ball court that could date to Natividad or an earlier period (Spores 1967:44–45; Byland and Pohl 1994:90–91).

Another potentially significant geographical pattern is that large plazas and sites with multiple plazas were found overwhelmingly in one area, a belt extending from Magdalena Peñasco to Tlaxiaco. Eleven sites had plazas, many of them quite large.

New civic-ceremonial construction was substantial but spotty. Teposcolula and Achiutla had the most new construction. The western side of the Nochixtlán Valley and Tlaxiaco had the least. The obvious suggestion would be that capitals having substantial Las Flores construction required the least new investment and newly established centers had to construct new buildings. In the Valley of Oaxaca there was less construction in Monte Albán V compared to earlier periods, even at the power centers of Cuilapan and Macuilxochitl, but rather spectacular new buildings were constructed at the rising centers of Mitla and Yagul.

We see two types of subregional-scale hierarchies based on civic-ceremonial architecture. One consisted of a leading center, barrios, and border or shrine sites. These are relatively small and compact territorial units such as Achiutla and Tlacotepec. They may correspond to the ñuu of the sixteenth century. Tlaxiaco may have been like this, having several barrios and either Cerro de la Virgen or El Vergel as a leading center. A second type added secondary towns between the level of the Pueblo Viejo and the barrios. Teposcolula and Magdalena Peñasco are examples.

The civic-ceremonial hierarchies just described correspond to the settlement hierarchies and clusters of settlements discussed above. These civic-ceremonial and settlement units we identify from the survey are the material manifestations of the ñuu, the "potentially autonomous state" and its constituent *siqui, siña,* or *dzini* (Terraciano 2001:347–348), three local terms corresponding to barrio. From the archaeological survey (not the documentary history) the hierarchically organized, potentially autonomous states were Jazmín, Nejapilla, Tilantongo, Teposcolula, perhaps Yolomécatl, perhaps Yucuxaco, Huamelulpan/Tayata, Achiutla, Yucuañe, Tlacotepec, Amoltepec, Magdalena Peñasco, Dzinicahua, and Tlaxiaco. The aceph-alous, dependent subregions were Nuñu, Yucunama, Nduayaco, San Juan Achiutla, and the northeastern and southeastern Tlaxiaco peripheries. Some subregions were split by our survey boundary and could have been either acephalous and dependent or potentially autonomous ñuu: Yodocono, Tidaá, and Nundichi/Ñumi. Two sub-regions, Yodobada and Lagunas, were divided between the cacicazgos of Teposco-lula and Tamazulapan. Yodobada was dependent and not autonomous. The status of Lagunas is ambiguous.

Variation in these units is interesting. Subregions varied in the proportion of sites having mounds. Tlaxiaco, the Achiutla-Tlacotepec-Yucuañe area, and most of greater Teposcolula had higher-than-average proportions of sites with mounds. All the subregions we surveyed on the western flank of the Nochixtlán Valley had relatively few mound sites. (Fortified sites have an approximately similar distribu-tion—heaviest around Tlaxiaco, Teposcolula, and the south, and lightest in the Nochixtlán Valley.) If low-ranking mound sites were associated with local-level elite, border, or shrine activities, the pattern suggests differences in their centraliza-tion or dispersal.

In the Peñoles survey area (the mountains between the Nochixtlán Valley and the Valley of Oaxaca), Postclassic sites with one or a few mounds were very com-mon (Smith 1993), as in many of our subregions west of the Sierra de Nochixtlán. If mounds were often shrines and shrines were part of a nexus of patrilocal group formation and land rights as they are today in Peñoles, the implication would be that land rights were kept more closely by local groups in Postclassic Peñoles, Tlaxiaco, Achiutla, and greater Teposcolula than in the Nochixtlán Valley. This surmise remains untested.

Our interpretation of the civic-ceremonial hierarchy, taking into account the difficulties mentioned above, is that there was substantial similarity and few differ-ences between Natividad and Las Flores. Las Flores had two of the same types of subregional hierarchies, center-and-barrios and barrios only. The only structural difference is whether there was a tier of secondary towns within the subregion. Whether that type was present in Las Flores might be debated.

In Natividad as well as Las Flores states grew outward by incorporating sub-regions. Some incorporated subregions had leading centers that became the secondary centers of the larger state. Others were less urbanized and remained organized as barrios or local communities.

In some respects Natividad civic-ceremonial functions were more centralized than in Las Flores. Natividad capitals tended to have single focal architectural groups. Las Flores capitals often had multiple architectural groups at different places. At the basic levels of community and barrio civic-ceremonial architecture and border or shrine sites, there was virtually no difference between Las Flores and Natividad aside from the fact that in many places in Natividad old mounds were used instead of new ones being constructed, which of course argues for continuity as well.

In Natividad, boundaries between settlement clusters and subregions were fuzzy and permeable, as was the case in the Valley of Oaxaca in the Late Postclassic. The width of uninhabited buffer zones between cacicazgos was reduced compared to Las Flores times. In some areas affiliation seems problematic. For example, were Amoltepec and Tlacotepec part of the same polity as Dzinicahua? What was the status of Yodocono vis-à-vis Tilantongo and Jazmín? Where was the boundary between Teposcolula and Huamelulpan and between Teposcolula and Tejupan? Likewise we found no discrete breaks or sharp boundaries in ceramic type distributions. People in different cacicazgos participated in larger, common ceramic-distribution networks.

Boundaries identified as less inhabited buffer zones may have been ambiguous, yet there were scores of special border sites. Magdalena Peñasco had border sites with small mound groups at the four cardinal directions. There are border sites with mounds or shrines on the heights above the Teposcolula Valley, Achiutla, Nuñu, Tlacotepec, and elsewhere.

Ball courts have two locations: in cacicazgo centers and at the presumed edges of territories. The Nduayaco, El Vergel, and perhaps the Mogote del Cacique ball courts were at the edges of territories.

We recorded fifteen sites as fortified with defensive walls, ditches, or gates. (Other sites were defensible too because of hilltop location or the way terrace retaining walls were built.) Five are at the northern and southern ends of the greater Teposcolula cacicazgo; four ring Tlaxiaco; and there is a string of three running from the western edge of Achiutla to Yucuañe, suggesting conflict between this cacicazgo and the polities of the Peñascos.

Within subregions and between subregions there was more differentiation and interdependence in Natividad than in prior periods, including Las Flores, for which we have described increased integration over the Ramos period. There was considerable diversity in site size, site population density, and evidence for different activities. Natividad had the widest ranges of site settings, from valley floor to the upper reaches of barrancas in the Yanhuitlán beds to small mountain gorges and ridge crests. The range of elevations where settlements were found was typically greater in each subregion than in prior periods and there were more sites in the mountains. But judging from sheer numbers of sites and the situations of larger settlements, the agricultural emphasis was on intensive use of the Yanhuitlán Formation soils and opportunities for irrigation. Teposcolula, for example, had a strong bias toward valley-edge locations where floodwater and canal irrigation could have been carried out. The diversity of site locations is evidence of differentiation of economic activities. More than in any period since Cruz, settlement locations were oriented toward maximizing production. Security and strategic concerns were the main factor at relatively few sites.

Another sign of increasing integration was the disappearance of gaps between settlement clusters within and between subregions. Lagunas, for example, had always had clumps of settlement separated by gaps of unoccupied land but in Natividad the whole subregion was occupied.

The artifactual evidence also suggests economic integration. Although we propose some general patterns, sample biases and small sample sizes place limits on our conclusions, which should instead be seen as openings for future research. We describe distributional evidence for obsidian, local chipped stone, groundstone, and ceramics.

Obsidian was more abundant in Natividad than in prior periods. Most is assumed to have come from Central Mexico. This study area has more obsidian than does the Valley of Oaxaca. We recorded flakes, including thick flakes, more often than in the Valley of Oaxaca. Some obsidian may have come to the Mixteca Alta in large blocks. Prismatic blades were the most common end result but other products were made, including PPKs and other items.

Obsidian was not limited to major centers or ritual sites; it was widespread in sites large and small. Gray obsidian was slightly more common than green, and black was least frequent. However, not all places followed the general pattern. Nuñu sites seemed to have relatively small amounts of obsidian.

We found high-density scatters of obsidian blades, flakes, and sometimes a few exhausted cores at twelve sites (SPP 1 and 4, SMX 3, SDT 5, SAL 9, SJA 13, SMA 1 and 2, SDH 9, ODA 2, SIP 5, and YOS 8). Because of disturbance and varying visibility this list probably does not exhaust the corpus of obsidian work areas. Of the twelve sites, only SMA 2, SMX 3, and YOS 8 have other periods in addition to Natividad. We think the concentration of gray flakes and pieces at SMA 2 is potentially not Natividad (it may be Early Ramos); the large quantity of obsidian at SMX 3 may be Las Flores, Natividad, or both.

The Natividad obsidian concentrations represent various site types. SIP 5 and SPP 1 were the centers of their polities. SPP 4 was an important site close to the Teposcolula Pueblo Viejo. SMA 1, high on Cordón la Corona, was a boundary and ritual site of the Achiutla polity. SAL 9 was the second-largest settlement in Lagunas. SDT 5, SJA 13, ODA 2, SDH 9, and YOS 8 were otherwise undistinguished villages, more rural than urban but not isolated. The mean distance from these sites to the nearest large plaza was less than 3 km.

The evidence of obsidian working is diverse. At SAL 9 there was a 1 km long scatter of flakes, cores, and blades. SMA 1 had a very high-density concentration of secondary and tertiary flakes, a few blades, and several tools. SDH 9 had a concentration measuring 20 by 20 m with several hundred flakes. SIP 5 had a typical density of blade end-products but the evidence for production consists of some flakes, a blade core, and a non-blade core near the ball court and on several terraces near the site center. At ODA 2, YOS 8, SJA 13, and SDT 5 the evidence of reduction is not clear and the sites are distinguished only by high obsidian densities.

These sites where we noted higher densities of obsidian do not account for all obsidian working. Other sites have blades, flakes, and cores in lower densities. In Achiutla, for example, we found two exhausted blade cores and flakes at two other sites besides the two with high densities just described.

Hard, grainy volcanic rock suitable for manos, metates, and other groundstone tools does not occur everywhere. We found possible evidence for the movement of a distinctive pink groundstone either as raw material or finished product from the Huendio locality to other places perhaps as distant as Lagunas and Yosojica. Sites in Teposcolula, Amoltepec, Tlacotepec, and Magdalena Peñasco had evidence for working basalt in the form of flake scatters and finished tools.

Local chipped stone was generally common. Chert flakes were almost ubiquitous. Sources of chert were numerous and widespread. The quality of the materials was often quite suitable for knapping. The most common color was white but other colors were locally available. Chert color does not distinguish source. Other materials included a fine, milky or translucent white chalcedony that is sometimes made into blades and unifacially or bifacially flaked. Quartz was relatively rare (it was more common in Peñoles, which has much more metamorphic rock). Coarse-textured greenstone was found flaked for large tools or sometimes ground.

Expedient working of chert must have been almost ubiquitous. More specialized working for exchange or for use in some other activity took place where we found high concentrations of chert debris. Numerous chert-working sites with abundant materials covering many hectares were in Yolomécatl, Yucuxaco, and Lagunas; other substantial concentrations were at sites in Teposcolula, Tilantongo, Amoltepec, La Estancia, and Achiutla.

In Yucuxaco and Yolomécatl we found four types of chert-working areas: quarries with primary reduction, secondary reduction at special non-residential sites, concentrations indicating secondary reduction within settlements, and flake and tool concentrations within residential sites but without specific evidence of early-stage reduction. Bifaces could have been made for exchange but other formal tools are uncommon and the bulk of the industry would appear to be expedient. Specialized chert working in Yucuxaco and Yolomécatl took place at upland sites on the fringes of more urbanized Teposcolula. This archaeologically visible evidence may indicate production of stone tools and materials specifically for exchange; it may also be a by-product of the production and exchange of other upland goods destined for urban areas. There were large plazas nearby in Huamelulpan, Yucuxaco (PMY 12), Yolomécatl (YOL 26), and Teposcolula (SMX 3). Chert working is the best of the relatively meager direct evidence for specialized craft production in this part of the Mixteca Alta. Additional studies could be designed to specify the reduction and flow of chert products.

Regarding the pottery economy, we have four summary observations on ceramic specialization, the relative production cost of assemblages, the extent of ceramic spheres, and the social distribution of costlier types.

We found no direct evidence of pottery making. We found no pottery-making tools or sites, no unusual concentrations of particular wares that might indicate production, and almost no kiln wasters. This is in contrast to the Valley of Oaxaca where similar regional surveys found many pottery production sites. We believe almost all pottery we saw was made within the study area. We believe there were specialized producers as it would have been most unlikely that each household in this urbanized society made its own pots.

Certain technological characteristics strongly suggest specialized potters and a degree of scale and intensity in production. One is the large repertoire of fairly standardized vessel forms and shapes (many shapes and sizes of bowls, cooking pots, storage jars, water jars, pitchers, shoe-shaped pots, comals, ladles, braziers, incense burners, figurines, supports, handles, and pichanchas or coladeros). Another feature of Natividad pottery suggesting professional production is that the texture of pastes was fairly uniform. Pastes followed the general Mixteca Alta Natividad trend (Spores 1972) toward fine pastes for serving vessels. Fine Cream wares were most frequent. Fine Gray like Miguelito Hard Gray of Nochixtlán was rare, perhaps indicating that west of the Sierra de Nochixtlán potters were less concerned with higher-temperature reduction firing.

The overwhelming bulk of pottery from this survey, the follow-up controlled surface collections by Heredia, and the household excavations by Pérez was plain Chachoapan Sandy Cream for utility vessels and Yanhuitlán Fine Cream for serving vessels (or local variants of these general wares). There were quite a few vessel forms and sizes so in practical terms typical household assemblages were not impoverished. But decorated sherds may have been less than 5 percent of a household's assemblage. Excavations at Nicayuju found that painted and Cacique Burnished wares made up only 1.67 percent of the domestic assemblage (Pérez 2003; see Lind 1979 for wealthier contexts).

Ceramic wares and specific vessel and decorative types had broad ranges of distribution. A ceramic sphere is the geographical range of a pottery ware, regardless of how many producers or places made it. The same wares and types occur over the 55 km length of the study area and beyond (their frequencies vary). Ceramic spheres crossed political boundaries and were thus much more extensive than subregional or cacicazgo territories. Whether by the fashion-following of multiple potters in many places or by direct distribution from a limited number of production sites, markets were likely to have been the key institutional mechanism behind the ceramic sphere.

Social differences in access to decorated pottery existed but the patterns were complex, quantitative, multidimensional, and indicative of a continuous range of wealth stratification. Our field observations and opportunistic collections are not adequate to address this issue specifically but we can sketch broad outlines that will help in designing future research. Major centers had more decorated (especially painted) types and unusual, costly vessel forms than other sites. Teposcolula's Pueblo Viejo, Cerro Jazmín, and SIP 5 are examples. At Teposcolula (SPP 1) there were specific residential zones that had many decorated types (Stiver Walsh 2001, 2005). Conversely, small and rural settlements away from centers generally had lower frequencies of decorated wares. This is a quantitative not a qualitative pattern and there are many small rural sites with decorated pottery. For example, in the Nduayaco uplands peripheral to Teposcolula people had access to obsidian and decorated pottery, and the amounts of decorated wares and elaborate forms do not suggest impoverishment. In Jazmín we could see no difference in decorated pottery occurrences between residential areas in the city and in large villages. It is not known how strong the urban/rural or major center/minor settlement dichotomy would be if variation in sample size, surface visibility, and length of occupation were controlled. In other words some of the apparent difference in decorated type frequencies could be due to sampling biases.

The role wealthy people or petty nobility had in local or border-site rituals has yet to be addressed archaeologically. Our survey shows that the elaborate Mixteca Alta ladle censers and braziers are often found around civic-ceremonial mounds. So were obsidian blades and painted pottery. Censers, braziers, obsidian blades, and painted pottery also occur in residential areas away from mounds. At some mounds we found (on the surface) few or none of these items. The ritual activities involving censers and braziers were not confined to public architectural contexts.

Many Natividad sites, large and small, were rich and abundant in artifacts; others, especially smaller ones, have low artifact densities. Longevity of occupation and site formation processes play a role. Other factors such as proximity to major centers and proximity to markets remain to be investigated.

The settlement system we describe here was a Late Postclassic phenomenon. The Early Postclassic is poorly represented and poorly known. Our Early Natividad assignments are uncertain. Sites we thought might be Early Natividad were widely dispersed on the western side of the Nochixtlán Valley, in Achiutla, Yosojica, and scattered sites around Tlaxiaco, Nduayaco, and Lagunas. None of these occupations was securely dated by ceramics.

A late development of the Late Natividad system would be consistent with what is known from excavations and surveys across highland Oaxaca. In many parts of Mesoamerica the Epiclassic was a time of decline and reorganization. In the Central Mixteca Alta, if Postclassic development were late, it would add centuries to the time of hiatus and population decline. The trough between the Early Classic and Late Postclassic peaks could have lasted a maximum of 800 years, from AD 500 to 1300.

A long hiatus in such a rich area in the heart of Mesoamerica confronts us with a chronological problem or a problem in cultural evolution. We think the hiatus involves both archaeological recognition and a real phenomenon.

The Las Flores and Natividad ceramic and radiocarbon chronology is weak in the Mixteca Alta. There have been few excavations at Late Las Flores, Epiclassic, and Early Postclassic to date. There have been few excavations because there are few sites of the kind that lure archaeologists. Highland Oaxaca does not have a Tula, Xochicalco, or Chichén Itzá. Chronology must be strengthened through work at smaller, less spectacular sites and at larger sites where the Late Classic through Early Postclassic components are overshadowed by earlier or later occupations. For example, Yucuñudahui and Yucuita in the Nochixtlán Valley have Late Las Flores occupations. In the eastern Mixteca Alta region of Peñoles there are quite a few sites with Epiclassic and Early Postclassic ceramic assemblages. Given the Late Classic, Epiclassic, and Early Postclassic sites in Peñoles, we should be able to recognize similar components in the Central Mixteca Alta if they were present in force.

Our current assessment, which we will be happy to change if it is contradicted by new information, is that there really was a hiatus of unknown duration in large parts of the Mixteca Alta and that our chronological problems are in large measure because of that hiatus. Perhaps where there was settlement, populations were small, not organized as states with major capitals or urban centers, and not very visible given our current archaeological discernment. Decline in fertility rates (due to a factor like economic depression) would be sufficient to make a demographic and settlement hiatus even with no emigration or change in mortality.

Collapse is something that civilizations (or parts thereof) are known for. A hiatus in the Central Mixteca Alta during the Las Flores/Natividad transition would have been similar to the abandonment and reorganization during Late Ramos. It would have been part of larger processes of political and economic disintegration, decline, and reorganization in the greater Mesoamerican macroregion.

A significant implication of a such a collapse concerns the strong continuity in the form of state institutions between the Early Classic and the Late Postclassic. The evidence presented in this volume shows close similarities in the scale and vertical complexity of Early Classic and Late Postclassic states. State institutions persisted elsewhere in Mesoamerica after the Classic, to be brought back to the Central Mixteca Alta in the Late Postclassic (just as in the Terminal Formative political institutions continued at Yucuita, Huamelulpan, and Dzinicahua while other places were abandoned). Culture is, after all, a macroregional phenomenon. The small state was also a tried-and-true adaptation for the Mixteca Alta. Even Late Cruz polities had some of the same elements. So even if the small state (the ñuu) were not re-introduced after the hiatus as the political form of the time in Mesoamerica, an institution of its scale and integration would have formed again because it worked.

CHAPTER ELEVEN

The Ñuu in Anthropological Perspective

Thus far our discussion has been involved with the particulars of the Mixteca Alta. Here we place the archaeological results into a more general Mesoamerican and comparative perspective. In this final chapter we reach five major conclusions. These concern the method of archaeological survey, the societies of the Formative period, the nature of the state, episodes of decline and abandonment, and a form of urbanism that is primarily agrarian.

SURVEY

Survey is early homonin behavior: more or less upright posture, hands free, bipedal locomotion, visual attention to surroundings, in touch with nearby comrades, on the lookout for wild dogs, searching for food. Survey is late homonin activity too: thought, pattern recognition, comparing visual input to cognitive models, talking about what is seen.

As method, systematic, regional surface survey is a practical, efficient, low-cost means of locating, describing, and dating archaeological sites and their components. Such surveys deliver new research questions and hypotheses and frame the context for further investigations at smaller scales. In Mesoamerica, survey works in the mountains as well as in valley settings.

We found 999 sites (1,670 components) in 1,622 km². Many of these sites are spectacular in their degree of preservation of artifacts, architecture, subsurface deposits, and their setting. More detailed investigations, revisits, and excavations will show that there is much more to the archaeological record than we report here.

In spite of erosion, plowing, looting, and neglect the archaeological record of the Mixteca Alta still leaves experienced archaeologists standing in wonder. Some of the sites of the Central Mixteca Alta are among the largest of their time periods known in Oaxaca. The Early Formative occupations at Tayata, Diuxi, and Xacañi cover over 50 ha each. The Middle Formative site of La Providencia at Tilantongo spreads over 90 ha. Monte Negro, the most famous Late Formative site in the Mixteca Alta, has an area of 78 ha and its contemporary at Cerro Jazmín was just as large. The Terminal Formative urban complex at Huamelulpan sprawled over more than 2 km². Early Classic Cerro Jazmín had 230 ha of dense urban occupation and it grew to over 577 ha in the Postclassic. There are not many major towns as awesomely fortified as Yucuninde. The Pueblo Viejo at Teposcolula is one of the most impressive Postclassic capitals in Oaxaca. Few major sites in Oaxaca can match Cerro de la Peña Grande at San Mateo Peñasco for its spectacular setting and daring architecture.

The total extent of the archaeological sites we mapped is 125.8 km² or 7.8 percent of the project's land area. For just the Postclassic sites the total site area is 105.5 km² or 6.3 percent compared to 3.7 percent for the Postclassic in the Valley of Oaxaca (Kowalewski et al. 1989:755) and 6.2 to 12.5 percent for the Basin of Mexico (Smith 2002:110).

This is the first systematic study of the archaeology of the Central Mixteca Alta. It is the current baseline for cultural resource management and heritage interpretation in that area. The data reported here provide an empirical starting point for framing and testing new research models. Nevertheless, this study must be considered preliminary to and not a substitute for studies of intrasite variability, systematic study of artifacts, and excavations as in the research carried out by Pérez (2003) and Heredia (2005) and the projects underway at Tayata (Balkansky) and Teposolula Pueblo Viejo (Spores and Robles 2006).

Given the methodological efficiencies demonstrated in several dozen full-coverage regional surveys since the 1970s, there is now little justification for unsystematic, reconnaissance-style survey in Mesoamerica. We are not asserting that all archaeological surveys should be like this one because, depending on research, design methods will vary in grain, intensity, and scale of area, but unsystematic reconnaissance may entail costs equivalent to a well-managed full-coverage survey and produce less information. As discussed in Chapter 1, this project made certain improvements in field and lab procedures relative to previous surveys in highland Mesoamerica: better paperwork and data organization in the field and lab, daily data entry and checking in a relational database, and use of GIS in early stages of the project.

Improvements need to be made in our field and lab methods: better knowledge of diagnostic ceramics by each field crew, better recognition of component boundaries in the field, assignment of architecture and artifacts to components earlier in the data management process, getting field notes into electronic files at the end of each day, more use of digital cameras, and faster production of written reports for the local and scientific communities. Innovations in these areas should improve data quality and the frustrating lag time between fieldwork and final publication.

Our results are limited by the unsatisfactory coarseness of the archaeological chronology. With good collections we can recognize ten ceramic phases covering almost 3,000 years (Appendix 1). Our phases are too long, especially the Postclassic Natividad. The Late Classic and Early Postclassic are not well understood. The failure to refine chronology in highland Oaxaca is due to the plainness and conservatism of the pottery and to the poor deployment, reporting, and analysis of chronometric dating. The overly broad chronological framework adversely affects all behavioral interpretations of survey and excavation data. Yet interestingly there are relatively few ceramic-bearing sites in this study area that we could not assign to a period. We have nineteen undated sites with undiagnostic ceramics. This is a smaller proportion of undated sites than in the Peñoles area, peripheral to the Valley of Oaxaca (Finsten 1996).

Several colleagues who have seen some of the data in this volume have expressed reservations about our population estimates, feeling that they are too high in some cases. For example, our estimate for Cerro Jazmín in the Natividad period is a range of 21,004 to 42,988 inhabitants, which is higher than the estimate for Monte Albán at its largest. Our estimation procedures (Chapter 1) are similar to those used in other highland Mesoamerican surveys. The difference between the Cerro Jazmín and Monte Albán estimates is that we used 50 to 100 people per ha for residentially terraced areas and for Monte Albán Blanton used a figure similar to Sanders's 25 to 50 people per ha for compact settlements (Sanders 1965:50; Blanton 1978:29–30). Blanton had derived a similar range by dividing the total flat area of terraces by 312 m², an estimate of the space taken up by one household, quite close to the household areas excavated by Pérez in the Mixteca Alta (Pérez 2003:101).

However, there is evidence pointing to higher densities in town and urban contexts in Oaxaca. Our counts of houses on well-preserved terraced sites in the Mixteca Alta show house densities that project into the 50 to 100 person/ha range if not more in some cases. We found other examples of high densities of domestic units on terraced sites in the Valley of Oaxaca (described in Chapter 1). Also in the Valley of Oaxaca, intensive mapping and excavation by Feinman and Nicholas (Feinman et al. 2002; Feinman and Nicholas 2004) show variation in intrasite residential density with the built-up sectors of terraced sites such as El Palmillo definitely in the 50 to 100 person/ha range.

In their times of greatest size hilltop terraced sites in both the Mixteca Alta and the Valley of Oaxaca probably had population densities higher than the 25 to 50 person/ha estimate used for the Monte Albán survey. Not all sectors within a site's boundaries had the same population density. The procedures for estimating population used in the present study attempt to account for varying intrasite densities by assigning different ranges to fractions of the total area for sites in which there is surface evidence for doing so. If one believes that our population estimates for terraced sites are still too high, one might choose to use the lower end of the range.

FORMATIVE SOCIETIES

The Mixteca Alta was a core region in the Early and Middle Formative. This environment offered relatively low-risk opportunities for early farmers. One of its natural advantages compared to lower valleys was access to water. The Mixteca Alta generally has a slightly higher mean annual rainfall than, for example, the Valley of Oaxaca. It is our impression that the Central Mixteca Alta has more places with permanent flowing water.

The Mixteca Alta had as many or more large sites and population densities as high or greater than other places in Mesoamerica thought to be important nuclei for the development of ranked society. The Early and Middle Formative centers of the Mixteca Alta were the peers of sites such as Paso de la Amada in Chiapas and centers in the Valley of Mexico or the Amatzinac Valley in Morelos (Smith 2002:106–218). Places in the Central Mixteca Alta such as Dzinicahua, Tayata, Teposcolula, Yanhuitlán, and Tilantongo had head villages that were important nodes in Mesoamerica-wide exchange, just as in Oaxacan sites that have received more attention such as Yucuita, Etlatongo, and San José Mogote.

The basic sociopolitical unit in the Early and Middle Formative was a cluster of settlements consisting of a head village and smaller satellite villages and hamlets. Such clusters were separated from one another by uninhabited space.

Early Formative settlement hierarchies consisted of head villages and their smaller satellites. We do not know much about a civic-ceremonial hierarchy at this stage but presumably most central functions took place in special buildings at the head village.

In the Middle Formative, population grew and expanded territorially. This expansion happened in a particular way. The older original settlement clusters appear to have added "daughter" settlement clusters in adjacent valleys. In other words the viable social unit, new or old, was the cluster of nearby villages and hamlets—not the village. Middle Formative settlement hierarchies continued the same pattern as in the Early Formative but they added a new hierarchical level with the subordinate settlement clusters. There was a two-tiered hierarchy of central places above the level of the hamlet in core settlement clusters, with relatively undifferentiated subordinate settlement clusters surrounding the core. Head towns of the super-clusters emerged as regionally important centers.

What kind of chiefdoms (?) were Early-Late Formative societies in the Mixteca Alta? An answer would be premature for little is known about institutions. We have settlement pattern data but little else. The settlement data show hierarchies of one level above the common village in the earliest phase and two or three levels in the Middle Formative. The autonomous political unit was not the village but the settlement cluster. These might be termed chiefdoms but we know little about the form of the institutions, status differentiation, or rulership; nothing is known about their individualizing or collectivizing character.

Why were people integrated at the scale and complexity that they were, in the head-and-satellite-village clusters? This pattern was widespread across Mesoamerica. Chalcatzingo was the head town for smaller settlements in its vicinity (Hirth 1987a, 1987b); San Lorenzo Tenochtitlán was the center of a cluster of small sites (Symonds and Lunagómez 1997). From an internal point of view settlement clusters would have optimally distributed labor to resources, thus minimizing risks and labor costs. People would have been located within an easy day's round-trip of a central place that was a single hub of exchange. Populations of these clusters were sufficiently high for long-term viability. To do well in interregional competition and exchange local populations would have concentrated their efforts into a single portal to the outside. Interregional exchange would strongly encourage participating societies to integrate at the scale and complexity of their peers.

A benefit of surveying more and more contiguous area is the opportunity to see interregional patterns in new ways. Having empirical sequences for multiple contiguous regions can free one from the essentialist conceptualizations and limited vocabularies of culture history. A multi-regional perspective can replace single-focus questions such as how the "Zapotec state" "influenced" the "Mixtecs" (Balkansky et al. 2004). We can take advantage of variation to look for dimensions of patterning other than "Mixtec" and "Zapotec."

The Mixteca Alta shares with the largely Zapotec Valley of Oaxaca a concordant sequence of changes in pottery design and technology, although the clay bodies, many styles, and the archaeologically designated types were different. For example, Early Formative pottery in both areas used residual upland clays that were not usually winnowed (such as Fidencio Coarse and Leandro Gray of the Valley of Oaxaca; Flannery and Marcus 1994:149–180). The Atoyac Yellow-White of the Valley of Oaxaca is matched by Reyes White in the Mixteca Alta. Channel rims are found in the Terminal Formative and Transición phases in both areas. In short, at every phase there were correspondences in design, technology, and fashion transmitted through social exchange. The stylistic sharing and concordant change are strong evidence of intensive, systematic, and frequent interaction among commoners as well as traders and elite.

To come to our point here, each settlement cluster was embedded as a component of a greater, multilingual cultural system. The Early and Middle Formative settlement cluster of head-village-and-satellites is a very common pattern in Mesoamerica. That commonality reflects a shared political economy, a common set of socially determined objectives and modes of exchange. The Mixteca Alta did not originate this mode of political economy any more than did any of the other contemporary polities, but its societies participated in, reproduced, and thereby helped create the Mesoamerican macroregional system.

Formative political economies created regional and macroregional landscapes of difference. People and valuable goods concentrated more or in varying combinations in some places rather than others. These differences became important causes in cultural dynamics. By the Late Formative there emerged major differences between the Valley of Oaxaca and the Mixteca Alta in how societies were put together and integrated.

In the late Middle Formative (Late Cruz, Monte Albán Early I) the Valley of Oaxaca began to become more integrated as a regional system than it had been earlier and more integrated than the Mixteca Alta. This might have been in response to competition from its many neighbors, including the populous places we have been describing in the Mixteca Alta. During this time the Mixteca Alta retained relatively high populations but it did not develop the institutions for larger-scale regional integration like those in the Valley of Oaxaca.

In the Late and Terminal Formative, warfare increased all across Oaxaca. The Valley of Oaxaca stepped up its march toward greater integration and centralization. The Mixteca Alta became especially militarized and fragmented. Every subregion in the Mixteca Alta was affected, most settlements were abandoned, and people took to fortified hilltowns. The settlements varied in size but whether they formed a central-place hierarchy is doubtful because the climate of hostilities preempted stable political and economic relationships. This militarized mode was not the most optimal for production, prosperity, or stability. After a century or two it had collapsed. Archaeologists have written about a similar (although larger-scale) process of abandonment, consolidation, competition, and further abandonment, coalescence, and the creation of new institutions in the Greater Southwest after AD 1250 (LeBlanc 1998; Wilcox et al. 2001; Hill et al. 2004). In the Mixteca Alta the difficult times of the Late and Terminal Formative also led to innovations in political forms. Urban Huamelulpan became the successful adaptation that led to the state in the Mixteca Alta. In contrast Monte Negro appears to have created a different form not seen elsewhere, but it did not last.

The sudden change from valley-floor settlement clusters to fortified hilltowns created institutions of community integration and governance that endured beyond the original conditions of Late Formative times (Kowalewski et al. 2006). The hill villages were not simply fortified settlements to be understood solely as a response to military threat. They were also collectively organized communities. Heredia's research (2005) shows that hilltowns in the Mixteca Alta were not as socially stratified as other towns and cities in Oaxaca. It is possible but not proven that when conditions changed in the Early Classic this collective community structure lived on in the hilltowns, perhaps even to the Postclassic. Hilltowns may have had a different legal standing than communities consisting of more dispersed settlement. Alternatively, the historical experience of the hilltowns endured in corporate institutions of barrios and local communities whether these were nucleated or dispersed. In the Mixteca Alta they lasted as compact settlements through the Postclassic. In the Valley of Oaxaca compact hilltowns of the Classic became dispersed settlements in the Postclassic.

The chiefdom-to-state and urban transformation in the Valley of Oaxaca, the militarization of the Mixteca Alta, and changes in other regions such as the Mixteca Baja (Rivera 1999) and the Lower Verde on the Oaxaca coast (Joyce 1991, 2003) were particular manifestations of a wider macroregional shakeup. This was not a matter of chiefs at Monte Albán figuring out all by themselves how to become kings, as if in a pristine glass case in which they were the sole center of attention. Instead, within the same macroregion there were differences among polities that were accentuated and exploited by numerous actors. The actions of people in the Valley of Oaxaca (and elsewhere) had consequences that only the most magical of chiefs could have foreseen.

By the Terminal Formative there were states in the Mixteca Alta—centralized, internally complex, and urban. These (Yucuita, Huamelulpan, and probably centers in places yet to be surveyed) were the effective peers of Monte Albán and others Mesoamerican centers. (In the Terminal Formative the Huamelulpan subregion had about 17,000 people and Monte Albán and its immediate hinterland had about 15,000; Kowalewski 1989:756). The Terminal Formative timing is interesting in light of the earlier development of deep hierarchy, urbanism, and integrated regional institutions (the state) in the Valley of Oaxaca in Late Formative Late Monte Albán I. Other scholars (see, e.g., Marcus and Flannery 1996) tend to place state origins in Terminal Formative Monte Albán II but we take note of the rapid transformation of the Valley of Oaxaca in Late I (Blanton et al. 1999).

Compared to Classic and Postclassic states in Oaxaca the earliest states in the Valley of Oaxaca and in the Mixteca were remarkably centralized and primate. They lacked the horizontal complexity of later states. In our view these states shared similar forms because they were components embedded in a wider cultural system with a common political-economic structure, even though the constituent societies differed in languages, customs, dress, and many other aspects of culture.

THE ÑUU AND THE STATE

The Mixteca Alta is not a single well-delimited river valley or highland basin but a mosaic of mountain ridges and little valleys. These little valleys are behaviorally significant places—small natural and cultural regions—with their own settlement histories. They are the physical homes of ñuu, the "potentially autonomous state" (Terraciano 2001:347–348). The ñuu was larger than a community, as this term is usually understood; it was a multi-community grouping. The ñuu was an integral autonomous unit or an integral component of a larger polity. It was not dissolved in a more centralized solution. It retained its integrity even when drawn into alliances or core-periphery relationships.

Ethnohistorically, below the level of the ñuu were groups of households known as siqui or barrios that had land and other rights and could be considered the local communities. Archaeologists have paid a lot of attention to the household scale and to regional settlement patterns but less has been done with the middle level. Siqui may be archaeologically visible. For example, at Nicayuju, originally surveyed by Stiver Walsh (2001) and then excavated by Pérez (2003), the people who lived on residential terraces on the hillsides had a temple and plaza at the top of the hill. Our regional survey found scores of Classic and Postclassic barrio centers with small, one- or two-mound arrangements like those at the top of Nicayuju.

In simplified form, polities of the Classic and Postclassic Mixteca Alta had a four-tiered settlement and civic-ceremonial hierarchy. Households were grouped in barrios suggested by numerous small public buildings. Communities were formed of several barrios. Each valley had a polity composed of at least one and usually multiple communities, one of which generally but not always was the primary center. Multi-valley aggregates and their centers were the fourth hierarchical level. But this ideal model passes over considerable variation. Subregions could differ from one another because of their positions in the larger political-economic field. They also differed in population size. In the Classic, single-valley populations ranged between 2,000 and 20,000 people; Postclassic populations ranged between 2,000 and 40,000.

When was the origin of the ñuu? It is described in sixteenth-century historical accounts. It was the form of the state in the Mixtec codices, which deal mainly with Postclassic times. In this book we have described the prehispanic settlement-pattern manifestation of the ñuu. We have shown that settlement and civic-ceremonial groupings having the scale, complexity, and form of the Postclassic ñuu were present in the Early Classic.

Early Classic settlement hierarchies often had an outstanding primate center followed by secondary and tertiary places, all above the level of the non-central village. The public buildings and plazas suggest a four-level civic-ceremonial hierarchy. The pattern of boundary sites found first in the Ramos period continued in the Classic. The diversity of environmental settings and site functions strongly suggests greater horizontal and vertical complexity compared to earlier periods. We do not have direct evidence of markets or market systems but by analogy and from the numerous plazas potentially suitable for markets we infer that centers were also differentiated by their importance in market systems. Hierarchical relationships again developed between core and peripheral subregions.

The ñuu of the Postclassic were thus not the result of a Balkanization or breakup of larger regional states of the Classic because the latter had always been small— they were ñuu too. Postclassic settlement complexity developed in the same mold as in Classic times but in some cases with greater horizontal complexity. Settlement hierarchies varied by position in core-periphery relationships, with greater vertical complexity in core subregions and lesser vertical complexity in peripheries. Typically there was a major urban center and secondary and tertiary towns and villages. We identified local barrios, ñuu, and major cacicazgo centers. Rulers' palaces were sometimes but not always located in the largest towns. Shrines and boundary sites were common. Defense was probably a subregional concern. Settlements differed considerably in environmental situation, suggesting considerable horizontal complexity. We hypothesize that land and labor were allocated through institutions at the community and subregional scale. There is indirect evidence for systems of markets, which created more differentiation and complexity. Individual market areas were likely to have coincided with entire subregions or large sectors of the larger subregions.

Subregions and their ñuu formed larger spheres of civic-ceremonial and marketing exchange. We found the archaeological settlement pattern evidence of these aggregations or alliances centered on Teposcolula, Jazmín-Yanhuitlán, Achiutla, Huamelulpan, Tilantongo, and Tlaxiaco. In the sixteenth century the alliances of ñuu under the rulership of a royal pair was called a "yuhuitaiyu" (Spores 1984; Terraciano 2001:158–197). The larger aggregations of subregions display core-periphery characteristics with peripheral ñuu having less vertical complexity than core ñuu. In the economic realm, patterns of chipped stone tool debris suggest ways in which peripheral and core communities were bound together in differentiated exchange. Control over more manpower and more effective offense and defense would have been advantageous for the core. These aggregations were bounded, with fortified sites fairly common on their edges. Special boundary sites identified by small mounds with little residential occupation are frequently located on high points around the edges of ñuu, much like the named points around the compass of cacicazgos in Colonial period *lienzos* (maps).

Was the ñuu a descendent of the older head-village-with-satellites polity of the Early and Middle Formative? The ñuu was vertically and horizontally more complex, was larger in population scale, and had a greater volume of exchange and interaction between subregions than the Early and Middle Formative polity. But like the ñuu, the Early and Middle Formative head village with satellites was a hierarchically organized, enduring polity on the subregional scale, it was the fundamental political unit, and larger clusters were formed by a hierarchical relationship between central and outlying head-and-satellite systems. One difficulty with positing a relationship of descent from the Early and Middle Formative polity to the Classic state is the double disjunction between these periods—the rapid abandonment of most valley settlements in favor of fortified hill villages in the Late Formative and then the abandonment of these in favor of the urban agglomerations of the Terminal Formative.

What was the role of outside powers in determining the course of cultural evolution in the Mixteca Alta? Did the state centered at Monte Albán expand its dominion into the Mixteca Alta in the Late Formative at Monte Negro (Flannery 1983:99) or in the Late Classic around Tilantongo or elsewhere (Byland and Pohl 1994)? We have discussed why we think the evidence for outside intrusion and replacement is weak (Balkansky 1998a; Balkansky et al. 2004). The regional surveys reported here show strong local continuities in architecture and ceramics and conversely no evidence of intrusions or outposts durable enough to leave a material imprint. Currently there is even less evidence of Teotihuacan in the Mixteca Alta than there is in the Valley of Oaxaca. In the Late Postclassic we recovered Aztec-style ceramics from several cacicazgo centers. These sherds may be associated with the imperial expansion described in historical sources. Generally, however, the cultural sequence in the Mixteca Alta shows strong in-situ continuity and an early and persistent development of distinctive institutions, which were of course members of and subject to the political economy of the larger macroregional cultural system.

When we proposed this project we hypothesized that cacicazgos in the Mixteca Alta might have developed from the Balkanization of large states, from formations developed in core areas elsewhere, or as clients or colonies like those that tend to develop on the frontiers or peripheries between major core areas or empires. We can now reject all three of these alternative ideas. The small state and the ñuu were not residual products of the breakup of large regional states or empires because there were no big empires here. The cacicazgos in this region had their roots in the Early Classic or even the Terminal Formative. States in the Central Mixteca Alta were not secondary copies of original states somewhere else because they grew out of the distinctive military collectives of the Late Formative Mixteca Alta; they exhibit a long in-situ continuity in scale, complexity, and specific forms of public architecture and boundary marking. They were not client states and colonies on the frontiers between imperial blocks because there is no evidence of clientage or colonization from outside. They were not the creatures of a political or economic periphery because the Mixteca Alta itself had considerable economic power based on intensive agriculture, high population density, and political autonomy.

The state in the Mixteca Alta was territorially small. Early Classic Teposcolula, including its peripheral subregions, measured less than 25 km across; it had a population in the low tens of thousands. Greater Teposcolula in the Postclassic was somewhat larger and had a population of perhaps 60,000. Most states in the Mixteca Alta were smaller. The large alliances did not transform or dissolve their subordinate or constituent ñuu but left them largely intact.

At the time of the Spanish conquest Mesoamerican states took the form of hereditary kingdoms that had somewhat limited bureaucratic development (Berdan et al. 1996). These states were numerous and territory sizes were small—100 km^2 to a few thousand km^2. Yucatán had about fifteen autonomous provinces (Roys 1957). Outside of its core area in the Valley of Mexico the Aztec state did not fundamentally alter the form of governance in its conquered provinces. The Mesoamerican state in 1520 was generally a petty kingdom, which might be drawn into a larger group but such alliances or empires tended to be historically ephemeral and did not develop centralizing institutions that altered the structure of local kingdoms. In the Classic period in the Maya lowlands there were as many as sixty or eighty petty kingdoms. Apparently, these were brought by conquest or alliance into larger territorial blocks ruled from major cities, although these larger aggregates were not enduring (Grube 2000; Marcus 2003). At the upper end, the Late Classic Calakmul state is said to have covered 8,000 km^2 (Folan et al. 1995).

Most Classic period states of the Mesoamerican highlands were like the territorially small polities of the Maya lowlands. For the Classic period state, attention is usually drawn to Teotihuacan (Millon 1981; Cowgill 1997) but Teotihuacan was the odd (but magnificent) exception. The city had 125,000 inhabitants yet its own hinterland, the Valley of Mexico (5,000 km^2), was almost emptied of population. Teotihuacan had under its direct control a radius of about 90 km. Some areas within this radius were only lightly populated; there was no lattice of strong secondary and tertiary centers. The nearest large cities, such as Cholula and Cantona, are thought to have been independent (Smith 2002).

In sum, the ñuu of the Mixteca Alta were akin to the small polities elsewhere in Mesoamerica. Larger states or empires could be formed by the joining of smaller polities under a single ruler or alliance but they did not develop the bureaucratic apparatus capable of penetrating and transforming their constituent polities and they did not last long. Beyond this comparative observation, however, we hasten to insist that Mesoamerica's states were variable and that this variation should not be swept aside by over-generalization.

The small state was remarkably resilient and persistent. It was not transitional, ephemeral, or peripheral. It persisted through times of growth, collapse, and regional abandonments only to be re-instituted again in much the same form. If Mesoamerica was fragmented politically, what held it together? Why was there a Mesoamerica? States were only one actor in this play. Other important actors were market institutions, cities apart from their roles as capitals of states, other elite interactions, diplomacy, long-distance trade, pilgrimages and shrines, and ideological movements. Characterizing the Mesoamerican social systems primarily by the form of governance misses the complexity generated by these other institutions.

These conclusions about small states inevitably raise questions about the city-state concept (Nichols and Charlton 1997; Hansen 2000, 2002). Hansen's concept of "city-state culture," based on numerous cross-cultural cases, merits attention. "City-state culture" refers to the macroregional phenomenon of a multi-state, often multi-lingual, complex social system formed from many different kinds of exchange that cross city-state political boundaries. Lind (2000) describes the Late Postclassic petty kingdoms of the Mixteca Alta in Hansen's terms. On the other hand, a seminar of American scholars of the archaic state (Feinman and Marcus 1998) that included several prominent Mesoamericanists voiced skepticism about the applicability of the city-state concept to Mesoamerica on the grounds that "city-state" was supposed to be a term for the polis and Mesoamerica had nothing like the Greek polis. We think that the prevalence and viability of the small state in Mesoamerica warrants cross-cultural comparison and that city-state culture is a reasonable description of the matrix of Mesoamerica's small states.

Gat (2003) retains the concept of city-state and also speaks of rural small states that were not especially urbanized but were still more complex in various ways than chiefdoms. In the Mixteca Alta, polities with lesser urbanization—Gat's "rural petty states"—were not a separate phenomenon but instead were border, frontier, client, backwater, or peripheral polities vis-à-vis core urban states. Places sometimes shifted from core to peripheral status or vice versa between the Classic and Postclassic. Yet regional indices of urbanization stayed high for both the Classic and the Postclassic in the Mixteca Alta, with no secular trend (62 percent of the population—Classic and Postclassic—lived in places of over 1,000 inhabitants; cf. 76 percent urban in the Late Aztec eastern and southern Basin of Mexico [Hodge 1994]). Gat (2002) has argued that war was the main factor that made macroregions with multiple city-states. But that explanation does not account for the political economy that maintained macroregional cultural integration for centuries and reproduced city-state culture. Mesoamerican petty kingdoms were woven together not by a simple tribute mode of production but by a complex intertwining of market, tribute, and long-distance trading institutions. This was a differentiated and specialized political economy, not monetized but still capable of transferring value over long distances, and thus integrated at regional and interregional levels (Smith 2002).

Whether Mesoamerican polities were city-states is a typological not a processual question (Heredia 2005). Calling a polity a "city-state" would not explain variation and change. One approach to understanding variation among polities is to identify key, more or less exogenous variables. In our case the physical distribution of intensifiable resources was clearly one such factor. We have also suggested that ñuu varied depending on their place in regional and macroregional systems.

Here we outline another approach. It is dialectical in the sense that social formations at various scales are the products of classes and interests that compete and cooperate. We draw on the historical and ethnographic record of Oaxaca to identify objectives and strategies of actors at each level of integration. Since the objectives of people at different levels are sometimes conflicting and a single actor may have contradictory aims, a rather fluid game results. One aim is to breathe life into typological names like "state" and "city-state." We also want to avoid a purely top-down approach to the state by drawing attention to the middle levels of organization between the throne and the dooryard and to the place of the state in its larger matrix. Our approach follows that of multiscalar explanations (Wu and Loucks 1995) in which to understand a phenomenon at one scale (the state, for instance) one needs to comprehend processes operating at one or two levels below (constituent ñuu and communities or barrios) and above (the Oaxaca cultural region, Mesoamerica). In a dialectical approach, variation is explained by the strength or weakness of social forces at different levels of integration. In this way the particulars from archaeology or native documents can be attached to a general model. Although the following sketch is based on historical and ethnographic facts, when we apply it to the archaeological past it is speculative and we will mark it as hypothesis by using the present tense.

Households of commoners have loyalties to barrios and communities, which are corporate groups that guarantee land and other rights. Individuals or families access land and livelihood through their membership in these first-level local groups. Individuals in the main support the objectives of their barrios or communities because these shield them from excessive labor demands and are the primary defenders of land rights. Barrios and communities organize collective labor for internal purposes and for the cacique's use. They are jealous of their territorial boundaries.

However, marketing, specialized or increased agricultural production, personal clientage to nobles, and participation in cults offer outside opportunities for individuals or households to advance their interests in ways that bypass the barrio or community. Such activities are in conflict with the closed corporate aims of the community. The corporate group can attempt to prevent individual aggrandizement by institutions of internal sharing, feasting, drinking, and other obligations. Yet outside, non-corporate activities can reward individuals and result, for example, in greater household size, a benefit in peasant societies because more people means more labor. Successful households accumulate minor capital holdings or estates by incremental labor investments in agave plants, agricultural terraces, water management, fruit trees, houses, and other facilities. Kin or local groups may have their own shrines.

Barrios and communities attempt to suppress individualism when that behavior conflicts with barrio allegiance. For example, individuals who shirk the burden of collective labor (tequio) create more work for others, so free riding is not allowed. Barrios have symbolic activities and material features including temples and boundary shrines. In theory the barrio has its own collective leadership but rulers may subvert this by insisting on a noble patriarch. Despite their closure, barrios and communities are not economically self-sufficient. Not only may trade, marketing, defense, the overlord, and long-distance ritual events constantly call individuals away, but many goods of daily and ritual consumption are not produced locally. The barrio must be part of a wider exchange network. And as jealous of its prerogatives as it may be, over the long run there will be times when it must rely on outside powers to sanction its claims.

Several barrios and communities are bound together in a political institution, here called the "ñuu." A local community is too small to be viable by itself. But a handful of them together might have several thousand people. This is the potentially autonomous state and the level at which there is a noble ruling family and its house, a palace, petty or grand. (A more democratic or council-led ñuu is conceivable but real cases are hard to come by in the Oaxacan historical record.) Hereditary lords (caciques) of the ñuu are owed tribute, mainly in labor but also in kind, including symbolically important food items. Other sources of hereditary lords' wealth are long-distance trade, market advantages, war, and their role in shrines and pilgrimage centers. Caciques foster marketplaces. Caciques are able to organize the largest capital projects, such as big canal irrigation systems. They are glory-seeking militarists. Descent and alliance reckoning justify their authority. They are network players but at times it is in their interest to promote the internal corporate solidarity of the ñuu because they need the wealth and manpower generated by harmonious home production. Much of ñuu ideology is localist, tied to specific places on the local landscape, but rulers seek external legitimation.

Caciques and barrios or communities are at odds over land and labor. Cacique power is not absolute; it is checked by local corporate groups and peer competition. Lords have their own domains, often worked by dependents, perhaps landless laborers. Caciques that make excessive demands may see a fall in overall production and exchange. They do not have large bureaucracies; instead they rely on kin for high-level positions in military, priestly, and mercantile affairs, and tribute labor for repetitive tasks. An administrative bureaucracy conflicts with the caste and class principles of the cacique system.

Caciques attempt to weave together large states. Some of these attempts are the subjects of legends. But since every cacique may be trying to do the same thing, the competition lowers the chances of any one succeeding. Subordinate ñuu must be held by rewarding or punishing their lords or by dealing directly with their populace, but too much meddling may be counterproductive.

Caciques may also attempt to build power by circumventing corporate communities. They create and manipulate a class of landless workers with fewer rights than the members of the barrios. In the Mixteca, landless laborers were called "*tay situndayu*" but Terraciano notes that this is but one category of dependent workers and that dependent workers may not have had a legal status clearly distinguished from other commoners (2001:140–145). The ambiguity suits a dialectical model as it represents a matter of contestation. We need to know more archaeologically about landless laborers.

To see how larger states or empires could (or could not) be built out of a city-state landscape, we can turn to the Aztec case. To the extent that the Aztecs began to build a large empire, which included the Mixteca Alta, how did they operate? One factor was the intensifiable resource advantage of the Basin of Mexico lakes. Another was that as the empire grew, the Aztecs manipulated production and exchange of specialized products in greater volume by using the tribute and pochteca systems. Unlike the short-lived alliances and conquests of Eight Deer Tiger Claw in the Mixteca, the Aztecs began to build bureaucracy in the core and fostered cadres independent of barrios and communities. The Aztecs also created a new corporate, universalizing ideology that transcended the localisms of city-states.

In this dialectical model the main political-economic strategies, identified by the shorthand terms individualizing/collective or network/corporate (Blanton et al. 1996), alternate by level of integration: individual—collective—individual—collective. Individuals have a tendency to seek opportunities outside as well as inside through multiple channels and therefore can be network operators when conditions are right. Barrios and communities are corporate groups. Caciques are network actors. Empire builders promote universalist ideologies. But there are also contradictory tendencies at every level. Individuals, insofar as their livelihood depends on access to land and their status is determined by their local standing, will make each other adhere to corporate values. Corporate communities can become instruments of individual aggrandizers—caciques in the modern sense. The hereditary rulers, quintessential network operators, nevertheless promote internal collectivism as a means to generate revenue and hold onto labor power—provided that the communities in their domains do not become too powerful and challenge their authority. Empire builders may try to transcend their local roots, but at base they are still caciques, factional leaders in a world of factions.

This interleaved structure opens many possibilities for variation, change, growth, and collapse. Political-economic weaknesses at one level allow for the expansion of groups immediately above or below. This suggests, for instance, that in the ñuu peripheral to a major cacicazgo, such as Nduayaco in its relationship to Teposcolula (Chapter 3), the hereditary lord will be weak but the barrios or communities will be strong. More opportunities for market exchange promote individual status enhancement and social stratification at the expense of local corporate groups. This may be part of what Heredia (2005) found in her comparison of Nochixtlán Valley centers and Tlaxiaco centers: the former had better access to markets and were more wealth-stratified.

At times households and the state establish a feedback circuit of agricultural intensification: the state provides security for markets and people and in turn receives increased revenues; households benefit as long as labor demands are reasonable and the security bargain is kept. Stiver Walsh (2001) and Pérez (2003) describe this association between prosperous households and an intensively developed agricultural landscape at Nicayuju in the core of a strong state, Teposcolula. Local corporate groups have a role in blocking or resisting this circuit if the lord expands his private agricultural domains at their expense. A class-based alliance of landed peasants and landless laborers is a threat to the hereditary aristocracy. Evidence of such conflict is harder to find archaeologically but the court records of Colonial times have many instances of conflict between caciques and villages in their domains.

An interesting test for further archaeological and historical research would be the fascinating case of Tlaxiaco. This was a major cacicazgo in the sixteenth century. Yet we found no large city or palatial remains at Tlaxiaco. The demographic and economic heartland of the Tlaxiaco cacicazgo was instead in the inner basin where a half-dozen strong and wealthy ñuu clustered next to each other. What kind of cacicazgo was this? What were the dynamics between central power and the separate ñuu?

Local groups can benefit in principle if a petty state is weak, but if states fail completely, there can be a breakdown of integration resulting in violence or collapse. If disintegration and violence persist, it may be impossible for local groups to survive. In the Mixteca Alta there was a collapse in the Late Classic/Epiclassic, but it is not well understood.

REGIONAL ABANDONMENTS

The settlement history of this part of the Mixteca Alta has two major gaps in an otherwise continuous sequence. The two gaps are the Terminal Formative and the Late Classic/Epiclassic. Two alternative explanations are that the hiatuses are abandonments of substantial portions of the Mixteca Alta or that we are failing to see occupation because of chronological problems that are due to ceramic conservatism (or our imbecility).

For reasons discussed earlier in this book we think that many subregions really were devoid of occupation in the Terminal Formative (Late Ramos) and the Late Classic/Epiclassic (Late Las Flores) and that the gaps in the sequence are (mostly) not artifacts of poor chronological control. For the Terminal Formative we have excellent and very recognizable ceramic collections from two major centers (Huamelulpan and Dzinicahua) and a number of smaller sites. We do not have assemblages of Late Classic/Epiclassic pottery from our project area, but just to the east in the Nochixtlán Valley, Spores (1983:155–158), Plunket (1983:383–391), and Byland and Pohl (1994:66–67, e.g.) describe Late Classic occupations at Yucuñudahui, Yucuita, and other places, and Etlatongo may have a Late Classic component (Blomster 1998). We thus have reason to conclude that if there had been more than the most ephemeral of occupations we would have detected them.

Is it unusual that a potentially bountiful land like the Mixteca Alta could lie unoccupied for a century or more? Other resource-rich places in the world had no human occupation for long periods of time. Blanton (2000) summarizes the data on the fairly common regional hiatuses in the Mediterranean. Beginning in Pueblo III and continuing in Pueblo IV large areas of the Southwest did not have permanent occupation sites (Hill et al. 2004). Smith's (2002) analysis of all regional surveys in the Mesoamerican highlands west of the Isthmus of Tehuantepec shows that both periods in question, the Terminal Formative and the Late Classic/Epiclassic, were fairly chaotic and had declining macroregional integration.

Recall that what made the Mixteca Alta bountiful in the eyes of the sixteenth-century Spanish was not just nature but a tremendous amount of persistent human labor: "Lo que transformaba a la sierra inhóspita en un jardín era el trabajo de los agricultores" (Pastor 1987:38). Labor was not carried out by hypothetically free individuals. It was organized according to the prevailing mode of production and in the prevailing climate of physical and market security. If the region was too dangerous or if households could not be reasonably assured of access to markets for their harvests and their needs, the institutions of community, siqui, and ñuu may not have been viable. Parts of the Mixteca Alta, especially the smaller subregions, indeed may have suffered from the broader political-economic disintegration during the periods in question. This explanation for the regional abandonments might be called the Great Depression hypothesis.

An intriguing problem of descent versus replacement is that of continuity across periods of regional abandonment. The hierarchically organized subregional polity was essentially the same in the Postclassic as it had been in the Classic, yet a large part of the Mixteca Alta, especially west of the Sierra de Nochixtlán, was apparently unoccupied for several centuries in between. The institutional form of the state lived on and continued to be reproduced elsewhere in Mesoamerica. From what places were abandoned subregions re-colonized? Presumably older, core subregions in the Nochixtlán Valley or elsewhere in the Mixteca persisted and attracted people from weaker, disintegrating places and then later became the sources for re-colonization. Most definitely the abandonment problem needs further study.

AGRARIAN URBANISM

The Mixteca Alta was a very productive place for intensive agriculture. It was more urbanized than most regions in highland Mesoamerica (Smith 2002:189). Its population size and density, urbanization indices, and central place densities were comparable to those of other world civilizations (a few references are given in Kowalewski

1990; see also Blanton 1985 on market densities). We conclude this book with a discussion of the functions of urbanism in the Mixteca Alta and Mesoamerica. We propose that cities were key brokers in an agrarian economy. The proposal is neither novel nor complete but it may serve as a basis for designing interesting archaeological research.

What activities were particularly characteristic of cities in the Mixteca or Mesoamerica generally? Durable craft production is usually not assigned a leading causal role in Mesoamerican urbanism as it is in Chinese civilization. Urbanized regional systems in this part of the world did not have intensive animal raising as in Mesopotamia or Africa; shipbuilding and shipping were not a great economic force (as in Europe). If these factors were absent or of lesser importance, what made Mesoamerican urbanism?

Some archaeologists have emphasized the ceremonial and regal functions of Mesoamerican cities, perhaps because these institutions have left obvious remains—temples, palaces, or carved stone monuments (Sanders and Webster 1988; comments by Smith 1989). Without denying that ceremonial and rulership functions were significant in Mesoamerican urbanism we suggest that more attention be given to urban economic functions. Pérez (2003:1) has written about the cacicazgos of the Mixteca as "agricultural powerhouses." Agriculture in this context refers to far more than the domestic economy, subsistence, and the simple rural life of an undifferentiated peasantry. In prehispanic Mesoamerica, agriculture meant the full panoply of producing food, fiber, and fuel; the transformation of primary products into highly differentiated goods; their exchange; and their consumption. Agriculture in urbanized Mesoamerica was intensive, diversified, and market-driven in the sense that people produced all sorts of things for exchange in market institutions and that production decisions depended on extra-household economic demand.

Cities were the central nodes of these agricultural powerhouses (Heredia et al. 2004). As central places for regional economies, Mesoamerican cities had functions and institutions involved with coordinating the activities of this most important sector. Labor organization, regulation, taxation, dispute resolution, land and water allocation, information exchange, new projects, wholesaling, retail trade, coordination of local and long-distance exchange, fairs and festivals, and judicial functions all must have been functions whose apex or first order resided in institutions located in cities. We attribute the greater degree of wealth stratification seen in top-ranked Mesoamerican cities to the multiple economic opportunities available in these places.

Caciques and temples played a role in these affairs but so did markets, middle-level institutions such as the siqui, and other institutions that are difficult to study because they were not of great interest to Spanish chroniclers or they leave few archaeological remains. Future research should be specifically designed to examine activities and institutions at this middle level between household and state. We suggest a model in which cities of the Mixteca Alta were demographically large and socially differentiated places in large part because their inhabitants carried out activities central to intensive and diverse agrarian economies.

Craft specialization has a very low profile in our survey data. Compared to other surveyed regions in Oaxaca such as the Tlacolula and Ocotlán arms of the Valley of Oaxaca, the Central Mixteca Alta has strikingly little evidence of craft specialization. One should not conclude that there were not specialists, for example, in pottery or textiles. Instead, such specialties were apparently not very intense in this region.

We hypothesize that economic integration was not based on differentiation in non-agricultural sectors but on intensified and differentiated agricultural production. We are reminded of the Javanese "agricultural involution" described by Geertz (1963). The Mixteca Alta was capable of producing larger and larger yields through labor-intensive terracing, irrigation, and crop specialization. In this situation integration was not a matter of exchanging products among butchers, bakers, and candlestick makers; it was a matter of allocating labor, negotiating land rights, adjudicating claims, and marketing surpluses for long-distance exchange. Urban institutions, including markets and the ñuu, performed these functions; such institutions were probably also the actors in the structural conflicts between nobility, communities, and barrios.

Our claim is that Mixteca Alta urbanism was fundamentally agrarian and that cities performed the central place functions necessary to integrate an intensive agricultural economy. Integration and interaction imply flows and movement of energy, matter, information, and people. What moved in our case? If we are correct in saying that this was an agrarian urbanism, what moved was people (labor), agricultural products, and information about land, labor, and farm products. In these movements urban institutions were the key nodes.

Monaghan (1995) showed in great detail how food was exchanged in late twentieth-century Mixteca Alta village ceremonial institutions. Garvin (1994) provides excellent descriptions of small-scale but almost constant inter-household exchange of labor in agriculture and household maintenance at another village in the Mixteca Alta. These are the kinds of low-level movements that archaeologists need to be looking for. We also need to investigate the roles of barrios, the ñuu, and cities as nodes and actors in the agrarian economy.

This economy was built on milpas, agaves, and fruit trees. These crops in turn derived their nutrients from the good water and fertile soils, which people retained and concentrated on terraces. Human population depended on this agroecosystem. Human labor was key—the more labor, the richer the yields. It was a regime capable of absorbing increasing amounts of labor. Limits to this positive feedback system could have come from pests, climate fluctuation, or political-economic disruption. In a sense the limits were spatial—land intensification might proceed until at some point one ran out of room. Or the limits came from the demand side—falling demand, internal or external, created surplus labor.

Human labor was the crucial input in this agroecosystem but people were also the safety valve. The Late Postclassic movement of people from the Mixteca Alta into the Valley of Oaxaca is well known (Bernal 1966; Paddock 1966). Today the Mixteca Alta is known for exporting its people; emigration of "surplus" people may have been a long-standing pattern.

The work of holistic anthropologists like Alfonso Caso and Ron Spores made known the significant place of the Mixteca Alta in Mesoamerican civilization. More of the details of the cultural sequence leading to its states and urbanism are now known. In addition the combined studies in central Oaxaca, including the Mixteca Alta, the Valley of Oaxaca, and their neighboring regions, now offer an unusual multi-regional or macroregional perspective on long-term cultural evolution. The challenges are to place this knowledge in greater global perspective and to use the macroregional advantage to build better theory.

CHAPTER TWELVE

Resumen en Español

En este libro presentamos los resultados de un recorrido arqueológico sistemático realizado en la Mixteca Alta Central y una serie de estudios sobre el surgimiento y desarrollo de su civilización. En el siglo XVI la Mixteca fue descrita como una región rica, próspera y densamente poblada. Los datos arqueológicos sugieren que esta región fue una de las más importantes y densamente pobladas en la Mesoamérica Postclásica. En la actualidad, la región está severamente erosionada, lo que ha dejado a varias comunidades con pocos suelos cultivables, además de que gran parte de su escasa población ha tenido que emigrar por falta de oportunidades económicas. ¿Cómo es que surge una civilización en una región que puede considerarse ambientalmente marginal? ¿Cómo se convierte una región ambientalmente marginal en una región rica? ¿Cómo se convierte una región rica en un lugar agrícolamente pobre y erosionado? ¿Qué nos puede decir el caso de la Mixteca Alta acerca del funcionamiento de las sociedades complejas? Los estudios que presentamos buscan dar respuesta a estos y otros cuestionamientos.

En el primer capítulo presentamos una introducción a nuestro trabajo, sus objetivos y metodología. Nuestros objetivos fueron: (1) localizar y describir todos los yacimientos arqueológicos en el área de estudio; (2) describir los contextos ambientales de los sitios (topografía, suelos y su uso, agua, vegetación, recursos especiales); (3) fechar los sitios y sus distintos sectores mediante el uso de la tipología de cerámica establecida; (4) medir, elaborar mapas y describir elementos agrícolas y arquitectónicos; (5) examinar los perfiles de áreas erosionadas o cortes de carretera para buscar evidencia de sitios y paleo suelos; (6) recolectar cerámica y artefactos líticos para estudiar la variación estilística, funcional y cronológica presente.

Los datos recopilados se sumaron a aquellos obtenidos en recorridos previos realizados por Stiver Walsh en Teposcolula y por Balkansky en Huamelulpan. Como resultado obtuvimos información sobre un área contigua de 1,668 km², la cual es aledaña a otras regiones previamente estudiadas como Tamazulapam, Jaltepec, la porción oeste del Valle de Nochixtlán, la sierra de Peñoles y el Valle de Oaxaca. En base a estos estudios presentamos la historia de la ocupación humana y del desarrollo de sociedades complejas en la Mixteca Alta, a partir del período Arcaico hasta el siglo XVI.

En los capítulos del 2 al 6 se presenta en detalle la secuencia de ocupación humana desde el período Arcaico al Posclásico para las distintas subregiones y localidades del área de estudio. De esta manera, el capítulo 2 se enfoca en la subregión localizada al oeste de la sierra de Nochixtlán, el 3 en la subregión de Teposcolula, el 4 en la localidad de Huamelulpan, el 5 en el área central que se extiende entre Achiutla, Tlacotepec, Yucuañe, y Dzinicahua y, finalmente, el 6 describe la región de Tlaxiaco y sus periferias. En estos capítulos presentamos referencias detalladas y mapas de distribución de asentamientos para cada subregión y fase prehispánica.

El capítulo 7 toma en cuenta los datos de todas las subregiones del área de estudio para describir los resultados y patrones identificados para las unidades políticas del Preclásico Temprano y Medio. A esta discusión se añaden resultados de estudios adicionales realizados acerca de la asociación que hubo entre asentamientos humanos y suelos propios para la agricultura; la asociación espacial entre sitios y terrazas agrícolas y el grado de acceso o restricción a los complejos arquitectónicos y lo que esto revela acerca de la organización socio-política de la época. Dentro del Preclásico se encontró una fuerte asociación entre los asentamientos humanos y la distribución de suelos de los tipos denominados Yanhuitlán y Jaltepec. El estudio sobre la distribución regional de terrazas agrícolas (lama-bordo) y asentamientos humanos sugiere que la asociación entre los sitios y las terrazas posiblemente se remonta al Preclásico Medio, predatando de esta manera a los primeros centros urbanos y sociedades estatales en la región.

El capítulo 8 discute las transformaciones y patrones identificados para la fase Ramos, la cual se refiere al surgimiento del estado en la Mixteca. Los asentamientos humanos de la fase Ramos no siguen la distribución de los mejores suelos agrícolas, lo cual sugiere que la localización de dichos asentamientos se debe a otros factores no ambientales. Por otra parte, un estudio de sintaxis espacial encontró que hubo un aumento en el número de espacios arquitectónicos restringidos del Preclásico Medio al Tardío y del Preclásico Tardío al Clásico. Esto se interpreta como una manifestación material de un proceso social en el cual se desarrolló una autoridad religiosa y política más formal y más separada de la población general. La fase Ramos se refiere a un período de transformación en el que se establecieron nuevos asentamientos urbanos en sitios protegidos o de defensa, al mismo tiempo en que los antiguos centros eran abandonados. Este período marca el inicio de la vida urbana y posiblemente el de las organizaciones estatales en la región.

El capítulo 9 trata de la Mixteca Alta y los *ñuu* de la época Clásica. El ñuu era un estado potencialmente autónomo y más grande que una comunidad individual. Los datos regionales sugieren que los asentamientos Clásicos no siempre se localizaron en los mejores suelos agrícolas. A diferencia de otras regiones Mesoamericanas, la Mixteca nunca desarrolló una estado grande o centralizado que rigiera sobre toda la región, más sin en cambio se identificaron una serie de pequeños estados localizados en las montañas y valles. Presentamos aquí los resultados de un estudio que investigó la integración política y económica entre los distintos asentamientos y subregiones, mismo que sugiere que a partir de la época Clásica temprana, estas subregiones se integraron en jerarquías de asentamiento que se extendían más allá de la subregión individual. Esta integración a través de áreas mayores caracterizaba la estructura de los cacicazgos Posclásicos (o *yuhuitayu*). Encontramos entonces que las organizaciones políticas Posclásicas pudieran tener sus orígenes en la época Clásica.

Nos enfocamos en la distribución de tipos cerámicos no utilitarios o exóticos para estudiar la naturaleza de la organización política de la Mixteca Clásica. Esta investigación sugiere que las entidades políticas del Clásico estuvieron marginalmente estratificadas y que su organización política fue distinta a la de los cacicazgos Posclásicos, ya que estos últimos centralizaban el poder en la figura del cacique y la élite que controlaba la distribución de materiales exóticos.

El capítulo 10 se enfoca en la Mixteca Alta y los ñuu Posclásicos, en donde describimos sus características y distribución regional. Dentro del Posclásico se encontró una fuerte asociación entre los asentamientos humanos y la distribución de suelos de tipo Yanhuitlán y Jaltepec. Esta fuerte asociación también se ve reflejada en la distribución de asentamientos humanos y terrazas agrícolas. Se presentan resultados de excavaciones de terrazas agrícolas Posclásicas, la importancia de su uso y método de construcción, así como su papel dentro de la organización social. En general, en este capítulo resumimos los datos de patrones de asentamiento para hablar acerca de los ñuu Posclásicos y su organización social, económica, política y regional.

En el capítulo 11 presentamos una serie de conclusiones relativas al ñuu dentro de una perspectiva antropológica. Estas conclusiones se basan en los datos recopilados por este proyecto y en lo que éstos revelan acerca del desarrollo de su civilización. Nuestras conclusiones integran una perspectiva macro-regional. A continuación presentamos un resumen de las conclusiones principales de este libro.

Contrario a lo que se esperaba, se encontró que la Mixteca Alta era una región principal durante el Preclásico Temprano y Medio. La región presentaba oportunidades ambientales para los primeros grupos agricultores y su población fue igual o mayor a la de otras regiones principales de Mesoamérica.

Uno de los hallazgos de este estudio fue que la unidad socio-política del Preclásico Temprano y Medio no fue una sola aldea, sino una agrupación de asentamientos consistentes de una aldea principal y varias aldeas o rancherías satélites. La población creció y se extendió del Preclásico Temprano al Medio. Las agrupaciones de asentamientos iniciales, las del Preclásico Temprano, se añadieron a otras agrupaciones 'hijas' establecidas en zonas cercanas o adyacentes a la agrupación inicial. Con esta innovación se crearon dos niveles jerárquicos por encima de la aldea común. Este nivel de jerarquía podría considerarse una jefatura, aunque hace falta saber más acerca de las instituciones y del sistema político. Las capitales o aldeas principales de estas súper-agrupaciones emergen como centros regionales importantes. Al parecer este patrón no sólo se encuentra en la Mixteca, sino en toda Mesoamérica, lo cual sugiere que la macro-región compartía una economía política.

Hacia el Preclásico Tardío y Terminal existe evidencia macro-regional de la presencia de conflicto y de una marcada militarización de la Mixteca Alta. Cada subregión de la Mixteca se vió afectada y los viejos asentamientos fueron abandonados, al mismo tiempo que se establecieron nuevos centros urbanos en cimas fortificadas. Este modo de vida militarizado no fue estable y después de uno o dos siglos colapsó. Aunque en la Mixteca Alta nunca surgió un estado grande y centralizado como Teotihuacan o Monte Albán, no encontramos evidencia de una invasión o influencia directa por parte de estos estados sobre la región durante la época Clásica.

Por lo general, la secuencia cultural de la Mixteca Alta muestra una fuerte evidencia de continuidad autónoma y un persistente y temprano desarrollo de instituciones distintivas que fueron miembros o sujetos de un sistema cultural macro-regional (mesoamericano) mayor. La Mixteca Alta no es una región físicamente monolítica, sino un compuesto de montañas y pequeños valles. Cada uno de estos valles tienen sus particularidades ambientales y cada uno tuvo su propia historia de asentamiento humano. En nuestra área de estudio distinguimos 27 subregiones, que fueron agrupaciones multicomunitarias y hogares de los ñuu, cada una con una superficie de 50 a 100 km².

¿Cuándo surgió el ñuu? La organización social del ñuu fue descrita en las crónicas del siglo XVI y se le denominó estado en los códices mixtecos que datan principalmente de la época Postclásica. En base a datos regionales concluimos que el ñuu y su manifestación en cuanto a sus patrones de asentamiento datan del Clásico Temprano. No obstante, su escala, complejidad y forma sobrevive y aumenta en la época Postclásica. Las jerarquías de asentamiento del Clásico Temprano contaban con un sitio primario seguido por sitios secundarios y terciarios que conformaron tres niveles jerárquicos por encima de la aldea común. La distribución y configuración de la arquitectura pública sugiere también una jerarquía cívico-ceremonial de cuatro niveles.

Los ñuu Posclásicos no surgieron como resultado de la desintegración de los estados regionales de la época Clásica ya que consideramos que estos estados

Clásicos fueron pequeños ñuu. La complejidad de asentamientos Posclásicos surge del patrón Clásico, aunque llega a mostrar una mayor complejidad horizontal. En áreas centrales encontramos evidencia de una mayor complejidad vertical, una estructura compuesta por centros urbanos capitales, pueblos y aldeas secundarias y terciarias. Identificamos barrios locales, ñuu y capitales de cacicazgos, aunque los palacios de los caciques no siempre se localizaban en los pueblos más grandes. Fueron además comunes los sitios fronterizos y rituales. Los asentamientos se encontraban en una gran diversidad de ambientes y contextos naturales, lo que sugiere un grado considerable de complejidad horizontal. Recursos como la tierra, la población y su labor fueron distribuidos a través de instituciones comunitarias en una escala también comunitaria. Existe además evidencia indirecta que sugiere la presencia de sistemas de mercado que crearon a su vez una mayor diferenciación y complejidad social.

¿Fueron los ñuu descendientes de las unidades sociales del Preclásico Temprano y Medio? En comparación con las entidades identificadas en la época Preclásica, los ñuu fueron más complejos, su escala y población fue mayor, al igual que el volumen de su intercambio e interacción con otras regiones. Pero, al igual que el ñuu, las aldeas mayores y los satélites de la época Preclásica estaban organizados de manera jerárquica y formaban una entidad política a una escala subregional. Estos grupos de asentamientos fueron la unidad política fundamental y formaron una relación jerárquica de grupos principales y periferias. Es difícil establecer una continuidad entre estas entidades políticas Preclásicas y los estados Clásicos y los ñuu, ya que hubo periodos de abandono y reorganización en torno a sitios fortificados.

A raíz de este estudio argüimos que los estados en la Mixteca Alta fueron pequeños, como lo fueron la mayoría de los estados Clásicos y Posclásicos de Mesoamérica. El estado de Teposcolula durante el Clásico Temprano midió menos de 25 kilómetros de extremo a extremo, incluyendo su periferia. El estado de Teposcolula durante el Posclásico fue un poco más grande y tuvo una población de cerca de 60,000 habitantes. La mayoría de los estados mixtecos fueron de menor tamaño. Aunque los ñuu estaban integrados a unidades políticas o alianzas mayores como Teposcolula e imperios como el Azteca, éstos no se transformaron ni se disolvieron, sino que siguieron intactos aunque subordinados.

Al inicio, cuando comenzamos este proyecto, propusimos que los cacicazgos mixtecos pudieron haberse desarrollado a partir de la separación de estados Clásicos. Estos cacicazgos se habrían originado en las zonas centrales de los estados Clásicos o en las áreas fronterizas o periferias. En base a este proyecto podemos ahora rechazar esa idea. Los ñuu no fueron producto de la disolución de grandes estados o de imperios, porque tales nunca existieron en la Mixteca Alta. Los cacicazgos mixtecos tuvieron sus raíces en la época Clásica Temprana e incluso pudieron tener sus orígenes a finales de la época Preclásica. Los estados de la Mixteca Alta no fueron copias secundarias de estados originales de otras regiones, sino que se desarrollaron a partir de las comunidades y colectividades militares del Preclásico Tardío, por lo que exhiben una larga continuidad *in situ*. Estas entidades políticas no fueron colonias o estados subordinados a bloques imperiales, ya que no encontramos evidencia de colonización externa. Por otro lado, en el transcurso de su historia, la Mixteca Alta fue una región con alta densidad de población, autonomía política y poder económico basado en la agricultura intensiva.

Los datos del recorrido muestran dos interrupciones en una secuencia de ocupación casi continua, durante el Preclásico Terminal y la época Clásica Tardía, para lo cual existen dos posibles explicaciones: (1) que hubieron períodos de abandono en grandes porciones de la Mixteca Alta o (2) que no fue posible identificar ocupaciones debido a problemas cronológicos relacionados a la secuencia cerámica.

Por razones que discutimos en detalle en esta monografía pensamos que muchas subregiones en verdad fueron abandonadas en el Preclásico y Clásico Tardío y que estos patrones no son el resultado de una pobre cronología cerámica. Contamos con excelentes colecciones cerámicas de material de diagnóstico para el Preclásico Terminal provenientes de Huamelulpan, Dzinicahua y otros sitios menores. Más allá de estos sitios no encontramos cerámica del Preclásico Tardío en el área de estudio. No encontramos materiales del Clásico Terminal dentro de nuestra área de estudio, sin embargo, al este en el Valle de Nochixtlán hay evidencias de ocupaciones del Clásico Tardío en Yucuñudahui, Yucuita, y Etlatongo, entre otros. Concluimos que si hubieran existido ocupaciones significativas en nuestra área de estudio, las hubiéramos podido registrar.

¿Es inusual que una tierra tan rica como la Mixteca Alta hubiera sido abandonada por más de un siglo? Existen casos de regiones similarmente favorecidas que han sido desocupadas por largos períodos, tal es el ejemplo de la zona del Mediterráneo y partes del Suroeste de los Estados Unidos. Los periodos Preclásico Terminal y el Clásico Tardío o Epiclásico fueron, en las tierras altas de Mesoamérica, épocas caóticas en las que hubo una marcada desintegración socio-política a nivel macroregional y en varios casos incluso hubo abandono de regiones enteras.

Cabe recordar que lo que convirtió a la Mixteca Alta en una tierra rica ante los ojos de los cronistas españoles, no fue la naturaleza sino la gente y su trabajo. Esta labor no fue realizada por individuos hipotéticamente libres, sino que fue organizada por el modo de producción dentro de un clima político y económico existente. Las comunidades, ñuu o *siqui* (barrio) no pudieron haber sobrevivido en un clima político que convertía a la región en un lugar inseguro para los agricultores, si los sistemas de mercados eran interrumpidos o si la gente común tenía problemas de abastecimiento, consecuentemente, partes de la Mixteca Alta pudieron haber sufrido una desintegración política y económica durante estos períodos.

Existe un problema interesante en cuanto a la continuidad y reemplazo de población en épocas posteriores a los abandonos. Como hemos dicho, las entidades políticas del Posclásico son esencialmente las mismas que las de la época Clásica, sin embargo grandes porciones de la Mixteca Alta, en especial áreas al oeste de la Sierra de Nochixtlán estuvieron desocupadas por varios siglos. ¿En dónde continuaron o sobrevivieron estas formas políticas ancestrales? ¿De dónde provino la gente que repobló las áreas abandonadas? Es posible que subregiones en el Valle de Nochixtlán y otras áreas aún no estudiadas hayan perdurado, atrayendo a poblaciones de las áreas inseguras y de las entidades políticas que se desintegraban para después exportar su población a las áreas abandonadas. Este es un problema que sin duda requiere mayor estudio.

La Mixteca Alta fue un lugar que estuvo urbanizado por 1,500 años antes de la Conquista. Como en otros lugares de Mesoamérica, su población, tamaño y densidad fueron comparables a otros lugares y civilizaciones. Concluimos este libro con una discusión sobre las funciones del urbanismo en la Mixteca Alta y en Mesoamérica. Proponemos que los centros urbanos fueron los principales negociadores y actores en los conflictos sociales de una economía agrícola. Aunque esta propuesta no es una novedad, pudiera servir de base para originar futuras investigaciones arqueológicas.

En comparación con otras regiones Mesoamericanas, en la Mixteca hubo una fuerte asociación entre los centros poblacionales y los suelos aptos para la agricultura, los suelos de la formación Yanhuitlán. Por otra parte, los datos de recorrido no sugieren producción especializada a comparación con el Valle de Oaxaca. En la Mixteca Alta tenemos muy poca evidencia de producción especializada y esto es notable. No pensamos que no haya habido productores especializados de textiles o cerámica en la región, sino que dicha producción, que sin duda tuvo lugar, fue de menor escala e intensidad.

Proponemos que el urbanismo mixteco fue fundamentalmente agrario y que los centros urbanos sirvieron las funciones necesarias para la integración de una economía agrícola intensiva. Esta integración implicó el desplazamiento humano, labor, técnicas, productos agrícolas e información sobre las tierras. En este movimiento las instituciones urbanas actuaron como nódulos centrales. Sin embargo, también queda la necesidad de investigar el papel que desempeñaron los barrios, ñuu y ciudades como nódulos y actores en una economía agrícola dinámica.

Dentro del urbanismo Mesoamericano las actividades referentes a la producción de objetos perdurables no son consideradas como centrales. En esta parte del mundo el urbanismo tampoco fue influenciado por la crianza de animales de carga, la construcción de navíos ni el intercambio mediante la utilización de redes marítimas. Entonces, ¿qué factores influyeron en la formación del urbanismo Mesoamericano?

Algunos estudiosos se han enfocado en las funciones ceremoniales y gubernamentales de las ciudades Mesoamericanas, tal vez porque estas instituciones dejaron restos impresionantes como templos y palacios. Sin negar las funciones rituales y políticas del urbanismo Mesoamericano, proponemos que se debe prestar mayor atención a las funciones económicas de los centros urbanos y a los cacicazgos como poderíos agrícolas. En este contexto nos referimos a la agricultura como algo más que la economía doméstica, la producción para subsistencia y la vida rural de los campesinos. En la Mesoamérica prehispánica la agricultura consistió en una serie de actividades como la producción de comida, fibras y combustible, la transformación de productos primarios en objetos especiales de valor económico, social y ritual, su intercambio y consumo. La agricultura que se llevaba a cabo dentro del urbanismo Mesoamericano fue intensiva, diversificada y enfocada hacia los mercados.

Con este trabajo esperamos contribuir a la larga y distinguida historia de trabajo arqueológico en Oaxaca y la Mixteca Alta. Pensamos que este trabajo ha generado un volumen importante de información acerca de la secuencia cultural de la Mixteca Alta, el origen de la vida sedentaria, de las sociedades estatales y de la organización política de ñuu. Sin embargo, reconocemos que este estudio debe sumarse a otros realizados en Oaxaca y otras regiones para seguir construyendo una visión multi y macro regional acerca de la evolución cultural de las civilizaciones Mesoamericanas. El reto será aplicar esta visión a una perspectiva global que nos revele algo significativo acerca de la naturaleza de las sociedades humanas en el presente y en el pasado.

Ceramic Chronology

The Mixteca Alta ceramic chronology was initially outlined following stratigraphic excavations covering multiple time periods in Tamazulapan-Tejupan, Coixtlahuaca, and Nochixtlán, including the sites of Yatachio, Las Pilitas, Iglesia Vieja, Yucuñudahui, and Monte Negro (Caso 1938, 1942; Bernal 1949; Paddock 1953). With his Nochixtlán Valley regional survey and excavations, Spores (1972, 1974) established the basic five-period sequence used here and in all contemporary studies in the Mixteca Alta (Table 1.2) and published ware and type descriptions. We also draw on pottery descriptions and chronological adjustments from subsequent studies (Byland 1980; Plunket 1983; Gaxiola 1984; Lind 1987; Zárate 1987; Robles 1988; Byland and Pohl 1994; Spores 1996; Winter 1997). Cross-ties confirm substantial interregional communication and provide crucial evidence for dating. The Valley of Oaxaca ceramic studies are especially valuable: Caso et al. (1967); Drennan (1976, 1983); Kowalewski et al. (1978); Whalen (1981); Flannery and Marcus (1994); Martínez López et al. (2000). See also Joyce (1991) for Formative coastal Oaxaca;

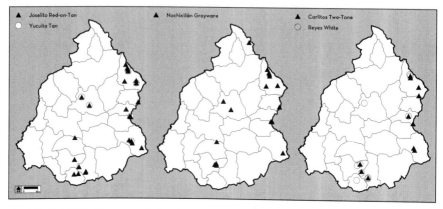

A1.1 *Early/Middle Cruz ceramic distributions.*

Spencer and Redmond (1997, 2001) for the Cuicatlán Cañada; and MacNeish et al. (1970) for the Tehuacan Valley. The relationships of the Mixteca Alta phases and their ceramics to those of neighboring areas are critically reviewed in detail by Stiver Walsh (2001:59–83).

The current sequence relies heavily on cross-ties and associations; the Mixteca Alta needs more stratigraphic excavations and many more radiocarbon dates. The dates for phases set forth in this book must be considered provisional and not definitive.

This appendix summarizes the chronological sequence of known phases and their ceramic indicators (see Stiver Walsh 2001 for a fuller treatment). The illustrations are from our surface collections. Measurements, ware and type information, and proveniences for the sherds shown in the photographs are given in Table A1.1. The figures showing spatial distributions of the major wares are for the 1999 survey area (not Huamelulpan or Teposcolula).

EARLY/MIDDLE CRUZ

Buff and red-on-buff pottery characterize the first part of the Early Formative (1400 to 1150 BC). Early Cruz has Etlatongo Buff wares including a plain and a red-painted variety. Paste is buff or light tan. Our collections have thin-walled Etlatongo Buff cylindrical and hemispherical bowls and jars. Vessels are usually well burnished and slipped red, though brown and black slips occur and fine-line incising may also occur. The sherds are rare in surface collections. We combined Early and Middle Cruz into one phase from 1400 to 700 BC to avoid defining components based on very few diagnostics.

We have more material from the latter portion of the period, 1150 to 700 BC (Figure A1.1). Yucuita Red-on-Tan, Joselito Variety, is characteristic of Early/Middle Cruz (Figure A1.2:1–14). The tan to brown clay body contains abundant inclusions,

A1.2 Early/Middle Cruz sherds (Joselito Red-on-Tan, Jazmín Red and White, and others) (see Table A1.1).

often quite large. Forms include everted and flaring-rim jars, bottles, tecomates, and hemispherical, cylindrical, outleaned-wall, and other types of bowls. Jars and bowls may have red, or less frequently orange, slip or paint, which is sometimes applied heavily, sloppily, or in bands around the vessel. Burnishing is common and occasional decoration includes incised lines, scratching, raking, rocker stamping (Figure A1.2:15), and Olmec horizon excised "X" motifs. When no slip can be detected tanwares are classified as Yucuita Tan. There are tanware figurine heads with flat, elongated faces, and slanting eyes.

Jazmín Red and White wares are excellent markers for the Early/Middle Cruz phase, with two varieties, Carlitos Two-Tone and Reyes White. The tan or brown paste is generally finer than in Joselito Red-on-Tan vessels. Carlitos Two-Tone bowls are found with outleaned walls, flared, everted, or other rim profiles, with red or orange slip and white slip (Figure A1.2:16, Figure A1.3:1–6). A contrasting band is often applied around the rim of the vessel. Rims are frequently incised, including the double-line break. White-slipped Reyes White has jars, bottles, and most typically bowls (Figure A1.3:7–9). Bowl forms include outleaned-wall, hemispherical, cylindrical, and flaring to everted-rim bowls. Our collections have examples with incised lines, shallow grooves, and incised "X" motifs along the rim.

Nochixtlán Graywares are well represented, with flaring, cylindrical, hemispherical and other bowls, and occasionally jars and tecomates. Graywares tend to have a fine clay body and small inclusions. Decoration includes incised lines, double-line breaks, "X" motifs, excising, and raking (Figure A1.3:10–11, 13–17). Burnishing and slipped surfaces were noted, including red or black, sometimes specular, or whitish slips.

LATE CRUZ

In the Middle Formative (ca. 700 to 300 BC), all wares are widespread throughout the region (Figure A1.4). The Filemón Red-on-Tan variety of Yucuita Tan, with finer clay body and inclusions than the earlier Joselito variety, is a dominant ware. Its forms include jars, bottles, tecomates, comals, and bowls (Figures A1.5:1–15 and A1.6). Jar rims often are flaring or everted; upright-necked jars and other profiles also are present. Bowl profiles vary from everted, flaring, or outleaned to cylindrical, hemispherical, occasionally incurving, or composite-silhouette (Figure A1.7). Bolstered and eccentric rims (Figure A1.5:7) and pedestal bases sometimes were found. Slips range from garnet red to red to red-orange to orange, with pale or streaky slips to heavily applied paint. A few vessels have black on red or simply black slips. Incised decoration is not uncommon on bowl rims but unusual on jars and includes lines, double-line break, saw tooth, scallops, and more rarely a checkerboard or crosshatching design. There are distinctive waxy red-painted, narrow-necked bottles (Figure A1.8).

Polished Brown refers to a diagnostic slipped and burnished serving ware (Figure A1.9:1–10). Clay body is brown to tan, generally finer and more consistent than Yucuita Tanwares, and the slip is usually black. Brown, red, orange, and other colors also appear. Single or multiple lines, double-line breaks, zigzags, and other elements typically are incised through the slip around an everted or flaring, bolstered rim (Figure A1.10). Incised patterns vary widely, eccentric rims with scallops

A1.3 Early/Middle Cruz sherds (Jazmín Red and White and Nochixtlán Gray) (see Table A1.1).

or crenulations are not unusual, and other decoration such as pattern burnishing occurs on some examples. Bowls often have composite silhouettes, sometimes with pedestal bases (Figure A1.11).

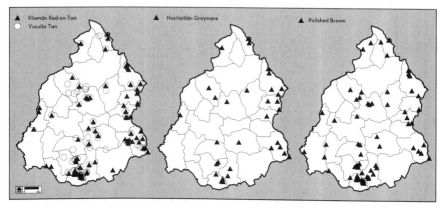

A1.4 Late Cruz ceramic distributions.

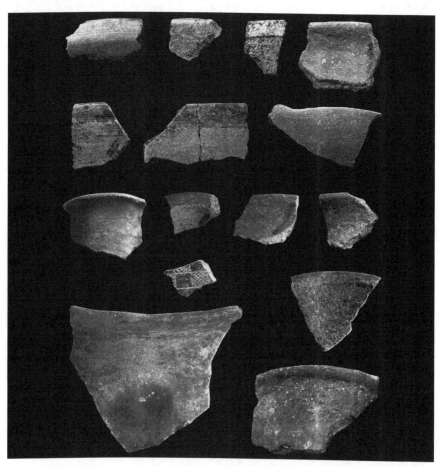

A1.5 Late Cruz sherds (Yucuita Tan and Filemón Red-on-Tan) (see Table A1.1).

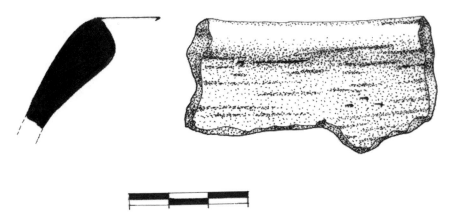

A1.6 Yucuita Tan tecomate from YBA 1B (drawn by Roberto Santos Pérez).

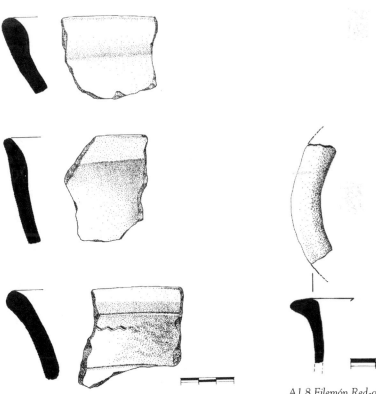

A1.7 Three burnished Filemón Red-on-Tan bowls from YBA 1B (drawn by Roberto Santos Pérez).

A1.8 Filemón Red-on-Tan bottle from YBA 1B (drawn by Roberto Santos Pérez).

A1.9 Late Cruz sherds (Yucuita Polished Brown and Nochixtlán Gray) (see Table A1.1).

We found a few gray bowls incised with the "pennant motif" (Figure A1.9:16). Other gray pottery displays the incised lines and other patterns typical on Late Cruz tanware vessels (Figures A1.9:11–15, A1.12, A1.13).

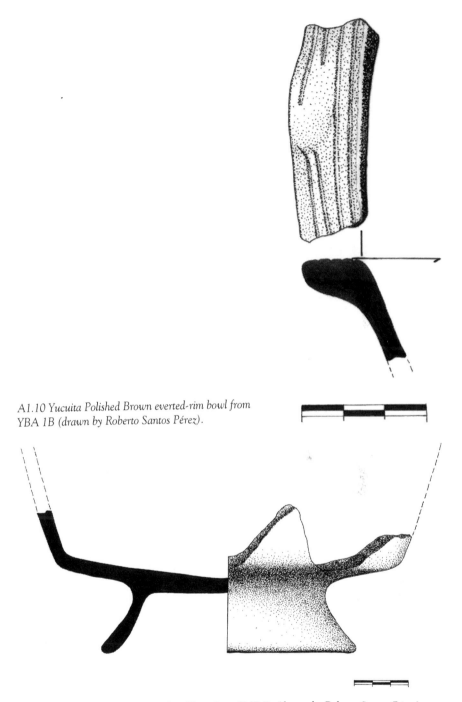

A1.10 *Yucuita Polished Brown everted-rim bowl from YBA 1B (drawn by Roberto Santos Pérez).*

A1.11 *Yucuita Polished Brown pedestal base from SMP 7a (drawn by Roberto Santos Pérez).*

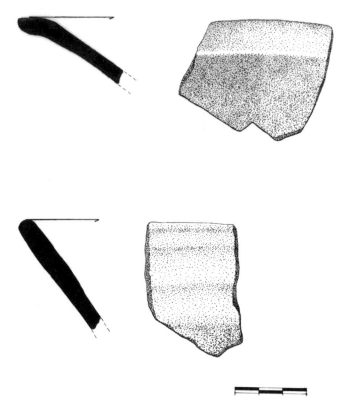

A1.12 Two Nochixtlán Gray bowls from YBA 1B (drawn by Roberto Santos Pérez).

Sherds from the subsequent Early Ramos phase did not often co-occur with Late Cruz types on survey sites. This chronological division is quite discrete throughout the study area.

EARLY RAMOS

The Early Ramos phase is dated from 300 to 150/100 BC. It is distinctive and well represented in the Central Mixteca Alta (Figure A1.14). The utilitarian ceramics of the Ramos period are dominated by Filemón Red-on-Tan ollas (Figure A1.15:11–17). They resemble earlier examples but often have a darker brown clay body and everted rims with a sharp rim to neck angle that was not characteristic in the Cruz period. Flaring rim jars also are common and upright-necked jars and tecomates appear. Waxy "garnet-red"-slipped bottles present in some Late Cruz assemblages are found occasionally in Ramos contexts and serve as markers for Early Ramos. Red-slipped comals (Figure A1.15:9–10) are typical throughout the Ramos period; those with handles are characteristic of Early Ramos.

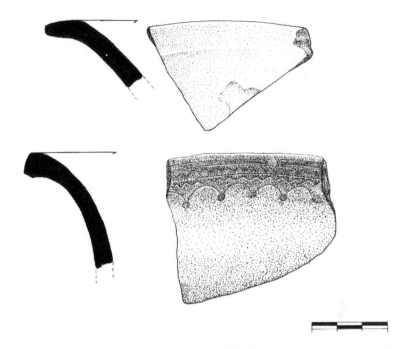

A1.13 Two Nochixtlán Gray everted-rim bowls from YBA 1B (drawn by Roberto Santos Pérez).

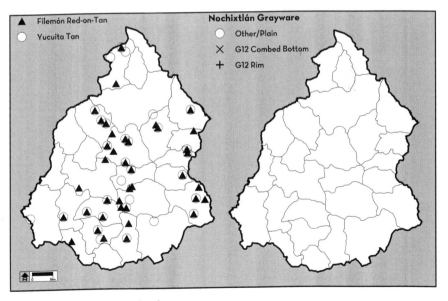

A1.14 Early Ramos ceramic distributions.

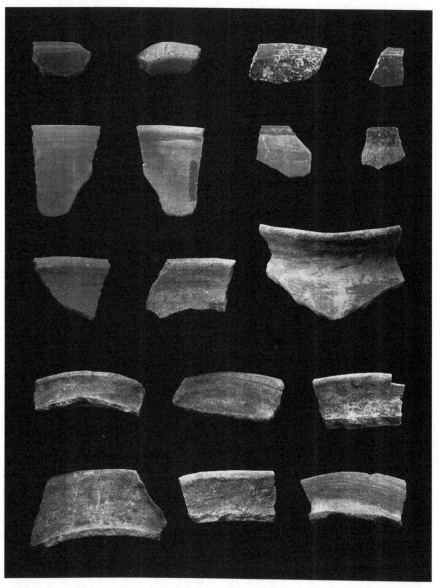

A1.15 *Ramos sherds (Filemón Red-on-Tan) (see Table A1.1).*

Early Ramos Filemón Red-on-Tan bowls come in various profiles including hemispherical, outleaned wall, cylindrical, and flaring (Figure A1.15:1–4, 7–8). Composite-silhouette and pedestal-base bowls are less common. Eccentric rims occur rarely on jars, bottles, and bowls. Fine-line incised horizontal lines and other designs like those of the Late Cruz occur but are far less frequent and varied, and

A1.16 Ramos sherds (Filemón Red-on-Tan, Nochixtlán Gray, and Yucuita Tan) (see Table A1.1).

bolstered, everted rims give way to down-turned exterior rim flanges. In some cases the "flange" is reduced to a slight ridge, occasionally scalloped or notched.

Slips are seldom anything but red. Infrequent examples with black, orange, brown, and specular red slip do appear and a small subset of our Filemón Red-on-Tan category has both red and black slip, sometimes separated by unslipped bands, often with scratched-through incising (Figures A1.15:1, A1.16:1–2).

Yucuita Tan includes tanware sherds that did not fit the Filemón Red-on-Tan definition, including unslipped sherds, those whose slip had eroded away completely, and black-slipped tanwares. In some instances graphite slip was applied. A similar assortment of jar, bowl, and comal forms are represented. Decorative attributes such as fine-line and more rarely scratch-incising, exterior rim flanges, and occasionally eccentric rims and burnishing occur. Burnished outleaned-wall bowls with the interior base decorated with "jab and drag" or wavy line incised designs resemble Valley of Oaxaca G-12 combed bottoms but in tan paste. Like the exterior rim flanges, incised bases are good Early Ramos markers. (Figure A1.16:12–14). Other unusual vessels include a cylindrical effigy vessel; a red-on-orange slipped, flaring bowl, which is a C-7 analog; and a flaring bowl and a cylindrical bowl with red-on-brown slips that are C-13 analogs.

A few gray types carry over from Cruz, such as fine-incised vessels like the Valley of Oaxaca G-15 and G-16. Mixteca Alta G-12-like bowls generally have flaring to everted rims with two parallel, incised lines (infrequently three lines), and fine combing on the interior base in a pattern of concentric circles and wavy lines (Figure A1.16:4–11). G-17 and G-25 bowls also appear, associated with Early Ramos tanwares. In the Mixteca Alta there are low, composite-silhouette gray vessels with wide-line incised parallel lines below the exterior rim and a basal angle or slight flange that is sometimes notched or decorated with a concentric half-circle motif. Highly burnished gray bridge-spout jars are another marker.

Ramos Nochixtlán Grayware clay body is fine and compact with small inclusions; the paste does not match most Ramos tan ceramics. Manufacturing was not simply a matter of reducing typical tanwares.

LATE RAMOS

Late Ramos is well represented at Huamelulpan and Dzinicahua. But it is much less common and even absent in many places in the Central Mixteca Alta as shown in Figure A1.17. Late Ramos assemblages, roughly dated between 150/100 BC and AD 200, are characterized by a heavy predominance of red-slipped tanware vessels. Polished Brown bowls and other pottery and attributes with strong continuity from the Late Cruz phase drop out. Filemón Red-on-Tan jars usually have everted or flaring rims; bottles and tecomates do occur. Bowls include flaring-rim, outleaned-wall, and hemispherical forms, in some cases with pedestal bases. Slipped vessels often tend toward red-orange coloration (Figure A1.15:5–6) and a few are orange with a red stripe or other design painted over that. Several examples have a black slip. Late Ramos comals usually are slipped red. Plain Yucuita Tanwares are less numerous and varied than red-slipped pottery. Graywares are not common but the G-21-like bowl rim is one type that does occur.

TRANSICIÓN LAS FLORES

We can sometimes distinguish the initial phase of the Las Flores period, termed

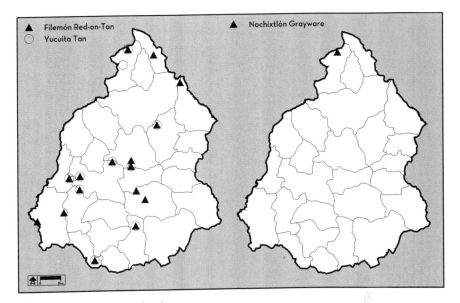

A1.17 *Late Ramos ceramic distributions.*

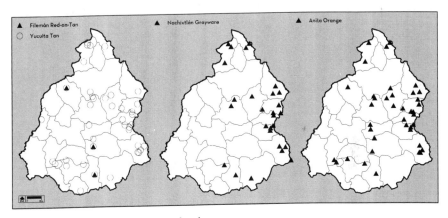

A1.18 *Transición/Las Flores ceramic distributions.*

Transición Las Flores, which begins at the end of Ramos, AD 200, and ends at perhaps AD 350. Its Yucuita Tan and Anita Orange markers are widespread (Figure A1.18). Transición is included in Early Las Flores in this book.

The onset of Las Flores is signaled by a color shift toward orange. Tan to brown clay body and the previously typical red slip become increasingly orange. As the once-standard red-slipped, low-necked jars become less frequent, red-orange and orange-slipped tan ollas with taller upright necks and flaring rims become more typical (Figure A1.19:3–11). Because they did not possess the typical Filemón Red-

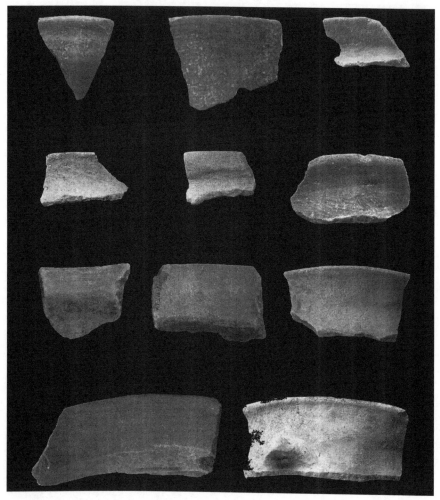

A1.19 Las Flores sherds (Yucuita Tan) (see Table A1.1).

on-Tan characteristics, we classified most Classic period tan to brown jars, bowls, comals and other vessel forms as Yucuita Tan. Orange, red-orange, and red slips were applied frequently to all forms; only a few examples of black slip and gray slip occur in survey collections. The first examples of everted-rim floreros appear. Bowl profiles include hemispherical, outleaned wall, and flaring rims, the rare pedestal base, and rims with a shallow groove or channel (Figure A1.19:1–2). Channel-rim bowls and jars are common. Scraped, raked, and rough exteriors become popular but fine-line incising declines significantly. Streaky burnishing and smoothing is done, often to bowl interiors whereas the exterior surface treatment is rough. Nubbin supports and handles and mica temper are introduced.

A1.20 Las Flores sherds (Anita Orange) (see Table A1.1).

Fine-paste orangewares emerge as a dominant constituent of Las Flores assemblages. These are Chachoapan Orange, including the common Anita Fine Orange Variety and Susana Thin Orange, rare and probably imported. We use the name Anita Orange to avoid any confusion with Mesoamerican Fine Orange pottery. In Transición Las Flores components, Anita Orange vessels are mostly bowls, although jars and small numbers of floreros, plate-like comals, and ladles are represented. Jars are generally flaring or everted and rarely slipped, they may have burnished or rough exteriors, and necks occasionally exhibit vertical smoothing strokes, a diagnostic trait of Transición (Figures A1.20:9–10, A1.21:2–3). Bowls have a variety of profiles, surface treatments, and decoration (Figure A1.20:1–8). Survey collections include hemispherical, outleaned-wall, flaring, and everted rim, cylindrical, and composite-silhouette bowls. Channel rims are frequent (Figure A1.20:3, 7) and slab supports are represented. We note orange slips, red-orange slips or paint, red-on-orange and streaky red-and-orange slips or paint, an orange-painted stripe, and in a few instances black or gray slips. Burnishing and scraped exteriors also occur.

Nochixtlán Graywares include bowls and thin-walled floreros. Outleaned-wall, hemispherical, and flaring-rim gray bowls are common. A few G-12-style incised rims still are seen and a few G-23-style carved designs appear for the first time. Other decorative attributes include channel rims, burnishing and streaky burnishing, and scraped and rough exteriors. Slipping is rare; orange slips are the most common.

EARLY LAS FLORES

Ceramic types and trends present in Transición continue during the Early Las Flores phase (ca. AD 350 to 550). Yucuita Tan and Anita Orange are especially widespread and graywares also occur (Figure A1.22). Slipped Yucuita Tan jars, bowls, and comals typically have orange or red-orange slip. Some have been fired and slipped orange. Only a few have red slips; even fewer have black slips. Upright-neck, flaring, and everted-rim jar profiles are common. Brushed or raked exteriors become frequent on jars. One orange-fired and slipped bottle and several floreros are found in survey samples. Comals are plain or slipped. Many have a plate-like profile particular to the Las Flores period. Slipped urns are represented (Figure A1.21:9). Early Las Flores Yucuita Tan bowls include flaring-rim, outleaned-wall, hemispherical, cylindrical, and other profiles. Classic period attributes on bowls include ring bases (Figure A1.21:1), slab supports, G-23-style carving, micaceous temper, streaky burnishing, and rough exterior.

Upright-necked and flaring-rim Anita Orange jars occur with plain, streaky burnished, orange-slipped exterior, but the fine paste orangeware was predominantly used for bowls. Varied surface treatments were applied to bowls: orange, red-orange, or red slip, specular red and/or specular orange slip, red or orange paint stripes, burnishing, and G-23-style carving. Bowl profiles also vary (Figures A1.23, A1.24) and include outleaned-wall, cylindrical, hemispherical, flaring-rim, everted-rim, or pinched-rim bowls, some of them with ring bases. Unusual orangeware forms include a "plate-comal," a ladle, a handled sahumador, and figurines with moveable limbs. Some bowls have micaceous inclusions. More rarely, very thin orange pottery with white inclusions is found in the Central Mixteca Alta—Susana Thin Orange.

Early Las Flores Nochixtlán Graywares are mostly unslipped flaring, outleaned-wall, hemispherical, or cylindrical bowls (Figure A1.21:4–6) and excised G-23 bowls (Figure A1.21:8). Surface finishing ranges from fine burnishing to rough scraping and wall thickness varies from under 5 to over 10 mm. We found several grooved chilmoleros or molcajetes (Figure A1.21:7). Whereas gray sherds during previous periods have a distinctly finer paste than most tanware sherds, Las Flores orange-

A1.21 Las Flores sherds (Anita Orange, Nochixtlán Gray, and others) (see Table A1.1).

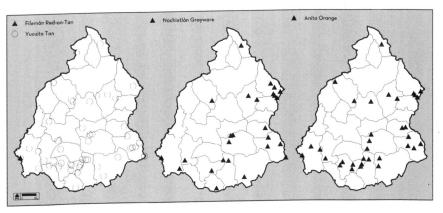

A1.22 Early Las Flores ceramic distributions.

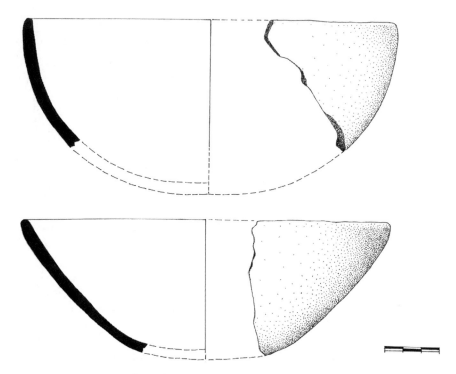

A1.23 Two Anita Orange hemispherical bowls from TOP 1A (drawn by Roberto Santos Pérez).

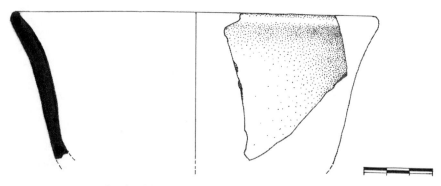

A1.24 Anita Orange deep bowl from Top 1A (drawn by Roberto Santos Pérez).

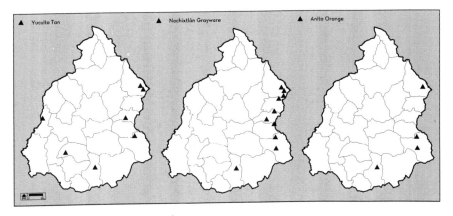

A1.25 Late Las Flores ceramic distributions.

wares regularly match the fine clay body of Las Flores grays. Colors can range from gray to taupe, tan, and orange, and some vessels are incompletely reduced graywares or incompletely oxidized orangewares with gray and orange zones. Gray jars and bowls were sometimes slipped orange, and the occasional orange vessel has a gray slip. Reduction firing to produce gray pottery may be a common practice in the Mixteca Alta during Las Flores.

LATE LAS FLORES

Late Las Flores pottery (ca. AD 550 to 900/950) was found in relatively small quantities on relatively few sites, often mixed among larger collections of Transición and Early Las Flores types (Figure A1.25). Suggestive attributes are thick-walled, scraped tan or gray bowls, including outleaned-wall and cylindrical profiles, bolstered rims and rough exteriors on bowls and jars, spiked or hourglass braziers and early censers, and vessels that appeared transitional to Postclassic types.

NATIVIDAD

Pottery pertaining to this period (AD 900/950 to 1520/1535) is abundant and readily identified. Creamwares are distributed everywhere, graywares are more common in the east, Graphite-on-Orange is more common in the south, and polychromes seem to have a patchy distribution (Figure A1.26).

Light-colored creamwares dominate both cookware and serving vessel types. Chachoapan Sandy Cream jars are ubiquitous (Figure A1.27:1–2). Most are unslipped, cream to light brown, with white or sandy inclusions, or occasionally mica tempered. Some have a cream or more rarely orange slip, and some are fired orange. Sandy Cream jars are well smoothed and have everted or flaring rims, sometimes an upright-necked profile, often with a thick, rounded lip. Many ollas have

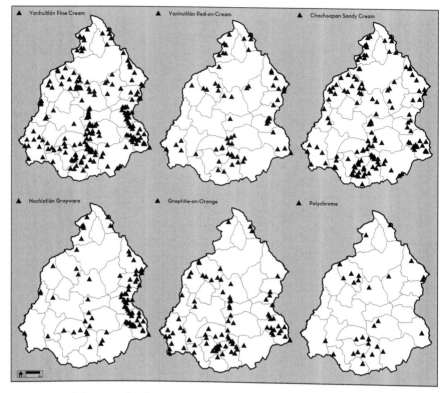

A1.26 *Natividad ceramic distributions.*

strap handles. In just a few collections, scraped, raked, and rough exterior Sandy Cream jars predominate, possibly indicating an Epiclassic occupation. Other vessel forms that appear periodically include flat-bottom ladles or cucharas, ladle censers, tecomates, huge basins or apaxtlis, a pedestal or brazier base, an effigy vessel and a large, deeply incised cylinder vessel.

Comals and bowls come with a range of cream paste from coarse (Chachoapan Sandy Cream) to very fine (Yanhuitlán Fine Cream). Most comals have burnished interiors with obvious burnishing strokes, uniformly roughened exteriors, very thin walls, and an easily recognized rim profile (Figure A1.27:8–9). Often they exhibit tan and dark gray to black areas from oxidation and reduction during firing. A small number were described as possible Epiclassic comals, including some orange-slipped examples.

Unslipped bowls fall into two main groups. One (Sandy or Fine Cream) is hemispherical with a tapered or "pinched" lip. Profiles often are sufficiently sinuous to be considered composite-silhouette. Bowl interiors and exterior rims generally are smooth but most of the exterior is crudely finished, sometimes with visible finger

A1.27 Natividad sherds (Chachoapan Sandy Cream, Yanhuitlán Fine Cream, and Yanhuitlán Red-on-Cream) (see Table A1.1).

marks. They may be differentially fired to produce orange or light tan rims and/or interiors with the remainder of the bowl reduced to dark gray or black (Figure A1.27:10). Paste may be fine or hold many inclusions, sherds may be quite thick

A1.28 *Natividad sherds (Yanhuitlán Red-on-Cream, Nochixtlán Gray, Graphite-on-Orange, Polychrome, and others) (see Table A1.1).*

to very thin, and surfaces may appear carefully or carelessly finished. A small number of unburnished bowls have different profiles (outleaned walls, flaring rims, or incurved rims), and a few have orange slips that may indicate an earlier date.

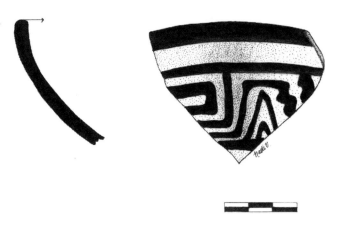

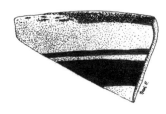

A1.30 Yanhuitlán Red-on-
Cream hemispherical bowl
from SJG 11F (drawn by Naoli
Victoria Lona).

The other main group of unslipped bowls is the Yanhuitlán Fine Cream category. These have highly burnished interior and exterior surfaces, normally with obvious horizontal burnishing strokes (Figure A1.27:11). They usually have light tan and dark gray to black areas, sometimes differentially fired with intentionally patterned reduction and oxidation. Rim profiles range from composite-silhouette to sinuous hemispherical profiles with a tapering lip. Some thin-walled bowls have a distinctive composite silhouette and are referred to as "candy dishes."

Fine Cream pottery also includes ladles (Figure A1.27:3), censers, miniatures, figurines, a flute, and other forms. The ladle censer cover is another distinctive form. Censer covers are made from fine to sandy cream paste, in rare instances with mica temper, or from a sandy orange paste seldom seen in any other form. They may be incised, painted, or appliquéd and may have thin tabular supports (with the fine cream clay body) or thick triangular tripod supports with or without hollow rattles (Figure A1.27:4–6). Figurines in survey collections include mold-made females wearing huipils as well as figures with earspools indicating noble status.

Yanhuitlán Red-on-Cream bowls are common. They have bands and delicate curvilinear and geometric designs painted in red over a cream slip (Figures A1.27:12–14, A1.28:1–6). Designs painted in brownish red and black occur periodically. The

A1.31 Yanhuitlán Red-on-Cream hemispherical bowl from SJG 11F (drawn by Naoli Victoria Lona).

A1.32 Two Yanhuitlán Red-on-Cream hemispherical bowls from SJG 11F (drawn by Naoli Victoria Lona).

bowl profile may be hemispherical (Figures A1.29–32), composite-silhouette (in the sinuous Postclassic style), flaring, incurved, outleaned wall, or cylindrical. A few red-on-cream ladles appear. A subset of highly polished, sometimes unslipped bowl sherds with concentric bands around the rim, often incurving with a rounded lip, may be temporally significant (Figure A1.28:4, 6). Background color and painted designs tend to be darker in color.

Graphite-on-Orange pottery often shares some of the Red-on-Cream characteristics, including the polished surface and aspects of form. Typically, graphite designs are painted on orange slipped, sinuous, composite-silhouette, hemispherical, or flaring bowls (Figure A1.28:10–12). Variations include vessels with interior or exterior surfaces entirely covered with graphite slip and vessels with fine-line or scratch-incised designs that may be applied after the slip. Occasionally we see sherds with graphite on red slip or graphite and red painted on orange slips (Figure A1.28:13); these may actually be polychrome.

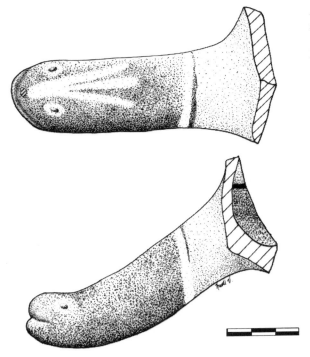

A1.33 Polychrome effigy support from TIL 24Y (drawn by Naoli Victoria Lona).

Fine, compact paste distinguishes the Miguelito Hard Gray variety of Nochixtlán Gray. Its forms include thin jars and pitchers with strap handles, in some cases slipped orange, red, or cream, "candy dish" composite-silhouette bowls, chilmoleros, and stamped-bottom tripod bowls. Most vessels are bowls (Figure A1.28:7–9). Hemispherical, sinuous, composite-silhouette, incurved, outleaned-wall, and flaring profiles appear, usually well burnished with tapered rims, and occasionally with cream, orange, or black slip. Other decoration includes differential firing, fine-line incising, or post-firing scratching.

Compared to creamwares, Mixtec Polychrome vessels are relatively uncommon. Forms include fancy jars and cylindrical, outleaned-wall, flaring, incurving, everted, hemispherical, and tripod bowls (Figure A1.28:14). Hollow supports may be conical or have the form of a serpent or other creature (Figure A1.33). Censers and other forms may also be polychrome.

Aztec Black-on-Orange (Figure A1.28:15) and burnished Texcoco Red types appear in small numbers in eleven Natividad collections, six of which are in the Tlaxiaco core subregion.

Flaked and Ground Stone

Stone artifacts are an important part of the archaeological record in the Mixteca Alta. With proper study they can be informative for understanding chronology and the past economy. Our field observations and collections were not designed to investigate the lithic industries. Current collecting procedures for regional settlement pattern survey are not compatible with what is needed to study lithic reduction strategies or regional lithic economies. Many sites are multicomponent, making it difficult with the surface evidence to examine change over time in stone technology. However, our data will be useful in designing future research to test hypotheses about stone working and the role of stone in other economic activities.

Chert is found in nodular and tabular form in numerous deposits in the Mixteca Alta. Flaked chert is nearly ubiquitous on archaeological sites. In the 1999 survey area, flaked stone—almost always chert—was reported at 580 sites (more than 77 percent). In contrast, in the Valley of Oaxaca local flaked stone was found on less than a third of the sites (Kowalewski et al. 1989:34).

Quartz is abundant in the Peñoles region and common in the Valley of Oaxaca, and quartz artifacts are commonly found in those areas. But quartz and quartz artifacts are rare in the Central Mixteca Alta.

The most common chert color is white. Almost every other color imaginable can also be found. Chert colors are not specific to particular sources. Some sources are ancient gravel deposits that contain chert nodules in great varieties of colors and textures. We identified no specific localities to which a particular color, texture, or knapping quality could be traced; instead, cherts of similar visual properties are available at multiple locations and chert specimens from a single source can be quite variable.

Chert was intensively worked in many places. We found quarries and sites devoted to chert reduction; we also found habitation sites with abundant accumulations of chert debris. Northwest of Huamelulpan and west of Teposcolula (i.e., Yolomécatl and Yucuxaco) the artifactual remains of chert working are especially abundant. Chert was undoubtedly worked in all periods but it was most intensively used in Natividad. Many chert-reduction sites have Natividad as the only ceramic phase.

Figure A2.1 illustrates examples of cores, blades, flakes, and expedient tools (see Table A2.1 for details on all artifacts illustrated in this appendix). Chert was occasionally heat treated. Bifacial reduction was most common. High-quality chert (or chalcedony) was sometimes handled like obsidian in that we find prepared cores, prismatic blades, and unifacial retouch. Formal tools other than PPKs are rare. Note the variety of "scrapers" in Figure A2.2.

Of the projectile point/knives (PPKs) that can be assigned to a time period most are Natividad. For example, the relatively large, thin, parallel-sided or triangular, side-notched points in Figure A2.3:3 and 5 are similar to Postclassic Texcoco points of central Mexico (MacNeish et al. 1967:74–77; Tolstoy 1971). Natividad arrow points (Figure A2.3:1, 7) are like the small Teotihuacan or Harrel points of Aztec times (MacNeish et al. 1967:74–77; Tolstoy 1971). Many of the broken points we found were thin, were light in weight, and had forms consistent with these types.

Fewer PPKs can be assigned to the Classic. The stemmed points in Figure A2.4:13 and 14 are similar in form to the obsidian points in burials at the Templo Viejo de Quetzalcoatl in the Ciudadela, Teotihuacan (Sugiyama 1991). Those burials date to Miccoatli to Early Tlamimilolpa, about AD 200–300 (Sugiyama 1989), corresponding to Transición or Early Las Flores.

The Formative is apparently not well represented by PPKs. Figure A2.4 has several contracting stem points (9–11; see also A2.5:7) found in Ramos contexts, but in each case Natividad is also present. We have no clear examples of the small stemmed points made on blades that were found in a Rosario phase tomb at San José Mogote (Parry 1987:120–122). Unfortunately, we found no points at Monte Negro, the essentially single-component Early Ramos town, and the Monte Negro excavation report mentions only two ovate blades (Acosta and Romero 1992:122–125). Some of the PPKs in our collections could date to the Formative but there are none that we could assign to that period with complete confidence.

A2.1 *Miscellaneous chipped-stone artifacts.*

Two points may date to pre-Formative times (Figure A2.5:12, 13). They are from SPP-NDU-NDU 23, a site we think is Archaic, and TLA-NUN-NUN 1, an undated lithic scatter. Both PPKs are relatively long, broad, and heavy compared to later types. Figure A2.5:12 is carefully worked and has a broad stem. It may compare to the Pedernales type (cf. Hole 1987:figs. 6.29–6:31). Figure A2.5:13 is a

A2.2 Scrapers.

thick biface resembling a Trinidad point (MacNeish et al. 1967:61–62; Hole 1987: fig. 6.27).

Obsidian is more abundant in the Mixteca Alta than in the Valley of Oaxaca or Peñoles. That is to be expected given the Mixteca's proximity to the central Mexican sources. We recorded obsidian at 252 sites (34 percent) in the 1999 survey

A2.3 *Side-notched and square-based projectile point/knives.*

area; Stiver Walsh found it at 90 sites (55 percent) in the Teposcolula survey area
(2001:347–349). In contrast, obsidian was recorded on only 23 percent of Valley
of Oaxaca *components* (the percentage of *sites* is even less in the Valley of Oaxaca
since occurrences are counted multiple times in multicomponent sites) (Kowalewski
et al. 1989:34). Likewise, Mixteca Alta sites have greater frequencies of obsidian

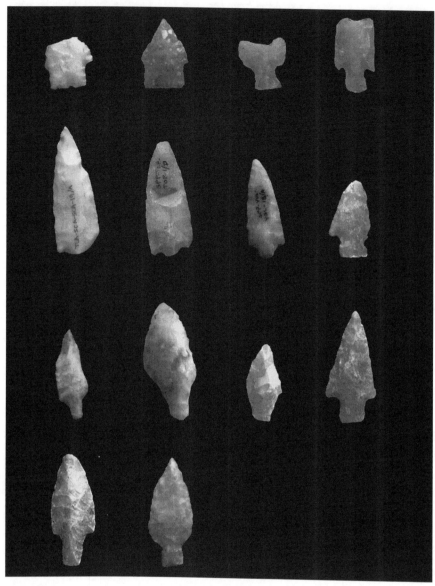

A2.4 *Corner-notched and stemmed projectile point/knives.*

cores, flakes, and expedient tools than Peñoles or the Valley of Oaxaca. Prismatic blades are still the most common form. Obsidian is most common on Natividad sites. Green and gray obsidian have very similar regional distributions. Both colors are widespread and occur in all subregions. Black obsidian is much less frequent and has a more restricted distribution.

A2.5 Miscellaneous and possible Archaic projectile point/knives.

We recorded manos, metates, celts, axes, scrapers, and several miscellaneous items (Figure A2.6). For the 1999 survey area we recorded ground stone at 117 sites (16 percent). In the Valley of Oaxaca groundstone was found at a roughly comparable number of sites (Kowalewski et al. 1989:34). Stone suitable for manos, metates, axes, and celts is available in the Central Mixteca Alta but good-quality

A2.6 *Groundstone artifacts.*

stone is not ubiquitous. What we called "basalt" (dense volcanic rock) is probably available in several locations. Streambeds such as those near Huendio and Junta del Río have cobbles that can be made into tools fairly easily. We did not locate other quarries. Pink and dark gray basalt may have been obtained and made into manos and metates locally and traded to other places, as it has been recently. We identified no places of intensive quarrying or reduction for groundstone tools.

References Cited

Acosta, Jorge R., and Javier Romero
  1992 *Exploraciones en Monte Negro, Oaxaca: 1937–1938, 1938–1939 y 1939–1940.* Instituto Nacional de Antropología e Historia, México, D.F.

Alavez Chávez, Raúl G.
  1988 *Toponimia Mixteca.* Centro de Investigaciones y Estudios Superiores en Antropología Social and Ediciones de la Casa Chata, México, D.F.

Alvarez, Luis Rodrigo
  1998 *Geografía General del Estado de Oaxaca.* 3rd ed. Carteles Editores, Oaxaca.

Balkansky, Andrew K.
  1998a Settlement Pattern Studies in the Mixteca Alta, Oaxaca, 1966–1996. In *Fifty Years since Virú: Recent Advances in Settlement Pattern Studies in the Americas,* edited by Brian R. Billman and Gary M. Feinman, pp. 191–202. Smithsonian Institution Press, Washington, D.C.
  1998b Urbanism and Early State Formation in the Huamelulpan Valley of Southern Mexico. *Latin American Antiquity* 9:37–76.

395

Balkansky, Andrew K., Verónica Pérez Rodríguez, and Stephen A. Kowalewski
    2004   Monte Negro and the Urban Revolution in Oaxaca, Mexico. *Latin American Antiquity* 15:33–60.

Berdan, Frances F., Richard E. Blanton, Elizabeth Hill Boone, Mary C. Hodge, Michael E. Smith, and Emily Umbarger
    1996   *Aztec Imperial Strategies*. Dumbarton Oaks, Washington, D.C.

Bernal, Ignacio
    1949   Exploraciones en Coixtlahuaca, Oax. *Revista Mexicana de Estudios Antropológicos* 10:5–76.
    1966   The Mixtecs in the Archaeology of the Valley of Oaxaca. In *Ancient Oaxaca*, edited by John Paddock, pp. 345–366. Stanford University Press, Stanford, California.

Blanton, Richard E.
    1978   *Monte Albán: Settlement Patterns at the Ancient Zapotec Capital*. Academic Press, New York.
    1985   A Comparison of Early Market Systems. In *Markets and Marketing*, edited by Stuart Plattner, pp. 399–416. University Press of America, Lanham, Maryland.
    2000   *Hellenistic, Roman and Byzantine Settlement Patterns of the Coast Lands of Western Rough Cilicia*. BAR International Series 879. Archaeopress, Oxford.

Blanton, Richard E., Gary M. Feinman, Stephen A. Kowalewski, and Linda M. Nicholas
    1999   *Ancient Oaxaca: The Monte Albán State*. Cambridge University Press, Cambridge.

Blanton, Richard E., Gary M. Feinman, Stephen A. Kowalewski, and Peter N. Peregrine
    1996   A Dual-Processual Theory for the Evolution of Mesoamerican Civilization. *Current Anthropology* 37:1–14.

Blanton, Richard E., Stephen A. Kowalewski, Gary Feinman, and Jill Appel
    1982   *Monte Albán's Hinterland*, Part 1: *The Prehispanic Settlement Patterns of the Central and Southern Parts of the Valley of Oaxaca, Mexico*. 2 vols. Memoirs No. 15. Museum of Anthropology, University of Michigan, Ann Arbor.

Blomster, Jeffrey Paul
    1998   At the Bean Hill in the Land of the Mixtec: Early Formative Social Complexity and Interregional Interaction at Etlatongo, Oaxaca, Mexico. Unpublished Ph.D. dissertation, Department of Anthropology, Yale University, New Haven, Connecticut.

Borah, Woodrow W., and Sherburne F. Cook
    1960   *The Population of Central Mexico in 1548: An Analysis of the Suma de Visitas de Pueblos*. Ibero-Americana 43. University of California Press, Berkeley.

Braudel, Fernand
    1972   *The Mediterranean and the Mediterranean World in the Age of Philip II*. 2 vols. Translated by Siân Reynolds. Harper & Row, New York.

Burgoa, Francisco de
    1989   *Geográfica Descripción*. 2 vols. Editorial Porrua, México, D.F.
    [1674]

Butterworth, Douglas
1975   *Tilantongo: Comunidad Mixteca en Transición.* Instituto Nacional Indigenista and Secretaría de Educación Pública, México, D.F.

Byland, Bruce E.
1980   Political and Economic Evolution in the Tamazulapan Valley, Mixteca Alta, Oaxaca, México: A Regional Approach. Ph.D. dissertation, Department of Anthropology, Pennsylvania State University, University Park.

Byland, Bruce D., and John M.D. Pohl
1994   *In the Realm of Eight Deer: The Archaeology of the Mixtec Codices.* University of Oklahoma Press, Norman.

Carta de Climas
1970   *San Pedro Pochutla 14P-(11), Oaxaca 14Q-VIII.* Dirección de Planeación, Comisión de Estudios del Territorio Nacional y Planeación, México, D.F.

Caso, Alfonso
1938   *Exploraciones en Oaxaca, Quinta y Sexta Temporadas, 1936–1937.* Publicación No. 34. Instituto Panamericano de Geografía e Historia, México, D.F.
1942   *Resumen del Informe de las Exploraciones en Oaxaca durante la 7a y la 8a Temporadas, 1937–1938 y 1938–1939.* Actas del XXVII Congreso Internacional de Americanistas, 1939, 2:159–187. México, D.F.
1977   *Reyes y Reinos de la Mixteca.* Fondo de Cultura Económica, México, D.F.

Caso, Alfonso, Ignacio Bernal, and Jorge R. Acosta
1967   *La Cerámica de Monte Albán.* Memorias XIII. Instituto Nacional de Antropología e Historia, México, D.F.

Chamblee, John Francis
2000   The Classic-Postclassic Transition in the Central Mixteca Alta, Oaxaca. Unpublished Master's report, Department of Anthropology, University of Arizona, Tucson.

Cook, Sherburne F.
1949   *Soil Erosion and Population in Central Mexico.* Ibero-Americana 34. University of California Press, Berkeley.

Cook, Sherburne F., and Woodrow W. Borah
1968   *The Population of the Mixteca Alta 1520–1960.* Ibero-Americana 50. University of California Press, Berkeley.

Cowgill, George
1997   State and Society at Teotihuacan, Mexico. *Annual Review of Anthropology* 26: 129–161.

Dahlgren de Jordán, Barbro
1954   *La Mixteca: Su Cultura e Historia Prehispánicas.* Imprenta Universitaria, México, D.F.

Drennan, Robert D.
1976   *Fábrica San José and Middle Formative Society in the Valley of Oaxaca.* Memoirs No. 8. Museum of Anthropology, University of Michigan, Ann Arbor.

1983   Appendix: Radiocarbon Dates from the Oaxaca Region. In *The Cloud People: Divergent Evolution of the Zapotec and Mixtec Civilizations*, edited by Kent V. Flannery and Joyce Marcus, pp. 363–370. Academic Press, New York.

Feinman, Gary M., and Joyce Marcus (editors)
1998   *Archaic States*. School of American Research Press, Santa Fe, New Mexico.

Feinman, Gary M., and Linda M. Nicholas
2004   *Hilltop Terrace Sites of Oaxaca, Mexico: Intensive Surface Survey at Guirún, El Palmillo, and the Mitla Fortress*. Fieldiana Anthropology new series No. 37. Field Museum of Natural History, Chicago.

Feinman, Gary M., Linda M. Nicholas, and Helen R. Haines
2002   Houses on a Hill: Classic Period Life at El Palmillo, Oaxaca, Mexico. *Latin American Antiquity* 13:251–277.

Finsten, Laura M.
1996   Periphery and Frontier in Southern Mexico: The Mixtec Sierra in Highland Oaxaca. In *Pre-Columbian World-Systems*, edited by Peter N. Peregrine and Gary M. Feinman, pp. 77–96. Prehistory Press, Madison, Wisconsin.

Flannery, Kent V.
1983   Monte Negro: A Reinterpretation. In *The Cloud People: Divergent Evolution of the Zapotec and Mixtec Civilizations*, edited by Kent V. Flannery and Joyce Marcus, pp. 99–102. Academic Press, New York.

Flannery, Kent V., and Joyce Marcus
1983   Urban Mitla and Its Rural Hinterland. In *The Cloud People: Divergent Evolution of the Zapotec and Mixtec Civilizations*, edited by Kent V. Flannery and Joyce Marcus, pp. 295–300. Academic Press, New York.
1994   *Early Formative Pottery of the Valley of Oaxaca*. Memoirs No. 27. Museum of Anthropology, University of Michigan, Ann Arbor.

Folan, William J., Joyce Marcus, Sophia Pincemin, María del Rosario Domínguez Carrasco, Laraine Fletcher, and Abel Morales López
1995   Calakmul: New Data from an Ancient Maya Capital in Campeche, Mexico. *Latin American Antiquity* 6:310–334.

García García, Angel
1998   *Oaxaca: Distritos, Municipios, Localidades y Habitantes*. Angel García García, Oaxaca, Oaxaca de Juárez.

Garvin, Richard D.
1994   Modern and Prehispanic Agriculture in the Sierra Mixteca, Oaxaca, Mexico. Ph.D. dissertation, Department of Archaeology, University of Calgary, Calgary, Alberta.

Gat, Azar
2002   Why City-States Existed? Riddles and Clues of Urbanisation and Fortifications. In *A Comparative Study of Six City-State Cultures: An Investigation Conducted by the Copenhagen Polis Centre*, edited by Mogens Herman Hansen, pp. 125–139. The Royal Danish Academy of Sciences and Letters, Copenhagen.
2003   Rural Petty-State and Overlordship. *Anthropos* 98:127–142.

Gaxiola González, Margarita
1984   *Huamelulpan. Un Centro Urbano de la Mixteca Alta.* Colección Científica No.
        114. Instituto Nacional de Antropología e Historia, México, D.F.

Geertz, Clifford
1963   *Agricultural Involution: The Process of Ecological Change in Indonesia.* University
        of California Press, Berkeley.

Gerhard, Peter
1993   *A Guide to the Historical Geography of New Spain.* Revised edition. University of
        Oklahoma Press, Norman.

Grube, Nikolai
2000   The City-States of the Maya. In *A Comparative Study of Thirty City-State Cul-
        tures: An Investigation Conducted by the Copenhagen Polis Centre,* edited by Mo-
        gens Herman Hansen, pp. 547–566. The Royal Danish Academy of Sciences
        and Letters, Copenhagen.

Hansen, Mogens Herman (editor)
2000   *A Comparative Study of Thirty City-State Cultures: An Investigation Conducted by
        the Copenhagen Polis Centre.* The Royal Danish Academy of Sciences and Let-
        ters, Copenhagen.
2002   *A Comparative Study of Six City-State Cultures: An Investigation Conducted by the
        Copenhagen Polis Centre.* The Royal Danish Academy of Sciences and Letters,
        Copenhagen.

Heredia Espinoza, Verenice Y.
2003   Administración y Gobierno en Centros Secundarios del Periodo Clásico en la
        Mixteca Alta, Oaxaca, México. Submitted to the Consejo de Arqueología, In-
        stituto Nacional de Antropología e Historia. Manuscript on file, Centro INAH
        Oaxaca, Oaxaca de Juárez.
2005   The Nature of Governance in Secondary Centers of the Classic Period, Mixteca
        Alta, México. Unpublished Ph.D. dissertation, Department of Sociology and
        Anthropology, Purdue University, West Lafayette, Indiana.

Heredia Espinoza, Verenice Y., Stephen A. Kowalewski, and Verónica Pérez Rodríguez
2004   Cerro Jazmín: The Morphology of an Urban Center in the Mixteca Alta. Paper
        presented at the Cuarta Reunión del Proyecto El Urbanismo en Mesoamérica,
        Pennsylvania State University, University Park.

Hill, J. Brett, Jeffrey J. Clark, William H. Doelle, and Patrick D. Lyons
2004   Prehistoric Demography in the Southwest: Migration, Coalescence, and Popu-
        lation Decline. *American Antiquity* 69:689–716.

Hirth, Kenneth G.
1987a   Formative Period Settlement Patterns in the Río Amatzinac Valley. In *Ancient
        Chalcatzingo,* edited by David C. Grove, pp. 343–367. University of Texas Press,
        Austin.
1987b   Río Amatzinac Survey: Site Descriptions. In *Ancient Chalcatzingo,* edited by
        David C. Grove, pp. 509–524. University of Texas Press, Austin.

Hodge, Mary G.
1994   Polities Composing the Aztec Empire's Core. In *Economies and Polities in the Aztec Realm*, edited by Mary G. Hodge and Michael E. Smith, pp. 43–71. Institute for Mesoamerican Studies, University at Albany, State University of New York, Albany.

Hole, Frank
1987   Chipped-Stone Tools. In *Guilá Naquitz: Archaic Foraging and Early Agriculture in Oaxaca, Mexico*, edited by Kent V. Flannery, pp. 97–140. Academic Press, Orlando, Florida.

Instituto Nacional de Estadística, Geografía, e Informática [INEGI]
1984   Carta Geológica 1:250,000, Oaxaca E14-9. México, D.F.
1988   Carta Topográfica 1:50,000, Yolomécatl E14D35. México, D.F.

Jansen, Maarten, and Luis Reyes García (editors)
1997   *Códices, Caciques, and Comunidades*. Cuadernos de Historia Latinoamérica No. 5. Asociación de Historiadores Latinoamericanistas Europeos.

Joyce, Arthur A.
1991   Formative Period Occupation in the Lower Río Verde Valley, Oaxaca, Mexico: Interregional Interaction and Social Change. Ph.D. dissertation, Rutgers University. University Microfilms, Ann Arbor, Michigan.
2003   Imperialism in Pre-Aztec Mesoamerica: Monte Albán, Teotihuacan, and the Lower Río Verde Valley. In *Ancient Mesoamerican Warfare*, edited by M. Kathryn Brown and Travis W. Stanton, pp. 49–72. Alta Mira Press, Walnut Creek, California.

Kirkby, Michael
1972   *The Physical Environment of the Nochixtlán Valley, Oaxaca*. Publications in Anthropology No. 2. Vanderbilt University, Nashville, Tennessee.

Kowalewski, Stephen A.
1976   Prehispanic Settlement Patterns of the Central Part of the Valley of Oaxaca, Mexico. Unpublished Ph.D. dissertation, Department of Anthropology, University of Arizona, Tucson.
1990   The Evolution of Complexity in the Valley of Oaxaca. *Annual Review of Anthropology* 19:39–58.
2003a   Backcountry Pots. *Ancient Mesoamerica* 14:65–75.
2003b   Scale and the Explanation of Demographic Change: 3,500 Years in the Valley of Oaxaca. *American Anthropologist* 105:313–325.

Kowalewski, Stephen A., Gary Feinman, Laura Finsten, Richard E. Blanton, and Linda Nicholas
1989   *Monte Albán's Hinterland*, Part 2: *Prehispanic Settlement Patterns in Tlacolula, Etla, and Ocotlán, the Valley of Oaxaca, Mexico*. 2 vols. Memoirs No. 23. Museum of Anthropology, University of Michigan, Ann Arbor.

Kowalewski, Stephen A., Gary M. Feinman, Linda M. Nicholas, and Verenice Y. Heredia
2006   Hilltowns and Valley Fields: Great Transformations, Labor, and Long-Term History in Ancient Oaxaca. In *Labor in Cross-Cultural Perspective*, edited by E.

Paul Durrenebreger and Judith Marti, pp. 197–216. Altamira Press, Lanham, Maryland.

Kowalewski, Stephen A., Verenice Y. Heredia Espinoza, Andrew K. Balkansky, Laura R. Stiver Walsh, John F. Chamblee, Thomas J. Pluckhahn, Verónica Pérez Rodríguez, Charlotte A. Smith, Dmitri Beliaev, and Roberto Santos Pérez
    2006   Resultados del Recorrido Regional de la Mixteca Alta Central, Oaxaca. Submitted to the Consejo de Arqueología, Instituto Nacional de Antropología e Historia, México, D.F.

Kowalewski, Stephen A., Charlotte A. Smith, Verenice Y. Heredia Espinoza, and John F. Chamblee
    2004   The Highland Mesoamerican Classic: Small States. Paper presented at the Third International Conference "Hierarchy and Power in the History of Civilizations," Moscow.

Kowalewski, Stephen A., Charles Spencer, and Elsa Redmond
    1978   Ceramic Appendix. In *Monte Albán: Settlement Patterns at the Ancient Zapotec Capital*, by Richard E. Blanton, pp.167–193. Academic Press, New York.

LeBlanc, Steven A.
    1998   Settlement Consequences of Warfare during the Late Pueblo III and Pueblo IV Periods. In *Migration and Reorganization: The Pueblo IV Period in the American Southwest*, edited by Katherine A. Spielmann, pp. 115–136. Anthropological Research Papers No. 51. Arizona State University, Tempe.

Lind, Michael D.
    1977   Mixtec Kingdoms in the Nochixtlán Valley: A Preconquest to Postconquest Archeological Perspective. Unpublished Ph.D. dissertation, Department of Anthropology, University of Arizona, Tucson.
    1979   *Postclassic and Early Colonial Mixtec Houses in the Nochixtlán Valley, Oaxaca*. Publications in Anthropology No. 23. Vanderbilt University, Nashville, Tennessee.
    1987   *The Sociocultural Dimensions of Mixtec Ceramics*. Publications in Anthropology No. 33. Vanderbilt University, Nashville, Tennessee.
    2000   Mixtec City-States and Mixtec City-State Culture. In *A Comparative Study of Thirty City-State Cultures: An Investigation Conducted by the Copenhagen Polis Centre*, edited by Mogens Herman Hansen, pp. 567–580. The Royal Danish Academy of Sciences and Letters, Copenhagen.

MacNeish, Richard S., Antoinette Nelken-Terner, and Irmgard W. Johnson
    1967   *The Prehistory of the Tehuacan Valley*, Vol. 2: *Nonceramic Artifacts*. University of Texas Press, Austin.

MacNeish, Richard S., Frederick A. Peterson, and Kent V. Flannery
    1970   *The Prehistory of the Tehuacan Valley*, Vol. 3: *Ceramics*. University of Texas Press, Austin.

Marcus, Joyce
    2003   Recent Advances in Maya Archaeology. *Journal of Archaeological Research* 11(2): 71–148.

Marcus, Joyce, and Kent V. Flannery
1996   Zapotec Civilization: How Urban Society Evolved in Mexico's Oaxaca Valley. Thames and Hudson, London.

Martínez López, Cira, Robert Markens, Marcus Winter, and Michael D. Lind
2000   Cerámica de la Fase Xoo (Epoca Monte Albán IIIB–IV) del Valle de Oaxaca. Centro INAH Oaxaca, Oaxaca de Juárez.

Matadamas Díaz, Raúl
1991–   Rescate Arqueológico en Yucunama, Mixteca Alta de Oaxaca. Notas Meso-
1992   americanas 13:163–176.

Millon, Rene
1981   Teotihuacan: City State and Civilization. In Archaeology, edited by Jeremy A. Sabloff, pp. 198–243. Supplement to the Handbook of Middle American Indians, vol. 1, Victoria Reifler Bricker, general editor. University of Texas Press, Austin.

Monaghan, John
1994   Irrigation and Ecological Complementarity in Mixtec Cacicazgos. In Caciques and Their People: A Volume in Honor of Ronald Spores, edited by Joyce Marcus and Judith Francis Zeitlin, pp. 143–162. Anthropological Papers No. 89. Museum of Anthropology, University of Michigan, Ann Arbor.
1995   The Covenants with Earth and Rain: Exchange, Sacrifice, and Revelation in Mixtec Sociality. University of Oklahoma Press, Norman.

Nichols, Deborah L., and Thomas H. Charlton
1997   The Archaeology of City-States: Cross-Cultural Approaches. Smithsonian Institution Press, Washington, D.C.

Paddock, John
1953   Excavations in the Mixteca Alta. Mesoamerican Notes 3. Mexico City College, México, D.F.
1966   Mixtec Ethnohistory and Monte Albán V. In Ancient Oaxaca, edited by John Paddock, pp. 367–385. Stanford University Press, Stanford, California.

Palerm, Angel, and Eric R. Wolf
1957   Ecological Potential and Cultural Development in Mesoamerica. In Studies in Human Ecology, pp. 1–37. Social Science Monographs 3. Anthropological Society of Washington and Pan American Union, Washington, D.C.

Parry, William J.
1987   Chipped Stone Tools in Formative Oaxaca, Mexico: Their Procurement, Production and Use. Memoirs No. 20. Museum of Anthropology, University of Michigan, Ann Arbor.

Pastor, Rodolfo
1987   Campesinos y Reformas: La Mixteca 1700–1856. El Colegio de México, México, D.F.

Pérez Rodríguez, Verónica
2003   Household Intensification and Agrarian States: Excavation of Houses and Terraced Fields in a Mixtec Cacicazgo. Unpublished Ph.D. dissertation, Depart-

ment of Anthropology, University of Georgia, Athens. Electronic document, http://dbs.galib.uga.edu, accessed June 25, 2004.

Plunket, Patricia Scarborough
1983   An Intensive Survey in the Yucuita Sector of the Nochixtlán Valley, Oaxaca, Mexico. Ph.D. dissertation, Tulane University, New Orleans. University Microfilms, Ann Arbor, Michigan.

Pohl, John M.D., John Monaghan, and Laura R. Stiver
1996   Religion, Economy, and Factionalism in Mixtec Boundary Zones. In *Códices y Documentos sobre México: Segundo Simposio*, vol. 1, edited by Salvador Rueda Smithers, Constanza Vega Soza, and Rodrigo Martínez Baracs, pp. 205–232. Instituto Nacional de Antropología e Historia and Consejo Nacional para la Cultura y las Artes, México, D.F.

Rabin, Emily
1979   The War of Heaven in Codices Zouche-Nuttall and Bodley: A Preliminary Study. *Actes du XLII Congrés International des Américanistes* 7:171–182.

Rivera Guzmán, Angel Iván
1999   El Patrón de Asentamiento en la Mixteca Baja de Oaxaca: Análisis del Area de Tequixtepec-Chazumba. Unpublished M.A. thesis, Department of Anthropology, Escuela Nacional de Antropología, México, D.F.

Robles García, Nelly M.
1988   *Las Unidades Domésticas del Preclásico Superior en la Mixteca Alta*. BAR International Series 407. British Archaeological Reports, Oxford.

Romero Frizzi, María de los Angeles
1990   *Economía y Vida de los Españoles en la Mixteca Alta: 1519–1720*. Instituto Nacional de Antropología and Gobierno del Estado de Oaxaca, México, D.F.

Romney, Kimball, and Romaine Romney
1966   *The Mixtecans of Juxtlahuaca, Mexico*. John Wiley and Sons, New York.

Roys, Ralph L.
1957   *The Political Geography of the Yucatan Maya*. Publication 613. Carnegie Institution of Washington, Washington, D.C.

Sanders, William T.
1965   The Cultural Ecology of the Teotihuacán Valley. Preliminary Report of the Results of the Teotihuacán Valley Project. Manuscript on file, Department of Anthropology, Pennsylvania State University, University Park.

Sanders, William T., Jeffrey R. Parsons, and Robert S. Santley
1979   *The Basin of Mexico: Ecological Processes in the Evolution of a Civilization*. Academic Press, New York.

Sanders, William T., and David Webster
1988   The Mesoamerican Urban Tradition. *American Anthropologist* 90:521–546.

Sepúlveda y Herrera, María Teresa
1999   *Procesos por Idolatría al Cacique, Gobernadores y Sacerdotes de Yanhuitlán, 1544–1546*. Instituto Nacional de Antropología e Historia, México, D.F.

Smith, Charlotte A.
1993   Prehispanic Mixtec Social Organization: The Architectural Evidence. Unpublished M.A. thesis, Department of Anthropology, University of Georgia, Athens.
2002   Concordant Change and Core-Periphery Dynamics: A Synthesis of Highland Mesoamerican Survey Data. Unpublished Ph.D. dissertation, Department of Anthropology, University of Georgia, Athens. Electronic document, http://dbs .galib.uga.edu, accessed March 4, 2005.

Smith, Mary Elizabeth
1973   *Picture Writing from Ancient Southern Mexico: Mixtec Place Signs and Maps.* University of Oklahoma Press, Norman.
1998   *The Codex López Ruiz: A Lost Mixtec Pictorial Manuscript.* Publications in Anthropology No. 51. Vanderbilt University, Nashville, Tennessee.

Smith, Michael D.
1989   Cities, Towns, and Urbanism: Comment on Sanders and Webster. *American Anthropologist* 91:454–460.

Spencer, Charles S., and Elsa M. Redmond
1997   *Archaeology of the Cañada de Cuicatlán, Oaxaca.* Anthropological Papers No. 80. American Museum of Natural History, New York.
2001   The Chronology of Conquest: Implications of New Radiocarbon Analyses from the Cañada de Cuicatlán, Oaxaca. *Latin American Antiquity* 12:182–202.

Spores, Ronald
1967   *The Mixtec Kings and Their People.* University of Oklahoma Press, Norman.
1969   Settlement, Farming Technology, and Environment in the Nochixtlán Valley. *Science* 166:557–569.
1972   *An Archaeological Settlement Survey of the Nochixtlán Valley, Oaxaca.* Publications in Anthropology No. 1. Vanderbilt University, Nashville, Tennessee.
1974   *Stratigraphic Excavations in the Nochixtlán Valley, Oaxaca, Mexico.* Publications in Anthropology No. 11. Vanderbilt University, Nashville, Tennessee.
1983   Yucuñudahui. In *The Cloud People: Divergent Evolution of the Zapotec and Mixtec Civilizations,* edited by Kent V. Flannery and Joyce Marcus, pp. 155–159. Academic Press, New York.
1984   *The Mixtecs in Ancient and Colonial Times.* University of Oklahoma Press, Norman.
1996   Informe Final del Proyecto Recorrido Arqueológico de la Región Mixteca Alta Central y Oeste. Submitted to the Consejo de Arqueología, Instituto Nacional de Antropología e Historia. Manuscript on file, Centro INAH Oaxaca, Oaxaca de Juárez.
2005   El Impacto de la Política de Congregaciones en los Asentamientos Coloniales de la Mixteca Alta, Oaxaca: El Caso de Tlaxiaco y su Región. *Cuadernos del Sur* 22:7–16.

Spores, Ronald, and Nelly Robles García
2006   El Pueblo Viejo de Teposcolula Yucuda, Proyecto Arqueológico: Primera Temporada (2004). Submitted to the Consejo de Arqueología, Instituto Nacional de Antropología e Historia. Fundación Alfredo Harp Helú, Oaxaca. Electronic

document, http://www.fundacionharpoaxaca.org.mx/pueblo_viejo.pdf, accessed November 1, 2006.

Stiver Walsh, Laura R.
1997   Investigaciones Arqueológicas, Etnohistóricas, y Etnográficas de los "Mercados de Raya" y las Economías Tempranas de la Región Mixteca, Oaxaca. Informe Técnico Parcial submitted to the Consejo de Arqueología, Instituto Nacional de Antropología e Historia. Manuscript on file, Centro INAH Oaxaca, Oaxaca de Juárez.
2001   Prehispanic Mixtec Settlement and State in the Teposcolula Valley of Oaxaca, Mexico. Unpublished Ph.D. dissertation, Department of Anthropology, Vanderbilt University, Nashville, Tennessee.
2005   Mixtec Urbanism: Architecture and Artifact Distribution Patterns at a Postclassic Center. Paper presented at the 70th annual meeting of the Society for American Archaeology, Salt Lake City.

Sugiyama, Saburo
1989   Burials Dedicated to the Old Temple of Quetzalcoatl at Teotihuacan, Mexico. *American Antiquity* 54:85–106.
1991   Descubrimientos de Entierros y Ofrendas Dedicadas al Templo Viejo de Quetzalcóatl. In *Teotihuacan 1980–1982: Nuevas Interpretaciones*, edited by Rubén Cabrera Castro, Ignacio Rodríguez García, and Noel Morelos García, pp. 275–326. Instituto Nacional de Antropología e Historia, México, D.F.

Symonds, Stacey C., and Roberto Lunagómez
1997   Settlement System and Population Development at San Lorenzo. In *Olmec to Aztec: Settlement Patterns in the Ancient Gulf Lowlands*, edited by Barbara L. Stark and Philip J. Arnold III, pp. 144–173. University of Arizona Press, Tucson.

Tamayo, Jorge L.
1950   *Geografía de Oaxaca*. Comisión Editora de El Nación, México, D.F.

Terraciano, Kevin
2001   *The Mixtecs of Colonial Oaxaca: Ñudzahui History, Sixteenth through Eighteenth Centuries*. Stanford University Press, Stanford, California.

Tolstoy, Paul
1971   Utilitarian Artifacts of Central Mexico. In *Archaeology of Northern Mesoamerica*, part 1, edited by Gordon F. Ekholm and Ignacio Bernal, pp. 270–296. *Handbook of Middle American Indians*, vol. 10, Robert Wauchope, general editor. University of Texas Press, Austin.

Whalen, Michael E.
1981   *Excavations at Santo Domingo Tomaltepec: Evolution of a Formative Community in the Valley of Oaxaca, Mexico*. Memoirs No. 12. Museum of Anthropology, University of Michigan, Ann Arbor.

Wilcox, David R., Gerald Robertson Jr., and J. Scott Wood
2001   Organized for War: The Perry Mesa Settlement Systems in West-Central Arizona. In *Deadly Landscapes: Case Studies in Prehistoric Southwestern Warfare*, ed-

ited by Glen E. Rice and Steven A. LeBlanc, pp. 141–194. University of Utah Press, Salt Lake City.

Winter, Marcus C.
1976   The Archaeological Household Cluster in the Valley of Oaxaca. In *The Early Mesoamerican Village*, edited by Kent V. Flannery, pp. 25–31. Academic Press, New York.
1986   Templo-Patio-Adoratorio: Un Conjunto Arquitectónico No-Residencial en el Oaxaca Prehispánico. *Cuadernos de Arquitectura Mesoamericana* 7:51–59. Facultad de Arquitectura, Universidad Nacional Autónoma de México.
1994   The Mixteca Prior to the Late Postclassic. In *Mixteca-Puebla: Discoveries and Research in Mesoamerican Art and Archaeology*, edited by H. B. Nicholson and E. Quiñones Keber, pp. 201–221. Labyrinthos, Culver City, California.
1997   Primer Taller: Cerámica Arqueológica de Oaxaca. Manuscript on file, Centro INAH Oaxaca, Oaxaca de Juárez.

Winter, Marcus C., Margarita Gaxiola, and Gilberto Hernández
1984   Archeology of the Otomanguean Area. In *Essays in Otomanguean Culture History*, edited by J. Kathryn Josserand, Marcus Winter, and Nicholas Hopkins, pp. 25–64. Publications in Anthropology No. 31. Vanderbilt University, Nashville, Tennessee.

Winter, Marcus, Alicia Herrera Muzgo T., Ron Spores, and Vilma Fialko
1991   Exploraciones Arqueológicas en Huamelulpan, Mixteca Alta, Oaxaca: Informe Temporada 1990. Manuscript on file, Centro INAH Oaxaca, Oaxaca de Juárez.

Wu, Jianguo, and Orie L. Loucks
1995   From Balance of Nature to Hierarchical Patch Dynamics: A Paradigm Shift in Ecology. *Quarterly Review of Biology* 70:439–466.

Zárate Morán, Roberto
1987   *Excavaciones de un Sitio Preclásico en San Mateo Etlatongo, Nochixtlán, Oaxaca, México.* BAR International Series 322. British Archaeological Reports, Oxford.

Table 1.1. Twentieth-Century Jurisdictions, Populations, and Site Prefixes.

Distrito	Muncipio	Agencia/Localidad	Site Prefix	Abbr	Pop 1990	Total Municipio Pop 1960	Total Municipio Pop 1990
Nochixtlán	San Juan Diuxi	San Juan Diuxi	NO-SJD-SJD	SJD	1,676	1,288	1,790
Nochixtlán	San Pedro Tidaá	San Pedro Tidaá	NO-SPT-SPT	SPT	1,002	2,209	1,002
Nochixtlán	Santiago Tilantongo	Buenavista	NO-TIL-BV	BV	131		
Nochixtlán	Santiago Tilantongo	Guadalupe Hidalgo	NO-TIL-GHO	GHO	525		
Nochixtlán	Santiago Tilantongo	La Paz	NO-TIL-LPZ	LPZ	285		
Nochixtlán	Santiago Tilantongo	Las Palmas	NO-TIL-LPS	LPS	435		
Nochixtlán	Santiago Tilantongo	Santiago Tilantongo	NO-TIL-TIL	TIL	409	3,507	4,272
Nochixtlán	Santiago Tillo	Santiago Tillo	NO-TLO-TLO	TLO	342	932	499
Nochixtlán	Santo Domingo Yanhuitlán	La Cieneguilla	NO-YAN-CIE	CIE	31		
Nochixtlán	Santo Domingo Yanhuitlán	Xacañi	NO-YAN-XAC	XAC	273		
Nochixtlán	Yodocono de Porfirio Díaz	Yodocono de Porfirio Díaz	NO-YPD-YPD	YPD	822	1,220	1,311
Teposcolula	San Andrés Lagunas	San Andrés Lagunas	SPP-SAL-SAL	SAL	339	1,128	670
Teposcolula	San Andrés Lagunas	San Isidro Lagunas	SPP-SAL-SIL	SIL	276		
Teposcolula	San Bartolo Soyaltepec	San Pedro Añañe	SPP-SPA-SPA	SPA	215		
Teposcolula	San Juan Teposcolula	Refugio de Morelos	SPP-SJT-MOR	MOR	220		
Teposcolula	San Juan Teposcolula	San Juan Teposcolula	SPP-SJT-SJT	SJT	548	2,683	1,457
Teposcolula	San Pedro Topiltepec	San Pedro Topiltepec	SPP-TOP-TOP	TOP	238	1,582	527
Teposcolula	San Pedro Topiltepec	Santa María Tiltepec	SPP-TOP-TIP	TIP	289		
Teposcolula	San Pedro y San Pablo Teposcolula	Guadalupe Tixa	SPP-SPP-GTX	GTX	73		
Teposcolula	San Pedro y San Pablo Teposcolula	San Felipe Ixtapa	SPP-SPP-SFI	SFI	222		

continued on next page

Table 1.1—*continued*

Distrito	Municipio	Agencia/Localidad	Site Prefix	Abbr	Pop 1990	Total Municipio Pop 1960	Total Municipio Pop 1990
Teposcolula	San Pedro y San Pablo Teposcolula	San Miguel Tixa	SPP-SPP-SMX	SMX	207		
Teposcolula	San Pedro y San Pablo Teposcolula	San Pedro y San Pablo Teposcolula	SPP-SPP-SPP	SPP	1,355	4,489	3,694
Teposcolula	San Pedro y San Pablo Teposcolula	Santa Catarina Río Delgado	SPP-SPP-CAT	CAT	78		
Teposcolula	San Pedro y San Pablo Teposcolula	Santo Domingo Tlachitongo	SPP-TOP-TGO	TGO	96		
Teposcolula	San Pedro y San Pablo Teposcolula	Santo Tomás Tecolotitlán	SPP-SPP-TEC	TEC	199		
Teposcolula	San Pedro y San Pablo Teposcolula	Yucumesa	SPP-SPP-YCM	YCM	229		
Teposcolula	San Pedro Yucunama	San Pedro Yucunama	SPP-YUC-YUC	YUC	236	484	262
Teposcolula	San Vicente Nuñu	Anama	SPP-SVN-ANM	ANM	80		
Teposcolula	San Vicente Nuñu	San Vicente Nuñu	SPP-SVN-SVN	SVN	392	1,046	591
Teposcolula	San Vicente Nuñu	San José de Gracia	SPP-NDU-SJG	SJG	187		
Teposcolula	Santa María Nduayaco	Santa María Nduayaco	SPP-NDU-NDU	NDU	194	1,998	756
Teposcolula	Santa María Nduayaco	Santo Domingo Ticu	SPP-NDU-TIC	TIC	148		
Teposcolula	Santa María Nduayaco	Unión Paz y Progreso	SPP-NDU-UPP	UPP	90		
Teposcolula	Santiago Nejapilla	Santiago Nejapilla	SPP-NEJ-NEJ	NEJ	335	776	335
Teposcolula	Santiago Yolomécatl	Santiago Yolomécatl	SPP-YOL-YOL	YOL	1,453		
Teposcolula	Santo Domingo Tlatayapam	Santo Domingo Tlatayapam	SPP-SDT-SDT	SDT	175	513	175
Teposcolula	Tejupan Villa de la Unión	Tejupan Villa de la Unión	SPP-TDU-TDU	TDU	995	2,740	2,317
Teposcolula	Tejupan Villa de la Unión	Tierra Blanca	SPP-TDU-TBA	TBA	128		
Teposcolula	Tejupan Villa de la Unión	Yodobada Peñasco	SPP-TDU-YBA	YBA	238		
Tlaxiaco	Heroica Ciudad de Tlaxiaco	Cañada Alejandro	TLA-TLA-CAL	CAL	207		

Tlaxiaco	Heroica Ciudad de Tlaxiaco	Heroica Ciudad de Tlaxiaco	TLA-TLA-TLA	TLA	9,555	13,484	22,813
Tlaxiaco	Heroica Ciudad de Tlaxiaco	Llano de Guadalupe	TLA-TLA-LLG	LLG	606		
Tlaxiaco	Heroica Ciudad de Tlaxiaco	Ojo de Agua	TLA-TLA-ODA	ODA	894		
Tlaxiaco	Heroica Ciudad de Tlaxiaco	Santa Lucrecia	TLA-TLA-SLC	SLC	331		
Tlaxiaco	Heroica Ciudad de Tlaxiaco	Santo Domingo Huendio	TLA-TLA-SDH	SDH	260		
Tlaxiaco	Magdalena Peñasco	Cabacoa	TLA-SMP-CAB	CAB	101		
Tlaxiaco	Magdalena Peñasco	Ignacio Zaragoza	TLA-SMP-ZAR	ZAR	532		
Tlaxiaco	Magdalena Peñasco	Magdalena Peñasco	TLA-SMP-SMP	SMP	437	2,920	3,185
Tlaxiaco	Magdalena Peñasco	San Isidro Peñasco	TLA-SMP-SIP	SIP	655	1,211	824
Tlaxiaco	San Agustín Tlacotepec	San Agustín Tlacotepec	TLA-SAT-SAT	SAT	245		
Tlaxiaco	San Agustín Tlacotepec	Yosojica	TLA-SAT-YOS	YOS	140		
Tlaxiaco	San Bartolomé Yucuañe	San Bartolomé Yucuañe	TLA-SBY-SBY	SBY	575	990	575
Tlaxiaco	San Cristóbal Amoltepec	San Cristóbal Amoltepec	TLA-SCA-SCA	SCA	559	1,443	1,221
Tlaxiaco	San Juan Achiutla	San Juan Achiutla	TLA-SJA-SJA	SJA	553	1,031	656
Tlaxiaco	San Juan Ñumi	El Río Ñumi	TLA-SJN-ERN	ERN	349		
Tlaxiaco	San Juan Ñumi	Monte Negro Ñumi	TLA-SJN-MNN	MNN	103		
Tlaxiaco	San Juan Ñumi	San Pedro Ñumi	TLA-SJN-SPN	SPN	451		
Tlaxiaco	San Martín Huamelulpan	Morelos	TLA-SMH-MRS	MRS	36		
Tlaxiaco	San Martín Huamelulpan	Plan de Guadalupe	TLA-SMH-PDG	PDG	190		
Tlaxiaco	San Martín Huamelulpan	San Martín Huamelulpan	TLA-SMH-SMH	SMH	136	1,258	1,220
Tlaxiaco	San Martín Huamelulpan	Totonundo	TLA-SMH-TTN	TTN	344		
Tlaxiaco	San Mateo Peñasco	San Mateo Peñasco	TLA-SMO-SMO	SMO	727	1,416	1,573
Tlaxiaco	San Miguel Achiutla	San Miguel Achiutla	TLA-SMA-SMA	SMA	950	1,574	1,198
Tlaxiaco	San Miguel Achiutla	San Sebastián Atoyaquillo	TLA-SMA-ATY	ATY	248		
Tlaxiaco	San Pedro Mártir Yucuxaco	Cañada María	TLA-PMY-CMA	CMA	469		
Tlaxiaco	San Pedro Mártir Yucuxaco	El Progreso	TLA-PMY-EPO	EPO	81		
Tlaxiaco	San Pedro Mártir Yucuxaco	Guadalupe Hidalgo	TLA-PMY-GPE	GPE	306		
Tlaxiaco	San Pedro Mártir Yucuxaco	Las Peñas	TLA-PMY-LPE	LPE	168		
Tlaxiaco	San Pedro Mártir Yucuxaco	San Pedro Mártir Yucuxaco	TLA-PMY-PMY	PMY	407	1,859	1,620
Tlaxiaco	Santa Catarina Tayata	Cuauhtemoc	TLA-SCA-CUA	CUA	334		

continued on next page

409

Table 1.1—*continued*

Distrito	Muncipio	Agencia/Localidad	Site Prefix	Abbr	Pop 1990	Total Municipio Pop 1960	Total Municipio Pop 1990
Tlaxiaco	Santa Catarina Tayata	Santa Catarina Tayata	TLA-SCT-SCT	SCT	89	863	748
Tlaxiaco	Santa Cruz Tayata	La Estancia Tayata	TLA-SZT-LET	LET	231		
Tlaxiaco	Santa Cruz Tayata	Santa Cruz Tayata	TLA-SZT-SZT	SZT	299	901	530
Tlaxiaco	Santa María del Rosario	La Unión Vista Hermosa	TLA-SMR-UVH	UVH	104		
Tlaxiaco	Santa María del Rosario	Santa María del Rosario	TLA-SMR-SMR	SMR	108	867	445
Tlaxiaco	Santiago Nundichi	Cañada Tierra Blanca	TLA-NUN-CTB	CTB	146		
Tlaxiaco	Santiago Nundichi	Hidalgo	TLA-NUN-HID	HID	266		
Tlaxiaco	Santiago Nundichi	Santiago Nundichi	TLA-NUN-NUN	NUN	173	909	1240
Totals					37,531	57,321	57,506

Notes: Affiliations and spellings: official sources including Instituto Nacional de Estadística, Geografía, e Informática (INEGI) censuses and municipios themselves. Populations: García 1998, which is from INEGI censuses. Populations of San Felipe Ixtapa and Yosojica interpolated.

Table 1.2. Archaeological Chronology for the Mixteca Alta and the Valley of Oaxaca.

Time	Mesoamerica	Valley of Oaxaca	Mixteca Alta
AD 1500	Historic		
1400			
1300	Late Postclassic	(Late)	(Late)
1200		Monte Albán V	Natividad
1100		(Early)	(Early)
1000	Early Postclassic		
900			
800	(Epiclassic)	Monte Albán IV	
700	Late Classic		Late Las Flores
600		Monte Albán IIIb	
500			
400	Early Classic	Monte Albán IIIa	Early Las Flores
300			(Transición)
200			
100	Terminal Formative	Monte Albán II	Late Ramos
1			
100			
200	Late Formative	Monte Albán Late I	Early Ramos
300			
400		Monte Albán Early I	
500			Late Cruz
600		Rosario	
700	Middle Formative		
800		Guadalupe	
900			Middle Cruz
1000		San José	
1100			
1200	Early Formative		
1300		Tierras Largas	Early Cruz
1400			
BC 1500		Espiridión	

Table 2.1. Early/Middle Cruz Sites in Jazmín.

Site	Toponym	Elev (m)	Area (ha)	Min Pop	Avg Pop	Max Pop	Strs	Pz	% Terr
SPP-SPA-SPA-2		2,252	5.9	59	104	148			
SPP-TOP-TIP-9		2,392	0.1	5	8	10			
SPP-TOP-TIP-10		2,179	0.3	5	8	10			
SPP-TOP-TIP-12	Loma de Nuyó	2,139	4.9	49	85	121			
SPP-TOP-TIP-16		2,143	4.5	45	79	112			
NO-YAN-XAC-4		2,220	43.5	435	761	1,087			
NO-YAN-XAC-6		2,280	21.6	216	378	541			
NO-YAN-XAC-7		2,240	9.1	91	160	228			

Table 2.2. Late Cruz Sites in Jazmín.

Site	Toponym	Elev (m)	Area (ha)	Min Pop	Avg Pop	Max Pop	Strs	Pz	% Terr
SPP-SPA-SPA-1		2,230	6	60	106	151			
SPP-SPA-SPA-3		2,270	5.8	58	101	144			
SPP-SPA-SPA-6		2,200	3.1	31	55	78			
SPP-TOP-TIP-5		2,240	4	40	70	100			
SPP-TOP-TIP-10		2,153	6.3	63	109	156			
NO-TLO-TLO-7		2,100	5.3	53	92	132	1		
NO-YAN-XAC-6		2,200	21.6	216	379	541			
NO-YAN-XAC-7		2,221	9.1	91	160	228			

Table 2.3. Ramos Sites in Jazmín.

Site	Toponym	Elev (m)	Area (ha)	Min Pop	Avg Pop	Max Pop	Strs	Pz	% Terr
NO-YAN-CIE-3		2,560	1.5	15	27	38			
SPP-SPA-SPA-6		2,200	0.1	5	8	10			
SPP-TOP-TIP-1	Cerro Jazmín	2,445	79.7	3,983	5,974	7,965	10	5	100

Table 2.4. Las Flores Sites in Jazmín.

Site	Toponym	Elev (m)	Area (ha)	Min Pop	Avg Pop	Max Pop	Strs	Pz	% Terr
SPP-TOP-TIP-1	Cerro Jazmín	2,416	229.1	11,453	17,180	22,906	10		100
SPP-TOP-TIP-2		2,240	20.2	202	353	504			
SPP-TOP-TIP-5		2,360	4	40	70	100			
SPP-TOP-TIP-10		2,153	6.3	63	109	156			
SPP-TOP-TIP-12	Loma de Nuyó	2,160	26.9	269	470	672			
SPP-TOP-TIP-14		2,220	13.9	139	243	347			
SPP-TOP-TIP-16		2,180	10.2	102	179	255			
NO-TLO-TLO-1		2,100	14.7	147	258	368			
NO-TLO-TLO-3	Loma Yusandicana	2,100	9.1	91	158	226	5		
NO-TLO-TLO-4	Cerro de Tillo	2,100	10.2	102	179	255			
NO-TLO-TLO-5		2,133	23.7	237	415	592			
NO-TLO-TLO-7		2,100	5.3	53	92	132	1		
NO-TLO-TLO-9		2,112	2.7	27	46	66			
NO-YAN-XAC-2		2,235	0.1	5	8	10			

Table 2.5. Natividad Sites in Jazmín.

Site	Toponym	Elev (m)	Area (ha)	Min Pop	Avg Pop	Max Pop	Strs	Pz	% Terr
NO-YAN-CIE-1		2,400	0.5	5	8	10			
NO-YAN-CIE-2		2,405	0.8	8	13	19			
NO-YAN-CIE-3		2,559	1.5	15	27	38			
SPP-SPA-SPA-1		2,230	8	80	139	199			
SPP-SPA-SPA-2		2,252	5.9	59	104	148			
SPP-SPA-SPA-3		2,270	5.8	58	101	144			
SPP-SPA-SPA-4		2,419	1.7	17	29	42			
SPP-SPA-SPA-5		2,446	0.1	5	8	10			
SPP-SPA-SPA-6		2,237	14.7	147	258	368			
SPP-TOP-TIP-1	Cerro Jazmín	2,420	577	21,004	31,996	42,988	12	5	66

continued on next page

Table 2.5—continued

Site	Toponym	Elev (m)	Area (ha)	Min Pop	Avg Pop	Max Pop	Strs	Pz	% Terr
SPP-TOP-TIP-2		2,175	93.7	937	1,640	2,343			
SPP-TOP-TIP-3		2,321	3.4	34	59	84			
SPP-TOP-TIP-4		2,204	16.3	163	286	408			
SPP-TOP-TIP-5		2,240	4	40	70	100			
SPP-TOP-TIP-7		2,243	20.7	207	362	517			
SPP-TOP-TIP-8		2,320	3.7	37	66	94			
SPP-TOP-TIP-10		2,160	15.6	156	273	390			
SPP-TOP-TIP-11		2,374	1.3	13	22	31			
SPP-TOP-TIP-12	Loma de Nuyó	2,175	48.5	485	849	1,213			
SPP-TOP-TIP-13		2,357	2.2	22	38	54			
SPP-TOP-TIP-14		2,220	3.3	34	59	84			
SPP-TOP-TIP-15		2,321	1.5	15	27	38			
SPP-TOP-TIP-16		2,140	10.2	102	179	255			
SPP-TOP-TIP-17		2,360	1.9	19	34	48			
NO-TLO-TLO-1	Loma Yusandicana	2,118	14.7	147	258	368			
NO-TLO-TLO-2		2,100	14.3	143	250	357			
NO-TLO-TLO-3	Cerro de Tillo	2,081	9.1	91	158	226	5		
NO-TLO-TLO-4		2,103	10.2	102	179	255			
NO-TLO-TLO-5		2,134	23.7	237	415	592			
NO-TLO-TLO-7		2,100	25	250	438	626	1		
NO-TLO-TLO-8		2,095	2.2	22	39	55			
NO-TLO-TLO-9		2,103	9.8	98	172	245			
NO-YAN-XAC-1		2,220	18	180	315	450			
NO-YAN-XAC-2		2,259	20.8	208	365	521			
NO-YAN-XAC-3		2,257	8.4	84	146	209			
NO-YAN-XAC-4		2,212	85.1	851	1,489	2,127			
NO-YAN-XAC-5	Cerro Endesacao	2,400	7.8	78	136	194			
NO-YAN-XAC-6		2,214	28.2	282	494	705			
NO-YAN-XAC-7		2,221	9.1	91	160	228			

Table 2.6. Cruz Sites in Nejapilla.

Site	Toponym	Elev (m)	Area (ha)	Min Pop	Avg Pop	Max Pop	Strs	Pz	% Terr
SPP-SDT-SDT-1EMC		2,206	1.9	19	33	47			
SPP-NEJ-NEJ-5		2,324	1.5	15	27	38			
SPP-SDT-SDT-2		2,208	3.8	38	66	94			
SPP-SDT-SDT-7		2,220	2.8	28	49	70	1		
SPP-TOP-TGO-1		2,139	3.1	31	55	78			
SPP-TOP-TOP-3	Topiltepec	2,160	1	10	18	25			

Table 2.7. Ramos Sites in Nejapilla.

Site	Toponym	Elev (m)	Area (ha)	Min Pop	Avg Pop	Max Pop	Strs	Pz	% Terr
SPP-SDT-SDT-12	Loma Xatacahua (Loma del Baño)	2,460	11.2	560	840	1,120			100
SPP-TOP-TOP-1	Cerro de Topiltepec	2,307	10.4	520	780	1,040	6	1	100
SPP-TOP-TOP-2		2,140	0.1	5	8	10			

Table 2.8. Las Flores Sites in Nejapilla.

Site	Toponym	Elev (m)	Area (ha)	Min Pop	Avg Pop	Max Pop	Strs	Pz	% Terr
SPP-NEJ-NEJ-1		2,320	8.2	82	144	205			
SPP-NEJ-NEJ-4		2,729	0.5	5	9	12			
SPP-NEJ-NEJ-6		2,600	0.3	5	8	10			
SPP-SDT-SDT-12	Loma Xatacahua (Loma del Baño)	2,429	11.2	560	840	1,120			100
SPP-SDT-SDT-2		2,208	3.8	38	66	94			
SPP-TOP-TGO-1		2,260	7.9	79	138	197			
SPP-TOP-TGO-1		2,180	7.9	79	138	197			
SPP-TOP-TOP-1	Cerro de Topiltepec	2,202	66	2,640	4,001	5,362	6	1.5	75
SPP-TOP-TOP-2		2,100	23.7	237	415	592			
SPP-TOP-TOP-3	Topiltepec	2,060	1	10	18	25			

Table 2.9. Natividad Sites in Nejapilla.

Site	Toponym	Elev (m)	Area (ha)	Min Pop	Avg Pop	Max Pop	Strs	Pz	% Terr
SPP-NEJ-NEJ-1		2,280	8.2	82	144	205			
SPP-NEJ-NEJ-11		2,380	5.5	55	96	137			
SPP-NEJ-NEJ-13		2,363	10.4	104	182	260			
SPP-NEJ-NEJ-3		2,323	28	280	490	700			
SPP-NEJ-NEJ-5		2,324	7.7	77	135	192			
SPP-NEJ-NEJ-6		2,634	0.3	5	8	10			
SPP-NEJ-NEJ-7		2,331	2.9	29	52	74			
SPP-NEJ-NEJ-9		2,544	9.8	98	172	246			
SPP-SDT-SDT-1		2,218	12.9	129	226	322			
SPP-SDT-SDT-12	Loma Xatacahua (Loma del Baño)	2,452	0.1	5	8	10			
SPP-SDT-SDT-2		2,200	11.3	113	197	281			
SPP-SDT-SDT-3		2,345	9.3	93	162	231			
SPP-SDT-SDT-4		2,504	0.2	5	8	10			
SPP-SDT-SDT-5		2,358	4.3	43	75	107			
SPP-SDT-SDT-6		2,320	3.4	34	59	84			
SPP-SDT-SDT-7		2,220	2.8	28	49	70	1		
SPP-SDT-SDT-8		2,240	7	70	123	175			
SPP-SDT-SDT-9		2,285	18.9	189	330	472			
SPP-TOP-TGO-1		2,197	132.2	1,322	2,314	3,305			
SPP-TOP-TGO-2		2,200	145.7	1,457	2,550	3,643			
SPP-TOP-TOP-1	Cerro de Topiltepec	2,240	31.9	957	1,475	1,993			
SPP-TOP-TOP-2	Topiltepec	2,140	23.7	237	415	592			
SPP-TOP-TOP-3		2,160	1	10	18	25			

Table 2.10. Early/Middle Cruz Sites in Yodocono.

Site	Toponym	Elev (m)	Area (ha)	Min Pop	Avg Pop	Max Pop	Strs	Pz	% Terr
NO-SPT-SPT-7		2,320	7.3	73	129	184			
NO-YPD-YPD-5		2,334	0.3	5	8	10			
NO-YPD-YPD-14		2,368	0.5	5	8	10			

Table 2.11. Late Cruz Sites in Yodocono.

Site	Toponym	Elev (m)	Area (ha)	Min Pop	Avg Pop	Max Pop	Strs	Pz	% Terr
NO-YPD-YPD-5		2,340	5.3	53	92	131			
NO-YPD-YPD-19		2,400	5.9	59	103	147			
NO-YPD-YPD-20		2,586	3.4	34	59	84			

Table 2.12. Ramos and Las Flores Sites in Yodocono.

Site	Toponym	Elev (m)	Area (ha)	Min Pop	Avg Pop	Max Pop	Strs	Pz	% Terr
NO-YPD-YPD-6R		2,560	34.1	1,241	1,891	2,540	1		66
NO-YPD-YPD-1	Yucunee	2,820	5.2	262	392	523	10	2	100
NO-YPD-YPD-13		2,420	1.9	19	33	47			
NO-YPD-YPD-15		2,540	7.4	74	129	184			
NO-YPD-YPD-17		2,420	4.5	45	78	111			
NO-YPD-YPD-18		2,420	16.4	164	287	410			
NO-YPD-YPD-19		2,400	5.9	59	103	147			
NO-YPD-YPD-23		2,320	3.5	35	62	88			
NO-YPD-YPD-3		2,580	1	10	18	25			
NO-YPD-YPD-5		2,360	18.3	183	319	456	2		
NO-YPD-YPD-6		2,529	34.2	1,244	1,895	2,546	1		66
NO-YPD-YPD-8		2,440	6	60	105	150	1		

Table 2.13. Natividad Sites in Yodocono.

Site	Toponym	Elev (m)	Area (ha)	Min Pop	Avg Pop	Max Pop	Strs	Pz	% Terr
NO-SPT-SPT-7		2,320	7.3	73	129	184			
NO-YPD-YPD-1	Yucunee	2,777	0.2	5	8	10			
NO-YPD-YPD-2		2,313	11.4	114	200	285			
NO-YPD-YPD-3		2,586	1	10	18	25			
NO-YPD-YPD-4		2,560	4.3	43	75	107			
NO-YPD-YPD-5		2,327	18.3	183	319	456			
NO-YPD-YPD-7		2,400	0.5	5	9	12			
NO-YPD-YPD-8		2,389	2.5	25	43	61			
NO-YPD-YPD-9		2,460	0.4	5	8	10			
NO-YPD-YPD-10		2,380	1.3	13	22	31			
NO-YPD-YPD-11		2,398	0.2	5	8	10			
NO-YPD-YPD-12		2,540	1.5	15	27	38			
NO-YPD-YPD-13		2,394	1.9	19	33	47			
NO-YPD-YPD-15		2,480	7.4	74	129	184			
NO-YPD-YPD-16		2,424	1.6	16	28	40			
NO-YPD-YPD-17		2,411	4.5	45	78	111			
NO-YPD-YPD-18		2,420	16.4	164	287	410			
NO-YPD-YPD-19		2,400	21.6	216	377	539			
NO-YPD-YPD-21		2,383	2	20	35	50			
NO-YPD-YPD-22		2,360	2	20	35	50			
NO-YPD-YPD-23		2,340	3.5	35	62	88			

Table 2.14. Late Cruz Sites in Tidaá.

Site	Toponym	Elev (m)	Area (ha)	Min Pop	Avg Pop	Max Pop	Strs	Pz	% Terr
NO-SPT-SPT-9		2,390	13.5	135	237	338			
NO-SPT-SPT-11		2,324	0.1	5	8	10			

Table 2.15. Ramos Sites in Tidaá.

Site	Toponym	Elev (m)	Area (ha)	Min Pop	Avg Pop	Max Pop	Strs	Pz	% Terr
NO-SPT-SPT-3	Cerro Yucuayuxi	2,460	20.1	1,003	1,504	2,005	5	2	100
NO-SPT-SPT-10		2,371	0.3	5	8	10			

Table 2.16. Las Flores Sites in Tidaá.

Site	Toponym	Elev (m)	Area (ha)	Min Pop	Avg Pop	Max Pop	Strs	Pz	% Terr
NO-SPT-SPT-1		2,440	1.1	11	20	28			
NO-SPT-SPT-3	Cerro Yucuayuxi	2,447	20.1	1,003	2,005	2,005	5	2	100
NO-SPT-SPT-4		2,440	8.1	81	141	201			
NO-SPT-SPT-8		2,420	21.7	217	380	542			
NO-SPT-SPT-16		2,380	1	10	18	25			
NO-SPT-SPT-20		2,520	1.7	17	29	42			
NO-SPT-SPT-22		2,401	0.3	5	8	10			
NO-SPT-SPT-30		2,420	4.4	44	76	109	1		

Table 2.17. Natividad Sites in Tidaá.

Site	Toponym	Elev (m)	Area (ha)	Min Pop	Avg Pop	Max Pop	Strs	Pz	% Terr
NO-SPT-SPT-1		2,521	1.1	11	20	28			
NO-SPT-SPT-3	Cerro Yucuayuxi	2,387	0.1	5	8	10			
NO-SPT-SPT-4		2,432	8.1	81	141	201			
NO-SPT-SPT-5		2,307	2.5	25	44	62			
NO-SPT-SPT-6		2,340	9.6	96	169	241			
NO-SPT-SPT-8		2,410	21.7	217	380	542			
NO-SPT-SPT-9		2,390	13.5	135	237	338			
NO-SPT-SPT-11		2,332	2.1	21	36	51			
NO-SPT-SPT-12		2,340	3.5	35	61	87			
NO-SPT-SPT-14		2,320	0.3	5	8	10			
NO-SPT-SPT-16		2,380	1	10	18	25			
NO-SPT-SPT-18		2,540	1.3	13	22	31			
NO-SPT-SPT-20		2,519	1.7	17	29	42			
NO-SPT-SPT-24		2,398	11	110	192	274			
NO-SPT-SPT-26		2,380	3.7	37	64	92	1		
NO-SPT-SPT-30		2,379	16.8	168	294	420	1		

Table 2.18. Early/Middle Cruz Sites in Tilantongo.

Site	Toponym	Elev (m)	Area (ha)	Min Pop	Avg Pop	Max Pop	Strs	Pz	% Terr
NO-SJD-SJD-3		2,193	4.6	46	81	115			
NO-SJD-SJD-7		2,220	49.5	495	867	1,238			
NO-SJD-SJD-9		2,280	1.5	15	27	38			
NO-TIL-TIL-7	La Providencia	2,245	8.7	87	153	218	1		
NO-TIL-TIL-11		2,102	0.4	5	8	10			

Table 2.19. Late Cruz Sites in Tilantongo.

Site	Toponym	Elev (m)	Area (ha)	Min Pop	Avg Pop	Max Pop	Strs	Pz	% Terr
NO-TIL-BV-4		2,200	0.5	5	8	10			
NO-SJD-SJD-1		2,216	0.1	5	8	10			
NO-SJD-SJD-10		2,326	0.2	5	8	10			
NO-SJD-SJD-14		2,405	8.7	87	152	217			
NO-SJD-SJD-16		2,264	0.1	5	8	10			
NO-SJD-SJD-6		2,288	0.5	5	9	12			
NO-SJD-SJD-7		2,181	4.2	42	73	104			
NO-TIL-TIL-10		2,123	5.2	52	90	129			
NO-TIL-TIL-13		2,137	7.8	78	137	196	1		
NO-TIL-TIL-15		2,051	11.3	113	197	281			
NO-TIL-TIL-24	Pueblo Viejo de Tilantongo	2,215	14.5	145	253	361			
NO-TIL-TIL-3		2,082	1	50	75	100	3	1	100
NO-TIL-TIL-4		2,183	0.8	8	13	19			
NO-TIL-TIL-40		2,328	4.4	44	77	110			
NO-TIL-TIL-5		2,142	17.4	174	305	435			
NO-TIL-TIL-7	La Providencia	2,145	91.6	916	1,602	2,289	4		

Table 2.20. Ramos Sites in Tilantongo.

Site	Toponym	Elev (m)	Area (ha)	Min Pop	Avg Pop	Max Pop	Strs	Pz	% Terr
NO-TIL-BV-1	Buena Vista	2,380	0.1	5	8	10			
NO-TIL-BV-2		2,340	0.4	5	8	10			
NO-TIL-BV-3		2,311	1	10	18	25			
NO-SJD-SJD-2		2,520	1	10	18	25			
NO-TIL-TIL-1	Yucunoo (Monte Negro)	2,670	77.8	1,944	3,889	5,833	31	2	
NO-TIL-TIL-5		2,266	6.7	67	116	166	1		
NO-TIL-TIL-7	La Providencia	2,280	4.2	42	74	105			

Table 2.21. Las Flores Sites in Tilantongo.

Site	Toponym	Elev (m)	Area (ha)	Min Pop	Avg Pop	Max Pop	Strs	Pz	% Terr
NO-TIL-BV-1	Buena Vista	2,337	55	550	963	1,375	1		
NO-TIL-BV-2		2,332	0.4	5	8	10			
NO-TIL-BV-4		2,280	20	200	351	501			
NO-TIL-BV-5		2,304	0.1	5	8	10			
NO-SJD-SJD-2		2,340	13.9	416	642	867	2		
NO-SJD-SJD-5		2,160	0.8	8	13	19			
NO-SJD-SJD-7		2,220	49.5	495	867	1,238			
NO-SJD-SJD-9		2,280	1.5	15	27	38	1		
NO-SJD-SJD-18		2,562	17.6	176	307	439	1		
NO-SJD-SJD-20		2,500	36.4	364	637	910	1		
NO-TIL-TIL-3		2,280	12.1	363	559	756	3	1	50
NO-TIL-TIL-5		2,226	99.6	996	1,742	2,489	4		
NO-TIL-TIL-7	La Providencia	2,178	10	232	365	498	4		
NO-TIL-TIL-7	La Providencia	2,178	10	232	365	498	4		
NO-TIL-TIL-7	La Providencia	2,178	53.5	857	1,398	1,940	4		
NO-TIL-TIL-7	La Providencia	2,178	53.5	857	1,398	1,940	4		
NO-TIL-TIL-7	La Providencia	2,272	30.8	492	804	1,116			
NO-TIL-TIL-10		2,200	23.1	231	405	578			
NO-TIL-TIL-12		2,380	5.3	53	92	132			
NO-TIL-TIL-22		2,160	5	50	88	125			
NO-TIL-TIL-24	Pueblo Viejo de Tilantongo	2,219	53.3	1,236	1,944	2,651	1		
NO-TIL-TIL-24	Pueblo Viejo de Tilantongo	2,219	55	1,277	2,007	2,738	1		
NO-TIL-TIL-24	Pueblo Viejo de Tilantongo	2,091	2.5	25	44	63			
NO-TIL-TIL-25		2,260	3.9	39	67	96			
NO-TIL-TIL-41		2,380	3.4	34	59	84			
NO-TIL-TIL-43		2,400	31	310	543	775			

Table 2.22. Natividad Sites in Tilantongo.

Site	Toponym	Elev (m)	Area (ha)	Min Pop	Avg Pop	Max Pop	Strs	Pz	% Terr
NO-TIL-BV-1	Buena Vista	2,329	0.3	5	8	10			
NO-TIL-BV-1	Buena Vista	2,380	0.3	5	8	10			
NO-TIL-BV-1	Buena Vista	2,380	4.9	5	8	10			
NO-TIL-BV-1	Buena Vista	2,249	8.6	86	151	215			
NO-TIL-BV-1	Buena Vista	2,268	2.6	26	46	65			
NO-TIL-BV-1	Buena Vista	2,280	27	270	472	674			
NO-TIL-BV-3		2,320	1	10	18	25			
NO-TIL-BV-4		2,245	2	20	36	51			
NO-TIL-BV-5		2,311	15.8	158	276	395			
NO-SJD-SJD-1		2,202	1.5	15	25	36			
NO-SJD-SJD-2		2,509	13.9	416	642	867	2		
NO-SJD-SJD-3		2,193	4.6	46	81	115			
NO-SJD-SJD-4		2,852	0.1	5	8	10			
NO-SJD-SJD-5		2,145	0.8	8	13	19			
NO-SJD-SJD-7		2,180	24.7	247	433	618			
NO-SJD-SJD-8		2,289	1	10	18	25			
NO-SJD-SJD-10		2,326	0.2	5	8	10			
NO-SJD-SJD-12		2,333	0.8	8	13	19			
NO-SJD-SJD-14		2,405	8.7	87	152	217			
NO-SJD-SJD-16		2,260	3.9	39	68	97			
NO-TIL-TIL-1	Yucunoo (Monte Negro)	2,672	1	10	18	25			
NO-TIL-TIL-2		2,219	1	10	18	25			
NO-TIL-TIL-3		2,081	12.1	363	559	756	3		
NO-TIL-TIL-5		2,223	166.3	1,663	2,911	4,159	1	1	
NO-TIL-TIL-6		2,101	1	10	18	25			
NO-TIL-TIL-7	La Providencia	2,260	254.2	3,051	5,180	7,309	4		
NO-TIL-TIL-8		2,121	17.5	175	305	436			
NO-TIL-TIL-9		2,102	13.9	5	8	10			

continued on next page

Table 2.22—continued

Site	Topomym	Elev (m)	Area (ha)	Min Pop	Avg Pop	Max Pop	Strs	Pz	% Terr
NO-TIL-TIL-10		2,133	23.1	231	405	578			
NO-TIL-TIL-11		2,115	6.1	61	107	153			
NO-TIL-TIL-12		2,220	5.3	53	92	132			
NO-TIL-TIL-13		2,105	20	200	350	500	1		
NO-TIL-TIL-14		2,360	12.8	128	223	319			
NO-TIL-TIL-17		2,063	35.5	355	621	887			
NO-TIL-TIL-18		2,251	10	100	174	249			
NO-TIL-TIL-22		2,160	5	50	88	125			
NO-TIL-TIL-24	Pueblo Viejo de Tilantongo	2,158	181.6	2,542	4,222	5,902	1		
NO-TIL-TIL-25		2,039	3.9	39	67	96			
NO-TIL-TIL-40		2,328	4.4	44	77	110			
NO-TIL-TIL-41		2,380	3.4	34	59	84			
NO-TIL-TIL-42		2,380	0.1	5	8	10			
NO-TIL-TIL-43		2,384	31	310	543	775			

Table 3.1. Early/Middle Cruz Sites in Teposcolula.

Site	Topomym	Elev (m)	Area (ha)	Min Pop	Avg Pop	Max Pop	Strs	Pz	% Terr
SPP-SPP-SFI-3		2,201	8.8	44	66	88			
SPP-SJT-SJT-4		2,360	3.1	31	55	78			
SPP-SPP-SMX-3		2,240	2.4	24	42	60			
SPP-SPP-SPP-24		2,222.5	0.6	6	8.5	11			
SPP-SPP-SPP-24		2,250	1.1	14	21	28			
SPP-SPP-SPP-53		2,260	5.3	53	92	131			
SPP-SPP-TEC-4		2,264	0.8	8	14	20			
SPP-SPP-TEC-4		2,230	11	110	193	275		1	
SPP-SPP-YCM-4		2,407	4.3	21	32	43			

Table 3.2. Late Cruz Sites in Teposcolula.

Site	Toponym	Elev (m)	Area (ha)	Min Pop	Avg Pop	Max Pop	Strs	Pz	% Terr
SPP-SPP-CAT-1		2,426	2.8	28	48	69			
SPP-SPP-CAT-3		2,476	2.4	24	43	61			
SPP-SPP-CAT-6		2,240	1	10	18	25			
SPP-SPP-CAT-7		2,168	3.5	35	62	88			
SPP-SPP-CAT-7		2,346	12	60	90	120			
SPP-SPP-CAT-8		2,311	8	80	140	200			
SPP-SPP-SFI-1		2,309	0.1	5	8	10			
SPP-SPP-SFI-3		2,185	26	130	195	260			
SPP-SPP-SFI-6		2,220	0.5	5	9	13			
SPP-SPP-SFI-6		2,154	13.8	138	241	344			
SPP-SPP-SFI-7		2,179	22.5	113	169	225			
SPP-SPP-SFI-7		2,222	0.8	8	14	19			
SPP-SPP-SFI-7		2,340	0.9	9	17	24			
SPP-SPP-SFI-7		2,140	1.5	15	27	38			
SPP-SJT-SJT-4		2,360	5.5	55	97	138	2		
SPP-SPP-SMX-3		2,240	3.4	34	60	85	1		
SPP-SPP-SMX-3		2,317	9.3	93	162	231	2		
SPP-SPP-SPP-5		2,232	0.3	5	8	10			
SPP-SPP-SPP-14		2,380	3.4	34	60	85			
SPP-SPP-SPP-15		2,380	0.1	5	8	10			
SPP-SPP-SPP-16		2,400	0.1	5	8	10			
SPP-SPP-SPP-24		2,204	17	170	298	425			
SPP-SPP-SPP-24		2,300	1.2	12	21	30			
SPP-SPP-SPP-28		2,197	1.6	16	29	41			
SPP-SPP-SPP-29		2,300	4.3	43	75	106	9	1	
SPP-SPP-SPP-53		2,263	16.3	163	285	406	1		
SPP-SPP-TEC-1		2,243	1	10	18	25			
SPP-SPP-TEC-3		2,280	0.3	5	8	10			
SPP-SPP-TEC-4		2,273	26.5	265	464	663	8		
SPP-SPP-YCM-4		2,360	0.3	5	8	10		1	

425

Table 3.3. Ramos Sites in Teposcolula.

Site	Toponym	Elev (m)	Area (ha)	Min Pop	Avg Pop	Max Pop	Strs	Pz	% Terr
SPP-SPP-CAT-7		2,324	29	725	1,088	1,450	5	1	
SPP-SPP-GTX-15		2,486	2.1	21	37	53	1		
SPP-SJT-SJT-20		2,431	32.3	968	1,452	1,935	11	1	
SPP-SPP-SMX-3		2,325	5.3	26	40	53	12		
SPP-SPP-SMX-3		2,239	1.4	69	104	138			
SPP-SPP-SPP-1		2,365	2.9	29	51	72	34	2	
SPP-SPP-SPP-2		2,346	7	350	525	700	5	1	
SPP-SPP-SPP-3		2,320	25.8	1,288	1,932	2,575	2	1	
SPP-SPP-SPP-26		2,320	1	10	18	25	3	2	
SPP-SPP-SPP-29		2,299	5.4	54	95	135	9	1	
SPP-SPP-SPP-33		2,400	3.3	33	57	81	4		
SPP-SPP-SPP-39		2,560	4.5	45	79	113	1		
SPP-SPP-SPP-53		2,268	6.8	34	51	68	1		
SPP-SPP-SPP-54		2,287	6.3	63	110	156			
SPP-SPP-SPP-55		2,530	30.6	1,532	2,298	3,063	20	1	
SPP-SPP-TEC-4		2,225	15.3	381	572	763	8	1	

Table 3.4. Las Flores Sites in Teposcolula.

Site	Toponym	Elev (m)	Area (ha)	Min Pop	Avg Pop	Max Pop	Strs	Pz	% Terr
SPP-SPP-CAT-2		2,480	1	10	18	25			
SPP-SPP-CAT-4	Yodonde	2,277	3	30	53	75			
SPP-SPP-CAT-5		2,407	12.3	123	216	308	1		
SPP-SPP-CAT-6		2,240	1.8	18	31	44			
SPP-SPP-CAT-7		2,264	33	825	1,238	1,650	5	1	
SPP-SPP-CAT-8		2,303	4.8	48	84	119			
SPP-SPP-CAT-10		2,320	1	10	18	25			
SPP-SPP-GTX-5		2,320	0.1	5	8	10			

continued on next page

SPP-SPP-GTX-6	2,314	9	90	158	225		1
SPP-SPP-GTX-8	2,220	0.9	9	16	22		
SPP-SPP-GTX-10	2,354	7.8	78	136	194		
SPP-SPP-GTX-13	2,314	1.4	14	25	35		
SPP-SPP-GTX-14	2,340	2.5	25	44	63		
SPP-SPP-GTX-15	2,500	2.1	21	37	53	1	
SPP-SPP-SFI-1	2,320	23.6	236	414	591		
SPP-SPP-SFI-3	2,247	7.4	37	56	74		
SPP-SPP-SFI-5	2,320	2.4	24	42	60		
SPP-SPP-SFI-6	2,311	2.8	14	21	28		
SPP-SPP-SFI-6	2,158	20.5	205	359	513		
SPP-SPP-SFI-7	2,360	21.1	106	159	211		
SPP-SPP-SFI-7	2,194	60.1	301	451	601		
SPP-SJT-SJT-2	2,400	0.8	8	14	19		
SPP-SJT-SJT-4	2,360	6.5	65	114	163		
SPP-SJT-SJT-5	2,420	2.1	21	37	53		
SPP-SJT-SJT-20	2,415	38.5	1,155	1,733	2,310	4	1
SPP-SJT-SJT-21	2,480	1.9	19	33	47		
SPP-SPP-SMX-3	2,312	14	70	105	140	13	
SPP-SPP-SMX-3	2,231	29	870	1,305	1,740		
SPP-SPP-SPP-1	2,370	9	90	158	225	34	2
SPP-SPP-SPP-2	2,317.3	29	870	1,305	1,740	7	2
SPP-SPP-SPP-3	2,320	34.8	1,043	1,564	2,085	2	1
SPP-SPP-SPP-5	2,220	0.3	5	8	10		
SPP-SPP-SPP-6	2,260	0.3	5	8	10		
SPP-SPP-SPP-10	2,460	0.5	5	9	13		
SPP-SPP-SPP-14	2,380	0.8	8	14	19		
SPP-SPP-SPP-17	2,460	0.2	5	8	10		
SPP-SPP-SPP-23	2,460	0.6	6	10	14		
SPP-SPP-SPP-24	2,278	0.6	6	10	14		

Table 3.4—continued

Site	Toponym	Elev (m)	Area (ha)	Min Pop	Avg Pop	Max Pop	Strs	Pz	% Terr
SPP-SPP-SPP-26		2,320	11.5	115	202	288		2	
SPP-SPP-SPP-27		2,280	3.8	38	66	94			
SPP-SPP-SPP-29		2,294	13.3	663	994	1,325			
SPP-SPP-SPP-32		2,580	0.3	5	8	10			
SPP-SPP-SPP-33		2,400	3.4	34	60	85	4		
SPP-SPP-SPP-37		2,320	1.8	18	31	44			
SPP-SPP-SPP-38		2,448	3.3	33	57	81			
SPP-SPP-SPP-39		2,570	4.5	23	34	45			
SPP-SPP-SPP-53		2,278	9.8	98	171	244			
SPP-SPP-SPP-54		2,321	15.3	153	267	381			
SPP-SPP-SPP-55		2,439	63	3,150	4,725	6,300	20	1	
SPP-SPP-SPP-58		2,480	0.1	5	8	10			
SPP-SPP-TEC-4		2,263	31	775	1,163	1,550	8	1	

Table 3.5. Natividad Sites in Teposcolula.

Site	Toponym	Elev (m)	Area (ha)	Min Pop	Avg Pop	Max Pop	Strs	Pz	% Terr
SPP-SPP-CAT-1		2,426	2.8	28	49	70			
SPP-SPP-CAT-2		2,487	1	10	17.5	25			
SPP-SPP-CAT-3		2,494	9	90	157	224	1		
SPP-SPP-CAT-5		2,416	0.5	5	9	12			
SPP-SPP-CAT-6		2,200	29.4	147	221	294			
SPP-SPP-CAT-7		2,210	12.5	125	219	313	5	1	
SPP-SPP-CAT-7		2,300	0.5	5	8	10			
SPP-SPP-CAT-7		2,376	0.8	5	8	10			
SPP-SPP-CAT-7		2,352.3	12.3	61	92	123			

Sample						
SPP-SPP-CAT-7	2,320	1.2	6	9	12	
SPP-SPP-CAT-7	2,340	1.8	9	14	18	
SPP-SPP-CAT-8	2,311	9.4	94	165	235	
SPP-SPP-CAT-9	2,248	0.2	5	8	10	
SPP-SPP-CAT-10	2,428	1	10	18	25	1
SPP-SPP-GTX-1	2,480	3.7	37	66	94	
SPP-SPP-GTX-2	2,330	0.1	5	7.5	10	
SPP-SPP-GTX-3	2,440	0.3	5	7.5	10	
SPP-SPP-GTX-4	2,283	0.1	5	7.5	10	
SPP-SPP-GTX-5	2,320	1.8	18	31	44	
SPP-SPP-GTX-6	2,320	0.8	5	8	10	3
SPP-SPP-GTX-7	2,307	1	10	18	25	1
SPP-SPP-GTX-8	2,204	9.1	46	69	91	
SPP-SPP-GTX-9	2,294	3.1	31	55	78	
SPP-SPP-GTX-10	2,368	6.3	63	110	156	
SPP-SPP-GTX-11	2,280	1.5	15	27	38	
SPP-SPP-GTX-12	2,400	0.7	7	12	17	
SPP-SPP-GTX-13	2,328	0.3	5	8	10	
SPP-SPP-GTX-14	2,352	2.5	25	44	63	
SPP-SPP-SFI-1	2,251	23	115	173	230	
SPP-SPP-SFI-2	2,140	0.1	5	8	10	
SPP-SPP-SFI-3	2,180	41.9	209	314	419	1
SPP-SPP-SFI-4	2,378	0.4	5	8	10	
SPP-SPP-SFI-5	2,315	4.1	21	31	41	
SPP-SPP-SFI-6	2,185	59.3	296	445	593	
SPP-SPP-SFI-7	2,235	147.6	738	1,107	1,476	1
SPP-SJT-SJT-1	2,400	0.4	5	8	10	
SPP-SJT-SJT-2	2,400	0.8	8	14	19	
SPP-SJT-SJT-3	2,512	0.1	5	8	10	
SPP-SJT-SJT-4	2,368	83.3	833	1,457	2,081	5

continued on next page

Table 3.5—continued

Site	Toponym	Elev (m)	Area (ha)	Min Pop	Avg Pop	Max Pop	Strs	Pz	% Terr
SPP-SJT-SJT-5		2,420	6	60	105	150			
SPP-SJT-SJT-6		2,420	3	15	23	30			
SPP-SJT-SJT-7		2,412	1.5	15	27	38			
SPP-SJT-SJT-8		2,420	1	10	18	25			
SPP-SJT-SJT-9		2,402	2.5	13	19	25			
SPP-SJT-SJT-10		2,382.5	3	15	23	30			
SPP-SJT-SJT-11		2,317	5.5	55	97	138			
SPP-SJT-SJT-12		2,339	0.3	5	8	10			
SPP-SJT-SJT-13		2,320	18	90	135	180			
SPP-SJT-SJT-14		2,440	0.8	8	14	19			
SPP-SJT-SJT-15		2,316	5.3	26	40	53			
SPP-SJT-SJT-16		2,440	0.3	5	8	10			
SPP-SJT-SJT-17		2,369	3.3	33	57	81			
SPP-SJT-SJT-18		2,260	0.3	5	8	10			
SPP-SJT-SJT-19		2,387	0.3	5	8	10			
SPP-SJT-SJT-20		2,412	68.8	344	516	688	8	1	
SPP-SJT-SJT-21		2,400	440.8	4,408	7,714	11,019	7		
SPP-SPP-SMX-1		2,363	0.1	5	8	10			
SPP-SPP-SMX-2		2,432	9.6	48	72	96			
SPP-SPP-SMX-3		2,240	116.1	1,161	2,032	2,903	13		
SPP-SPP-SPP-1		2,324	289.3	2,893	5,062	7,231	34	7	
SPP-SPP-SPP-2		2,274	45.9	459	803	1,147	7	2	
SPP-SPP-SPP-3		2,298	64.9	649	1,136	1,622	2	1	
SPP-SPP-SPP-4		2,420	5.9	29	44	59			
SPP-SPP-SPP-5		2,220	0.3	5	8	10			
SPP-SPP-SPP-6		2,260	0.3	5	8	10			
SPP-SPP-SPP-7		2,280	0.3	5	8	10			
SPP-SPP-SPP-9		2,460	1	10	18	25			
SPP-SPP-SPP-10		2,460	0.5	5	9	13			

SPP-SPP-SPP-11	2,455	1.1	11	20	28	
SPP-SPP-SPP-12	2,460	1.1	11	20	28	
SPP-SPP-SPP-13	2,460	0.5	5	9	13	
SPP-SPP-SPP-14	2,380	3.4	34	60	85	
SPP-SPP-SPP-16	2,400	0.1	5	8	10	
SPP-SPP-SPP-17	2,387	0.2	5	8	10	
SPP-SPP-SPP-18	2,280	2	10	15	20	
SPP-SPP-SPP-19	2,180	0.1	5	8	10	
SPP-SPP-SPP-20	2,170	0.2	5	8	10	
SPP-SPP-SPP-21	2,160	0.5	5	8	10	
SPP-SPP-SPP-22	2,232	13.8	69	104	138	
SPP-SPP-SPP-23	2,450	9.8	49	74	98	
SPP-SPP-SPP-24	2,212	76	760	1,330	1,900	4
SPP-SPP-SPP-25	2,300	14.9	74	112	149	4
SPP-SPP-SPP-26	2,278	104.8	1,048	1,834	2,619	2
SPP-SPP-SPP-27	2,281	23.9	239	418	597	
SPP-SPP-SPP-28	2,212	31.1	311	545	778	1
SPP-SPP-SPP-29	2,278.5	21	210	368	525	11
SPP-SPP-SPP-30	2,292	0.6	5	8	10	
SPP-SPP-SPP-31	2,280	0.9	5	8	10	
SPP-SPP-SPP-32	2,560	0.3	5	8	10	
SPP-SPP-SPP-33	2,400	7.1	36	54	71	
SPP-SPP-SPP-37	2,320	9.3	46	70	93	
SPP-SPP-SPP-38	2,460	11.8	59	89	118	1
SPP-SPP-SPP-39	2,560	3.9	39	68	97	
SPP-SPP-SPP-40	2,546	0.5	5	9	13	1
SPP-SPP-SPP-41	2,217	0.1	10	15	20	
SPP-SPP-SPP-42	2,241	0.1	5	8	10	
SPP-SPP-SPP-43	2,275	0.6	6	11	15	
SPP-SPP-SPP-44	2,352	0.1	5	8	10	

continued on next page

Table 3.5—continued

Site	Toponym	Elev (m)	Area	Min Pop	Avg Pop	Max Pop	Strs	Pz	% Terr
SPP-SPP-SPP-45		2,277	0.5	13	20	27			
SPP-SPP-SPP-46		2,320	0.6	16	24	32	1		
SPP-SPP-SPP-47		2,326	1.5	8	12	15			
SPP-SPP-SPP-48		2,476	5.3	26	40	53			
SPP-SPP-SPP-49		2,359	78.6	786	1,376	1,966	5	1	
SPP-SPP-SPP-50		2,294	0.1	5	8	10			
SPP-SPP-SPP-51		2,240	1	25	38	50			
SPP-SPP-SPP-52		2,376	18.8	94	141	188			
SPP-SPP-SPP-53		2,253	130	1,300	2,275	3,250	1		
SPP-SPP-SPP-54		2,364	28.6	143	215	286			
SPP-SPP-SPP-55		2,320	32.6	163	245	326	4	1	
SPP-SPP-SPP-55		2,413	0.4	5	8	10			
SPP-SPP-SPP-56		2,265	76.4	764	1,337	1,910	1		
SPP-SPP-SPP-57		2,420	0.3	5	8	10			
SPP-SPP-TEC-1		2,215	45.3	226	340	453			
SPP-SPP-TEC-2		2,220	1.1	11	20	28			
SPP-SPP-TEC-3		2,271	11.5	58	87	115			
SPP-SPP-TEC-4		2,263	57.8	289	434	578	3		
SPP-SPP-YCM-1		2,295	0.6	5	8	10			
SPP-SPP-YCM-2		2,300	0.3	5	8	10			
SPP-SPP-YCM-3		2,260	2.5	25	44	63			
SPP-SPP-YCM-4		2,420	55.6	556	974	1,391		1	
SPP-SPP-YCM-5		2,367	0.4	5	8	10			

Table 3.6. Late Cruz Sites in Nuñu.

Site	Toponym	Elev (m)	Area (ha)	Min Pop	Avg Pop	Max Pop	Strs	Pz	% Terr
SPP-SVN-ANM-6	Ticoteo	2,720	0.1	5	8	10			
SPP-SVN-SVN-4	Arroyo Nuñu	2,340	21.1	211	369	527			
SPP-SVN-SVN-15		2,420	0.4	5	8	10			
SPP-SVN-SVN-17		2,440	0.1	5	8	10			

Table 3.7. Ramos Sites in Nuñu.

Site	Toponym	Elev (m)	Area (ha)	Min Pop	Avg Pop	Max Pop	Strs	Pz	% Terr
SPP-SVN-SVN-4	Arroyo Nuñu	2,340	21.1	211	369	527			
SPP-SVN-SVN-10	Ndicaynu	2,480	4.6	230	344	459			100
SPP-SVN-SVN-11		2,280	3.4	34	59	84			
SPP-SVN-SVN-13	Cerro Ayodo	2,460	10.9	543	815	1,086	5		100
SPP-SVN-SVN-21		2,442	0.9	5	8	10			100

Table 3.8. Las Flores Sites in Nuñu.

Site	Toponym	Elev (m)	Area (ha)	Min Pop	Avg Pop	Max Pop	Strs	Pz	% Terr
SPP-SVN-SVN-2		2,320	11.3	11	20	28			
SPP-SVN-SVN-3		2,380	1.6	16	29	41			
SPP-SVN-SVN-6		2,400	1.5	15	27	38			
SPP-SVN-SVN-10	Ndicaynu	2,480	16	798	1,198	1,597	2	1	100
SPP-SVN-SVN-11		2,260	3.4	34	59	84			
SPP-SVN-SVN-12	Totojano	2,540	11.4	114	200	286			
SPP-SVN-SVN-13	Cerro Ayodo	2,447	62.2	2,289	3,485	4,681	6	1	67
SPP-SVN-SVN-14		2,424	2.2	110	165	220	2		100
SPP-SVN-SVN-19		2,520	3.8	38	66	94			
SPP-SVN-SVN-23	Tiandacoo, La Muralla	2,780	11.3	11	20	28	3		
SPP-SVN-SVN-32	Diquindiyi or Nuutende	2,473	20.4	490	768	1,046	6	2	
SPP-SVN-SVN-34		2,680	0.3	5	8	10			

Table 3.9. Natividad Sites in Nuñu.

Site	Toponym	Elev (m)	Area (ha)	Min Pop	Avg Pop	Max Pop	Strs	Pz	% Terr
SPP-SVN-ANM-1		2,669	0.4	5	8	10			
SPP-SVN-ANM-2		2,788	0.1	5	8	10			
SPP-SVN-ANM-5		2,664	0.6	6	11	16			
SPP-SVN-ANM-6	Ticoteo	2,720	11.3	113	197	281			
SPP-SVN-SVN-1		2,380	41.1	411	720	1,028	1		
SPP-SVN-SVN-3		2,360	1.6	16	29	41			
SPP-SVN-SVN-4	Arroyo Nuñu	2,320	0.1	5	8	10			
SPP-SVN-SVN-4	Arroyo Nuñu	2,328	0.1	5	8	10			
SPP-SVN-SVN-4	Arroyo Nuñu	2,379	9.8	5	8	10			
SPP-SVN-SVN-5		2,320	0.1	5	8	10			
SPP-SVN-SVN-6		2,368	1.5	15	27	38			
SPP-SVN-SVN-7		2,255	0.2	5	8	10			
SPP-SVN-SVN-9		2,294	3	30	53	75			
SPP-SVN-SVN-10	Ndicaynu	2,475	4.7	236	353	471			100
SPP-SVN-SVN-12	Totojano	2,522	11.4	114	200	286			
SPP-SVN-SVN-13	Cerro Ayodo	2,413	0.6	5	8	10			
SPP-SVN-SVN-13	Cerro Ayodo	2,585	0.3	5	8	10	1		
SPP-SVN-SVN-13	Cerro Ayodo	2,620	5	5	8	10			
SPP-SVN-SVN-15		2,420	0.4	5	8	10			
SPP-SVN-SVN-16		2,460	0.3	5	8	10			
SPP-SVN-SVN-18		2,440	2.8	28	48	69	1		
SPP-SVN-SVN-19		2,511	22.9	229	401	573			
SPP-SVN-SVN-20		2,457	2.9	143	215	286	2		100
SPP-SVN-SVN-21		2,457	0.9	45	68	90	5		100
SPP-SVN-SVN-22		2,436	17.8	178	312	446			
SPP-SVN-SVN-24		2,550	0.3	5	8	10			
SPP-SVN-SVN-27		2,484	0.3	5	8	10			
SPP-SVN-SVN-29		2,380	1.9	19	33	47			
SPP-SVN-SVN-30		2,408	0.1	5	8	10			
SPP-SVN-SVN-31		2,299	0.3	5	8	10			
SPP-SVN-SVN-38		2,512	4.6	46	81	115			

Table 3.10. Early/Middle Cruz Sites in Yodobada.

Site	Toponym	Elev (m)	Area (ha)	Min Pop	Avg Pop	Max Pop	Strs	Pz	% Terr
SPP-TDU-YBA-1	·	2,226	0.3	5	8	10			
SPP-TDU-YBA-2		2,260	7.5	75	131	187	1		

Table 3.11. Late Cruz Sites in Yodobada.

Site	Toponym	Elev (m)	Area (ha)	Min Pop	Avg Pop	Max Pop	Strs	Pz	% Terr
SPP-SJT-MOR-4		2,372	25.4	254	444	634			
SPP-SJT-MOR-7		2,424	1.4	14	25	35	1		
SPP-SJT-MOR-8		2,340	1	10	18	25			
SPP-TDU-TBA-2		2,576	0.6	6	10	14			
SPP-TDU-YBA-1		2,223	21.1	211	369	527	2	1	
SPP-TDU-YBA-2		2,260	6.5	65	114	162	1		

Table 3.12. Ramos Sites in Yodobada.

Site	Toponym	Elev (m)	Area (ha)	Min Pop	Avg Pop	Max Pop	Strs	Pz	% Terr
SPP-TDU-TBA-5		2,372	1.5	15	27	38	3	1	
SPP-TDU-YBA-2		2,260	5.4	268	402	536	1		100

435

Table 3.13. Las Flores Sites in Yodobada.

Site	Toponym	Elev (m)	Area (ha)	Min Pop	Avg Pop	Max Pop	Strs	Pz	% Terr
NO-YPD-YPD-1	Yucunee	2,820	5.2	262	392	523	10	2	100
NO-YPD-YPD-3		2,580	1	10	18	25			
NO-YPD-YPD-5		2,360	18.3	183	319	456	2		
NO-YPD-YPD-6		2,529	34.2	1,244	1,895	2,546	1		66
NO-YPD-YPD-8		2,440	6	60	105	150	1		
NO-YPD-YPD-13		2,420	1.9	19	33	47			
NO-YPD-YPD-15		2,540	7.4	74	129	184			
NO-YPD-YPD-17		2,420	4.5	45	78	111			
NO-YPD-YPD-18		2,420	16.4	164	287	410			
NO-YPD-YPD-19		2,400	5.9	59	103	147			
NO-YPD-YPD-23		2,320	3.5	35	62	88			

Table 3.14. Natividad Sites in Yodobada.

Site	Toponym	Elev (m)	Area (ha)	Min Pop	Avg Pop	Max Pop	Strs	Pz	% Terr
SPP-SJT-MOR-1		2,357	10.8	108	188	269			
SPP-SJT-MOR-2	Llano de Satayuco	2,359	6.9	69	121	173	2		
SPP-SJT-MOR-3		2,360	18.1	181	317	453			
SPP-SJT-MOR-4		2,360	0.3	5	8	10			
SPP-SJT-MOR-5		2,300	0.1	5	8	10			
SPP-SJT-MOR-6		2,296	9.9	99	174	248			
SPP-SJT-MOR-7		2,432	3.8	19	29	38	1		
SPP-SJT-MOR-8		2,360	2.1	21	37	53			
SPP-SJT-MOR-9		2,353	9.1	91	160	228			
SPP-SJT-MOR-11		2,320	2.8	28	48	69			
SPP-SJT-MOR-13		2,337	11.8	118	206	294			
SPP-SJT-MOR-15		2,340	0.1	5	8	10			
SPP-TDU-TBA-1		2,564	3.6	36	62	89			

Site	Elev (m)	Area (ha)	Min Pop	Avg Pop	Max Pop	Strs	Pz	% Terr
SPP-TDU-TBA-2	2,576	0.6	6	10	14			
SPP-TDU-TBA-3	2,568	4.7	47	83	118			
SPP-TDU-TBA-4	2,620	0.3	5	8	10		1	
SPP-TDU-TBA-5	2,422	0.3	5	8	10	3		
SPP-TDU-TDU-1	2,140	35.3	353	618	882			
SPP-TDU-TDU-2	2,167	35.4	354	620	885			
SPP-TDU-YBA-1	2,223	21.1	211	369	527	2		
SPP-TDU-YBA-2	2,260	35.5	355	621	887	1	1	
SPP-TDU-YBA-3	2,270	11.3	113	198	283			
SPP-TDU-YBA-4	2,332	2.5	25	44	62			
SPP-TDU-YBA-5	2,340	13	130	228	325			
SPP-TDU-YBA-6	2,291	32	320	560	800			

Table 3.15. Cruz Sites in Yucunama.

Site	Elev (m)	Area (ha)	Min Pop	Avg Pop	Max Pop	Strs	Pz	% Terr
SPP-YUC-YUC-21	2,420	22.9	229	401	572	1		
SPP-YUC-YUC-24	2,500	0.5	5	9	13			
SPP-YUC-YUC-30	2,540	2.5	25	44	63			
SPP-YUC-YUC-39	2,400	0.1	5	8	10			
SPP-YUC-YUC-46	2,414	1.1	11	20	28			
SPP-YUC-YUC-50	2,400	0.3	5	8	10			
SPP-YUC-YUC-51	2,414	0.1	5	8	10			
SPP-YUC-YUC-59	2,460	0.5	5	9	13			
SPP-YUC-YUC-61EMC	2,460	1	10	18	25			
SPP-YUC-YUC-61	2,460	2.3	23	40	56			

Table 3.16. Ramos Sites in Yucunama.

Site	Toponym	Elev (m)	Area (ha)	Min Pop	Avg Pop	Max Pop	Strs	Pz	% Terr
SPP-YUC-YUC-16		2,540	26.5	265	464	663	6	1	
SPP-YUC-YUC-20		2,560	7.1	357	535	713	9	2	
SPP-YUC-YUC-45		2,422	1.1	11	20	28			
SPP-YUC-YUC-56		2,500	0.9	9	16	22			
SPP-YUC-YUC-61		2,464	2.3	23	40	56			

Table 3.17. Las Flores Sites in Yucunama.

Site	Toponym	Elev (m)	Area (ha)	Min Pop	Avg Pop	Max Pop	Strs	Pz	% Terr
SPP-YUC-YUC-5		2,538	0.6	6	11	16			
SPP-YUC-YUC-7		2,473	1.4	14	25	35			
SPP-YUC-YUC-11		2,422	0.4	5	8	10			
SPP-YUC-YUC-13		2,501	1	10	18	25			
SPP-YUC-YUC-16		2,550	29.6	1,482	2,223	2,963		1	
SPP-YUC-YUC-20		2,560	13	650	975	1,300		2	
SPP-YUC-YUC-23		2,520	0.4	5	8	10			
SPP-YUC-YUC-24		2,515	14.1	141	247	353			
SPP-YUC-YUC-32		2,460	0.9	9	17	24			
SPP-YUC-YUC-34		2,420	1	10	18	25			
SPP-YUC-YUC-38		2,560	2.3	23	40	56		1	
SPP-YUC-YUC-47		2,560	3	30	53	75			
SPP-YUC-YUC-52		2,420	3.8	38	66	94			
SPP-YUC-YUC-53		2,464	0.6	6	11	16			
SPP-YUC-YUC-54		2,570	3.3	33	57	81			
SPP-YUC-YUC-58		2,460	0.1	5	8	10			

Table 3.18. Natividad Sites in Yucunama.

Site	Toponym	Elev (m)	Area (ha)	Min Pop	Avg Pop	Max Pop	Strs	Pz	% Terr
SPP-YUC-YUC-1		2,480	0.1	5	8	10			
SPP-YUC-YUC-2		2,620	0.1	5	8	10			
SPP-YUC-YUC-3		2,559	0.1	5	8	10			
SPP-YUC-YUC-4		2,505	0.9	9	16	23			
SPP-YUC-YUC-5		2,540	0.6	6	11	16			
SPP-YUC-YUC-6		2,461	0.1	5	8	10			
SPP-YUC-YUC-7		2,476	1.4	14	25	35			
SPP-YUC-YUC-8		2,540	0.1	5	8	10			
SPP-YUC-YUC-9		2,471	0.2	5	8	10			
SPP-YUC-YUC-10		2,540	0.1	5	8	10			
SPP-YUC-YUC-11		2,430	0.4	20	30	40			
SPP-YUC-YUC-13		2,497	2.2	22	39	55			
SPP-YUC-YUC-14		2,489	0.1	5	8	10			
SPP-YUC-YUC-15		2,478	0.6	5	8	10			
SPP-YUC-YUC-16		2,550	26.6	266	466	666	6	1	
SPP-YUC-YUC-17		2,457	0.5	5	9	13			
SPP-YUC-YUC-18		2,519	0.1	5	8	10			
SPP-YUC-YUC-19		2,505	0.1	5	8	10			
SPP-YUC-YUC-20		2,555	6.5	65	114	163	9	2	
SPP-YUC-YUC-21		2,420	22.9	114	172	229			
SPP-YUC-YUC-22		2,482	0.1	5	8	10			
SPP-YUC-YUC-24		2,520	18	90	135	180			
SPP-YUC-YUC-26		2,408	0.3	5	8	10			
SPP-YUC-YUC-27		2,440	0.1	5	8	10			
SPP-YUC-YUC-28		2,520	0.1	5	8	10			
SPP-YUC-YUC-30		2,540	2.5	25	44	63			
SPP-YUC-YUC-31		2,491	0.1	5	8	10			
SPP-YUC-YUC-32		2,472	0.9	9	17	24			

continued on next page

Table 3.18—continued

Site	Toponym	Elev (m)	Area (ha)	Min Pop	Avg Pop	Max Pop	Strs	Pz	% Terr
SPP-YUC-YUC-33		2,477	0.1	5	8	10			
SPP-YUC-YUC-34		2,429	4	40	70	100			
SPP-YUC-YUC-35		2,469	4.5	23	34	45			
SPP-YUC-YUC-36		2,417	2.5	13	19	25			
SPP-YUC-YUC-37		2,400	2	20	35	50			
SPP-YUC-YUC-38		2,560	1	5	15	25	5	1	
SPP-YUC-YUC-39		2,400	1.9	19	33	47			
SPP-YUC-YUC-40		2,400	1.5	15	27	38			
SPP-YUC-YUC-41		2,400	4	20	30	40			
SPP-YUC-YUC-42		2,420	1.4	14	25	35			
SPP-YUC-YUC-43		2,420	1.4	7	11	14			
SPP-YUC-YUC-44		2,420	2.5	13	19	25			
SPP-YUC-YUC-45		2,429	1.1	11	20	28			
SPP-YUC-YUC-46		2,411	9.3	93	162	231			
SPP-YUC-YUC-47		2,548	3.5	18	27	35			
SPP-YUC-YUC-48		2,540	0.9	9	17	24			
SPP-YUC-YUC-49		2,382	0.2	9	8	10			
SPP-YUC-YUC-50		2,400	0.3	5	8	10			
SPP-YUC-YUC-51		2,425	6.4	32	48	64			
SPP-YUC-YUC-52		2,423	5	25	38	50			
SPP-YUC-YUC-53		2,460	0.6	5	8	10			
SPP-YUC-YUC-54		2,571	3.6	18	27	36			
SPP-YUC-YUC-56		2,500	0.9	5	8	10			
SPP-YUC-YUC-57		2,520	0.5	5	8	10			
SPP-YUC-YUC-58		2,463	0.3	5	8	10			
SPP-YUC-YUC-59		2,460	0.5	5	9	13			
SPP-YUC-YUC-60		2,488	0.1	5	8	10			
SPP-YUC-YUC-61		2,454	3	30	53	75			

Table 3.19. Late Cruz Sites in Lagunas.

Site	Toponym	Elev (m)	Area (ha)	Min Pop	Avg Pop	Max Pop	Strs	Pz	% Terr
SPP-SAL-SIL-6	Cerro la Culebra	2,500	3.6	36	63	90			
SPP-SAL-SIL-13		2,395	0.1	5	8	10			

Table 3.20. Ramos Sites in Lagunas.

Site	Toponym	Elev (m)	Area (ha)	Min Pop	Avg Pop	Max Pop	Strs	Pz	% Terr
SPP-SAL-SAL-16	Ñunducha	2,480	13	165	248	330	2	2	
SPP-SAL-SAL-28		2,480	0.6	6	11	15	4	1	
SPP-SAL-SIL-1	Cerro Verde	2,520	9.3	463	694	925			100
SPP-SAL-SIL-3		2,440	0.1	5	8	10			
SPP-SAL-SIL-6	Cerro la Culebra	2,520	5.6	56	97	139	2		
SPP-SAL-SIL-11		2,380	10.3	103	179	256			

Table 3.21. Las Flores Sites in Lagunas.

Site	Toponym	Elev (m)	Area (ha)	Min Pop	Avg Pop	Max Pop	Strs	Pz	% Terr
SPP-SAL-SAL-2	Yu'undu	2,360	1	50	75	100			
SPP-SAL-SAL-16	Ñunducha	2,457	13	165	248	330	2	2	
SPP-SAL-SAL-28		2,442	0.6	6	11	15	4	1	
SPP-SAL-SIL-1	Cerro Verde	2,520	43.1	862	1,374	1,886			100
SPP-SAL-SIL-3		2,440	0.1	5	8	10			
SPP-SAL-SIL-4		2,380	10.2	102	179	256	2		
SPP-SAL-SIL-6	Cerro la Culebra	2,540	15.5	155	272	388	2		
SPP-SAL-SIL-7		2,340	2.1	21	37	53	2		
SPP-SAL-SIL-15		2,469	1.5	15	27	38	2		

Table 3.22. Natividad Sites in Lagunas.

Site	Toponym	Elev (m)	Area (ha)	Min Pop	Avg Pop	Max Pop	Strs	Pz	% Terr
SPP-SAL-SAL-1	Yu'undu	2,360	57.3	573	1,003	1,432	1		50
SPP-SAL-SAL-2		2,368	9.9	297	457	618			
SPP-SAL-SAL-3		2,500	1	10	18	25			
SPP-SAL-SAL-4		2,460	0.1	5	8	10			
SPP-SAL-SAL-5		2,359	33.9	339	593	847			
SPP-SAL-SAL-6		2,448	16.2	162	284	406			
SPP-SAL-SAL-7		2,404	30.7	307	536	766			
SPP-SAL-SAL-8	Cerro Yucuñuvis	2,535	1	10	18	25			
SPP-SAL-SAL-9		2,306	63.1	631	1,104	1,577			100
SPP-SAL-SAL-10		2,424	0.5	5	9	12	1		
SPP-SAL-SAL-11		2,361	2.9	29	50	72			
SPP-SAL-SAL-12		2,492	4.4	220	329	439	1		
SPP-SAL-SAL-14		2,446	0.1	5	8	10			
SPP-SAL-SAL-15		2,470	1.5	15	27	38			
SPP-SAL-SAL-16	Ñunducha	2,457	0.6	10	15	20			
SPP-SAL-SAL-17		2,440	3	30	53	75			
SPP-SAL-SAL-18		2,409	27	270	473	675			
SPP-SAL-SAL-20		2,400	4	40	70	100			
SPP-SAL-SAL-22		2,416	4.7	47	83	118			
SPP-SAL-SAL-24		2,363	10.8	108	188	269			
SPP-SAL-SAL-26		2,460	3	30	53	75			
SPP-SAL-SAL-28		2,454	9.1	91	159	227	4	1	
SPP-SAL-SAL-35		2,433	1	10	18	25	2		
SPP-SAL-SIL-1	Cerro Verde	2,462	43.1	690	1,126	1,562	2	1	
SPP-SAL-SIL-2		2,360	17.9	179	313	447			
SPP-SAL-SIL-3		2,410	5	50	87	125			
SPP-SAL-SIL-5		2,360	0.3	5	8	10			
SPP-SAL-SIL-6	Cerro la Culebra	2,520	15.5	155	272	388			
SPP-SAL-SIL-7		2,326	2.1	21	37	53			

Site	Elev (m)	Area (ha)	Min Pop	Avg Pop	Max Pop	Strs	Pz	% Terr
SPP-SAL-SIL-8	2,440	5.1	51	89	127	1		
SPP-SAL-SIL-9	2,299	0.1	5	8	10			
SPP-SAL-SIL-11	2,397	10.3	103	179	256			
SPP-SAL-SIL-13	2,424	21.3	213	372	531			
SPP-SAL-SIL-15	2,480	1.5	15	27	38		2	

Table 3.23. Late Cruz Sites in Yolomécatl.

Site	Toponym	Elev (m)	Area (ha)	Min Pop	Avg Pop	Max Pop	Strs	Pz	% Terr
SPP-YOL-YOL-6		2,100	8.1	81	141	201	1		
SPP-YOL-YOL-9		2,155	6.5	65	114	162			
SPP-YOL-YOL-23		2,144	8.2	82	143	205			
SPP-YOL-YOL-30		2,082	3.6	36	62	89			
SPP-YOL-YOL-40		2,219	4.4	44	76	109			
SPP-YOL-YOL-42		2,310	1	10	18	25			
SPP-YOL-YOL-45		2,247	5.4	54	94	134			

Table 3.24. Ramos Sites in Yolomécatl.

Site	Toponym	Elev (m)	Area (ha)	Min Pop	Avg Pop	Max Pop	Strs	Pz	% Terr
SPP-YOL-YOL-4		2,298	9.9	99	173	247	1		
SPP-YOL-YOL-8	Cerro Yucuniñi	2,178	22.3	357	584	810	4	2	
SPP-YOL-YOL-13		2,220	0.1	5	8	10			
SPP-YOL-YOL-35		2,404	0.1	5	8	10			
SPP-YOL-YOL-37	Cerro Cuate	2,428	15.8	787	1,181	1,575	4	1	100

Table 3.25. Las Flores Sites in Yolomécatl.

Site	Toponym	Elev (m)	Area (ha)	Min Pop	Avg Pop	Max Pop	Strs	Pz	% Terr
SPP-YOL-YOL-2	Río Novadavi	2,240	10.8	108	189	270	4		
SPP-YOL-YOL-4		2,291	12.4	124	218	311	1		
SPP-YOL-YOL-6		2,100	9.3	93	163	233	1		
SPP-YOL-YOL-8	Cerro Yucuniñi	2,140	5.7	57	100	143	1		
SPP-YOL-YOL-16		2,300	5.7	171	264	356	1		
SPP-YOL-YOL-18		2,180	5.1	101	161	221			
SPP-YOL-YOL-19		2,180	0.3	5	8	10			
SPP-YOL-YOL-20		2,120	7.6	76	133	190	2		
SPP-YOL-YOL-23		2,141	15.2	152	267	381	1		
SPP-YOL-YOL-24		2,200	17.5	175	307	438	3		
SPP-YOL-YOL-25		2,160	5.6	56	98	140			
SPP-YOL-YOL-26		2,160	4.3	43	74	106	3	2	
SPP-YOL-YOL-27	Cerro Yucudavico	2,251	27.9	1,397	2,095	2,793	4	1	100
SPP-YOL-YOL-37	Cerro Cuate	2,436	8.5	424	636	848			100
SPP-YOL-YOL-40		2,240	11.1	111	195	278	3		
SPP-YOL-YOL-43		2,251	10.7	107	186	266	3		
SPP-YOL-YOL-44		2,388	0.8	8	13	19			

Table 3.26. Natividad Sites in Yolomécatl.

Site	Toponym	Elev (m)	Area (ha)	Min Pop	Avg Pop	Max Pop	Strs	Pz	% Terr
SPP-YOL-YOL-1	Río Novadavi	2,176	6.9	69	120	171	1		
SPP-YOL-YOL-2		2,176	10.8	108	189	270			
SPP-YOL-YOL-3		2,141	0.8	8	13	19			
SPP-YOL-YOL-4		2,254	122.6	1,226	2,145	3,064	4		
SPP-YOL-YOL-5		2,160	0.3	5	8	10			
SPP-YOL-YOL-6		2,097	22.4	224	392	560	1		
SPP-YOL-YOL-9		2,155	6.5	65	114	162			
SPP-YOL-YOL-10		2,300	12.6	126	221	316	3		

SPP-YOL-YOL-11	Río Mixteco	2,154	12.5	125	218	311	
SPP-YOL-YOL-12		2,241	17.1	86	128	171	
SPP-YOL-YOL-13		2,211	44.6	446	781	1,116	
SPP-YOL-YOL-15		2,240	7.4	74	130	186	
SPP-YOL-YOL-16		2,280	5.7	171	264	356	2
SPP-YOL-YOL-17		2,160	8.3	83	146	208	1
SPP-YOL-YOL-18		2,300	5.1	101	161	221	
SPP-YOL-YOL-19		2,200	16.6	166	291	416	2
SPP-YOL-YOL-20		2,110	7.6	76	133	190	1
SPP-YOL-YOL-21		2,130	5.2	52	90	129	1
SPP-YOL-YOL-22		2,120	0.4	5	8	10	
SPP-YOL-YOL-23		2,137	31	310	543	776	3
SPP-YOL-YOL-24		2,200	17.5	175	307	438	
SPP-YOL-YOL-25		2,160	5.6	56	98	140	
SPP-YOL-YOL-26		2,140	4.3	43	74	106	3
SPP-YOL-YOL-29		2,173	0.3	5	8	10	
SPP-YOL-YOL-30		2,082	3.6	36	62	89	
SPP-YOL-YOL-31		2,170	0.1	5	8	10	
SPP-YOL-YOL-32		2,220	0.4	5	8	10	
SPP-YOL-YOL-33		2,140	3.2	32	55	79	1
SPP-YOL-YOL-34		2,134	0.1	5	8	10	
SPP-YOL-YOL-35		2,412	3.5	35	62	88	
SPP-YOL-YOL-36		2,117	0.1	5	8	10	
SPP-YOL-YOL-38		2,107	0.1	5	8	10	
SPP-YOL-YOL-39		2,136	1.5	15	27	38	
SPP-YOL-YOL-40		2,227	11.1	111	195	278	3
SPP-YOL-YOL-41		2,280	4.1	41	72	102	
SPP-YOL-YOL-42		2,297	12.6	126	220	315	
SPP-YOL-YOL-44		2,380	6.1	61	106	151	
SPP-YOL-YOL-45		2,247	5.4	54	94	134	
SPP-YOL-YOL-46		2,160	2.7	27	48	68	
SPP-YOL-YOL-47		2,178	0.8	8	13	19	

Table 3.27. Early/Middle Cruz Sites in Nduayaco.

Site	Toponym	Elev (m)	Area (ha)	Min Pop	Avg Pop	Max Pop	Strs	Pz	% Terr
SPP-NDU-NDU-15		2,320	2.5	25	44	63			
SPP-NDU-TIC-9		2,240	1	10	18	26			

Table 3.28. Late Cruz Sites in Nduayaco.

Site	Toponym	Elev (m)	Area (ha)	Min Pop	Avg Pop	Max Pop	Strs	Pz	% Terr
SPP-NDU-NDU-17		2,316	0.3	5	13	20			
SPP-NDU-TIC-6		2,256	2	20	34	49			
SPP-NDU-TIC-10		2,272	0.5	5	8	10			
SPP-NDU-TIC-19		2,300	1.5	5	8	10			
SPP-NDU-TIC-20		2,400	1.4	10	15	20			
SPP-NDU-TIC-20		2,394	1.4	15	23	30			
SPP-NDU-UPP-5		2,343	0.1	5	8	10			

Table 3.29. Ramos Sites in Nduayaco.

Site	Toponym	Elev (m)	Area (ha)	Min Pop	Avg Pop	Max Pop	Strs	Pz	% Terr
SPP-NDU-NDU-5		2,375	2.2	22	39	56			
SPP-NDU-NDU-20		2,220	0.9	9	15	22			
SPP-NDU-NDU-21		2,293	5.4	268	403	537	9	1	100
SPP-NDU-SJG-11		2,420	19.2	300	450	600	2	1	
SPP-NDU-TIC-3		2,440	5.7	57	100	142			
SPP-NDU-TIC-6		2,240	2	20	34	49			
SPP-NDU-TIC-7		2,282	2.3	23	39	56			
SPP-NDU-UPP-2		2,420	3.1	156	234	312			100
SPP-NDU-UPP-4		2,380	1.1	11	20	28			
SPP-NDU-UPP-6		2,380	0.1	5	8	10			

Table 3.30. Las Flores Sites in Nduayaco.

Site	Toponym	Elev (m)	Area (ha)	Min Pop	Avg Pop	Max Pop	Strs	Pz	% Terr
TLA-SZT-LET-3		2,300	7.6	76	134	191			
TLA-SZT-LET-5		2,348	0.5	5	8	10			
TLA-SZT-LET-7		2,240	0.2	5	8	10			
SPP-NDU-NDU-1		2,340	3.7	37	66	94			
SPP-NDU-NDU-2		2,340	3	30	53	76			
SPP-NDU-NDU-6		2,400	1.3	13	22	31			
SPP-NDU-NDU-14		2,544	1.3	10	18	25	1	1	
SPP-NDU-NDU-21		2,271	6.3	317	476	634	2	1	100
SPP-NDU-NDU-22		2,734	0.8	8	13	19			
SPP-NDU-SJG-1		2,386	1.9	19	33	47			
SPP-NDU-SJG-2		2,400	12.6	379	584	789	2	1	50
SPP-NDU-SJG-5		2,460	0.5	5	8	10			
SPP-NDU-SJG-9		2,500	2.7	27	46	66			
SPP-NDU-SJG-11		2,394	1.5	77	116	154			
SPP-NDU-SJG-14		2,480	0.1	5	8	10			
SPP-NDU-TIC-3		2,440	5.7	57	100	142	2		100
SPP-NDU-TIC-11		2,260	1.1	11	20	28			

Table 3.31. Natividad Sites in Nduayaco.

Site	Toponym	Elev (m)	Area (ha)	Min Pop	Avg Pop	Max Pop	Strs	Pz	% Terr
TLA-SZT-LET-1		2,250	2.6	26	46	66			
TLA-SZT-LET-2		2,260	0.9	9	16	23			
TLA-SZT-LET-3		2,268	7.6	76	134	191			
TLA-SZT-LET-4		2,305	0.9	9	15	22			
TLA-SZT-LET-6		2,233	0.6	6	11	16			
TLA-SZT-LET-8		2,231	9.8	98	171	245			
TLA-SZT-LET-9		2,243	2.5	25	44	62			
TLA-SZT-LET-11		2,240	3.6	36	63	90	2		
SPP-NDU-NDU-1		2,332	3.8	38	66	94			
SPP-NDU-NDU-2		2,340	5.8	58	101	145			
SPP-NDU-NDU-3		2,509	15.5	565	861	1,157	5	1	66
SPP-NDU-NDU-4		2,499	1	10	18	25			
SPP-NDU-NDU-5		2,372	3.1	31	54	77			
SPP-NDU-NDU-6		2,401	1.3	13	22	31			
SPP-NDU-NDU-7		2,376	3.5	35	61	87			
SPP-NDU-NDU-8		2,460	2	5	8	10			
SPP-NDU-NDU-9		2,460	8.6	86	151	215	1		
SPP-NDU-NDU-11		2,357	0.5	5	9	12			
SPP-NDU-NDU-12		2,581	1.1	5	8	10	3		
SPP-NDU-NDU-13		2,320	0.9	9	16	23			
SPP-NDU-NDU-16		2,486	0.4	5	8	10			
SPP-NDU-NDU-18		2,340	3.1	31	55	79			
SPP-NDU-NDU-19	Cerro Dicatijui	2,442	6.7	67	117	167	1		
SPP-NDU-NDU-20		2,214	0.9	9	15	22			
SPP-NDU-NDU-21		2,300	0.3	5	8	10		1	
SPP-NDU-NDU-21		2,281	0.3	5	8	10			
SPP-NDU-SJG-3		2,380	0.1	5	8	10			
SPP-NDU-SJG-4		2,491	8.2	82	143	204	1		
SPP-NDU-SJG-5		2,445	0.5	5	8	10			

Site	Name	Elevation					
SPP-NDU-SJG-6		2,500	6.6	66	116	165	3
SPP-NDU-SJG-7		2,391	0.1	5	8	10	
SPP-NDU-SJG-8		2,310	0.1	5	8	10	
SPP-NDU-SJG-9		2,500	2.7	27	46	66	
SPP-NDU-SJG-10		2,440	0.8	8	13	19	1
SPP-NDU-SJG-11		2,400	19.2	308	502	697	2
SPP-NDU-SJG-12		2,494	1.7	17	20	42	
SPP-NDU-SJG-13		2,445	6.5	65	113	162	
SPP-NDU-SJG-14		2,474	0.1	5	8	10	
SPP-NDU-SJG-15		2,460	1	10	18	25	
SPP-NDU-TIC-1	Yucu Tindu	2,479	1.9	19	32	46	
SPP-NDU-TIC-2	Cerro Yucudavi	2,508	6	60	105	150	
SPP-NDU-TIC-3		2,456	5.7	57	100	142	1
SPP-NDU-TIC-4		2,314	0.3	10	15	20	
SPP-NDU-TIC-5		2,300	1.5	15	27	38	
SPP-NDU-TIC-6		2,256	2	20	34	49	
SPP-NDU-TIC-8		2,260	3.3	33	58	82	
SPP-NDU-TIC-10		2,272	0.5	5	8	10	
SPP-NDU-TIC-12		2,320	0.6	6	11	16	
SPP-NDU-TIC-13		2,260	1.5	15	27	38	
SPP-NDU-TIC-14		2,270	0.9	9	16	23	
SPP-NDU-TIC-15		2,356	15.9	159	277	396	
SPP-NDU-TIC-16		2,273	0.9	9	16	23	
SPP-NDU-TIC-17		2,273	0.1	5	8	10	
SPP-NDU-TIC-18		2,240	1.5	15	27	38	
SPP-NDU-TIC-19		2,300	1.5	15	27	38	
SPP-NDU-TIC-20		2,395	10.6	106	185	265	
SPP-NDU-UPP-1		2,333	0.1	5	8	10	
SPP-NDU-UPP-3		2,321	3.1	31	54	77	
SPP-NDU-UPP-5		2,343	0.1	5	8	10	
SPP-NDU-UPP-6		2,380	0.1	5	8	10	
SPP-NDU-UPP-7		2,290	0.3	5	8	10	

Table 4.1. Late Cruz Sites in Yucuxaco.

Site	Toponym	Elev (m)	Area (ha)	Min Pop	Avg Pop	Max Pop	Strs	Pz	% Terr
TLA-PMY-PMY-12		2,374	0.1	5	8	10			
TLA-PMY-PMY-12		2,320	0.1	5	8	10			
TLA-PMY-PMY-13		2,202	1.9	9	14	19			
TLA-PMY-PMY-14		2,220	13.3	133	232	332	1		
TLA-PMY-PMY-15		2,200	0.5	5	8	10			
TLA-PMY-PMY-16		2,211	0.5	5	9	12			
TLA-PMY-PMY-17		2,256	0.3	5	8	10			
TLA-PMY-PMY-19		2,253	0.5	5	8	10			
TLA-PMY-PMY-20		2,349	0.5	15	23	31			50

Table 4.2. Ramos Sites in Yucuxaco.

Site	Toponym	Elev (m)	Area (ha)	Min Pop	Avg Pop	Max Pop	Strs	Pz	% Terr
TLA-PMY-LPE-2	Cerro Las Peñas	2,704	0.5	5	8	10			
TLA-PMY-PMY-8		2,248	7	98	163	228	1		10
TLA-PMY-PMY-9		2,210	1.8	9	14	18			
TLA-PMY-PMY-12		2,397	21	965	1,453	1,941			
TLA-PMY-PMY-20		2,374	12.4	570	858	1,146	5	1	90
TLA-PMY-PMY-21		2,300	3.5	17	26	35			90
TLA-PMY-PMY-23		2,237	0.1	5	8	10			

Table 4.3. Las Flores Sites in Yucuxaco.

Site	Toponym	Elev (m)	Area (ha)	Min Pop	Avg Pop	Max Pop	Strs	Pz	% Terr
TLA-PMY-GPE-17		2,380	17.5	175	307	439			
TLA-PMY-PMY-10		2,220	0.1	5	8	10			
TLA-PMY-PMY-12		2,336	8.6	361	546	731	7	2	80
TLA-PMY-PMY-17		2,265	8.6	257	396	535	3	1	50
TLA-PMY-PMY-18		2,300	2.1	21	36	52			
TLA-PMY-PMY-20		2,356	3.1	128	194	260			80
TLA-PMY-PMY-24		2,220	0.1	5	8	10			

Table 4.4. Natividad Sites in Yucuxaco.

Site	Toponym	Elev (m)	Area (ha)	Min Pop	Avg Pop	Max Pop	Strs	Pz	% Terr
TLA-PMY-CMA-2		2,446	3.1	31	54	77			
TLA-PMY-CMA-4		2,466	4	40	71	101			
TLA-PMY-EPO-1		2,320	9.8	98	172	246			
TLA-PMY-EPO-3		2,427	0.3	5	8	10			
TLA-PMY-EPO-5		2,584	1	10	18	25			
TLA-PMY-GPE-5		2,200	3	30	53	76			
TLA-PMY-GPE-9		2,212	17.6	176	309	441			
TLA-PMY-GPE-11		2,234	1.5	15	27	38			
TLA-PMY-GPE-13		2,234	19.4	194	340	486			
TLA-PMY-GPE-17		2,351	17.5	175	307	438			
TLA-PMY-GPE-19		2,259	17	170	297	424			
TLA-PMY-LPE-2	Cerro Las Peñas	2,359	7.8	78	137	195			
TLA-PMY-LPE-4		2,320	1.3	13	22	31			
TLA-PMY-PMY-2	Cerro Montezacate	2,760	3.6	36	63	90			
TLA-PMY-PMY-4		2,260	2.4	24	41	59			
TLA-PMY-PMY-7		2,485	0.4	5	8	10			
TLA-PMY-PMY-8		2,280	1.1	5	8	11			
TLA-PMY-PMY-10		2,220	1	5	8	10			
TLA-PMY-PMY-11		2,220	1	5	8	10			
TLA-PMY-PMY-12		2,399	46.2	2,124	3,197	4,271	2		90
TLA-PMY-PMY-13		2,206	2.6	13	20	26			
TLA-PMY-PMY-15		2,205	0.2	5	8	10			
TLA-PMY-PMY-16		2,273	16.8	707	1,068	1,430			80
TLA-PMY-PMY-17		2,271	18	540	832	1,124			50
TLA-PMY-PMY-18		2,300	1.9	10	14	19			
TLA-PMY-PMY-20		2,360	3.6	182	273	364			100
TLA-PMY-PMY-22		2,209	3.8	38	66	94			
TLA-PMY-PMY-23		2,224	1.4	7	10	14			
TLA-PMY-PMY-24		2,220	1.5	8	11	15			

Table 4.5. Cruz Sites in Huamelulpan.

Site	Toponym	Elev (m)	Area (ha)	Min Pop	Avg Pop	Max Pop	Strs	Pz	% Terr
TLA-SMH-MRS-1EMC		2,225	0.5	5	8	10			40
TLA-SMH-MRS-1		2,280	0.5	5	8	10			
TLA-SMH-MRS-2		2,194	0.1	5	8	10			
TLA-SMH-SMH-1		2,249	4.1	106	165	224			
TLA-SMH-SMH-1		2,214	0.5	5	8	10			
TLA-SMH-SMH-2		2,294	0.1	5	8	10			
TLA-SMH-SMH-4		2,270	3.1	16	23	31			
TLA-SMH-SMH-5		2,295	0.5	5	8	10			
TLA-SMH-SMH-14		2,151	0.1	5	8	10			
TLA-SMH-SMH-19		2,359	1.3	6	9	12			
TLA-SMH-SMH-19		2,236	0.5	5	8	10			
TLA-SMH-SMH-24		2,180	0.1	5	8	10			
TLA-SMH-SMH-26		2,140	15.8	79	119	158			
TLA-SMH-SMH-27		2,100	0.1	5	7.5	10			
TLA-SMH-TTN-1		2,242	18.3	475	739	1,004	2		40

Table 4.6. Ramos Sites in Huamelulpan.

Site	Toponym	Elev (m)	Area (ha)	Min Pop	Avg Pop	Max Pop	Srs	Pz	% Terr
TLA-SMH-MRS-1		2,247.5	16	738	1,111	1,484	3		90
TLA-SMH-PDG-1		2,146	0.1	5	8	10			
TLA-SMH-PDG-2		2,140	0.1	5	8	10			
TLA-SMH-PDG-4		2,160	0.1	5	8	10			
TLA-SMH-PDG-5		2,148	0.1	5	8	10			
TLA-SMH-PDG-6		2,145	0.1	5	8	10			
TLA-SMH-PDG-7		2,219	0.8	5	8	10			
TLA-SMH-SMH-1		2,320	67.2	2,789	4,201	5,612	20		80
TLA-SMH-SMH-2		2,250	44.7	2,058	3,098	4,138		7	90
TLA-SMH-SMH-3		2,283	18.2	838	1,262	1,685			90
TLA-SMH-SMH-4		2,280	14.5	666	1,003	1,339			90
TLA-SMH-SMH-5		2,300	25	738	1,137	1,537	3		50
TLA-SMH-SMH-6		2,360	0.1	5	8	10			
TLA-SMH-SMH-7		2,329	0.1	5	8	10			
TLA-SMH-SMH-8		2,368	0.1	5	8	10			
TLA-SMH-SMH-9		2,301	3.5	106	164	221	3		50
TLA-SMH-SMH-10		2,236	11.6	163	271	378	1		10
TLA-SMH-SMH-11		2,297	0.1	5	8	10			
TLA-SMH-SMH-12		2,280	0.1	5	8	10			
TLA-SMH-SMH-15		2,160	0.1	5	8	10			
TLA-SMH-SMH-18		2,340	21	966	1,454	1,942	3	1	90
TLA-SMH-SMH-19		2,412	39.4	1,812	2,727	3,643	3		90
TLA-SMH-SMH-19		2,238	3.1	143	215	287			90
TLA-SMH-SMH-21		2,290	0.1	5	8	10			
TLA-SMH-SMH-23		2,191	5.3	27	40	53			

Table 4.7. Las Flores Sites in Huamelulpan.

Site	Toponym	Elev (m)	Area (ha)	Min Pop	Avg Pop	Max Pop	Strs	Pz	% Terr
TLA-SMH-MRS-1		2,272	2.5	25	43	62			
TLA-SMH-MRS-2		2,180	0.1	5	8	10			
TLA-SMH-PDG-1		2,147	0.1	5	8	10			
TLA-SMH-PDG-2		2,140	0.1	5	8	10			
TLA-SMH-PDG-4		2,160	0.1	5	8	10			
TLA-SMH-PDG-5		2,148	0.1	5	8	10			
TLA-SMH-PDG-6		2,154	0.1	5	8	10			
TLA-SMH-PDG-7		2,212	2.5	13	19	25			
TLA-SMH-SMH-1		2,224	67.2	2,282	3,998	5,713	20		80
TLA-SMH-SMH-2		2,300	5.4	271	407	542			100
TLA-SMH-SMH-3		2,278	3.3	100	153	207			50
TLA-SMH-SMH-4		2,265	7.4	221	341	461			50
TLA-SMH-SMH-5		2,307	3.1	104	159	214			60
TLA-SMH-SMH-11		2,308	0.1	5	8	10			
TLA-SMH-SMH-12		2,258	0.1	5	8	10			
TLA-SMH-SMH-15		2,160	0.1	5	8	10			
TLA-SMH-SMH-16		2,160	0.1	5	8	10			
TLA-SMH-SMH-17		2,209	4.7	47	82	117			
TLA-SMH-SMH-18		2,372	3.4	157	237	316	2	1	90
TLA-SMH-SMH-19		2,321	1.5	15	27	38			
TLA-SMH-SMH-19		2,400	10.4	104	182	260			
TLA-SMH-SMH-20		2,339	2.4	118	178	237	1		100
TLA-SMH-SMH-23		2,186	0.5	5	8	10			

Table 4.8. Natividad Sites in Huamelulpan.

Site	Toponym	Elev (m)	Area (ha)	Min Pop	Avg Pop	Max Pop	Strs	Pz	% Terr
TLA-SMH-MRS-1		2,280	0.3	5	8	10			
TLA-SMH-MRS-2		2,180	0.1	5	8	10			
TLA-SMH-PDG-3		2,140	0.1	5	8	10			
TLA-SMH-PDG-6		2,149	0.1	5	8	10			
TLA-SMH-SMH-1		2,249	58.1	2,440	3,707	4,973			80
TLA-SMH-SMH-2		2,267	7.7	383	575	766			100
TLA-SMH-SMH-3		2,307	6.6	198	306	413			50
TLA-SMH-SMH-4		2,259	11.5	530	798	1,066			90
TLA-SMH-SMH-4		2,220	2.3	117	175	233			100
TLA-SMH-SMH-5		2,316	2.2	22	39	55			
TLA-SMH-SMH-6		2,360	0.1	5	8	10			
TLA-SMH-SMH-8		2,380	0.1	5	8	10			
TLA-SMH-SMH-9		2,329	0.5	25	38	50			100
TLA-SMH-SMH-10		2,203	0.1	5	8	10			
TLA-SMH-SMH-11		2,318	0.1	5	8	10			
TLA-SMH-SMH-13		2,147	0.1	5	8	10			
TLA-SMH-SMH-14		2,148	0.1	5	8	10			
TLA-SMH-SMH-15		2,160	0.1	5	8	10			
TLA-SMH-SMH-19		2,238	143.9	4,137	6,295	8,454	3		50
TLA-SMH-SMH-21		2,313	1.7	85	128	171			100
TLA-SMH-SMH-22		2,299	2.7	137	205	273			100
TLA-SMH-SMH-23		2,181	0.5	5	8	10			
TLA-SMH-SMH-24		2,188	0.1	5	8	10			
TLA-SMH-SMH-25		2,197	0.1	5	8	10			
TLA-SMH-SMH-26		2,140	11.5	58	86	115			
TLA-SMH-SMH-27		2,106	6.2	31	47	62			
TLA-SMH-SMH-28		2,247	0.5	5	8	10			
TLA-SMH-TTN-1		2,227	17.4	453	706	959	2		40
TLA-SMH-TTN-2		2,184	3.8	19	29	38			

Table 4.9. Early/Middle Cruz Sites in Tayata.

Site	Toponym	Elev (m)	Area (ha)	Min Pop	Avg Pop	Max Pop	Strs	Pz	% Terr
TLA-SCT-CUA-5		2,140	2.2	11	17	22			
TLA-SCT-CUA-12		2,140	0.1	5	8	10			
TLA-SCT-SCT-6		2,100	0.1	5	8	10			
TLA-SZT-SZT-10		2,220	0.5	5	8	10			
TLA-SZT-SZT-11		2,141.5	2.4	24	41	59			
TLA-SZT-SZT-11		0	21.9	219	383	547			
TLA-SZT-SZT-12		2,120	0.5	5	8	10			

Table 4.10. Late Cruz Sites in Tayata.

Site	Toponym	Elev (m)	Area (ha)	Min Pop	Avg Pop	Max Pop	Strs	Pz	% Terr
TLA-SCT-CUA-1		2,175	1	10	18	25			
TLA-SCT-CUA-3		2,131	0.1	5	8	10			
TLA-SCT-CUA-4		2,235	0.1	5	8	10			
TLA-SCT-CUA-5		2,133.5	14.9	75	112	149			
TLA-SCT-CUA-6		2,140	7.1	35	53	71			
TLA-SCT-CUA-7		0	1.5	8	11	15			
TLA-SCT-CUA-11		2,175	10.1	50	76	101	1		
TLA-SCT-CUA-12		2,120	11.9	59	89	119	1		
TLA-SCT-SCT-2		2,135	12.8	435	666	896	1		60
TLA-SCT-SCT-4		2,060	11.6	116	204	291			
TLA-SCT-SCT-5		2,118	11.2	56	84	112			
TLA-SCT-SCT-6		2,098	0.1	5	8	10			
TLA-SCT-SCT-7		2,083	12	60	90	120			
TLA-SCT-SCT-8		2,100	0.1	5	8	10			

continued on next page

457

Table 4.10—continued

Site	Toponym	Elev (m)	Area (ha)	Min Pop	Avg Pop	Max Pop	Strs	Pz	% Terr
TLA-SMR-SMR-2		2,217	7.5	37	56	75			
TLA-SMR-SMR-2		2,197	0.1	5	8	10			
TLA-SMR-SMR-2		2,240	6.1	110	170	244			20
TLA-SMR-SMR-2		2,138	0.3	5	8	10			
TLA-SMR-SMR-2		2,202	0.1	5	8	10			
TLA-SMR-SMR-2		2,180	8.3	42	62	83			
TLA-SMR-SMR-2		2,177	0.1	5	8	10			
TLA-SMR-SMR-2		2,160	16.5	83	124	165			
TLA-SMR-SMR-2		2,200	0.1	5	8	10			
TLA-SZT-SZT-1		2,259	2	50	75	100	1		
TLA-SZT-SZT-10		2,216	0.5	5	8	10	2		
TLA-SZT-SZT-11		2,151	67.7	1,218	1,963	2,708	3		20
TLA-SZT-SZT-12		2,120	9	127	210	294			10
TLA-SZT-SZT-13		2,123	0.1	5	8	10			
TLA-SMR-UVH-1		2,214	2.5	25	45	64			

Table 4.11. Ramos Sites in Tayata.

Site	Toponym	Elev (m)	Area (ha)	Min Pop	Avg Pop	Max Pop	Strs	Pz	% Terr
TLA-SMR-SMR-3		2,440	0.4	30	45	60	2		
TLA-SZT-SZT-1		2,242	12.8	213	345	476.5	9		
TLA-SZT-SZT-2		2,185	0.5	5	8	10			
TLA-SZT-SZT-4		2,244	0.4	5	8	10			
TLA-SZT-SZT-8		2,276	1.8	55	84	114			50
TLA-SZT-SZT-10		2,200	7.4	221	341	461	2	2	50
TLA-SMR-UVH-2		2,386	4.8	240	360	480	2		100

Table 4.12. Las Flores Sites in Tayata.

Site	Toponym	Elev (m)	Area (ha)	Min Pop	Avg Pop	Max Pop	Strs	Pz	% Terr
TLA-SCT-SCT-3		2,078	0.1	5	8	10			20
TLA-SCT-SCT-6		2,111	7.4	133	214	295	2	1	20
TLA-SCT-SCT-8		2,100	16.1	289	466	643			80
TLA-SMR-SMR-2		2,180	19.6	824	1,245	1,667			
TLA-SMR-SMR-2		2,125	0.1	5	8	10			
TLA-SZT-SZT-8		0	16.1	482	744	1,005	2		50
TLA-SZT-SZT-10		2,158	8.6	325	494	663		2	70
TLA-SZT-SZT-11		2,149	0.1	325	494	663			
TLA-SMR-UVH-1		2,200	1.5	15	27	38	1		

Table 4.13. Natividad Sites in Tayata.

Site	Toponym	Elev (m)	Area (ha)	Min Pop	Avg Pop	Max Pop	Strs	Pz	% Terr
TLA-SCT-CUA-1		2,200	10	100	174	249			100
TLA-SCT-CUA-2		2,154	0.1	5	8	10			
TLA-SCT-CUA-4		2,245	0.3	13	19	25			
TLA-SCT-CUA-5		2,140	0.3	5	8	10			
TLA-SCT-CUA-5		2,160	5.2	52	92	131			
TLA-SCT-CUA-6		2,140	5.3	53	92	131	1		50
TLA-SCT-CUA-7		2,140	1.7	50	77	104			
TLA-SCT-CUA-8		2,120	4.5	22	34	45			
TLA-SCT-CUA-9		2,120	1.7	8	12	16			
TLA-SCT-CUA-10		2,120	1	5	8	10			
TLA-SCT-CUA-11		2,140	1	5	8	10			
TLA-SCT-CUA-12		2,140	1	10	18	25			

continued on next page

Table 4.13—*continued*

Site	Toponym	Elev (m)	Area (ha)	Min Pop	Avg Pop	Max Pop	Strs	Pz	% Terr
TLA-SCT-CUA-12		2,120	5.5	55	97	138	1		70
TLA-SCT-SCT-2		2,143	12.8	487	740	993			
TLA-SCT-SCT-3		2,084	1.8	9	13	18			
TLA-SCT-SCT-4		2,061	0.1	5	8	10			
TLA-SCT-SCT-5		2,059	1	5	8	10			
TLA-SCT-SCT-6		2,100	1.9	10	14	19			
TLA-SCT-SCT-7		2,080	0.1	5	8	10			
TLA-SCT-SCT-8		2,090	9.5	48	71	95			
TLA-SMR-SMR-1		2,270	10.7	107	188	268			
TLA-SMR-SMR-2		2,199	176.9	5,084	7,737	10,390	3		50
TLA-SMR-SMR-3		2,432	0.4	30	20	10			
TLA-SMR-SMR-4		2,383	0.1	5	8	10			
TLA-SMR-SMR-5		2,560	0.8	5	8	10	3	1	
TLA-SMR-SMR-6		2,400	0.1	5	8	10	1		
TLA-SZT-SZT-1		2,240	3.1	31	54	77			
TLA-SZT-SZT-2		2,210	0.1	5	8	10			
TLA-SZT-SZT-3		2,234	1.5	15	27	38			
TLA-SZT-SZT-5		2,240	0.1	5	8	10			
TLA-SZT-SZT-6		2,152	3.7	37	64	92			
TLA-SZT-SZT-7		2,220	2.9	29	51	73			
TLA-SZT-SZT-8		2,264	7.3	218	337	455			50
TLA-SZT-SZT-9		2,149	1.2	6	9	12			
TLA-SZT-SZT-10		2,200	34.1	1,294	1,967	2,640	1	2	70
TLA-SZT-SZT-11		2,160	0.4	5	8	10			
TLA-SZT-SZT-12		2,120	8.3	42	62	83			
TLA-SMR-UVH-1		2,200	15	150	263	375			
TLA-SMR-UVH-2		2,389	0.1	5	8	10			

Table 5.1. Late Cruz Sites in San Juan Achiutla.

Site	Toponym	Elev (m)	Area (ha)	Min Pop	Avg Pop	Max Pop	Strs	Pz	% Terr
TLA-SJA-14		2,040·	2	20	35	50			
TLA-SJA-25		2,226	13	130	227	324			

Table 5.2. Ramos Sites in San Juan Achiutla.

Site	Toponym	Elev (m)	Area (ha)	Min Pop	Avg Pop	Max Pop	Strs	Pz	% Terr
TLA-SJA-SJA-1		2,220	13.6	271	432	593	2		
TLA-SJA-SJA-10		2,373	3.2	162	243	324	3	1	100
TLA-SJA-SJA-18		2,200	1.6	16	28	40	2		

Table 5.3. Las Flores Sites in San Juan Achiutla.

Site	Toponym	Elev (m)	Area (ha)	Min Pop	Avg Pop	Max Pop	Strs	Pz	% Terr
TLA-SJA-1		2,202	1	10	18	25			
TLA-SJA-11		2,056	1.1	11	20	28			
TLA-SJA-12		1,972	18.1	181	317	453			
TLA-SJA-13		2,080	0.5	5	8	10			
TLA-SJA-14		2,040	2	20	35	50			
TLA-SJA-15		2,075	0.8	8	13	19			
TLA-SJA-17		2,066	1.5	15	27	38			
TLA-SJA-19		2,100	1.1	11	20	28			
TLA-SJA-2		2,108	9	90	157	225			
TLA-SJA-21		2,132	0.8	8	13	19			

continued on next page

Table 5.3—continued

Site	Toponym	Elev (m)	Area (ha)	Min Pop	Avg Pop	Max Pop	Strs	Pz	% Terr
TLA-SJA-SJA-23		2,041	7.1	71	123	176			
TLA-SJA-SJA-27		2,382	0.3	5	8	10			
TLA-SJA-SJA-29		2,193	5.6	56	99	141			
TLA-SJA-SJA-3		2,080	0.5	5	8	10			
TLA-SJA-SJA-4		2,073	1	10	18	25			
TLA-SJA-SJA-7		2,081	1.5	15	27	38			
TLA-SJA-SJA-8		2,377	2.8	28	49	70	1		
TLA-SJA-SJA-9		2,194	11.1	111	193	276	1		

Table 5.4. Natividad Sites in San Juan Achiutla.

Site	Toponym	Elev (m)	Area (ha)	Min Pop	Avg Pop	Max Pop	Strs	Pz	% Terr
TLA-SJA-SJA-2		2,100	9	90	158	225			
TLA-SJA-SJA-5		2,220	3	30	53	75			
TLA-SJA-SJA-6		2,391	0.9	9	16	23			
TLA-SJA-SJA-9		2,220	0.3	5	8	10			
TLA-SJA-SJA-13		2,080	0.5	5	8	10			
TLA-SJA-SJA-20		2,134	2	20	35	50			
TLA-SJA-SJA-22		2,079	1.5	15	27	38			
TLA-SJA-SJA-31		2,145	7	70	123	176	1		

Table 5.5. Late Cruz Sites in Achiutla.

Site	Toponym	Elev (m)	Area (ha)	Min Pop	Avg Pop	Max Pop	Strs	Pz	% Terr
TLA-SMA-ATY-1		1,927	0.1	5	8	10			
TLA-SMA-ATY-1		1,887	6.5	65	113	162			
TLA-SMA-ATY-2		1,990	2	20	35	50			
TLA-SMA-ATY-5		1,960	0.1	5	8	10			
TLA-SMA-SMA-33		2,030	2.9	29	51	72			
TLA-SMA-SMA-38		2,062	0.3	5	8	10			
TLA-SMA-SMA-41		1,974	1	10	18	25			
TLA-SMA-SMA-42		1,964	0.1	5	8	10			

Table 5.6. Ramos Sites in Achiutla.

Site	Toponym	Elev (m)	Area (ha)	Min Pop	Avg Pop	Max Pop	Strs	Pz	% Terr
TLA-SMA-ATY-1		2,000	13	130	227	324	5	1	
TLA-SMA-ATY-1		1,940	13	647	971	1,295	3		100
TLA-SMA-ATY-4		2,047	5.5	55	97	138			
TLA-TLA-SDH-4		1,900	0.1	5	8	10			
TLA-TLA-SDH-4		1,900	0.1	5	8	10			
TLA-SMA-SMA-1	Cordon la Corona	2,200	2.1	107	161	214			100
TLA-SMA-SMA-2	Cordon la Corona	2,383	3.6	178	266	355	3	1	100
TLA-SMA-SMA-3	La Casa del Sol	2,220	6.9	69	121	173	1		
TLA-SMA-SMA-5		1,860	1	10	18	25			
TLA-SMA-SMA-11	Cerro El Moral	2,036	1.3	13	22	31			
TLA-SMA-SMA-31		2,150	11.2	560	840	1,120	1	1	100
TLA-SMA-SMA-40		2,020	1	10	18	25			

463

Table 5.7. Las Flores Sites in Achiutla.

Site	Toponym	Elev (m)	Area (ha)	Min Pop	Avg Pop	Max Pop	Strs	Pz	% Terr
TLA-SMA-ATY-1		1,893	3.1	31	54	77			
TLA-SMA-ATY-1		1,949	3.1	31	53	76			
TLA-SMA-ATY-2		2,004	13.4	134	234	335			
TLA-SMA-SMA-3	La Casa del Sol	2,220	12.3	123	214	306	4	1	
TLA-SMA-SMA-4	Pueblo Viejo de Achiutla	2,000	1.6	16	28	40	1		
TLA-SMA-SMA-5		1,860	1.3	13	22	31			
TLA-SMA-SMA-30		2,060	2.5	25	43	62			
TLA-SMA-SMA-31		2,156	11.2	560	839	1,119	1	1	100
TLA-SMA-SMA-32		2,114	1	10	18	25			

Table 5.8. Natividad Sites in Achiutla.

Site	Toponym	Elev (m)	Area (ha)	Min Pop	Avg Pop	Max Pop	Strs	Pz	% Terr
TLA-SMA-ATY-1		1,929	248.8	1,244	1,866	2,488	13	2	
TLA-SMA-ATY-2		2,000	16.8	168	294	420			
TLA-SMA-ATY-3		1,986	49.5	495	867	1,238	2		
TLA-SMA-ATY-4		2,049	17.7	177	309	442			
TLA-SMA-ATY-5		1,971	118.8	1,188	2,078	2,969	1		
TLA-SMA-ATY-6		2,040	19.1	191	335	478	1		
TLA-TLA-SDH-4		1,890	16.9	169	295	422	2	1	
TLA-SMA-SMA-1	Cordon la Corona	2,200	22.3	112	167	223	2		
TLA-SMA-SMA-2	Cordon la Corona	2,400	16.8	168	293	419			
TLA-SMA-SMA-3	La Casa del Sol	2,216	1	10	18	25			
TLA-SMA-SMA-4	Pueblo Viejo de Achiutla	1,979	14.4	718	1,077	1,436	11		100
TLA-SMA-SMA-5		1,860	1	10	18	25			
TLA-SMA-SMA-6		1,920	5.5	27	41	55	1		
TLA-SMA-SMA-7		1,920	0.1	5	8	10			
TLA-SMA-SMA-8		1,940	0.1	5	8	10			

Site	Toponym	Elev (m)	Area (ha)	Min Pop	Avg Pop	Max Pop	Strs	Pz	% Terr
TLA-SMA-SMA-9		2,020	0.5	5	8	10			
TLA-SMA-SMA-10		2,020	0.1	5	8	10			
TLA-SMA-SMA-11	Cerro El Moral	2,040	0.1	5	8	10			
TLA-SMA-SMA-30		2,027	2.5	25	43	61			
TLA-SMA-SMA-32		2,112	27.4	274	480	685			
TLA-SMA-SMA-33		2,060	104.9	1,049	1,835	2,622			
TLA-SMA-SMA-34		2,062	31.1	311	544	777			
TLA-SMA-SMA-35		2,016	8.7	87	153	218			
TLA-SMA-SMA-36		1,948	4	40	69	99			
TLA-SMA-SMA-38		2,062	0.3	5	8	10			
TLA-SMA-SMA-40		2,026	5.2	52	91	130	1		
TLA-SMA-SMA-41		1,974	8.4	84	147	210			
TLA-SMA-SMA-42		1,982	50	500	876	1,251			
TLA-SMA-SMA-43		2,019	4.5	45	78	111	1		

Table 5.9. Late Cruz Sites in Yucuañe.

Site	Toponym	Elev (m)	Area (ha)	Min Pop	Avg Pop	Max Pop	Strs	Pz	% Terr
TLA-SBY-SBY-2		1,920	1.3	13	22	31			
TLA-SBY-SBY-6		2,047	1.7	17	29	42			
TLA-SBY-SBY-14		1,842	3.2	32	55	79			

Table 5.10. Ramos Sites in Yucuañe.

Site	Toponym	Elev (m)	Area (ha)	Min Pop	Avg Pop	Max Pop	Strs	Pz	% Terr
TLA-SBY-SBY-3	Yucuañe	2,247	6.7	337	506	674	2		100
TLA-SBY-SBY-8		1,968	0.5	5	8	10			
TLA-SBY-SBY-11		2,100	5.5	277	415	553	2		100

Table 5.11. Las Flores Sites in Yucuañe.

Site	Toponym	Elev (m)	Area (ha)	Min Pop	Avg Pop	Max Pop	Strs	Pz	% Terr
NO-TIL-GHO-1		1,948	34.8	348	608	869	3		
NO-TIL-GHO-3		2,020	26.6	266	465	664	1		
NO-TIL-GHO-5		1,840	1	10	18	25	1		
NO-TIL-LPS-1		2,260	16.1	161	281	402	3		
NO-TIL-LPS-3		2,329	0.2	5	8	10			
NO-TIL-LPS-7		2,403	0.8	8	13	19			
NO-TIL-LPZ-2		2,675	2.7	27	46	66			
TLA-SBY-SBY-3	Yucuañe	2,237	22.8	1,140	1,710	2,280	7		100
TLA-SBY-SBY-7		1,953	0.1	5	8	10			
TLA-SBY-SBY-8		1,969	0.5	5	8	10			
TLA-SBY-SBY-11		2,108	5.3	265	398	531	2		100
TLA-SBY-SBY-16		1,781	0.5	5	8	10			
TLA-SBY-SBY-18		1,940	2.6	26	46	66			
TLA-SBY-SBY-20		1,918	2.7	27	48	68			
TLA-SBY-SBY-22	Cerro Yucunuviso	2,165	32.3	1,613	2,419	3,226	3		100
TLA-SBY-SBY-28		2,093	3.7	37	65	93	2		

Table 5.12. Natividad Sites in Yucuañe.

Site	Toponym	Elev (m)	Area (ha)	Min Pop	Avg Pop	Max Pop	Strs	Pz	% Terr
NO-TIL-GHO-3		1,966	26.6	266	465	664	1		
NO-TIL-GHO-5		1,833	1	5	8	10	1		
NO-TIL-GHO-7		1,800	16.5	165	289	413	3		
NO-TIL-LPS-5		2,326	1.1	11	20	28	1		
NO-TIL-LPS-9		2,285	0.2	5	8	10			
NO-TIL-LPZ-1		2,468	15.3	153	267	382			
TLA-SBY-SBY-1		1,974	1.5	15	27	38			
TLA-SBY-SBY-2		1,920	14.4	144	251	359			
TLA-SBY-SBY-3	Yucuañe	2,150	80.2	4,012	6,018	8,024	1		100
TLA-SBY-SBY-4		1,784	6.7	67	118	168			
TLA-SBY-SBY-5		1,958	7.9	79	137	196			
TLA-SBY-SBY-6		2,047	1.4	14	25	36			
TLA-SBY-SBY-10		1,860	0.3	5	8	10			
TLA-SBY-SBY-18		1,921	2.6	26	46	66			
TLA-SBY-SBY-22	Cerro Yucunuviso	2,097	6.8	339	508	677			100
TLA-SBY-SBY-24		1,978	9.6	96	168	240			
TLA-SBY-SBY-26		1,866	0.5	5	8	10			

Table 5.13. Early/Middle Cruz Sites in Tlacotepec.

Site	Toponym	Elev (m)	Area (ha)	Min Pop	Avg Pop	Max Pop	Strs	Pz	% Terr
TLA-SAT-SAT-1	Pueblo Viejo de Tlacotepec	1,960	0.2	5	8	10			
TLA-SAT-SAT-16		2,000	2	20	35	50			
TLA-SAT-SAT-2		2,072	0.1	5	8	10			
TLA-SAT-SAT-28		1,970	4.5	45	79	112			
TLA-SAT-SAT-6		1,980	0.1	5	8	10			

Table 5.14. Late Cruz Sites in Tlacotepec.

Site	Toponym	Elev (m)	Area (ha)	Min Pop	Avg Pop	Max Pop	Strs	Pz	% Terr
TLA-SAT-SAT-1	Pueblo Viejo de Tlacotepec	2,026	0.2	5	8	10			
TLA-SAT-SAT-12		1,961	4.3	43	76	108			
TLA-SAT-SAT-13		1,877	0.1	5	8	10			
TLA-SAT-SAT-16		1,980	2	20	35	50			
TLA-SAT-SAT-17		1,807	0.3	5	8	10			
TLA-SAT-SAT-2		2,073	1.5	15	27	38	2	1	
TLA-SAT-SAT-38		2,320	0.5	5	8	10			
TLA-SAT-SAT-39		1,833	6.5	65	115	164	6		
TLA-SAT-SAT-6		2,094	0.1	5	8	10			
TLA-SAT-SAT-8		1,915	0.4	5	8	10			
TLA-SAT-SAT-9		1,980	0.6	5	8	10	1		
TLA-TLA-SDH-16		1,920	1.5	15	27	38			

Table 5.15. Ramos Sites in Tlacotepec.

Site	Toponym	Elev (m)	Area (ha)	Min Pop	Avg Pop	Max Pop	Strs	Pz	% Terr
TLA-SAT-SAT-7		1,822	0.1	5	8	10			
TLA-SAT-SAT-9		2,220	0.4	5	8	10			
TLA-SAT-SAT-9		1,906	0.4	5	8	10	2	2	
TLA-SAT-SAT-9		1,957	0.1	5	8	10			
TLA-SAT-SAT-9		1,943	0.2	5	8	10			
TLA-SAT-SAT-19		2,222	2.4	24	42	60	1		
TLA-TLA-SDH-1	Cerro Yucuñushiño	2,125	18.3	917	1,375	1,834	2		100
TLA-TLA-SDH-2	Cerro Yucuñucu	2,062	27.8	1,388	2,081	2,775	1		100
TLA-TLA-SDH-12		1,873	0.8	8	13	19			
TLA-TLA-SDH-24		1,843	0.2	10	15	20			

Table 5.16. Las Flores Sites in Tlacotepec.

Site	Toponym	Elev (m)	Area (ha)	Min Pop	Avg Pop	Max Pop	Strs	Pz	% Terr
TLA-SAT-SAT-11		2,045	2.6	26	42	65	1		
TLA-SAT-SAT-14		1,988	20.6	206	360	514			
TLA-SAT-SAT-16		1,941	7.7	77	135	193			
TLA-SAT-SAT-21	Yucunoo	2,475	13	652	978	1,304	6	1	100
TLA-SAT-SAT-3		2,141	0.3	5	8	10			
TLA-SAT-SAT-4		1,980	0.1	5	8	10			
TLA-SAT-SAT-8		1,942	3.7	37	65	93			
TLA-TLA-SDH-1	Cerro Yucuñushiño	2,125	8.8	439	659	878	2		100
TLA-TLA-SDH-16		1,920	1.5	15	27	38			
TLA-TLA-SDH-3		1,900	0.9	9	16	22			
TLA-TLA-SDH-8		1,917	1.8	18	32	45			

Table 5.17. Natividad Sites in Tlacotepec.

Site	Toponym	Elev (m)	Area (ha)	Min Pop	Avg Pop	Max Pop	Strs	Pz	% Terr
TLA-SAT-SAT-1	Pueblo Viejo de Tlacotepec	2,053	4.1	41	72	103			
TLA-SAT-SAT-15		1,803	0.3	5	8	10			
TLA-SAT-SAT-16		1,956	20.8	208	363	519			
TLA-SAT-SAT-17		1,794	3.8	38	67	95		2	
TLA-SAT-SAT-21	Yucunoo	2,490	0.6	6	11	15			
TLA-SAT-SAT-23	Yucunoo	2,582	8.4	420	631	841	1	1	100
TLA-SAT-SAT-28		1,973	17.5	175	307	439			
TLA-SAT-SAT-3		2,137	3.1	31	54	77	1		
TLA-SAT-SAT-39		1,824	16.4	164	287	410	6		
TLA-SAT-SAT-4		2,096	0.1	5	8	10			
TLA-SAT-SAT-5		2,052	0.3	5	8	10			
TLA-SAT-SAT-8		1,931	6.3	63	109	156			
TLA-SAT-SAT-9		2,035	237.7	2,377	4,159	5,941	2		
TLA-TLA-SDH-1	Cerro Yucuñushiño	2,105	24.8	124	186	248	1		
TLA-TLA-SDH-10		1,960	0.5	5	9	12			
TLA-TLA-SDH-11		1,882	2.4	24	42	60			
TLA-TLA-SDH-13		1,860	0.1	10	10	10			
TLA-TLA-SDH-15		1,919	0.2	5	8	10			
TLA-TLA-SDH-17		2,000	6.6	66	116	165	3		
TLA-TLA-SDH-18		1,831	20.4	204	358	511			
TLA-TLA-SDH-19		1,971	4.5	45	79	113			
TLA-TLA-SDH-2	Cerro Yucuñucu	2,052	10.8	54	81	108	7		
TLA-TLA-SDH-20		1,840	0.1	5	8	10			
TLA-TLA-SDH-21		1,980	8.8	88	155	221			
TLA-TLA-SDH-22		1,864	8.6	43	64	86			
TLA-TLA-SDH-23		1,920	1	10	18	25			
TLA-TLA-SDH-3		1,896	0.9	9	16	22			
TLA-TLA-SDH-5		1,889	0.5	5	9	12			
TLA-TLA-SDH-6		1,833	0.2	5	8	10			
TLA-TLA-SDH-9		1,863	0.9	9	16	22			

Table 5.18. Cruz Sites in Amoltepec.

Site	Toponym	Elev (m)	Area (ha)	Min Pop	Avg Pop	Max Pop	Strs	Pz	% Terr
TLA-SCA-SCA-2		2,220	0.3	5	8	10			
TLA-SCA-SCA-5EMC		2,180	0.3	5	8	10			
TLA-SCA-SCA-5LC		2,173	2.5	25	44	62			
TLA-SMP-ZAR-2		2,055	1.3	5	8	10			

Table 5.19. Ramos Sites in Amoltepec.

Site	Toponym	Elev (m)	Area (ha)	Min Pop	Avg Pop	Max Pop	Strs	Pz	% Terr
TLA-SCA-SCA-2		2,140	1	10	18	25			
TLA-SCA-SCA-2		2,143	36.6	659	1,061	1,464	2	1	20
TLA-SCA-SCA-3		2,241	0.6	6	11	16			
TLA-SCA-SCA-5		2,173	2.5	25	44	62			
TLA-SCA-SCA-9		2,226	0.8	8	14	20			
TLA-SCA-SCA-14	Yucuñucoo	2,429	0.1	5	8	10	1		
TLA-SCA-SCA-16		2,340	1	50	75	100			100

Table 5.20. Las Flores Sites in Amoltepec.

Site	Toponym	Elev (m)	Area (ha)	Min Pop	Avg Pop	Max Pop	Strs	Pz	% Terr
TLA-SCA-SCA-2		2,232	3.9	39	69	98			
TLA-SCA-SCA-4		2,440	1.8	89	134	178	3	1	100
TLA-SCA-SCA-6		2,499	2.4	24	42	60	3		
TLA-SCA-SCA-12		2,031	8.6	86	151	216			
TLA-SCA-SCA-13		2,333	24.8	248	434	620			
TLA-SCA-SCA-14	Yucuñucoo	2,460	7.5	375	563	750	4	1	100
TLA-SCA-SCA-15		2,304	1.7	17	30	43			
TLA-SCA-SCA-16		2,330	2.3	59	91	124			
TLA-SCA-SCA-19		2,320	13.4	134	235	335			
TLA-SMP-ZAR-1		2,040	0.5	5	8	10			

Table 5.21. Natividad Sites in Amoltepec.

Site	Toponym	Elev (m)	Area (ha)	Min Pop	Avg Pop	Max Pop	Strs	Pz	% Terr
TLA-SCA-SCA-1		2,200	0.7	7	11	16	2	1	
TLA-SCA-SCA-2		2,141	239	2,390	4,183	5,976	3	1	
TLA-SCA-SCA-4		2,407	1.8	18	31	44			
TLA-SCA-SCA-5		2,172	1	10	18	25			
TLA-SCA-SCA-6		2,435	1.8	18	32	45			
TLA-SCA-SCA-7		2,200	1.3	13	23	32			
TLA-SCA-SCA-10		2,337	10.5	105	183	262			
TLA-SCA-SCA-11		2,172	5.4	54	94	134			
TLA-SCA-SCA-12		2,027	0.1	5	8	10			
TLA-SCA-SCA-15		2,316	0.2	5	8	10			
TLA-SCA-SCA-16		2,335	0.1	5	8	10			
TLA-SCA-SCA-18		2,237	0.8	8	14	20			
TLA-SCA-SCA-19		2,295	13.4	134	235	336			
TLA-SCA-SCA-20		2,300	0.1	5	8	10			
TLA-SMP-ZAR-1		1,858	0.5	5	13	20			
TLA-SMP-ZAR-2		2,055	1.3	13	22	31			
TLA-SMP-ZAR-3		2,060	2.9	29	51	73			
TLA-SMP-ZAR-4		1,920	1.3	13	22	31			

Table 5.22. Early/Middle Cruz Sites in Magdalena Peñasco.

Site	Toponym	Elev (m)	Area (ha)	Min Pop	Avg Pop	Max Pop	Strs	Pz	% Terr
TLA-SMP-SMP-3		2,180	0.3	5	8	10			
TLA-SMP-SMP-6		2,100	4	40	70	100			
TLA-SMP-SMP-10		2,140	2.3	23	40	57			
TLA-SMP-SMP-23		2,080	0.1	5	8	10			

Table 5.23. Late Cruz Sites in Magdalena Peñasco.

Site	Toponym	Elev (m)	Area (ha)	Min Pop	Avg Pop	Max Pop	Strs	Pz	% Terr
TLA-SMP-CAB-5		2,452	0.5	5	8	10			
TLA-SMP-SMP-10		2,101	2.3	23	40	57			
TLA-SMP-SMP-12		2,033	1.1	11	20	28			
TLA-SMP-SMP-18		2,108	0.1	5	8	10			
TLA-SMP-SMP-2		2,048	0.1	5	8	10			
TLA-SMP-SMP-23		2,065	0.1	5	8	10			
TLA-SMP-SMP-32		2,481	4.2	42	73	105			
TLA-SMP-SMP-5		2,149	0.1	5	8	10			
TLA-SMP-SMP-6		2,060	4	40	70	100			
TLA-SMP-SMP-7		1,973	0.1	5	8	10			

Table 5.24. Ramos Sites in Magdalena Peñasco.

Site	Toponym	Elev (m)	Area (ha)	Min Pop	Avg Pop	Max Pop	Strs	Pz	% Terr
TLA-SMP-SMP-11		2,345	0.3	5	8	10			
TLA-SMP-SMP-12		2,033	1.1	11	20	28			
TLA-SMP-SMP-13	Yucuñucuiñe (Cerro del Tigre)	2,280	7.8	391	586	781	2		100
TLA-SMP-SMP-14	El Gachupin	2,560	4	40	71	101	9	3	

Table 5.25. Las Flores Sites in Magdalena Peñasco.

Site	Toponym	Elev (m)	Area (ha)	Min Pop	Avg Pop	Max Pop	Strs	Pz	% Terr
TLA-SMP-CAB-1	Yucudiqui	2,596	6.1	61	107	153	2		
TLA-SMP-CAB-2	Cerro Tucutinuno	2,724	1.7	17	30	43	3		
TLA-SMP-SIP-5	Pueblo Viejo	2,477	6.4	64	111	159			
TLA-SMP-SMP-2		2,120	6.9	69	121	173			
TLA-SMP-SMP-11		2,460	11.4	570	854	1,139	2	2	100
TLA-SMP-SMP-12		2,038	0.1	5	8	10			
TLA-SMP-SMP-14	El Gachupin	2,560	4.3	43	75	107	9	3	
TLA-SMP-SMP-22		1,980	9.4	94	165	236			
TLA-SMP-SMP-25		2,032	1.8	18	31	44			
TLA-SMP-SMP-26		1,940	0.3	5	8	10			
TLA-SMP-SMP-27		1,920	5.1	51	90	128			
TLA-SMP-SMP-31	Cerro Yucuyuyu	2,500	0.4	5	8	10	1	1	
TLA-SMP-SMP-32		2,540	65.7	657	1,149	1,641			
TLA-SMP-SMP-35	Yucudzanini or Cerro la Colmena	2,364	32.7	327	573	818	4	1	

Table 5.26. Natividad Sites in Magdalena Peñasco.

Site	Toponym	Elev (m)	Area (ha)	Min Pop	Avg Pop	Max Pop	Strs	Pz	% Terr
TLA-SMP-CAB-3		2,572	0.1	5	8	10			
TLA-SMP-CAB-4		2,526	1.6	16	27	39			
TLA-SMP-CAB-6		2,425	3	30	53	75			
TLA-SMP-SIP-1		2,082	0.1	5	8	10			
TLA-SMP-SIP-2		2,204	7.8	78	137	196			
TLA-SMP-SIP-3		2,295	3.1	80	120	160			
TLA-SMP-SIP-5	Pueblo Viejo	2,300	129	3,870	5,966	8,062	7	3	

Site	Name								
TLA-SMP-SMP-1		2,003	2.8	28	48	69			
TLA-SMP-SMP-2		2,048	6.8	68	118	169			
TLA-SMP-SMP-3		2,196	0.5	5	8	10		2	100
TLA-SMP-SMP-4		2,218	23.5	329	546	763	2		
TLA-SMP-SMP-5		2,017	0.5	5	8	10			
TLA-SMP-SMP-6		2,060	4	40	70	100			
TLA-SMP-SMP-7		1,973	0.1	5	8	10			
TLA-SMP-SMP-8		1,980	0.7	7	13	18			
TLA-SMP-SMP-9		2,080	0.1	5	8	10			
TLA-SMP-SMP-10		2,101	2.3	23	41	58			
TLA-SMP-SMP-11		2,348	11.3	563	845	1,126	2	2	
TLA-SMP-SMP-12		2,001	18	180	316	451	9		
TLA-SMP-SMP-14	El Gachupin	2,544	4.1	41	72	102		3	
TLA-SMP-SMP-15		2,054	3.2	32	56	80			
TLA-SMP-SMP-16		2,188	1.5	15	27	38			
TLA-SMP-SMP-17		2,060	2.8	28	48	69			
TLA-SMP-SMP-18		2,108	0.1	5	8	10			
TLA-SMP-SMP-19		2,022	16.9	169	295	421			
TLA-SMP-SMP-20		2,015	3.4	34	59	84			
TLA-SMP-SMP-21		1,984	0.6	6	10	14			
TLA-SMP-SMP-22		1,967	9	90	158	226			
TLA-SMP-SMP-23		2,065	5.6	56	98	140			
TLA-SMP-SMP-24		2,057	2	20	35	50			
TLA-SMP-SMP-26		1,919	0.3	5	8	10			
TLA-SMP-SMP-27		1,884	5	50	88	125			
TLA-SMP-SMP-31	Cerro Yucuyuyu	2,492	0.4	5	8	10	1		
TLA-SMP-SMP-32		2,455	66.7	667	1,168	1,668		1	
TLA-SMP-SMP-33		2,084	1	10	18	25			
TLA-SMP-SMP-34	La Cumbre	2,380	9.1	91	159	227			
TLA-SMP-SMP-35	Yucudzanini or Cerro la Colmena	2,469	5.1	51	90	128	4		
TLA-SMP-SMP-36		2,336	1.3	13	22	31		1	

Table 5.27. Early/Middle Cruz Sites in Dzinicahua.

Site	Toponym	Elev (m)	Area (ha)	Min Pop	Avg Pop	Max Pop	Strs	Pz	% Terr
TLA-SAT-YOS-7		2,023	1.5	15	27	38			
TLA-SAT-YOS-11		1,993	0.1	5	8	10			

Table 5.28. Late Cruz Sites in Dzinicahua.

Site	Toponym	Elev (m)	Area (ha)	Min Pop	Avg Pop	Max Pop	Strs	Pz	% Terr
TLA-SAT-SAT-41		1,918	28	280	491	701			
TLA-SAT-SAT-42		1,900	45.7	457	801	1,144	4		
TLA-SMO-SMO-3		1,920	11.7	396	606	816			60
TLA-SAT-YOS-1		1,961	73.5	735	1,287	1,838	1		
TLA-SAT-YOS-4		2,022	7.4	74	129	184			
TLA-SAT-YOS-5		2,034	5.2	52	90	129			
TLA-SAT-YOS-8		1,980	6.1	61	107	153	1		
TLA-SAT-YOS-10		1,989	12	120	210	300			
TLA-SAT-YOS-11		1,911	38.5	385	673	961			
TLA-SAT-YOS-13		1,952	5.9	59	103	147			
TLA-SAT-YOS-14		1,932	4.8	48	85	121			
TLA-SAT-YOS-15		2,127	2	20	35	50	1		
TLA-SAT-YOS-16		2,140	1	10	18	25			

Table 5.29. Ramos and Las Flores Sites in Dzinicahua.

Site	Toponym	Elev (m)	Area (ha)	Min Pop	Avg Pop	Max Pop	Strs	Pz	% Terr
TLA-SMO-SMO-1LR	Cerro Peña Grande	2,483	16.1	375	586	800	5	1	80
TLA-SMO-SMO-1	Cerro Peña Grande	2,483	16.1	375	586	800	5	1	80
TLA-SMO-SMO-3		1,905	4.6	46	81	115	6	1	
TLA-SAT-SAT-41		1,935	12.3	123	216	308			

Table 5.30. Natividad Sites in Dzinicahua.

Site	Toponym	Elev (m)	Area (ha)	Min Pop	Avg Pop	Max Pop	Strs	Pz	% Terr
TLA-SAT-SAT-41		1,900	0.1	5	8	10			
TLA-SMO-SMO-1	Cerro Peña Grande	2,624	37.34	1,160	1,818	2,475			
TLA-SAT-YOS-1		2,026	88.9	889	1,556	2,222			
TLA-SAT-YOS-2		1,991	1.3	13	22	31			
TLA-SAT-YOS-3		2,055	2.8	28	48	69			
TLA-SAT-YOS-4		2,022	7.2	72	125	179			
TLA-SAT-YOS-5		2,034	5.2	52	90	129			
TLA-SAT-YOS-6		2,035	0.1	5	8	10			
TLA-SAT-YOS-7		2,023	1.5	15	27	38			
TLA-SAT-YOS-8		1,980	6.1	61	107	153	1		
TLA-SAT-YOS-9		2,071	0.1	5	8	10			
TLA-SAT-YOS-10		1,989	12	120	210	300			
TLA-SAT-YOS-11		1,898	0.1	5	8	10			
TLA-SAT-YOS-11		1,944	21.4	214	375	536			
TLA-SAT-YOS-12		1,919	6.5	65	113	162			
TLA-SAT-YOS-14		1,932	4	40	70	100			
TLA-SAT-YOS-15		2,127	2	20	35	50	1		
TLA-SAT-YOS-16		2,149	4.1	41	72	103			

Table 6.1. Late Cruz Sites in Tlaxiaco.

Site	Toponym	Elev (m)	Area (ha)	Min Pop	Avg Pop	Max Pop	Strs	Pz	% Terr
TLA-TLA-CAL-2		2,194	1	10	18	25	2		
TLA-TLA-TLA-43		2,125	0.1	5	8	10	3		

Table 6.2. Ramos Sites in Tlaxiaco.

Site	Toponym	Elev (m)	Area (ha)	Min Pop	Avg Pop	Max Pop	Strs	Pz	% Terr
TLA-TLA-CAL-6		2,260	3.8	188	281	375			100
TLA-TLA-TLA-1	Cerro Encantado	2,100	1	50	75	100	5	2	100

Table 6.3. Las Flores Sites in Tlaxiaco.

Site	Toponym	Elev (m)	Area (ha)	Min Pop	Avg Pop	Max Pop	Strs	Pz	% Terr
TLA-TLA-CAL-3		2,257	0.2	5	8	10	1	1	
TLA-TLA-CAL-4		2,240	0.2	5	8	10	2		
TLA-TLA-CAL-5		2,140	1.9	19	33	47			
TLA-TLA-CAL-6		2,260	3.8	188	281	375	6	1	100
TLA-TLA-CAL-7		2,227	3.4	34	60	85			
TLA-TLA-SLC-2	Cerro El Jabali	2,351	5.7	57	99	142	3		
TLA-TLA-TLA-1	Cerro Encantado	2,178	41.7	2,086	3,129	4,172	5	2	100
TLA-TLA-TLA-24		2,215	11.8	589	884	1,178	1		100
TLA-TLA-TLA-26		2,600	30.7	307	538	768	2	1	
TLA-TLA-TLA-28	Cerro El Tambor	2,620	3	30	53	75	2		
TLA-TLA-TLA-31		2,140	0.2	5	8	10	1		
TLA-TLA-TLA-32		2,180	1	50	75	100	3	1	100
TLA-TLA-TLA-33		2,287	2.2	112	168	224	5	2	100
TLA-TLA-TLA-36	El Vergel	2,120	12.6	629	943	1,257	20	2	100
TLA-TLA-TLA-40		2,099	10.6	106	185	265	1		
TLA-TLA-TLA-41		2,313	17.4	174	305	435	1		
TLA-TLA-TLA-42	Cerro de la Virgen	2,254	61.6	3,082	4,623	6,164	1	2	100
TLA-TLA-TLA-43		2,157	1.8	18	31	44	3		
TLA-TLA-TLA-44		2,264	4.3	212	319	425	2	1	100

Table 6.4. Natividad Sites in Tlaxiaco.

Site	Toponym	Elev (m)	Area (ha)	Min Pop	Avg Pop	Max Pop	Strs	Pz	% Terr
TLA-TLA-CAL-1		2,179	3.7	37	65	93	2		
TLA-TLA-CAL-2		2,180	9	90	158	225	2		
TLA-TLA-CAL-4		2,230	0.2	5	8	10	6		
TLA-TLA-CAL-6		2,239	10	252	393	535		1	38
TLA-TLA-CAL-7		2,231	3.4	34	60	85			
TLA-TLA-SLC-1		2,280	0.1	5	8	10			
TLA-TLA-SLC-3		2,344	0.9	5	8	10			
TLA-TLA-SLC-3		2,280	0.9	5	8	10			
TLA-TLA-SLC-4		2,233	3.6	36	62	89			
TLA-TLA-SLC-5		2,169	0.4	5	8	10			
TLA-TLA-SLC-6		2,177	5.8	291	436	581	1		100
TLA-TLA-TLA-1	Cerro Encantado	2,210	0.6	30	45	60			100
TLA-TLA-TLA-25		2,146	2.3	112	169	225	1		100
TLA-TLA-TLA-26		2,367	30.9	309	540	772	2	1	
TLA-TLA-TLA-27		2,120	1.5	15	27	38			
TLA-TLA-TLA-28	Cerro El Tambor	2,591	3	30	53	75	2		
TLA-TLA-TLA-29		2,196	6.1	61	106	152	4	1	
TLA-TLA-TLA-31		2,136	0.2	5	8	10	1		
TLA-TLA-TLA-32		2,162	1	50	75	100	3	1	100
TLA-TLA-TLA-36	El Vergel	2,121	12.6	629	943	1,257	20	2	100
TLA-TLA-TLA-42	Cerro de la Virgen	2,241	65.1	3,255	4,883	6,511	5	1	100
TLA-TLA-TLA-43		2,160	11.1	111	195	278			
TLA-TLA-TLA-44		2,275	9	450	675	900	2	1	100
TLA-TLA-TLA-48		2,100	10.7	107	186	266	4	2	

Table 6.5. Late Cruz and Ramos Sites in Northeast Tlaxiaco.

Site	Toponym	Elev (m)	Area (ha)	Min Pop	Avg Pop	Max Pop	Strs	Pz	% Terr
TLA-TLA-TLA-6		2,113	2	20	35	50			
TLA-TLA-TLA-15		2,416	0.5	5	8	10	5		
TLA-TLA-TLA-17LC		2,338	1.5	15	27	38			

Table 6.6. Las Flores Sites in Northeast Tlaxiaco.

Site	Toponym	Elev (m)	Area (ha)	Min Pop	Avg Pop	Max Pop	Strs	Pz	% Terr
TLA-TLA-TLA-2		2,280	1	10	18	25			
TLA-TLA-TLA-7		2,160	0.1	5	8	10			
TLA-TLA-TLA-9		2,280	0.5	5	9	13			
TLA-TLA-TLA-11		2,260	0.3	5	8	10	2		
TLA-TLA-TLA-14		2,202	0.6	10	15	20			
TLA-TLA-TLA-23		2,271	4.4	89	141	194	1		
TLA-TLA-TLA-45		2,243	1	50	75	100	1		100
TLA-TLA-TLA-46		2,343	1	50	75	100	1		100
TLA-TLA-TLA-47		2,404	8.4	419	628	838	2	1	100
TLA-TLA-TLA-49		2,437	0.1	5	8	10			

Table 6.7. Natividad Sites in Northeast Tlaxiaco.

Site	Toponym	Elev (m)	Area (ha)	Min Pop	Avg Pop	Max Pop	Strs	Pz	% Terr
TLA-TLA-TLA-3	La Purisima	2,260	6	60	104	149			
TLA-TLA-TLA-4	La Purisima	2,300	11	110	193	275	4	1	
TLA-TLA-TLA-7		2,160	0.1	5	8	10			
TLA-TLA-TLA-8		2,126	0.1	5	8	10			
TLA-TLA-TLA-9		2,272	0.5	5	9	13			
TLA-TLA-TLA-10		2,329	0.1	5	8	10			

Site	Elev (m)	Area (ha)	Min Pop	Avg Pop	Max Pop	Strs	Pz	% Terr
TLA-TLA-TLA-11	2,245	0.3	5	8	10			
TLA-TLA-TLA-12	2,262	0.1	5	8	10			
TLA-TLA-TLA-13	2,215	1.5	15	27	38			
TLA-TLA-TLA-14	2,213	0.1	5	8	10			
TLA-TLA-TLA-18	2,318	1	10	18	25			
TLA-TLA-TLA-19	2,380	3.2	32	55	79			
TLA-TLA-TLA-20	2,482	1.8	18	31	44			
TLA-TLA-TLA-21	2,312	9	90	158	225			
TLA-TLA-TLA-47	2,403	8.3	415	623	831	2		100
TLA-TLA-TLA-50	2,373	6.6	66	116	165			

Table 6.8. Late Cruz Sites in Southeast Tlaxiaco.

Site	Toponym	Elev (m)	Area (ha)	Min Pop	Avg Pop	Max Pop	Strs	Pz	% Terr
TLA-TLA-ODA-5		2,203	0.5	5	8	10	1		
TLA-TLA-ODA-10		2,388	0.3	5	8	10		2	

Table 6.9. Ramos Sites in Southeast Tlaxiaco.

Site	Toponym	Elev (m)	Area (ha)	Min Pop	Avg Pop	Max Pop	Strs	Pz	% Terr
TLA-TLA-LLG-3		2,576	9.1	112	190	267	4		
TLA-TLA-LLG-4		2,400	3.3	33	58	83			
TLA-TLA-ODA-10		2,360	15.9	794	1,192	1,589	6		100
TLA-TLA-ODA-11		2,400	0.1	5	8	10			

Table 6.10. Las Flores and Natividad Sites in Southeast Tlaxiaco.

Site	Toponym	Elev (m)	Area (ha)	Min Pop	Avg Pop	Max Pop	Strs	Pz	% Terr
TLA-TLA-ODA-1LF		2,280	6.1	306	459	612	1	1	100
TLA-TLA-LLG-1		2,579	1.8	18	32	45	1		
TLA-TLA-LLG-2		2,444	8	400	600	800	1	1	100
TLA-TLA-LLG-4		2,388	3.9	39	68	97			
TLA-TLA-ODA-1		2,275	6.1	306	459	612	1	1	100
TLA-TLA-ODA-2		2,262	1.5	15	27	38			
TLA-TLA-ODA-3		2,240	7	70	122	174			
TLA-TLA-ODA-4		2,442	6.6	93	154	215	2	2	
TLA-TLA-ODA-10		2,402	41.1	411	720	1,028	6		
TLA-TLA-ODA-11		2,381	6.1	304	456	608	1	1	100
TLA-TLA-ODA-12		2,393	4.9	49	85	121	1		
TLA-TLA-ODA-13		2,361	2.7	27	47	67			

Table 6.11. Late Cruz Sites in Nundichi/Ñumi.

Site	Toponym	Elev (m)	Area (ha)	Min Pop	Avg Pop	Max Pop	Strs	Pz	% Terr
TLA-SJN-ERN-7		2,202	1.3	13	22	32			
TLA-NUN-NUN-2		2,101	0.1	5	8	10			
TLA-NUN-NUN-3		2,064	0.6	6	10	14			
TLA-SJN-SPN-32		2,151	4	40	70	100	3	1	

Table 6.12. Ramos Sites in Nundichi/Ñumi.

Site	Toponym	Elev (m)	Area (ha)	Min Pop	Avg Pop	Max Pop	Strs	Pz	% Terr
TLA-NUN-HID-2		2,120	0.1	5	8	10			
TLA-SJN-SPN-36		2,120	0.3	5	8	10			

Table 6.13. Las Flores Sites in Nundichi/Ñumi.

Site	Toponym	Elev (m)	Area (ha)	Min Pop	Avg Pop	Max Pop	Strs	Pz	% Terr
TLA-SJN-ERN-1		2,177	15.8	158	277	395			
TLA-SJN-ERN-2		2,500	2.4	24	43	61			
TLA-SJN-ERN-3		2,220	1.9	19	33	47			
TLA-SJN-SPN-32		2,151	4	40	70	100	3	1	
TLA-SJN-SPN-34		2,162	13.3	267	425	584	5	1	

Table 6.14. Natividad Sites in Nundichi/Ñumi.

Site	Toponym	Elev (m)	Area (ha)	Min Pop	Avg Pop	Max Pop	Strs	Pz	% Terr
TLA-NUN-CTB-1		2,163	4.2	42	74	106			
TLA-NUN-CTB-2		2,149	5.5	55	96	137	2		
TLA-SJN-ERN-1		2,185	4.1	41	72	103			
TLA-SJN-ERN-3		2,253	1.9	19	33	47			
TLA-SJN-ERN-5		2,183	0.1	5	8	10			
TLA-SJN-ERN-7		2,182	5.7	57	100	143			
TLA-NUN-HID-1	Cerro Yucutisuchi	2,270	4.5	45	79	113			
TLA-NUN-HID-2		2,125	0.1	5	8	10			
TLA-SJN-MNN-1		2,228	0.1	5	8	10			
TLA-NUN-NUN-3		2,064	0.6	6	10	14			
TLA-NUN-NUN-4		2,231	0.1	5	8	10			
TLA-NUN-NUN-23		2,022	2.3	23	39	56	1	1	
TLA-SJN-SPN-2		2,264	2.2	22	39	55			
TLA-SJN-SPN-30		2,163	37.3	373	653	933			
TLA-SJN-SPN-32		2,148	10.8	108	189	270			
TLA-SJN-SPN-34		2,162	0.5	5	10	14			
TLA-SJN-SPN-36		2,124	0.3	5	8	10			
TLA-SJN-SPN-38		2,120	6.3	63	110	157			

Table 7.1. Early/Middle Cruz Sites in the Central Mixteca Alta.

Subregion	Min Pop	Max Pop	Avg Pop	Occupied Area (ha)	Component Count
Amoltepec	5	10	8	0	1
Dzinicahua	20	48	34	2	2
Huamelulpan	5	10	8	1	1
Jazmín	905	2,257	1,581	90	8
Magdalena Peñasco	73	177	125	7	4
Nduayaco	35	89	62	4	2
Nejapilla	19	47	33	2	1
Tayata	273	668	471	27	7
Teposcolula	311	734	523	37	9
Tilantongo	649	1,619	1,134	65	5
Tlacotepec	80	192	136	7	5
Yodobada	80	197	138	8	2
Yodocono	83	204	144	8	3
Yucunama	10	25	18	1	1
Totals	2,548	6,277	4,412	257	51

Table 7.2. Components and Component Area by Surface Geology.

Geol Unit	Description	Project Area (%)	Early/Middle Cruz Rel Freq (%)	Comp Area (%)	Late Cruz Rel Freq (%)	Comp Area (%)	Ramos Rel Freq (%)	Comp Area (%)	Las Flores Rel Freq (%)	Comp Area (%)	Natividad Rel Freq (%)	Comp Area (%)
Q(al)	Quarternary alluvium	3.0	0.0	2.0	2.3	2.5	0.0	0.0	0.6	1.0	0.7	2.1
Q(re)	Quaternary residual	0.2	0.0	0.0	0.0	0.0	0.0	0.0	0.0	0.0	0.0	0.0
Ts(ar-ti)	Upper Tertiary sandstone/tuff	5.0	0.0	0.0	2.3	0.4	2.6	1.5	1.7	0.3	2.0	1.3
Tom(Ta)	Oligocene/Miocene acidic tuff	0.1	0.0	0.0	0.0	0.0	0.0	0.0	0.3	1.1	0.0	0.1
Tom(A)	Oligocene/Miocene andesite	22.5	15.7	8.0	16.8	14.0	29.9	40.4	26.7	31.5	24.4	18.7
Tom(Ti)	Oligocene/Miocene intermediate tuff	4.8	0.0	0.0	0.9	0.2	2.6	0.4	2.3	2.9	2.2	0.7
Ti(cg)	Lower Tertiary conglomerate	1.9	0.0	0.0	1.4	0.6	1.3	0.1	2.9	2.7	1.7	0.9
Ti(cz)	Lower Tertiary limestone	2.9	0.0	0.5	1.4	1.2	2.6	3.3	3.5	2.6	3.9	3.1
Ti(ar)	Lower Tertiary sandstone	1.4	0.0	0.1	0.9	0.8	2.6	1.9	2.0	1.1	2.2	0.5
Ti(ar-cg)	Lower Tertiary sandstone/conglomerate	15.6	33.3	33.1	28.2	39.4	15.6	11.7	17.7	22.1	23.9	31.4
Ti(lm-ar)	Lower Tertiary siltstone/sandstone	12.5	45.1	54.6	34.1	32.7	16.2	11.3	19.5	15.0	20.2	24.4
Ki(cz)	Lower Cretaceous limestone	26.9	5.9	1.6	9.5	7.4	22.7	27.1	19.8	17.4	16.9	12.3
Ki(cz-lu)	Lower Cretaceous limestone/shale	1.8	0.0	0.0	1.8	0.8	3.2	2.2	2.6	1.1	1.3	3.9
Js(cz)	Upper Jurassic limestone	0.8	0.0	0.0	0.5	0.0	0.6	0.1	0.3	1.2	0.5	0.7
Js(cz-lu)	Upper Jurassic limestone/shale	0.0	0.0	0.0	0.0	0.0	0.0	0.0	0.0	0.0	0.0	0.0
Ji(lu-ar)	Lower Jurassic shale/sandstone	0.6	0.0	0.0	0.0	0.0	0.0	0.0	0.0	0.0	0.1	0.1
P(E)	Paleozoic schist	0.0	0.0	0.0	0.0	0.0	0.0	0.0	0.0	0.0	0.0	0.0
		100.0	100.0	100.0	100.0	100.0	100.0	100.0	100.0	100.0	100.0	100.0

485

Table 7.3. Late Cruz Sites in the Central Mixteca Alta.

Subregion	Min Pop	Max Pop	Avg Pop	Occupied Area (ha)	Component Count
Achiutla	144	349	246	13	8
Amoltepec	35	82	59	4	3
Dzinicahua	2,697	6,569	4,633	242	13
Huamelulpan	726	1,519	1,123	45	14
Jazmín	612	1,530	1,071	61	8
Lagunas	41	100	71	4	2
Magdalena Peñasco	146	350	248	13	10
Nduayaco	65	149	107	7	7
Nejapilla	122	305	213	12	5
Northeast Tlaxiaco	15	38	27	2	1
Nundichi	63	156	110	6	4
Nuñu	226	557	391	22	4
San Juan Achiutla	149	374	262	15	2
Southeast Tlaxiaco	10	20	15	1	2
Tayata	2,652	5,742	4,197	215	29
Teposcolula	1,580	3,781	2,681	186	30
Tidaá	140	348	244	14	2
Tilantongo	1,732	4,293	3,012	168	16
Tlacotepec	193	468	331	18	12
Tlaxiaco	15	35	25	1	2
Yodobada	559	1,397	978	56	6
Yodocono	145	362	253	14	3
Yolomecatl	370	925	648	37	7
Yucuañe	61	152	106	6	3
Yucunama	313	775	544	30	9
Yucuxaco	187	444	316	17	9
Totals	12,998	30,820	21,909	1,207	211

Table 7.4. Lama-Bordos Directly Adjacent to Settlements.

Period	Total L-B	Single Period Association	E/M Cruz	L Cruz	Ramos	Las Flores	Natividad
E/M Cruz	7	0	—	4	0	2	6
Late Cruz	30	8	4	—	4	1	22
Ramos	35	15	0	1	—	15	12
Las Flores	61	17	2	4	15	—	36
Natividad	151	90	6	22	12	36	—

Table 7.5. Scale of Mixteca Alta and Valley of Oaxaca Polities.

Late Cruz/Early I

Mixteca Alta			*Valley of Oaxaca*		
Unit	Length (km)	Avg Pop Est	Unit	Length (km)	Avg Pop Est
Teposcolula super-cluster	19	4,000	Etla	24	4,000
Tayata super-cluster	23	6,000	Monte Albán & Central	18	7,000
Dzinicahua super-cluster	18	5,000	Tlacolula	38	2,000
Total CMASPP area	1,622 km²	22,000	Valle Grande & Ocotlán	36	2,000
			Etla, M.A., & Central	34	11,000
			Total Valley of Oaxaca	2,150 km²	15,000

Early Ramos/Late I

Mixteca Alta			*Valley of Oaxaca*		
Unit	Length (km)	Avg Pop Est	Unit	Length (km)	Avg Pop Est
Greater Teposcolula	22	15,000	Etla	24	12,000
Greater Huamelulpan	14	6,000	Monte Albán & Central	18	23,000
Jazmín	?	6,000	Tlacolula	38	6,000
Tilantongo	?	4,000	Valle Grande & Ocotlán	36	9,000
Total CMASPP area	1,622 km²	48,000	Etla, M.A., & Central	34	35,000
			Total Valley of Oaxaca	2,150 km²	50,000

Late Ramos/II

Mixteca Alta			*Valley of Oaxaca*		
Unit	Length (km)	Avg Pop Est	Unit	Length (km)	Avg Pop Est
Greater Huamelulpan		20,000	Etla	24	11,000
Total CMASPP area	1,622 km²	25,000	Monte Albán & Central	18	15,000
			Tlacolula	38	8,000
			Valle Grande & Ocotlán	36	7,000
			Etla, M.A., & Central	34	26,000
			Total Valley of Oaxaca	2,150 km²	41,000

Table 8.1. Ramos Sites in the Central Mixteca Alta.

Subregion	Min Pop	Max Pop	Avg Pop	Occupied Area (ha)	Component Count
Achiutla	1,788	3,720	2,754	59	12
Amoltepec	763	1,697	1,230	43	7
Dzinicahua	375	800	588	16	1
Huamelulpan	11,108	22,449	16,778	270	25
Jazmín	4,003	8,013	6,008	81	3
Lagunas	797	1,675	1,236	39	6
Magdalena Peñasco	447	920	684	13	4
Nduayaco	871	1,812	1,341	42	10
Nejapilla	1,085	2,170	1,627	22	3
Northeast Tlaxiaco	25	60	43	2	2
Nundichi	10	20	15	0	2
Nuñu	1,022	2,166	1,594	41	5
San Juan Achiutla	449	957	703	18	3
Southeast Tlaxiaco	945	1,949	1,447	28	4
Tayata	769	1,612	1,190	28	7
Teposcolula	5,628	11,380	8,504	179	16
Tidaá	1,008	2,015	1,511	20	2
Tilantongo	2,083	6,174	4,128	91	7
Tlacotepec	2,371	4,758	3,564	51	10
Tlaxiaco	238	475	356	5	2
Yodobada	283	574	429	7	2
Yodocono	1,241	2,540	1,891	34	1
Yolomecatl	1,253	2,652	1,953	48	5
Yucuañe	619	1,237	928	13	3
Yucunama	665	1,482	1,074	38	5
Yucuxaco	1,670	3,388	2,529	46	7
Totals	41,515	86,694	64,104	1,234	154

Table 9.1. Las Flores Sites in the Central Mixteca Alta.

Subregion	Min Pop	Max Pop	Avg Pop	Occupied Area (ha)	Component Count
Achiutla	940	2,071	1,506	49	9
Amoltepec	1,076	2,434	1,755	67	10
Dzinicahua	545	1,223	884	33	3
Huamelulpan	3,511	8,302	5,906	114	23
Jazmín	12,927	26,589	19,758	376	14
Lagunas	1,381	3,076	2,229	87	9
Magdalena Peñasco	1,986	4,671	3,328	152	14
Nduayaco	1,080	2,336	1,708	51	17
Nejapilla	3,734	7,814	5,774	130	10
Northeast Tlaxiaco	648	1,320	984	17	10
Nundichi	508	1,187	847	37	5
Nuñu	3,931	8,153	6,042	125	12
San Juan Achiutla	245	607	426	24	8
Southeast Tlaxiaco	306	612	459	6	1
Tayata	2,403	4,994	3,698	69	9
Teposcolula	11,590	23,995	17,793	548	51
Tidaá	1,387	2,962	2,174	58	8
Tilantongo	6,627	15,535	11,081	498	22
Tlacotepec	1,489	3,172	2,331	61	11
Tlaxiaco	7,707	15,786	11,746	214	19
Yodobada	1,613	3,605	2,609	94	9
Yodocono	2,153	4,687	3,420	104	11
Yolomecatl	3,207	7,003	5,105	158	17
Yucuañe	3,947	8,349	6,148	152	16
Yucunama	2,467	5,093	3,780	75	16
Yucuxaco	952	2,037	1,495	40	7
Totals	78,360	167,613	122,986	3,343	341

Table 10.1. Natividad Sites in the Central Mixteca Alta.

Subregion	Min Pop	Max Pop	Avg Pop	Occupied Area (ha)	Component Count
Achiutla	7,172	16,864	12,018	796	29
Amoltepec	2,835	7,085	4,960	282	18
Dzinicahua	2,827	6,624	4,725	201	20
Huamelulpan	8,710	17,778	13,244	278	29
Jazmín	26,522	56,783	41,652	1,128	39
Lagunas	4,727	11,408	8,068	407	34
Magdalena Peñasco	6,727	14,804	10,766	353	38
Nduayaco	2,481	5,830	4,156	193	61
Nejapilla	5,420	13,144	9,282	477	23
Northeast Tlaxiaco	850	1,904	1,377	49	16
Nundichi	884	2,198	1,541	86	18
Nuñu	1,709	4,022	2,866	147	31
San Juan Achiutla	659	1,641	1,150	66	18
Southeast Tlaxiaco	1,731	3,805	2,768	90	11
Tayata	8,029	16,642	12,335	331	39
Teposcolula	21,117	50,884	36,001	2,457	121
Tidaá	984	2,454	1,719	98	16
Tilantongo	10,906	26,153	18,530	931	42
Tlacotepec	4,249	10,271	7,260	410	30
Tlaxiaco	5,928	12,302	9,115	192	24
Yodobada	2,708	6,747	4,728	271	25
Yodocono	1,102	2,748	1,925	109	21
Yolomecatl	4,373	10,767	7,570	427	40
Yucuañe	5,406	11,331	8,369	193	17
Yucunama	1,195	2,747	1,971	148	56
Yucuxaco	4,748	10,145	7,447	209	29
Totals	144,000	327,081	235,541	10,329	845

Table 10.2. Most Fertile Soils, Population, and Urbanization.

Subregion	Area (km²)	Yanhuitlán & Jaltepec Soils (km²)	Early/Middle Cruz Pop	Late Cruz Pop	Late Cruz Pop in Sites >1,000	Ramos Pop	Ramos Pop in Sites >1,000	Las Flores Pop	Las Flores Pop in Sites >1,000	Natividad Pop	Natividad Pop in Sites >1,000
Tilantongo	76.3	40.3	1,134	3,012	53%	4,128	94%	14,481	49%	18,530	66%
Jazmín	70.6	38.1	1,581	1,071	0%	6,008	99%	36,938	93%	41,652	84%
Amoltepec	53.7	36.9	8	59	0%	1,230	86%	1,755	0%	4,960	84%
Tayata	93.9	36.5	471	4,197	47%	1,535	0%	3,698	34%	12,335	79%
Yucuxaco	55.3	31.3	0	316	0%	2,529	57%	1,495	0%	7,447	57%
Magdalena Peñasco	52.1	29.9	125	248	0%	684	0%	3,328	35%	10,766	66%
Teposcolula	156.3	28.0	523	2,681	0%	8,504	80%	17,793	73%	36,001	74%
Nejapilla	36.1	27.0	33	213	0%	1,627	0%	10,615	75%	9,282	68%
Tlacotepec	56.9	23.3	136	331	0%	4,939	98%	2,331	0%	7,260	57%
Yucuañe	115.2	18.6	0	106	0%	928	0%	6,429	64%	8,369	72%
Achiutla	86.9	17.8	0	246	0%	2,875	0%	1,506	0%	13,884	63%
Dzinicahua	31.2	15.5	34	4,633	28%	0	0%	6,915	96%	2,908	53%
Huamelulpan	36.1	14.9	8	1,123	0%	16,778	95%	5,906	68%	13,244	76%
Tidaá	41.7	13.8	0	244	0%	1,511	100%	2,174	69%	1,719	0%
Yodobada	37.7	13.4	138	978	0%	429	0%	2,834	47%	4,728	0%
Yodocono	31.2	11.7	144	253	0%	1,891	100%	3,739	51%	1,925	0%
Nduayaco	84.4	11.5	62	107	0%	1,341	0%	1,708	0%	4,156	0%
Nuñu	70.3	11.1	0	391	0%	1,594	0%	6,042	78%	2,866	0%
Yucunama	35.4	10.0	18	544	0%	1,074	0%	3,780	59%	1,971	0%
Lagunas	58.4	10.0	0	71	0%	1,930	0%	3,603	76%	8,068	40%
Yolomecatl	67.7	6.8	0	648	0%	1,953	60%	5,105	41%	7,570	28%
Nundichi	40.9	5.4	0	110	0%	15	0%	1,273	0%	1,541	0%
San Juan Achiutla	45.5	2.2	0	262	0%	703	0%	426	0%	1,150	0%
Southeast Tlaxiaco	34.5	1.7	0	15	0%	1,447	82%	459	0%	2,768	0%
Tlaxiaco	96.9	0.0	0	25	0%	713	0%	11,746	66%	9,509	51%
Northeast Tlaxiaco	56.3	0.0	0	27	0%	43	0%	984	0%	1,377	0%

492

Table A1.1. Descriptions, Proveniences, and Measurements of Photographed Sherds.

Early/Middle Cruz Ware/Type	Fig	No	Description	Ht (cm)	Site/Coll
Joselito Red-on-Tan	2.1	1	Jar (ext.)	5.1	YPD 14A
Joselito Red-on-Tan	2.1	2	Jar	6.7	YPD 14A
Joselito Red-on-Tan	2.1	3	Jar (ext.)	5.7	YPD 14A
Joselito Red-on-Tan	2.1	4	Jar	4.3	SDT 1A
Joselito Red-on-Tan	2.1	5	Jar, red paint	3.0	YPD 14A
Joselito Red-on-Tan	2.1	6	Jar	3.3	SDT 1A
Joselito Red-on-Tan	2.1	7	Jar, red paint	2.9	YPD 14A
Joselito Red-on-Tan	2.1	8	Tecomate (int.)	3.4	YPD 14A
Joselito Red-on-Tan	2.1	9	Bowl (ext.)	4.5	TIP 12A
Joselito Red-on-Tan	2.1	10	Bowl, red paint	4.8	YPD 14A
Joselito Red-on-Tan	2.1	11	Bowl (ext.)	5.8	TIP 12A
Joselito Red-on-Tan	2.1	12	Flaring bowl (int.)	10.2	XAC 7A
Joselito Red-on-Tan	2.1	13	Hemispherical bowl	7.9	SDT 1A
Joselito Red-on-Tan	2.1	14	Bowl (ext.)	3.8	TIP 12A
Other	2.1	15	Tan jar, rocker stamping	3.8	XAC 4A
Jazmín Red and White	2.1	16	Outleaned bowl (int.)	6.0	SJD 7A
Jazmín Red and White	2.2	1	Carlitos Two-Tone bowl (int.)	2.2	SAT 1A
Jazmín Red and White	2.2	2	Carlitos Two-Tone bowl, incised (int.)	6.1	YPD 14A
Jazmín Red and White	2.2	3	Carlitos Two-Tone bowl, incised (int.)	5.9	YPD 14A
Jazmín Red and White	2.2	4	Carlitos Two-Tone bowl (ext.)	5.2	YPD 14A
Jazmín Red and White	2.2	5	Carlitos Two-Tone outleaned bowl (int.)	9.0	XAC 4C
Jazmín Red and White	2.2	6	Carlitos Two-Tone bowl, incised (int.)	3.5	TIP 12A
Jazmín Red and White	2.2	7	Reyes White bottle (int.)	9.1	XAC 7A
Jazmín Red and White	2.2	8	Reyes white bowl, incised (int.)	4.9	XAC 6B
Jazmín Red and White	2.2	9	Reyes white bowl, incised (int.)	3.8	XAC 6B
Nochixtlán Graywares	2.2	10	Everted-rim bowl, incised (int.)	3.7	SCA 5A
Nochixtlán Graywares	2.2	11	Cylinder base, excised	3.7	TIC 9C
Nochixtlán Graywares	2.2	12	White-rimmed black bowl (int.)	6.2	SMP 6A
Nochixtlán Graywares	2.2	13	Cylinder, incised	5.0	XAC 4B

Nochixtlán Graywares	2.2	14	Everted eccentric rim bowl (int.)	7.6	XAC 4C
Nochixtlán Graywares	2.2	15	Everted-rim bowl (int.)	5.3	XAC 4A
Nochixtlán Graywares	2.2	16	Everted-rim bowl (ext.)	3.8	TIP 12A
Nochixtlán Graywares	2.2	17	Everted-rim bowl, incised (int.)	3.4	XAC 6B

Late Cruz Ware/Type	Fig	No	Description	Ht (cm)	Site/Coll
Yucuita Tan	2.3	1	Everted-rim bowl, incised	3.9	SAT 2A
Yucuita Tan	2.3	2	Comal (int.)	3.7	SAT 39B
Yucuita Tan	2.3	3	Comal (ext.)	4.8	SAT 2A
Yucuita Tan	2.3	4	Jar, red paint (ext.)	6.0	TIL 7E
Filemón Red-on-Tan	2.3	5	Bowl, red paint (ext.)	5.7	SDT 2A
Filemón Red-on-Tan	2.3	6	Tecomate, red paint (int.)	5.6	NEJ 5A
Filemón Red-on-Tan	2.3	7	Bowl, eccentric rim	5.2	XAC 7A
Filemón Red-on-Tan	2.3	8	Jar, red paint (ext.)	5.7	SDT 2A
Filemón Red-on-Tan	2.3	9	Bottle	3.6	SMP 10A
Filemón Red-on-Tan	2.3	10	Jar, red paint (ext.)	4.7	YBA 1B
Filemón Red-on-Tan	2.3	11	Jar, red paint (ext.)	4.9	YBA 1B
Filemón Red-on-Tan	2.3	12	Jar, red paint, zoned cross-hatch incising	3.2	TIL 7I
Filemón Red-on-Tan	2.3	13	Comal, red paint	7.0	SAT 6A
Filemón Red-on-Tan	2.3	14	Jar, red paint	12.7	SMP 10A
Filemón Red-on-Tan	2.3	15	Jar, red paint (ext.)	7.8	TIL 7E
Yucuita Polished Brown	2.7	1	Bowl, everted rim, incising	9.5	ZAR 2A
Yucuita Polished Brown	2.7	2	Bowl, everted rim, incising	5.2	SAT 2A
Yucuita Polished Brown	2.7	3	Bowl, everted rim, incised (int.)	4.2	SJD 7A
Yucuita Polished Brown	2.7	4	Bowl, everted rim, eroded (ext. of previous)	4.2	SJD 7A
Yucuita Polished Brown	2.7	5	Bowl, everted rim, incising	4.1	SVN 4A
Yucuita Polished Brown	2.7	6	Bowl, everted rim, incised (int.)	5.2	SJD 7A
Yucuita Polished Brown	2.7	7	Bowl, everted rim, eroded (ext. of previous)	5.2	SJD 7A
Yucuita Polished Brown	2.7	8	Bowl, everted rim, incising, eroded	4.6	SVN 17A
Yucuita Polished Brown	2.7	9	Bowl, everted rim, incising	5.7	XAC 7A

continued on next page

Table A1.1—continued

Late Cruz Ware/Type	Fig	No	Description	Ht (cm)	Site/Coll
Yucuita Polished Brown	2.7	10	Bowl, everted rim, incising	3.3	SVN 4A
Nochixtlán Graywares	2.7	11	Everted-rim bowl, incised (int.)	4.0	SAT 2A
Nochixtlán Graywares	2.7	12	Everted-rim bowl, incised	2.6	SMP 7A
Nochixtlán Graywares	2.7	13	Bowl, everted rim, burnished (ext.)	4.4	YBA 1B
Nochixtlán Graywares	2.7	14	Bowl, thickened rim (ext.)	4.2	YBA 1F
Nochixtlán Graywares	2.7	15	Bowl, incised (int.)	3.1	YBA 1F
Nochixtlán Graywares	2.7	16	Outleaned-wall bowl, incised pennant motif	4.6	XAC 7A

Ramos Ware/Type	Fig	No	Description	Ht (cm)	Site/Coll
Filemón Red-on-Tan Bowls	2.12	1	Bowl, black and red paint, incising	2.6	SJG 11C
Filemón Red-on-Tan Bowls	2.12	2	Bowl, everted rim, red paint, incising	2.5	SJG 11C
Filemón Red-on-Tan Bowls	2.12	3	Flaring bowl, red paint, incised lines	3.0	YOL 4B
Filemón Red-on-Tan Bowls	2.12	4	Flaring bowl, brown slip, red paint, incised lines	2.9	YOL 4B
Filemón Red-on-Tan Bowls	2.12	5	Flaring bowl, streaky red paint, post-firing scratching	6.7	TLA 15A
Filemón Red-on-Tan Bowls	2.12	6	Ext. of previous, Late Ramos	6.7	TLA 15A
Filemón Red-on-Tan Bowls	2.12	7	Flaring bowl (int.)	3.8	SMP 14A
Filemón Red-on-Tan Bowls	2.12	8	Bowl, red paint (int.)	3.1	TOP 1A
Filemón Red-on-Tan Comal	2.12	9	Comal	4.7	SJG 11C
Filemón Red-on-Tan Comal	2.12	10	Comal, red paint	4.5	SAT 9F
Filemón Red-on-Tan Jars	2.12	11	Jar neck, red paint	7.0	TIL 1A
Filemón Red-on-Tan Jars	2.12	12	Jar neck, red paint (ext.)	3.4	SAT 9F
Filemón Red-on-Tan Jars	2.12	13	Jar neck, red paint (ext.)	3.7	SAT 9F
Filemón Red-on-Tan Jars	2.12	14	Jar neck, red paint	4.2	TIL 1B
Filemón Red-on-Tan Jars	2.12	15	Jar neck, red paint	6.1	TIL 1B
Filemón Red-on-Tan Jars	2.12	16	Jar neck, red paint (ext.)	3.9	TIL 1A
Filemón Red-on-Tan Jars	2.12	17	Jar neck, black and red paint, incising	4.0	SAT 9F
Filemón Red-on-Tan Jars	2.13	1	Jar body, black, black and red paint, incising	5.8	SAT 9F
Filemón Red-on-Tan Jars	2.13	2	Jar body, black and red paint	4.2	TIL 1A
Filemón Red-on-Tan Jars	2.13	3	Everted rim bowl, broad incising	4.8	TIP 1A
Nochixtlán Graywares	2.13				

Ware/Type	Fig	No	Description	Ht (cm)	Site/Coll
Nochixtlán Graywares	2.13	4	G-12 bowl rim	5.7	SAT 9F
Nochixtlán Graywares	2.13	5	G-12 bowl rim	4.9	SAT 9F
Nochixtlán Graywares	2.13	6	G-12 bowl rim	9.7	SJG 11C
Nochixtlán Graywares	2.13	7	G-12 bowl rim	2.7	SAT 9F
Nochixtlán Graywares	2.13	8	Fine-combed bowl base	6.1	SJG 11C
Nochixtlán Graywares	2.13	9	Fine-combed bowl base	4.7	SAT 9F
Nochixtlán Graywares	2.13	10	Fine-combed bowl base	7.0	TIL 1A
Nochixtlán Graywares	2.13	11	Fine-combed bowl base	4.2	TIP 1A
Yucuita Tan Bowls	2.13	12	Combed bowl base	6.8	TIL 1B
Yucuita Tan Bowls	2.13	13	Fine-combed bowl base	5.2	TIL 1A
Yucuita Tan Bowls	2.13	14	Fine-combed bowl base	4.7	TIP 1A

Las Flores Ware/Type	*Fig*	*No*	*Description*	*Ht (cm)*	*Site/Coll*
Yucuita Tan Bowls	2.14	1	Outleaned-wall bowl, burnished (ext.)	6.2	YOL 20A
Yucuita Tan Bowls	2.14	2	Outleaned-wall bowl, red slip (int.)	7.0	YBA 1E
Yucuita Tan Jars	2.14	3	Jar neck, flaring rim (ext.)	3.7	YPD 15B
Yucuita Tan Jars	2.14	4	Jar neck, flaring rim (ext.)	4.0	YPD 15B
Yucuita Tan Jars	2.14	5	Jar neck, flaring rim (ext.)	4.1	YPD 15B
Yucuita Tan Jars	2.14	6	Flaring-rim jar neck (ext.)	5.2	YOL 24A
Yucuita Tan Jars	2.14	7	Jar neck, flaring rim (int.)	5.5	NEJ 1A
Yucuita Tan Jars	2.14	8	Jar neck, everted rim (int.)	5.7	NEJ 1A
Yucuita Tan Jars	2.14	9	Jar with vertical neck, flaring rim	5.5	SAT 11A
Yucuita Tan Jars	2.14	10	Everted-rim jar (int.)	6.7	SVN 10B
Yucuita Tan Jars	2.14	11	Jar with vertical neck, orange slip	6.2	YOL 4A
Anita Orange	2.15	1	Outleaned-wall bowl, orange slip (ext.)	9.0	SVN 13C
Anita Orange	2.15	2	Outleaned-wall bowl (int. of previous)	9.0	SVN 13C
Anita Orange	2.15	3	Flaring bowl, channel rim (int.)	4.4	SVN 10B
Anita Orange	2.15	4	Flaring bowl (int.)	5.2	TLO 3A
Anita Orange	2.15	5	Flaring bowl (int.)	5.0	TLO 3A
Anita Orange	2.15	6	Flaring bowl (int.)	4.9	SJD 7A

continued on next page

495

Table A1.1—continued

Las Flores Ware/Type	Fig	No	Description	Ht (cm)	Site/Coll
Anita Orange	2.15	7	Flaring bowl, channel rim (int.)	4.8	TIP 1A
Anita Orange	2.15	8	Flaring bowl (int.)	6.2	TIP 1A
Anita Orange	2.15	9	Flaring-rim jar, vertical neck w/ smoothing	6.0	SVN 10B
Anita Orange	2.15	10	Flaring-rim jar (ext.)	4.2	SVN 10B
Anita Orange	2.16	1	Ring base (bottom view)	6.2	SVN 13C
Anita Orange	2.16	2	Cántaro, vertical neck, smoothing	6.7	SJG 11F
Anita Orange	2.16	3	Cántaro, vertical neck, smoothing	5.1	SJG 11F
Nochixtlán Graywares	2.16	4	Outleaned-wall bow, G-35 style (ext.)	9.5	SVN 13C
Nochixtlán Graywares	2.16	5	Outleaned-wall bow, G-35 style (ext.)	5.6	YOL 20A
Nochixtlán Graywares	2.16	6	Cylindrical bowl	7.4	SVN 13D
Nochixtlán Graywares	2.16	7	Molcajete/chilmolero	3.9	TIP 1C
Nochixtlán Graywares	2.16	8	Outleaned-wall bowl, G-23 excising (ext.)	6.6	SJG 11C
Other	2.16	9	Fragment of box from urn, orange	4.0	SPT 4A

Natividad Ware/Type	Fig	No	Description	Ht (cm)	Site/Coll
Chachoapan Sandy Cream	2.19	1	Jar (ext.)	5.5	ATY 1C
Chachoapan Sandy Cream	2.19	2	Jar	10.0	TIP 1B
Chachoapan Sandy Cream	2.19	3	Ladle	3.7	ODA 1A
Yanhuitlán Fine Cream	2.19	4	Brazier	6.0	YOL 24A
Yanhuitlán Fine Cream	2.19	5	Brazier	5.5	SCA 2A
Yanhuitlán Fine Cream	2.19	6	Brazier cover support	5.5	TIP 1A
Yanhuitlán Fine Cream	2.19	7	Ollita	5.1	TIP 1X
Yanhuitlán Fine Cream	2.19	8	Comal	4.4	YBA 1B
Yanhuitlán Fine Cream	2.19	9	Comal	2.8	SMA 1A
Yanhuitlán Fine Cream	2.19	10	Differentially fired bowl	5.3	TIP 1A
Yanhuitlán Fine Cream	2.19	11	Composite silhouette bowl	3.8	TIP 1A
Yanhuitlán Red-on-Cream	2.19	12	Hemispherical bowl (ext.)	4.5	TIP 1B
Yanhuitlán Red-on-Cream	2.19	13	Hemispherical bowl (int. of previous)	4.5	TIP 1B
Yanhuitlán Red-on-Cream	2.19	14	Outleaned-wall bowl	3.4	YBA 1B

Ware		No.	Description	%	Code
Yanhuitlán Red-on-Cream	2.20	1	Hemispherical bowl (ext.)	5.9	TIP 1B
Yanhuitlán Red-on-Cream	2.20	2	Hemispherical bowl (int. of previous)	5.9	TIP 1B
Yanhuitlán Red-on-Cream	2.20	3	Composite silhouette bowl (int.)	8.5	ATY 5A
Yanhuitlán Red-on-Cream	2.20	4	Hemispherical bowl (int.)	3.2	TIC 15A
Yanhuitlán Red-on-Cream	2.20	5	Hemispherical bowl (ext.)	4.6	TLO 5A
Yanhuitlán Red-on-Cream	2.20	6	Bowl (int.)	2.3	YOL 13B
Nochixtlán Graywares	2.20	7	"Candy dish" (int.)	5.7	TIP 1B
Nochixtlán Graywares	2.20	9	Hemispherical bowl (int.)	5.8	TGO 2A
Nochixtlán Graywares	2.20	8	Flaring-rim bowl (ext.)	6.1	YPD 17B
Graphite-on-Orange	2.20	10	Bowl (ext.)	7.8	SMP 7A
Graphite-on-Orange	2.20	11	Bowl (int. of previous)	7.8	SMP 7A
Graphite-on-Orange	2.20	12	Flaring-wall bowl	6.5	TIL 26A
Graphite-on-Orange	2.20	13	Hemispherical bowl, red and gray-blue paint (int.)	5.3	SJA 1A
Polychrome	2.20	14	Bowl; red, white, orange, black paint; hollow support	7.1	TLO 5A
Other	2.20	15	Aztec Black-on-Orange style bowl (int.)	3.6	TLA 27A

Table A2.1: Descriptions, Proveniences, and Measurements of Illustrated Stone Tools.

Fig	No	Description	Site/Coll	Periods	Length (cm)
7.1	1	Amorphous core	SMH 1A		5.3
7.1	2	Prismatic core	TIL 7A		3.7
7.1	3	Biface that could not be thinned	YOL 13B		6.3
7.1	4	Point broken during manufacture	YOL 6B		6.5
7.1	5	Blade flake	YPD 3A		5.3
7.1	6	Blade flake	TLO 5A		5.8
7.1	7	Blade flake	TLA 40A		5.9
7.1	8	Drill	SJA 24A		4.1
7.1	9	Adze-shaped biface	GPE 9A		4.9
7.1	10	Biface thinning flake	GPE 9A		3.7
7.1	11	Biface thinning flake	SAT 38A		2.2
7.1	12	Unifacially retouched flake	YPD 15A		6.6
7.1	13	Unifacially retouched flake	SAT 28A		9.2
7.1	14	Flake	SMA 30A		3.0
7.1	15	Flake	TIL 3B		3.1
7.1	16	Flake	GPE 9A		3.5
7.1	17	Flake	GPE 1A		3.1
7.1	18	Flake	TIL 3A		3.8
7.2	1	Scraper fragment	TLA 24H		4.0
7.2	2	Scraper fragment	NDU 22A		2.7 (vertical)
7.2	3	Scraper fragment	TIL 3A		2.5 (vertical)
7.2	4	Steep-edged scraper, a reworked core	YPD 3A		3.5
7.2	5	Steep-edged scraper, reworked core or flake	TGO 1A		3.7 (vertical)
7.2	6	Steep-edged scraper	TGO 1		6.0
7.2	7	Steep-edged scraper	SAT 16A		4.4 (vertical)
7.2	8	Thumbnail scraper	TGO 1A		3.2
7.2	9	Unifacial scraper	TIL 3A		4.4
7.2	10	Unifacial scraper/adze	YOL 40		12.8
7.2	11	Steep-edged unifacial scraper	YOL 4A		7.9 (vertical)
7.2	12	Steep-edged scraper	ATY 1C		7.2 (vertical)
7.3	1	Side-notched point	LPE 2A	N	2.8
7.3	2	Side-notched point	HID 1A	N	3.8
7.3	3	Side-notched point	YOL 12A	N	2.6 (vertical)
7.3	4	Side-notched point	GPE 13A	N	4.3
7.3	5	Side-notched point	PMY 6A	Undated	3.6
7.3	6	Side-notched point	SJA 16A	Undated	3.8
7.3	7	Side-notched point	YOL 48A	Undated	2.1 (vertical)
7.3	8	Side-notched point	YOL 16A	LF, N	4.3
7.3	9	Side-notched point	BV 1C	LF, N	3.1
7.3	10	Side-notched point	TLA 26A	LF, N	2.5 (vertical)
7.3	11	Side-notched point	SMA 40A	R, N	3.7
7.3	12	Side-notched point	TIL 5C	C, LF, N	3.0
7.3	13	Side-notched point	CAL 2A	C, N	1.4 (vertical)
7.3	14	Side-notched point	TIL 40A	C, N	2.7 (vertical)
7.3	15	Side-notched point	XAC 6B	C, N	3.7

continued on next page

Table A2.1—*continued*

Fig	No	Description	Site/Coll	Periods	Length (cm)
7.3	16	Side-notched point	TIP 1A	R, LF, N	3.6
7.3	17	Square-based point	YOL 19A	N	3.0 (vertical)
7.3	18	Square-based point	YOL 46A	N	5.1
7.3	19	Square-based point	YOL 16A	LF, N	4.8
7.3	20	Square-based point	YOL 6B	C, LF, N	3.3
7.4	1	Broad, square-stemmed point	CAL 1A	N	2.4
7.4	2	Broad, square-stemmed point	MNN 1A	N	3.2
7.4	3	Corner-notched point	SDH 18A	N	2.4
7.4	4	Corner-notched point	SPN 34A	LF, N	3.4
7.4	5	Corner-notched point	SCA 19A	LF, N	5.8
7.4	6	Corner-notched point	TOP 1D	LF, N	5.2
7.4	7	Corner-notched point	YOL 18A	LF, N	4.5
7.4	8	Corner-notched point	SJD 2A	R, LF, N	3.5
7.4	9	Stemmed point	UVH 2A	R, N	4.1
7.4	10	Stemmed point	SDH 2A	R, N	5.3
7.4	11	Stemmed point	ATY 1G	R, N	3.5
7.4	12	Stemmed point	YPD 5D	C, LF, N	5.1
7.4	13	Stemmed point	SJD 2A	R, LF, N	5.1
7.4	14	Stemmed point	ERN 1A	LF	5.0
7.5	1	Point	GPE 9A	N	3.5
7.5	2	Point	SMA 6A	N	3.7
7.5	3	Point	YOL 10A	N	3.7
7.5	4	Point	SPN 34A	LF, N	3.3
7.5	5	Point	TOP 1D	LF, N	4.0
7.5	6	Point	SJD 2A	R, LF, N	2.9
7.5	7	Point	SJD 2A	R, LF, N	3.4
7.5	8	Point	TLA 40A	LF	3.7
7.5	9	Point	SAT 11A	LF	4.1
7.5	10	Point	SCA 14A	R, LF	5.8
7.5	11	Heavily resharpened point	PMY 6A	Undated	4.5
7.5	12	Point, cf. Pedernales or Shumla	NDU 23A	Undated	6.7
7.5	13	Point, cf. Trinidad	NUN 1A	Undated	5.7
7.6	1	Basalt SJG 1A			5.5 (vertical)
7.6	2	Desfibrador de maguey	SDH 19A		9.3
7.6	3	Hammerstone	YBA 2B		6.2
7.6	4	Greenstone ax	TIL 7C		4.6 (vertical)
7.6	5	Orange stone disk (pendant broken at hole?)	SPT 26A		5.1 (vertical)

Index